Mechthild Leutner,
Nicola Spakowski (Eds.)

Women in China

Berliner China-Studien

44

Herausgegeben von
Mechthild Leutner

Redaktion: Nicola Spakowski

Ostasiatisches Seminar
der Freien Universität Berlin

LIT

Mechthild Leutner,
Nicola Spakowski (Eds.)

Women in China

The Republican Period
in Historical Perspective

LIT

Bibliographic information published by Die Deutsche Bibliothek
Die Deutsche Bibliothek lists this publication in the Deutsche
Nationalbibliografie; detailed bibliographic data are available in the
Internet at http://dnb.ddb.de.

ISBN 3-8258-8147-4

©LIT VERLAG Münster   2005
Grevener Str./Fresnostr. 2   48159 Münster
Tel. 0251-62 03 20   Fax 0251-23 19 72
e-Mail: lit@lit-verlag.de   http://www.lit-verlag.de

Distributed in North America by:

Transaction Publishers
New Brunswick (U.S.A.) and London (U.K.)

Transaction Publishers   Tel.: (732) 445-2280
Rutgers University   Fax: (732) 445-3138
35 Berrue Circle   for orders (U. S. only):
Piscataway, NJ 08854   toll free (888) 999-6778

Contents

Introduction Mechthild Leutner, Nicola Spakowski — 7

Questions of Theory and Methodology

Hsiung Ping-chen, *Seeing Neither the Past Nor the Future: The Trouble of Positioning Women in Modern China* — 14

Wen-hsin Yeh, *The Paradox of Autonomy: Nation, Revolution, and Women through the Chinese Looking Glass* — 40

Mechthild Leutner, *Women's, Gender and Mainstream Studies on Republican China: Problems in Theory and Research* — 57

Women and the State/Women and the Nation

Gotelind Müller, *Knowledge Is Easy – Action Is Difficult: The Case of Chinese Anarchist Discourse on Women and Gender Relations and Its Practical Limitations* — 86

Louise Edwards, *Opposition to Women's Suffrage in China: Confronting Modernity in Governance* — 107

Nicola Spakowski, *Women's Military Participation in the Communist Movement of the 1930s and 1940s: Patterns of Inclusion and Exclusion* — 129

Helen Praeger Young, *Threads from Long March Stories: The Political, Economic and Social Experience of Women Soldiers* — 172

Political Women and Their Posthumous Careers

Sabine Hieronymus, *Qiu Jin (1875-1907) – A Heroine for All Seasons* — 194

Natascha Vittinghoff, *Jiang Qing and Nora: Drama and Politics in the Republican Period* — 208

Little Traditions and Discourses of Otherness

Maria Jaschok, Shui Jingjun, *Gender, Religion and Little Traditions: Henanese Women Singing* Minguo   242

Jens Damm, *Contemporary Discourses on Homosexuality in Republican China: A Critical Analysis of Terminology and Current Research*   282

Women in Social and Economic Life: Discourses and Experiences

Tani E. Barlow, *Wanting Some: Commodity Desire and the Eugenic Modern Girl*   312

Bryna Goodman, *Unvirtuous Exchanges: Women and the Corruptions of the Shanghai Stock Market in the Early Republican Era*   351

Zang Jian, *"Women Returning Home" – A Topic of Chinese Women's Liberation*   376

Du Fangqin, *Women and Gender in the Rural Modernization Movement: A Case Study of Ding County (1912-1937)*   396

Christina K. Gilmartin, Isabel Crook, *Marriage Reform, Rural Women and the Chinese State during World War II*   422

Women's Education

Harriet T. Zurndorfer, *Gender, Higher Education, and the "New Woman": The Experiences of Female Graduates in Republican China*   450

Yu Chien-ming, *Female Physical Education and the Media in Modern China*   482

Contributors   507

Introduction

In the past ten years or so, the period of the Chinese Republic (1911-1949) has taken on a new significance in sinological research. The successful reforms of the People's Republic of China have led to a new perception of the Mao Zedong era as a mere pause in a modernization trend that started long before the late 1970s. Historiographers studying China have discovered continuities and breaks in various areas of Chinese history that contradict the conventional view of its epochs and call for a new periodization. In addition, parallels between the period of the Republic and the current phase of reform have become increasingly apparent, with both periods now being understood as times of transformation. Solutions for social problems that have developed during the current upheaval are now being sought with direct recourse to the period of the Republic.

The new relevance of the Republican period in historical research is also having an effect on women's studies in the Chinese context. Both in the West and in China, research is being done on the many different realities of Chinese women during this period. After the early phase of a women's movement in the late nineteenth century initiated by men, the Republican period can be described as a highpoint of the Chinese women's movement. During this period, women themselves began to agitate for their rights and were also able to secure concrete gains in many different areas. The women's movement saw different phases and suffered internal divisions that reflect the social differences and political polarizations during the period of the Republic. In terms of women's realities, urban China has experienced a deep-reaching transformation, during which women have increasingly entered into the public sphere, either through their profession or through political or social engagement. The basis for this transformation was a systematic effort to educate women and girls, but also a change in mentality among the urban elite that reaches even further back. This class encouraged their daughters to participate in society in order to demonstrate their progressive thinking. Because the gender question became an important part of public discourse during the period of the Republic, extensive sources are available on the situation of women from different social classes. This is also true, particularly for the period of the 1930s and 1940s, for women among the peasantry, whose lives changed dramatically as a result of the war with Japan and with the systematic spread of the revolution into China's provinces. Rural China also underwent social and political changes that have affected the lives of China's rural population up until today.

Research on women in Republican China is being carried out under new conditions. There is clearly an attempt underway to overcome a period of stagnation in the field that had been felt well into the 1990s. This renaissance can be attributed to at least two different factors. Firstly, there is a much better base of sources available due to better access to archives and libraries, extensive source editions, and diverse oral history projects that have been undertaken in the People's Republic of China. Secondly, new topics and new theoretical approaches and methodologies have been developed in which impulses from the wider field of women's studies have played an important role.

The conference at the Free University of Berlin in October 2002 entitled "Women in Republican China" was intended as a forum for honoring this upturn in research and for simultaneously creating the conditions for more direct exchange of the new research being done. The contributions to this conference are compiled here. This anthology reflects the manifold perspectives, approaches, and questions that have come to distinguish this area of research since its inception. It also points to future directions that promise to further our knowledge.

The introductory chapters in this volume address basic theoretical and methodological issues in studies on women in Republican China. Women's studies has had difficulties in becoming accepted within Chinese studies and in bringing a gender perspective into the mainstream approaches within the field. And women's studies research related to China is itself influenced by diverse discourses, both Western and Chinese, that have been developed within distinct cultural and political contexts and which have opened up a complex field of theoretical possibilities. *Hsiung Ping-chen* demonstrates the problematic aspects in women's studies' approaches to China by examining the contradictory images of women in Late Imperial and modern China conjured in the field to date. Her solution to "The Trouble of Positioning Women in Modern China" is to give up modern Western and feminist categories of analysis and to take up an approach that situates women's history within a broader social history and takes into account areas that have not yet been sufficiently explored, for example religion, concepts of the body, ethics and aesthetics. *Wen-hsin Yeh* addresses "The Paradox of Autonomy" for women in contemporary China in relation to their past. In women's efforts to gain independence from Western and Orientalist – as well as Chinese revolutionary – discourses, in a paradoxical way political classifications have been reversed and simultaneously limitations accepted from those discourses whose influence one is trying to leave behind. And finally, *Mechthild Leutner* considers the successes and the remaining deficits in endeavors to integrate a gender perspective into the general historiography of Republican China. Using examples from influential work on this period, she demonstrates that women's studies has been able to situate gender issues within a general social context, but that broader studies have hardly taken up questions of gender relations.

Women's relationship to the state and nation have long been a central concern of Chinese feminism. As the following articles show, the evaluation of this relationship has been interpreted in various ways and its results have been differently put into practice depending upon the historical period, political context and political affiliations. In her article, *Gotelind Müller* comes to the conclusion that "Knowledge is Easy – Action Is Difficult," thereby pointing to the practical limitations of anarchist discourse. Concerning the question of what role women and gender relations have played in this discourse, she shows that a form of anarcho-feminism developed during the late Qing period in the Chinese group active in Tokyo, and in particular with He Zizhen. But this tradition was not taken up later on the Chinese mainland. *Louise Edwards* thematizes the "Opposition to Women's Suffrage in China," beginning with the question of why the demand for women's right to vote was granted comparatively quickly in China.

She points to the specific context of the suffrage movement in Republican China, where women's right to vote was part of a modernization imperative, against which the conservatives' alternative agendas could not hold sway. Two articles focus on the women who fought in the Communist revolution. In "Women's Military Participation in the Communist Movement of the 1930s and 1940s," *Nicola Spakowski* explores the general patterns of women's involvement in the military. She demonstrates that in different political-military contexts, women had the choice of a more or less broad range of military roles. She then identifies the motivations that led women to take on one role or another. *Helen Young* explores "The Political, Economic and Social Experience of Women Soldiers," in particular those women who took part in the Long March. The article is based on interviews with women veterans of the Long March and considers the gender specific aspects in the biographical backgrounds and the experiences of those women who participated in it.

The women of the Chinese revolution are interesting not only because of their fates and the circumstances of their lives, but also – particularly in the very famous examples – because of the images of them through which they became known to later generations. It is impossible to separate their authentic experiences from those that were later attributed to them, which is apparent from the examples of Qiu Jin and Jiang Qing. *Sabine Hieronymus* describes Qiu Jin as a "A Heroine for All Seasons," basing this judgment in part on the fact that Qiu Jin stylized her own image during her lifetime and thereby contributed to what later became a myth nurtured by very different interests. The case of Jiang Qing is quite similar. *Natascha Vittinghoff* introduces us to the Shanghai phase of Jiang Qing's life (1934-37), showing that her self-stylization during her lifetime merged with later views of her in which her role in the Cultural Revolution is projected back into the Republican period.

The next two articles are devoted to traditions and discourses of social groups not represented in mainstream discourses. *Maria Jaschok* and *Shui Jingjun* show how difficult the reconstruction of these marginalized cultures is in their contribution on "Gender, Religion and Little Traditions," in which they explore the traditions of

Muslim women in Henan Province. These traditions were influenced by an Islamic "New Culture Movement" that articulated its ideas about the "new Chinese Muslim woman." These traditions are also reflected in the contributions of intellectual Muslim women and are preserved for example in the *jingge*, or popular songs, which were an important part of women's mosque culture. *Jens Damm* examines "Contemporary Discourses on Homosexuality in Republican China," looking in particular at the relationship between international discourses and indigenous traditions. He demonstrates that new concepts of sexuality in the Republican period were due not only to Western influences but also to the tradition of Late Imperial China, a period during which there were significant transformations in the conceptualization of sexuality.

The Republican period was a phase in which the economic and social possibilities for women were greatly extended as the result of a large number of reform efforts. At the same time, the images of and social discourses on women who participated in society and the economy reflect social projects and fears that raise questions beyond that of women's emancipation. In her article "Commodity Desire and the Eugenic Modern Girl," *Tani Barlow* elucidates the relationship between the new type of female consumer, general discourses on modernity, and consumer culture of the 1920s. The "natural woman," a product of a vernacular sociology committed to "modernity," was simultaneously the target of commercial products (for example women's hygiene products) distributed by transnational enterprises in China. Criticism of modernity could also be transmitted in images of women. In "Unvirtuous Exchanges," *Bryna Goodman* addresses the perception of the Shanghai stock exchange as represented in novels of the 1920s and determines that the figure of woman symbolized the loss of virtue in what was seen as an empty, selfish, Westernized and decadent world. Examining the motto of "Women Returning Home" (*funü huijia*), *Zang Jian* shows how over the period of almost one hundred years leading up to the present, the issue of working women was repeatedly a subject of debate. She distinguishes three different periods in these debates, which she then elucidates with reference to the specific economic and political backgrounds of each period.

Reform projects aimed directly at the status of women or affecting women are discussed in the following two articles. In her case study of Ding County in Hebei Province, *Du Fangqin* explores the issue of "Women and Gender in the Rural Modernization Movement." She is interested in the role that male reformers prescribed for women and shows that women were neglected as potential agents of rural modernization, but that they profited from the new educational projects, which enabled them to later gain greater independence. *Christina Gilmartin* and *Isabel Crook* explore "Marriage Reform, Rural Women and the Chinese State during World War II" in a case study of a rural township in Sichuan Province that was under the influence of the Guomindang in the early 1940s. They show that the state's efforts to reform traditional marriage practices through laws and propaganda campaigns were only moderately successful and that real changes were more the indirect result of factors related to the war.

This anthology concludes with a section on the subject of education – an area that initiated many of the changes in women's realities during the Republican period. In "Gender, Higher Education, and the 'New Woman,'" *Harriet Zurndorfer* shows by looking at women's access to higher education that reforms in the education sector were limited and concepts of women's education were tinged with conservatism. The relationship between "Female Physical Education and the Media in Modern China" is the focus of *Yu Chienming's* article. She posits that the media functioned as a mouthpiece for the government in its efforts to promote sports as a means for strengthening the nation, while at the same time satisfying audiences' need for entertainment.

We have chosen the title "Women in China: The Republican Period in Historical Perspective" due to our conviction that the contributions to this anthology pose questions that are relevant to women's studies research on China as well as to research with other points of focus. The questions raised here throw light on China's Republican period as well as on the continuities and breaks in Chinese history in general.

We would like to thank all those who supported us and helped to make this publication possible. Special thanks to Carola Krüger who helped edit the texts and whose patience and attention to detail ensured consistency throughout the texts. Helen Young revised the English version of those articles originally written in Chinese. Ingrid Dammalage-Kirst and Jens Damm created one manuscript out of the many contributions. The conference was funded by the German Research Foundation and the publication of this book was made possible by funds from the Department of History and Cultural Studies at the Free University of Berlin. We are sincerely thankful to all these persons and institutions.

Berlin, August 2004

Mechthild Leutner, Nicola Spakowski

Seeing Neither the Past Nor the Future: The Trouble of Positioning Women in Modern China

Hsiung Ping-chen

It does not take too expert a pair of eyes to detect a curious discrepancy between the existent knowledge of the life and culture of women in Late Imperial China to that of their experience and situation in the modern era. Anybody who throws themselves at the task of teaching the subject for any period of time will find himself or herself experimenting with any number of means to close up the gap, as he or she is compelled first to introduce the facts and details of the extraordinary cultivated world of Ming-Qing talented women *(cainü)*, only to be dashed away by the "harsh reality" of tens of millions of oppressed and suppressed females (physically immobile, socially subjugated, with few opportunities for education or employment, almost no liberty over their mate or fate) presented from the late nineteenth century and onward.[1] Granted that there were questions of methodology (i.e. for the Late Imperial period, researchers in history and literature rely heavily on textual evidence that documented the world of gentry ladies, whereas for the modern period statistical data, anthropological reports and contemporary surveys yield information about conditions of women in the rural, lower classes),[2] and granted

---

[1] Scholars on the historical heritage of Ming-Qing talented women fully acknowledge the intellectual connection between modern Western feminist concerns (which may be "completely unconnected with China") and their excavation of the female culture in the past. Furthermore, most of them are also fully aware of and thus pay due attention to the politics and rhetorics of Chinese modernism as represented by the late Qing reformers, revolutionaries and the May Fourth iconoclasts as the immediate local background and ideological burden that they and their works have to wrestle with (see Widmer 1997:4-6, 13 and Ko 1994:1-28).

[2] Reviews of European women's history also discover a disparity in perspectives, with the works on earlier periods showing a sympathetic view toward the gender system in the past whereas those on the modern times showing a future-oriented

that both have served as forceful rebuttal to many crude Western-centric views on women's history in general or elsewhere (namely that women in premodern societies did not all live under dark, savage regimes waiting to be enlightened and rescued, and that much of the agency of change in women's lives can come from local subjectivity, intertwined with perhaps but not led by imported ideas or forces),[3] it may still be worthwhile to examine once more what each of these discursive representations is made of, how it has come about, and whether or how the two may be considered as connected or disjointed.

Bringing forth revealing and exciting discoveries as they have, recent studies in Chinese women's history did not develop as an organized effort or a planned field. Other than obvious lapses between areas of investigation (e.g. that between cultural history and socio-economic history, that between public political and private life, and religious activities), the unintended gap thus far produced concerning the women's world in the Late Imperial period and (the same or a different world) for the Republican and modern period can be a staggering and bewildering one. To put it succinctly, the wonderful realm of women's culture made up of women of letters, readers, writers, curious urban consumers, able and enabling gentry mothers, learned and cultivated wives and daughters lively and persuasively presented by scholars in Ming-Qing literature, society, and culture (Widmer/Sun Chang Kang-i 1997; Mann 1997; Ko 1994) could hardly be squared with the struggling factory workers, and impoverished peasant women discussed no less movingly by scholars from the field of late nineteenth- and early twentieth-century China (Honig 1986; Gilmartin et al. 1994). As each speaks past one another, how are their readers to conjure up any overall picture of women or gender over the

---

analysis toward their subjects. See Bridenthal et al. 1987:3 and chapters 1, 3, 5, 6 as opposed to chapters 11, 12, 13, and 15.

[3] There is a broad consensus in the women's history field that its growth and expansion in the academia in most countries of the world owe a clear and direct debt to the latest wave of feminist movements since the 1970s. The professional performance and intellectual substance of the subject has also benefited, as pointed out, from the development of interdisciplinary studies in the humanities and social sciences in this same period of time. See, for instance, Blom 1991:xiii-xvi and Offen et al. 1991:xix-xli.

last few centuries of that complicated history? Shall one incline to, or be persuaded by the feminist agenda and China's modern revolutions, more to believe in the earlier history as one burdened with an oppressive patriarchal orthodoxy in gender relations that was finally undermined and turned around as the country was introduced to the impact of modern Western progressive discourse (e.g. women's liberation)? Or shall one turn more to the premodernist story, in taking note of a significantly different gender construction as formulated in Late Imperial Chinese society which may even promise some kind of an alternative experience and explanation for then and later? Before responding to any specific quibbles, we may begin by looking at how each of these fields of discovery has been established and the intellectual or political implications of what had been disclosed.

Checking the Scenes

Whether as a direct correction or as a causal patching-up, modern scholars' uncovering and reconnection with the Ming-Qing elite women was a powerful retrieval happening at a prime time and put forth in an opportune fashion. Regardless of the fact that these educated, thinking, writing, publishing and traveling women that they unearthed were mostly gentry daughters, wives, and mothers from the Jiangnan region, thus representing numerically and proportionately but a small minority (less than 10 percent of the females or 1-5 percent of the total population, although equivalent to as much as one quarter or more of affluent local society),[4] the existence and activities of over 3,500 published female authors and their entourage, both women and men, dealt an effective blow to whatever was left over from people's stereotypical image of a victimized, passive second sex living out dark lives under insurmountable oppression. Works by Dorothy Ko, Susan Mann, Kang-i Sun Chang, and Ellen Widmer on the broader social institutional environment that gave rise to, and sustained, the cultivated pursuits of these educated, active female writers,

---

[4] See Rawski 1979:140: "Information from the mid- and late nineteenth century suggests that 30-45 percent of the men and from 2-10 percent of the women in China knew how to read and write."

painters, and teachers would have dispelled even Chinese reformers' vehement attacks on their helpless and hopeless country women as epitomizing the social ills of China's feudal past. To their credit, most of these scholarly investigations never denied that the works of women's poetry, fiction, commentaries, *tanci* theatrical composition, or paintings and calligraphy were carried out while they continued fulfilling their obligations as respectful daughters, dutiful wives and laboring mothers, and almost all moved about on bound feet. In other words, there was never any doubt or denial of their operating under restricted, "unliberated" conditions; in fact, the very limited nature and particular configuration that the lives and accomplishments of these *cainü* (talented women) and *guixiu* (virgin) women demonstrated gave more food for thought than modern Chinese critics or those with Western feminist misgivings suspected. In any event, their scholarly discoverers, while joyful in their uncovering and reacquaintance with this lost world of elegance and beauty, could hardly be mindless of the brilliance under bondage that their subjects represented less they become forgetful of the feminist quest of their own search. Ingenious female agency and cleverly navigated individual subjectivity borne out and illustrated by these gentry ladies who tried to and succeeded in carving out an active social space of their own characterized not an exceptional story of miraculous escape but the very significance of incomplete deliverance laboriously devised.

Revealingly, many studies, though offering strikingly different pictures of modern Chinese women from those of premodern female elites may in fact be envisioned and anchored by a similarly searching and argumentative modern (mostly also Western) feminist thrust. Since scholars disagreed that Chinese women lacked any agency, or subjectivity on their own before the coming of foreign ideas, imported enlightenment, or simply Western capitalism, marked by industrialization, and urbanization, they went out and found evidence of their subjects in roles and activities that could hardly confirm them in the role of vulnerable victims to patriarchal hierarchy, despotic oppression, or retarded developments. Even though, at an expense, Chinese women's past was painted bleak and cast as necessarily oppressive, rendering this more recent history and contemporary struggles of Chinese women as showing ample reasons for a supportive sympathy. As a result Emily Honig's insightful work on women in the Shanghai cotton mills in the first part of the twentieth century is an example of sophisticated and intriguingly positioned scholarship that can either confirm suspected sufferings of the subjects or lead to self-questioning of the on-lookers. Thinking through such intricately nuanced studies, few readers could close the book with any doubt in the mind that "Shanghai women workers had ever been passive victims" of industrial poverty, capitalist exploitation, their patriarchal past or imported present (Honig 1986:248). To her credit, on the other hand, more than enough details were also made manifest from the same disclosure, of the same women's ordering of their lives by old local affinities, forging sisterhood as one another's protection and in mutual aid (ibid. 209-216). Localism, traditional hierarchies, or premodern styles in fashioning intimate bonds and social relations can therefore function and be understood as not necessarily antithetical to modern consciousness or forces of adoption and change (ibid. 249).

The question is given a potentially disparate narrative, are these scholars of Late Imperial *cainü* culture and those of modern, striving women actually speaking of a related story? That is, other than separated by time, did the Ming-Qing educated and writing women and their low-status, low-income female compatriots that attracted political and intellectual attentions one or two hundred years later make up part of the same world of Chinese women, or not? Argumentatively, can we imagine how might Honig or Hershatter think of the *guixiu* ladies from the same Jiangnan region that they study, who in their more fortunate or unfortunate existence had not been pressed to become social entertainers or migrant workers? Or hypothetically, what, if anything, did the elite women or female workers have to say or think of each others' stations in life? Given that class in many instances operates more compellingly than gender, on the other hand, what may we say about Dorothy Ko's or Susan Mann's ideas about the over 40-60 percent of women in their region who could not read or write and therefore had to act upon their agency through non-literary means? Surely the intellectual gap that we are trying to gauge here has more to it than simply the nature of source materials, quantitative versus qualitative analysis, different methodological approach, or some changing characters of history. For although people well realize that women made up about half of China's rural and illiterate population in the premodern society, more could and should be explored about their daily laboring, frustration and accomplishments through material artifacts, legal papers, medical records, the physical set-up of family and local economy (special arrangements for instance for production and consumption of commercialized or self-used commodities), and religious activities, but this has not been so. Causal perusals of twentieth-century social, political, and intellectual history also confirm that educated and seriously-minded women continued to live through or perish under China's modern regime. We know that before marrying the linguist Zhao Yuanren (1892-1982), Yang Buwei (1889-1981) was a Japanese trained physician who operated a new hospital in Beijing (Yang Puwei 1967) and that Chen Hengzhe (1890-1976), with her American education, continued to teach as the first female professor of Western history at Beijing University after her marriage to the chemist Ren Hongjuan (1886-1961) (Chen Hengzhe 1924; Jen Hung-chun 1993). Whereas Lin Huiyin (1904-1955) demonstrated her gift as an erudite and devoted architecture historian, (Liang Congjie 1999; Fairbank 1994) and Fei Xiaotong's (1910-) first wife Wang Tonghui (1911-1935) showed early budding in a promising career as a field social anthropologist (Arkush/Dong Tianmin 1985:49-57), these educated women as wives, when pursued further, may not represent as much of a completely unprecedented phenomenon or "new" females as people believed. Because they not only revealed local traditions of intellectual cultivation and strong family support, but also represented literally the tip of a huge iceberg of the long-standing sociocultural commitment for female education and the broader networking behind women's individual "public" dedication situated in a drastically changing environment.[5] Experiences and stories like theirs compel us

---

[5] In this regard, it is actually important to understand the earlier generations of the most radically "new women" such as Qiu Jin (1875-1907) and other seemingly rebellious daughters, wives, and mothers in the older context of "gentry activism." Read, for instance, Qiu's classical lyric *Qiu deng ke shi tu (Poetry*

to gather more systematic information and collect our thoughts about the vocational development for Chinese women in the modern era, including the elitist, professional kind (such as professors, medical doctors, authors, artists, lawyers, bankers[6] as well as the more ordinary but massive categories (such as factory workers, midwives, teachers, street venders or agricultural laborers).

So, fully recognizing the social and cultural dynamics of the May Fourth iconoclasts' espousal both of a "total condemnation of tradition" and "complete manipulation of the past to serve the present" (Gilmartin et al. 1994:11), the revisiting and reappraisal of Chinese women's history by its modern investigators cannot be devoid of or detached from their own latter day contemporary feminist agenda. In the search for the women's voice, female agency and women's subjectivity as embodied in the writers, readers, or virtuous mothers and chaste wives of Ming-Qing Jiangnan gentry, or reexamination of stages of women's emancipation, delineating gender difference from gender discrimination, deliberation over the separation and relatedness between gender hierarchy and patriarchal social regime, modern scholars cannot but be tantalized by the twentieth-century quest for equality and liberty (or liberation), lurking behind these academic activities. Opportunities of female education, income-earning vocational employment outside the family, freedom to love, personal selection of marriage partners, individual rights over one's body and sexuality, legal protection on one's physical safety and material property, in other words, remain the burning issues that inform and instigate people's intellectual inquiries, for most everything else continues to fall to the margins of concern, unattended, disengaged, appearing insignificant, scattered, disconnected. This might not look as natural or logical if either modern (Western or global) feminism or Chinese modernity turns out to be surprising and promises us something other than its most familiar features. That is, if feminist thinking proves

---

Instruction under the Autumn Lantern) remembering her mother's influence on her. See also Hsiung Ping-chen 2002.

[6] The poet Xu Zhimo's (1896-1931) first wife Zhang Youyi educated herself to become a banker after their high-profile divorce (Chang 1996:179-180). See also Chang Pang-Mei/Tan Chia-yu 1996.

capable of bringing forth a few characteristics besides those of the modern or Western type, that modernity somehow reveals a different evolution for Chinese women in the area of gender issues than is the case for their counterparts in the Western hemisphere of the nineteenth and twentieth centuries, or still more bafflingly, in the event that there appears a possibility of conceiving, observing, and analyzing the "women's question" from a standpoint that is neither modern (e.g. postmodern?), nor feminist (by its usual Western, or modern standard), much of the substance and critiques that we have accumulated at hand thus far can be considerably shaken. But in their stead, what will these other findings or arguments be like, and how is it to be done from where we stand?

Random Notes on Scattered Attempts

It is partly with these disturbing propositions in mind that I would like to have us consider here three sets of potential initiatives toward a Chinese women's history, repositioned once again: (1) those founded on a shifting definition of human sentiments and material and carnal desires vis-à-vis (mostly Confucian or Neo-Confucian) orthodox culture in Late Imperial and modern China; (2) those regarding the understanding and performances of body and sexuality in gendered domains; and (3) those about the non-fixing and constantly evolving character of gender acting out and posted against temporality and locality. First of all, with regard to the characterization of the old Confucian patriarchal and patrilineal orthodoxy that the "oppression hypothesis" is identified as the arch evil for Chinese women and China's past, newer studies have reintroduced people to its inner workings to show how women were by no means victims, helpless, hopeless, voiceless. Mostly represented by scholarship on the Late Imperial era, historians and literary scholars demonstrate through the social reproduction of motherhood, self-empowerment as a housewife, or conscientious readers and writers, Ming-Qing Chinese women learned to navigate their way, not without either constant frustration *or* considerable success, through ideological and institutional constraints to arrive at a fair share of legal, social, and cultural accomplishments for their right and status. Female agency or women's subjectivity, in other words, need not to be defined or gained through modern feminist means, nor can it be adequately measured by contemporary terms. Regardless of the question as to whether during those times and under that environment women might or might not be gaining more comfort or become less obliging toward any subordination under the same patriarchal, dictatorial hierarchy, women of different classes and from different regions had allocated for themselves their own breathing space and manner of operating, arriving at similar goals of rights and protection through different channels, or understood in varying terms. There surely remain areas of frustration, places of want, room for improvement, but women in premodern China as a whole were far from miserable, ignorant sufferers in pitch darkness, awaiting for enlightenment and salvation from elsewhere, as the late Qing reformers, revolutionaries, or modern Western deliverers would have them, certainly not by comparison with the circumstances of their counterparts elsewhere at a comparable historical period (say compared with women's conditions in the advocating Western Europe or America) or even (questionably) with women's positions propagated by the "emancipated" modernists.

Situated and examined in this historical light, it becomes clear that much of what late Qing and early Republican social reformers identified as "women's problems" *(funü wenti)* concerned not only the welfare of the female population but many difficult issues relating to a sizable number of men at the time. Questions such as they had been raised about whether younger brothers-in-law were permitted, by Confucian propriety, to mourn for the death of their sisters-in-law who had virtually raised them in the role of surrogate mothers, or whether the essence of a wedding was to mark a woman's becoming the wife of her man or the daughter-in-law of his family clouded debates of serious high Qing philological circles because they were not just women's issues (Chang So-an 2001, chap. 2, 1999:125-178). In collaborating with and being supported by their fathers, husbands, brothers, sons, or male friends, furthermore, enough numbers of women were seen living and operating, across as well as, along gender boundaries. In other words, while it remains important to continue digging as much as we can on vocational women (such as healers, midwives, matchmakers, merchants, venders, even martial arts practitioners, bandits and pirates) or the liberty and validation of outdoor and out-of-the-house activities for high- or lowbrow women, we need not and ought not to be looking at women only for the purpose of ascertaining the conditions of the female gender. The impetus to do so only confirms the conviction of certain peculiar constructs in the modern feminist quest, which can be used to check the characteristics of the gender relations as they occurred before modern times or outside of the Western cultural sphere, but can better still be allowed an opportunity to be challenged, revised, and enriched by these "external" references.

When perceived as a platform for cross-gender debate and philosophical wrestling between fulfillment of human sentiment and reasonable desires on the one hand, and dated or rigidly formulated orthodox beliefs on the other, men and women in their Ming-Qing historical context could be seen as struggling and unpacking general sociocultural problems about gender equality and women's (or men's) liberation, but theirs could also be understood as a struggle about broader human inadequacy or cosmic disequilibrium. The connections between the engendered disputes among educated Jiangnan men and women (such as the seemingly calm but soon to appear fervently restless elites in Huizhou and other Jiangsu towns) and the increasingly irritated and irritating intellectuals in the coastal cities of the late nineteenth century and early twentieth century may thus be a cultural disruption embedded in and nourished by a profoundly and intentionally overlooked social continuum.

Similar comments may be made with regard to China's evolving culture of body, sexuality, and sensuality.[7] For the few initial explorations into Chinese body culture and traditions of sexuality reveal to us that people's universal essentialist assumptions, whether of the Confucianist humanist type that was epitomized in the eight-

---

[7] In posing the tantalizing question "Does a Sex Have a History?" Denise Riley reminds people that since women are historically and discursively constructed, they should always be remembered as subjects relative to other sociocultural categories which themselves change (see Riley 1996:11).

eenth-century progressive philosopher Dai Zhen (1723-1777) who called for "free expression of feelings and complete fulfillment of desires *(daqing suiyu)*" that anticipated China's iconoclasts of the twentieth century (Tai Chen 1978; Tuan Yu-Ts'ai 1971), or the modern feminist, liberationist type which rests its faith on a common human need and prevailing standard of bio-socially founded inalienable human rights and institutional equality between men and women, can be wildly ahistorical and thus substantively off the mark even if conceptually stimulating. As an important example of a premodern (therefore preanatomical) understanding and sociocultural system, for instance, Chinese medicine has creatively and confusingly allowed for a liberal mixture and interplay between the bio-physical body (as they then understood it) and people's sociocultural being. Charlotte Furth's study of traditional gynecology *(fuke)* and human cosmology (Furth 1999), Hsiung Ping-chen's look into male medicine *(nanke)* and masculine consciousness (Hsiung Ping-chen 1999), Matthew Sommer's examination of sodomy and masculinity (Sommer 2002:67-88), all point forward to an increased appreciation and daily conducting of people's physical existence within the boundary of family reproduction. They should not be interpreted in gender-segregated bipolar terms. Furthermore, research into popular religion and performing arts demonstrate that, in addition and complementary to medicine and law, Buddhism, Taoism, or familial and communal rites could all be manifestations and add-ons to this blurry yet potentially non-binary and therefore peculiarly liberating and maneuverable body culture (Yü Chün-fang 1983; Hwa Wei/Wang Ayling 1998). Many basic kernels of the modern bio-medical conceptualization of sexuality on which or against which global feminist thrust positions itself as a result can best function as an enticing hypothetical baseline for rebuttal and departure, but hardly any conceptual model for application or adaptation.

    Such reflections on the changing understandings and practices in sentiments, desires, body, and sexuality also make us realize the vitally important though equally bewitching character of feminist premises especially as they are played out across cultural boundaries, as in this instance it appears as a constant negotiation back and forth both between Western and Chinese categories and between Chinese women's issues in the past as opposed to those at the present or the foreseeable future.[8] Indeed in spite of repeated cautioning against the danger of polarizing the self-valorized present vis-à-vis its observed subject matter into "positive or negative versions" of approved standards, it is still fairly common to encounter intellectual creations of "universalized particularity" (Armstrong 1997:397). Among recent works in Chinese women's studies, it is not at all unusual to find examples of positing women's historical situations as some feudal shackles to be shattered by the liberating present or utopian future, as the political slogans had it. Similar observations can be made when we compare Chinese women's historical experience, past or present, vis-à-vis Western or global feminist ethos (if there is such a thing). Such liberal intellectual leaps across time and space become particularly problematic as recent unleashing of even more open-ended and wide range of bold experiments and drastic changes in post-1980's China confront researchers with waves of dazzling facts and puzzling possibilities. Information and trends, when either pressed against our familiar picture of China's distant or recent past (the traditional Ming-Qing or "modern" society by the old account) or considered under standard feminist inquiries, appear especially challenging. For ample data seem to suggest that traditional modes (of division of gender roles and labor, of customary codes of behavior or fundamental ethics) remain quite alive, though most probably under altered, revised, or mutated forms, such as "having men working in the industrial sector while women taking over agriculture production" *(nan gong nü geng)* in the remote country and underdeveloped regions, in place of or under the same terms as the old "men till and women weave" *(nan geng nü zhi)* ideal. Among young men and women in the urban population, a gush of enthusiasm in bourgeois romance, domestic sentimentality, and the "movement of returning home" *(huijia yundong)* impress their observers on the ironic turns of social tides, something not to be explained away with a simple claim of the oscillation in historicity. Such reminds us of the very double-edged nature of much of the modern feminist perspective; both fundamentally progres-

---

[8] In considering related issues, Tani E. Barlow once proposed the notion of "non-imperialist feminism" as a possible analytical stance (see Barlow 1996:48-50).

sive yet also fundamentally historical and therefore readily conservative (ibid. 422). If we follow Ellen Widmer's suggestion that we try abandoning such concepts as "domestic women," "companionate marriage," or "emotional compatibility," in the case of China thereby standing independent of such modern rhetoric of women's right, liberty, equality, or emancipation, may we be uncovering a newer, different Chinese society from the one modern theories or recent social movements imagined to be in need of subversion? Will it be at all useful, in other words, to go back to recapturing some of the basic features in the socioculturally grounded modern feminist thrusts that may or may not be born out by the totality of history, Chinese and other, past and present?[9]

An Interrogation on Academic Feminism

It might be worthwhile then to press the case one step further and imagine how the longer history of Chinese women may be turned around to precipitate a reconsidered and reinvigorated modern (Western) feminist outlook,[10] as this will show a clear need and special value in viewing together the gender relations both in their premodern Ming-Qing characters and in these modern (or postmodern) nineteenth- and twentieth-century developments. Here, I would like to take the topics of marriage, family, and reproduction as sites of creative contention. First of all, as late Qing and early Republican reformers set their prairie fire of social emancipation, pursuits of romantic love and freedom to choose one's marriage mate, they were

---

[9] Conscientious scholars in women's history have long taken notice of the tendency for studies on the West to universalize and essentialize the European and American historical experiences and to apply them to other societies. In such positive attempts to compose something akin to a world history on women to enhance international perspectives, such as the anthology of *Writing Women's History* whereby more than two dozen countries and areas are represented, there are still vital lapses, including the missing of the case of China (see Offen et al. 1991).

[10] Other historians have also encouraged scholars to come to terms with the potentially useful and productive tension between feminist history and the theories of feminism (see Scott 1996:5).

defining the essence of Chinese women's (and men's) liberation in both local history and global history terms. Identified and activated as a universal challenge to China's patriarchal regime, stirring slogans, dramatic plots and rational attacks spread from the country's urban elites to its rural constituency. In that agitation against arranged marriages, few had suspected that there may come times when marriage itself becomes a questionable choice for the population, one of the modern fads that catches up with Chinese men and women soon and real enough, which put the earlier solidarity in struggling for "self-determination in marriage" *(hunyin zizhu)* in quite a different light. What, may we ask, would the logical, sensible next step be in the question of marriage in an era when the validity of the marriage system itself as a social institution and personal choice appear to be taken away from under the feet both individually and collectively, first in the West but gradually also in the East? Surely in a society with long traditions of early universal marriage, nuptials continue on, at least statistically, under various editions of marriage laws. Yet ample sociological, demographic, community health, and anthropological evidence points also at a rapidly growing tread of increased divorce rates and single parenthood in the cities, and perennial existential spousal separation in the rural villages. What should "freedom in marriage" *(hunyin ziyou)* mean to anybody under these changing circumstances? What kind of a conceptual or pragmatic input can the liberationist or feminist ethos devise for people in the middle of this evolving current? Do these conditions not also cast a doubtful light upon the very character of the struggle the modernists used to have envisioned and continued to engage in? Can they thereby be pressing us to reevaluate and reappraise the socioeconomic implications of people's gender-related thinking and actions within China's Late Imperial marital regime (patrilineal, patrilocal, polygamous, universal) from some fresh angles different from those familiar ones precipitated by the enlightening feminist agenda?

What the strangely mutating understanding and operations of the family in its multiple variations in the premodern and modern Chinese context demand is probably an even more deeply stirring dialogue with the modern feminist mentality. For other than marital customs, if we turn our attention to domesticity, a wide host of Chinese social and cultural vocabularies roughly correlating to such Anglo-American terms (concepts) as the family, household, home, clan, kinship or even nest, and roof, for both the Late Imperial and modern Republican eras render any simple historical fact-seeking of the evolving concept or realities of this other area of life, where modernity and feminism join their progressive campaign, a forced and twisted case. The neither entirely public and certainly never completely private nature of the definitional and operational character of the Chinese family turns many hypothetical interpretation opaque either in their premodern European (say Victorian) analogy or in their twentieth-century myriad manifestations under modernist gaze. From this angle, the discovery of stubborn and surprisingly liberal, unconventional, non-conformist possibilities of women (and men) in the presumably oppressive Ming-Qing patriarchal regime, on the one hand, and the unfolding of stubborn "feudal ethics" (such as filiality or generational deference) that survive and thrive after waves of revolution purged over and beyond the twentieth century, on the other, asks us to be more prudent in pledging our analytical faith to the theoretical validity of the modernity thesis or the universalist tendency of the feminist approach in its association.

The issue becomes even more acute and complicated when it comes to the question of reproduction. Though clearly a means of self-empowerment, biological reproduction or begetting of sons for women in the premodern era under patrilineal terms has always been viewed with ambivalence for its modern feminist critics (Hsiung Ping-chen 1994:87-117). Family revolution and sex revolution in the twentieth century have indeed altered enough of the structural conditions under which reproductive decisions are weighed over and carried out at present and thereby extended to the past. Demographic, anthropological, and sociological studies on contemporary China bring forth additional complex information to a modern "foreign" take on this perennial issue (Lee/Wang Feng 1999; Judd 1994; Milwertz 1997). This indicates that in spite of, or precisely due to, state-enforced reproductive policy, reproduction and motherhood (or parenthood) at the micro-level can still be perceived and handled with an ever-changing rationality mingled with or understood under age-old personal and social ethics.[11] Together with the "voluntary" acceptance of the stern one-child policy, therefore, a myriad of strategies in family negotiation and socioeconomic improvements have been tested and devised (Milwertz 1997:150-160), which in turn set off many chain reactions in gender relations as an inseparable organic combination of the new and the old. While overall the role of a mother seems to be strengthened vis-à-vis that of a wife, in the urban sectors there are also ample suggestions of women (and men), seizing the rising opportunity to treat sexuality, marriage, and reproduction each as increasingly separate and independent choices (ibid. 160). Sex without marriage, marriage without reproduction, or reproduction devoid of either not only emerge as hip topics in mass media that cut through urban-rural and class boundaries, they also suggest themselves as practical options to the highly educated, high-paid younger generation in China's more developed regions. Which represents but one area of life that asks us to reconsider women's issues and the feminist agenda in more than one set of terms. Bio-physical reproduction, first of all, need hardly be fixed within the conjugal or familial contexts. Secondly, the relationship or disconnection between bio-physical and sociocultural reproduction is obviously in need of reexamination and reconsideration. Thirdly, current conflicts, debates, confusion, and difficulties Chinese women and men continue to have should be taken seriously as a comparison and contrast against the experiences individuals and societies have had at other times (in pre-1949 China to validate or undermine the "liberation" and "watershed" thesis) and in other places (e.g. with other Chinese populated societies such as Hong

---

[11] Cecilia Milwertz's study on population policy and China's reproductive culture shows that Chinese women's own thinking and managing of the situation has been in constant flux, which could hardly be appreciated from any fixed stance on women's questions. Hershatter and Honig also agree that the difficulties in analyzing many contemporary situations related to women's issues had to do with the contradiction and ambivalence Chinese women themselves continue to face and manifest in their everyday existence. But they could also arise or be exacerbated by congruous conceptual and theoretical positions that observers and researchers are armed with (see Milwertz 1997:150-152 and Honig/Hershatter 1988:157-160).

Kong, Taiwan, and other Asian countries or the rest of the "modernizing" nations), other than simply as failures or frustrations to the modernist's story of smooth growth and successful development (ibid. 158-159). Deeper skepticism than these will call people's attention to alternative views of life and reproduction that the broader Chinese experience represents, such as the Buddhist belief in reincarnation and endless suffering or the Taoist conviction of self-preservation and becoming-one with nature, which may play into the continuous adoption and self-invention of the reproductive culture of the Chinese people, both female and male. This alerts us again to the fact that reproductive self-determination understood in modern individualist or liberal terms may not be the most useful concept in deciphering or evaluating the mentality in this regard for those surrounded in a modernizing and Westernizing environment yet still immersed in a host of Chinese cultural assumptions. As long as women in China, like those everywhere else, continue to exercise choice and disclose their ongoing self-negotiation, something other than the kind of academic feminism that thinks and acts as a conceptual constant would have to be imagined.

Conclusion

> Seeing neither those of the past,
> Nor any in the future;
> Reminded of the vast vacuum (that exists) between heaven and earth;
> I alone shed a few tears.[12]

Whereas "becoming visible" continues to be a need and a goal in pursuits of women's history, the scope and the character of the vista that has emerged as a result of these myriad efforts may in fact produce a blurring fog or pose a stumbling block between the searching spirits and the object of their search. Reflecting on our present endeavor, therefore, there can be more than one kind of loneliness like the one alluded to by the Tang poet Chen Ziang (656-695) when he mused about his unwanted solitude against the vastness with which he

---

[12] Chen Ziang 1983:21a-21b.

craved in vain to make connections. With regard to our particular question of bringing together Chinese women's history in the Late Imperial and the modern eras, there are gaps in our knowledge on the conditions of Chinese women in two different time frames and there are problems of incongruity created out of unsound views and disjointed research methods.

So looking at these intellectual scenes, like a journey of self-questioning, oftentimes also means carrying on a conversation half-uttered, encountering at once travelers from the past and present, moving through landscapes already half-known or not yet imaginable. Glancing at the wonderful wonderings of women's history and gender studies thus far introduced and generated from Chinese studies, few of us can help but be amazed by how much previous authors through their bit-by-bit uncovering have illuminated the path, though what we gain in acquaintance as a result does nothing but to enhance our craving for more, which could hardly exist without these preliminary investigations, admittedly incomplete yet totally seductive. The very sketchy perusal of present scholarship on Chinese women's history, beginning with the seemingly incongruous picture produced by a motivated feminist rediscovery of a bustling Ming-Qing elite women's past and an ever-engaging women's liberation movement in the present, takes us to revisit the sites to which we have often transported ourselves, with their many hidden corners, to face again the potential in charting out a different contour in the future.[13]

In this overview of Chinese women's history and gender studies, what has happened to or what people think as occurring to the Chinese in the Republican era appears to be an increasingly critical nexus. There is little doubt that we need a thoroughly detailed, theoretically sophisticated, and intellectually straight forward re-working of many questions regarding women's experiences and the gender issue at that presumably transitional period, to figure out once again whether or what sort of a transformation had indeed taken place,

---

[13] Editors to one of the path-making anthology in European women's history, *Becoming Visible*, recognized as well the value of maintaining a long-term perspective when approaching and appraising issues in this area (see Bridenthal et al. 1987:1-15).

or what was really so very "traditional" or which kind of a tradition was in existence before. It will also be of crucial importance for us to take into consideration many bewildering phenomena unfolding before our own eyes all around us in women's lives as they connect with those of men and children, to recognize once again that the women's question, in China or elsewhere, was and will never be a onetime solution. What the intellectuals, social activists and politicians had seized upon, advocated and charged ahead with from before the turn of the nineteenth century assumes a better historical position with the advantage of gazing from the turn of the twentieth century. Among other matters, we are reminded of, as I hope this brief review serves to demonstrate, the completely inseparable nature between any investigation of women and gender questions with much of the other happenings in history. Any sound assessment of women's conditions is dependent on a fair grasp of the position of men and other related issues,[14] since gender issues are invariably tied with people's notions and practices not just in social organizations, economy, or law, but also in natural philosophy, religion, physical aspects, culture, ethics and aesthetics. It is time therefore that we propose to ourselves the study of women's history and gender studies, in the China field in particular, to look seriously at the question not merely from the area related to the bio-physical being of women or men but also how people's understanding of parallel categories such as female and male, femininity and masculinity, have been tangled up or worked through the by now jargonized category of yin and yang, or other manifestations of ordering forces which society has gone through and continue to be formulated.

Obviously I feel truly exhilarated and profoundly challenged, at a point where modern feminism of all manifestations continues to inspire but does not seem adequate as a basic frame of reference, that that conceptual value system itself be enriched and reconceived with substantial feedbacks from other areas of experience and expertise, including those from China and Chinese studies.

---

[14] Back in the 1970s, reflecting on the unfolding of European women's history, Natalie Zemon Davis made the plea that "we should be interested in the history of both women and men" (see Davis 1996:88).

References

Armstrong, Nancy, *Postface*: Chinese Women in a Comparative Perspective: A Response, in: Widmer/Sun Chang Kang-i 1997, pp. 397-422.
Arkush, R. David (Dong Tianmin, trans.), *Fei Xiaotong zhuan* (Biography of Fei Xiaotong), Beijing 1985.
Ayscough, Florence, *Chinese Women: Yesterday and Today*, Boston 1937.
Barlow, Tani E., Theorizing Woman: *Funü, Guojia, Jiating* (Chinese Women, Chinese State, Chinese Family), in: Scott 1996, pp. 48-75.
Blom, Ida, Foreword, in: Offen et al. 1991, pp. xiii-xvi.
Bray, Francesca, *Technology and Gender: Fabrics of Power in Late Imperial China*, Berkeley, Los Angeles, London 1997.
Bridenthal, Renate, Claudia Koonz, Susan M. Stuard, Introduction, in: Bridenthal et al. 1987, pp. 1-15.
Bridenthal, Renate, Claudia Koonz, Susan M. Stuard (eds.), *Becoming Visible: Women in European History*, Boston [2]1987 ([1]1977).
Casterline, John B., *The Determinants of Rising Female Age of Marriage in Taiwan, 1905-1976*, Ann Arbor 1985.
Chang Jung, *Wild Swans: Three Daughters of China*, New York 1991.
Chang, Pang-Mei Natasha, *Bound Feet and Western Dress: A Memoir*, New York 1996 (see Chang Pang-Mei, Chinese version).
Chang Pang-Mei (Zhang Bangmei) (Tan Chia-yu [Tan Jiayu], trans.), *Xiaojiao yu xizhuang: Zhang Youyi yu Xu Zhimo de jiabian* (Bound Feet and Western Dress: The Fair of Zhang Youyi and Xu Zhimo's Family), Taipei 1996 (see Chang, Pang-Mei Natasha, English version).
Chang So-an (Zhang Shouan), Sao shu wu fu, qing heyi kan? – "Qingdai yu renqing zhi chongtu" yili (A Case Study of Mourning Garment: The Conflict between Classic Ritual and Human Desire in Late Imperial China), in: Hsiung Ping-chen, Lu Miaw-fen (Xiong Bingzhen, Lü Miaofen) (eds.), *Lijiao yu qingyu: Qian jindai Zhongguo wenhua de houxiandaixing* (Neo-Confucian Orthodoxy and Human Desires: Post-Modernity in Late Imperial Chinese Cul-

ture), Taipei: Institute of Modern History, Academia Sinica, 1999, pp. 125-178.

Chang So-an (Zhang Shouan), *Shiba shiji lixue kaozhong de sixiang huoli: Lijiao lunzheng yu lizhi chongxing* (Debating Neo-Confucian Ritual Orthodoxy: Evidential Studies and the Reconstruction of Social Relations in Eighteenth-Century China), Taipei: Institute of Modern History, Academia Sinica, 2001.

Chen Hengzhe, *Xinzhi gaoji zhongxue jiaokeshu: Xiyang shi* (New High School Textbook: Western History), Shanghai 1924.

Chen Ziang, Deng Youzhou tai ge (A Song of a Gate Tower at Youzhou), in: Kang-hsi ([Emperor] Kangxi) (ed.), *Quan Tang shi* (The Three Hundred Poems of the Tang Dynasty), n.p. 1703, reprint Taipei 1983, vol. 83, pp. 21a-21b.

Chow, Rey, *Woman and Chinese Modernity: The Politics of Reading between West and East*, Minneapolis 1990.

Croll, Elisabeth, *Feminism and Socialism in China*, London 1978.

Croll, Elisabeth, *Women in Rural Development: The People's Republic of China*, Geneva: International Labour Office, 1980.

Croll, Elisabeth, *Chinese Women since Mao*, London 1983.

Croll, Elisabeth, *Changing Patterns of Rural Women's Employment: Production and Reproduction in China*, Geneva: International Labour Office, 1984.

Croll, Elisabeth, *Women and Rural Development in China: Production and Reproduction*, Geneva: International Labour Office, 1985.

Croll, Elisabeth, *Changing Identities of Chinese Women: Rhetoric, Experience and Self-Perception in Twentieth-Century China*, Hong Kong 1995.

Davin, Delia, *Woman-Work: Women and the Party in Revolutionary China*, Oxford 1979.

Davis, Natalie Zemon, "Women's History" in Transition: The European Case, in: Scott 1996, pp. 79-104.

Dikötter, Frank, *Sex, Culture, and Modernity in China: Medical Science and the Construction of Sexual Identities in the Early Republican Period*, London 1995.

Edwards, Louise, *Men and Women in Qing China: Gender in the Red Chamber Dream*, Leiden 1994.

Fairbank, Wilma, *Liang and Lin: Partners in Exploring China's Architectural Past*, Philadelphia 1994.

Furth, Charlotte, *A Flourishing Yin: Gender in China's Medical History, 960-1665*, Berkeley, Los Angeles, London 1999.

Gilmartin, Christina K., *Mobilizing Women: The Early Experiences of the Chinese Communist Party, 1920-1927*, PhD Dissertation, Ann Arbor 1989.

Gilmartin, Christina K., Gail Hershatter, Lisa Rofel, Tyrene White, Introduction, in: Gilmartin et al. 1994, pp. 1-24.

Gilmartin, Christina K., Gail Hershatter, Lisa Rofel, Tyrene White (eds.), *Engendering China: Women, Culture and the State*, Cambridge/MA, London 1994.

Hall, Christine, *Daughters of the Dragon: Women's Lives in Contemporary China*, London 1997.

Hemmel, Vibeke, Pia Sindbjerk, *Women in Rural China: Policy towards Women before and after the Cultural Revolution*, Malmö, London 1984.

Hoe, Susanna, *The Private Life of Old Hong Kong: Western Women in the British Colony, 1841-1941*, Oxford 1991.

Honig, Emily, *Sisters and Strangers: Women in the Shanghai Cotton Mills, 1919-1949*, Stanford 1986.

Honig, Emily, Gail Hershatter, *Personal Voices: Chinese Women in the 1980s*, Stanford 1988.

Hsiung Ping-chen, Constructed Emotions: The Bond between Mothers and Sons in Late Imperial China, in: *Late Imperial China* 15:1 (1994), pp. 87-117.

Hsiung Ping-chen, *Recipes for Planting the Seed and the Cult of Sleeping Alone: A Profile of Male Reproductive Culture in Imperial China*, paper delivered at "The Right to Family Planning, Contraception, and Abortion in Ten World Religions," Religious Consultation on Population, Reproduction Health and Ethics, Sugarloaf Conference Center, Philadelphia, 28 July-1 August 1999.

Hsiung Ping-chen, *Female Gentility in Transition and Transmission: Mother-Daughter Ties in Ming-Ch'ing China*, paper delivered at "Perceptions of Gentility in Chinese Literature and History", University of Durham, Durham, 21-23 March 2002.

Hwa Wei (Hua Wei), Wang Ayling (Wang Ailing) (eds.), *Ming Qing xiqu guoji yantaohui lunwenji* (Anthology of the International Conference on Drama in the Period of Ming Qing), Taipei: Institute of Chinese Literature and Philosophy, Academia Sinica, 1998.

Ishihara Akira, Howard S. Levy, *The Tao of Sex*, Tokyo 1968.

Jen Hung-chun (Ren Hongjuan), Wushi zishu (Self-Narrative at the Age of Fifty), in: Chang Peng-yuan (Zhang Pengyuan), Yang Tsui-hua (Yang Zuihua), Shen Sung-Chiao (Shen Songqiao), Pan Kuang-Je (Pan Guangzhe), *Ren Sun Yidou xiansheng fangwenjilu* (The Reminiscences of Mr. E-Tu Zen Sun), Taipei: Institute of Modern History, Academia Sinica, 1993, pp. 167-188.

Johnson, Kay Ann, *Women, the Family, and Peasant Revolution in China*, Chicago 1983.

Judd, Ellen R., *Gender and Power in Rural North China*, Stanford 1994.

Ko, Dorothy Yin-yee, *Towards a Social History of Women in Seventeenth-Century China*, PhD Dissertation, Stanford 1989.

Ko, Dorothy Yin-yee, Introduction: Gender and the Politics of Chinese History, in: Ko 1994, pp. 1-28.

Ko, Dorothy Yin-yee, *Teachers of the Inner Chamber: Women and Culture in Seventeenth-Century China*, Stanford 1994.

Ko, Dorothy Yin-yee, *Every Step a Lotus: Shoes for Bound Feet*, Berkeley, Los Angeles, London 2001.

Kung, Lydia, *Factory Women in Taiwan*, Ann Arbor 1978.

Lan Hua R., Vanessa L. Fong (eds.), *Women in Republican China: A Sourcebook*, Armonk 1999.

Lee, Ching Kwan, *Gender and the South China Miracle: Two Worlds of Factory Women*, Berkeley, Los Angeles, London 1998.

Lee, James Z., Wang Feng, *One Quarter of Humanity: Malthusian Mythology and Chinese Realities, 1700-2000*, Cambridge/MA 1999.

Lee, Lily Xiao Hong, *The Virtue of Yin: Studies on Chinese Women*, Honolulu 1994.

Liang Congjie (ed.), *Lin Huiyin wenji: Jianzhu juan* (The Anthology of Lin Huiyin: Volume on Architecture), Tianjin 1999.

Lin, Sylvia Li-chun, *The Discursive Formation of the "New" Chinese Women, 1860-1930*, Berkeley, Los Angeles, London 1998.

Liu Kwang-Ching (ed.), *Orthodoxy in Late Imperial China*, Berkeley, Los Angeles, London 1990.

Mann, Susan, *Precious Records: Women in China's Long Eighteenth Century*, Stanford 1997.

Mann, Susan, Cheng Yu-Yin, *Under Confucian Eyes: Writings on Gender in Chinese History*, Berkeley, Los Angeles, London 2001.

McAleavy, Henry, *That Chinese Woman: The Life of Sai-Chin-Hua*, London, New York 1959.

Milwertz, Cecilia Nathansen, *Accepting Population Control: Urban Chinese Women and the One-Child Family Policy*, Richmond, Surrey 1997.

Mohanty, Chandra T., Ann Russo, Lourdes Torres, *Third World Women and the Politics of Feminism*, Bloomington, Indianapolis 1991.

1950 nian de Zhongguo funü (Chinese Women in 1950), ed. by Quanguo minzhu funü lianhehui (All-China Democratic Women's Federation), Beijing 1950.

Offen, Karen, Ruth R. Pierson, Jane Rendall, Introduction, in: Offen et al. 1991, pp. xix-xli.

Offen, Karen, Ruth R. Pierson, Jane Rendall (eds.), *Writing Women's History: International Perspectives*, Bloomington, Indianapolis, Ind. 1991.

Ono Kazuko, *Chinese Women in a Century of Revolution (1850-1950)*, Stanford 1989.

Raphals, Lisa Ann, *Sharing the Light: Representations of Women and Virtue in Early China*, Albany/NY 1998.

Rawski, Evelyn S., *Education and Popular Literacy in Ch'ing China*, Ann Arbor 1979.

Raven, Arlene, *Crossing Over: Feminism and Art of Social Concern*, Ann Arbor 1988.

Riley, Denise, Does a Sex Have a History?, in: Scott 1996, pp. 17-33.

Ruan Fang Fu, *Sex in China: Studies in Sexology in Chinese Culture*, New York, London 1991.

Salaff, Janet W., *Working Daughters of Hong Kong*, Cambridge 1981.

Scott, Joan Wallach, Introduction, in: Scott 1996, pp. 1-13.
Scott, Joan Wallach (ed.), *Feminism and History*, Oxford 1996.
Semergieff, Kathleen B., *The Changing Roles of Women in the People's Republic of China, 1949-1967: With a Case Study of Ting Ling*, Ann Arbor 1982.
Sheridan, Mary, Janet W. Salaff, *Lives: Chinese Working Women*, Bloomington 1984.
Sidel, Ruth, *Women and Child Care in China: A Firsthand Report*, London ^{2}1974 (New York ^{1}1972).
Siu, Bobby, *Women of China: Imperialism and Women's Resistance, 1900-1949*, London 1981.
Smedley, Agnes, *Portraits of Chinese Women in Revolution*, Old Westbury/NY 1976.
Snow, Helen Foster, *Women in Modern China*, The Hague, Paris 1967.
Sommer, Matthew H., Dangerous Males, Vulnerable Males, and Polluted Males: The Regulation of Masculinity in Qing Dynasty Law, in: Susan Brownell, Jeffrey N. Wasserstrom (eds.), *Chinese Femininities/Chinese Masculinities: A Reader*, Berkeley, Los Angeles, London 2002, pp. 67-88.
Spivak, Gayatry C., *In Other Worlds: Essays in Cultural Politics*, London, New York 1987.
Spence, Jonathan D., *The Death of Woman Wang*, New York 1978.
Tai Chen (Dai Zhen), *Mengzi ziyi shuzheng* (Commentary on the Works of Mencius), n.p. 1774, reprint Taipei 1978.
Tuan Yu-Ts'ai (Duan Yucai), *Dai Dongyuan (Zhen) xiansheng nianpu* (The Biography of Dai [Zhen] Dongyuan), Hong Kong 1971.
T'ien Ju-k'ang, *Male Anxiety and Female Chastity: A Comparative Study of Ethical Values in Ming-Ch'ing Times*, Leiden 1988.
Tsung Fan Shiu-Kuen, *Moms, Nuns and Hookers: Extrafamilial Alternatives for Village Women in Taiwan*, PhD Dissertation, Ann Arbor 1978.
Wang Ping, *Aching for Beauty: Footbinding in China*, Minneapolis 2000.
Wang Zheng, *Women in the Chinese Enlightenment: Oral and Textual Histories*, Berkeley, Los Angeles, London 1999.

Watson, Rubie S., Patricia Buckley Ebrey (eds.), *Marriage and Inequality in Chinese Society*, Berkeley 1991.
Wei, Karen T., *Women in China: A Selected and Annotated Bibliography*, Westport/CT 1984.
Widmer, Ellen, Introduction, in: Widmer/Sun Chang Kang-i 1997, pp. 1-14.
Widmer, Ellen, Sun Chang Kang-i (eds.), *Writing Women in Late Imperial China*, Stanford 1997.
Wile, Douglas, *Art of the Bedchamber: The Chinese Sexual Yoga Classics Including Women's Solo Meditation Texts*, Albany/NY 1992.
Wolf, Margery, *The House of Lim: A Study of a Chinese Farm Family*, New York 1968.
Wolf, Margery, *China and Gendered Anthropology: Some Notes Toward Integration*, Durham: Asian/Pacific Studies Institute, Duke University, 1985a.
Wolf, Margery, *Revolution Postponed: Women in Contemporary China*, Stanford 1985b.
Wolf, Margery, Roxane Witke (eds.), *Women in Chinese Society*, Stanford 1975.
Yang Pu-wei (Yang Buwei), *Yige nüren de zizhuan* (Autobiography of a Woman), Taipei 1967.
Yü Chün-fang, Kuan-yin: *The Chinese Transformation of Avalokitesvara*, New York 1983.
Zhong Xueping, Wang Zheng, Bai Di (eds.), *Some of Us: Chinese Women Growing Up in the Mao Era*, New Brunswick/NJ 2001.
Zhong Xueping, Masculinity Besieged? Issues of Modernity and Male Subjectivity in Chinese Literature of the Late Twentieth Century, Durham, London 2000.
Zurndorfer, Harriet T. (ed.), *Chinese Women in the Imperial Past: New Perspectives*, Leiden 1999.

The Paradox of Autonomy: Nation, Revolution, and Women through the Chinese Looking Glass

Wen-hsin Yeh

In the early 1980s, after nearly three decades of centralized state planning and socialist management, the Chinese economy underwent significant changes as it diversified forms of ownership and reoriented itself towards market incentives. Prostitutes appeared again on Chinese streets after a hiatus of decades (Pang Ruiyin et al. 1989:1-67). Gender displaced class as the main category in the discussion of social differences among the people. The All-China Women's Federation (*Quangguo funü lianhehui*), a mass organization under the Chinese Communist Party (CCP), reorganized branch offices and set up research institutions at various locations both to represent women's interest and to collect materials that reflect women's condition. A growing number of writers and researchers, women of urban educated background, began publishing on the subject of Chinese women. This new development did not escape the attention of Western scholars of modern China. A decade later an active field emerged and the study of women attained growing prominence as a subject in the field of modern Chinese history.

This cross-cultural discussion of Chinese women, as it cuts across the discursive boundaries fashioned in the context of national traditions, encompasses divergent approaches over issues and agenda. Many Western scholars of China have steadfastly resisted the liberal bias in media presentations that used women to encode the authoritarian backwardness in Communist China: the abduction and sale of rural women into prostitution, the forced implementation of the one-child policy, the high rate of female infanticide, the abuse of young mothers who gave birth to girls rather than boys, the revival of feudal customs in the countryside, and the like. Gender identities and issues of subjectivity – forms of self-understanding that define modernity – nonetheless remain central in scholarly examinations of the condition of the Chinese women. Much scholarly energy has gone not only into a search for women's agency but also into the narration of a gendered and contested history of modern China (Gilmartin et al. 1994). Endeavors along those lines are, in comparison, by and large missing in Chinese historical works.

Chinese researchers in China, in contrast, found themselves embroiled in a debate in the early 1980s over whether it was legitimate to engage in "women's studies" in a Marxist context. It was the Communist Party's long-standing claim that socialism had either eliminated the injustice of gender inequity or redefined its intractability. It was the reopening of the market in the reform era that had occasioned the reintroduction of some of the old problems (Li Xiaojiang et al. 1997:346-360). No wholesale borrowing of Western theories in feminist studies, then, would apply. Interpretive descriptions of women's conditions in China need to begin with a better appreciation of the country's recent history and a deeper understanding of the role of the socialist state and its policies.

Unlike the capitalist West, where women find themselves in an overly sexualized relationship that is at the same time unequal, Chinese women have been liberated by decades of socialism and have attained structural equality with men. This equality, however, is predicated upon a unisex approach that does not sufficiently address the differences between men and women. The challenge facing Chinese women, if we follow this line of argument, was thus not to demolish a gendered inequality that did not exist, but to seek recognition of women as separate and distinct in accordance with their endowed biological quality.

It was the Women's Federation that had represented Chinese women under socialism. This was also the entity that had been the sole beneficiary of Party-state support in terms of resources and opportunities. But who would or should rightfully speak for women in China's reform era? Did the problems confronting Chinese women stem from their conditions under socialism? Or did women have more to fear from the newly emergent market forces? Was there any theory beyond Marxism-Leninism, propagated and upheld by the Federation that should guide such discussions? Or should the women researchers in provincial universities be allowed to form their own networks and pursue their own agenda? Whether the issues pertained to the problems that women faced or the organizations that claimed to represent their best, two themes were prominent in this cross-cultural discussion: the role of the state versus the market, and the comparison between desexualized equality versus gendered hierarchy.

Women or Nation?

It is a belief long held by the CCP that its version of socialist revolution has liberated Chinese women from feudal authority and brought them social equality. Chairman Mao was famously known to have stated, as early as 1927, that Chinese women had been oppressed by the combined power of state, religion, lineage, and patriarchy (Mao Zedong 1991, 1:31-34). Shortly after taking power in 1949, the new Communist Government issued its version of Marriage Law and banned polygamy, concubinage, and the sale of women. It outlawed marriage without the consent of the partners and granted women their right to sue for divorce. Women were also granted their right to property and inheritance and guaranteed equal treatment at employment, including equal pay for equal work. Other legislations were adopted in the mid-1950s, entitling women to childcare facilities and maternity leave and giving them limited access to abortion and contraceptives (White 1994; Woo 1994).

Much in the Communists' Marriage Law was in fact comparable to what the Nationalist Government had spelled out in its Marriage Law in the 1930s (Glosser 2003:167-195; Diamont 2000). The two laws, bridging the 1949 divide, shared a common goal to place all men and women directly under the law of the state instead of the authority of the clan or the lineage. Women were further liberated, in that sense, in the late 1950s when the CCP pursued a policy of socialization of private enterprises and pushed the rural collectivization campaign to a high gear. Millions of rural women were brought out of their homes and organized into production brigades in the local communes (Johnson 1983). These women, like their urban counterparts in the factories, were assigned work along with men.

They were compensated, as men did, on the basis of the work points they earned. They were, furthermore, lauded for their contribution to socialist construction as well as stepping beyond the bounds of traditional womanhood. During the height of the collectivization, private kitchens were shut down and families ate in communal dining halls. Communes organized communal childcare that further spared women from household chores and enabled them to work in the field. As a result of collectivization, an estimated 70-80 percent of rural women eventually worked outside their homes for nearly half the time during the year. This massive participation by women in agricultural campaigns in the late 1950s liberated women from the routines of the households and loosened the grip of patriarchal authority. During the Cultural Revolution, women were told that they held up half the sky. Propaganda campaigns lauded as exemplary women workers who took on jobs conventionally held by males, such as working as the operators of tractor machines. This process of state-orchestrated socialization broadened the exposure of rural women to communal society and eventually prepared them for cadre responsibilities at the local level.

The 1950s were thus a time of momentous changes in the lives of a vast number of Chinese women. But these changes were open to a different understanding. Poster images of liberated women, like all propaganda propositions, too often depicted fiction rather than reality. Collectivization measures had not been launched with the emancipation of women as their primary goals. Nor did they seek to challenge the sex biases embedded in the social practices of peasant families. Such bias continued to kill on a gender-specific basis. More girls than boys were allowed to die, for example, of malnutrition during the famine that followed the Great Leap Forward. In the reform era state enforcement of the one-child policy was performed ultimately on female bodies rather than male ones. Whatever feminist vision there was in the early Chinese Communist movement, the Party, on its way to power, had abandoned urban women in favor of rural men who controlled the countryside (Stacey 1983; Wolf 1989).

We may agree or disagree over the assessment of women's gains and losses in the first three decades under the rule of the CCP.

What seems notable is how this discussion, in the final analysis, has turned, wittingly or unwittingly, on an evaluation of the effect of CCP policies. Socialist women in China have had their share of progress and autonomy, some Chinese scholars have argued, whether this had come in forms readily recognized by women in capitalist society. Subtly but significantly, this insistence on autonomy thus turns a conversation on "women" into a dialogue over the contrastive features between socialist states and capitalist societies.

During the reform era women in China confronted circumstances engendered by uncertain market forces. Chinese researchers, drawing on their surveys and interviews in the field, reported that there had been an all-out feminization of the Chinese agrarian economy, which was happening especially in industrializing areas (Li Xiaojiang et al. 1997:171-186). In a scenario reminiscent of the Taiwanese countryside in the 1960s, large numbers of able-bodied men have migrated out to take up employment in industrial enterprises and construction sites either in the towns or in the cities. In the absence of their men, women stepped in to fill positions thus left vacant, and became the mainstay of agrarian labor force and de facto heads of households. This, then, represented both an upgrading and a further integration of women into a larger work force outside the home.

Unmarried women in the villages, meanwhile, were just as likely to join the outflow of rural labor force as able-bodied men were. Women workers constituted, for example, majority work force in export processing industries in the Special Economic Zones in the southeastern coast (Lee Ching Kwan 1998). In the outskirts of a fast-growing metropolis such as Shanghai, women launched businesses and ran township enterprises located inside the industrializing villages as their men went off to places as far away as Hong Kong, Japan, and Australia (Li Xiaojiang et al. 1997:187-204). On the peripheries of Beijing, the 1990s witnessed the transformation of dusty dirt-packed villages into bustling red-brick townships within the span of less than a decade, thanks to a "one family, two systems" division of labor between husbands and wives. In case after case the resident husbands, as township Communist cadres, mobilized their administrative resources and networks to control the labor and promote the products manufactured under the supervision of their enterprising wives. The latter, in turn, combined their chores as housewives with that of private entrepreneurs, employing teenage workers from even poorer districts to manufacture in garage-shop condition handbags and suitcases. In some spectacular cases of success, these home-made products, built on images copied off television screens and measured according to specifications transmitted via the internet, garnered tens of thousands of *yuan* in profits and fulfilled export orders destined for markets as far away as Eastern Europe, Russia, and Korea (Yeh 2002). This contrasted sharply with the conditions elsewhere in North China, where the economy had lagged and women were asked once again to go home while their husbands and sons sought work (Woo 2002:308-329; Jacka 1997).

The benefits of the economic reform were thus substantial. They were also undeniably uneven. A second effect of the market orientation was thus regional disparity in economic conditions that situated the "Chinese women" in varying conditions. It was the discipline and the imperatives of the socialist state that had produced, through institutional mechanisms and administrative actions, the uniformity of the "Chinese women." In the reform era this uniformity has now been fragmented by the divergence in market opportunities and social prospects. The irony here is that just as the Party is trying to set aside the whole notion of "class," class distinctions have become perhaps more pronounced than ever before (Lu Xueyi 2002). This disparity is too often masked, in Chinese writings, as regional differences that presumably would resolve themselves as reform policies deepen the effects on Chinese society. Those who have embraced the reform are thus able to describe the changes at a place like Beijing as a picture of China's future.

Surveys conducted by the Women's Federation show that in Beijing, the reform has brought enormous improvement to the status of women. Beijing parents now value daughters and sons alike. Married couples often choose to live close to the wife's parents rather than the husband's. Couples share decision-making in finance and children, and a growing number of young husbands share housework and child-care while their wives, often just as well educated, hold jobs outside the home (Li Xiaojiang et al. 1997:221-243). The proactive state, meanwhile, has legislated that all private enterprises provide childcare and maternity leave, which are believed to benefit working women. "Socialism with Chinese characteristics" and its market economy, in short, have not only sustained the socialist equality between men and women, but have also given gender-specific recognition to women's role as mothers.

But the rosy picture offered by the Women's Federation contains not only an urban bias but also an age or generation restriction. Nearly one third of Chinese women born in the 1950s and 1960s are illiterate, and have been trapped in stagnant conditions for decades. These are peasant women in poor areas, who live among illiterate family members and work in conditions that require little literacy. The de-collectivization of agriculture has returned them firmly to the control of their husbands at home (ibid. 205-221). Domestic violence and abusive cadres seem to be the norm rather than the exception. Few have, statistically, opted even for prostitution, which appeared to be pursued mainly by middle school educated women of younger generations from better located towns, driven to search for a different way of life elsewhere (ibid. 262-297). The reform has done little to ameliorate the condition of tens of millions of women in China's interior. It has, in fact, left them even more vulnerable to the unregulated forces of the liberalized economy and patriarchal authority.

Those who insist that Chinese women, or at least some of them, had made substantial gains during the reform era were thus again addressing the subject of the action of the Party-state rather than that of women. Whether with policies of socialist planning or market capitalism, the Communist Party-state in China is seen to have prepared Chinese women to hold their ground. In the 1995 Fourth World Conference on Women, Chinese delegates acceded to the wish of the state to glorify the status of Chinese women rather than to present their lists of identified problems. Discussions of women in China in the international arena, in that regard, have become less a cross-cultural dialogue concerning "women" as they are exchanges on women as products of the Chinese "nation."

Women or Revolution?

In the 1990s, with the gathering momentum of the Pudong Project and the physical reconstruction of the city, Shanghai emerged, once again, as a metropolis of maritime connections and global consumerism. Overseas capital poured in and a combination of cranes, bulldozers, and spotlights transformed the city into a seething construction site. By the mid-decade over two thousand new high-rise buildings had arisen. Like a ridge of skyscrapers, this chain of concrete and glass encircled the old foreign concessions of the Republican period, transforming the skyline and redefining the topography as it reconfigured the human flow on the ground.

Nostalgia took hold, meanwhile, just as the old city was receding relentlessly into the past. In printed pages as well as in advertised images, in literary journals as well as on roadside billboards, the "Old Shanghai" of the 1930s returned with the full force of its presumed charm and glamour. Poster images abound, beaming the smiles of young women fashioned in understated sexuality and pampered materiality. What was once denounced in Republican period left-wing campaigns as comprador-bourgeois decadence had now become, thanks to the passage of time, the tamed past of a prospering city that had stepped out of the shadow of its own history (Yeh 2001:3-7). It was in this context that a group of Chinese women historians turned their attention to Republican Shanghai in the first half of the twentieth century, and focused their attention on women who had lived through that earlier time.

What they show, first of all, is that Chinese women, with impressive facility, were gaining access to higher education and modern professions at the beginning of the century, doing so virtually at the same time along with Chinese men. This was accomplished on the women's own initiatives, while receiving the blessing of an enlightened elite. There was, in other words, a remarkable openness among traditional Chinese elite to progressive ideas and women's rights (Luo Suwen 1996; Wang Zheng 1999). This reading of the "feudal" order of traditional Shanghai contrasts sharply with what the

Communists of an earlier time have been denouncing as characteristic of that elite.

But the centerpiece of this revisionist historiography is the bourgeois nuclear family in the 1930s, which emerged in Shanghai under the watch of British and French colonial authorities. These nuclear families were the home of middle-class women of taste and education, who were the true mistresses of their private domain. Unlike their mothers, these women had bobbed hair and put on high heels, make-up, and Western-style clothing. They had chosen their own husbands and now cared for their children. Away from the control of their in-laws and extended lineage in the countryside, they led a life of leisure and autonomy, and were able to patronize theaters and shops in the company of female friends (Luo Suwen 2001; Yeh 1995, 1997; Glosser 2003). The city, with its department stores and charitable societies, was their city. The public space of old Shanghai was both pleasurable and safely feminine for these women who were their own mistresses.

There were, of course, problems with a gendered division of labor, and the discrimination of women at the workplace. Chinese women historians, in an unabashed affirmation of the bourgeois life style, often chose, however, to overlook these points. What they focused upon, instead, were matters such as the availability of disposable leisure and personal space, and a distinct style of being feminine. "Modernity" in this sense meant a service industry that attended to the daily needs of the household, plus conveniences that would spare the housewife the drudgery of work around the house. Middle-class homes, in these writings, became havens of privacy and tranquility. This image held a particular appeal to urban residents in the 1990s, who had to make do with congested living quarters and to share intimate moments on park benches after sunset.

The unalloyed admiration of bourgeois family might strike some as conservative and conventional. But what it performed, in the context of the political history of the 1990s, was a veiled critique of the entrenched Party line.

Beginning in the 1930s, against the backdrop of global economic depression, a left-wing discourse emerged, in which bourgeois family was simply declared to be an institution doomed to perish (Yeh 1992). No family unit, according to the left wing, could possibly survive either the attack of the Japanese on China, or escape the effect of economic exploitation by Western imperialism. Middle-class men must thus set aside their career goals for personal advancement, and join the struggle for national survival. They should prepare to sacrifice themselves for the Party, displaying "feminine" virtues of self-denial and dedication. Middle-class women, who had been represented as dependent on their men, were urged, on the other hand, to leave the comfort of their homes and join the national salvation movement, attaining self-reliance by becoming a woman warrior (Pickowicz 2000). By the 1940s, two stereotypes have taken hold. Women with bobbed hair, make-up, silk gowns and high heels were coded as the mistresses of collaborators, speculators, corrupt officials, and reactionaries of other sorts. Those with short hair, cloth shoes, clean face and military uniform, meanwhile, were coded as patriotic fighters who stood by their male comrades. Romance and family had no place in the lives of these women, who were dedicated to the nation and the revolution. A distinct shift took place, separating the sexually charged bourgeois women of the 1930s from the desexualized guerilla fighters of the following decade. Women activists of the 1940s rallied around the slogan, "Our real enemies are the Japanese invaders and not the Chinese men in our lives who share our fate." Certain equality was achieved, one may say, in the representation of men and women in the militarized atmosphere of the War of Resistance. This was, however, orchestrated by a revolutionary party, which then proceeded to break up the family units and reconstitute men and women alike into members of a socialist system under the paternalistic watch of the Party-state in the 1950s.

    The aspiration for bourgeois women and their middle-class life style in the 1990s, seen against this past, represented a major departure from a clichéd Party line. In its affirmation of domesticity and femininity, revisionist historians sought to undo the Party's politicization of personal space in the past half century. They sought to redefine the terms of the good life by placing women in the context of a market economy of accumulation and consumption. By doing so – and by stressing the market rather than the statist dimension of the reformed Party line – these researchers rejected the Party's earlier treatment of women as primary objects of political campaigns of mobilization.

One may well wish to raise questions about this revisionist reading of middle-class women. It is problematic, for instance, to see the representations of these women in contemporary journals of the 1930s as images of reality, rather than the products of a commercialized print media designed to help sell certain goods. It is also problematic to overlook the cultural dynamics that were fashioning Shanghai's middle-class men, who had sought a new sense of manhood vis-à-vis their fathers in the provinces, and had supported their women in a joint pursuit of new life (Yeh 1997).

Those who urged Chinese women scholars to adopt a more critical stance towards Westernized bourgeois value often found themselves, nonetheless, answered with bemused tolerance. The idea was unappealing less because it lacked merit, but because it seemed like a dead end in modern Chinese political history. Attack on bourgeois femininity was reminiscent of the clichéd rhetoric of the CCP at an early point in the past century. Early feminist agenda, thus understood, had not only been appropriated by the Party, but had also been subverted by it in subsequent decades. The history of the CCP yields the insight that revolution does not always lead to emancipation. If history offers any lesson at all, Chinese women scholars of the 1990s seemed to be saying, one might be better off by simply pursuing an alternative course of action that started with an unabashed enamor with the privacy and sanctity of feminine domesticity.

What have appeared to be historical projects on Republican Shanghai women then turned out to be just as much reflections on the history of the Chinese Communist revolution.

The Paradox of Autonomy

In the Jiangnan region in the 1870s, there were charitable homes for widows from impoverished gentry families. Acceptance into these homes entailed the acceptance of certain rules. Among them, there were rules restricting the freedom to leave, to travel unaccompanied, or to spend a night away. Visiting activities were similarly restricted. A woman might receive her mother or mother-in-law in her chambers twice a month. All other visitors were to be turned away, including sons over the age of thirteen, who must only speak with their widowed mothers from the distance of the middle courtyard on the other side of the inner gate. All other male visitors must remain on the other side of the second gate that was at least forty feet away. These rules were adopted, incidentally, to help prevent the abduction of marriageable widows. There was a bridal price attached to such women in the marriage market. Widows from gentry households, so the reasoning went, needed the protection of such charitable establishments to safeguard themselves from the unscrupulous who might otherwise sell them for a price.

From a start like that in the 1870s, Chinese women have come a long way over the course of the next hundred years. Late nineteenth-century impetus for change often came not from women but from men. Compelled by a sense of national crisis and mindful of the practices in other countries, elite reformers conjured up the "Chinese women" and gave them a new role in the newly fashioned Chinese nation (Judge 2002). Women activists who had contributed to this message, for their part, by and large did not seek a clear separation between a concern for the status of women and a desire to help the Chinese nation. A group of women activists stunned the nation in 1913 when they resorted to the use of force in the National Assembly to demand voting rights for women. But by and large women did not seek to reset the reform agenda for women.

Over the course of the Republican decades women have, meanwhile, become increasingly visible in the public space. These "women in public," whether by virtue or transgression, gained visibility either in representation or in person as writers, students, workers, soldiers, professionals, courtesans, socialites, or prostitutes. A large number of women, under a variety of circumstances, became involved in historical moments of national importance. At least 1.6 million women joined the women's bureau and the peasant bureau of the Northern Expedition Army during the Nationalist revolution of 1927 (Gilmartin 1995). Before the massive mobilization of peasant women for agricultural work in the late 1950s, numerous others before them had already had a taste of a semi-military existence as they joined the campaigns for resistance during the war against Japan.

Did women, then, have their Chinese revolution? Recent scholarship from China, whether in an effort to look backward in time or outward towards other societies, has consistently insisted upon the increasing autonomy enjoyed by Chinese women over the course of China's twentieth century.

But there is a paradox to this autonomy. First, for outsiders looking in, China's modern history of Communist rule has turned the Chinese situation into a kind of looking glass with a mirror effect, in which the relative positioning of the "left" and the "right" has been transposed and reversed. A seemingly old-fashioned liberal conservative affirmation of the bourgeois nuclear family, with its material comfort and feminine aspirations, functions contextually in fact as an emancipating position as it is set against a state-sponsored ideology of revolution and liberation. Similarly, in discussions about the condition of Chinese women, a seemingly progressive socialist position turns out to serve a nationalist agenda after all, especially when situated within the context of an international dialogue.

Thanks to the work of women writers, historians, and social science researchers, gender has become an important area in post-Mao theoretical reformulation of a number of issues, including the nature of Chinese modernity and the possibility for civil society. It has stimulated research into earlier periods in Chinese culture and history. It has provided an avenue for a reevaluation of traditional Chinese society. It has opened up the field of Chinese studies for comparative studies, for example, with post-socialist transformation in Eastern European countries (Gal/Kligman 2000).

But with national culture and revolutionary legacy as the issues that framed the subtext, the paradox of autonomy operates in yet another sense. It was discursively imperative that Chinese scholars paint a positive picture when writing about the bourgeois episode in Republican Shanghai. This is because a negative assessment of what they uncover would have placed their work in the tradition of decades of well-rehearsed Communist tracts produced by the Party's ideologues. Similarly, it was also discursively imperative that Chinese scholars insist on Chinese women's gains when writing about their lives under socialism. A negative assessment would have placed their writings in the company of the large body of Orientalist or liberal critique of the authoritarianism and backwardness of Communist regime and Chinese society. The autonomy in this regard is thus the outcome of a historical logic of entrapment. It was out of a desire to escape the clichéd and predictable past either in the Orientalist or the revolutionary discourse that Chinese writers insist upon the themes of autonomy. Yet this very insistence on autonomy seems just as much the product of the discursive dynamics that have restricted their options in the first place.

References

Chen Xiaomei, Growing Up with Posters in the Maoist Era, in: Harriet Evans, Stephanie Donald (eds.), *Picturing Power in the People's Republic of China: Posters of the Cultural Revolution*, Lanham 1999, pp. 101-122.

Chen Xiaomei, *Acting the Right Part: Political Theater and Popular Drama in Contemporary China*, Honolulu 2002.

Chow Hsu-chi, *1910-1920 niandai duhui xin funü shenghuo fengmao: Yi Funü zazhi wei fenxi shili* (Life Style of Urban New Women in the 1910s and 1920s: A Case Analysis Based on The Ladies' Journal), Taipei 1996.

Chow, Rey, *Woman and Chinese Modernity: The Politics of Reading between West and East*, Minneapolis 1991.

Clements, Barbara Evans, *Bolshevik Women*, Cambridge, New York, Melbourne 1997.

Croll, Elizabeth, *Chinese Women since Mao*, Armonk 1983.

Diamont, Neil, *Revolutionizing the Family: Politics, Love, and Divorce in Urban and Rural China, 1949-1968*, Berkeley 2000.

Gal, Susan, Gail Kligman, *The Politics of Gender after Socialism*, Princeton 2000.

Gilmartin, Christina K., *Engendering the Chinese Revolution: Radical Women, Communist Politics, and Mass Movement in the 1920s*, Berkeley, Los Angeles, London 1995.

Gilmartin, Christina K., Gail Hershatter, Lisa Rofel, Tyrene White (eds.), *Engendering China: Women, Culture, and the State*, Cambridge/MA, London 1994.

Glosser, Susan, *Chinese Visions of Family and State, 1915-1953*, Berkeley 2003.

Goldman, Merle, Elizabeth J. Perry (eds.), *Changing Meanings of Citizenship in Modern China*, Cambridge/MA 2002.

Hershatter, Gail, *Dangerous Pleasures: Prostitution and Modernity in Twentieth Century Shanghai*, Berkeley 1997.

Hershatter, Gail, Emily Honig, Susan Mann, Lisa Rofel (comps./eds.), *Guide to Women's Studies in China*, Berkeley 1998.

Honig, Emily, Gail Hershatter, *Personal Voices: Chinese Women in the 1980s*, Stanford 1988.

Jacka, Tamara, *Women's Work in Rural China: Change and Continuity in an Era of Reform*, Cambridge, New York, Melbourne 1997.

Johnson, Kay Ann, *Women, the Family, and Peasant Revolution in China*, Chicago 1983.

Judd, Ellen, *Gender and Power in Rural North China*, Stanford 1994.

Judge, Joan, Citizens or Mothers of Citizens: Gender and the Meaning of Modern Chinese Citizenship, in: Goldman/Perry 2002, pp. 23-43.

Kerber, Linda K., *Toward an Intellectual History of Women*, Chapel Hill, London 1997.

Landes, Joan B., *Women and the Public Sphere in the Age of the French Revolution*, Ithaca, London 1988.

Lee Ching Kwan, *Gender and the South China Miracle: Two Worlds of Factory Women*, Berkeley 1998.

Lee, Leo Ou-fan, *Shanghai Modern: The Flowering of a New Urban Culture in China, 1930-1945*, Cambridge/MA 1999.

Li Xiaojiang, Zhu Hong, Dong Xiuyu (eds.), *Pingdeng yu fazhan* (Equality and Progression), Beijing 1997.

Lu Xueyi (ed.), *Dangdai Zhongguo shehui jieceng yanjiu baogao* (Contemporary Chinese Social Stratifications: A Research Report), Beijing 2002.

Luo Suwen, *Da Shanghai: Shikumen, xunchang renjia* (Greater Shanghai: Ordinary Households behind the Rectangular Gates of Stone), Shanghai 1991.
Luo Suwen, *Nüxing yu jindai Zhongguo shehui* (Females and Modern Chinese Society), Shanghai 1996.
Luo Suwen, Dushi wenhua de shangyehua yu nüxing shehui xingxiang (The Commercialization of Urban Culture and the Social Images of the Female), in: Yeh Wen-hsin (ed.), *Shanghai bainian fenghua* (A Century of Shanghai Glamour), Taipei 2001, pp. 55-110.
Mann, Susan, The Cult of Domesticity in Republican Shanghai's Middle Class, in: *Jindai Zhongguo funü shi yanjiu* 2 (1994), pp. 179-201.
Mao Zedong, *Mao Zedong xuanji* (Mao Zedong: Selected Works), 4 vols., Beijing 1991.
Ono Kazuko, *Chinese Women in a Century of Revolution, 1850-1950*, Stanford 1989.
Pang Ruiyin, Li You, Lu Xingsheng, He Jianhua, Zhang Lifen, Gao Xiaoyan, Xiang Ya, *Zhongguo changji xinsheng dai* (A New Generation of Chinese Prostitutes), Hong Kong 1989.
Pickowicz, Paul, Victory as Defeat: Postwar Visualizations of China's War of Resistance, in: Yeh, Wen-hsin (ed.), *Becoming Chinese: Passages to Modernity and Beyond*, Berkeley 2000, pp. 365-398.
Rofel, Lisa, *Other Modernities: Gendered Yearnings in China after Socialism*, Berkeley 1999.
Scott, Joan, *Gender and the Politics of History*, New York 1988.
Scott, Joan Wallach, *Only Paradoxes to Offer: French Feminists and the Rights of Man*, Cambridge/MA 1996.
Stacey, Judith, *Patriarchy and Socialist Revolution in China*, Berkeley 1983.
Stranahan, Patricia, *Yan'an Women and the Communist Party*, Berkeley 1983.
Wang Zheng, *Women in the Chinese Enlightenment: Oral and Textual Histories*, Berkeley, Los Angeles, California 1999.
White, Tyrene, The Origins of China's Birth Planning Policy, in: Gilmartin et al. 1994, pp. 250-278.

Wolf, Margery, *Revolution Postponed: Women in Contemporary China*, Stanford 1989.

Woo, Margaret Y.K., Chinese Women Workers: The Delicate Balance between Protection and Equality, in: Gilmartin et al. 1994, pp. 279-295.

Woo, Margaret Y.K., Law and the Gendered Citizen, in: Goldman/Perry 2002, pp. 308-329.

Yang Dali, *Calamity and Reform in China: State, Rural Society, and Institutional Change since the Great Leap Famine*, Stanford 1996.

Yeh, Catherine Vance, Creating the Urban Beauty: The Shanghai Courtesan in Late Qing Illustrations, in: Judith Zeitlin, Lydia Liu, Ellen Widmer (eds.), *Writing and Materiality in China*, Cambridge/MA 2003, pp. 397-447.

Yeh, Wen-hsin, Progressive Journalism and Shanghai's Petty Urbanites: Zou Taofen and the Shenghuo Enterprise, in: Frederic Wakeman, Wen-hsin Yeh (eds.), *Shanghai Sojourners*, Berkeley 1992, pp. 186-238.

Yeh, Wen-hsin, Corporate Space, Communal Time: Everyday Life in Shanghai's Bank of China, in: *American Historical Review* 100:1 (1995), pp. 97-122.

Yeh, Wen-hsin, Shanghai Modernity: Commerce and Culture in a Republican City, in: *The China Quarterly* 150 (1997), pp. 375-394.

Yeh Wen-hsin (ed.), *Shanghai bainian fenghua* (Shanghai: One Hundred Years of Glamour), Taipei 2001.

Yeh Wen-hsin, Field Trip to Baigou, Hebei, unpublished notes, July 2002.

Women's, Gender and Mainstream Studies on Republican China: Problems in Theory and Research

Mechthild Leutner

In the past three decades women's and gender studies have considerably strengthened their position within and outside China. In this respect, the struggle to establish the field on its own has been successful. Yet, at the same time, it must be stressed that women's and gender studies still essentially exist only as a part of Chinese studies and as an independent supplement to so-called mainstream Chinese studies. This situation is connected with different methodological approaches: one which supports the establishment of women's studies as an independent, albeit interdisciplinary discipline, and another which supports changes within disciplines from an overall gender perspective (see Eichler 1995:305). Moreover, some scholars might practically argue that not enough research has been done yet on women themselves, and therefore, our first task at the moment is still primarily to focus on women, their status, and their position in the family, in society, in the military, in political circles and religious associations and, in this way, to promote and encourage women's studies; later, we can discuss the question of engendering the whole period. In my view, however, we should not only concentrate on women's and gender studies, but at the same time also make an effort to engender the history of the Republican period or Chinese history in general in every aspect. This means that every historical analysis should consider the male and the female factor equally and take gender relations into account as a possible driving force of history (Perrot 1989:25). Or, to put it another way, the "dynamics of social gender relations and their regulation within a society is part of the universal/general historical process" and need to be studied as such (Wunder

---

This essay was already published in an earlier version in the Taiwanese journal *Jindai Zhongguo funüshi yanjiu (Research on Women in Modern Chinese History)* 10 (December 2002), pp. 117-145.

1992:132). Such a call for engendering was made by feminist studies already in the early 1980s, but so far we have not been able to develop a practical strategy for doing this. Thus, in practical research, only a few studies (generally written by female academics who concentrate on women's and gender studies) have engendered certain periods or aspects of Republican history. But they have hardly had any effect on the so-called mainstream study and research of the Republican period, that is, on the whole picture of the Republican period which still predominates the field.

So my first question is why hardly any or only a very slow integration of the findings from women's history studies into non-gendered "mainstream" studies on the Republican period has taken place. My second question is how we can further promote women's and gender history studies and at the same time develop strategies to engender the whole history, that is, using the gender category as we use other central concepts, such as class, to study Chinese Republican history.[1] I would like, from a very practical point of view, to make some observations on three points:

1. I will briefly outline the development of women's and gender history which deals with the Republican period: the dominant methodological approaches, paradigms, and its academic institutionalization.
2. I will discuss five reasons for the non-integration of women's and gender studies and "mainstream history" and point out possible strategies for overcoming the marginalization of women's and gender studies and for promoting the integration of the gender perspective in Republican history studies in general.

---

[1] I will not enter into the ongoing theoretical debates concerning gender and I will not argue why I do not agree with Judith Butler and a poststructural approach questioning the practicability and usefulness of the category "gender." Moreover, I will not be able to plunge into the debates on postmodernism and feminism, on the "linguistic turn" and the "cultural turn" or on recently made calls for a materialist feminism. In this essay I use the terms "women" and "gender" not from a postmodern and cultural perspective but from a perspective of feminist historical materialism, which takes gender as a hierarchical social division between women and men rather than simply a cultural distinction (Delphy 1993). See also Jackson 2001:285 who follows the arguments made by Delphy 1993.

3. I will present two examples to show how women and gender are depicted in mainstream studies.

The Development of Women's and Gender History Dealing with the Republican Period

Three distinct periods can be identified:

First: The Period of Feminist Socialism in the 1970s

This period was influenced by the new feminist movement in the West, which brought the contemporary situation of Chinese women, their historical process of liberation from the traditional patriarchal family and society into the focus of Western female scholars. The Western women's movement and studies on Chinese women were therefore closely interrelated. These studies were connected with the then prevalent perception of the liberation of Chinese women as a model for Western women[2] – parallel to the perception of Maoist China as a model for socialism and revolution in the West and in the Third World. Embedded in the whole process of socialist revolution, women's history was depicted as an integral part of the emancipation movement in modern China. Theoretically and methodologically, Chinese women's studies were closely connected with critical theory and an approach influenced by Marxist and Maoist theories. The dominant approach can be described as compensatory and contributory, that is, women were "discovered" as historical subjects and objects and added – at that time – mostly to political history, and their role as actors in history and their significant contribution to revolutionary history and the liberation process were

---

[2] The history of how Chinese women have been perceived in European travel books and European writings on China in general since the time of Marco Polo is in itself complex, ranging from very positive images to the construction of very negative images. One of the most prevalent aspects regarding the perception of Chinese women since the times of the Jesuits (sixteenth century) is the role of women as victims which certainly also had a great influence on scholarly approaches (see Leutner 1999:79-95, which depicts the changing and sometimes contradictory images of Chinese women in Europe since the times of Marco Polo).

highlighted.³ Examples of this kind of approach were "pioneering monographs related to a gender analysis of the Chinese Communist Party's march to power" (Gilmartin 1995:233), such as Elisabeth Croll's *Feminism and Socialism in China* (1978), Delia Davin's *Woman-Work: Women and the Party in Revolutionary China* (1976) and Bobby Siu's *Women of China: Imperialism and Women's Resistance* (1983). Women in these studies were presented as either traditional or revolutionary, the history of the Republican period was a prelude to the People's Republic, and in this sense, seen as a road to victory, a process of liberation, in which women played an integral part. In this period when Chinese studies, in general, were very weak in the West, only very few female scholars and graduate students started with women's history studies.⁴ The male-dominated scientific community in the China field in the West was very reluctant to accept the new topic and even rejected it. In mainland China women's studies at that time were not a topic at all, whereas in Taiwan the first publications on women's studies appeared. Lü Xiulian's book *On New Feminism (Xin nüxingzhuyi)* dominated the debate (Spakowski 1995:50-60).

Second: The Period of Critical Feminism in the 1980s

The disillusionment about socialism in China on one hand, the access to more information and the development of new modes of analysis in feminist studies on the other, resulted, on the whole, in more elaborated studies of women's history in the Republican period. The relationship between women's studies and Marxist-Maoist studies

---

3   In this respect I do not agree with Wang Zheng's statement that studies in the 1970s and 1980s – "largely because of the inaccessability of primary source material" and because the major works drew on official documents for an interpretation of Chinese women's history – "tend to reduce Chinese women to obscure entities with little significance in historical process" and that "the women in these works do not appear as agents for social change" (Wang Zheng 1999:2).

4   In Germany the first conference on Chinese women's studies was held in 1991 at Free University of Berlin, where the state of the field was evaluated and proposals were made on how to promote gender studies (see for instance Gransow 1992:17-24; Leutner 1992:25-38; and Übelhör 1992:39-48).

was replaced by a more independent feminist position, which was generally critical towards male and mainstream positions, including Marxist theory. The dominant conceptual framework employed by historians of the Republican period was the incompatibility of Marxism and feminism (Gilmartin 1995:4). The compensatory and contributory approach was still widespread, but now the paradigm had been radically reversed: the entirety of Chinese history in the twentieth century, including women's history, was no longer depicted as a revolutionary process and liberation, rather, conversely, as a process of hindering liberation, hindering a "real revolution," or sacrificing women to a so-called revolution. Thus, sharp critics of the Cultural Revolution turned into sharp critics of the Chinese Communist Party (CCP) and its policies on women. Women continued to be victims even in the liberation movement. An example of this trend was Judith Stacey's *Patriarchy and Socialist Revolution in China* (1983). Using the category "patriarchy" and following a social history approach, Stacey nevertheless was successful in integrating "women's history" as a structural part in the whole process of Chinese development. The number of women's studies in the China field increased and more detailed research was done on the Republican period, which slowly replaced the "revolution" paradigm with the "modernization" paradigm. The China field in the West still did not in general pay much attention to women's history.

In Taiwan the feminist periodical *Awakening (Funü xin zhi)* was started in 1982 and this was the start of a broader development of women's studies using a feminist perspective (Spakowski 1995:60-76). In China itself during the latter half of the 1980s, starting with Li Xiaojiang,[5] the issue of women's studies was raised, some conferences were organized, a few female historians started paying attention to this new topic. Women's studies in China in the late 1980s was a direct outcome of the so-called "women's question," that is, all the social problems women had to face after market reforms started replacing state socialism (Spakowski 1993; Frick 1995).

---

[5] For an elaborate study on Li Xiaojiang's concepts see Sausmikat 1995.

Third: The Period of More Diversified "Academic" Women's and Gender Studies in the 1990s

This period is characterized by several new tendencies. In some respects, it yielded a more sophisticated, scholarly approach to Chinese women's history and more detailed analysis, from both Western and Chinese scholars. The close relationship between women's studies and the feminist movement loosened, in part due to harsh criticism that the true value of history may become ideologized or politicized through excessive gender history (Smith 1998:2) and the connection between studies on Chinese women and emancipatory theories, including the feminist critique of male and mainstream works, was no longer inevitable. The category "women," moreover, was often replaced by the category "gender." This "gender turn," in some respects, marked a more academic approach and a less political-minded, critical feminist approach.

Moreover, the revolution paradigm was replaced by the modernization paradigm and the contributory approach, i.e. women's contribution to the history of mankind, was once again underscored by depicting the active and positive elements of contribution. But "contribution" now meant not only contribution to political history and to the cause of liberation, but to all aspects of women's lives. A de-victimization of Chinese women took place. Readers learned much more about "how women responded to, coped with, struggled against, or maneuvered to change the circumstances around them, or what role women played in the relations of power in social, political, or domestic arenas" (Wang Zheng 1999:2). Even for the so-called premodern period, it was pointed out that Chinese women had not only been victims, but had also acted as agents for historical change. They were not longer depicted merely as obedient daughters and wives in patriarchal families, suppressed by the patriarchal system and Confucian ideology, but also as self-conscious agents in social networking and part of a flourishing women culture, as for example in Dorothy Ko's *Teachers of the Inner Chambers* (1994) and Patricia Ebrey's *The Inner Quarters* (Song period) (1993). As a result, a historicization took place which analyzed women in their respective historical periods, in their respective social and family status; and to a certain extent, the term "woman" was deconstructed. But women were still often depicted as an entity, irrespective of class, social and political status. The emphasis on the agency of women and the evaluation of this agency per se as positive without regarding the character of this agency in relation to their role in society is something I would like to question here. Take a historical figure such as Song Meiling, for example, who belonged to the network of Guomindang (Nationalist Party, GMD) leadership and who, of course, actively supported GMD policy in every period. Her political role is more likely different from the political role of Qiu Jin (1875-1907) or other prominent women in the May Fourth period.

Moreover, the gender turn, which in theory means that the analytical category "gender" should replace the category "women," in practical research, however, tends to focus on women rather than on both men and women. This may be due to the nature of practical research which demands a focus on workable topics. Researchers in general do not use gender as a starting point in the sense of taking both women and men into account as distinctive agents of history and depicting both women's and men's historical role and point of view. Nevertheless, these studies have successfully linked the history of women to social history, family history, cultural history and political history, and, moreover, have shown – like Christina K. Gilmartin in her book *Engendering the Chinese Revolution* (1995) and Wang Zheng in her *Women in the Chinese Enlightenment* (1999) – how the gender perspective can add not only to knowledge on women and their contribution to history and thus enrich the picture of the so-called main perspective on revolution, but can also change the whole picture. From a feminist perspective they tried "to reconfigure" the history of a whole period and sought "to break male monopoly of a contested site" (Wang Zheng 1999:4-5).

The arguments raised by female academics who challenged white women's dominance in feminist studies influenced yet another important tendency. Western female scholars began to develop a self-critical attitude towards Eurocentric or Westerncentric feminist approaches in evaluating the history of Chinese women in the twentieth century. There was a "break with a universalist outlook that presumes that only one type of female emancipatory experience, that based on Western criteria, can be deemed truly feminist" (Gilmartin 1995:6). Instead, they demanded that Chinese women's history should be contextualized and evaluated from its own point of view. Examples of this approach are Elisabeth Croll's *Changing Identities of Chinese Women* (1995) and, published in 1994, the book *Engendering China*, edited by Christina K. Gilmartin, Gail Hershatter, Lisa Rofel and Tyrene White, and, last but not least, Christina Gilmartin's *Engendering the Chinese Revolution* (1995). Besides, Maria Jaschok and Shui Jingjun presented a striking example of cooperative research between "Western feminists" and "Other women" in their book *The History of Women's Mosques in Chinese Islam* (2000b).[6]

Finally, women's studies began flourishing in China itself, both male and female historians participated, centers for women's studies were established at several academic institutions, and valuable source material on the women's movement, women's periodicals and autobiographies, and studies on women's history in the Republican period were published[7]. The Fourth World Conference on Women in 1995 in Peking as well as the funding of centers and research by American foundations interested in promoting trends of Westernization contributed to this flourishing of women's studies (Spakowski 2000). The promotion of women's studies, however, has decreased in the meantime because of diminishing financial support and reluctant acceptance. Nevertheless, in the People's Republic of China (PRC) as well as in Taiwan and in Western countries, the issue of women's and gender studies and women's history have been accepted to the extent that conferences hold special gender panels, research foundations give funding to gender issues, and courses on gender issues have been accepted in university curricula. And of course the conference held in Berlin and the present volume demonstrate the state of the field.

---

[6] On their methodological reflections on this cooperation see also Jaschok/Shui Jingjun 2000a:33-58.

[7] For an overview see Zang Jian 1995:119-126.

Five Reasons for the Non-Integration of Women's and Gender Studies into "Mainstream History"

As I pointed out in the first part of this essay, historical women's and gender studies increasingly integrate the history of women with the social, cultural and political development of each respective period and have demonstrated the usefulness of this approach in challenging the findings of male and mainstream histories and reconfiguring the picture of the whole historical process. From this angle the integration of the particular history of women into a "general history" has started.[8]

The question is why so-called mainstream studies have not reacted to this challenge and made efforts to engender their narratives and stories. Admittedly, some changes have occurred in comparison with earlier studies and "any work on the era that omits discussion of gender is considered parochial and incomplete" (Wang Zheng 1999:4). Therefore, one result of the establishment of women's and gender studies is that gender and women are now included and added to the stories which are told, a result of greater awareness in this respect. But up to now gender as an analytical category and as a specific perspective has not really been accepted by the still male-dominated field.[9] This is not only the case with male Chinese historians, who at a recent conference on family history ridiculed and openly attacked the gender

---

[8] The subject of engendering history is also discussed within the category of combining the particular and the general when writing the histories of women and men. Women's history is depicted here as micro-level and gender history as macro-level. "With its higher claim to generality, gender history can be the bridge that connects the particulars discovered by women's history with wider social contexts, and therefore with the space occupied by general history" (Pomata 1998:117). From a different perspective, Karin Hausen gives examples of how a deficiency in research, not only in the area of women's history but especially also in the area of men's history, hinders a general history conceived to be a gender history. Rather than constructing a "diversity of history" she thinks it makes more sense to conceive a "unity of history" as a historiographic program and construct "multi-faceted relevances" (Hausen 1998:35-55).

[9] In a similar way, class as a category does not often find its way into studies; so it is still necessary to deconstruct "the Chinese" or "Peking" when speaking of the Chinese government or the CCP.

approach as a means of dealing with this topic; this is also the case with Western studies, including studies by female scholars who in theory accept gender as an analytical category. There seems to be a certain tension between being a researcher in the field of Republican history (for instance) and being a researcher in the field of gender studies (see Budde 1997:125-150).[10] And there is an economic reason for this attitude as well: women and gender studies, if taken as a separate subject, have low status in terms of career opportunities.

Gender studies are still put in a specific niche and research findings from gender studies only slowly trickle their way into mainstream studies.[11] In consequence, what the gender approach demands, that is, an expansion of methods, a revision of concepts, the formulation of new research questions and research aims (ibid. 131) as well as a deconstruction of prevalent (non-gendered) images of history, has not yet taken place.

Gender studies and so-called mainstream studies and reference works on the Republican period are separate; for the most part the discourses and debates are also separate. "Her-story" can sometimes be read in a "separatist way" apart from the mainstream. More or less the only links are mainly constituted by persons working in both fields. The source material is different and research aims are not interconnected. A scholar might do research on women's issues on one hand and on, for example, political history without taking the gender perspective into consideration, on the other. These include female researchers who are willing to use the gender approach. They see the need to engender history and are aware of the potential of this approach to deepen our knowledge of history, but they still do not necessarily apply this approach to all their studies. So tension often arises between a researcher who applies certain disciplinary (mainstream) approaches and a researcher who also applies feminist approaches. As Marcia Westkott (1979:422) and, taking up her argument, also Leigh Leslie and Donna Sollie (1994:1-2) had pointed out, women as insiders (to the mainstream) also felt that at the same time

---

[10] For reflections on this problem see Sollie/Leslie 1994.
[11] Budde (1997:126) came to the same conclusions concerning the engendering of German history.

they were outsiders both to their particular discipline and to the Western intellectual tradition in general. "This tension rooted in the contradiction of women's belonging and not belonging, provides the basis for knowing deeply and personally that which we criticize. A personally experienced, culturally based contradiction means that in some fundamental way we as critics also oppose ourselves, or at least that part of us that continues to sustain the very basis of our own estrangement. Hence, the personal struggle of being both insider and outsider is not only a source of knowledge and insight, but also a source of self-criticism" (Westkott 1979:422).

What are the reasons for the non-integration of mainstream studies and gender studies?

First: The Problem of the Heavy Impact and Dominance of Already Established Theories, Paradigms and Master Narratives

"In Western iconography," and I would add, in Chinese iconography as well, "the knowing subject – along with the historically important objects the mirror serves up for scrutiny – is usually male, adding complexity to what seems a simple image" (Smith 1998:2). This statement was made by Bonnie Smith, who herself undertook a sophisticated analysis of how universality of history has been constructed in the process of developing the discipline and how claims of universality also in so-called abstract disciplines were accompanied by the elevation of men and a devaluation of women. It can also be applied to our field of research. On the whole, therefore, as well as on different levels of methodology, once-established theories, paradigms, and master narratives have a very strong influence on the ongoing research and study of a subject.[12] A very heavy burden in this respect is the old and still strong notion that the core of history is politics and that the core of politics means power, which is male-defined (see also Pomata 1998:110).

To bridge the gap between gender/women's studies and mainstream studies, I think it is necessary to show much more concretely than we have in the past the male bias of the theories and paradigms

---

[12] One well-known example is the impact-response paradigm established by the Fairbank school which, despite Paul Cohen's criticism, is still influential today.

used in mainstream studies. A critical evaluation of these studies (including those written by ourselves) in respect to how they depict gender relations and gender hierarchies, and how they legitimate, reproduce and reestablish gender hierarchies,[13] may help us to find a way out of this dilemma. We need to adopt a critical attitude towards the dominant paradigms and master narratives of the field and should try to change the situation actively from within the field and, in some respects, against the field, and not from outside or from the niche of women's and gender studies. The master narrative of Chinese women as victims, for instance, still prevails in mainstream studies despite the de-victimization narrative now dominant in Chinese women's history.

Second: The Problem of Scholarly Acceptance of the Gender Perspective

Wholehearted acceptance by so-called mainstream Chinese studies and by influential male and female scholars still does not exist. For them, gender is not an analytical category of the same value as class or race. They do not regard the category "gender" as a methodological tool for doing research and are not aware of the potential in working with this category. What we can do to promote their willingness to integrate the gender perspective into their research is to continue pointing out issues and topics and to show how an engendering is possible. Maybe we need to change the perspective: starting not with women and asking how we can depict their historical role in distinctive historical events and periods, but starting from the master narratives prevalent in the field and asking for female and male agency and non-agency in every institution, decision, policy etc.

The problem of individual acceptance is, to be sure, closely related to the social practices of knowledge production and mechanisms of positional, symbolic and collective (networking) power, control of publication, and funding, which, I dare say, is still male and mainstream-dominated. Of course, nowadays the situation is not the same as in the field of history in the late nineteenth and early twentieth centuries, when attempts were made to keep women from getting

---

[13] See Fox Keller/Longino 1996 who claim this as a task for feminist cultural studies.

jobs and when "men were envisioned as members of the brotherhood, as scholars and colleagues; women, as something other" (Smith 1998:191). There are much more subtle instruments for keeping "the community" male-oriented and closed to women, especially those women perceived to be "feminist." In claiming that those academics who follow a gender approach are critical towards the mainstream, I am assuming that the gender perspective per se still means having an emancipatory intent and being anti-hegemonic and opposing dominant attitudes with respect to political and social questions as well.[14]

Third: The Problem of Institutional Political and Academic Acceptance

I think another reason for the marginalization of women's and gender studies is the institutional weakness of Chinese studies in general at European universities and at most North American universities, which have no special Chinese studies program or have only a small area studies department. There is a fixed set of curricula concentrating on major developments in politics, economics, culture and ideology etc., let us say, a basic set of knowledge on China. The topics are much broader than your own research so you have to use the available studies as reference and teaching material – which is not engendered. In this situation it is hardly possible for anyone to do the process of "engendering" on their own while teaching. This is how mainstream knowledge and approaches – already forming a canon of knowledge and a master narrative about the Republican period – are transmitted from one generation to the next. These still include the books by John K. Fairbank and *The Cambridge History of China*.

Starting from my view of the European state of the field, I would suggest three ways to overcome this situation. First: we should try to include in our teaching – much more than we have already – critics of the dominant paradigms in the field. We should incorporate into our teaching discussions on the construction and transmission of

---

[14] I would not – as Sandra Harding, for instance, did for sociology – make sharp distinctions for the China field between three feminist epistomologies: empiricism, postmodernism, and standpoint theory, even if I myself would argue in favor of standpoint theory and thereby avoid a claim of objectivity which seems to be outdated. See the debate about these distinctions in sociology in Witz 1998.

knowledge pertaining to China research, on methodology, which itself is an outcome of male dominance,[15] and on the tension of claiming objectivity and a value-free science on the one hand while having a gender, class or race bias on the other. Second: it would be worthwhile to make an effort to prepare new teaching material which is engendered and is not only adding "women" to an ungendered history. This would include thinking about training methods and ways of overcoming the widespread assumption among students that gender studies or a gender perspective are of a low value[16] and the perception that they present opinions rather than facts. Third: we should encourage at least our PhD students to achieve a threefold qualification: a qualification in the basic discipline, that is, history; a qualification in the area of China research; and an additional qualification in gender studies. This may lead to a disciplinary/China/gender tension in the field of Republican history which, once revealed, may also become an effective methodological tool.

Fourth: The Problem of "Difficult" Topics and Non-gendered Source Materials

It seems that some topics and issues are more difficult to engender than others. At first glance it seems that this is related to the historical source material. But upon closer scrutiny it is obvious that

---

[15] Compare, for instance, the debate on statistical science and its male bias (Hughes 1995). See Bonnie Smith's excellent book on male bias in the field of history, which proposes "that the development of modern scientific methodology, epistomology, professional practice, and writing has been closely tied to evolving definitions of masculinity and femininity" (Smith 1998:1). A book on the development of sinology and of Chinese studies and its male bias still has to be written.

[16] See, for instance, the research report about gender inclusiveness of a women's history curriculum in secondary education by ten Dam/Teekens 1997, which states that in the eyes of students and even teachers "women's history is exclusively associated with values, in terms of opinions, whereas the regular issues that are treated in the 'traditional' history curriculum are seen as knowledge, in terms of fact" (1997:72). Even nowadays in the European age of "gender mainstreaming", exclusively undertaking feminist/gender research is not a "good" career move and – if one focuses on Chinese gender studies – will inevitably lead to academic marginalization or, if one is not already established as an academic, might be the means for being pushed aside by male competitors.

(Chinese) history as a whole has been constructed for many centuries as having two spheres: one which is a valued and important male sphere of activity and another, which seems to be a negligible female and familial sphere (see also Smith 1998:197). The latter named generated the initial subject matter of gender studies. Up to now they have concentrated on fields such as political movements, cultural history, and social history, or on specific subjects: the status and role of women in the family and in society, women's work, issues which obviously relate to women's questions such as marriage, family, children, footbinding, sexuality, demographic development. These are not only depicted as "female spheres" but at the same time the source material is arranged according to that. In the source materials available on these topics, there is evidence of the specific historical roles and functions women played. It is not very difficult to find these materials and conduct the respective research, including a critical evaluation of the male bias of the sources. In this regard, studies on women's history have done a very good job in discovering new material or reading already well-known material from a new perspective.

In the so-called male sphere of history, however, there are some topics that are much more difficult to "engender," such as economic history, political history, and international relations (on a macro base), or the history of ideas or discourses. Quite a different type of source material exists for these topics, which at a first glance does not reveal an obvious gender distinction but instead implies seemingly non-gendered information. The specific character of this source material, collected or left behind mainly by men, has a male bias and often does not differentiate class, race, generation, profession, or, especially, gender, thus contributing to the difficulties historians have and should not be underestimated. How to deal with these texts? One strategy is to supply what these texts do not: namely, oral histories of women as a corrective.[17] Oral histories, of course, are a very good means of reconstructing not only the subject position of women in history, but also of men, especially those of the lower classes. But collecting oral histories is only possible to a limited extent. In my view, it is still necessary

---

[17] See Wang Zheng 1999:7 who used oral histories of women to counter male-dominant written sources.

that we ourselves uncover the male bias and learn and then teach our students how to read source materials[18] in an indirect way in order to explore and reveal men and women as different actors, or how to discuss the respective issues from a gender perspective. In this way we can attempt to engender topics which are based on this male-biased "non-gendered" material, where only non-gendered persons and institutions appear, and for the writer and the reader this means "men."

Let us examine the history of the relations between Comintern and the CCP or the GMD in the 1920s and 1930s, for example. In this material on political history and the history of Russian-Chinese relations, "gender" is not visible. The great bulk of the available source material contains, in some way, gender-neutral information, speaking of peasants, workers, party members, institutions, "the party," party conferences and sessions. For those who left these materials behind as working reports, decisions, or proposals the characteristic "worker" or "party" was much more important than the characteristic "men" or "women." Women are put in a special niche apart from the mainstream when some sources specifically relate to the women's movement as part of the revolutionary movement, but also, in some respects, as something different. Apart from this, women are mentioned or enter the stage as historical actors only in very special cases. Even women as victims rarely appear.

But do these "ungendered" perceptions of those years really demonstrate that "gender" in relation to the concept "class" or "peasant" might be placed second or third when evaluating the political development of the Republican period? Certainly, the motives for political strategies and the outcomes of their policies at first seem difficult to analyze from a gender perspective. To be sure, there are no gender-neutral topics and issues, but I have to stress that we must still work on finding methods and ways of implementing the processes of engendering history, especially on macro-level topics.

One strategy for overcoming the difficulties with male-biased texts might be to deconstruct and evaluate anew the central texts and

---

[18] See also Gallagher et al. 2001:8, who claim that in interdisciplinary approaches the "(re)interpretation of sources" is most important.

categories of twentieth-century history on "revolution," "identity," "modernization," "nation-building", CCP and GMD from the gender perspective. On the discursive level we may start asking what the functions and outcomes of prevalent gender constructions in narratives or so-called non-gendered narratives of the Republican period are. Is there a difference between Chinese discourse and Western discourse? How can we engender the collective memory both from the actor's and the perception's perspective? Or let us examine "nation," for example. How is the construction of "nation" related to the construction of "gender" in the Republican period? Do men represent the nation and the national level, whereas women represent the imagined community, the symbolic level only and have no relation to this national agency?[19] On the history level we may ask: What were the differences or similarities in the perception of nation and revolution by men and women, in the motives for joining or not joining the national or the revolutionary movements, the outcomes, the strategies in dealing with revolution and the historical roles that males and females played? In what way was the concept of national identity and the "nation-building" process of the Republic a gendered one? Were male and female roles ascribed to complementary roles and identities as they were in European countries?[20]

Fifth: The Problem of "Ranking" the Gender Category as Compared with Other Analytical Categories

One big methodological and practical question still lies in determining the relationship of the category "gender" to other concepts and analytical categories, such as "class," "race," "generation," "religion," "ethnicity," or "nation." I would suggest viewing this relationship not as a fixed one, but as one dependent on the issue and the period. I argue that it is an interactional, reciprocal relationship which may undergo changes in the processes of interactions. Therefore, we need to find out and evaluate what categories are predominant in what topics or in which ways categories and practical politics

---

[19] This at least is assumed for European countries (see Wenk/Eschebach 2002:27-28).

[20] See Planert 2000:9 who discusses this in terms of Europe.

are related to one another. For instance, in the field of Japanese history, one thesis postulates that in the process of establishing a modern society the category "gender" replaced the category "status" as a predominant category of social stratification (Getreuer-Kargl 1997:21).[21] Works on the Chinese Republican period do not go so far: Wang Zheng, however, made the point that "gender equality [...] was a principle of modern society" and that talking about women's emancipation was an easy way to express an identification with the New Culture Movement and with the idea of a modern citizenship (Wang Zheng 1999:13). To give another example: in studying educational problems or political participation, women of the upper classes – in my view – have much more in common with men of the upper classes than with women of the lower classes. But in studying gender relations in families, women of both upper and lower classes share more features than what divides them by class distinctions. So when talking about the relationship between gender and class, for instance, it is necessary to distinguish the respective contexts. The relationship is not a constant one which remains the same in every context, but is a changing one.

Women and Gender in Mainstream Studies: Two Examples

I would like to present two examples here of the treatment of women and gender in mainstream studies, which to some extent represent the field and are widely used – I assume – in teaching Chinese Republican history:
First, women are invisible, conceptualized as victims, and briefly tacked on to the narrative.
In *China: A New History* by John K. Fairbank and Merle Goldman (the expanded 1998 edition, first edition 1992), women are almost invisible[22] in the narrative with two exceptions. The first is that

---

[21] Furthermore, in Europe the category "gender" is an invention of modern society from the eighteenth century, before that it meant all females and males, living and dead, and not restricted to one generation (Wunder 1992:132-133).

[22] This invisibility of women is, firstly, due to the fact that their actions in history were not perceived as significant and important and, secondly, the questions

women play an important role in the conceptual framework of the book insofar as the inferior position ascribed to them by Confucian (male) moralists serves as a means of revealing the character of the Chinese state and society. The second is the issue of footbinding, which is elaborated at considerable length to show women as victims on one hand and their passivity on the other. In this way, the depiction of women is more an instrument of Fairbank's and Goldman's narrative rather than a part, not even a very small part, of the narrative.

The book gives a short description of the history from 1912 to 1949 in about ninety pages (Fairbank/Goldman 1998:255-342). According to one reviewer, it "will serve for decades to come as a standard reference and text book"[23] and indeed it proclaims to be an authoritative history of China and has had significant influence in constructing a specific image of China. For the Republican period, the index in the category "women" boasts two entries with respect to the "emancipation of women." Mao Zedong, for instance, is mentioned on twenty-three pages referring only to the Republican period. The reference to "footbinding" covers the pre-Republican period with six entries, covering eight pages. There are five entries for the period after 1949 and ten entries for the pre-Republican period with respect to women. In addition, there are twelve pictures for the Republican period, which are all of men with two exceptions: Sun Yatsen is shown accompanied by his wife Song Qingling, and Song Meiling is shown sewing bandages in a wartime hospital: several other women are sewing in the background.

The conceptual framework for the interpretation of women in Chinese history is laid out in the introduction which aims to serve as a guideline (ibid. 18-19): Women's positions are closely linked and interpreted within a hierarchical structured family and family system, a state in miniature, a microcosm parallel with the macrocosm of society and state. A Chinese woman "had no economic independence," had an "inferior social status," which was "merely one manifestation of the hierarchic nature of China's entire social code and cosmology."

---

historians have posed do not expect or allow space for women in the answer; see also Gallagher et al. 2001:2-3.
[23] Robert L. Worden, front cover of the paperback edition 1998.

While male and female are both viewed as necessary and complementary, one element, the female one, has been depicted by nature as passive toward the other. Chinese male moralists worked out "the behavior pattern of obedience and passivity that was expected by women." And here the narrative stops, leaving the reader alone in equating these ideas, which have been passed on in the China field for decades, with historical reality. None of the findings from historical women's studies has been taken into consideration. The authors later exemplify the subjection of women in Late Imperial China by presenting the case of footbinding as an incomparably cruel social practice (ibid. 173-176), mentioning in particular that Manchu women did not bind their feet (ibid. 148).[24] These statements are the only ones concerning women during this period, except for pointing out the segregationist tendencies of the Taiping and that they gave "special scope to women, who supported and sometimes served in the army and ran the palaces in place of eunuchs" (ibid. 210).

The first entry concerning the Republican period says: "Ideas of several kinds of socialism, of the emancipation of women, and the rights of labor versus capitalists swept around the globe and flooded into Republican China" (ibid. 267). First, this statement has to be evaluated in the context of the above-mentioned framework of women's subjection and the pattern of their obedience and passivity. It exemplifies the paradigm of a dichotomy between tradition and modernity which also relates to women. Second, in connection with this paradigm, we see the outdated "impact-response paradigm" in the image that ideas, including the idea of women's emancipation, flooded into China, implying that China's scholar-elite were mainly responsive objects who took over tasks from the West, thereby neglecting their own agency, to say nothing of women being depicted as historical subjects, as agents. Third, far more space in the short chapter on the New Culture Movement is devoted to the attacks on the writing system than to referring – at least – to the situation of women;

---

[24] This is also a good example of how women, rather than being represented in their own right as women, are defined in terms of their relationship to men; see also Gallagher et al. 2001:3, where this tendency is depicted as prevalent in many mainstream histories.

they do not – at this point of the narrative – even show up as victims. Women are invisible and, if they are mentioned, then only ideas about them, presented by men, play a historical role.

This can also be clearly seen with the second entry on women. It specifies that it was "the anarchists" who "eloquently put forward ideas of egalitarianism, especially the emancipation of women from family bonds and of the peasantry from exploitation, that would become part of the Chinese vocabulary of revolution" (ibid. 275). Women were objects of political action, not historical agents; anarchists – without gender distinction – were assumed to be men.

Second, women are added as agents, but as separate entities. Furthermore, men represent women, but women do not represent men.

John Fitzgerald's *Awakening China: Politics, Culture, and Class in the Nationalist Revolution*, published in 1996, is an example of the contributory approach I have just described, which follows the narrative of women's agency in contributing to the "awakening" trope, but separates them from other social groups. The "separation" of women from other social entities, such as peasants or revolutionary thinkers, is combined with a methodological approach with a non-gendered concept of "awakening" in which women are represented by men, but men are not represented by women.

This book presents a new approach to that period and to the topic of revolution, influenced by methodological positions embedded in the "linguistic and cultural turn." It is one of the mainstream books covering a broader spectrum of the political and cultural history from this period that also includes women in its narrative. One can find in the index the categories "women" and "emancipation of women," "Women's Bureau, Central," "Women's Bureau, City," "Women's Bureau, Provincial," "women's cooperatives," "women's movement," "Women's Movement Training Institute," "Women's Patriotic Comrades of Tianjin," "Women's Weekly" and "Women's Voice." Altogether, according to the index, excluding the mention of "women" in the footnotes, women are mentioned on eighteen out of 348 pages. The category "men" is missing in the index. As acting women Qiu Jin, He Xiangning, Ding Ling, Isabella Bird, Pearl Buck, Vera Vladimirovna Vishniakova-Akimova and Deng Yingchao are mentioned. They are included not as representatives of women but because they are exceptional and outstanding women (Fitzgerald 1996).

The master narrative of this book centers around "awakening" as a topic of intellectual discourse, subjective perception, political goal, mobilizing force, manifested in architecture, literature, politics, institutions and parties. In the end, it turns out to be a history centering around intellectual history that broadens its scope to other layers of historical development. Therefore a few pages are dedicated to outlining the specific role of women's institutions on this topic. Furthermore, the author clearly describes the role and function of women in the perception and politics of awakening. He points out that the figures of the New Citizen and the New Woman were generic icons of nationalism in the propaganda of both Nationalist and Communist parties (ibid. 22). He claims that the trope of awakening was used by different interest groups, study societies and political factions, including the women's movement. It was namely Qiu Jin who "turned the awakened lion to the service of the women's movement" (ibid. 31). The role of Ibsen's play "Nora" and its function in the emancipation narrative is related by the author as well (ibid. 99-101). And, last but not least, Fitzgerald states that in the perception of foreign writers on China as well as in the perception of Chinese intellectuals such as Liang Qichao, Chinese women have been depicted as the most oppressed members of Chinese society and that the "female condition served as an indisputable sign of the unredeemed barbarity of the people of Asia" (ibid. 132). And as a consequence, women became the symbol of awakening (and I would add: of liberation) (ibid. 284), but both female and male "recognized themselves in the symbol of the awakening female, and both invested in her struggle to free the suppressed hopes of a captive nation" ibid. 284).

To summarize: In terms of methodology, women play a role in Fitzgerald's perception and narrative of Republican history in four respects: First: several active women contribute to history as agents by participating in the master narrative of those years: the awakening issue. This "adding" of women to the picture of history is on the level of "contributory history."

Second: "women's issues," "women's problems," and the "emancipation narrative" were depicted as part of the awakening trope alongside issues such as "nation," "youth," "peasants" and "workers." This, of course, is partly due to the materials Fitzgerald analyzed, in which women as special subjects are separated and appear as a special social entity at the same level as other subjects. The problem is that Fitzgerald followed the sources in this respect, not asking why women – together with youth, peasants and workers – have been given this specific role in the awakening narrative, and why men and women alike have been depicted without gender difference in their function as youth, peasants or workers. So he uncritically placed women (as a construct) separate from youth, peasants and workers, while the latter – one might conclude – were perceived (and constructed) as gender-neutral, which, in general, means as male. The compensatory function of women and women's issues in history, which is clearly seen in the relevant source material, is continued in Fitzgerald's narrative. He does not step away from his male-biased sources in order to include gender.

Third, the leading concept of the study, "awakening," is discussed in many aspects and in many relations, but Fitzgerald does not deconstruct or engender the meaning, the content itself, such as the meaning of class, race, nationalism, Marxism. The study assumes that these concepts and the reality behind these concepts embrace people, masses, proletariat, activists, and revolutionary thinkers (ibid. 320) and does not take into consideration that "awakening" of the "masses" mean different things for men and women. Gilmartin's finding, for instance, that in the 1920s it was necessary for He Xiangning to wrap the CCP Women's Department programs in a nationalist cloak (Gilmartin 1994:224) hints at the way in which the concept of nation has been understood by female activists. It was merely a conceptual tool to promote their material interests. Therefore, one has to ask whether the narrative of awakening – as Fitzgerald suggests – was used in the same way by male and female revolutionaries, whether there was a difference of content and meaning and, last but not least, in the way it was connected with feminist narratives of that time.

Fourth, it is interesting to note that, for instance, Qiu Jin is cited only when especially addressing the awakening of women, but is not when addressing "revolutionary thinkers," which – at least according to the following quotations – means male revolutionary thinkers. As this example reveals, it is assumed that male revolutionary thinkers also represent female thinkers, but female revolutionary thinkers are assumed to represent only women, and not male thinkers.

Conclusions

First, we should promote the engendering of the history of the Republican period in China from within the field rather than establish Chinese gender studies as a supplement to mainstream studies. This includes making women visible in history and at the same time developing new approaches "to doing history in ways which not only challenge women's invisibility but also avoid reproducing other forms of social inequality"(Gallagher et al. 2001:5).

Second, I suggest strengthening our criticism of dominant paradigms, master narratives, and the male bias of the field from a gender perspective by deconstructing ungendered agency and institutions in mainstream works and exposing the reasons for the continuation of non-gendering approaches. We need to look at the particular ways in which women have been represented (ibid. 2001:5) and how these representations are being transferred.

Third, I further recommend emphasizing the need to work on new engendered teaching materials and interdisciplinary study programs which include women's and gender studies. In this respect women's networking and the strengthening of collaborative, interdisciplinary research is of utmost importance.

Fourth, last but not least I recommend that we consider gender studies and the integration of gender studies into the mainstream not merely as an academic task, but also as a means of empowering women, as a task connected with political aims, such as implementing the political and social emancipation of women in China and in the West.

Studying and engendering Chinese Republican history in this way may become a kind of personal and academic "journey" similar to that of Donna Sollie and Leigh Leslie, when in compiling their book they asked contributors to describe the process of studying their topics (Sollie/Leslie 1994:263). Writing history in this sense might be understood as a creative journey of interweaving feminist and gender standpoints with professional paths as scholars in academia.

References

Annuß, Evelyn, Grenzen der Geschlechterforschung, in: *Feministische Studien* 1 (1999), pp. 91-102.
Budde, Gunilla-Friederike, Das Geschlecht der Geschichte, in: Thomas Mergel, Thomas Welskopp (eds.), *Geschichte zwischen Kultur und Gesellschaft*, München 1997, pp. 125-150.
Cheng Ying, Bettina Gransow, Mechthild Leutner (eds.), *Frauenstudien. Beiträge der Berliner China-Tagung 1991*, München 1992.
Croll, Elisabeth, *Feminism and Socialism in China*, London 1978.
Croll, Elisabeth, *Changing Identities of Chinese Women: Rhetoric, Experience and Self-Perception in Twentieth-Century China*, London, Atlantic Highlands/NJ 1995.
Croll, Elisabeth, New Spaces, New Voices: Women Organizing in Twentieth-Century China, in: Hsiung Ping-chun, Maria Jaschok, Cecilia Milwertz (eds.), *Chinese Women Organizing: Cadres, Feminists, Muslims, Queers*, Oxford, New York 2001, pp. 25-40.
Davin, Delia, *Woman-Work: Women and the Party in Revolutionary China*, Oxford 1976.
Delphy, Christine, Rethinking Sex and Gender, in: *Women's Studies International Forum* 16:1 (1993), pp. 1-9.
Ebrey, Patricia Buckley, *The Inner Quarters: Marriage and the Lives of Chinese Women in the Sung Period*, Berkeley, Los Angeles, London 1993.
Eichler, Margrit, *Feminist Methodology*, Toronto 1995.
Fairbank, John K., Merle Goldman, *China: A New History*, enlarged edition, Cambridge/MA, London 1998.

Fitzgerald, John, *Awakening China: Politics, Culture, and Class in the Nationalist Revolution*, Stanford 1996.

Fox Keller, Evelyn, Helen E. Longino (eds.), *Feminism and Science*, Oxford, New York 1996.

Frick, Heike, "Frauenwissenschaft" als Diskurs zwischen Theorie und Praxis: Tendenzen der Frauenforschung in der VR China, in: Frick et al. 1995, pp. 11-42.

Frick, Heike, Mechthild Leutner, Nicola Spakowski (eds.), *Frauenforschung in China. Analysen, Texte, Bibliographie*, München 1995.

Gallagher, Ann-Marie, Cathy Lubelska, Louise Ryan, Introduction, in: Ann-Marie Gallagher, Cathy Lubelska, Louise Ryan (eds.), *Representing the Past: Women and History*, Harlow 2001, pp. 1-20.

Getreuer-Kargl, Ingrid, Geschlechterverhältnis und Modernisierung, in: Ilse Lenz, Mae Michiko (eds.), *Getrennte Welten, gemeinsame Moderne? Geschlechterverhältnisse in Japan*, Opladen 1997, pp. 19-58.

Gilmartin, Christina K., Gail Hershatter, Lisa Rofel, Tyrene White (eds.), *Engendering China: Women, Culture, and the State*, Cambridge/MA, London 1994.

Gilmartin, Christina K., *Engendering the Chinese Revolution: Radical Women, Communist Politics, and Mass Movements in the 1920s*, Berkeley, Los Angeles, London 1995.

Gransow, Bettina, Frauen in der (China-) Wissenschaft: "Marginal Women"?, in: Cheng Ying et al. 1992, pp. 17-24.

Hausen, Karin, Die Nicht-Einheit der Geschichte als historiographische Herausforderung. Zur historischen Relevanz und Anstößigkeit der Geschlechtergeschichte, in: Medick/Trepp 1998, pp. 15-55.

Hawkesworth, Mary, Analyzing Backlash: Feminist Standpoint Theory as Analytical Tool, in: *Women's Studies International Forum* 22:2 (1999), pp. 135-155.

Hughes, Donna M., Significant Differences: The Construction of Knowledge, Objectivity, and Dominance, in: *Women's Studies International Forum* 18:4 (1995), pp. 395-406.

Jackson, Stevi, Why a Materialist Feminism Is (Still) Possible – and Necessary, in: *Women's Studies International Forum* 24:3-4 (2001), pp. 283-293.

Jaschok, Maria, Shui Jingjun, "Outsider within": Speaking to Excursions across Cultures, in: *Feminist Theory* 1 (2000a), pp. 33-58.

Jaschok, Maria, Shui Jingjun, *The History of Women's Mosques in Chinese Islam*, Richmond, Surrey 2000b.

Ko, Dorothy, *Teachers of the Inner Chambers*, Stanford 1994.

Leslie, Leigh A., Donna L. Sollie, Why a Book on Feminist Relationship Research?, in: Sollie/Leslie 1994, pp. 1-15.

Letherby, Gayle, Jen Marchbank, Why Do Women's Studies? A Cross England Profile, in: *Women's Studies International Forum* 24:5 (2001), pp. 587-603.

Leutner, Mechthild, Bilder chinesischer Frauen von Marco Polo bis zur Gegenwart, in: *Berliner China-Hefte* (Free University Berlin) 16 (1999), pp. 79-95.

Leutner, Mechthild, Chinabezogene Frauenforschung und geschlechterspezifischer Ansatz, in: Cheng Ying et al. 1992, pp. 25-38.

Leutner, Mechthild, Nicola Spakowski, "Die Komplexität der Realität". Chancen und Rückschritte von Frauen im Transformationsprozess Chinas, in: *asien, afrika, lateinamerika* 24 (1996), pp. 253-285.

Logan, Mary Ellen, Helen Huntley, Gender and Power in the Research Process, in: *Women's Studies International Forum* 24:6 (2001), pp. 623-635.

Lutter, Christina, Feministische Forschung, Gender Studies und Cultural Studies – Eine Annäherung, in: Waniek/Stoller 2001, pp. 21-32.

Medick, Hans, Anne-Charlott Trepp (eds.), *Geschlechtergeschichte und Allgemeine Geschichte. Herausforderungen und Perspektiven*, Göttingen 1998.

Pelkner, Anna-Katharina, How to "Discipline" Women's Studies? Über die Institutionalisierung Feministischer Wissenschaft(skritik) im kanadischen Hochschulsystem, in: *Feministische Studien* 2 (1998), pp. 125-134.

Perrot, Michelle (ed.), *Geschlecht und Geschichte. Ist eine weibliche Geschichtsschreibung möglich?*, Frankfurt/M. 1989.

Planert, Ute, Nationalismus und weibliche Politik: Zur Einführung, in: Ute Planert (ed.), *Nation, Politik und Geschlecht. Frauenbewegun-*

gen und Nationalismus in der Moderne, Frankfurt/M., New York 2000, pp. 9-14.

Pomata, Gianna, Close-Ups and Long Shots: Combining Particular and General in Writing the Histories of Women and Men, in: Medick/Trepp 1998, pp. 99-124.

Puff, Helmut, Männergeschichten/Frauengeschichten. Über den Nutzen einer Geschichte der Homosexualitäten, in: Medick/Trepp 1998, pp. 127-169.

Sausmikat, Nora, *Nichtstaatliche Frauenforschung in der VR China. Eine Diskussion der Frauenwissenschaft Li Xiaojiangs*, Münster 1995.

Schissler, Hanna (ed.), *Geschlechterverhältnisse im historischen Wandel*, Frankfurt/M., New York 1993.

Siu, Bobby, *Women of China: Imperialism and Women's Resistance*, London 1983.

Smith, Bonnie G., *The Gender of History: Men, Women, and Historical Practice*, Cambridge, London 1998.

Sollie, Donna L., Leigh A. Leslie, Feminist Journeys: Final Reflections, in: Sollie/Leslie 1994, pp. 263-283.

Sollie, Donna L., Leigh A. Leslie (eds.), *Gender, Families and Close Relationships: Feminist Research Journeys*, Thousand Oaks/CA, London, New Delhi 1994.

Spakowski, Nicola, "Frauenforschung chinesischer Prägung"? Ursprung, Themen und Theorien der aktuellen Frauenforschung in China, in: *Newsletter Frauen und China* (Free University Berlin) 4 (1993), pp. 13-27.

Spakowski, Nicola, Zuerst Mensch oder zuerst Frau sein? Positionen der taiwanesischen Frauenbewegung und Frauenforschung seit den 70er Jahren, in: Frick et al. 1995, pp. 43-81.

Stacey, Judith, *Patriarchy and Socialist Revolution in China*, London 1983.

ten Dam, Geert, Hanneke Farkas Teekens, The Gender Inclusiveness of a Women's History Curriculum in Secondary Education, in: *Women's Studies International Forum* 20:1 (1997), pp. 61-75.

Tinkler, Penny, Introduction to Special Issue: Women, Imperialism and Identity, in: *Women's Studies International Forum* 21:3 (1998), pp. 217-222.

Übelhör, Monika, Das Bild der Frau im traditionellen China. Einige Überlegungen zu Möglichkeiten der Aussage von Malerei und Literatur, in: Cheng Ying et al. 1992, pp. 39-48.

Wang Zheng, *Women in the Chinese Enlightenment: Oral and Textual Histories*, Berkeley, Los Angeles, London 1999.

Waniek, Eva, Silvia Stoller, Verhandlungen des Geschlechts – Ein Vorwort, in: Waniek/Stoller 2001, pp. 7-17.

Waniek, Eva, Silvia Stoller (eds.), *Verhandlungen des Geschlechts. Zur Konstruktivismusdebatte in der Gender-Theorie*, Wien 2001.

Wenk, Silke, Insa Eschebach, Soziales Gedächtnis und Geschlechterdifferenz. Eine Einführung, in: Insa Eschebach, Sigrid Jacobeit, Silke Wenk (eds.), *Gedächtnis und Geschlecht. Deutungsmuster in Darstellungen des nationalsozialistischen Genozids*, Frankfurt/M., New York 2002, pp. 13-38.

Westkott, Marcia, Feminist Criticism of the Social Sciences, in: *Harvard Educational Review* 49:4 (1979), pp. 422-430.

Witz, Anne, Was tun Feministinnen, wenn sie Soziologie betreiben?, in: *Feministische Studien* 2 (1998), pp. 46-61.

Wunder, Heide, Geschlechtsidentitäten. Frauen und Männer im späten Mittelalter und am Beginn der Neuzeit, in: Karin Hausen, Heide Wunder (eds.), *Frauengeschichte – Geschlechtergeschichte*, Frankfurt/M., New York 1992, pp. 131-153.

Zang Jian, Frauengeschichte: Themen und Charakteristika, in: Frick et al. 1995, pp. 119-126.

Knowledge Is Easy – Action Is Difficult: The Case of Chinese Anarchist Discourse on Women and Gender Relations and Its Practical Limitations

Gotelind Müller

The problematic relationship of Chinese communism and feminism has been dealt with in several studies and is still much of a debate. Much less attention, however, has been paid to the one-time primary ideological rivals of the Chinese Communists: the anarchists, and their stance on gender issues, even though Chinese anarchists have been generically hailed as pioneers in women's and gender issues.

This essay tries to fill in part of this lacuna. The period covered extends from 1907 to the early 1930s because, arguably, the proposed time-span of 1911-1949 does not make much sense in the case of Chinese anarchism. The basis of anarchist discourse on women and gender issues was laid before 1911 and by 1949 the anarchist movement had long lost its hold on China. Special attention will be paid here to the specific relationship between anarchist rhetoric and social practice at given times. Because of space limitation, I will only highlight the more general points.[1]

Taking the development of Chinese anarchism and its deliberations on women and gender as a whole, one may individuate four relevant phases:[2]

I would like to thank all those who commented on earlier drafts of this paper. Special thanks to Ed Krebs who shared his thoughts and helped me improve the paper's style as well.

[1] For more detailed information on the Chinese anarchist movement in general, named proponents and journals, the reader may refer to my recent extensive book on the subject (Müller 2001).

[2] These phases partly coincide with established ways of historical periodization but are not only derived from the general context. Rather they are linked to specific groups of people, their publications and actions with regard to gender issues.

1. The initial phase, basically the last years of the Qing (1907-1912), when the first anarchist journals (*Tianyi [Natural Justice]* in Tokyo, *Xin shiji [New Century]* in Paris) appeared. Here the emphasis is on the "founding" rhetoric.
2. The first years of the Republic (1912-1915/16) when (Liu) Shifu and his group were active. Here the emphasis lies on the contradictory nature of rhetoric and social practice.
3. The New Culture/May Fourth period (1917-mid-1920s). On the ideological side I will focus on the introduction of Emma Goldman and her feminism to the Chinese reading public, on the practical side on the various experiments in terms of "new life-styles."
4. The late 1920s and early 1930s. Here the emphasis lies on the disintegration of rhetoric and social practice.

The Last Years of the Qing (1907-1911)

Anarchism was one of the first brands of socialism that held sway in modern China. As is now well established (Bernal 1968; Zarrow 1990; Dirlik 1991; Müller 2001), anarchism was very much in vogue during the first two decades or so of the twentieth century. This attractiveness depended not only on the anarchist critique of power structure in the political sense, but was grounded in the professed rejection of traditionally received life-styles as well. Part and parcel of this anti-traditionalism was a reformulation of gender issues.

The first Chinese anarchist groups were – significantly – located outside China: in Tokyo and in Paris. This certainly facilitated their assault on traditional life-styles which was integrated in the overall critique of power structures. Still, there were some differences in the respective stances between the Tokyo and the Paris group. The Tokyo group paid very much attention to gender issues – at least in the early phase – because the editor was a woman: He Zhen. Even though there had been several women's magazines and organizations led by Chinese women in Japan (Judge 2001, see esp. 795-796), including Qiu Jin, there was no figure comparable to He Zhen. She

---

They do not necessarily apply to a periodization of the history of Chinese anarchism as a whole. My views on the latter may be gleaned from Müller 2001.

stood out because of her radical anarcho-feminism, which did not even have a Japanese parallel. Although leading Japanese male socialists, namely Kōtoku Shūsui, were gravitating towards anarchism and had been instrumental in drawing the Chinese Tokyo group along, too, and even though e.g. Kōtoku's wife was an active feminist, nobody proposed outright anarcho-feminism at the time. Rather, the women in Kōtoku's circle limited themselves to agitating against official restrictions of women's political activities,[3] and the male core of Kōtoku's group confined itself to a more general socialist feminism.[4] Kōtoku himself seemed somewhat irritated by He Zhen's militant feminism (Kōtoku Shūsui 1966) which put gender issues at the center of the new journal *Tianyi (Natural Justice)*. Apparently as He Zhen lost dominance (and partly also redefined her views), the journal tuned down its feminism. With the following journal *Hengbao (Equity)* (1908) the topic practically disappeared.

He Zhen radically denied the right of men to speak "on women's behalf," explicitly including revolutionary men, and even declared women's wholesale "revenge".[5] This prospect of war between the sexes obviously appalled even revolutionary-minded male comrades and caused Zhang Ji, former member of the Tokyo group who then fled to Paris, to intervene through a letter from Europe pointing out that even Western anarchists did not support He Zhen's over-radical positions. Instead of "women's revenge" the anarchists should propagate "free love," he said.[6]

He Zhen not only asked for free choice in matters of marriage, public child-rearing, equal legal treatment of both sexes, a new naming practice,[7] abolition of prostitution, concubinage and the like

---

[3] A convenient survey on the Japanese feminist movement of the time is Sievers 1983.
[4] Sakai Toshihiko, for one, introduced Bebel's views on this subject.
[5] Her most important series of articles in *Tianyi* was consequently called "On Women's Revenge" (*Nüzi fuchoulun*) (He Zhen 1907b).
[6] The letter appeared in the following *Hengbao* (Zhang Ji 1908).
[7] As opposed to the later favored idea, common up to our days, of combining the natal (father's) and the husband's surname, He Zhen advocated the life-long use of mother's and father's surname. With this distancing from the husband's (and his family's) authority He Zhen on the other hand ironically cemented the

(all soon to become common-stock-positions, but at her time still very new and radical), but wanted to enforce an absolute equality. This basic concept of equality with heavy Buddhist underpinnings (Müller 2001:191-192) should in the end level all differences between the sexes. Therefore her understanding of equality differed decidedly from the common Western one. Her preoccupation with absolute equality was manifested also by her proposal of fixed rules e.g. with remarriage. Remarriage, which was traditionally ill-perceived in the case of women but totally acceptable for men, should be possible for both sexes, but only for partners who were in exactly the same position, i.e. who were both marrying the second time. Every imbalance, she feared, would lead to inequality. He Zhen reinforced her radical stance by suggesting the death penalty in cases of misconduct (He Zhen 1907c:3). These regulations betrayed an authoritarian strand in He Zhen's thinking that did not go unnoticed by Kōtoku and his friends (Müller 2001:183).

In terms of sexual life He Zhen proposed a rather puritanical ethic – even though this could be said of a large proportion of Western anarchists as well. (This value-conservative tendency in anarchism is often overlooked.) She analyzed prostitution not only as a result of economic exploitation, but also as moral bankruptcy.[8] Even worse, gender relations were in her eyes basically tainted by a sex-for-money deal (He Zhen 1907a). This implies that her criticism was directed not only against historically developed forms of gender relations but against gender relations as such. The only solution she could envisage would be the ideal anarcho-communist society.

Still, her simultaneous insistence on the economic aspects of women's oppression and her open denunciation of oppression of women by women (e.g. mother-in-law vs. daughter-in-law; main wife vs. concubine; mistress vs. maid) (He Zhen 1966b) revealed a double

---

authority of the natal family over women. In the end, though, she hoped to abolish surnames altogether. A recent treatment of He Zhen's views on naming practices is Sivers-Sattler 2001.

[8] In this regard Zarrow's assertion of the primacy of economics in He Zhen's anarchism should be qualified. Part of the problem lies in Zarrow's overlooking the strong Buddhist underpinnings. He acknowledges only the presence of Neo-Confucian aspects in her thinking.

conviction, namely that women on the one hand were definitely oppressed by "the system," but on the other hand were part of "the system" as well. In other words, women were not only victims but also actors. They were capable of the abuse of power (based on money, knowledge and brute force) as much as men and therefore every power-relation had to be abolished. On the basis of absolute equality every reformist way of ameliorating the problems in women's lives or even of fighting for participation in power-holding – which she deemed typical of Western feminism with its dominant women's rights approach (He Zhen 1991) – was clearly obsolete. He Zhen's point was, therefore, not to open up traditionally male spaces to women but to force men to give up their privileges. Only then would "true" communism, i.e. anarcho-communism, be possible, and this was the precondition for resolving gender inequalities (He Zhen 1966a).

The Paris group of Chinese anarchists, on the other hand, was composed only of men. Consequently, their anarchism did not start with gender issues, as did He Zhen's. Their emphasis was more on a general turn-over of Chinese society and in this context they attacked the family system and women's oppression, too. In other words, whereas He Zhen saw the gender problem as of primary importance, taking a decidedly female perspective, the Paris group's main focus rested on general evolutionary laws from which the answers to every single problem could be deduced.[9] Li Shizeng, the main spokesman, was a trained biologist.

He was preoccupied with China's being "retarded" – culturally *and* racially, and hoped to push evolution by enlightening his readership with the torch of science. He later professed the idea – actually somewhat reminiscent of Kang Youwei (see Kang Youwei 1936, part 4) – of improving the Chinese race by "mixed marriages" with Westerners (Müller 2001:241).[10] According to general scientific laws,

---

[9] This point leads to the question of a "male outlook" of science, but I do not want to go into this problem here.

[10] For more general information on questions of race in China, see Dikötter 1992 and Dikötter 1997, part 1. Li himself was the only one of the group who once – if briefly – chose a non-Chinese partner, though without procreating children with her.

he claimed, all human beings are basically equal (Li Shizeng 1947a). Therefore every institution that hinders the realization of this equality has to be demolished. For Chinese women the main obstacles were the social system, their economic dependence and – mainly – the traditional ideology (Li Shizeng 1947d; Li Shizeng 1947c) which had to be overcome by a modern, scientific education (Li Shizeng 1947b). Still, in terms of gender issues, Li was more preoccupied with free marriages and the abolishment of the family structure than with women per se. In other words, his "scientific" perspective actually betrayed a male one. In practice none of the Paris group lived out much of a revolution against the traditional family system (Müller 2001:240-241) even though they refrained from "bad habits" like concubinage, frequenting brothels etc. Their deliberations remained, therefore, mainly in the realm of theory about a better future.

The legacy of these "founding" discourses of the first generation of Chinese anarchists was mixed. He Zhen's anarcho-feminism largely disappeared, at least partly due to her "apostasy" in leaving the revolutionary camp and joining the Manchu side.[11] The Paris group's legacy was openly taken up by later anarchists. The Paris anarchists themselves continued their propaganda into the Republic, now focusing on educational programs. Their continuing on-principle support for new roles for women and a new gender system which they had again articulated in various morality societies in 1912,[12] now also expressed itself practically in their new educational programs. The preparatory school for students planning to study in France with their newly designed "frugal study program" was explicitly open to both sexes, hereby being the first Chinese-run coeducational facility in China.[13] Still, they chose to conceive of separate programs designed for female students going abroad, too (of which the outcome is not very clear), and retained some skepticism as to how far female students who were not supported by their families could earn a living

---

[11] The actual process is still unclear. For further information, see Müller 2001, part 2, chapter 3.
[12] These included the *Jindehui* (Society for the Advancement of Virtue) and the broader *Shehui gailianghui* (Society for the Improvement of Society). For the regulations in detail see Müller 2001:266-270.
[13] Female participants were few though (Müller-Saini 2001:198-199).

as they envisaged for poorer male students in the later work-study program.[14]

Basically, therefore, they remained rather passive in the case of women, on principle opening up new spaces to them but without much concrete effort. The women who did join the work-study program had to depend largely on themselves (Müller-Saini 2001:204).

The First Years of the Republic (1912-1915/16)

After the downfall of the Qing, anarchism also started to flourish in China proper. The main figure, Liu Sifu, who later called himself Shifu (explicitly rejecting any further use of his surname) took up the legacy of the Paris anarchists whose journal *Xin shiji (New Century)* he had read during his prison days following an assassination attempt. Shifu turned to anarchism during the days of the 1911 revolution and became the "soul" (Krebs 1998) or "personification" (Müller 2001) of Chinese anarchism. His journal *Minsheng (People's Voice)*[15] became the leading voice in disseminating anarcho-communism, i.e. the anarchism of Peter Kropotkin who was already the guiding spirit of the first generation of Chinese anarchists and – by the way – of the main faction of world anarchism at the time.

In his pre-anarchist days Shifu had already demonstrated an interest in women's issues by trying to start a girls' school in his home-district. He himself chose a young woman teacher as partner: Ding Xiangtian. She participated in his assassination corps shortly before the revolution and his turn to anarchism. Even though Shifu was already then the central figure of the corps, he did not stand out as clearly as he did later. During the days of the revolution Shifu became very disappointed with the realities of the new Republic and started his *Xinshe* (Heart Society) which basically tried to build a new China by way of new morals. With regard to gender issues, Shifu pleaded for a radical abolishment of the family, including an explicit rejection of

---

[14] Compare, e.g., Wu Zhihui's (one of the key figures of the old Paris group) lecture to female students interested in the work-study program (Wu Zhihui 1980; Müller-Saini 2001:204).

[15] 1913-1921, complete reprint Kyoto 1992.

marriage (Xinshe quyishu 1991; Shifu 1927a; Shifu 1927b). "Free love" in the anarchist sense (i.e. freedom of choice and freedom of ending a partnership without interference by any authorities, not libertinage) was the common catch-word, and Shifu practiced it with Ding in the sense that he never formally married her. His new anarchist group, the *Huimingshe* (Cockcrow Society), which would launch *Minsheng*, consisted mainly of his siblings and friends. Here, too, he proved to be unconventional, for women and men lived together in a kind of commune. Still, it is interesting to note that gender issues play almost no part in *Minsheng*. Even though Shifu held up the legacy of the former Paris group and even had contacts with Emma Goldman,[16] there was much less attention to gender issues than in the former *Xin shiji*. In other words, Shifu concentrated on purely ideological topics, introducing anarchist "orthodoxy" in China. Gender issues obviously did not count as part of the core of ideology. In fact, Shifu's idol Kropotkin, too, did not pay much attention to gender or women's issues, for which he was sometimes criticized by Emma Goldman who otherwise generally agreed with Kropotkin's views (Müller 2001:57, n. 34). Interestingly, Shifu the anarchist did not reveal any more profile in women's issues. Ding Xiangtian, who bore him a child, was practically left aside. Although she had actively cooperated in his earlier assassination corps, she had no voice in *Minsheng*. Shifu did not care much about her and the baby girl (Krebs 1998:116). If a woman comrade and partner had seemed useful, a wife and mother obviously was not, or rather was a burden (Müller 2001:542, n. 97).

In addition one may note that even the way Shifu led his group and published his journal did not mark him as a feminist. The group did live together but work was assigned in a typically gendered division (Krebs 1998:114). Shifu saw himself as a kind of teacher or missionary who was entitled to reserve all his energies for propaganda work. There was hardly any male member of the group whom he allowed to write or translate for *Minsheng*, let alone women. His own sisters were involved in the group but had to see only to the physical parts of publishing, i.e. binding, mailing and the like (Mo Jipeng

---

[16] *Minsheng* no. 21 did present Goldman, but emphasized her anarcho-communism, not her feminism.

1970:39b-40b). Even though Shifu left a long-term impression by his charismatic personality and contributed significantly to the popularity of anarchism in China, and even though his siblings and friends remained influential in the now developing Chinese anarchist movement, his legacy in terms of gender issues remains dubious. Actually he shifted the former affinity of anarchism to feminism present in the first generation to a "purer" ideological and theoretical stance. Ding Xiangtian, by the way, ended up in poverty, trying to sell some of Shifu's writings (Mo Jipeng 1970:63a-64a; Krebs 1998:239, n. 80).

The New Culture/May Fourth Period

Even though Shifu had somewhat brushed aside women's and gender issues in Chinese anarchism, due to the perceived urgency of ideological anarcho-communist propaganda, his followers picked up the thread left over by the first group of Chinese anarchists. This picking-up was done quite consciously as historical antecedents played an important role in anarchist ways of establishing legitimacy. Put in other words, this inclination to a genealogy of ideas was an integral part of anarchist self-understanding (elsewhere as in China).

The Chinese anarchists therefore joined in the developing discussion about women and their role in the new society. The crucial importance of the New Culture/May Fourth period for the development of the Chinese women's movement has long been acknowledged. Yet, the role anarchism and anarchists played has still not been fully understood.[17]

Turning first of all to the leading progressive journals of the time, one notes that several contributions to the discussion about

---

[17] This aspect deserves more attention. I confine myself here to naming a few people: Hua Lin, Yuan Zhenying (briefly addressed below), Zhu Qianzhi, Huang Lingshuang and later Wei Huilin, Mao Yibo, Lu Jianbo and Ba Jin (for the last two also see below). Interestingly, even the recent translations of "influential" articles of the period (Lan Hua/Fong 1999) stick to the questionable criterion of defining "importance" by choosing authors who became influential *later*. Partly due to the translators' taking a similar Chinese collection from 1981 as guideline, most authors turn out to be later Communists. With Wang Zheng's (1999) study, at least the liberal women's movement has started to be put back into place now.

women were written by authors with an anarchist background. Besides, more general contributions by those authors there were also explicitly anarchist ones which, of course, set the tone in the consciously anarchist press.

I want to focus here on the introduction of Emma Goldman's feminism to Chinese readers. Goldman was the major exponent of anarcho-feminism in the West. Browsing through the history of Western anarchism, one rarely finds outstanding women and, of those, only a few who actively engaged in women's issues. With Goldman the case was different. As already noted she followed the anarcho-communism of Kropotkin and contributed a lot to the propagation of this ideal, but her life-long engagement in women's issues marked her as the central figure of anarcho-feminism. Goldman polemicized against the bourgeois feminist movement, especially against the suffrage movement, because as an anarchist she denied any value to parliaments and politics. On the other hand she was only partly supportive of the movement led by Margaret Sanger, who propagated birth control and who would also tour China in 1922. In Goldman's eyes birth control was necessary and she herself took many risks by making speeches on this and related topics; still this was not the whole answer to her. If birth control would not be integrated into a reformulation of gender relations and of society in general, the movement would easily become a technical one (teaching methods of birth control) at best, an upper-class one at worst.

Goldman, who had become famous for her propagation of the often misunderstood slogan "free love" (even if it did not originate with her) agitated against the institution of marriage, because in her eyes it was not really different from prostitution, i.e. sex for money. Women should be independent economically and – like men – free to choose partners and to leave them. Nothing and nobody should interfere with these personal decisions. There was no hatred of men in general in Goldman's feminism, rather she identified "the system" as the arch-enemy. She herself lived with several partners during her life and because of this and her public assaults on the institution of marriage, sanctioned by the state and the church, she became the target of vehement attacks in the United States, where she lived most of her life. In 1919 she was expelled from the United States and, as a Russian-born Jew, forcefully repatriated to the Soviet Union. Here she became very critical of state-communism in general and the fate of women in this "revolutionary" country in particular. Still, she believed that only "true" communism, i.e. anarcho-communism, would finally resolve the problem of women's oppression – and also that of men. In this regard her outlook resembled that of the Marxist communists. Feminism would have to be integrated into the overarching system of ideology. Anything else she termed "bourgeois."

Goldman's name had not been totally unfamiliar to the Chinese reading public before the New Culture Movement. As early as 1903, Su Manshu, who later was connected to the Tokyo group of Chinese anarchists, had written a short presentation of Goldman (Su Manshu 1968), but then she was conceived of primarily as a radical activist (connected with her alleged involvement in the assassination of US-president McKinley), not as a feminist. In the anarchist press of the first generation, as with Shifu, she figured primarily as a female "hero" of anarcho-communism, and much of what was written later about her stuck to this view. Furthermore, in the 1920s her personal experiences and indictments of Soviet rule would be much publicized. But in the May Fourth period her feminism, too, was introduced to China. The catchword "free love" was a well-established motto used by very different people who did not always realize the anarcho-feminist background. In 1917, the anarchist Yuan Zhenying began to present Goldman's feminism in *Xin qingnian (New Youth)* by translating her views on marriage and love (Goldman/Yuan Zhenying 1962).[18] He went on to translate other central articles of Goldman's on prostitution,[19] the futility of suffrage,[20] the "hypocrisy of puritanism"[21] and the "tragedy of woman's emancipation."[22] The latter she perceived in

---

[18] Goldman's article "Marriage and Love" is to be found in Goldman 1969.
[19] "The Traffic in Women," in: ibid.
[20] "Woman's Suffrage," in: ibid.
[21] In: ibid.
[22] In: ibid. The Chinese translations by Yuan Zhenying of all these articles during the May Fourth years were again published together with the other articles of Goldman's *Anarchism and Other Essays* as a *Collection of Goldman's Writings*

those women who claimed to be economically independent and without husbands, while in their heads still clinging to conventional gender relations. Because Yuan did his earliest translations in the classical language, Lu Jianbo, for one, would retranslate some of Goldman's articles in the vernacular.[23] Later on Lu, Qin Baopu and Ba Jin would keep Goldman popular, but only Lu Jianbo highlighted her views on gender questions.[24]

Besides this theoretical introduction to anarcho-feminism, the New Culture/May Fourth period abounded in practical experiments with new gender roles. Couples living freely together became increasingly common among the student generation in the big cities. In general, therefore, the involved people were very young. Some had already entered arranged marriages; most only faced this prospect. Emancipation of the family called for alternatives (consider Lu Xun's question about where Nora could go after leaving home) (Lan Hua/Fong 1999:176-181). One alternative could be a commune, a lifestyle suitable to anarchist-oriented people. Even though anarchists were not always directly involved, the craze for communes that developed around 1920 had decidedly anarchistic underpinnings.[25] On the other hand, these experiments were usually of short duration. Emancipation from one's family (often also expressed in the rejection of surnames) was not that easy, but even more difficult was the living-out of these new gender roles. Sometimes emotional attachments were seen as a crucial factor in the demise of the communes (Yeh Wen-hsin 1996:195-196, 199-200). "Free love" was obviously a tricky thing. From the outside there was always strong pressure against this kind of free social intercourse of sexes (even though Chinese communes tended to keep some organizational distinction between the sexes).

(Gaoman nüshi wenji) in the mid-1920s. See the review of Yi Wenbin (Yi Wenbin 1926).

[23] See e.g. Lu Jianbo's retranslation of "Marriage and Love" (*Jiehun yu lian'ai*) (Goldman/Lu Jianbo 1927). He later added the translation of Hippolyte Havel's biographical sketch of Goldman (included in Goldman 1969) (Havel/Lu Jianbo 1927).

[24] Lu Jianbo collected some of her work in translation and published it as *Ziyou de nüxing (Free Women)* (Ge Maochun et al. 1991, 2:1084; Lu Zhe 1990:167).

[25] A more extensive treatment of this point can be found in Müller 2001:370-388.

The blame usually fell on the women, who were depicted by outsiders as "promiscuous." This kind of "bad" reputation has been repeatedly seen by women as haunting (Wang Zheng 1999:163-164, 169, 183-184; Gilmartin 1995:103, 142-143, 197). Whereas men turned away from these experiments disillusioned (e.g. [Shi] Cuntong 1920), for women the way "back" into society was definitely more difficult. Even in those cases where outright women's groups were formed, none could endure (Liu Jucai 1989:459-464). This was, of course, also an outcome of the problem of financing. Not only did women students get much less support from their families, they also had more difficulties in landing jobs and also often had less expertise in job-relevant knowledge and training. (This became very clear in the case of those women who participated in the work-study program in France, which was initially devised by the old Paris group of Chinese anarchists) (Müller-Saini 2001; Barman/Dulioust 1987).

In the explicitly anarchist press of the May Fourth period, on the other hand, gender issues remained alive but did not really go beyond what had been formulated in the "founding" discourses. Women remained a subspecies of those "oppressed" to be awakened to emancipate themselves.

Concluding this phase one may briefly mention a rather curious contribution by southern anarchists in the journal *Minxing (Fujian Star)* (1919-1920). Here the basic feature of equality was spelled out for the sexes in a totally utopian way, but starting from a very concrete problem (not only often met with by anarchists): If a man loves a woman, but that woman loves another man and lives with him, she has realized her freedom. But what about the freedom of the first man? The solution could lie only in groups of men loving groups of women (Chen Qiulin 1919).

The Late 1920s and Early 1930s

In the 1920s, as is well known, free partnerships were very much in vogue among the young Chinese intelligentsia. Very often these relationships were extremely idealistic – and often without the problematic presence of children. The anarchist-nihilist Zhu Qianzhi, for one, even proposed a conscious rejection of procreation (Zhu Qianzhi 1921:229ff.). This situation was partly due to young age, of course, but it also reflected a view of life. In the bid to overcome the institution of family, children were hard to integrate. Still it is noteworthy that even in the 1920s when gender issues were much on the agenda even in society in general, Chinese anarchists did not produce any significant female representative. We are informed about women having participated in various groups, but since the times of He Zhen no woman of any influence can be discerned.

Chinese anarchist feminism was still a male endeavor. In the mid-/late 1920s two individuals became more prominent: Lu Jianbo and Ba Jin. Lu Jianbo often contributed to *Xin nüxing (New Woman)*, a progressive journal, though not an anarchist one. In the journal various developments of women's movements in other countries, including the Soviet Union, were dealt with. Lu published also separately on women[26] and was unusual again in the sense that he had married and wanted his wife to be a partner even in propaganda. (Some of his publications on women's issues were actually coauthored by her.) This was a far cry from Shifu, who had had no place for women, be it his lover or his sisters, in propaganda work. Still, even though much of Lu's work is hard to find today, it is even more difficult with contributions of his wife Deng Tianyu. Furthermore, in the puritanical atmosphere of Chinese anarchism in the 1920s, Lu's open affirmation of being attracted to the other sex was disturbing to many comrades and forced him to "explain" himself (Lu Jianbo 1994:138).[27]

---

[26] Some of his publications are listed in Ge Maochun et al. 1991, 2:1084.
[27] By the way, this feature of celibacy had been more common in the earlier years of the New Culture Movement (Wang Zheng 1999:280), but with the anarchists

This atmosphere can be gleaned from some of Ba Jin's writings. Ba Jin who – like Lu Jianbo – admired Emma Goldman, entertained an extremely idealistic relationship with women. Actually, in the case of Goldman, he did not really seize on her feminism,[28] but preferred to call her (e.g. in his letters to her), quite tellingly, his "spiritual *mother*." Lu Jianbo, on the other hand, did take up Goldman's feminist views. Ba Jin was long said to be "immune" to women. He himself later explicitly refuted rumors that he had formed a group with two other comrades to swear off love relationships (Ba Jin 1985a:339). When he married, he was already forty and it took some years, almost into the times of the People's Republic of China (PRC), until he lived a "normal" family life.

Ba Jin's reluctance in terms of love relationship – in spite of his reputation as a "romantic" author – can be explained by his obvious fear that love distracts one from the important mission of propaganda (Ba Jin 1985b:356, n. 1). In his trilogy *Love (Aiqing de sanbuqu)* he actually blamed his comrades for betraying anarchism by starting a family.[29] In fact, many anarchists were active in the movement as youngsters. Coming more of age they dropped out. This process was significantly accelerated by the critical developments since the mid-1920s. Anarchists had lost out to the Marxist communists especially after the May Thirtieth Incident (1925) and the Northern Expedition (1926-1928). These developments had caused a deep division in anarchist circles, epitomized by the split in 1927 between the anarchist "right" who joined the GMD of Jiang Kaishek (including most of the old Paris group), and the anarchist "left" around Lu Jianbo. Ba Jin was somewhere in between, basically tending to the left. Still, in his account of the downfall of Chinese anarchism, Ba Jin blamed internal factors much more than external ones, and of these

---

it seems to have stuck more deeply than with anybody else, mainly due to their moral impetus, but probably partly due also to their delicate position between the Chinese Communist Party (CCP) and the Nationalist Party (Guomindang, GMD).

[28] He stated explicitly that he did the retranslation of Goldman's "The Tragedy of Women's Emancipation" only at Goldman's personal request (Müller 2001:541, n. 94).

[29] He made this point clearly in his long preface to the trilogy (Ba Jin 1985a, see esp. 307-308).

internal factors loss of interest and commitment was central (Müller 2001:615-616). This he attributed to "bourgeoization" through marriage, because marriage led to financial responsibilities and consequently to vulnerability. In other words, petty day-to-day problems ate up revolutionary fervor. Because of these financial pressures, comrades had to renounce their propaganda work for paying alternatives. This meant that the "burden" of marriage led to an acquiesement to "the system."

Ba Jin's charges were not totally out of place. Bi Xiushao, one of the most wavering figures in the Chinese anarchist movement, more or less explicitly explained his going back and fro between anarchists and Nationalists with the need to feed his big family (Bi Xiushao 1991). Ba Jin did not blame women in general as culprits, but wanted them to be mere partners or comrades. In his view, anarchist gender relations had to remain untainted by overt desire and building-up of extra-ideological commitments. He wrote a lot about romantic involvements, but these should not be allowed to take the first place in the life of "comrades." Therefore he subscribed to friendship as the primary human relationship. This included women, for sure, but in an idealistic way, not a sexual one. In the movement people had, above all, to be "pure."

Final Remarks

Chinese anarchists have been credited as being among China's first feminists (Zarrow 1990:2) and there is certainly some truth to this. Still, in view of this reputation, it is amazing that in browsing through collections of anarchist materials – be it the over 1,000 pages of the *Collection of Materials on Anarchist Thought (Wuzhengfuzhuyi sixiang ziliaoxuan)* (Ge Maochun et al. 1991), be it the 12-volume-collection published in Japan (Sakai/Saga 1994) – one finds only a single female author: He Zhen. She was certainly a remarkable case in many ways, but it is even more noteworthy that this single woman was not central to the anarchist movement in China. She seems to have had hardly any impact on later developments. On the other hand, even though anarchism was very popular until the early 1920s and many women were drawn into social activities especially during May Fourth, there is virtually no outstanding anarchist woman in China. This holds true not only for authorship which – more than with other ideologies – in anarchism was *the* means of gaining visibility, because publications were to a degree a substitute for organization; it holds also true at the level of other activities. Even in memoirs of and interviews with male anarchists, at least, women are rarely mentioned.

To be sure, even Western anarchism was not rich in great female figures, and in Japan they were few, too, but still there were at least some. Chinese communism has often been criticized for lack of gender equality, but in terms of women's voice and the general visibility of women, their record is decidedly better than the anarchist one. About the reasons for this "lack" one can only speculate. Women reportedly participated in anarchist activities and groups, but why did they remain without any profile? The often underground activity was certainly a limiting factor, but this holds partly true for Chinese Communists as well. The lack of organization could be another factor, as at least in the Communist movement the need to build up a "women's department" or "women's bureau" called for some women to come to the fore, even though in Communist publications female contributions were very rare, too. In the case of communism, as has been demonstrated (Gilmartin 1995:48, 67-68, 122, 142), being the wife of an important leader was usually the precondition for gaining visibility. Anarchists were often young and single, but even when they had wives or partners, these remained rather obscure. This suggests a significant lack of will or support, but it also could be interpreted in terms of anarchist logic: nobody would do for women, if they did not do it for themselves.

In sum, anarchist rhetoric raised hopes that were not fulfilled in social practice. The paradigmatic case is Shifu. He started with a mildly feminist agenda and ended up – putting it in a somewhat exaggerated way – as an ideological patriarch. In his case the driving force seems to have been a deep sense of mission to propagate the truth of anarcho-communism. Even though he professed to live up to his faith, this did not extend to a comprehensive practical reformulation of gender relations. Rather, women's roles remained ephemeral to the "central" ideological tenets of anarcho-communism and in practice women were not granted an active part in propaganda work. In spite of continuing feminist rhetoric, this was to be basically men's business in later decades as well.

References

Ba Jin, "Aiqing de sanbuqu" zongxu (General Preface to the Trilogy "Love"), (written in 1935), in: Li Cunguang 1985a, vol. 1, pp. 305-348.
Ba Jin, "Aiqing de sanbuqu" zuozhe de zibai (Confession of the Author of the Trilogy "Love"), (written in 1935), in: Li Cunguang 1985b, vol. 1, pp. 349-361.
Barman, Geneviève, Nicole Dulioust, Un groupe oublié: Les étudiantes-ouvrières chinoises en France, in: *Études chinoises* 6:2 (1987), pp. 9-46.
Bernal, Martin, The Triumph of Anarchism over Marxism, 1906-1907, in: Mary C. Wright (ed.), *China in Revolution: The First Phase, 1900-1913*, New Haven, London 1968, pp. 97-142.
Bi Xiushao, Wo xinyang wuzhengfuzhuyi de qianqian houhou (The Whole Story about My Believing in Anarchism), (interview in 1982), in: Ge Maochun et al. 1991, vol. 2, pp. 1022-1038.
(Chen) Qiulin, Nannü xingyu wenti de jieda (The Solution to the Problem of Sexual Desire between the Sexes), in: *Minxing* 7 (1919), pp. 9-12.
Dikötter, Frank, *The Discourse of Race in Modern China*, London 1992.
Dikötter, Frank (ed.), *The Construction of Racial Identities in China and Japan: Historical and Contemporary Perspectives*, London 1997.
Dirlik, Arif, *Anarchism in the Chinese Revolution*, Berkeley, Los Angeles, Oxford 1991.
Ge Maochun, Jiang Jun, Li Xingzhi (eds.), *Wuzhengfuzhuyi sixiang ziliaoxuan* (Collection of Materials on Anarchist Thought), 2 vols., Beijing ²1991 (¹1984).
Gilmartin, Christina K., *Engendering the Chinese Revolution: Radical Women, Communist Politics, and Mass Movements in the 1920s*, Berkeley, Los Angeles, London 1995.

Goldman, Emma, *Anarchism and Other Essays*, New York 1969 (^{1}1910).
Goldman, Emma ([Lu] Jianbo, trans.), Jiehun yu lian'ai (Marriage and Love), in: *Xin nüxing* 2:1 (1927), pp. 81-92.
Goldman, Emma ([Yuan] Zhenying, trans.), Meiguo Gaoman nüshi: Jiehun yu lian'ai (The American Mrs. Goldman: Marriage and Love), in: *Xin qingnian* 3:5 (1917), reprint Tokyo 1962, 9 pp.
Havel, Hippolyte ([Lu] Jianbo, trans.), Aima Gaodeman zhuan (Biography of Emma Goldman), in: *Xin nüxing* 2:3 (1927), pp. 269-284.
He (Yin) Zhen, Diwang yu changji (Emperor and Courtesan), in: *Tianyi* 1 (1907a), pp. 13-14.
He (Yin) Zhen, Nüzi fuchoulun (On Women's Revenge), in: *Tianyi* 2-10 (1907b).
He (Yin) Zhen, Nüzi xuanbushu (Women's Declaration), in: *Tianyi* 1 (1907c), pp. 1-7.
(He) Zhen, Lun nüzi dang zhi gongchanzhuyi (Women Should Know about Communism), in: *Tianyi* 8-10 (1907), partial reprint Tokyo 1966a, pp. 229-232.
(He) Zhen, Lun Zhongguo nüzi suo shou zhi candu (On the Cruel Treatment Received by Chinese Women), in: *Tianyi* 15 (1908), partial reprint Tokyo 1966b, pp. 443-450.
(He) Zhen, Nüzi jiefang wenti (The Problem of Women's Emancipation), in: *Tianyi* 7-10 (1907), reproduced in: Ge Maochun et al. 1991, vol. 1, pp. 98-107.
Judge, Joan, Talent, Virtue, and the Nation: Chinese Nationalisms and Female Subjectivities in the Early Twentieth Century, in: *American Historical Review* 106 (2001), pp. 765-803.
Kang Youwei, *Datongshu* (Book of the Great Unity), Shanghai ^{2}1936 (^{1}1935).
(Kōtoku Shūsui), Xingde Qiushui lai han (Letter from Kōtoku Shūsui), in: *Tianyi* 3 (1907), partial reprint Tokyo 1966, pp. 51-52.
Krebs, Edward S., *Shifu: Soul of Chinese Anarchism*, Lanham 1998.
Lan Hua R., Vanessa L. Fong, (eds.), *Women in Republican China: A Sourcebook*, Armonk, London 1999.
Li Cunguang (ed.), *Ba Jin yanjiu ziliao* (Materials for the Study of Ba Jin), vol. 1, Fuzhou 1985.

Li Shizeng (pseud. Zhen), Nannü zhi geming (Gender Revolution), in: *Xin shiji* 7 (1907), reprint Shanghai 1947a, pp. 3-4.
Li Shizeng (pseud. Zhen), Nüjie geming (Revolution in the World of Women), in: *Xin shiji* 5 (1907), reprint Shanghai 1947b, pp. 2-3.
Li Shizeng (pseud. Zhen), Sangang geming (Revolution of the Three Followings), in: *Xin shiji* 11 (1907), reprint Shanghai 1947c, pp.1-2.
Li Shizeng (pseud. Zhen), Xu nannü geming (Further on Gender Revolution), in: *Xin shiji* 8 (1907), reprint Shanghai 1947d, p. 1.
Liu Jucai, *Zhongguo jindai funü yundongshi* (A History of the Women's Movement in Modern China), Liaoning 1989.
Lu Jianbo, You ci de qiangwei (Thorny Roses), Shanghai 1936 (preface dated 1928), reproduced in: Sakai/Saga 1994, vol. 12.
Lu Zhe, *Zhongguo wuzhengfuzhuyi shigao* (Outline of the History of Chinese Anarchism), Fuzhou 1990.
Mo Jipeng, *Huiyi Shifu* (Remembering Shifu), unpublished manuscript, ca. 1970.
Müller, Gotelind, *China, Kropotkin und der Anarchismus: Eine Kulturbewegung im China des frühen 20. Jahrhunderts unter dem Einfluß des Westens und japanischer Vorbilder*, Wiesbaden 2001.
Müller-Saini, Gotelind, Chinesische Frauen zwischen Bildung und Geld: Ideal und Realität der Werkstudentinnen in den frühen Jahren der Republik, in: Monika Übelhör (ed.), *Zwischen Tradition und Revolution: Lebensentwürfe chinesischer Frauen an der Schwelle zur Moderne*, Marburg 2001, pp. 196-217.
Sakai Hirobumi, Saga Takashi, *Genten chūgoku anakizumu shiryō shūsei* (Collection of Original Historical Materials on Chinese Anarchism), 12 vols. with explanatory booklet, Tokyo 1994.
(Shi) Cuntong, "Gongdu huzhutuan" di shiyan he jiaoxun (The Experiment of the "Work-Study Mutual Aid Group" and Its Lessons), in: *Xingqi pinglun* 48 (1920), part 7, pp. 1-4.
Shifu, Fei hunyin zhuyi (Against Marriage), 1912, in: Tiexin 1927a, pp. 107-114.
Shifu, Fei jiazu zhuyi (Against the Family), 1912, in: Tiexin 1927b, pp. 115-125.
Sievers, Sharon L., *Flowers in Salt: The Beginnings of Feminist Consciousness in Modern Japan*, Stanford 1983.

Sivers-Sattler, Gabriele von, He Zhens Forderungen zur Namensgebung von Frauen im vorrevolutionären China: Untersuchung zur anarchistischen Zeitschrift *Tian Yi* („Naturgemäße Rechtlichkeit"), 1907-1908, in: Gimpel, Denise, Melanie Hanz (eds.), *Cheng – All in Sincerity [sic]: Festschrift in Honour of Monika Übelhör*, Hamburg 2001, pp. 275-284.

(Su Manshu) (pseud. Zigu), Nüjie Guoerman (The Heroine Goldman), in: *Guomin riribao huibian* (Collection of the People's Daily) 3 (1903), reprint Taipei 1968, pp. 0801-0803.

Tianyi, 1907-1908, partial reprint Tokyo 1966. (No. 1 and parts of no. 2 by courtesy of the University of Marburg.)

Tiexin (pseud.) (ed.), *Shifu wencun* (Writings of Shifu), Guangzhou 1927.

Wang Zheng, *Women in the Chinese Enlightenment: Oral and Textual Histories*, Berkeley, Los Angeles, London 1999.

Wu Zhihui, Nüzi qingong jianxue (Women's Diligent Work and Frugal Study), in: Dagongbao, 3, 8 November 1919, reproduced in: Zhang Yunhou, Yin Xuyi, Li Junchen (eds.), *Liu Fa qingong jianxue yundong* (The Movement of Diligent Work and Frugal Study in France), Shanghai 1980, vol. 1, pp. 301-302.

Xinshe quyishu (What the Heart Society Wants), in: Shehui shijie 5 (November 1912), reproduced in: Ge Maochun et al. 1991, vol. 1, pp. 235-239.

Yeh Wen-hsin, *Provincial Passages: Culture, Space and the Origins of Chinese Communism*, Berkeley, Los Angeles, London 1996.

Yi Wenbin, Gaoman nüshi wenji (Writings of Mrs. Goldman), in: *Xin nüxing* 1:10 (1926), pp. 754-756.

Zarrow, Peter, He Zhen and Anarcho-Feminism in China, in: *Journal of Asian Studies* 47:4 (1988), pp. 796-813.

Zarrow, Peter, *Anarchism and Chinese Political Culture*, New York 1990.

(Zhang Ji), Zhang Ji jun you Lundun lai han (Mr. Zhang Ji's Letters from London), in: *Hengbao* 4 (1908), p. 2.

Zhu Qianzhi, *Geming zhexue* (Revolutionary Philosophy), Shanghai 1921.

Opposition to Women's Suffrage in China: Confronting Modernity in Governance

Louise Edwards

This essay explores the opposition faced by the women's suffrage movement in China to their campaign to have equal participation in parliamentary politics for both men and women – *funü canzheng yundong*. The essay explains the comparative rapidity of the women's suffrage victories in China – albeit fragmented and patchy in coverage – as resulting in part from the ineffectiveness of the anti-suffrage lobbyists. While the success of the campaigns is primarily due to the strategic perseverance of the women's suffrage activists, it is also important to consider the strength of the opposition the women faced in any analysis of the comparative success of their movement to appreciate its full historical significance. Brian Harrison argues that the study of anti-suffragism places the suffrage campaigns "firmly into context" (Harrison 1978:14). Moreover, in her 1994 article on the state of academic research on women's suffrage, Carole Pateman raised the concern that little was known about struggles for suffrage outside of the Western world. She also pointed out that there was equally little known about the nature of the opposition to women's suffrage across cultures (Pateman 1994:346). How does a specific cultural and historical context affect the nature of the public debates about women's participation in politics? This essay aims to contribute to what will no doubt be the ongoing and lengthy procedure of filling this gap.

Specifically, the essay argues that the "anti's" cause was undermined by the constant state of political, social, economic and military chaos that China was experiencing during the first three decades of the Republic. The system of Republican representative

---

This research was made possible by the generous support of the Australian Research Council. The author would also like to thank the participants of the Berlin conference for their most useful advice.

democracy that the "antis" aimed to "preserve" or "consolidate" was a clear failure. By dismantling the monarchy with the overthrow of the Qing dynasty in 1911 the reformist intellectuals debating women's suffrage had embraced radical social change as a solution to current problems thus rendering "consolidation" a less attractive option. Moreover, the modernity imperative that drove much social and political debate during the 1910s, 1920s and 1930s ensured that women's suffrage – which women's suffrage activists had effectively presented as an emblem of modernity – was difficult for the "antis" to counteract. Ultimately, the "antis" found themselves in the untenable position of opposing Chinese modernization. Even provocative arguments based on physiological, "natural" differences between men and women were unable to win the case for the "antis."

In the context of the reformist-elite's desire for modernity, the Chinese "antis" were less effective at stalling women's suffrage than their counterpart organizations had been in the West. The essay narrates the major arguments posed by the "antis" in China and draws comparisons with those posed by the "antis" in the West. In so doing, it becomes clear that there were many considerable points of similarity among the "antis" around the globe. However, these same arguments against women's suffrage were less effective in the Chinese context for specific social and political reasons.

Modernity and Suffrage

Over the course of the first three decades of the twentieth century, China's women's suffrage activists facilitated a major shift in the perception of their goal – women's suffrage was not dangerous radicalism, but representative of women's desire to work on behalf of the nation, the new Republic of China, as dedicated citizens. The shift in perceptions was made possible by their public espousal of the place of women's suffrage within the Chinese modernity project.

Leo Lee describes modernity as being associated with a "new linear consciousness of time and history [...] derived from a social Darwinist concept of evolution" (Lee 2000:31). The suffrage activists, within a global suffrage movement, strategically placed themselves in this linear consciousness. China's political leaders of the early Republican decades began to perceive of their task as moving along a tangent between the backwardness of dynastic China and modern constitutional nationhood. In order not to slip further back, social and political reforms had to be made. The composition of the exact detail of these reforms was the contentious issue. Indeed, modernity in governance necessarily incorporated some elements of tradition and, as Leo Lee notes, some Chinese around the May Fourth period saw a mixture of Chinese tradition and Western modernity as the appropriate path (ibid. 34). Women's suffrage activists occupied this complex discursive space – winning gains for women while simultaneously buttressing the perceived traditional and inherently *Chinese* gendered social values. China's "suffragettes" presented themselves as good Chinese in a new nation that was coming to terms with its global status.

During these early decades of the twentieth century China's suffrage activists emerged as self-sacrificing, loyal political workers whose goal lay not in wresting power from men for selfish political gain. Rather, their goals were to modernize the nation, to rebuild the nation and to win international respectability for the nation. This "loyal patriot suffragette" invoked sufficient connotations of the self-sacrificing virtuous women of the past that she was "traditional" while also being very "modern." The link between suffrage and modernity strengthened as nationalist discourse gradually emerged. As Yeh Wen-hsin has noted, "the valorization of the nation and public opened up new spheres for women's activities" (Yeh Wen-hsin 2000:25). This new space enabled women to challenge their subordination to familial patriarchy while simultaneously embracing a "modern" role as good sisters, daughters and wives to the (patriarchal) nation-state. This modern feminine space included participation in supporting the modern nation-state and its accompanying nationalist discourse in governance. Women's participation in party, provincial and national politics was a loyal, virtuous and noble performance of dedication to the nation. In this respect, the Chinese "antis" were in the invidious position of arguing against an increasingly strengthening nationalist discourse that included virtuous women's labor and noble self-sacrifice as integral to its system of governance. Many were the stories and journal articles on the "new woman" and her importance to the creation of a new China. As Duara has explained, even the conservatives within this elite agreed that China's women needed renovation; however, their nationalist project envisaged a modern woman who also maintained the essential traditional Chinese womanly attribute – the spirit of self-sacrifice (Duara 2000:347). It is within this nexus that China's women's suffragists were able to successfully operate – modern nationalistic workers for the rebuilding of China.

In 1912, just after the establishment of the Republic of China, one of the less radical women's suffrage groups, the "Shenzhou Women's Assistance Society" (*Shenzhou nüjie gonghe xiejishe*), wrote a letter to the interim president, Sun Yat-sen, in which their discursive position in the new Republican nation-state is explained. Prominent Revolutionary Alliance member Zhang Mojun (also known as Zhang Shaohan) (1883-1965) led the group. Their letter spoke of the importance of gender equality for rebuilding the strength of the nation. They stressed that women had been active in the revolution that led to the formation of the Republic and through these actions had demonstrated women's patriotic feelings for the "fatherland" (Shenzhou nüjie gonghe xiejishe 1936:61-63). Later suffragists mobilized similar arguments. Between 1919 and 1921, the major federation of women's suffrage groups, the "United Women's Association" (UWA) (*Nüjie lianhehui*), was linked explicitly with the national revolution cause. The constitution of the Guangdong UWA stated from the outset that it aimed to "encourage women to exert themselves for the national revolution, to promote the realization of [Sun Yatsen's] Three Principles of the People, to encourage a women's movement and to safeguard women's rights" (Guangdong nüjie lianhehui 1936:97-104). Even more left-wing radical groups of this period enunciated their campaign for political rights within the context of national service. The "Beijing Women's Right's League" (*Nüquan yundong tongmenghui*), which maintained close membership links with the Chinese Communist Party (CCP), declared in its manifesto: "In this era of people's revolution we women should participate in such a revolutionary movement. This is not only our duty but also our right" (Nüquan yundong tongmenghui 1936:121-122). Thus, throughout the 1910s and 1920s, China's aspiring women politicians were patriotic and nationalistic and publicly espoused a "culture of service" and womanly sacrifice.

In addition, the Chinese women's suffrage campaign was part of an international "modernizing" trend that eventually reconfigured citizenship along universalistic and individualistic lines wherein distinctions between men and women were inappropriate. This is not to say that China's suffrage movement was the passive beneficiary of this increasingly "universal norm." Rather the women's campaigns in China formed part of the international trend *towards* this "norm." Ramirez et al. (1997:735) have convincingly demonstrated that "during the twentieth century national factors have grown less important to this struggle as the locus of debate has become internationalized." However, they point to the 1930s as the turning point: "By the 1930s the localized national movements and their organizational infrastructure were overshadowed by transnational influences that eventually dictated a particular model of citizenship in which women held the franchise" (ibid.). As will be discussed in the section below, the crucial first victories for China's suffrage activists came in the early 1920s and it is clear that national concerns and domestic debates are of paramount importance to the success of this movement. Nonetheless, China's suffrage movement and the emerging and strengthening public narrative creating the Chinese modern nation-state were enmeshed in the global. As contributors to this global trend towards women's suffrage normalization, China's participants in political debate – both pro and anti women's suffrage – demonstrated China's increasingly stable "imagined nation." This is precisely because in their discussions about women's citizenship they engaged in a process of defining China against the more well-established nations of Europe and the Americas. In the view of the time countries like Germany, France, the United States of America, and Britain were perceived as "advanced" and "modern" with constitutions that guaranteed their prosperity and success. Andrew Nathan argued that the active modernizers of China during this period held constitutionalism paramount and "their models were the Western nations and Japan, where constitutions and national power seemed conspicuously linked" (Nathan 1976:9). As we will see below, China's women's suffrage activists successfully insinuated themselves into a growing nationalist discourse that took pride in China's potential as a modern nation. The women's suffrage activists in the 1910s and 1920s were loyal women to the Chinese nation as it faced tough comparisons with the powerful, modern nations either side of the Atlantic.

Women's Campaigns for Suffrage in China: An Overview

The feminist movement for suffrage rights in China began as soon as the Republic was being formed in the closing months of 1911. Socialist party activist Lin Zongsu formed the "Women's Suffrage Comrades' Alliance" (*Nüzi canzheng tongzhihui*) on 12 November 1911 in Shanghai – only weeks after the collapse of the Qing dynasty. Their goal was to "enhance women's knowledge of politics, nurture women's political strength, and to win the rights to political participation due full citizens" (Lin Zongsu 1912). A few months later, in February 1912, Tang Qunying formed the "Alliance for Women's Participation in Politics" (*Nüzi canzheng tongmenghui*), co-opting one of the alternative names for Lin's 1911 group for her new association (Nüzi canzheng tongmenghui 1911). Tang's group served as an umbrella organization drawing Lin Zongsu's and five other women's rights groups together in the campaign to enshrine gender equality in the first constitution of the Republic. This umbrella organization engaged in numerous controversial activities over the month of March – including storming parliament, smashing windows, assaulting parliamentary security guards. They also deployed more conventional methods such as organizing rallies and marches, letter writing, petitioning and lobbying. However, their attempts to ensure that women were recognized as full citizens resulted in failure when by the end of March the constitution failed to reflect their demands. Although these women struggled on for another eighteen months, their campaign came to a close along with several other democratic organizations as Yuan Shikai's increasingly draconian laws prohibited their activities. This period of activism by women on suffrage issues between 1911 and 1913 is known as the "first wave."

The women's suffrage movement revived in the late 1910s, as part of the general politicization of China resulting from the May Fourth Movement. However, this so-called "second wave" also gained impetus from the provincial independence movement that was sweeping southern China during the four years from 1918. The inability of the Beijing-based government to maintain legitimacy, the existence of the competing government in Guangzhou led by Sun Yat-sen, and the continued military instability resulted in an enthusiasm for individual provinces to organize their own political structures. This included the writing of a constitution and the establishment of elected parliaments. The women's suffrage activists saw the opportunity to move quickly to win gender equality in these provincial constitutions. They were successful in several important provinces winning rights to political participation in Hunan in June 1921, Zhejiang in September 1921, Guangdong in December 1921, and Sichuan in 1923 (Edwards 2002a). This success was comparatively early and comparatively rapid in global terms. Nonetheless, despite these successes at the provincial level, the goal for recognition in a national constitution remained elusive. However, the power of the "antis" diminished quickly from the mid-1920s with the successes at the provincial level.

During the 1920s, national reunification was the major concern for most politically active Chinese – both men and women. The successful conclusion of the Northern Expedition in unifying China was undermined by the right wing of the Nationalist Party (Guomindang, GMD) with the brutal expulsion of the CCP during 1927 and 1928. Over the course of the next decade, the energies of the women's movement were divided between those who supported the CCP and those who remained within the GMD-controlled areas. Not all of the latter were supporters of the GMD and many of these women forged productive liaisons with women activists in the CCP during the 1930s. The competition for credibility between the CCP and the GMD helped promote women's rights as neither party wanted to alienate the politically active women. Consequently, in both GMD- and CCP-controlled areas constitutions emerged that trumpeted gender equality in political rights. In the GMD-controlled areas this appeared first in the "Tutelage Constitution" of 1931 and was formalized in the "Double Fifth Constitution" of 1936. The 1936 document was the forerunner of the 1946 "Constitution of the Republic of China" ratified by the GMD prior to its defeat in the civil war. From 1931 onwards, women participated in politics with confidence that their position was legally legitimate. In the CCP-controlled areas 1931 is a similarly significant year. Electoral laws for the Ruijin Township Soviet confirmed the principle of gender equality and women's rights and by 1933 gender equality was confirmed in election laws for the entire Jiangxi Soviet. This convention expanded to include each of the CCP's base areas.

As the war with Japan intensified from the late 1930s, women of all political persuasions moved to enshrine set minimum quotas for women in the constitution. This campaign was waged largely within the war-time parliament – which included both CCP and GMD members – and victory was confirmed in the 1946 "Constitution of the Republic of China" which guaranteed women a set minimum of 10 percent of seats (Edwards 1999). From 1949, with the defeat of the GMD, this constitutional arrangement was isolated on the island of Taiwan and the provisions for women's quotas are still maintained today. In the rest of China, the CCP's victory saw the reaffirmation of gender equality with the first "Constitution of the People's Republic of China" in 1954.

The major problem for the women's suffrage activists in China was that for the most part their victories remained theoretical. Although women voted and stood for election for a brief period in the 1920s (for example, women were elected to the Hunan provincial parliament the winter of 1921), and again in 1946, democracy evaded China for decades. Nonetheless, the constitutional provisions, even in the absence of parliamentary democratic elections and structures, served to legitimize women's participation in the wide variety of political bodies that have existed in China and on Taiwan (until the lifting of martial law in 1987) for many decades.

Women's engagement in formal politics should not only be valorized if it appears in a Western-style democratic structure. Moreover, the history of women's successful engagement with politics should not ignore the stories of those women who fought for suffrage in nations that have not embraced "voting" in the Western democratic sense (Edwards 2000). Triumphalist narratives of democratic histories wherein histories of women's suffrage in New Zealand or Australia can be mobilized to celebrate the legitimacy of the political status quo are not available to support the excavation of histories of women's suffrage in the Republic of China (ROC) and the People's Republic of China (PRC). Their history is nonetheless worthy and the debates that they engaged with in mobilizing public support for their campaigns provide us with much useful information about the role, status and expectations of women in China in the first half of the twentieth century. The obverse is also true. The history of the "antis" reveals much about women's status in pre-1949 Republican China.

Contextual Problems for the Chinese "Antis"

Three overarching conditions rendered the Chinese "antis" less effective than their European and American counterparts. First, the Chinese suffrage activists were not as easily divided by other political loyalties as the British or American suffragists had been. The Chinese women lobbied consistently from the platform of "gender equality" until they had won suffrage in 1936 and in the absence of a politicized male working-class or peasant political lobby, they were not subject to problems of splits occurring on class or race grounds. Schisms between the advocates of universal adult suffrage, adult male suffrage and the equal suffrage for men and women did not occur in the early part of the Chinese women's suffrage campaign. These had caused enormous divisions within the British and American women's suffrage movements. There was no competing movement to enfranchise all adult males regardless of education or property requirements in China as there had been in Britain and America (DuBois 1980). The "antis" had exploited these divisions effectively in the West whereas in China, where the women's suffrage movement had been unequivocally based on "equal rights," the "antis," who were all part of the educated elite, had no class or race sensitivities to exploit as wedges to divide the suffrage movement. The elitism of the small group of China's population with political aspirations, both male and female, ensured that "gender equality" was problematic on one dimension only. The educated men in the first assembly of the Republic were not driven to include illiterate, working-class or peasant men any more than they were keen to see their sisters and mothers enter parliament. This elitism, when coupled with the undeveloped state of the labor movement in China until the 1920s, ensured that the early women's suffrage campaign was not fraught with class tensions. By the 1920s, with the rise in influence of the Soviet Union on the CCP and the GMD, the political elites who would preside over changes to suffrage laws were sufficiently astute to espouse a comparatively "universal" suffrage.

In the first wave of 1911-1913, women suffrage activists had effectively accepted the limited, elitist franchise of the 1912 electoral laws by arguing exclusively for women's rights. They waged no campaigns to overturn the education and property qualifications of the laws that would have resulted in universal adult suffrage, although this would have dovetailed with their invocation of the natural rights to equality of all humans. Their campaign was premised on gender equality and they cautiously upheld that line. As China's national political discourses shifted more to the left during the May Fourth Movement the women's movement simply maintained its platform of "gender equality" regardless of the specific legislation. They had no objections to universal adult male suffrage – they simply wanted whatever rights granted men to be extended to women as well. The simplicity of their premise then removed a weapon for those who opposed women's participation in politics in China that had been particularly effective in America and Europe. This flexibility was not always found among the more fragmented suffrage movements in the United States, for example. There we see the women's suffrage movement split along lines of both class and ethnicity making unity on gender lines difficult (Edwards 2002b).

Second, women's suffrage activists in China had a more fluid ideological environment within which to function. During the first half of the twentieth century an epistemic shift occurred among China's politically active elite – one that took "Chineseness" as conceived along Confucian lines of venerating tradition to one that conceived of "Chineseness" as "aspirational" modernity in radical, albeit often superficial, opposition to this Confucian reverence for tradition. In most of Europe, but particularly in Britain, the "antis" appealed to conserving the traditions that had resulted in the "glorious empire" that "Britains" were currently enjoying. The argument ran along the lines that Britain's current prosperity would be threatened by a radical change such as that represented by women's suffrage. In China, by contrast, the reformist-intellectuals who dominated public debate were increasingly convinced that the old structures required overhaul because it was precisely these relics of past systems of governance that had rendered China so weak and vulnerable. A narrative of Chinese modernity emerged within the overarching campaign to revive and strengthen China. Appeals to the glorious traditions of Confucian monarchy were unconvincing within a situation of political chaos.

The third factor weakening the campaign waged by the Chinese "antis" was the intimate link between the women's suffrage activists and patriotic movements to revive China. Women's suffrage activists in China presented themselves as "super-patriots" – in part this was aided by the almost constant state of war and military instability during the period of their struggle. Their cause was repeatedly enunciated within a discourse of national strengthening and national revival. Modernization would revive China's strength and women's suffrage was an emblem of modernity. Women's engagement in political affairs would harness the energies of women to the nation-building cause, the latest nation-unifying military campaign, or the latest anti-foreign aggression campaign. China's women's suffrage activists did not engage with pacifism – as had their counterparts in Italy and Germany. In these latter countries women's suffrage activists were labeled "traitors" for their advocacy of peaceful conflict resolution. China's suffrage activists, like Christabel Pankhurst in Britain during World War I, became militaristic super-patriots. Moreover, their active involvement in various military campaigns and their advocacy of women's participation in the military, reiterated their claim to full citizenship rights and willingness to shoulder full citizenship responsibilities.

Within this context then, what were the major arguments waged against the women's suffrage activists' bids for political power?

"Natural Rights" or "Natural Order"

The women's movement in China from the late 1890s on had emerged from within the philosophical framework provided by the Enlightenment concept of "natural rights." The argument ran that women were human beings and therefore deserved equality and liberty alongside men. This notion came into direct conflict with the Chinese "antis'" arguments about a biological "natural order" that resulted in different social roles for men and women. Women, it was argued, were naturally suited to domestic work within the home whereas men were naturally suited to public work outside the home. Moreover, women had child-bearing responsibilities – to reproduce the race-nation – and these were anathema to public political duties. Alterations to this pattern, it was feared, would cause untold chaos and disorder. Indeed, to the Chinese "antis," the very fabric of the nation was at threat by women's proposed involvement in affairs of state. The centuries-old antipathy to women's involvement in government served as a check on women's suffrage campaigns. The iconographical significance of the supposed chaos of Wu Zetian's rule and the instability caused by Yang Guifei's influence on court during the Tang continued to undermine women's involvement in politics into the twentieth century.

A typical example of this type of argument is provided by a commentator who wrote under the penname "Kong Hai" (Empty Sea) in 1912. Kong Hai raised three main objections to the case for gender equality in political rights. "First, we must examine the abilities of men and women. Second, we must research the special natures of men and women. Third, we must consider its effects on social order." Of the first s/he stated that those who have the right to participate in politics must have knowledge about politics and the ability to participate in politics. Since not even all the men of China had these abilities how could women have these skills? Women have been preoccupied solely with household [literally: "inner" (*nei*)] matters and thereby have no understanding of affairs external to the household. On the second point, relating to the special natures of men and women, Kong Hai argued that the special characteristics of men were to concentrate on financial matters beyond the confines of the house and to ensure that these external affairs are well managed. A woman's special nature is to manage the household and to bear and raise sons – all her activities should be centered on the inner domestic realm. "These distinctions evolved through nature and one cannot force the [genders] into similarity." S/he continued saying, if women undertake tasks that are against their nature then there is no possibility of a successful outcome, just as it would be impossible for men to bear sons. Indeed, it would be as futile as trying to "teach a hen to crow at dawn." On the third point, the consequences of women's suffrage on social stability, Kong Hai reproduced a classic Confucian maxim – s/he stressed that the family was the foundation of society and that harmony in society grew from harmony in the family. If women engage in politics, they will argue with men and vie for power with men. This would cause chaos in society because it would cause chaos in the family. Women would be assuming roles that were not in their nature, the family would no longer be a foundation for society and consequently society would descend into chaos. In sum, according to Kong Hai, women had neither the education nor the natural talents for participation in politics, and if China were to allow women's suffrage, then Chinese culture and society would be certain to decline as a result (Kong Hai 1912a, published on 28 February).

This single article generated a flurry of responses. On 5 March, Yang Jiwei replied to Kong Hai. Yang pointed out that if knowledge of politics were to be a prerequisite for suffrage, as Kong Hai had asserted, then many men would be eliminated from participation as well. Without gender equality only women were being explicitly excluded from demonstrating their competencies in political affairs. On the matter of the special characteristics of the two sexes, Yang argued that there is very little that cannot be taught and learned by human beings and indeed, turned into talent. On Kong Hai's third point about the potential for social chaos, Yang stressed that women were already performing a far greater range of roles than Kong Hai had acknowledged. The manner in which they organize their families is their own concern and need not be legislated. She concluded by pointing out that the improvement in the status of women would raise the standard of the nation as a whole (Yang Jiwei 1912). In an article published immediately below Yang's, Kong Hai replied: if women's nature had included the skill in politics then how is it that for thousands of years they have not demonstrated this skill?

S/he argued that it was not just the Confucian East which "revered men and denigrated women" and spoke of women being inner and men being outer. The West never had an egalitarian ideology either. Kong Hai dismissed the examples of Queen Victoria and Empress Wu Zetian as extremely special circumstances (Kong Hai 1912b).

Four days later a reaction came from Zhang Renlan who had recently returned from studying in America. She declared that women's rights activists were misinterpreting the system of separate spheres for men and women, where women govern the household while men govern the outside. She argued that separate spheres are not "unequal" and in fact result merely from natural differences between the genders. "Men have men's natural abilities and women have women's natural abilities." The existence of separate spheres does not mean there is no equality, rather that there is mutual cooperation in roles. Moreover, she argued if the "no husband-ism" views of the women's rights activists were propagated, then within a few years there would be a sadly diminished Chinese race. Zhang described the women's suffrage activists and their supporters as being so uncivilized that they are "neither Western nor Eastern, neither male nor female, and neither monk nor nun" (Zhang Renlan 1912).

The arguments about women's "natural" ability appealed to the close link between education and moral authority to rule tempered in the centuries of Confucian notions of governance. The Chinese "antis" aimed to stall or prevent women's suffrage by insisting that women's educational level was as yet insufficiently advanced to cope with affairs of the state. In an anonymous two-part article published in

Dagongbao (Dagong News) during March of 1912 one commentator argued that women's special strength lies in their domestic and child-rearing skills and for women to enter in an area of weakness – politics – would result in poor politics. Women have neither the education, experience nor the natural ability to engage in political work. Moreover, if they enter political life they will be unable to perform their vital functions in the family. People cannot live alone and if the family is in chaos then the country will be in chaos. Men cannot possibly manage the household, because it runs counter to their natural abilities (Nüzi canzheng lun 1912).

By the 1920s, although the occasional commentator did invoke the "different-but-equal natural abilities" arguments, the main thrust of debate shifted to a discussion of the importance of modernization in governance and the power of "change" to improve China. Moreover, discussion of "natural" gender differences such as those discussed above inevitably invoked notions of unchanging essences – which in turn hinted of tradition and inability to change. As we see in the section below, "change" increasingly carried a positive imperative for aspirants of modernity.

Change as a "Risk" or Change to Guarantee "Modernity"

By 1918 women's suffrage activists, and other advocates of political reform, began to query the legitimacy and structure of the current system. For some, this crisis of faith in the current system resulted in an embracing of a Marxist solution – the formation of the CCP was the natural consequence of this sentiment. For the women's suffrage activists – who were by definition advocates of a parliamentary democracy – the chaos of the first decade of the Republic suggested that reform of the system was required and that change should involve women's equal political participation. China's Republic was under threat – the men who claimed to know how to "do politics" were clearly failing in their duties. The conservatives' espousal of the notion of separate gendered spheres of competency did not reflect well on Chinese men. The tension emerged between conservative elements that regarded change as a risk and those who saw change as a guarantee of modernity. Denise Gimpel has explained in the context of China's early twentieth-century literary magazines that "modern and modernity [...] refer to the sense of living in a changing world, of reconsidering past attitudes and examining new possibilities of thought and action" (Gimpel 2001:18). Change was construed as an inherent part of modernity, but China's "antis" nonetheless attempted to mobilize arguments about the importance of maintaining the status quo in order to stabilize the nation and establish the best possible circumstances for prosperity. In contrast, China's women's suffrage advocates argued that a change in political regulations was central to guaranteeing success for China's modernity.

During the debate about including women's suffrage in the Hunan constitution in 1921 one of the members of the constitutional drafting committee, Cheng Xiluo, wrote to the newspapers expressing his concerns about women's suffrage. Cheng was worried about social change and asserted that social problems had emerged in the European and American nations that had granted women full suffrage rights. He did not specify the exact nature of these problems and his vague references to "problems" were to draw ridicule from respondents to his letter. He also took the dangerous step of insulting the abilities of women in his province. Cheng declared that while it was true that in Europe and America women had assumed positions of responsibility in a range of careers, few women in Hunan would be capable of performing well alongside men – only one or two in a hundred. He continued his provocative argument with the assertion that political chaos would result from such unenlightened government. Women in Europe and America had the vote because these are advanced nations whereas China was a mere "beginner" and could not risk granting women the vote. Moreover, he asserted, throwing women into the hurley-burley of political life would jeopardize the safety of women. "Would such a move be respectful of women or is it sacrificing them?" he asked. Finally, he doubted the wisdom of women's participation on the grounds that they are physically incapable of maintaining political activities simply because of limitations imposed by their physiology (Cheng Xiluo 1921, published on 16 May).

A quick response to Cheng's article came from Jiang Zhaoxiang the following day. Jiang called for Cheng to provide evidence of the "problems" caused by women's suffrage elsewhere in the world asserting that Cheng's claims were complete fabrications. Jiang reiterated the importance of embracing change and accepting that uncertainty of outcomes is an integral part of politics. Jiang continued: "So Mr. Cheng, how many hundred years would it take for you to feel comfortable before allowing women to vote with a democratic constitution?" The barrage continued with Jiang asking if Cheng also felt that the men of Hunan Province compared unfavorably with foreign men. After all, the chaos of China over the past decade hardly indicates competence in the ruling men. Moreover, Jiang argued, Cheng's arguments about protecting women from the rough and tumble of political life is complete nonsense (Jiang Zhaoxiang 1921).

> Have women not suffered untold hardship during the tumultuous period? And yet, what of the suffering of politicians during this same period? [...] Looking at politicians during this same period we can see that they are not to be pitied at all. The ones that should be pitied are the millions of women who have been trapped in the inner chambers. They have not exercised political power, and yet with every change of political circumstance they are subject to hardship; now we want to ease or even erase this suffering. (Jiang Zhaoxiang 1921)

A joint letter of opposition came from students at the "Number One Girls' Normal School." They also queried Cheng's assertion about the effects of women's suffrage in Europe and America had been problematic writing that extensive research on the topic has shown that women's suffrage has overwhelmingly positive results. On the charge that Hunan's women were incapable of political leadership because they lacked the requisite education level, the students argued that illiteracy was a problem across the entire rural sector but there were sufficient numbers of adequately educated women to participate productively in political life. Cheng's fears that women's physiology was unsuited to politics, they argued, should be allayed by the experience of women in Europe and America. Their reaction to his purported concern for women's welfare contained the most venom.

> Your concerns about the safety of women are repulsive given the fact that for so many years women have been trampled on by men. Is being subjected to this sort of hardship your idea of "protection"? [...] Your suggestion that we should wait until after the national revolution is successfully completed is abhorrent and such promises have been made in the past and have come to naught. We women have waited long enough and we will not wait any longer. We want to participate in the building of this new system. (Di yi nüzi shifan di qi quanti tongxue 1921)

In contrast to the start of the Republican era, by the 1920s there was no question in the readers' and authors' minds that a new system was required – indeed, a new system was inevitable.

The importance of international comparisons was a crucial deciding factor in the debate on women's suffrage during these years. Importantly, political regulations had changed around the world within many of its most powerful and modern nations. To both the women's suffrage advocates and the reformist intellectuals these activists aimed to influence, it was increasingly evident that a new political structure was central to the development of modern governance and national strength. In the first wave of suffrage activism women could point to only a handful of small countries, like Australia and New Zealand, as examples of nations where women participated equally with men in politics. These were not nations to which China likened herself. However, by the 1920s many of the world's great powers had gender equality in suffrage rights – including Germany, Britain and the United States of America. To many intellectuals of the New Culture period it was inevitable that China, with its democratic and "modern" pretensions, should proceed down this path. Typical of the sentiment is Wu Yuxiu's article where she describes women's suffrage as an inevitable international trend for the twentieth century. With nations like Britain already recognizing women's right to vote and stand for election there should be no doubt that China should not follow suit (Wu Yuxiu 1921). Another commentator reiterated the link between modernity in governance and women's suffrage suggesting that the granting of women's suffrage was part of the path towards modernity and not a reward for modernity. Yi Chuheng asked Mr. Cheng if there would ever be anyone capable of deciding when China would be sufficiently advanced to permit women to vote (Yi Chuheng 1921).

The "antis" were in the invidious position of having to argue against the intellectual enthusiasm for change. Modern nations around the world showed that change was an integral part of modernity in their evolving political structures. Modernization required adaptation, reform and to some thinkers, revolution. Conservatism was discredited as an option because of the chaos of the current political and social situation and the perceived bankruptcy of the past. Where appeals to the glorious status quo had been effective in halting women's suffrage in Europe, this was impossible in China during the 1920s when aspirations to modernity were the driving force. As Duara has identified, "Modern societies are dominated by the discourse on evolutionary history and the conception of linear time it embodies. The anxiety produced by a conception of time that has potentially no end, goal or moral purpose generates as much a need for faith in the future (progress), as for a secure identity symbolized by the unchanging essence" (Duara 2000:345). It was desire for this time/space trajectory that was emerging as the dominant discourse in China during the early twentieth century. China's women's suffrage activists presented their cause as steps along this path that progressed to the glorious future where China was once again among the world leaders. Thus, the modernity imperative of linear time, with change inherent as time progressed, undermined their detractors' arguments and confirmed the women's suffrage cause as an integral part of "modernity in politics."

Conclusion

Women's suffrage activists in China linked their cause closely to the broader quest for "modernity." Indeed, women's suffrage became an emblem of modernity. The women also positioned their movement with sufficient credibility within the rhetoric of service to the nation to invoke traditional female virtues of sacrifice and industriousness. The consolidating Chinese nation-state required just such (modern) loyal sisters, daughters and wives. Moreover, when confronted with the reformist elite's widespread and overwhelming desire for modernity in governance, the "antis'" appeals to political "conservation" and "stasis" were ineffective. The comparative brevity of the Chinese women's suffrage movement in international terms – a mere quarter of a century – in part results from the political activist elite's extensive enthusiasm for social change and the desire for a vision of linear historical progress stretching towards a strong, stable and modern China. Ultimately, however, due credit must be paid to those women who dared to challenge the commonplace understandings about women's roles in society by persevering with their bid for access to formal political power. China's women's suffrage activists performed important symbolic and practical roles in creating the possibility for the dramatic improvement in women's status that was to occur over the course of the twentieth century.

References

Cheng Xiluo, Bu zuzhang nüzi canzheng (Opposition to Women's Participation in Politics), in: *Dagongbao*, 16 May 1921.

Di yi nüzi shifan di qi quanti tongxue (Class Seven of the Number One Girls' Normal School), Zhi Cheng Xiluo shu (Reply to Cheng Xiluo), in: *Dagongbao*, 18 May 1921.

Duara, Prasenjit, Of Authenticity and Woman: Personal Narratives of Middle-Class Women in Modern China, in: Yeh Wen-hsin 2000, pp. 342-364.

DuBois, Ellen Carol, *Feminism and Suffrage: The Emergence of an Independent Women's Movement in America, 1848-1869*, Ithaca ^{2}1980 (^{1}1978).

Edwards, Louise, From Gender Equality to Gender Difference: Feminist Campaigns for Quotas for Women in Politics, in: *Twentieth Century China* 24:2 (1999), pp. 69-105.

Edwards, Louise, Women's Suffrage in China: Challenging Scholarly Conventions, in: *Pacific Historical Review* 69:4 (2000), pp. 617-38.

Edwards, Louise, Co-opting the Chinese Women's Suffrage Movement for the Fifth Modernisation – Democracy, in: *Asian Studies Review* 26:3 (2002a), pp. 285-307.

Edwards, Louise, Narratives of Race and Nation in China: Women's Suffrage in the Early Twentieth Century, in: *Women's Studies International Forum* 29:6 (2002b), pp. 619-30.

Gimpel, Denise, *Lost Voices of Modernity: A Chinese Popular Fiction Magazine in Context*, Honolulu 2001.

Guangdong nüjie lianhehui (Guangdong United Women's Association, UWA), Guangdong nüjie lianhehui zhangcheng (Constitution of the Guangdong UWA), 1919, reproduced in: Tan Sheying 1936, pp. 97-104.

Harrison, Brian, *Separate Spheres: The Opposition to Women's Suffrage in Britain*, London 1978.

Jiang Zhaoxiang, Bo Cheng Xiluo jun de buzhang nü canzheng (Reply to Mr. Cheng Xiluo's Opposition to Women's Suffrage), in: *Dagongbao*, 18-19 May 1921. The quotation comes from the 19 May section.

Kong Hai, Duiyu nüzi canzheng quan zhi huaiyi (My Concerns about Women's Participation in Politics), in: *Minlibao*, 28 February 1912a.

Kong Hai, Fu Yang Jiwei nüshi han (Reply to Madam Yang Jiwei's Letter), in: *Minlibao*, 5 March 1912b.

Lee, Leo Ou-fan, The Cultural Construction of Modernity in Urban Shanghai: Some Preliminary Explorations, in: Yeh Wen-hsin 2000, pp. 31-61.

Lin Zongsu, Nüzi canzheng tongzhi hui huiyuan Lin Zongsu xuanyan (Declaration by Women's Suffrage Comrades' Alliance Member Lin Zongsu), in: *Tianduobao*, 24 January 1912.

Nathan, Andrew, *Peking Politics, 1918-1923: Factionalism and the Failure of Constitutionalism*, Berkeley, Los Angeles, London 1976.

Nüquan yundong tongmenghui (Women's Rights League), Nüquan yundong tongmenghui xuanyan (Manifesto of the Women's Rights League), 1922, reproduced in: Tan Sheying 1936, pp. 121-124.

Nüzi canzheng lun (Discussion on Women's Suffrage), in: *Dagongbao*, 27-28 March 1912.

Nüzi canzheng tongmenghui (Alliance for Women's Participation in Politics), Nüzi canzheng tongmenghui jianzhang (Regulations of the Alliance for Women's Participation in Politics), in: *Tianduobao*, 3 December 1911.

Pateman, Carole, Three Questions about Womanhood Suffrage, in: Daley, Caroline, Melanie Nolan, *Suffrage and Beyond: International Feminist Perspectives*, Auckland 1994, pp. 331-348.

Ramirez, Francisco O., Yasemin Soysal, Suzanne Shanahan, The Changing Logic of Political Citizenship: Cross-National Acquisition of Women's Suffrage Rights, 1890 to 1990, in: *American Sociological Review* 62:5 (1997), pp. 735-745.

Shenzhou nüjie gonghe xiejishe (Shenzhou Women's Assistance Society), Shenzhou nüjie gonghe xiejishe (Shenzhou Women's Assistance Society), 1912, reproduced in: Tan Sheying 1936, pp. 61-63.

Tan Sheying (ed.), *Zhongguo funü yundong tongshi* (A General History of the Chinese Women's Movement*)*, Nanjing 1936.

Wu Yuxiu, Nüzi yingyou canzheng quan de wo jian (My Opinion on Why Women Ought to Have the Right to Participate in Politics), in: *Dagongbao*, 25-27 May 1921.

Yang Jiwei, Yang Jiwei nüshi lai han (Letter from Madam Yang Jiwei), in: *Minlibao*, 5 March 1912.

Yeh Wen-hsin, Introduction: Interpreting Chinese Modernity, 1900-1950, in: Yeh Wen-hsin 2000, pp. 1-30.

Yeh Wen-hsin (ed.), *Becoming Chinese: Passages to Modernity and Beyond*, Berkeley, Los Angeles, London 2000.

Yi Chuheng, He Cheng Xiluo xiansheng bu zhuzhang nüzi canzheng de shangliang (Joining the Discussion about Mr. Cheng Xiluo's Opposition to Women's Participation in Politics), in: *Dagongbao*, 30-31 May 1921, 1-2 June 1921.

Zhang Renlan, Zhang Renlan nüshi lai han (Letter from Madam Zhang Renlan), in: *Minlibao*, 9 March 1912.

Women's Military Participation in the Communist Movement of the 1930s and 1940s: Patterns of Inclusion and Exclusion

Nicola Spakowski

Studies of women's military participation usually draw a picture of women's exclusion from the armed forces. Although it is not disputed that examples of fighting women can be found throughout history, these are considered to be individual cases and exceptions that prove the rule of male dominance in the field of the armed forces.[1] Furthermore, women's access to military roles – and to combat roles, in particular – is directly connected with the empowerment of women, no matter whether "empowerment" is defined as enfranchisement, as access to public roles or as an attack on patriarchal society.[2]

In the field of Chinese studies, Judith Stacey is a prominent supporter of this "right to fight" view. In her book, women's exclusion from the Red Army during the Republican period is an integral part of "patriarchal socialism." Although she admits that there was "room for exceptional women to participate in direct combat" (Stacey 1983:151) and that women's war service in the base areas posed "challenges" to

---

This article presents the findings of parts of a research project on women's military participation in the Communist movement between 1925 and 1949.

[1] See DeGroot 2000:12: "In all these cases, the women's contribution did not inspire a reconsideration of patriarchal social order because they did not threaten masculine stereotypes or contradict feminine ones."

[2] See Peach's discussion of feminist attitudes towards women in combat roles. According to the "ethic of justice" as one line of argument, women's contributions to national defense and their participation in regular armies are prerequisites for gaining the status of full citizens with equal rights (Peach 1997:100). See also DeGroot 2000:4: "Since the early 1970s, military service, and particularly participation in combat, has been seen by some feminists as one of the most important bastions of patriarchy. To knock it down, it seems, would leave the entire edifice of male domination fatally weakened."

"male domination" (ibid. 152), she also contends that the "limitations of those challenges" reveal the true nature of the Communist army as a "patriarchal army" and a "male preserve" (ibid. 147, 151). According to Stacey, male dominance in the armed forces was the general pattern from the 1920s to the 1940s and it even affected the political culture of the People's Republic.[3] This theory of women's exclusion from the armed forces by patriarchal structures has recently been offered support by Lily Lee and Sue Wiles in their study of women on the Long March. Relating the biographies of three prominent women and their instrumentalization by individual male leaders, they create a narrative of the victimization of women at an individual level (Lee/Wiles 1999).

However, the case of the Chinese Communist revolution might also be used as evidence for a different pattern of women's military participation. Comparative studies argue that women's military participation was (and is) more acceptable in revolutionary wars – especially in those cases where women's liberation is an integral part of a revolutionary ideology – and in guerilla war. Underlying this argument is the assumption that liberation wars are based on a strong ideological bond shared by men and women alike. Furthermore, the structures of revolutionary armies tend to be less rigid and less hierarchical than those of national armies. As for guerilla wars, the fighting and auxiliary functions of soldiers tend to be leveled down.[4]

Claims of women's exclusion and victimization have also been contested by studies that focus on the subject position of women. From Helen Young's oral history study of women on the Long March, we know that women soldiers viewed their roles in a much more posi-

---

[3] See Stacey 1983:155: "This was to have inestimable significance for the structure of Chinese Communist Party (CCP) leadership and the future nature of Chinese Communist society. The revolutionary process of protracted guerilla warfare resulted in a predominance of military men in the ranks of highest leadership."

[4] Yuval-Davis 1999:28, 35. For a discussion of the Chinese Communist revolution as an example of this particular pattern of women's military participation, see DeGroot 2000:12.

tive light than the term "patriarchal socialism" would suggest.[5] The stories told in her book reveal that military structures alone – particularly where the "right to fight" is the criterion of military participation – do not account for the experiences of women in the military.

The focus of this article is on both military structures and women's agency. It aims to explore the dynamics between mobilization policy and women's interests: What was the mobilization policy of a particular period and how did gender figure in this policy? What were the motives and expectations of the women who strove for military participation? What were the typical problems and conflicts between these two levels and how were they resolved? What I would like to show is that with regard to women's military participation, Communist policy and practice was neither strictly exclusive nor entirely inclusive. There was scope for both, women's exclusion or instrumentalization and women's inclusion and agency due to

a) changing historical circumstances that called for different military and political approaches, each of which assigned women a particular role in revolution and
b) ambiguities and contradictions in Communist gender norms[6] and regulations on women's military participation which made role allocations negotiable.[7]

Based on sources such as the memoirs of women soldiers and women activists, political directives, contemporary reports on the women's movement and contemporary articles in newspapers and journals, I would like to establish the following patterns of mobilization policy in the periods under discussion:

---

[5] See Young 2001:160: "When women are mentioned in standard histories, the usual focus is on the suffering of the women. However, the women interviewed did not view themselves as victims but believed that their work on the Long March was essential. The work they did was the meat of their own stories, a substantial part of the broader history."

[6] See also Gilmartin 1995:206 on the "paradoxical and contradictory nature of Chinese Communist gender politics" in the 1920s.

[7] For a historicist approach to the assessment of the relationship between gender and the armed forces, see Hagemann 1998 who claims ambivalences and paradoxes to be the "normal" case in this field of study.

1. Women's inclusion under a People's War approach which was typical of comparatively stable circumstances as in the soviets of the early 1930s and in consolidated base areas in the War of Resistance. Although women were primarily designated for supporting roles, these very roles were considered an important part of the revolution.
2. Women's exclusion in times of crisis when evacuation moves called for a reduction of the Communist movement to its military core, i.e. to male combatants. The Long March is the most outstanding example of this pattern.
3. A "feminization" during the Three-Year Guerrilla War from 1934 to 1937 and in guerrilla zones in earlier and later periods. Here political and military activities depended largely on the support of women because they were less conspicuous than men. In addition to this, the less rigid organizational structures pertaining to guerrilla warfare gave women greater opportunities for military participation.

There were, of course, variations to these patterns, especially in the early years when Communist policies had not yet been standardized. What is more important, however, is that these patterns were challenged by the women themselves when their expectations were not met. This occurred with regard to two quite distinctive groups of women:

1. Young rural women in the early 1930s who were not content with part-time service within local boundaries but wanted to join the Red Army as a mobile and full-time force.
2. Young urban educated women in the War of Resistance who did not want to be assigned to mass work but called for a "right to fight."

As we shall see, there was scope for negotiation, and some women – either as individuals or as groups – asserted themselves against the narrow definitions of gender roles.

The article is divided into three sections, each of which covers a distinctive period of the Communist revolution: (1) the Soviet movement of the early 1930s, (2) the Long March and the Three-Year Guerrilla War from 1934 to 1937, and (3) the War of Resistance from

1937 to 1945. In my conclusion, I shall come back to the theories listed in the introduction and discuss their applicability to the case of the Chinese revolution.

The Soviets of the Early 1930s – Young Peasant Women Joining the Army as an Escape from Repressive Family Structures

By the early 1930s, the focus of the Communist movement had shifted to rural China and peasants were regarded as the main social force of revolution.[8] The construction and defense of the soviets in South China had become the major task for both army and party, but due to Chiang Kai-sheks encirclement campaigns the military situation was rather unstable. The Red Army, which had been founded in 1927, was the mobile force of the Chinese Communist Party (CCP) which, at local level, was assisted by local militias: the "Red Guards" (*Chiweidui*) or the "Young Vanguards" (*Shaoxiandui*) – depending on the age of their members. These local defense units were not to be withdrawn from production work. In this early phase of Communist military engagement the pattern of relying on the masses which was later to be known as "People's War" (*Renmin zhanzheng*) was already established. The Red Army depended to a great extent on mass support and on local knowledge that only the masses could provide. So-called supporting roles which were chiefly performed by women were thus of vital importance to the Communist cause. This also holds true for the non-combatant tasks Red Army soldiers had to perform such as doing propaganda work, mobilizing and organizing the masses, since armed battle and political work were considered to be equally important parts of the revolution. As we shall see, however, this pattern changed in times of crisis when the Red Army was forced to evacuate an area; the movement was then reduced to its military core and, as a result, the status of non-combatants became insecure. Furthermore, mobilization policy and patterns of inclusion and exclusion varied between soviets because Communist policy during this early period was less uniform and less standardized than it was later on.

---

[8] For a general account of Communist policy in the early 1930s, see Ch'en 1991.

One *common* feature was a gendered policy of military mobilization which was based on an essentialist understanding of gender where women were regarded as physically weak.[9] In addition, it would have been unrealistic to try to mobilize women for tasks that fundamentally contravened traditional role allocations in rural China in the first place. The general policy, therefore, was to mobilize men to join the Red Army and to mobilize women for supporting roles which would keep them within their local boundaries. A broad range of military campaigns was indicative of this particular role for women, such as the campaign for the "enlargement of the Red Army" (*kuoda Hongjun*), where women mobilized their husbands and sons for military service; the campaign for "showing gratitude towards the Red Army" (*weilao Hongjun*), where women supported soldiers by washing their clothes, making straw sandals, singing and dancing etc.; the campaign for "supporting the Red Army" (*bangzhu Hongjun*), where women were organized into washing teams, transport teams, teams performing medical duties etc.; and the campaign for "preferential treatment of Red Army dependents" (*youdai Hongjun jiashu*), where women assisted the families of Red Army soldiers in doing farm work (Zhonggong suqu zhongyang ju 1991:229; Zhongguo gongchandang zhongyang weiyuanhui, Zhonghua suwei'ai gongheguo renmin weiyuanhui 1991:364).

Women were encouraged to join local defense units (the Red Guards or the Young Vanguards) that were not to be withdrawn from production work.[10] There is even evidence of units with a majority of women members (Nuo Jie 1991:378). These local defense units were assigned tasks such as standing sentry, spying, making enquiries, doing transport work, guarding the political bodies of the soviet or doing support work in battle (ibid.). In some areas women were even encouraged to engage in battle.[11] There were so-called "assault groups" (*chongfengdui*) some of which were entirely made up of

---

[9] This was the justification for women's exclusion from the army (see, for instance, Tuan Xiang-Gan shengwei qingfubu 1991:318).

[10] See Zhu Changxie 1991:81 on Southwest Jiangxi and Xiang-E-Gan sheng chise zhigong lianhehui nügong bu 1991:348 on the Xiang-E-Gan Soviet.

[11] See Zhu Changxie 1991:81 on the women's movement in Southwest Jiangxi in 1930.

women.[12] In addition, many reports on the local situation of women's participation give examples of other forms and individual cases of women's support to the army and of women taking part in armed battles.[13] On the whole, women's military participation was marked by local and regional varieties.

As to women's participation in the Red Army as a mobile and full-time force, there was a general trend to prevent women from joining. It is uncertain, however, whether there was an explicit rule on women's admission to the Red Army that applied to all the soviets for the whole period. A report from October 1930 on the women's movement in Southwest Jiangxi says: "In the Red Army there are women shouldering arms. However, since women used to be banned from the Red Army there is only a very small number of them now" (Zhu Changxie 1991:82). In some areas, however, there were even entire detachments of women that were formally part of the Red Army (see below).

There is no doubt that in certain areas women were willing to join the revolution and to join auxiliary and regular forces. This is particularly true of young women from an extremely poor social background. Liu Jian, who was head of the Women's Department of the Party Committee in the Sichuan-Shaanxi Soviet characterized the members of the "Women's Independent Battalion" (see below) as follows:

> The oldest among these women soldiers of the Red Army were about twenty years old, the youngest were only thirteen or fourteen and were called "baby girl soldiers" (*nüwa bing*). All of them had gone through extremely hard experiences. Some had been maids to rich landlords, some had been beaten and scolded as child brides, some of them were

---

[12] Ibid. It is not explained whether these groups were organized from above or on the women's own initiative.
[13] See, for instance, Gan xinan funü gongzuo baogao 1991:85 and Tuan Xiang-Gan shengwei qingfubu 1991:318.

orphans who were not backed by anyone. All of them came from the lowest stratum of society. (Liu Jian 1987:194)[14]

These women's motives for joining were social, but first and foremost negative, i.e. joining the revolution for them meant escaping from oppressive family structures and extreme forms of poverty. Positively, they were attracted by the Red Army's propaganda, which claimed that the Red Army was the advocate of the poor and especially of women. To them, the Red Army was an institution that was grounded on an ideology that promised women's liberation from the very structures they wanted to escape.[15]

As we shall see below, many women did apply to join the army as a mobile force. In contrast to the urban educated women, however, who joined the army in the War of Resistance, the peasant women of the 1930s were obviously not attracted by military life as such.[16] The moment of becoming a soldier and the adjustments women had to make to conform to military life are not usually mentioned in their memoirs. Some sources even reveal that most of them were unwilling to cut their hair und unbind their feet, because short hair, in their view, was ugly and unbinding one's feet meant that there would be no way back into marriage. Squad leaders had to persuade and finally force them to do it.[17] Given their wish to leave their families, the army, for them, was probably a substitute institution which could lead them away from their villages. The kind of work they would perform was secondary; or rather the hierarchy between combatant and non-combatant roles at that time was not very distinct.[18] In any case, women obviously found their work essential

---

[14] A high proportion of child brides is also reported with regard to the "Women's Worker-Soldier Battalion" (*Funü gongbingying*) which was also attached to the Fourth Front Army, see Lin Yueqin 1987:231, 234-235.

[15] On the social background and motives of these women, see Young 2001:131ff.

[16] Women cadres, however, who wanted to join the "Women's Independent Regiment" one year after it had been founded seem to have asked to take part in the defense of the soviet (Ding Wenjian 1993:7).

[17] See, for instance, Lin Jiang 1987:206-207.

[18] See also Young 2001:245: "For many of these women, joining the army was not an event. They were simply subsumed into the military as political soldiers,

and did not complain about the tasks they were assigned (Young 2001:160).

Conflicts of military practice arose where there was a considerable number of women who wanted to join the Red Army. For example, around 1,000 women volunteered to join the Red Army in the Hunan-Jiangxi border region in one year.[19] One solution to this problem was to direct them into part-time units with local defense tasks.[20] Another solution which came closer to compromise was the establishment of all-women detachments.[21] These offered women a more formalized means of military participation, were more likely to operate outside their home villages, were more likely to co-operate with regular forces, and in many cases were the starting point for a revolutionary career either within local boundaries or at national level.[22] Depending on the general policy of different soviets, these detachments differed in nature and were more or less wide-spread.

---

cadres, working in jobs in a military setting. The line between party and army was muddy in several ways."

[19] See Tuan Xiang-Gan shengwei qingfubu 1991:318 on the situation in the Hunan-Jiangxi area in 1932: "Within the last half year, more than 1,000 [women] applied to join the Red Army. They were particularly determined to go to the front. In the end, the Red Army did not accept them for physical reasons (*yinwei tamen tili shang de guanxi*). Only in the Political Department of the 'First Independent Division' (which is now the 23rd Division of the Eighth Red Army), is there a platoon to protect the Department which is made up exclusively of young women. In Yongxin there is a Red Security Guard which is made up exclusively of young women. In all the other places, young women have joined the Red Security Guards too."

[20] One directive of April 1931 concerning women's work in Northwest Anhui claimed: "If the women's masses should demand to participate in armed [units], they can be as far as possible integrated into the Red Guards or the Young Vanguards to receive military and political training which will enable them to take charge of supporting and safeguarding the political power of the local soviets. But they need not be withdrawn from production work. Neither is there any need for them to join the Red Army in great numbers" (Wan xibei tewei 1991:171). See also Zhonggong Xiang-Gan shengwei 1991:242 on the Hunan-Jiangxi border area.

[21] See, for instance, ibid.

[22] See Young 2001:246 on the women who had joined the Long March.

The most famous among them is the so-called "Red Women's Battalion" (*Hongse niangzi jun*) of Qiongya, because it provided the plot for the model opera of the same name in the 1960s. It is said to be the "first regular women's armed force under the leadership of the Communist Party." Founded in 1930 as an official part of the Red Army, it was made up of 120 women who received military training, had to protect the organs of the Qiongya Soviet, were to perform supporting roles such as assisting the local population in farming and doing propaganda work, and finally took part in battle. It was dissolved in August 1932 after the Fourth Encirclement Campaign when warlord troops inflicted great losses upon the detachment (Zhongguo funü yundong shi 1989:319-320).

The "Women Volunteers' Detachment" (*Nüzi yiyongdui*) in Ruijin had 180 members but was typical for the restrictions on women's military service in the Central Soviet. It was founded in 1932 when local women who had performed transport and medical duties for the Red Army demanded to be accepted as regular soldiers. However, although these women did receive military training, the detachment was not made an official part of the Red Army. From the beginning it was intended for the training of political cadres who after six months' instruction should be sent to the villages to do women's work or to the Red Army's hospital to do medical work.[23]

Women's military participation in the Sichuan-Shaanxi Soviet, on the other hand, reflected the more progressive situation of the women's movement and the more tolerant attitude of party and army leaders there. So-called "Women's Independent Regiments" (*Funü duli tuan*) were established in different counties (Ding Wenjian 1993:4-5). The most outstanding among them was the "Women's Independent Regiment" of Tongjiang County which was founded in March 1933.[24] This was notable, firstly, because it was directly attached to the headquarters of the Fourth Front Army and thus formally belonged to the Red Army. Secondly, with its 300 to 2,000

---

[23] On the history and function of the "Detachment," see Cai/Zhang 1995:127 and Kang Keqing 1987:129-131.

[24] For the history of the "Women's Independent Regiment," see Ding Wenjian 1993; Su Feng 1987; Tao Wanrong 1993 and He Ziyou 1987.

members it was exceptionally large. And thirdly, it was not as short-lived as other groups – according to Chinese authors, it continued to exist throughout the Long March until the end of the Western Route Army in March 1937 (ibid. 4). The "Regiment" was founded at a time of military engagement when men were mobilized to fight at the front and local defense became precarious. In a first stage, 300 women – among them 100 cadres and 200 women who had been active in various local defense units – were recruited to join the Regiment.[25] However, the material provisions were poor: the women had to produce their uniforms themselves and they were only issued with a small number of rifles (He Ziyou 1987:201-202). At first, the range of tasks they had to fulfill was limited: military training, protection of the Province Committee and its organs, transport, and fighting against so-called "bandits" – i.e. any sort of armed resistance to Communist rule (ibid. 202). The situation changed as a result of good performance and military activities initiated by the women themselves. In May 1933, while on a mission to transport grain, the women suddenly met with a regiment of warlord soldiers who had lost their way and were smoking opium while taking a rest. The women decided to take the opportunity offered and captured up to several hundred rifles. They were praised by military leaders, were allowed to keep the guns and from that point on were regarded as a fighting unit (Tao Wanrong 1993:44; Ding Wenjian 1993:6). However, the status, size and tasks of the "Women's Independent Regiment" changed according to military needs. It was disbanded at one point, refounded and enlarged to a division of 2,000 women at another point. The Regiment took part in battle, but auxiliary tasks – transport, medical duty – had priority. After down-sizing to 1,000 soldiers, the Regiment took part in the Long March. It participated in battle but mainly performed auxiliary duties which at that point comprised mass work as well (Ding Wenjian 1993:7ff.; He Ziyou 1987:203).

Though women in some soviets did join the Red Army, their status remained precarious. From one memoir of a Red Army woman soldier who depicted military life in 1928 we know that the hardships of frequent evacuation moves – which were also common practice in

---

[25] At that time it was called the "Women's Independent Battalion."

the early 1930s – made male soldiers hostile towards women. Zeng Zhi recalls:

> The soldiers began to complain and vent their rage on the women comrades. They mocked them and made ironic remarks, discriminated against them and insulted them. We were utterly furious, but it couldn't be helped. We had to bottle up our anger. (Zeng Zhi 1996:185)

At a conference of political and military personnel, according to Zeng Zhi, one soldier claimed:

> Our troops are not sufficiently reduced. Women, in particular, some of who are pregnant or in poor physical condition, are not only a burden on the troops but also absorb the energy of instructors. Since an underground organization does exist here, we should leave behind those women comrades who are physically weak. (ibid.)

Other male soldiers even demanded that all women be left behind. Zeng Zhi accused these soldiers of murder, since women who had to stay behind were bound to be killed as a result of the hostile military situation and the very weak structures of the underground organization in that area. Although Mao Zedong was furious with Zeng Zhi and called her an "empress" (*nühuang*), in the end the women were allowed to stay (ibid.).

To sum up, mobilization policy in the soviets of the early 1930s was determined by the People's War approach which made distinctions between combatant and non-combatant roles fluid, and considered both defense and political work as integral parts of the revolution. Due to an essentialist definition of gender and a concept of a gendered division of tasks, women were basically designated for supporting roles which they were to perform within local boundaries. However, the Soviet movement was marked by heterogeneity and a lack of standardization of gender policy, so that individual soviets offered women greater scope for military participation. Young peasant women who volunteered for service in the Red Army were assembled in women's detachments, the status and functions of which, again, differed from soviet to soviet. The "Women's Independent Regiment" is an example of formal affiliation to the army and an extension of tasks as a result of military engagements initiated by the women themselves. Although some of these detachments actually participated in fighting, the "right to fight" view does not apply to this period because women's motives for joining the army were first and foremost social, i.e. the army provided a means of escape from repressive family life and poverty. Women's participation in the army was not challenged until evacuation moves called for a "reduction" of the army.

The Long March and the Three-Year Guerrilla War from 1934 to 1937 – How Did Women Fare in a Period of Crisis?

The years between 1934 and 1937 were the most difficult in the history of the Communist movement and its Red Army. What was later to be called the "Long March" was the evacuation of the Red Army and parts of the political personnel from the soviets in South China to the more secure areas of the Northwest. Its complement was the Three-Year Guerrilla War for those left behind.[26] Both parts of the movement were on the defensive against Guomindang (Nationalist Party, GMD) troops and their allies among the warlords. Faced with the threat of annihilation, military defense became a priority and revolution became a matter of mere survival. Whereas the Long March was an evacuation move which was based on the reduction of the revolution to its military core, the Guerrilla War called for a complete reorganization of political and military work, decentralization, and a shift to underground work and guerrilla activities that were to be carried out from the guerrilla bases in the mountain areas.

However, neither the Long March nor the Guerrilla War were homogenous movements in terms of leadership and policies. As to the Long March, the diversity of the soviets resulted in a variety of different armies ranging from Mao Zedong's highly disciplined First Front Army, with only thirty women among a total of 80,000 soldiers and no children allowed to be taken on the march;[27] to Zhang Guotao's

---

[26] For the complementary nature of the Long March and the Three-Year Guerilla War and the characterization of both movements, see Benton 1995.

[27] For the numbers see Young 2001:187, 199. For the discipline of the First Front Army and regulations on children, see ibid. 159 and 162.

Fourth Front Army[28] with several thousand women among a total of 80,000 soldiers and no restrictions on keeping children.[29] "Difference" is even more obvious with regard to the Guerrilla War. Here policies differed regionally, and individual guerrilla groups were scattered over large areas operating independently and flexibly and often lacking any contact with the party organization. It is no wonder, therefore, that not one single pattern of women's military participation can be discerned during this period.

As we shall see below, the Long March and the Guerrilla War were complementary movements also from a gender perspective. The Long March was characterized by a reduction of the Communist movement to the Red Army, i.e. to male regular forces that were engaged in regular warfare, with only a very small number of women performing supporting tasks. In the guerrilla areas, on the other hand, after the departure of male soldiers the proportion of women increased and their contribution became more important because guerrilla warfare to a great extent relied on women's "special functions." Thus in different contexts, women's prescribed gender role could lead to more central or to more marginal roles.

To gain an understanding of the patterns of women's military participation, the first question one has to answer concerns the grounds on which people were selected to join the March or to stay behind. Here, policies differed from army to army. In the First Front Army that departed from the Central Soviet, women's participation was the exception. Thirty women were allowed to join, half of them on the grounds of affiliation to a political or military leader plus revolutionary experience, half of them in order to perform supporting tasks. This latter group was selected according to revolutionary experience and physical constitution.[30] Obviously, military and party

---

[28] Zhang Guotao was the head of the E-Yu-Wan Soviet and the Chuan-Shaan Soviet, where the Fourth Front Army had to move in 1932. Official army leaders were Xu Xiangqian and Chen Changhao.
[29] For general information on the number and functions of women soldiers in different armies, see Li/Liu 1991:1-9.
[30] For a list of the whole group of thirty women, see Lee/Wiles 1999:277-278, n. 18. I do not agree with the authors on the question of the criteria for selection. It is true that fifteen women were affiliated with party and military leaders but they

leaders were reluctant to admit women. Zhu De, looking back on the period of the soviets and the Long March, in an interview with Helen Foster Snow in 1937, gave discipline problems and women's physical constitution as the main reasons:

> Many women are very anxious to join the Red Army, but we can't take them in. The main problem is one of discipline. Then, too, the Red Army is so mobile that they cannot keep up with such fast marching as our maneuvering requires in fighting. Nor carry the necessary burdens easily, and also they get sick more often than men, as the life is extremely hard. However, their fighting spirit is good, and they would make good soldiers for any ordinary army. There have been many brave women in the partisan groups. In Kiangsi women were organized into fighting units, but never engaged in formal warfare, but only in sporadic skirmishes. They were good at capturing the enemy's supplies and arms and defeated one or two enemy regiments there. (Snow 1977:174)

The situation differed in the Fourth Front Army of the Sichuan-Shaanxi Soviet where women joined the main troops at an estimated number of several thousand.[31] Obviously, there was no gender-specific policy of selection. Neither was there prohibition of marriage

---

each had a remarkable record of revolutionary activities of their own. Neither were the other fifteen women, in my opinion, mere "token women" (Lee/Wiles 1999:25). According to Cai Chang (1987:119-120) the Organizational Department of the Central Committee decided that one woman should be selected from each province for support work on the March. These women, too, were cadres with a history of revolutionary activities. See Cai Chang 1987:120 who gives the position of each of the thirty women who joined the First Front Army. See also Young 2001:147.

[31] There is no consensus on the question of numbers, see Cheng Gengzheng 1996:2235-2236. In my view, a number of several thousand is realistic. As to the status of those who were joining the Fourth Front Army, most of them – at least 1,500 women – belonged to the "Independent Women's Regiment" (*Funü duli tuan*) and the "Women's Worker-Soldier Battalion" (*Funü gongbingying*) both of which formally belonged to the Fourth Front Army. Besides these, mixed groups with high numbers of women like the "General Hospital," the "Theatre Troupe" and various aid corps of the Army followed marching orders. And finally, women joined as members of the Women's Department, of local governments and of aid groups or factories that were not directly affiliated to the Army (see Liu Jian 1988:13). On the question of numbers, see also Helen Young, n. 1, in this volume.

or of taking newborns along on departure, as was the case in the First Front Army. Leaders of the Fourth Front Army thus continued to show their approval of women's military participation.

Being left behind was a fate women shared with other groups that were perceived as physically weak: "children, invalids, and old men" (Benton 1992:6). For women, staying behind was a fate hard to accept. There is evidence of women who tried to join the marchers despite the barriers to women's participation in the First Front Army (Li/Liu 1991:2). Women who were to stay behind perceived themselves as "left-behinders," i.e. as having lost contact with the main body of the movement and being left in a weaker position. Within a short time, the former soviets were occupied by GMD troops and women suffered badly: "Many were raped by members of the occupying army and the returning legions and sold to the brothels of Guangdong and the Nanyang or to Guomindang officers and soldiers" (Benton 1992:24).

All in all, 1934 was a year that left a deep scar in the memories of revolutionary women no matter whether they joined the March or were left behind.

Women's experiences on the Long March differed depending on which army they belonged to. Most of the women in all the armies – and all the women in the First Front Army – were assigned auxiliary tasks.[32] As to combat roles, again the Fourth Front Army was peculiar. There were several occasions when the "Women's Independent Regiment" was ordered to take part in fighting (Deng Hongcan et al. 1996:1651). Women in all the armies, however, ran the risk of being engaged in battle when they had to perform tasks that led them away from the main troops (Li/Liu 1991:53-54). This was particularly dangerous since women's work teams were only issued with a very small number of weapons (Liu Jian 1988:15).

Much can be said concerning the problems faced by women (and men) as a result of the hardships of marching.[33] My focus here is on occasions where the very participation of women was at stake. One

---

[32] On the fields of work women were assigned to, see Li/Liu 1991:73ff. and Young 2001:146ff.
[33] This aspect is very well covered by Young 2001 and Li/Liu 1991:9ff.

sort of conflict arose from women's prescribed roles as mothers. The CCP's gender concept did not release women from their responsibility for the offspring of relations and marriages between male and female comrades. In a situation where newborns were a heavy burden on the marchers, women were left alone with their conflicting private and political interests. Although women in the Fourth Front Army were allowed to keep their newborns they were still confronted with many difficulties when trying to take care of them. Military discipline in the First Front Army even forced women to leave their babies behind (the alternative being to stay behind together with the child and most probably be captured). The accounts of both groups (and even those of bystanders) provide us with powerful evidence of the physical hardships and emotional suffering endured by these women.[34]

The second kind of conflict arose from the precarious status of women in the army. Though women's work in their own view was essential, army leaders on several occasions showed that they thought the army could do without them. There were, for example, two instances when the seven women who were marching with the 25th Army were ordered to stay behind. In a political situation where staying behind meant being captured by GMD troops and at a stage in their lives where they had no families to return to, these women were determined to remain and in the end they succeeded in doing so (Li/Liu 1991:7-8).[35]

To understand how women fared in a time of absolute crisis, one has to turn to the fate of women in the Western Route Army which resumed marching in November 1936 after the main body of the Army had already settled in the base area of North Shaanxi.[36] The Western Route Army was made up of 21,000 soldiers mainly of the

---

[34] On the conflict and hardships of pregnancy and childbirth, see Young 2001:19ff. and Li/Liu 1991:23ff.

[35] Liu Xuezhi 1987, too, recalls the hard struggle between women soldiers and military leaders of the Fourth Front Army on the question whether women should remain in the army after the end of the Long March. As a result of their obstinate determination to do so, the women managed to stay on.

[36] For a general account of the Western Route Army, see Yang 1990:228ff. The fate of the women soldiers is covered in several memoirs collected in Sun Zhaoxia 1993.

Fourth Front Army; 1,300 of them were women (Ding Wenjian 1993:8). The plan was to pass the Gansu corridor and go further to the Xinjiang border to make contact with the Soviet Union. This was a plan that had long been fostered by Zhang Guotao but at that time it was also approved by Mao Zedong.

Conditions, however, were extremely bad: the Communist troops were constantly attacked by the armies of the Muslim warlords, Ma Buqing and Ma Bufang, and the Gansu corridor did not leave any escape route. Losses were high, and the five months' Western Route turned into the most terrible debacle of the Long March. Exact numbers of survivors do not exist. Around 1,000 soldiers managed to return to the Communist troops in Yan'an (Yang 1990:234). Around 1,100 survivors – of whom 400 were women – had to settle in the provinces of western China where most of them were forced to live in poverty and later, on repeated occasions, were persecuted for being "lackeys" of Zhang Guotao.[37] To date, survivors of the Western Route Army bear resentment against the CCP who was reluctant to rehabilitate them and give them material assistance.[38]

The Western Route Army is an example of the broader range of tasks women were assigned in times of military crisis. Women took part in numerous battles fulfilling auxiliary tasks *and* participating in fighting (Ding Wenjian 1993:10ff.). However, it is also an example of women's exclusion when the survival of the male "main" troops was at stake. On 13 March, at a time when the Western Route Army was already reduced to 2,000 soldiers (with 300 women among them) and when there seemed to be no way out for the Communist troops, the military leaders in Yan'an sent a telegram and gave instructions on how to deal with the situation.[39] Its essence was that Xu Xiangqian and Chen Changhao, the leaders of the Western Route Army, should decide by themselves whether to break out with all the troops or to disband into smaller guerrilla groups. In any case they should leave

---

[37] The numbers go back to a survey carried out in the western provinces in 1983 (see Ding Wenjian 1993:20).

[38] For the problems this group was facing after liberation, see Dong Hanhe 1991:3ff.

[39] For the numbers, see Yang 1990:234 and Tao Wanrong 1993:54.

the sick and the wounded behind.[40] On 14 March the Western Route Army's headquarters held a conference and opted for disbanding. This meant that the women and children lost the protection of the army. What is even more interesting is the way they disbanded: women were not only left to their fate but were actively prevented from joining the male groups who had better chances of survival. First of all, all soldiers had to give back their weapons. The Western Route Army was then split up into a "left" group, a "middle" group and a "right" group. The weapons were handed out to the all-male "left" and "right" groups who were each ordered to make their way down the mountain on a particular route. The "middle" group consisted of women, children and the sick and wounded. They were ordered to cover the "left" and "right" group by attracting the enemy and thus allowing the two other groups to escape (Tao Wanrong 1993:54-55; He Fuxiang 1993:105). Li Wenying gives the following account of events from the women's perspective:

> We women and the wounded made up one group and were told to take the opposite route to the first and second [i.e. the "left" and "right"] group. We wanted to follow the first and second group, [but] they set up posts on the mountain pass to block the way. They didn't let us follow. We could only take the path in the direction of Minle. (Li Wenying, quoted in: Dong Hanhe 1991:125)

As a result, the women were soon scattered and killed or captured by Ma-soldiers. Survivors were married to officers or soldiers of the Ma-troops. Only a few of those who managed to escape succeeded in rejoining the army. For the others, to marry and settle down in the western provinces, ironically, was the only escape.[41]

Whereas the Long March was obviously a male-centered undertaking, the Guerrilla areas, as a complement to this, became, in Gregor Benton's words, "feminized": "The Long March led to a feminization of the party in the old soviet bases. With the men gone,

---

[40] The text of the telegram is quoted in Dong Hanhe 1991:35.
[41] On the fate of the survivors, see Dong Hanhe 1991 and Sun Zhaoxia 1993.

violent struggle was replaced by milder and subtler tactics, and women's contribution became more important" (Benton 1995:126).[42]

The role of women was enhanced by their prescribed gender role. The Military and Political Commission of Minxi'nan (Southwest Fujian), in March 1936, called for the mobilization of women on the grounds of their "special functions" (*teshu zuoyong*):

> [...] those who in the present situation of guerrilla war think that "the function of women is small" or that "women are good for nothing" are taking the opportunistic standpoint of neglecting women's work and should be attacked without mercy. The Party has to pay the highest attention to striving for the recruitment of even more women masses[43] to participate in the whole struggle. It should not keep a single working woman out of the revolutionary struggle. In addition, the Party has to understand that under the present circumstances of most cruel fascist control, women masses have particular functions. No matter whether in struggle or in work, women are relatively colorless, they rarely attract the enemy's attention and can get in contact with us relatively easily. This is useful to us in performing our work, it is useful to use women to exert an influence on their husbands and sons, their relatives and friends to join us in our work. These particular functions should further attract our attention to women's work. (Minxinan junzheng weiyuanhui 1991:466)

Women's liberation in some regions remained party policy (Benton 1992:148, 170, 297), though little is known about details and results. Sources on the role women actually played in the guerrilla movement are scarce as well. We know that women did participate either by joining the guerrillas in the mountains or by supporting them from the villages (Zhongguo funü yundong shi 1989:374ff.). They were more likely to join in areas with a longer tradition of women's liberation and women's revolutionary activities. At an individual level, women with a personal history of revolutionary activities and women whose

---

[42] Benton gives the example of the Tingrui area in the border region of Fujian and Jiangxi where around 15 percent of party activists were women (Benton 1992:486-487).

[43] The term "women masses" (*funü qunzhong*) here is to be read as the plural of "women" (*funü*).

husbands or sons had departed for the Long March were most likely to either join or support the guerrillas.[44]

Women's support was – as the above-quoted directive indicated – essential for the survival of the guerrillas who badly needed food, materials, and intelligence on enemy positions. Thus, women took on the role of messengers and secret liaison – at the risk of being captured, tortured and killed. In addition to all this, women provided shelter for guerrillas in their homes and gave support to the guerrillas' families in the villages (ibid.).

There is little information on the extent to which women *formally* joined guerrilla groups. Some sources reveal that with regard to women's activities and experiences, the line between formally joining and performing supporting roles was fluid anyway.[45] There are examples of all-women guerrilla groups who, after the end of the war, were integrated into the New Fourth Army; and there is an example of a group with a majority of women (ibid. 375). But here again, some sources indicate that women guerrilla groups were mainly performing supporting tasks (Benton 1992:74). In areas with only a short history of revolution, women were mobilized for supporting roles only. Individual women became leaders or political instructors of guerrilla groups (Zhongguo funü yundong shi 1989:375), but these were exceptions. The term "feminization," therefore, is valid only in a relative sense.

---

[44] See Benton 1992:487: "Many young women who had become confident and 'politically aware' under the soviet cherished the rights they had gained through the revolution. Women were therefore more conspicuous in the Party in Gannan, Minbei, and Minxi than in Mindong, where there had been no Long March (and thus no shortage of young men) and no strong and rooted soviet to run night schools for young women." See also ibid. 148.

[45] See, for instance, the report on Dai Luying in the former Central Soviet: "Dai Liuying joined the revolution in 1931 and became the women's instructor with the soviet government in Anzhi Township. After the Red Army went to the North, she became a secret liaison for the Dingrui guerrilla force, passing enemy intelligence and gathering grains and other materials for the guerillas. During the six years of guerilla warfare, she often lived alone in forests and caves. In February 1940, she was captured while on a mission. She was cruelly tortured in the enemy prison, and finally killed in March" (Liu Zhonglu 1996:20-21).

The problems of guerrilla life resembled those of the Long March: physical hardships of hunger, thirst, cold. One woman described guerrilla life as one "similar to that of savages" (*yeren si de*) (Shi Yuqing 1987:324). Gendered problems of military life resulted from male prejudice against women. First of all, there is evidence that male guerrilla leaders had reservations about women's participation – but through personal contact came to appreciate them (Chen Maohui 1985). Secondly, under the physical hardships of life in the mountains, as on the Long March, pregnancy and childbirth became a problem for women. The few existing memoirs by women guerrillas all dwell on the conflicts resulting from pregnancy and childbirth.[46] Though there seem to have been no formal restrictions on marriage or on keeping children, women still felt forced to give up their newborns, either by killing them or by leaving them with local peasant families. According to Chen Maohui, a male guerrilla leader in Southwest Fujian, the main sources of pressure on women were male comrades who demanded that newborns be given up in order to avoid the guerrillas' being detected. Chen Maohui, in his report, tells the story of Fan Lechun, an outstanding woman member of his guerrilla group who had just given birth to a child. Fan Lechun held her ground against male demands that she abandon her child. Filled with rage, she declared that children were the descendants of the revolution and that giving them up was a crime. Fan kept her child (ibid. 173).

To sum up, the Long March and the Three-Year Guerrilla War proved that patterns of women's military participation changed in times of crisis. They have to be understood as complementary movements each of which offered – or rather, forced women into – different forms of participation. The Long March was an evacuation move that called for a reduction of the army to (male) combatants and, by and large, excluded women from joining. Again, with the participation of a rather wide range of revolutionary women, the Fourth Front Army

---

[46] Many women guerillas became pregnant, but only a very small number of newborns survived. Out of nine women guerillas in a guerilla group in northeastern Jiangxi, seven women gave birth to children, but none of the children stayed with their mothers: some died of hunger or sickness, some were given away and some were killed by their mothers to protect the guerilla group (see Zhongguo funü yundong shi 1989:376).

was an exception. However, the fate of those women who joined the Western Route Army shows that their status was still precarious: they were abandoned when the survival of the male "main" body was at stake. The Guerrilla War, on the other hand, depended on the support and liaison of locals and particularly of women because they were less suspect and therefore able to move around more freely. To a certain degree, this "special function" of women led to a "feminization" of the movement. It is true that due to the more informal structures of guerrilla war, women had access to combat roles. Yet even guerrilla war did not guarantee that the pattern of a gendered division of tasks would completely vanish. What both movements had in common was that in a situation of military crisis, mothers and children were not regarded as a legitimate part of the movement. Women soldiers thus were pressed to abandon newborns in favor of revolution.

The Anti-Japanese War of 1937 to 1945 – Young Urban Patriotic Women and the Question of Women's "Right to Fight"

The Anti-Japanese War of Resistance opened up a new front for the Communist troops while at the same time, at least temporarily, bringing an end to the civil war with the GMD.[47] The concept of a united front against Japan applied to social groups as well: rural and urban Chinese, men and women should all contribute to national defense. Authorized by the national government, the former Red Army was reorganized into the Eighth Route Army (8RA) and the New Fourth Army (N4A) which engaged in anti-Japanese fighting in North and Central China respectively. As regular and full-time forces they were placed at the top of a "linked hierarchy of military power reaching downward into local society" (Van Slyke 1991:192). At the bottom were the local militias (*minbing*) which, like the local defense units in the early soviets, were not to be withdrawn from production work (ibid. 191).[48] Again, mass support was central to the Communist

---

[47] For an account of the Communist movement during this period, see Van Slyke 1991.
[48] The middle layer were local forces (*difang jun*) which were full-time forces but operated at local or regional level (ibid. 191).

strategy of People's War and the support of local women was indispensable for maintaining Communist activities in guerrilla zones especially in the years between 1939 and 1943 when the military situation became extremely precarious.[49] Soldiers of the Communist armies, on the other hand, were not merely employed in fighting but had to perform a variety of tasks such as "combat, recruitment, political work and base area construction" (ibid. 240). Fighting and supporting roles obviously overlapped and were regarded as playing an equally important role for overall military success.

Mobilization policy in the Communist base areas during the War of Resistance basically followed the concept of a gendered division of tasks that had previously been implemented in the soviets, i.e. men were mobilized to join the N4A or the 8RA, women should perform supporting roles and replace men in local defense and production work. Many campaigns directed at rural women to encourage them to support the Communist troops resembled those of the early 1930s.[50] Women aged fifteen to forty-five were recruited into local militias which resembled those of the early 1930s except for the fact that men and women were now to join separate organizations.[51] Women's reluctance to join and their families' opposition made mobilization for the women's militias or "self-defense teams" (*funü ziweidui*) difficult and reports by women cadres were not entirely positive about the results of the campaign.[52] In the early 1940s, when women's contributions to production work became even more important, previous policies were criticized for having neglected the specific situation of rural women – the constraints imposed upon them by housework and by their physical constitution – and the mobilization of women into local militias came under special attack.[53] As we shall see below, this was because role allocations had become even more distinct by the 1940s.

---

[49] See, for instance, Wang Huixian et al. 1990:171ff.
[50] For a general account of women's contributions to war efforts in the Communist base areas, see Zhongguo funü yundong shi 1989:424ff.
[51] For sources that provide a general picture of activities and problems concerning the women militias, see Jin-Cha-Ji bianqu 1989:495-540.
[52] See, for instance, Yan 1989:507.
[53] For the general reorientation of mobilization policy and a criticism of the previous approach, see Zhongguo gongchandang zhongyang weiyuanhui 1991:647.

153

There are few reports by rural women on their motives for joining the movement. There is no doubt that rural women did participate in Communist war efforts and that their support – in guerrilla zones, in particular – was extremely important.[54] But these activities were limited to the local level. There are no examples of rural women striving to join regular armies and taking part in battle.[55]

However, the question of women's "right to fight" now came to the fore with regard to another group of women. They were the young urban female students who, motivated by patriotic feelings, were heading for the Communist base areas and especially for Yan'an and who were longing to be sent to the battlefields to fight the Japanese. Most of these young urban women had a family background of political activism, many of them had been active in the patriotic student movement of the 1930s, and many had read Edgar Snow's book *Red Star Over China* which was the main source of information on the Communists at that time.[56] It was the CCP's image of a truly patriotic force which fostered their wish to join the movement. To understand later conflicts about role allocations, it is necessary to take a closer look at their political attitudes.

First of all, the outlook of these women was patriotic in a very general sense. They did not have any profound knowledge of Marxism-Leninism[57] as the guiding principle of the Communist movement nor were they interested in the women's movement as an important

---

For a critical appraisal of women's work in the early 1940s, see Tian Xiujuan 1989. On the militias, see ibid. 458-462.

[54] For an account of the contributions by women from different social strata and in different phases of the war, see Zhongguo funü yundong shi 1989:386ff.

[55] To the contrary, reports on the women militias show that women were reluctant to join the militias because they were afraid of being forced to join the 8RA (see Yan 1989:507).

[56] For very typical biographies of that kind, see Su/Xu 1991.

[57] See, for instance, Ji Yu 1990:38 on her ideological background when entering the "Shanxi Women's Company" (*Shanxi nübinglian*): "At that time I was only full of enthusiasm to fight the Japanese and save the nation. I was no more than a simple-minded girl. With regard to revolutionary theory, I was a blank slate. [...] After half a year of studying, I had laid a foundation in the basic questions of Marxist-Leninist theory. At the same time, this was the beginning of a transformation of my world view [...]."

part of Communist activities.[58] Their patriotism had been fostered by songs and slogans that called for resistance to Japanese aggression, addressing men and women alike.[59] And examples of fighting women did exist, even in Communist propaganda (see below). These women, therefore, could hardly have foreseen that their role in the movement would be a gendered one.

Many memoirs reveal that it was the military as such that attracted these women. Their initiation into the army or into institutions of political and military training is depicted as a turning-point in their lives, dwelling on their pride at changing their names and being fitted out with a uniform:

> After registration I was sent to the 8th Team of the Instruction Team. The 8th Team was entirely made up of women soldiers. I put on a grey uniform, leg wrappings and a leather belt and put an army cap straight on my head. There was no mirror in the army, but seeing the mighty appearance of the others was like seeing oneself in the army uniform. Didn't I resemble the others? I was moved to tears. "Where are there girls who become soldiers? I had finally become a woman soldier with the N4A."[60]

---

[58] This even holds true for those who were teaching on questions of women's liberation. See, for instance, Dai Xinmin who was the political instructor of the Shanxi Women's Company: "[...] Before entering the 11th Company, I was particularly lacking in knowledge on the question of women's liberation (*funü wenti*) and on theories on the problems of imperialism. [...] After entering the 11th Company, my specific task was to teach classes on the question of women's liberation. At that time I had only read a small booklet (I can't remember its title) which comrade Luo Qiong had written on the question of women's liberation. But I didn't quite understand what the questions of women's liberation and the actual situation of Chinese women were like. I only knew that I did not have bound feet and pierced ears, because in my family I did not have to suffer the kind of oppression ordinary Chinese women had to endure" (see Dai Xinmin 1990:35-36).

[59] For the importance of songs, see Zhang Yan 1991:12. For the lines of a song appealing to both "brothers and sisters" to "take up your guns," see Ji Xichen 1997:534-535. There are many other examples of that kind. Interestingly, songs that were used to mobilize the rural population openly refer to men and women in their prescribed gender roles.

[60] See Chen Jing 1987:590. See also Lin Guo 1987:359 who recalled how, after entering the N4A, she and her friend chose names that better reflected their

Rifles, in particular, seem to have been of extremely high symbolic value to these women.[61] To go to the front and participate in fighting is presented in many sources as their common desire.[62]

The CCP's attitude towards this social group was rather ambiguous. Whereas in the early war years of 1937/1938 women were mobilized for tasks which were more directly linked to fighting (see Zhonggong zhongyang zuzhibu 1991), from 1939 on, role allocations became more distinctive.[63] Mobilizing rural women took priority because their support to the army and their contribution to production work were seen as vital for military success. In July 1939, Mao Zedong declared: "That day, on which the women of the entire nation rise up, will mark the victory of the Chinese revolution" (Mao Zedong 1991:150). As a result, mass work among rural women became a main focus of Communist activities and was put into the hands of the women's movement which was thought to be the natural domain of women.[64] Educated women, however, were quite reluctant to be appointed as cadres of the women's movement because this ran contrary to their original expectations. And it was a field of work that obviously lacked prestige (Zhang Yun 1991:718). These women were therefore subjected to an ideological reeducation that was intended to divert them from their military ambitions into mass work and particularly into the women's movement. In 1939, in order to train large numbers of women cadres, the "Chinese Women's University of Yan'an" (*Yan'an Zhongguo nüzi daxue* or *Nüda*) was founded, and many female students of the more military-oriented *Kangda*[65] were

---

revolutionary outlook. She stated: "From that point, our new names were passed on. Our new lives as revolutionary soldiers started there as well."

[61] See, for instance, Wang Yugeng 1987 who depicts her relation to her weapon in terms of a romantic attachment.

[62] See, for instance, Chen Muhua et al. 1991:88.

[63] This shift is most clearly reflected in Zhonggong zhongyang shujichu 1991.

[64] See, for instance, Peng Dehuai, who in Juni 1941 stated: "I think to participate in women's work is the natural task of women. If women do not perform women's work, who else should be put in charge of it? Although the liberation of women cannot be separated from the liberation of the working class and national liberation, it must not be mixed up with them" (Peng Dehuai 1991a:495).

[65] In full: *Zhongguo renmin kangRi junshi zhengzhi daxue*, i.e. Anti-Japanese Military-Political University of the Chinese People.

transferred to *Nüda* (Chen Muhua et al. 1991:88).[66] Though life at *Nüda* was militarized and *Nüda* students did receive some military training,[67] *Nüda* graduates were not designated for military service. On the occasion of the opening ceremony in July 1939, Wang Ming, who was president of *Nüda*, maintained:

> [...] to be victorious in the War of Resistance and the founding of the state, millions of the masses of women have to awake and rise. And to mobilize and organize millions of women, we need tens of thousands of both intelligent and brave women cadres. The reason why we founded *Nüda* was to train and steel women cadres of that kind. (Wang Ming 1991:153)

Quoting a phrase from the school hymn which read "We have to enter the battlefields bravely," Wang Ming declared:

> The meaning of the phrase "to enter the battlefields bravely" is: no matter how difficult the situation, no matter how hard the work, the pupils of *Nüda* must bravely shoulder any work that benefits the nation and society and any work that benefits the women's liberation movement. (ibid. 156-157)

It is true that military leaders were positive about women's contribution to defense. And there were a certain number of women doing service in the N4A and the 8RA.[68] Claims to a "right to fight," however, which obviously did exist, were rejected as "egalitarianism" (*pingjunzhuyi*) (Peng Dehuai 1991b:679). Women's access to combat roles thus never became an article of the women's movement. Instead, their role in the armed forces followed a concept of a gendered division of tasks which was based on an essentialist understanding of

---

[66] There are several volumes that document the history of *Nüda*, see Yan'an Nüda 1989 and Yanshui qing 1999.

[67] Women were obviously not exempted from the militarization that characterized the whole movement and symbolized discipline and dedication to war service of any kind. See Dai Ling 1983:114 on the training of women soldiers: "With regard to military education, we learn general military knowledge and technical skills of the lowest level. Particular emphasis is laid on developing a soldier's bearing and being steeled in military life."

[68] For women soldiers in the N4A, see Xiang Ying 1991. Sources on the 8RA are scattered.

gender roles. This is obvious from a statement made by the vice commander of the N4A, Xiang Ying, in 1940 on women soldiers in the N4A:

> At the beginning of our work there was a small number of women comrades who understood equality (*pingdeng*) as a form and requested that female and male comrades should be put in charge of the same kind of work. For example, they demanded to go to the front to participate in fighting etc. Neglecting men's and women's differences in physical strength and their different abilities with regard to work leads to their performing work that is unsuited to their physical constitution. One can thus by no means give full play to women's abilities and functions. [...] Women's liberation principally means to fight for the same rights and liberties enjoyed by men. With regard to work, one should, as far as is possible and suitable, practice cooperation with men based on a division of tasks. (Xiang Ying 1991:407)

Yet, to my knowledge, there was no regulation that definitely prohibited women from performing combat roles.[69] The reason for this was probably the CCP's ambiguity towards fighting women. Despite the leadership's reluctance to consent to women entering the battlefields, examples of individual women and women's detachments that had engaged in fighting formed part of Communist propaganda. One of these cases was the "Zhejiang" or "Shaoxing Women's Battalion" (*Zhejiang/Shaoxing funü ying*) which existed between May 1938 and summer 1940 and gained publicity in 1939 after taking part in an attack on a Japanese unit that was occupying a railway station. Zhou Enlai himself had visited the battalion, and in an interview which was reported in *Jiuwang ribao (Salvation Daily)* in May 1939 he said:

> All [the members of the battalion] are people from Hangzhou, Jiaxing, Huzhou[70] and South China who have always been considered as gentle and weak; and besides, they are women. That they were all able to get deep behind enemy lines and engage in battle proves that no matter where and which person – battle is always possible. (Fei 1991:255)

---

[69] There seems to have been a contemporary ban on accepting women soldiers in the N4A when the military situation became extremely tense in 1939 (Xiang Ying 1991:404).

[70] Three towns in northern Zhejiang.

According to Zhou's report, army leaders had been very interested in the case "and thought that if women from the most gentle and weak area can rise up and kill the enemy, can there still be Chinese who are not able to go to the front?" They had asked Zhou "to propagate [the example] everywhere in order to make the countrymen of the whole nation rise up upon hearing the news" (ibid.). This is a line of argument typical of Chinese appeals to patriotism: women give the most convincing examples of patriotism – particularly for men – because they traditionally represent the private which has to be overcome in favor of national interests (Spakowski 1999:205, 298). Another reason for eulogizing fighting women, of course, is that the Communists simply could not do without those individual women who, especially in guerrilla zones, were indispensable to the survival of the movement.

Conflicts of military practice consequently resulted from the unwillingness of political and military leaders to let women take part in battle or at least get close to the battlefields. Many women in their memoirs recount instances of being excluded from military training classes or of being left behind or delegated to the villages to do mass work when all the male comrades were sent to the front. Though training classes had been designed to provide women with a proper understanding of the overall strategy of Communist efforts, many women did not willingly follow party orders but asserted their wish to go to the battlefields. Some of those who were based in Yan'an even turned to Mao Zedong to gain his support.[71]

This was the case, for instance, when in December 1938 a training course for military advisers was established at *Kangda* but women were not allowed to join. Two female students of *Kangda* sent a petition to Mao Zedong claiming that "if male comrades could become military advisers, female comrades could do so, too." Mao Zedong approved their request and as a result a quota system was established according to which one woman should be appointed to each class of twelve students (Zeng Xianlan 1999:324).

One way of dealing with women's resistance was to subject them to "ideological work" (*sixiang gongzuo*) – the instrument most

---

[71] See, for instance, Chen Muhua et al. 1991:88.

typical of the Yan'an movement – and to appeal to party discipline. This was the case, for example, with Kang Daisha who, in contrast to her male comrades, missed several opportunities to go to the front because women were not supposed to do so. Later, the Party destined her to do political work in the white areas because her family background would allow her to contact persons of political relevance to the Communist cause. Kang was reluctant to consent, but Zhou Enlai and Deng Yingchao themselves, on several occasions, persuaded her to submit to the will of the Party. Kang finally agreed (Kang Daisha 1991:28-31).

In cases where the contribution of individual women was less important there was more scope for negotiation. Some women were accepted into male units after an examination of their physical constitution.[72] The essentialist argument of women's weakness in these cases proved to be incorrect with regard to individual women.

Besides, whether women were able to remain in more combat-linked functions depended also on the military circumstances. Again, access to combat roles was more likely in guerrilla zones than in consolidated areas. Li Lin, for example, a famous leader of guerrilla groups in Shanxi Province in the years between 1937 and 1940, at first encountered resistance from her male comrades but was eventually put in charge of organizing guerrilla groups. In a letter written in 1939, she recalled this particular situation in October 1937:

> It was decided that I should take charge of organizing guerrillas (*wuzhuang gongzuo*). No, in the beginning some comrades didn't approve and didn't let me take responsibility for organizing guerrillas. They

---

[72] See, for instance, sources on the Shanxi Women's Company: Those "iron girls" (*tie guniang*) who insisted on remaining in the mixed 12th Company instead of being transferred to the all-women 11th Company had to join the male soldiers in climbing walls and in running (see Luo Lan 1990:76). Those who later requested to join the "Dare to Die Corps" (*Juesidui*) in Shanxi Province had to do three extra laps of running to prove that they were physically fit (Gao Zhengxi 1990:95). When the main body of *Kangda* in 1939 was to be transferred behind enemy lines and the female students were ordered to stay in Yan'an because of "the inconveniences marching would impose on women comrades," some women who insisted on following the main body were accepted because "their constitution was relatively good" (see Chen Muhua et al. 1991:88).

always held that organizing guerrillas was a job that didn't really suit a woman. But apparently I had some self-confidence with regard to that work and I was interested in it. I always thought that in these times it was necessary that women, too, should learn about military affairs. I insisted on my request, and they could do nothing about it. They agreed that I should expand the local guerrilla work (*youjidui gongzuo*) in Pian'guan. (Li Lin 1990:204)

To sum up, Communist policy during the War of Resistance basically returned to the People's War approach of the early 1930s which attached high importance to supporting roles and political work that were considered as the natural domain of women. Differing from the early 1930s, mobilization policy became more and more standardized and evolved towards a concept of even more distinct role allocations with regard to both gender and social background: rural women were made the primary target group of mobilization which was placed in the hands of women cadres with an urban background. Yet the expectations of this group of young urban educated women were quite different. For the first time, they raised the question of women's "right to fight." Although military leaders rejected claims to a right to fight their attitude toward fighting women was quite ambiguous. Due to contradictions in Communist gender policy there was scope for negotiation and some women succeeded in gaining access to units which came closer to their idea of military service. Again, the less rigid organizational structures in guerrilla zones offered women a greater opportunity for fighting.

Conclusion

As we have seen, women's military participation in the Communist movement between the early 1930s and 1945 did not follow a single pattern of either inclusion or exclusion. Instead, historical sources reveal a picture of diversity which basically resulted from different approaches to revolution in different historical contexts. As a result of the concept of a gendered division of tasks, women were assigned duties that were basically non-combatant – but not necessarily insignificant to the Communist cause. Their contribution was highly regarded in the more stable situations of the early 1930s and the War of Resistance when the construction of soviets and base areas was based on both combatant and non-combatant roles. It was regarded even more highly in guerrilla zones where Communist activities depended on women's "special functions." And it became marginal in times of crisis when the movement was cut down to its military core of male combatants. However, women's experiences in the Shaanxi-Sichuan Soviet and the Fourth Front Army under Zhang Guotao indicate that there was a broader scope for women's military participation in some areas. It was not until the Yan'an years that under the leadership of Mao Zedong, the Communist movement became more centralized and these alternative traditions came to an end. In addition, mobilization patterns still left scope for negotiating and exceeding prescribed gender roles.

Obviously, the modern feminist "right to fight" view represented by Judith Stacey hardly applies to the whole period and to all groups of women discussed here. It was not until the late 1930s that young urban women wanted to enter the battlefields and assume combat roles. They were attracted by the military as such and – despite political leaders' statements to the contrary – felt that women's work was a domain of low prestige. Young peasant women in the early 1930s, however, volunteered for the army not as an institution of fighting but as an institution that stood for alternative social structures. Their standard of judgment was not the "right to fight" which probably is an explanation for the positive views most of them display in their memoirs.

What about the revolutionary war/guerrilla war argument raised in comparative studies? There is no doubt that Chinese women had access to a comparatively broad range of tasks in the period of revolution. Communist ideology and the importance attached to women's liberation certainly favored this trend. However, the concept of gender equality was not deeply rooted in the minds of military leaders and ordinary soldiers who were rather ambiguous in their attitudes towards fighting women. "Women comrades" (*nü tongzhi*) and "women soldiers" (*nübing*) in their minds were still a distinct category of revolutionary personnel that was to perform different tasks.

Apparently, even commitment to women's liberation did not guarantee the dissolution of gender segregation with regard to the military. Guerrilla war did foster women's military participation. Yet it was not guerrilla war as a strategy – which characterized Communist military operations throughout the entire period – but the less rigid structures in areas far from the political centre as well as sheer military necessity that accounted for women's access to combat roles in guerrilla zones.

Finally, how do these findings on women's military participation figure in a general history of the Communist revolution? First of all, they support recent studies that point to variations in Communist policy and argue for deconstructing the Communist movement and the Communist Party. This has been the case, for instance, with regard to the base areas of the War of Resistance[73] and with regard to the women's movement of the same period (Goodman 2000). Secondly, they show that political concepts do not necessarily reflect the political practice of a given period. After all, despite the CCP's commitment to gender equality, women's military participation was subject to military and political circumstances. Women's inclusion or exclusion, to a certain degree, even depended on individual male leaders' decisions in favor of or against women participating in military affairs.

References

Benton, Gregor, *Mountain Fires. The Red Army's Three-Year War in South China, 1934-1938*, Berkeley, Los Angeles, Oxford 1992.

Benton, Gregor, Under Arms and Umbrellas: Perspectives on Chinese Communism in Defeat, in: Tony Saich, Hans van de Ven (eds.), *New Perspectives on the Chinese Revolution*, Armonk, London 1995, pp. 116-143.

Cai Chang, Zai zhongyang suqu he changzheng lu shang (In the Central Soviet and on the Long March), in: *Nübing huiyilu* 1987, pp. 111-125.

---

[73] See the contributions to the special issue on the base areas in *China Quarterly* 140 (1994).

Cai Xiang, Zhang Yueming (eds.), *Zhongguo funü baike quanshu* (Encyclopedia on Chinese Women), Hefei 1995.

Changzheng dashi dian (Encyclopedia on the Major Events of the Long March), ed. by Changcheng dashi dian bianji weiyuanhui (Editorial Committee of the Encyclopedia on the Major Events of the Long March), vol. 2, Guiyang 1996.

Ch'en, Jerome, The Communist Movement, 1927-1937, in: Eastman et al. 1991, pp. 53-114.

Chen Jing, Zhandi sheying jizhe (A Press Photographer in the War Zone), in: *Nübing liezhuan* 1987, vol. 3, pp. 587-597.

Chen Maohui, Fan Lechun (Fan Lechun), in: *Nübing liezhuan* 1985, vol. 1, pp. 148-175.

Chen Muhua, Ding Xuesong, Hao Zhiping, Wei geming lixiang er douzheng (Fighting for the Ideals of Revolution), in: *Kangda xiaoyou huiyilu* 1999, pp. 84-98.

Cheng Gengzheng, Changzheng zhong de Hongjun nü zhanshi yanjiu zongshu (Summary of the Research on Women Soldiers on the Long March), in: *Changzheng dashi dian* 1996, pp. 2235-2237.

Dai Ling, Huoyue zai Jiangnan zhanchang shang de jiaodaodui nüshengdui (The Team of Female Students of the Instruction Team on the Battlefields of South China), in: Funü zhi lu (Women's Way) 9 (6 September 1940), reproduced in: *Funü zhi lu* (Women's Way), ed. by Chongqing shi funü lianhehui fuyunshi yanjiuzu (Group of Researchers at the Women's Federation of Chongqing Working on the History of the Women's Movement), internal publication, Chongqing 1983, vol. 1, pp. 113-121.

Dai Xinmin, Wo yu shiyi lian (Me and the 11th Company), in: *Shanxi nübinglian* 1990, pp. 35-36.

DeGroot, Gerard J., Introduction: Arms and the Woman, in: Gerard J. DeGroot, Corinna Peniston-Bird (eds.), *A Soldier and a Woman: Sexual Integration in the Military*, Harlow 2000, pp. 3-17.

Deng Hongcan, Liu Huiming, Wang Xiaomei, Hong sifangmian jun nü zhanshi zai changzheng zhong de zuoyong he gongxian chutao (Preliminary Discussion of the Functions and Contributions of Women Soldiers of the Fourth Front Army on the Long March), in: *Changzheng dashi dian* 1996, pp. 1649-1654.

Ding Wenjian, Jinguo beige – Ji hong sifangmian jun funü dulituan (Elegy on Women – Remembering the Women's Independent Regiment of the Fourth Front Army), in: Sun Zhaoxia 1993, pp. 4-21.

Dong Hanhe, *Xilujun nü zhanshi mengnan ji* (Report on the Capture of the Women Soldiers of the Western Route Army), Beijing ³1991 (¹1990).

Eastman, Lloyd E., Jerome Ch'en, Suzanne Pepper, Lyman P. Van Slyke (eds.), *The Nationalist Era in China 1927-1949*, Cambridge 1991.

Fei, Zhou Enlai xiansheng tan funüying sha di chuangju (Mr. Zhou Enlai Talks about the Pioneering Deed of Killing Enemies by the Women's Batallion), in: Jiuwang ribao, 12 May 1939, reproduced in: *Zhongguo funü yundong lishi ziliao (1937-1945)* 1991, pp. 254-256.

Fenghuo jinguo (Women in the Flames of War), ed. by Jin-Cha-Ji bianqu Beiyue qu funü kangRi douzheng shiliao bianji zu (Editorial Group for Historical Sources on the Anti-Japanese Struggle in the Beiyue Area of the Jin-Cha-Ji Border Area), Beijing 1990.

Gan xinan funü gongzuo baogao (Report on Women's Work in Southwest Jiangxi), October 1930, in: *Zhongguo funü yundong lishi ziliao (1927-1937)* 1991, pp. 84-86.

Gao Zhengxi, Beixian ji xin sheng (A New Sound Stirred by the Strings of Sadness), in: *Shanxi nübinglian* 1990, pp. 91-99.

Gilmartin, Christina K., *Engendering the Chinese Revolution: Radical Women, Communist Politics, and Mass Movements in the 1920s*, Berkeley, Los Angeles, London 1995.

Goodman, David S., Revolutionary Women and Women in the Revolution: The Chinese Communist Party and Women in the War of Resistance against Japan, 1937-1945, in: *China Quarterly* 164 (2000), pp. 915-942.

Hagemann, Karen, Venus und Mars. Reflexionen zu einer Geschlechtergeschichte von Militär und Krieg, in: Karen Hagemann, Ralf Pröve (eds.), *Landsknechte, Soldatenfrauen und Nationalkrieger. Militär, Krieg und Geschlechterordnung im historischen Wandel*, Frankfurt/M., New York 1998, pp. 13-48.

He Fuxiang, Nanwang de huiyi (Unforgettable Memories), in: Sun Zhaoxia 1993, pp. 102-109.

He Ziyou, Huiyi funü dulituan (Recalling the Women's Independent Regiment), in: *Nübing huiyilu* 1987, pp. 201-204.

Ji Xichen (ed.), *Zhanhuo qingchun* (Youth in the Flames of War), Beijing 1997.

Ji Yu, Nübinglian de qingchun huoli yong fang guang mang (The Youthful Vigor of the Women's Company Will Glow for Ever), in: *Shanxi nübinglian* 1990, pp. 37-40.

Jin-Cha-Ji bianqu funü kangRi douzheng shiliao (Historical Sources on the Anti-Japanese Struggle in the Jin-Cha-Ji Border Area,), ed. by Jin-Cha-Ji bianqu Beiyue qu funü kangRi douzheng shiliao bianji zu (Editorial Group for Historical Sources on the Anti-Japanese Struggle of Women in the Beiyue Area of the Jin-Cha-Ji Border Area), Beijing 1989.

Kangda xiaoyou huiyilu (Recollections by Kangda Alumni), ed. by Shanghai kangRi junzheng daxue yanjiuhui ji xiaoyou lianyihui (Shanghai Association for Research on the Anti-Japanese Military-Political University and Alumni Federation), vol. 1, internal publication, Shanghai 1999.

Kang Daisha, Yan'an zai xiang wo zhaohuan (Yan'an Called Me), in: Su/Xu 1991, pp. 20-35.

Kang Keqing, Juanke zai xintou de wangshi (Past Events Engraved on the Heart), in: *Nübing huiyilu* 1987, pp. 126-133.

Lee, Lily Xiao Hong, Sue Wiles, *Women of the Long March*, St Leonards 1999.

Li Anbao, Liu Lukai, *Nü Hongjun changcheng ji* (Report on the Long March of the Women Soldiers), Beijing 1991.

Li Lin, Letter to Zhang Qinqiu and Meng Qingshu, reproduced in: *Shanxi nübinglian* 1990, pp. 202-205.

Lin Guo, Yi Zhang Qian (Recalling Zhang Qian), in: *Nübing liezhuan* 1987, vol. 3, pp. 357-376.

Lin Jiang, Shi "Qionghua" ye shi "Xiaohua" ("Qionghua" as Well as "Xiaohua"), in: *Nübing huiyilu* 1987, pp. 205-210.

Lin Yueqin, Huiyi funü gongbingying (Recalling the Women's Worker-Soldier Battalion), in: *Nübing huiyilu* 1987, pp. 231-251.

Liu Jian, Wo zai Hongjun li (When I Was in the Red Army), in: *Nübing huiyilu* 1987, pp. 179-187.

Liu Jian (recorded by Sun Hong), Yi changzheng zhong hong sifangmian jun de funü gongzuo (Recalling Women's Work in the Fourth Front Army on the Long March), in: *Sichuan dangshi yuekan* 6 (1988), pp.13-16.

Liu Xuezhi, Yisan qian hou (Around the Time of Dismissal), in: *Nübing huiyilu* 1987, pp. 273-279.

Liu Zhonglu, History Will Never Forget Them – Ruijin Women (Part One), in: *Women of China* 10 (1996), pp. 18-21.

Luo Lan, Zai zhandou zhong chengzhang de shi'er lian (The 12th Company that Grew Up in Battle), in: *Shanxi nübinglian* 1990, pp. 69-77.

Mao Zedong zai Yan'an Zhongguo nüzi daxue kaixue dianli shang de jianghua (jielu) (Mao Zedong's Address at the Opening Ceremony of the Women's University at Yan'an [Extract]), in: Xin Zhonghuabao, 25 July 1939, reproduced in: *Zhongguo funü yundong lishi ziliao (1937-1945)* 1991, pp. 149-150.

Minxinan junzheng weiyuanhui guanyu funü gongzuo de jueding (Resolution of the Military-Political Commission of Southwest Fujian on Women's Work), 29 March 1936, in: *Zhongguo funü yundong lishi ziliao (1927-1937)* 1991, pp. 464-469.

Nübing huiyilu (Recollections of Women Soldiers), ed. by Xinghuo liaoyuan bianjibu (Editorial Department of the Collection *Xinghuo liaoyuan*), published as no. 5 of the collection *Xinghuo liaoyuan* (A Single Spark Can Start a Prairie Fire), Beijing 1987.

Nübing liezhuan (Biographies of Women Soldiers), ed. by Han Zi, vol. 1, Shanghai 1985.

Nübing liezhuan (Biographies of Women Soldiers), ed. by Han Zi, vol. 3, Shanghai 1987.

Nuo Jie, Zhonghua suwei'ai gongheguo de funü (The Women of the Chinese Soviet Republics), 29 March 1934, in: *Zhongguo funü yundong lishi ziliao (1927-1937)* 1991, pp. 376-384.

Peach, Lucinda Joy, Behind the Front Lines: Feminist Battles Over Women in Combat, in: Laurie Weinstein, Christie C. White (eds.),

Wives and Warriors: Women and the Military in the United States and Canada, Westport/CT, London 1997, pp. 99-135.

Peng Dehuai, Xie gei "Huabei funü" (Written for the [Journal] "Women of North China"), in: Huabei funü, 15 June 1941, reproduced in: *Zhongguo funü yundong lishi ziliao (1937-1945)* 1991a, pp. 494-496.

Peng Dehuai, Zai Jin Ji Lu Yu si qu dangwei fuwei lianxi huiyi bimu shi de jiangyan (Talk at the Closing Ceremony of the Joint Conference of the Party Committee and the Women's Committee in the Four Areas Jin, Ji, Lu, Yu), 22 April 1943, in: *Zhongguo funü yundong lishi ziliao (1937-1945)* 1991b, pp. 675-683.

Selden, Mark, *China in Revolution: The Yenan Way Revisited*, Armonk, London 1995.

Shanxi nübinglian (The Shanxi Women's Company), ed. by Shanxi sheng funü lianhehui and Shanxi xinjun shiliao weiji zhidaozu bangongshi (Women's Federation of Shanxi Province and Guiding Group Office for the Collection of Historical Sources on the New Army of Shanxi), Taiyuan 1990.

Shi Yuqing, She nü jiu zhanyou (Saving the Lives of One's Battle Companions by Abandoning One's Daughter), in: *Nübing huiyilu* 1987, pp. 324-326.

Snow, Helen Foster (Nym Wales), *Inside Red China*, New York [2]1977 ([1]1939).

Spakowski, Nicola, *Helden, Monumente, Traditionen. Nationale Identität und historisches Bewusstsein in der VR China*, Münster 1999.

Stacey, Judith, *Patriarchy and Socialist Revolution in China*, Berkeley 1983.

Su Feng, Nanwang de nübing shenghuo (The Unforgettable Life of a Woman Soldier), in: *Nübing huiyilu* 1987, pp. 188-193.

Su Ping, Xu Yuzhen (eds.), *Yan'an zhi lu* (The Way to Yan'an), Beijing 1991.

Sun Zhaoxia (ed.), *Xizheng zhong de Hongjun nü zhanshi* (The Women Soldiers of the Red Army on the Western Route), Lanzhou 1993.

Tao Wanrong, Wo de geming shengya (My Revolutionary Career), in: Sun Zhaoxia 1993, pp. 38-61.

Tian Xiujuan, 1943 nian qian Jin-Cha-Ji nongcun funü gongzuo de chubu guji (A Preliminary Appraisal of the Women's Work in the Villages of Jin-Cha-Ji before 1943), in: *Jin-Cha-Ji bianqu* 1989, pp. 450-465.

Tuan Xiang-Gan shengwei qingfubu (Department for Young Women of the Communist Youth League of Xiang-Gan), Xiang-Gan suqu tuan shengwei qingfubu baogao (Report by the Department for Young Women of the Communist Youth League of the Province Committee of the Xiang-Gan Soviet), 20 January 1933, in: *Zhongguo funü yundong lishi ziliao (1927-37)* 1991, pp. 317-321.

Van Slyke, Lyman P., The Chinese Communist Movement During the Sino-Japanese War, 1937-1945, in: Eastman et al. 1991, pp. 177-290.

Wan xibei tewei funü gongzuo jueyi an (Draft Resolution on Women's Work by the Special Committee of Northeast Anhui), April 1931, in: *Zhongguo funü yundong lishi ziliao (1927-1937)* 1991, pp. 168-172.

Wang Huixian, Deng Zhijian, Zhen Mingyu, KangRi zhanzheng zhong Ding bei xian de funü gongzuo (Women's Work in Northern Ding County in the Anti-Japanese War), in: *Fenghuo jinguo* 1990, pp. 166-176.

Wang Ming, Wang Ming zai Yan'an Zhongguo nüzi daxue kaixue dianli shang de baogao (Report of Wang Ming on the Occasion of the Opening Ceremony of the Chinese Women's University at Yan'an), in: Zhongguo Funü 1:1 (1939?), reproduced in: *Zhongguo funü yundong lishi ziliao (1937-1945)* 1991, pp. 152-163.

Wang Yugeng, Wang shi zhuozhuo (The Shining Glory of Past Events), in: *Nübing liezhuan* 1987, vol. 3, pp. 336-356.

Xiang-E-Gan sheng chise zhigong lianhehui nügong bu (Women's Department of the Association of Red Workers in Xiang-E-Gan Province), Xiang-E-Gan sheng zhigong hui ge xian nügong buzhang lianxihui shang de geming jingsai tiaoyue (Agreement on Revolutionary Competition Promulgated at the Joint Conference of the Heads of all Departments of Women Workers at County Level

Belonging to the Association of Workers and Staff Members of Xiang-E-Gan Province), 23 September 1933, in: *Zhongguo funü yundong lishi ziliao (1927-1937)* 1991, pp. 347-350.

Xiang Ying, Women de nü zhanshi (Our Women Soldiers), in: Kangdibao, 8 March 1940, reproduced in: *Zhongguo funü yundong lishi ziliao (1937-1945)* 1991, pp. 404-411.

Yan, Jin-Cha-Ji bianqu funü qunzhong wuzhuang – Funü ziweidui (Arming the Women Masses in the Jin-Cha-Ji Border Area – The Women Militias), in: *Jin-Cha-Ji bianqu* 1989, pp. 505-518.

Yan'an Nüda. Jinian Yan'an Zhongguo nüzi daxue jian xiao wushi zhou nian (1939-1989) (The Yan'an Women's University: Commemorating the Fiftieth Anniversary of the Founding of the Chinese Women's University at Yan'an [1939-1989]), ed. by Jinian Yan'an Nüda wushi zhou nian chouweihui (Preparation Committee for the Commemoration of the Fiftieth Anniversary of the Women's University at Yan'an), Beijing 1989.

Yanshui qing. Jinian Yan'an Zhongguo nüzi daxue chengli liushi zhou nian (Love for the Yan-River: Commemorating the Sixtieth Anniversary of the Founding of the Chinese Women's University at Yan'an), ed. by Yan'an Zhongguo nüzi daxue Beijing xiaoyou hui (Beijing Alumni Association of the Chinese Women's University at Yan'an), Beijing 1999.

Yang, Benjamin, *From Revolution to Politics: Chinese Communists on the Long March*, Boulder 1990.

Young, Helen Praeger, *Choosing Revolution: Chinese Women Soldiers on the Long March*, Urbana, Chicago 2001.

Yuval-Davis, Nira, Militär, Krieg und Geschlechterverhältnisse, in: Christine Eifler, Ruth Seifert (eds.), *Soziale Konstruktionen – Militär und Geschlechterverhältnis*, Münster 1999, pp. 18-31.

Zeng Xianlan, Yi Kangda di yi qi canmoudui nüshengban (Recalling the Women's First Year Class of the Military Advisers' Group at Kangda), in: *Kangda xiaoyou huiyilu* 1999, pp. 323-328.

Zeng Zhi, Yu Mao Zedong de jiaowang (Meeting Mao Zedong), in: Liu Qingxia, Tang Luo, Hua Sha (eds.), *Zhongguo nü Hongjun. Jinian changzheng shengli liushi zhou nian* (Chinese Women Soldiers: Commemorating the Sixtieth Anniversary of the Victory of the Long March), Xi'an 1996, pp. 180-196.

Zhang Yan, Dao geming shengdi qu (Going to the Sacred Place of Revolution), in: Su/Xu 1991, pp. 10-19.

Zhang Yun wei kaizhan funü gongzuo gei quanti nü tongzhi de yi feng xin (Letter from Zhang Yun to All Comrades Concerning the Development of Women's Work), in: Binhaibao, 25 September 1943, reproduced in: *Zhongguo funü yundong lishi ziliao (1937-1945)* 1991, pp. 717-720.

Zhonggong suqu zhongyang ju (Central Department of the Soviets of the CCP), Laodong funü daibiao huiyi zuzhi ji gongzuo dagang (Program Pertaining to Organization and Work Agreed at the Conference of Representatives of Working Women), 2 January 1932, in: *Zhongguo funü yundong lishi ziliao (1927-1937)* 1991, pp. 227-229.

Zhonggong Xiang-Gan shengwei (Province Committee of the CCP in Xiang-Gan), Quan sheng fuyun chongfeng ji gongzuo jihua (Work Schedule for the Women's Movement of the Entire Province for the Season of Assault), 3 July 1932, in: *Zhongguo funü yundong lishi ziliao (1927-1937)* 1991, pp. 241-244.

Zhonggong zhongyang shujichu guanyu kaizhan funü gongzuo de jueding (Resolution of the Central Committee of the CCP on Developing Women's Work), in: Xin Zhonghuabao, 6 March 1939, reproduced in: *Zhongguo funü yundong lishi ziliao (1937-1945)* 1991, pp. 136-137.

Zhonggong zhongyang zuzhibu (Organization Department of the Central Committee of the CCP), Funü gongzuo dagang (Program for Women's Work), September 1937, in: *Zhongguo funü yundong lishi ziliao (1937-1945)* 1991, pp. 1-7.

Zhongguo funü yundong lishi ziliao (1927-1937) (Sources on the History of the Chinese Women's Movement, 1927-1937), ed. by Zhonghua quanguo funü lianhehui funü yundong lishi yanjiushi (All-China Women's Federation, Department for Research on the History of the Women's Movement), Beijing 1991.

Zhongguo funü yundong lishi ziliao (1937-1945) (Sources on the History of the Chinese Women's Movement, 1937-1945), ed. by

Zhonghua quanguo funü lianhehui funü yundong lishi yanjiushi (All-China Women's Federation, Department for Research on the History of the Women's Movement), Beijing 1991.

Zhongguo funü yundong shi (A History of the Women's Movement of China), ed. by Zhonghua quanguo funü lianhehui (All-China Women's Federation), Beijing 1989.

Zhongguo gongchandang zhongyang weiyuanhui guanyu ge kangRi genjudi muqian funü gongzuo fangzhen de jueding (Resolution of the Central Committee of the CCP on the Guiding Principles for Women's Present Work in the Anti-Japanese Base Areas), 26 February 1943, in: *Zhongguo funü yundong lishi ziliao (1937-1945)* 1991, pp. 647-649.

Zhongguo gongchandang zhongyang weiyuanhui, Zhonghua suwei'ai gongheguo renmin weiyuanhui (Central Committee of the CCP and People's Committee of the Chinese Soviet Republic), Youdai Hongjun jiashu de jueding (Resolution on the Preferential Treatment of Red Army Dependants), 8 January 1934, in: *Zhongguo funü yundong lishi ziliao (1927-1937)* 1991, pp. 362-365.

Zhu Changxie guanyu Gan xinan fuyun baogao (Report by Zhu Changxie on the Women's Movement in Southwest Jiangxi), 23 October 1930, in: *Zhongguo funü yundong lishi ziliao (1927-1937)* 1991, pp. 81-83.

Threads from Long March Stories: The Political, Economic and Social Experience of Women Soldiers

Helen Praeger Young

During the Long March, the experiences of perhaps more than 8,000 women soldiers were as diverse as the women themselves and in many cases differed distinctly from those of the men soldiers. Women joined the Party and the Army for social and economic reasons, usually but not always, combined with political commitment. Many of them considered the Party and the Army as their new family, replacing the families they left in their villages. They accepted the male hierarchy in the Party and the Army, but, as they did in the family, they found ways to circumvent some of the consequences of patriarchal decisions even while following the political agenda of their male leaders. They were strongly affected by political conflict among the male leaders. Their marital relations were politicized. Their work on the March was gendered, especially their work on propaganda teams. They formed close relationships based on need and proximity: they were close to those with whom they worked and marched, while demonstrating strong bonds with other women. The men soldiers viewed them as suffering the most, especially pertaining to menstruation and childbirth; as keeping able-bodied men from fighting because they required help and protection; as objects of jealousy and targets of theft; as working well in caring for the wounded, gathering grain, recruiting bearers and soldiers. The women, while realistic about the nature of the ordeal, did not perceive themselves as victims. Finally, their participation on the Long March in many cases allowed them to move into positions of political responsibility in the national or provincial capitals, and to obtain higher social status and greater economic stability after 1949.

Background

In the late 1980s I had the privilege of interviewing twenty-three of the Long March women veterans from the First, Second and Fourth Front Armies. From the tapestry woven from their stories, I will pull threads that reveal their experiences on the Long March in three aspects: political, economic and social. Finding the threads is complicated by many factors, not the least of which is that in the minds of many Communists almost everything is political.

The twenty-three women, who came from seven different provinces, ranged in age from twelve to thirty-two when they began the Long March. Of the fifteen from poor families, all but one had been given or sold to another family as an infant or a young child. Nine had some education before the Long March and one studied at college level; the others were illiterate (Young 2001:4-5). Fourteen were seventeen years old or younger when they "joined the revolution," the term they used to describe their politicization. They participated in the Long March in three parts of the Red Army, which left at different times from different Chinese soviet base areas.

Three Strands of the Red Army

The First Front Army, which included such Chinese Communist Party (CCP) leaders as Zhou Enlai, Mao Zedong and Zhu De, left from the Jiangxi Soviet in October 1934 with about 86,000 troops (Zhongguo gongchangdang 1991:93; Saich 1996:523), and about thirty-five women (Harrison 1972:243; Li Xiaolin 1995:260). The Second Front Army, led by Generals He Long and Xiao Ke and Ren Bishi as Political Commissar, left the Hunan-Hubei-Sichuan-Guizhou Base in mid-November 1935 with about 20,000 troops (Harrison 1972:254; Yang 1990:203ff.) including twenty to twenty-four women (Jian Xianren, Jian Xianfo, Ma Yixiang interviews; Li Xiaolin 1995:261). The Fourth Front Army, with Zhang Guotao as Political Commissar, left the Sichuan-Shaanxi Base Area in April 1935 with over 80,000 troops, at least 2,000 and possibly as many as 8,000 of them women (Harrison 1972:248; Li Xiaolin 1995:261; Lin Yueqin interview).[1]

The three strands of the Red Army differed markedly, their special characteristics originating from the nature of both male and female leadership, and from provincial differences of the soldiers. For the women, these differences are apparent in the work they performed, in their political commitment and especially in their experiences with children and childbirth. The First Front Army was tightly disciplined. Before the Army left Jiangxi, all the women without exception had to place their children with families staying in the Base Area before they left on the Long March.[2] Xie Xiaomei was still in the hospital after childbirth when she received orders to prepare for departure. Her preparation included disposing of papers in her office, reassigning personnel, and finding a family with whom to leave her baby. Not only were babies and young children not allowed to accompany their parents on the Long March as a military precaution, but babies born along the way were left where they were born, hopefully with families who would care for them.[3]

In contrast, Jian Xianren, whose husband He Long was one of the Second Front Army generals, brought her twenty-day-old infant

---

[1] Troop numbers, which can only be estimates, vary depending on who is counting whom, when and where. The number of women is even more problematic than the number of men, since most histories of the Long March do not include numbers for women except those in the First Front Army. Li Xiaolin identified thirty-three women in the First Front Army. From the names given by the interviewees and other sources, I believe that thirty-five women left with the First Front Army on the Long March; two left the Army before they moved out of Jiangxi Province and three left in Guizhou. The official figure for First Front Army women on the Long March is thirty. Li Xiaolin identified twenty-four women in the Second Front Army; the Jian sisters both thought there were about twelve, and Ma Yixiang said not more than twenty. Li Xiaolin gives the figure for women soldiers in the Fourth Front Army as 8,000; Yan Jintang, Chief Researcher for the Long March in the Beijing Military History Museum put the number at over 2,000, the usual figure.

[2] He Zizhen, Mao Zedong's wife, was no exception. She placed her son with a local family in the Jiangxi Soviet before leaving on the Long March, and also left the baby born on the Long March with a local family.

[3] According to the interviewees from the First Front Army, Liao Siguang, He Zizhen, and Zeng Yu gave birth on the Long March.

with her, and most women in this Army who gave birth during the March carried their babies to Shaanbei (northern Shaanxi).[4] In addition, several female *xiaogui*[5] thirteen years old or younger, traveled with the Second Front Army.

The Fourth Front Army, which had so very many women soldiers, was different from the other two armies in many ways. In terms of including children, one interviewee described the Fourth Front Army as being "[...] just a mess! There were women and children everywhere." However, Jian Xianren found:

> In June [1936], the Second and Sixth Armies reached Ganzi in the Aba region where they met the Fourth Front Army. The Fourth Front soldiers, in a demonstration of "warm welcome" and "deep friendship," had spun yarn and knit woolen vests and socks for the tattered newcomers.

Wang Dingguo described preparations the Fourth Front Army made before greeting the Second Front Army and crossing the grasslands:

> Everyone was involved in the preparations. Young soldiers went to the river every day to wash the lamb's wool, dry it and pull it into pieces. The adults, both men and women made yarn from the wool. We used something like an onion to spin the yarn. We stuck a short stick in it and called it a spindle. Then we knit sweaters and socks, using two small sticks.

Jian Xianren continued:

> I saw women who were involved in political work, propaganda work, and those who were engaged in health care. They were all laboring women, mostly from Sichuan. Some of the women comrades who hadn't received much education were very capable. Those mainly engaged with propaganda work not only made speeches but sang songs and put on plays in order to enliven the life of the army. When they encountered the enemies in battle, they were very brave on the battlefield. They carried the wounded on stretchers. They carried the medicine kits. They dug trenches and carried grain. Both men and women who worked in the kitchen carried very big, heavy copper or bronze cooking pots. I didn't

---

[4] Chen Zongying, Jian Xianfo, Jian Xianren, Ma Yixiang interviews.
[5] An affectionate term for children in the Red Army; literally "little devils."

actually see the Women's Regiment because they had set off ahead of me.[6] I did see some women comrades holding babies.

Exactly how many women were in the Fourth Front Army and how many survived the Long March is still unknown.[7]

Many of the Fourth Front women had been recruited into the Red Army in Sichuan where opium was an important cash crop (Slack 2001:166, 172).[8] Lin Yueqin explained the situation this way:

> The men smoked opium and became addicted to it. Almost all the heavy labor was done by the women. The men stayed home, cooking and taking care of the children. When we wanted to recruit more soldiers, there were fewer males in this area to be recruited so we had to recruit women. [...] [The women] didn't smoke opium and become addicts.[9]

---

[6] The women in the Fourth Front Army were organized into independent battalions and regiments, including a Women's Engineering Regiment (*Funü gongbingying*).

[7] Yan Jintang, Chief Researcher for the Long March in the Beijing Military History Museum, was very supportive of the project to interview women Long March veterans, saying the researchers had "not had time to study the women." He said he was sure the work would contribute to the current meager knowledge about the women soldiers. Others concerned with the Fourth Front women soldiers include Wang Dingguo who began working in the 1970s to identify Fourth Front Army women captured after they transferred to the West Route Army, and to help them regain their status as Red Army veterans. Guo Chen, a journalist with the *Worker's Daily (Gongren ribao)* in Beijing, has also done extensive interviews with Fourth Front Army women.

[8] Slack's tables 7, 8 and 17, suggest that opium production was extremely lucrative. His tables 12 and 13 which show opium offenders by sex, bear out the large discrepancy in numbers of men and women. For a description of Communist efforts to eradicate opium usage, see Wang Dingguo's article (Wang Dingguo 1997:43-44).

[9] There were women addicts, of course, among them Li Yanfa's mother, who apparently died of an overdose, but clearly there were far fewer women than men who were addicted. I can only speculate about why fewer women became opium addicts. What immediately comes to mind is that women are often more diligent about funneling family resources to children rather than to themselves for their own use, a pattern suggested by the experience of microcredit loan grantors. They have found that women repay the loans at much higher rates than men, who are more apt to spend the money on their own pleasures, and reinvest it in small enterprises to benefit their families. It also seems to be that opium smoking was identified as a male habit. Slack depicts a male business and leisure culture in

Opium was important enough medically, economically and as a social issue, that twelve of the interviewees mentioned it when talking about their experiences before and during the Long March. They spoke of it in terms of male addiction affecting them personally: "My uncle had sold me for a couple ounces of opium," Liu Jian said, describing her childhood in Sichuan. They discussed the problems faced by the families of addicts in the Sichuan-Shaanxi Soviet Base Area, where opium-growing was outlawed and addicts were encouraged to break the habit. They reported the widespread use as cash crops which replaced food crops, as well as for personal usage in Hunan, Guizhou, Yunnan, Sichuan. Qian Xijun said that when the First Front Army reached a minority area after they crossed the grasslands in Northwest Sichuan, "Even pregnant women and little children were using opium." Two mentioned specific medical uses, for dysentery and for sprinkling on a wound. Several spoke of confiscating opium from landlords and five mentioned using it in lieu of cash to pay transport workers, or to leave for absent Tibetan landlords in exchange for grain. Describing opium addiction in the Nationalist Army, several said that the enemy soldiers had two guns – a rifle and a "smoking gun."

Political Commitment and Repercussions

The political commitment of the women when they began the Long March also reflected the differences in the armies and in the regions. All the interviewees in the First Front Army, three in the Second and three in the Fourth joined the revolution before the Long March. They worked in local CCP organizations either at school or in their villages, before becoming members of the CCP or the Youth League, depending on age. Their reasons for joining the revolution

---

China which grew around opium use in the 1920s and 1930s (Slack 2001:34-35, 40-41), reminiscent of present-day alcohol usage practices among Japanese businessmen. For example, Estelle Freedman states: "Microlending has improved the lives of poor women and their families. Women borrowers tend to reinvest their income in food, shelter, and schooling for their children" (Freedman 2002:185).

often spoke to their realization that their families were poor and therefore politically and economically impotent or, if they were from wealthier families and had been to school, that their country was poor and impotent politically and economically. They all expressed their determination to make revolutionary changes within the larger society. On the other hand, several who were members of revolutionary families simply slipped into their roles, often already targets of Nationalist enemies. Only the women in the Fourth Front Army underlined the liberation of women as a reason for joining the army, perhaps because of the situation in Sichuan, perhaps because of the large number of women already in the army, perhaps because it was an overt part of the recruiting propaganda of that army, or perhaps some part of all of these reasons.[10] Many, in addition to giving political reasons for running away to the army, or for joining the CCP organizations, also cited social factors. Many who joined when they were teenage *tongyangxi*[11] with no prospective husband in their foster family; they wanted to avoid being sent to a stranger's home as a wife, to become the lowest member of a family unless and until she produced a son. Ma Yixiang in the Second Front Army joined as a child to escape a murderous foster family; Zhang Wen in the Fourth was inducted along with other workers in a clothing factory. It was also a woman from the Fourth Front Army who frankly stated that the only reason she joined the army was economic. Li Yanfa said:

> Why did I join the revolution? Because my parents died young, and our family had nothing. We rented land from the landlord. Our ox died and the landlord didn't let us farm his land. My sister became a child bride at

---

[10] Maxine Molyneux develops the argument that political strategies linking gender interests with revolution must include practical gender interests to appeal to women. She states that "it is the politicization of these practical interests and their transformation into strategic interests that women can identify with and support which constitutes a central aspect of feminist political practice" (Molyneux 1985:234). Certainly the promise of equality between men and women had special appeal for women in Sichuan Province where opium addiction left the women to do the bulk of the agricultural work while they were often excluded from owning property or participating in political decisions.

[11] An affianced daughter-in-law; a girl who has been sold into another family in infancy or childhood, possibly as a mate for a son.

the age of five, my two older brothers ran away to become long-term tenants and I was the only one left at home. I joined the revolution in August 1933. I was actually 13, but we said 14 (*xu sui*).[12] Why did I join the revolution? To go find food to eat. There was no food at home.

Whether women joined the Party and the Army primarily for political, social or economic reasons, they finished the Long March with a strong political commitment. Their political commitment, however, did not seem to have an affect on their experiences with political campaigns. After entering the realm of the male-dominated Army and Party, women found it necessary to devise ways to survive and protect themselves, especially when they faced serious political difficulties having dire social and economic consequences. In the late 1920s and the early 1930s, there were CCP campaigns which "combed out" from the ranks people from questionable class backgrounds and those who might pose a counterrevolutionary threat (Harrison 1972:216-217; Saich 2001:lix). Five of the interviewees mentioned the campaigns and three were affected by it with greater or less severity.

He Manqiu came from an intellectual family that educated her to middle school. Before she joined the Fourth Front Army her uncle, a Red Army soldier, advised her not to reveal that she could read and write, persuading her to modify her behavior in an effort to be less visible during the campaigns. She followed his advice as she marched, working as a nurse in a field hospital until the Army reached western Sichuan and settled down long enough to open a medical school. When she had the opportunity to apply to take the entrance exam, she decided that becoming an army doctor sensitive to women's medical needs should supersede protecting herself from criticism.

Earlier, Lin Yueqin, daughter of an Anhui small-town merchant, was combed out of her leadership position in the Children's Bureau in the Fourth Front Army, just before the "small Long March" in 1932. This was probably during the Huangpo purge directed at the leadership of the Hubei-Henan-Anhui (E-Yu-Wan) Soviet Base Area (Guillermaz 1972:217). Believing she would be killed, or captured

---

[12] Age according to traditional Chinese reckoning in which a child is one year old at birth, and celebrates the next birthday on the following New Year's Day on the lunar calendar.

and sold, if she returned to her home area which had reverted to Nationalist control, she and others in like circumstances followed along behind the Army. In constant fear that they would be sent away, they did menial tasks for the soldiers in the hope of receiving some food. Worn out and hungry, they took turns carrying a comrade's baby until a peasant offered to help carry it for a while and disappeared with it. The small group of women eventually rejoined the Army as part of the propaganda team. Liao Chengzhi made the decision to reinstate them into the Army "probably after [Party] consideration," Lin said. Liao was a man whose political antecedents were impeccable, although Liao Zhongkai, his father, "was a big landlord," Lin Yueqin added with a laugh.

Ma Yixiang, who joined the Second Front Army at eleven or twelve years old to work in the hospital laundry, was combed out after a soldier joked about her hands, saying they had become so white she resembled a landlord's child. "Later," she said, "the rumor spread that I was probably really a child from a landlord's family." She continued:

> I wouldn't talk about this in the past. Now I want to tell all I have experienced. At that time there was a movement to eliminate the counter-revolutionaries when many people were wronged and killed. They went to leftist extremes and I became a target of the revolution. It was impossible that nine investigations out of ten would reach correct conclusions. The class struggle at that time was very complicated. They believed the rumor that I was from a landlord's family. Since my hometown had been occupied by the enemy, they couldn't go there to investigate and I was unable to find people who could prove who I was. Even though they knew I was a mistreated child bride, I couldn't explain myself clearly. One soldier from my hometown could, but one wasn't enough. I had to find a few more people to prove who I was, people who had been to my home. They wanted to drive me into the white area from the soviet area. I couldn't go to the white area or I would be caught by the bandits so I hid with the local people. I was lucky it ended when it did or I wouldn't be alive today [...].

Ma Yixiang stayed close to the Army, managing to survive with the help of the women in her group. When she learned that the Army was moving out, she followed along with others whose units had expelled them. She attached herself to a unit where her background was unknown, and continued marching until the investigation committee finally cleared her name.

Army and Party as the New Family

Within the army or following along after being combed out, what the interviewees feared most during the Long March was being left behind. This fear sprang partly from their belief that they would be captured and sold or killed at the hands of the Nationalists, and partly from more complicated factors. To be left behind in a place where one could not understand the local dialect, where there were no family ties, where the Communist Party was not in control, meant loss of the means of livelihood as well as loss of identity in relation to the local people. The dread of being abandoned was sometimes responsible for an interdependency among the women that was almost familial. Deng Liujin, a member of the work team in the First Front Army, relates an experience with a fellow worker on the Long March:

> I'll never forget the only time I was sick on the Long March. We were in Yunnan and I had dysentery with a temperature of about 39°. When I couldn't go on any further and dropped behind, they wanted me to stay with the local people but I absolutely refused. I told them I would rather die on the road than stay behind to be captured and killed by the Guomindang [Nationalist Party, GMD].
> Wei Xiuying stayed with me. She carried all of our things but, because I had one bout of diarrhea after another, I could only move on very slowly. I had no medicine. When it got dark, we just rested under a tree, back to back. I kept telling her to go on alone and catch up with the others or we would both die. She said, "If we die, we die together."
> By following the marks the troops left as they went along, we caught up with our unit after four days. I didn't look human – thin as a rail, and pale. Our Party Secretary, Dong Biwu, immediately gave me his food.

In mentioning the fatherly concern of the political leader of Deng Liujin's work group, she expressed what the women felt about their superiors, men and women, on the Long March. Many indicated in their stories that, in addition to providing a political cause in which they could believe, the Party and the Army had replaced the families they had left behind in social and economic aspects as well. Quan Weihua said, "I was born to my parents but raised by the Party," and Liu Ying: "The Party nurtured and educated me." The army was responsible for their livelihood, which on the Long March meant simply food, clothing and medical attention if available; the work the women did was often gendered, and always for the good of the whole, as it had been in the family; the military and Party hierarchy, male and female, was reminiscent of the family structure; moreover, the Army and the Party made personal decisions for them that affected their education, marriage and determined who would rear their children, echoing Chinese familial patterns.

Zhang Wen, who was inducted into the Fourth Front Army with other workers in her clothing factory, described in detail how the Party arranged her marriage. Toward the end of the Long March, just before the Fourth Front Army crossed the grasslands for the third time, the male leaders convinced Zhang Wen, who, she said, was "only a squad leader, nothing but an ordinary soldier," to marry the man whom she described as "Political Director of the Fourth Front Army." She felt that she was "too young at seventeen, and the time wasn't ripe." Zhang Wen continued:

> We were introduced by the Party Organization (*zuzhi*). As long as you hadn't done anything wrong politically, did your work well, had a strong revolutionary spirit [there was no problem]. Actually, when we joined the army there were three [requirements.] The first is not to be afraid of hardship (*chi ku*), second not to fear difficulties (*kunnan*), and third, to believe in the revolution. Our purpose in joining the revolution was to liberate the whole country and liberate women. So when we got married, our marriage was within the revolutionary army and based on revolutionary ideas.
> Someone [from the Party] introduced us. If they hadn't, there wouldn't have been any marriage. After all, there were some requirements based on your family background, your own political stance, your work. The Party had the final say.

As surrogate family, by arranging and legitimizing marriages with proper introductions, sending the young soldiers to school, freeing mothers to do revolutionary work, the Party took responsibility for many aspects of the lives of the interviewees, who in turn felt nurtured physically and emotionally. For example, Ma Yixiang said, she

> [...] felt very warm in this big army family. If I had stayed at home, they would have repeatedly sent me away as a child bride and I would have repeatedly been beaten. But here, nobody beat me and nobody cursed me. I was equal to everyone else. I had hoped I could find a way out when I came to join the Red Army. Although they sent me home several times and expelled me from the army, I didn't feel wronged. So long as they wouldn't drive me away when I caught up with them, so long as they wouldn't kill me.

And He Manqiu:

> I felt more warmth from them than I had in my own family. Although it was more comfortable at home with other people to cook and care for you and with parents and grandparents to love you, when I was among the army people I felt as if I were in a brand new world.

The closest friendships among the women without actual family relationships on the Long March arose among those who worked together. Leaders such as Li Jianzhen, head of the women's work team with the First Front Army, and Liu Ying, leader of her logistics group in the Political Department of the same Army, spoke of feeling close to the women who worked with them. At the same time, they emphasized that they could not be closer to one woman than to another without showing favoritism. Answering questions about friendships, the interviewees told stories about assisting at childbirth, picking the ubiquitous lice off each other, and being nurtured and encouraged by older or higher ranking women. Ma Yixiang was mothered by women in the Second Front Army, as was Zhong Yuelin, the youngest in the First Front Army, for whom He Zizhen knit a sweater before they crossed the grasslands.

Women's Work on the March

Clearly offering help and support to each other was something that both men and women soldiers did, as was other work they performed: decoding telegrams; carrying stretchers; caring for the wounded; recruiting; gathering grain; doing security, administrative and propaganda work. The gendered work they did included nursing and doing laundry in field hospitals; delivering and mothering babies, children and younger women, caring for their husbands.

Additionally, propaganda work had a gendered aspect. Propaganda teams persuaded peasants to sell them grain, to help transport the army goods for a few days, to join the army, or perhaps to take in a wounded soldier. The men encouraged the women to work in the propaganda teams because they believed women could interact more effectively with the peasants since they could more easily go into peasant homes and chat with women who would not perceive them as a threat. They could persuade peasant women to let their sons or husbands join the army, or be attached as transport workers for a limited time. (Neither the First nor the Second Front Armies recruited women as soldiers or transport workers during the March.) When searching for grain, they needed to discover where the landlords lived so they could raid the granaries. In the process, they often learned details of how the landlord oppressed the peasants and, if they were staying in a village long enough they would enact those stories in street drama to raise the consciousness of the peasants.[13] In the First Front Army, the women often took male roles, suggesting that all-women teams performed the street dramas.

Women soldiers who worked with the wounded carried medicine boxes weighing eighteen *jin* (nearly twenty pounds.) When the army stopped to rest, they first settled the wounded soldiers, ensuring they had food and water and tending their wounds before they themselves ate and rested. When there were not enough transport workers, they carried stretchers, often at night to avoid bombardment from enemy planes and troops, and up and down steep mountain paths. If they were not tall enough, two women replaced one man at the end of the stretcher. And if they were clumsy and dropped the stretcher, the

---

[13] Li Bozhao, who was initially with the First Front Army and transferred to the Fourth, was especially well known for writing these street dramas. In the final interview with Deng Liujin on 8 July 1986, she stated: "Last night we got together at the Capital Theater where two plays [written by Li Bozhao] were put on in memory of Li Bozhao."

wounded soldiers cursed them. The rough, mountainous terrain made it hard going for the carriers as well as those being carried, Deng Liujin said: "The wounded complained about us and even beat us with their sticks when we couldn't take good enough care of them. They beat us and cursed us [...] but we knew why they acted this way and we didn't blame them."

Another task women performed was identifying peasant families who would agree to care for severely wounded soldiers unable to continue the Long March. Wang Quanyuan told a story about having to leave some wounded soldiers in a Miao minority area in the mountains in Guizhou. Desperate at being left behind in an area so destitute that some families had only one set of clothing for all family members to share, wounded soldiers stole her clothes and blanket. Resourceful, Wang went to the field hospital for replacements.

Another sort of gendered work the women performed was caring for their husbands, a job with strong consequences for two First Front Army women. Li Guiying and Xie Xiaomei were detached and assigned to work at the local level in Sichuan and Guizhou shortly after the Zunyi Conference because both their husbands had been wounded in battle and were unable to continue with the Army. Just as marriage was a Party affair, so too was the belief that caring for wounded husbands was appropriate work for women soldiers.

Li Guiying's husband was, she said, "the head of the Propaganda Department, the Organization Department." Xie Xiaomei's husband was Luo Ming, whose report of a guerrilla battle in Fujian in 1933 was used by the Communist leadership at that time to attack Mao Zedong and his guerrilla warfare strategy. Reinstated at the Zunyi Conference, Luo Ming was wounded shortly after.

As Deng Liujin's story of being ill emphasized, the fear of being left behind was strong for everyone. Li Guiying said: "I'm telling the truth. I didn't want to go. It would have been better for all the *dajie*[14] to be together." Xie Xiaomei, whose stories were flatly understated and unemotional, said, "From the beginning, we thought that there would be a lot of difficulties if we stayed behind." After she

---

[14] *Dajie* was the term they all used for each other, as well as for the women in leadership positions.

left the First Front Army, Li Guiying became a guerrilla fighter in Sichuan and was captured by the Nationalists. She was released after the Communists and Nationalists formed a United Front to fight Japan and reunited with her Long March comrades in the New Fourth Army. Xie Xiaomei and Luo Ming were captured in Guizhou, escaped, then faced one hardship after another. Xie Xiaomei was not reinstated in the Party until the early 1980s.

Impacts of Political Decisions on Women

Other women and the work they did were also affected by political decisions the male leaders made. During the Long March, two major events effecting dramatic political changes among the leadership were the Zunyi Conference held by the First Front Army in January 1935, and the conflict between the leadership of the First and the Fourth Front Armies in western Sichuan in June and July 1935.

Liu Ying, the only interviewee educated at college level before the Long March, worked in the Political Department of the First Front Army, in charge of a logistics group. She described the situation before and after the Zunyi Conference:

> One night when we climbed a mountain in Hunan, there was a very heavy rain. The road was muddy, and even if we had been traveling light it would have been difficult. Six people carried a printing press on shoulder poles. How could they walk? One by one, people fell off the mountain and died. We could only cover five *li* in one night. Why did we carry these things which caused so many deaths?[15]
>
> After the Zunyi Conference, Zhang Wentian made a speech at a meeting for cadres. He told us he had criticized the erroneous line. I was very happy when I heard that because then we knew the line we had followed was wrong: the military tactics were wrong; the way we fought wasn't

---

[15] Benjamin Yang explains the decision to bring along equipment necessary for running the government as, "not just a thoughtless error. It was mainly due to the initial objective of the Long March that the Communists had brought with them printing machines, bank notes, large artillery, and heavy ammunition. At that time, none of the Communist leaders – Mao included – thought that they would have to move as far away as they eventually did, and they wanted to save these things for probable futures use" (Yang 1990:122).

right; trying to move all our things was wrong. Many had died, about 30,000, so we didn't have very many left. The Army was reorganized and from then on, Chairman Mao was our commander.

I was sent to the Center. Three people were in charge of the Central unit: Chairman Mao, Zhang Wentian, Wang Jiaxiang. This team was equal to the Central Government. Because of the reorganization, many soldiers were freed to fight at the front, making the Army more effective. Chairman Mao thought the women could do the work: manage the everyday living, raise the morale of the bodyguards, take notes during meetings. I was General Party Secretary for a while.[16]

Even though Liu Ying sat in on meetings after the Zunyi Conference, it is unclear to what extent she was involved in the decision-making process. During the conference itself, women whose husbands attended had little knowledge of or influence on the resultant decisions. Kang Keqing said:

I knew some of the decisions that everyone was entitled to know, but the secret ones I didn't know. I stayed in the house where the conference was held and they held the meeting in our rooms, but I was out collecting grain. Other women, like He Zizhen, stayed elsewhere, perhaps a day's walk away. Where we stayed was decided by headquarters.

Qian Xijun, Mao Zedong's sister-in-law, said that she knew some of what was happening from hearing the wives of other leaders talk about the conflict that precipitated the Zunyi meeting. She was "relatively close" to Mao Zedong's wife He Zizhen, she said. "When she came back from Chairman Mao's place, she told me everything. Sometimes we went to see Chairman Mao together."

When the First and the Fourth Front Armies met in western Sichuan, Mao Zedong and Zhang Guotao, the Political Commissar of the Fourth, held a meeting at which it became clear that Zhang Guotao would not accept the decisions made at the Zunyi Conference and was unwilling to grant authority to Mao Zedong. He would not allow the Fourth to accompany the First Front Army to Shaanbei. When she learned that the First Front Army was leaving to go north earlier than

---

[16] Zhang Wentian, also known as Luo Fu, was the man Liu Ying married after the Long March. He replaced Bo Gu as CCP General Secretary as a result of the Zunyi Conference.

planned, Qian Xijun prompted He Zizhen to go to her husband to find out why.

> The answer was that the Fourth Front Army had split from us, so we had to start off at three a.m. If we had started later, the Fourth Front Army was stronger and they would force us to go south. They would fight us.[17]

When Kang Keqing and her husband, Zhu De, transferred from the First to the Fourth Front Army before the split, Kang said that Zhang Guotao demoted her from Political Instructor and attached her to the Women's School. She explained:

> The two Armies joined together and my husband and I were assigned to the Fourth. When Zhang Guotao led the Fourth south, we couldn't do anything. Even though we didn't endorse it, he did it anyway. Commander-in-Chief Zhu didn't agree. He persistently tried to persuade Zhang Guotao to change his ideas. At that time, Zhang Guotao was Political Commissar. Zhu *laozong* was still the Commander of the whole Army, but the Political Commissar had the final word.

Although ill-informed and subject to the political and military decisions made by the male leaders, women found the means to protect each other. Liu Jian told a revealing story of women courageously and ingeniously countermanding a decision to abandon Kang Keqing when she became ill.

The Fourth Front Army had turned south in an attempt to establish another base area, fighting Nationalist troops back and forth across the snow mountains. The women had to "carry the stretchers, carry the wounded, carry guns and carry grain," Liu Jian said. When they were recrossing Jiajinshan, Kang Keqing, ill with typhoid (or perhaps malaria), ran a high fever. Advised by the leaders to abandon her in a ditch – a decision, Liu Jian implied, in which Zhang Guotao concurred – Kang Keqing's comrades in the Women's School and the

---

[17] In this candid remark, Qian Xijun offered a glimpse of the depth of the rift between Mao Zedong and Zhang Guotao. About the number of troops, Benjamin Yang believes that "a careful analysis of the most credible sources shows that the First Front Army had 10,000 to 15,000 men while the Fourth Front Army had 60,000 to 70,000. Their ratio was more or less 1:5, a considerable disparity of strength" (Yang 1990:147).

Women's Engineering Regiment devised a way to transport her over the mountain:

> Several people bent a tree down, whacked it with a rock until it fell down. When it was broken we cut off two branches. We were wearing leggings, so we took them off and used them to make a stretcher.

They carried the ill woman about forty *li* (twelve or thirteen miles), using snow to cool her fever, until they could report to Marshal Zhu De.

Perceptions of the Women's Ordeal

The men in the First Front Army were careful of the women, keeping them close to the well-protected headquarters as they marched. They may have resented the necessity of carrying ill women on stretchers or of providing horses or mules for those who were unwell, in the final stages of pregnancy or had recently delivered, but when the men spoke of the women who marched with them, it was with admiration for what they endured and pity for them for having greater suffering than the men (Yan Jintang interview).[18] The women did not perceive of themselves as victims, although they spoke sympathetically about women who, for instance, climbed the glacier mountains in their third trimester and bore babies on the Long March. Liu Ying said that when she visited the grasslands many years later she wondered how they had possibly made the crossing, but at the time they did what was necessary without question. Others explained that when they were on the Long March they did not think that enduring hardships was particularly heroic: they were young and strong, and they had a cause in which to believe.

Jian Xianren, who brought her infant daughter with her on the Long March in the Second Front Army, had no delusions about how difficult the Long March was, but like the other interviewees, gave no indication that she felt she deserved pity. Indeed, most of the women

---

[18] Yan Jintang said: "The Long March was not easy for a man soldier and even harder for a woman, especially during pregnancy and the births of their babies on the Long March. It's hard for us to imagine the difficulties."

who made the Long March regarded it as certainly a difficult ordeal, but only one of many they experienced during the years before Liberation. Zhong Yuelin said shortly after the end of the March, "One day I got married, and the next day I was out collecting grain." Near the time Zhong Yuelin married, Mao delivered the speech that propelled the Long March into legend.[19]

Conclusion

Although they did not give the Long March the heroic interpretation the men did, the women almost all lived very different lives than the women who stayed at home in their villages when the Red Army came through. At the end of the March, the illiterate interviewees were sent to school. Some married men in high leadership positions, and one divorced her husband. After Liberation, many held prestigious Party and government positions. They served in the Chinese People's Political Consultative Conference at the national or provincial level, on the board of the All-China Women's Federation and the China Children and Youth Fund, on the Party Central Commission for Inspecting Discipline; one became General Party Secretary of Guangdong Province (Huaxia funü 1988; Li Xiaolin 1995:240-271). Some stayed in the army; one became a lawyer,

---

[19] Mao Zedong, speaking at Wayaobao, Shaanxi, 27 December 1935, said: "For twelve months we were under daily reconnaissance and bombing from the skies by scores of planes, while on land we were encircled and pursued, obstructed and intercepted by a huge force of several hundred thousand men, and we encountered untold difficulties and dangers on the way; yet by using our two legs we swept across a distance of more than 20,000 *li* [about 6,000 miles] through the length and breadth of eleven provinces. Let us ask, has history ever known a long march to equal ours? No, never. The Long March [...] has proclaimed to the world that the Red Army is an army of heroes [...]. The Long March [...] has announced to some 200 million people in eleven provinces that the road of the Red Army is their only road to liberation. [...] In the eleven provinces [the Long March] has sown many seeds which will sprout, leaf, blossom and bear fruit, and will yield a harvest in the future. In a word, the Long March has ended with victory for us and defeat for the enemy" (Mao Zedong 1967:160).

another a novelist and several wrote their memoirs.[20] All the interviewees but one, who had been captured in Xinjiang Province and not reinstated as a Red Army veteran until 1989, moved physically from their native cities and villages, and most lived a far richer life than the one facing them before they joined the revolution.

References

Bartke, Wolfgang, *Who's Who in the People's Republic of China*, New York 1981.
Dai Keyu (ed.), *Bashu jingguo zhuangge: Hong si fangmian jun nüzhanshi geming douzheng shilu* (Glorious Songs of Ba Sichuan Heroines: A True Record of the Revolutionary Struggle of Women Soldiers in the Red Fourth Front Army), Chengdu 1993.
Freedman, Estelle B., *No Turning Back: The History of Feminism and the Future of Women*, New York, London 2002.
Guillermaz, Jacques, *A History of the Chinese Communist Party, 1921-1949*, New York 1972.
Harrison, James P., *The Long March to Power: A History of the Chinese Communist Party, 1921-1972*, New York 1972.
Huaxia funü mingren cidian (Dictionary of Famous Chinese Women), ed. by Huaxia funü mingren cidian bianweihui (Dictionary of Famous Chinese Women Composition Committee), Beijing 1988.
Li Xiaolin, *Women in the Chinese Military*, PhD Dissertation, Maryland/MD 1995.
Mao Zedong, *Selected Works of Mao Tse-tung*, vol. 1, Beijing 1967.
Molyneux, Maxine, Mobilization without Emancipation: Women's Interests, the State, and Revolution, in: *Feminist Studies* 11 (1985) pp. 227-254.
Saich, Tony with Benjamin Yang (eds.), *The Rise to Power of the Chinese Communist Party: Documents and Analysis*, Armonk 1996.

---

[20] During the Cultural Revolution, many, if not all, of the interviewees were undoubtedly required to write a narrative of their experiences, which may well have provided the basis for stories told to me during the interviews.

Slack, Edward R., Jr., *Opium, State, and Society: China's Narco-Economy and the Guomingdang, 1924-1937*, Honolulu 2001.

Wang Dingguo, The Fight to Ban Opium in the Soviet Areas of Sichuan, in: *Women of China* (October 1997), pp. 43-44.

Yang, Benjamin, *From Revolution to Politics: Chinese Communists on the Long March*, Boulder, San Francisco, Oxford 1990.

Young, Helen, *Choosing Revolution: Chinese Women Soldiers on the Long March*, Urbana 2001.

Zhongguo gongchangdang lishi dashiji, 1919-1990 (The History of the Chinese Communist Party: A Chronology of Events, 1919-1990), comp. by Zhonggong zhongyang dangshi yanjiushi (Party History Research Center of the Central Committee of the Chinese Communist Party), Beijing 1991.

Interviews of Women Soldiers

Chen Zongying	Beijing Foreign Studies University	6/87
Deng Liujin	Beijing, Friendship Hotel	6/86, 7/86
He Manqiu	Beijing Foreign Studies University	12/86, 3/87
Jian Xianren	Beijing Foreign Studies University	12/88
Jian Xianfo	Beijing, Xicheng, interviewee's home	9/88
Kang Keqing	Beijing Radio Building	1/87
Liao Siguang	Guangzhou, written report[21]	1/88
Li Guiying	Nanjing, friend's home	2/89
Li Jianzhen	Guangzhou, interviewee's home	1/88
Li Yanfa	Beijing, interviewee's home	6/88
Lin Yueqin	Beijing Museum of Military History	1/88
Liu Jian	Guangzhou, TV Hotel	1/88

---

[21] Liao Siguang became too ill just before the interview and sent a written report instead.

Liu Ying	Beijing Foreign Studies University	1/88
Ma Yixiang	Guangzhou, TV Hotel	1/88
Qian Xijun	Beijing, Dongcheng, interviewee's home	9/87
Quan Weihua	Beijing Foreign Studies University	12/86, 6/87
Wang Dingguo	Beijing, Chinese International Radio Press	6/86
Wang Quanyuan	Jiangxi, Taihe County Guest House	2/89
Wei Xiuying	Jiangxi, Nanchang, army hotel	2/89
Xie Fei	Beijing Foreign Studies University	12/88
Xie Xiaomei	Guangzhou, TV Hotel	1/88
Zhang Wen	Beijing Foreign Studies University	12/86, 6/87
Zhong Yuelin	Beijing Military History Museum	2/89

Other Interviews

Yan Jintang, Long March Researcher	Beijing Military History Museum	3/86
Guo Chen, Worker's Daily Reporter	Beijing Radio Building	6/86

Qiu Jin (1875-1907) – A Heroine for All Seasons

Sabine Hieronymus

The execution of Qiu Jin on 15 July 1907 marked the beginning of her posthumous career as national heroine. Her memory has since then been upheld in numerous articles, anthologies and monographs in the Republican period and later, in the People's Republic of China (PRC)[1] as well as in Taiwan and even in the West.[2]
Obviously since 1907, a need for a heroine like Qiu Jin has existed in China and in this respect, she has become a "heroine for all seasons." In secondary sources, she is listed under many different labels: as poet, anti-Manchu revolutionary, feminist, anarchist, terrorist, forerunner for women's education and martial arts, just to begin with.

Maybe Qiu Jin's success as national heroine can be explained by the fact that her life is better documented than that of her female contemporaries and that her writings and her actions perfectly reflect the thought and conditions of the prerevolutionary era. But it should be kept in mind that the creation and cultivation of the Qiu Jin myth also reflects the political ideals of later periods.

Qiu Jin: A Heroic Life and a Heroic Death

When Qiu Jin was sentenced to death, she became the martyr, the icon of the Xinhai revolution. Very few Chinese women equal her in respect of leaving so many traces in history. There are famous photographs showing a beautiful woman in men's clothing, carrying a short sword in a very determined manner.[3]

---

[1] See Chen Xianggong 1983:123-133; for a brief overview of research in the PRC on Qiu Jin see Zheng/Chen 1993.
[2] Examples for publications concerning Qiu Jin or Qiu Jin's works in Western Chinese studies: Giles 1913; 1917; Ayscough 1937; Rankin 1974, 1975, 1978; Gipoulon 1976; Spence 1985; Pao-Tao Chia-lin 1992; Hieronymus 1999; Martin 2000-2001.
[3] For photographs of Qiu Jin see Qiu Jin shiji 1991.

Her extant lyrics and pamphlets, invoking the need for revolution, are present in nearly every anthology of women's literature or literature of the late Qing dynasty and also in countless reminiscences of her by her contemporaries: Qiu Jin left enough evidence of her life and she was made of the stuff of cultural icons. And all this, in spite of her having lived in seclusion for twenty-nine years, before she started her "career as a national heroine." In fact, she actively pursued this way of life (which made her famous) only during the last three years of her life, until 1907.

Born into an old family of government officials in 1875,[4] Qiu Jin grew up in Xiamen where her grandfather held office as a prefect. Profiting from the classical education her parents allowed her to receive together with her sister and brother, she started very early producing lyrics. It is said that she even received training in horse riding and armor as a guest in her uncle's house. Although her education appears to have been liberal, in respect of her marriage, the family seems to have been very traditional: Qiu Jin was married in 1896 to Wang Tingjun, the son of a rich merchant from Hunan – a marriage that was far from happy.

Finally, in 1904, she decided to leave her husband and her two children: son Wang Yuande and daughter Wang Canzhi. She sold her jewelry to cover her expenses and made her way to join the groups of Chinese students in Tokyo. There, she started her political career with enormous energy: she became a member of several political organizations and even founded new ones together with others.[5]

In 1905, she traveled back to China, where, with the help of Tao Chengchang (1878-1912), she was introduced to the revolutionary and pedagogue Cai Yuanpei (1868-1940). In June, she met Xu

---

[4] On the discussion about her birth date (1875, 1877 or 1879) see Zheng/Chen 1993:268-269.

[5] She had contacts with the *Sanhehui* (Triad) of Yokohama, was a founding member of the *Yanshuo lianxihui* (Society for the Study of Political Speech), together with Chen Jiefen (1883-?); in 1905 she reorganized the *Gong'aihui* (Society of Mutual Love), a patriotic society of Chinese women (Lin Wei-hung 1975:248); in June 1905 she became a member of the *Guangfuhui* (Restoration Society) and was a founding member of the *Shirentuan* (Group of Ten). See Guo Yanli 1983:44-46 and Feng Ziyou 1977, 5:61-75.

Xilin (1873-1907), a distant cousin of hers from Shaoxing, with whom she would later prepare the uprisings in Henan and Zhejiang.

In the two years before her death, she was a political activist. She was editor of one of the first Chinese women's magazines, the *Zhongguo nübao (Chinese Women's Journal)*, wrote several poems and essays and started writing her pamphlet for women's rights (left unfinished at her death) *Jingwei shi (Stones of the Bird Jingwei)*,[6] written in the style of a *tanci*.[7] Moreover, she started organizing the revolution. After she was appointed leader of the rebellion in Zhejiang, she returned in November 1906 to Shaoxing where she taught at the "Datong School" (*Datong xuetang*) and at the "Mingdao Girls' School" (*Mingdao nüxuexiao*). These teaching activities were useful for two reasons: the training of revolutionary junior staff, especially the military training, and the fact that it was a perfect cover for her own revolutionary activities. But in her own individualistic way she was not a very good "undercover agent": on several occasions she provoked the inhabitants of Shaoxing with breathtaking public appearances, riding on horseback and wearing black clothes or military uniforms. When the planned revolts failed and Xu Xilin was executed for attempting to assassinate the governor of Anhui in Anqing, Qiu Jin deliberately ignored the opportunity to escape the government troops that were on their way to Shaoxing. On 13 July, she was arrested at the "Datong School" (Luo Jialun 1984, 1:97-140). After a short trial, she was sentenced to death and decapitated on 15 July 1907.[8] Her execution outraged people from all walks of life and it is said that public opinion, as a result, turned against the Manchu government and Qiu Jin finally became a martyr of the revolution.

---

[6] Qiu Jin ji 1985:121-164, trans. by Gipoulon 1976.

[7] A *tanci* is a literary genre, a story told with rhymed passages. There were many *tanci* written by women through Ming and Qing times. For a short introduction see Nienhauser 1986:747ff.

[8] For the exact date of her death see He Pingli 1983:313-315.

In Which Way Did Qiu Jin Herself Contribute to the Myth?

The heroine Qiu Jin had very good knowledge of the old myths of her culture, she knew how they worked and instrumentalized them – and thus created a myth of her own. She named herself *Jianhu nüxia* (warrior woman from the Jianhu/Jinghu; a lake near Shaoxing), and by doing so, deliberately placed herself in the tradition of Chinese heroines.

She lived up to her role models and in turn became one to many others after her death, as her self-created image conformed to ideas of a traditional Chinese heroine as well as that of a modern revolutionary woman. And she could be used in more ways than others because of all the different labels that were attached to her to make her an outstanding model for others.

Self-Presentation as a Warrior Woman

A very important element of Qiu Jin's presentation of herself was her sensational appearances in public. The "mise en scène" in the photographs mentioned above give only a small impression of her abilities in this respect. Whether in male clothing with a walking stick, in Japanese clothing with a short sword or in a markedly simple outfit – in order to show her sympathy to the ordinary people – Qiu Jin used visual means to underline her conviction. In the same way, her public appearances in Shaoxing intended to present her as a warrior woman, a *nüxia*.

These acts are mirrored in her writings where her poems and *tanci* uphold the memory of the Ming-loyalists Qin Liangyu (?-1645)[9] and Shen Yunying (1624-1661), the most famous being *Ti Zhi Kanji (Dedicated to Zhi Kanji)* (Qiu Jin ji 1985:55) and *Man jiang hong (The River is Red)* (Qiu Jin ji 1985:110).[10]

Those women had gone to war as substitutes for their male family members. They were acting as men and afterwards often

---

[9] On Qin Liangyu see Kehry-Kurz 1999.
[10] See the translations of Gálik 1979:92 and Pao Chia-lin, in: Lo/Schultz 1986:402-403.

returned to their traditional female role. But Qiu Jin's hunger for heroism was not satisfied by those heroines who were guided by filial piety, so she added male heroes too, especially those with a particular motivation for remonstrance against authorities, such as the poet Qu Yuan (340?-247 BC)[11] or Jing Ke (?-227 BC),[12] who intended to assassinate the King of Qin, the later emperor Shi Huangdi (reign 221-210 BC).

And the Song-loyalists Yue Fei (1103-1141) and Wen Tianxiang (1236-1283) can also be found among her heroes. They all fought against invading armies or foreign rulers. However, where the female models served as examples of female militancy or literacy, the male ones fought against authority by means of active or passive resistance. And we should not forget there were also foreign heroines whose biographies were published in the contemporary press, for instance the Girondist heroine of the French Revolution Mme Roland or the Russian anarchist Sophia Perovskaya, or the author of *Uncle Tom's Cabin*, Harriet Beecher-Stowe and last but not least, Jeanne d'Arc, to whom Qiu Jin referred in *Jingwei shi* (Qiu Jin ji 1985:122).

In 1907, the *Zhongguo nübao* published a picture of Qiu Jin which looks very much like the one of Sophia Perovskaya published earlier in the second issue of *Minbao (People's Journal)* in 1905. This picture shows a very ordinary and uncomplicated Qiu Jin, the hair is parted and combed back severely. Was this similarity intended? It certainly looks very different from the very gentrified woman of previous pictures.

Armed for Heroism

Knives and swords played a very important role in Qiu Jin's thought and self-presentation. She wrote many poems on weapons (also an old tradition)[13] and often carried a short sword. The blades were always symbols and tools for freeing her country from foreign intruders, i.e. the Manchu and foreign nations. Those blades returned

---

[11] See *Diao Qu Yuan (Mourning Qu Yuan)*, in: Qiu Jin ji 1985:74.
[12] See Bao dao ge (Song of a Precious Knife), in: ibid. 82.
[13] See Liu 1967:55-80. On heroic poetry see Lo 1971.

often as a topic, they were "clean" in opposition to the "dirty barbarians." She carried the blade in order to free her country, she was above others, a prophet, appointed by a higher power to save the country. The sword was hanging menacingly like the sword of Damocles above the head of the Manchu, ready to strike. The mystical swords she referred to were given by heaven, symbols of fight and hope. Their magical powers became apparent only when they were in the appropriate owners' hands. Again, in a clever move of Qiu Jin's, this can be compared to other famous swords, such as King Arthur's "Excalibur," Siegfried's "Nothung" in the *Nibelungen*, or "Snow in the clouds" (*Yun zhong xue*) of Hong Xiuquan (1813-1864), leader of the Taiping rebellion (1850-1864). Those swords all serve as symbols of divine legitimacy.

And so Qiu Jin fitted out herself as a heroine: she has ancestors – as the legendary heroes; she has inheritance – as the famous blades; she has colleagues – i.e. the assassin Wu Yue (aka Wu Tingfang, a member of the *Guangfuhui*, 1875-1905) whose obituary she wrote. Wu Yue was killed accidentally on 24 September 1905 by his own bomb with which he intended to kill five ministers of the Qing government (Feng Ziyou 1977, 3:197-204). In Wu Yue, she saw an instrument of the cause as she did in herself. She glorified his inattentiveness which caused his own death, calling it a "pure sacrifice." Maybe she saw her own refusal to escape and save her life in a similar way.

The difficult situation of China at that time needed special heroes. The outstanding qualities of the Chinese heroes were loyalty, piety and patriotism. But Qiu Jin had an innovative way of interpretation as to when and where those moral obligations fitted. Just as the ruler could be denied the mandate of heaven, husbands and fathers could be denied the right of filial and loyal behavior, which their wives and daughters were obliged to show them. So Qiu Jin left her husband because he did not deserve her loyalty, but her country was in urgent need of it.

At the end of the Qing dynasty, the whole society found itself in a period of upheaval. The failure of the reform movement and the death of Tan Sitong (1865-1898) had shown that on its way to a new and modern China, selfless martyrs were needed. Old values like loyalty and filial piety were again motivation for action, but they were only to serve the nation. They were losing their validity in the context of family ties. The stars of that time were military heroes and their weapons: blood and death were their companions. The Chinese public was to be prepared for a violent revolution.

Qiu Jin could very well understand this need and therefore her writings and her actions were full of reminiscences of warriors of former days. Heroes have influence and this potential should be used for revolution. Qiu Jin's calls to action and her appearances in which she showed her eagerness to fight and to die, had the desired effect: her execution made her a martyr and after her death, a flood of publications emerged praising her bravery (Pao Chia-lin 1974:173-174). Qiu Jin became the personification of "ready-to-fight" attitudes and her lyrics were lauded as "fanfares for the revolution" (Ding Ying 1946:92-101).

How to Bury and How to Remember a Martyr

The way in which the case of Qiu Jin was handled by the Qing officials was immediately discussed in the Chinese press. If the government officials had taken more time, and chosen a less violent and hasty method, public opinion may not have been stirred up quite so much. So the Qing officials Gui Fu and the governor of Zhejiang, Zhang Zengyang (1843-1921), responsible for her execution, were the obstetricians who brought to life the martyr Qiu Jin. Articles telling the news of her death could be found in several newspapers (Guo Yanli 1983:148).

There were two arenas for the creation of Qiu Jin's myth and one was in the public sphere of the newspapers and the magazines. But there is more to the martyr business than media bluff: you need a body and you need a grave.[14] Qiu Jin chose the place of her grave

---

[14] This holds also true for Christian martyrs where "initially official and private martyr cult took place next to the grave and mostly in the open air. But soon chapels were built that were later replaced by smaller or bigger basilisks [...]" (Klauser 1960:30).

herself. In March 1907, she made an excursion with her close friend Xu Zihua, the headmistress of the "Xunxi Girls' School" (*Xunxi nüxue*) in Nanxun, to the Xihu (West Lake) in Hangzhou. They visited Yue Fei's grave and each promised that whoever died first had to be buried by the other close to this place (Giles 1917:137).

But what really happened to Qiu Jin's corpse was an odyssey in no fewer than nine stages. First, no one dared to claim Qiu Jin's body after the execution. Then someone from a charitable society took her corpse and buried it in the foothills of a nearby mountain called Wolongshan. Around October, her brother took her coffin and buried her in Shaoxing. Then in early January 1908, Xu Zihua came to Shaoxing and secretly moved her coffin to the piece of land near Yue Fei's grave in Hangzhou that she and Qiu Jin's other close friend, the woman calligrapher Wu Zhiying (?-1935), had bought. In December 1908, the government ordered Qiu Jin's brother to bring the coffin back to Shaoxing in order to prevent too much publicity. Then Qiu Jin's fourteen-year-old son Wang Yuande carried out his deceased father's will and buried her in Xiangtan in Hunan in a joint burial with him – this was in autumn 1909. After the victory of the Xinhai revolution, the coffin was moved in the summer of 1912 to the Yuelushan in Changsha. Again, this time in autumn 1913, her remains were brought back to Hangzhou, where she was buried on the western side of Xiling Bridge in the vicinity of Yue Fei's temple and grave. In 1965, her grave was once more moved to the foothills of the Jilongshan in Hangzhou and finally in 1981, she found her last resting place on the eastern side of Xiling Bridge opposite of the Yue Fei Temple (Wang/Chen 1990:126-127; Guo Yanli 1983:148-150). Maybe this odyssey was one of the reasons why the memory of Qiu Jin has been upheld for so long.

On the occasion of Qiu Jin's funeral, at the Fenglin Temple in Hangzhou in spring 1908, Xu Zihua wrote an obituary and Wu Zhiying engraved it on a copper plate. In the same year, Xu Zihua, Chen Qubing and others founded the "Qiu Jin Society" (*Qiu she*). They met secretly and decided to meet every year on the sixth day of the sixth month of the Chinese lunar calendar to commemorate Qiu Jin's death on this day for a righteous cause (Xinhai geming huiyi lu 1981, 4:220).

In 1908 the poet Liu Yazi wrote a poem honoring Qiu Jin: *Diao Jianhu Qiu Jin shi shi (Mourning Poem on the Noble Qiu Jin of Jianhu)* (Chen Xianggong 1983:53). This is just one example of the way she inspired others, as indeed, she herself had been inspired by Wu Yue and others.

In 1912, the year of the fifth anniversary of Qiu Jin's death, the Qiu Jin cult had reached its zenith. A huge memorial ceremony was held in Hangzhou with more than a thousand guests. This event marks the first appearance of Qiu Jin relics: Wu Zhiying sent items of Qiu Jin's inheritance to the memorial hall, as she could not attend because of illness.[15] In Shanghai the "Jingxiong Girls' School" (*Jingxiong nüxue*)[16] was founded by Wang Jinfa in memory of Qiu Jin. In December, a memorial was held in Shaoxing with prominent guests. Sun Yatsen visited Qiu Jin's grave in Hangzhou and honored her memory with a large elegiac scroll *Jinguo yingxiong (Female Hero)*.

In 1920, a column for Qiu Jin was erected in Shaoxing.

During the Republican era, Qiu Jin survived as a role model for female revolutionaries. In a letter written by Lu Xun's student and later wife, Xu Guanping said that it would be a shame if no one else could measure up to Qiu Jin – a comment that provoked harsh criticism by Lu Xun, who had always had a very critical view of Qiu Jin's heroic death (Spence 1985:204).

Christina K. Gilmartin has stressed that the German socialist Rosa Luxemburg (1871-1919) was far more successful as a cult figure in the years after her death than Qiu Jin, and that Qiu Jin was ignored in the pantheon of revolutionary heroes (Gilmartin 1994:204-205). Maybe it was better to admire a foreign heroine and a very reasonable one too – less fiery and less eager to engender bloodshed – than to follow Qiu Jin, a female hero and model for the female soldiers of the 1911 revolution, who were so demoralized when disenfranchised by the formation of the Chinese Republican Government?

---

[15] For an overview of the activities holding up the memory of Qiu Jin see Chen Xianggong 1983:107-122.

[16] *Jingxiong* (Compete Male) was an honorary name that Qiu Jin took while she was in Japan.

In 1939 Zhou Enlai wrote when he traveled to Shaoxing: "Don't ever forget the tradition of the *Jianhu nüxia*, I hope that she will be honored even more" (Zhou Enlai, quoted in: Song Ruizhi 1995:113). In the 1940s, there seems to have been no time to cherish the memory of Qiu Jin and between the years 1949 to 1955, there were only few remarkable publications on Qiu Jin in the PRC, the most outstanding being Xia Yan's drama *Qiu Jin zhuan (The Story of Qiu Jin)* in the year 1950 (Xia Yan 1984). The year of 1956 marked the forty-fifth anniversary of the Xinhai revolution and the year of 1957, the fiftieth anniversary of Qiu Jin's death. These offered plenty of opportunities to honor her and subsequently, more than seventy publications commemorated her. In particular the article of Fan Wenlan in August 1956 "The Woman Revolutionary Qiu Jin" *(Nü gemingjia Qiu Jin)* was a remarkable catalyst for the revival of the Qiu Jin cult (Fan Wenlan 1956). This wave of public interest had slowed down by 1962. In the years before and during the Cultural Revolution, only a little work on Qiu Jin materialized. In 1977, the interest in Qiu Jin again gained momentum with the approach of the seventieth anniversary of her death. This interest had reached tremendous dimensions by 1983 and persists even to this day.

Conclusion

Qiu Jin was a martyr of the Xinhai revolution: she was sentenced to death in a trial that was considered unfair. Perhaps the officials in charge could have reacted in a more sympathetic manner, but they had to deal with treason and assassination. The opinion was voiced that the actions of Xu Xilin and Qiu Jin were highly individual and a threat to the revolutionary cause. But they had both learned their lesson by the example set by Tan Sitong, the martyr of the 1898 reform movement.

When the Qing government acted in the way it did – improper trial, quick death sentence and a broad public debate as a consequence – it showed that it had not done its homework since 1898. And its action damaged the image of the Qing jurisdiction and political system in a way nobody could have expected: had Qiu Jin been killed in a fight, or been imprisoned, or if she had killed herself, it could never have had a similar impact as her death sentence. The Qing government only weakened its position by letting political amateurs like Gui Fu help in producing a martyr. Qiu Jin's ambitious plan to die for her goals could not have been served better. She could die like Jeanne d'Arc – a pure and maybe innocent woman. Being a heroine, for Qiu Jin meant revolting against helplessness.

Becoming a heroine was the only means of gaining power. Unfortunately, this door to power remained closed for women who were alive, as the refusal of political participation of women in 1912 revealed.

But it seems that an interest in the dead female martyr had existed – even before Rosa Luxemburg could take this place. There was a willingness to accept Qiu Jin as a martyr and critical voices, such as that of Lu Xun, could not be heard before the 1920s. Lu Xun accused Qiu Jin of not having really constructive ideas for changes in China, and of fighting a struggle with fire and sword (Spence 1985:204). He also accused her of being too vain and said that she was "clapped to death" (ibid. 73).

Qiu Jin was a heroine of her time, as every era produces its heroes. Many factors contributed to her later popularity: without the important role of the press, her case would not have gained so much publicity. And there was the network of friends, relatives and revolutionaries who were interested in preserving her memory, and the politicians who wanted to benefit from her popularity and to gain kudos by paying tribute to her. She became a synthetic product, a celebrity, a person who was known for her popularity and a person who became a sort of polar star in the time after revolution. She was a woman who was killed by the evil Qing government, she was a revolutionary, she was a feminist, and she was everything that you could wish her to be: she was a role model. Heroes serve many purposes. Heroes are necessary for the success of popular movements.

References

Ayscough, Florence, *Chinese Women Yesterday and Today*, Boston, Cambridge/MA 1937.

Chen Xianggong (ed.), *Qiu Jin nianpu ji zhuanji ziliao* (Chronicle of Qiu Jin's Life and Biographical Materials), Beijing 1983.

Ding Ying, *Funü yu wenxue* (Women and Literature), Shanghai 1946.

Fan Wenlan, Nü gemingjia Qiu Jin (The Woman Revolutionary Qiu Jin), in: *Zhongguo funü* 8 (1956), pp. 20-21.

Feng Ziyou, *Geming yishi* (Fragments of a History of the Revolution), 5 vols., Taipei 1977.

Gálik, Marián, On the Literature Written by Chinese Women Prior to 1907, in: *Asian and African Studies* 15 (1979), pp. 65-99.

Giles, Lionel, The Life of Ch'iu Chin: Translated from the Chinese by Lionel Giles, in: *T'oung Pao* 14 (1913), pp. 211-226.

Giles, Lionel, Qiu Jin a Chinese Heroine, in: *Asiatic Review* 12:34 (August 1917), pp.125-146.

Gilmartin, Christina K., Gender, Political Culture, and Women's Mobilization in the Nationalist Revolution, 1924-1927, in: Christina K. Gilmartin, Gail Hershatter, Lisa Rofel, Tyrene White (eds.), *Engendering China: Women, Culture and the State*, Cambridge/MA, London 1994, pp. 195-225.

Gipoulon, Catherine, *Qiu Jin: Pierres de l'oiseau Jingwei, femme et révolutionnaire en Chine au XIXème siècle*, Paris 1976.

Guo Yanli, *Qiu Jin nianpu* (Chronicle of Qiu Jin's Life), Jinan 1983.

He Pingli, Qiu Jin xunnan ri zhiyi (About the Date of Qiu Jin's Death), in: *Jindai shi yanjiu* 1 (1983), pp. 313-315.

Hieronymus, Sabine, *Frauenvorbilder: Über fiktive und reale Heldinnen in der späten chinesischen Kaiserzeit am Beispiel von Meng Lijun und Qiu Jin*, PhD Dissertation, Ann Arbor 1999.

Hsu, C.Y., Ch'iu Chin: Revolutionary Martyr, in: *Asian Culture (Asian-Pacific Culture) Quarterly* 22:2 (1994), pp. 75-94.

Kehry-Kurz, Doris, Warum muß ein General ein Mann sein? Die Generalin Qin Liangyu und ihre Darstellung in biographischen Quellen des 17. bis 19. Jahrhunderts, in: Monika Übelhör (ed.), *Frauenleben im traditionellen China: Grenzen und Möglichkeiten einer Rekonstruktion*, Marburg 1999, pp. 60-95.

Klauser, Theodor, *Christlicher Märtyrerkult, heidnischer Heroenkult und spätjüdische Heiligenverehrung*, Köln 1960.

Lin Wei-hung, Activities of Woman Revolutionists in the Tung Meng Hui Period, 1905-1912, in: *Zhonghua xuebao* 2:2 (1975), pp. 245-299.

Liu, James, *The Chinese Knight Errant*, London 1967.

Lo, Irving Yucheng, *Hsin Ch'i-chi*, New York 1971.

Lo, Irving Yucheng, William Schultz (eds.), *Waiting for the Unicorn: Poems and Lyrics of China's Last Dynasty, 1644-1911*, Bloomington, Indianapolis 1986.

Luo Jialun (ed.), *Geming wenxian* (Documents of the Revolution), 2 vols., Taipei 1984.

Lu Xun (Yang Hsien-yi, Gladys Young, trans.), *Selected Works*, 4 vols., Beijing 1957.

Lu Xun quanji (Collected Works of Lu Xun), ed. by Lu Xun xiansheng jinian weiyuanhui (Committee in Commemoration of Mr. Lu Xun), Shanghai 1973.

Martin, Dorothea A.L. (guest ed.), Qiu Jin: A Female Knight-Errant; A True Woman Warrior, *Chinese Studies in History* 34:2 (2000-2001).

Nienhauser, William H., Jr. (comp.), *The Indiana Companion to Traditional Chinese Literature*, vol. 1., Bloomington 1986.

Pao Chia-lin, The Feminist Thought in the Hsing-hai Revolutionary Era, 1898-1911, in: *Zhonghua xuebao* 1:1 (1974), pp. 151-180.

Pao Chia-lin, Ch'iu Chin, in: Lo/Schultz 1986, pp. 399-403.

Pao-Tao Chia-lin, The Inception of the Women's Movement in China: xQiu Jin and Her Family, in: Philis Lan Lin, Winston Y. Chao, Terri L. Johnson, Joan Persell, Alfred Tsang (eds.), *Families: East and West*, Indianapolis 1992, pp. 1-142.

Qiu Jin ji (Anthology of Qiu Jin), ed. by Shanghai guji chubanshe (Shanghai Ancient Books Publishing House), Shanghai 1985.

Qiu Jin shiji (Historical Traces of Qiu Jin), ed. by by Shanghai guji chubanshe (Shanghai Ancient Books Publishing House), Shanghai 1991.

Rankin, Mary Backus, *Early Chinese Revolutionaries: Radical Intellectuals in Shanghai and Chekiang, 1902-1911*, Cambridge/MA 1974 ([1]1971).

Rankin, Mary Backus, The Emergence of Women at the End of the Ch'ing: The Case of Ch'iu Chin, in: Margery Wolf, Roxane Witke (eds.), *Women in Chinese Society*, Stanford 1975, pp. 39-66.

Rankin, Mary Backus, The Tenacity of Tradition, in: Mary Wright (ed.), *China in Revolution: The First Phase, 1900-1913*, New Haven, London 1978, pp. 319-364.

Song Ruizhi, *Zhongguo funü wenhua tonglan* (Survey of Chinese Women's Culture), Jinan 1995.

Spence, Jonathan D., *Das Tor des himmlischen Friedens: Die Chinesen und ihre Revolution, 1895-1980*, München 1985.

Wang Qubing, Chen Dehe, *Qiu Jin nianbiao (xibian)* (Chronological Tables on Qiu Jin [Detailed Volume]), Beijing 1990.

Xia Yan, Qiu Jin zhuan (The Story of Qiu Jin), in: *Xia Yan ju zuoji* (Collected Plays of Xia Yan) ed. by Zhongguo xiju chubanshe (Chinese Drama Publishing House), Beijing 1984.

Xinhai geming huiyi lu (Reminiscences of the Xinhai Revolution), ed. by Wenshi ziliao chubanshe (Documentary Materials Publishing House), 8 vols., Beijing 1981.

Zheng Yunshan, Chen Dehe, 1949 nian yilai dalu xueshujie de Qiu Jin yanjiu zongshu (Summary of Academic Research on Qiu Jin in the PRC since 1949), in: *Jindai Zhongguo funü shi yanjiu* 1 (1993), pp. 261-272.

Jiang Qing and Nora: Drama and Politics in the Republican Period

Natascha Vittinghoff

Jiang Qing, one of the main figures of the Cultural Revolution and last wife of Mao Zedong, is doubtless one of the most prominent and most controversially discussed women in modern Chinese history. Most life descriptions of Jiang Qing written in the People's Republic of China (PRC) apply two fundamental principles of the historiographic method of the Chinese Communist Party (CCP): one is to denounce a person with incorrect political positions as a fundamentally immoral person; and the second is to construct a life history which reveals the basic evil character of this person from the very beginning.[1] In Jiang Qing's case, these evil beginnings are to be found in Shanghai. Although her activities in Shanghai have rarely been studied from a sound historical perspective, they have become a central point of reference for later evaluations of her political career or for statements about her (evil) nature and character, which inevitably led to the national catastrophe of the Cultural Revolution. Jiang Qing's Shanghai sojourn lasted from 1934 to 1937, during which she was depicted superficially in many newspaper reports and articles either as a rather successful actress or a prominent social celebrity who had become the target of reports because of private scandals.

A major part of this essay is devoted to reconstructing the history of Jiang's "scandalous" life as the actress Lan Ping within the context of the rising cultural industry in Shanghai. Remapping the complex and winding routes of her activities in this period is especially difficult, as there is not much reliable material available.[2] By

---

[1] This method of course also functions in the inverse case, that is, if a positive figure has to be constructed, as can also be seen in the case of Jiang Qing.
[2] This is due to two reasons: one is that Jiang Qing herself attempted to keep this period in her life obscure. Moreover, for part of the CCP leadership it seemed appropriate to silence this part of Jiang Qing's past in order to save the face of

tracing contemporary news reports, I will attempt to sketch a picture of Lan Ping as she might have appeared to an audience in Shanghai that did not yet know about a future Jiang Qing. Jiang Qing's most famous role was the main protagonist Nora in the play by Ibsen; and the *Nora* theme seems to run through her life and the descriptions of her life. Contextualizing her activities and own statements in the cultural sphere of the mid-1930s in Shanghai shall help explain how she was attempting to dramatize herself in a very ambivalent manner, as a modern, progressive and (yet) attractive woman. This approach seems rewarding to me in two ways: on one hand it reveals the struggles and possibilities of survival for a – certainly strong-willed – independent individual woman in the very uncertain and ever-changing situation of the cultural industry in Shanghai in the 1930s. On the other hand it shows how differently these struggles can be evaluated from an *ex posto* perspective, depending on whether the subsequent life of the person is seen as a success or failure.

Biographical Writing on Jiang Qing

The best-known account of Jiang Qing is certainly Roxane Witke's semi-autobiographical record of Jiang's life (Witke 1977), which was quickly repudiated by academic scholarship and gives an unfiltered depiction of Jiang Qing as she wanted herself presented in the late years of the Cultural Revolution. As far as I know it was never translated as a whole into Chinese, but is often quoted in Chinese literature on Jiang Qing. [3] Chinese biographies or biographical

---

Mao, who – still evaluated as a predominantly correct Communist leader – should not have fallen into the trap of a charming but disastrous actress. On the other hand, later accounts of Jiang Qing in Shanghai greatly exaggerate and fantasize certain aspects of her life as an actress and present this as evidence of her evil and ambitious character.

[3] Accounts that followed in Western languages move between fictional and semi-fictional texts; one of the most prominent examples is Ross Terrill's biography *The White-boned Demon: A Biography of Madame Mao Zedong* (Terrill 1984), which contains footnotes but indulges in psychological interpretations which are not substantiated by references. A *neibu* (internal) translation of this book, translated by Ma Yuande, appeared in Chinese in 1988 as *Jiang Qing zhengzhuan*

sketches of Jiang Qing appeared from the start of the Cultural Revolution, many of them first published in Hong Kong. Among her first biographers are Zhong Huamin, whose *Jiang Qing zhengzhuan* (Zhong Huamin 1967a) was translated into English as *Madame Mao – A Profile of Jiang Qing* (Zhong Huamin/Miller 1968) and into Japanese as *Kōsei seiden* (Zhong Huamin 1967b), and Ding Wang, who compiled a short biography in the same year (Ding Wang 1967).[4] Publications from the PRC during the Cultural Revolution, such as the *Brief Introduction of Comrade Chiang Ch'ing* (1967), emphasize her devotion to Mao Zedong as political leader, while ignoring her marriage with him in Yan'an. Her contributions to the creation of the model operas are emphasized and legitimized by her experiences as an actress in the Lu Xun Academy in Yan'an, whereas her professional experience in Shanghai is not mentioned.

It is obvious that these Cultural Revolution sources attempt to construct a politically correct biography by focusing on her patriotism and subsequent turn to the revolutionary cause, her promotion of the "spirit of Yan'an," her immediate identification and support of the correct party line in the two-line struggle, her participation in the war of liberation (since she could not be merited for having taken part in the Long March) and her absolute obedience to Mao and Mao Zedong thought. Publications mentioning Jiang Qing's activities in Shanghai were banned in this period, such as the prominent film history by Cheng Jihua, *Zhongguo dianying fazhan shi (History of the Development of the Chinese Film)* (Cheng Jihua 1981),[5] and the rumor circulated for years that Mao had ordered the destruction of all her films after their marriage in Yan'an (Witke 1977:131). In her self-depiction, Jiang Qing is eager to either downplay her experiences as insignificant

---

(Authentic Biography of Jiang Qing). Its editorial preface stresses the accuracy of sources Terrill made use of but gives a different political evaluation of the events.

[4] These sources by China-observers are most often based on her own official speeches and reports from newspapers such as the *Renmin ribao (People's Daily)* or *Hongqi (Red Flag)*.

[5] The book was published in 1963. Different sources give different dates for its being banned, either in 1966 (Li Fengming 1969:132) or 1968 (Zhong Huamin/Miller 1968:21).

endeavors or integrate them into a narrative of her life-long dedication to the revolution (Witke 1977, chap. 1, *passim*), which was obstructed by the bourgeois cultural leaders of Shanghai.

Later sources, following her arrest in 1976, intend just the opposite: They discuss her dubious proletarian class background (The Criticism Group 1979) and her activities in Shanghai are singled out as examples of her vicious character (Jiang Qing shi qishi daoming de zhengzhi bashou 1976). Instead of her having been hindered by the "black line" (*heixian*) in Shanghai – which was her interpretation – it is claimed that she herself promoted the "black line" (Wen/Feng 1979:56-57). The main purpose of these reproaches was of course to undermine her authority in the cultural realm, which she allegedly had entirely controlled and homogenized through the model operas. Moreover, her ambitions as an actress were interpreted as her fundamental desire to appear in public and become a powerful public persona, just like the heroic roles she had played on stage. In this line of reasoning, her marriage with Mao was just a consistent step in her constant search for a significant role, which she – supposedly due to a lack of talent – could achieve only through the support and promotion of a powerful man. Evidence of this is provided by the sudden publication of excerpts from letters and articles she had published in Shanghai (Wang Hongwen 1976:87).[6]

Post-Mao party historiographers on the Cultural Revolution resolved the dilemma of how to explain the catastrophe of the Cultural Revolution by maintaining the picture of the great leader Mao Zedong and placing all the blame on the Gang of Four and especially Jiang Qing. Thus it was necessary to disintegrate the relationship between Mao and Jiang Qing on both a political as well as private level.[7] It

---

[6] In 1979, the Hong Kong *Mingbao yuekan (Mingpao Monthly)* also published two letters in full length, which were soon after translated into English. See footnotes 41 and 47 below.

[7] Arguing this case was one of the most difficult tasks for the official explanation of the Cultural Revolution. Jiang Qing, as the only member of the Gang of Four who did not show remorse for anything she had done, was quite aware of this political dilemma when she repeated time and again during the trial in November 1980 that she was nothing more than Mao Zedong's dog, who bit whomever it was ordered to bite.

became important to give a correct depiction of Mao Zedong's attitude towards Jiang Qing, which would attest to the fact that he was aware of Jiang Qing's evil character, yet unable to prevent her ambitious activities. Therefore, together with the "Resolution on Party History" (Resolution 1981) a handful of quotations by Mao were widely publicized, wherein he had criticized the conspiracies of the Gang of Four or had made remarks on Jiang Qing's *yexin* (mad ambitions).[8]

After this official verdict, official statements on Jiang Qing are rare. Most strikingly, the official reports of her suicide reveal the attempt of the Party to erase this person from the cultural memory of the people. The *Renmin ribao (People's Daily)* published only a few lines more than two weeks after her death (Renmin ribao, 5 June 1991:4); the party organ *Xinhua yuebao (New China Monthly)*, which has a special section for "deaths of important inland personages," did not list her. In the *Renmin ribao* article as well as in the PRC's *Zhongguo funü mingren lu (Biographical Dictionary of Famous Chinese Women)* (1988), her marriage with Mao is not mentioned.[9]

Nevertheless, Jiang Qing remained a source of inspiration for fictional texts in China as in the West, such as Lucien Bodard's novel describing in detail Jiang Qing's early romances before she lived in Yan'an (Bodard 1992). Anchee Min just recently came out with a novel on Madame Mao, which is allegedly based on historical archival material as well as diaries, letters and newspaper clippings (Min Anchee 2000).[10] The constant popular interest in the person Jiang Qing in China is reflected in numerous unofficial biographies and

---

[8] Seven of twenty-four Mao quotes contain this phrase in: *Jiang Qing shi qishi daoming de zhengzhi bashou* 1976:1-57.

[9] In the *Biographical Dictionary of Famous Chinese Women*, only the entry for Yang Kaihui contains the year of her marriage with Mao. He Zizhen is also not mentioned as one of Mao's wives (Zhongguo funü mingren lu 1988).

[10] The book was a bestseller when it first appeared in the United States. Regarding Jiang's life in Shanghai, Anchee Min seems to rely heavily on Ye Yonglie, as she mainly presents his version of Jiang Qing's life. Although both Terrill and Anchee Min emphasize their use of historical firsthand sources in an attempt to gain an "authentic" picture of "Madame Mao," they both have no qualms about developing fantasies about Jiang Qing's sexual desires and activities, for which, obviously, no historical sources are available. This reflects the strong connection between power and sex that is evident in the popular reception of Jiang Qing.

popular semi-fictional accounts of her life that had to a large part appeared in Hong Kong but were already available in China in the late 1980s and early 1990s. Many of these accounts attempt to substantiate the reproaches made against her in official post-Cultural Revolution documents by embedding them in fantasies about scandalous intrigues. One such example is Zhu Shan, a doctor in charge of high cadres before 1949, who, like Jiang Qing, lived in Moscow in the 1950s. Her first account *Jiang Qing yeshi (Unofficial History of Jiang Qing)* appeared as early as 1980 (Zhu Shan 1980), followed by another book in 1988, which was published under two different pseudonyms in Hong Kong and the PRC (Zhu Shan 1988a, 1988b). Written as a novel that lists no sources, it is of course of questionable historical merit. In contrast, popular historians such as Ye Yonglie and Cui Wanqiu present more material-based studies of Jiang Qing, which also focus on the early years of her life (Ye Yonglie 1988, 1993; Cui Wanqiu 1987).[11]

Apart from the mostly accurate sources, here too we find interpretations of her life that reflect the general verdict and present her as the active and evil (selfish) part of a historical tragedy in which Mao is a rather passive male counterpart who is overwhelmed, seduced and then deceived by her sexual charms. Again, the combination of sex and power is a central theme in these accounts and they can be read as direct counter-texts to Jiang Qing's own politically motivated self-presentation in Roxane Witke's account. Most striking is that all these depictions elaborate on a parallel argumentation of Jiang Qing's strategies as an actress in Shanghai and as part of the political elite in Yan'an. In both cases, whether because of her lack of talent in

---

[11] Ye Yonglie is well-known as an author of popular biographies of prominent party members (and his biography on Jiang Qing appears as part of a series on the members of the Gang of Four) and a presenter of inside accounts behind well-known historical events such as the Lushan Plenum. He wrote two biographies of Jiang Qing, in 1988 and 1993 (Ye Yonglie 1988, 1993). Cui Wanqiu was the editor of a literary supplement to the *Dawanbao (Grand Evening Post)* in Shanghai and personally acquainted with Jiang Qing (Ye Yonglie 1993:60-62). According to Ye Yonglie, Cui Wanqiu was a spy for the Guomindang (Nationalist Party, GMD) regime (Ye Yonglie 1988:76), but this is rejected by Terrill (Terrill 1984:75).

Shanghai or a lack of true revolutionary spirit in Yan'an, she is described as having had to functionalize men in power in order to achieve her goals.

In the following section I will contrast these narratives on Jiang Qing with reports and articles written by or about her, which seem to allow quite a different picture of her as an actress in Shanghai. By briefly discussing the various tasks and roles required of a "modern actress" and positioning Jiang Qing's statements and activities within these various, often contradictory claims, I would tend to argue that the strategies she chose in order to maintain a position on the new cultural market were just as common and, most importantly, as rationally chosen as those of many of her colleagues at the time. Jiang Qing seems an especially rewarding example by which to display the multifarious difficulties a modern actress had to face on the new public stages, to show the ambivalent social and political status of actresses as women, and to reveal the range of possible evaluations of their activities by contemporaries as well as later historians.

Jiang Qing's Long Road to Shanghai's Nora

When Jiang Qing performed *Nora* on Shanghai's Golden City Great Stage (*Jincheng da xiyuan*) on 27 June 1935, she was already closely integrated into a social network of dramatic and literary circles. She was asked to perform this role by the newly founded Shanghai Amateur Drama Association (*Shanghai yeyu juren xiehui*), which she had joined on recommendation of Tian Han (Guo Hua 1998, 1:171).[12] The association was one of the first professional drama troupes founded in the early 1930s. Its success marked a watershed in the development of modern Chinese drama (Eberstein 1983:112-114), partly due to its very successful performances of Ibsen's *Nora*, Ostrowski's *Storm* and Gogol's *Revisor*. It hosted important dramatists, directors and actors such as Tian Han, Yang Hansheng, Zhang

---

[12] The term "amateur" used by many theater troupes of the time did not necessarily indicate a non-professional, non-commercial nature of the group, but was often chosen for political reasons.

Min, Jin Shan, Zhao Dan, Wei Heling, Gu Erji, and Wang Ying, many of whom Jiang Qing had established contact with earlier.

Nora was directed by the renowned director Zhang Min. Star actor Zhao Dan, who had seen Jiang Qing in a previous performance through the invitation of Wei Heling, played the main protagonist Helmer.[13] Wei Heling, Wan Laitian and Wang Bosheng, who were also involved in the productions as actors or assistant directors, were acquaintances of Jiang Qing from her earlier years in Shandong (Ye Yonglie 1993:57).

The *Nora* performance was an instant success and ran for an unprecedented two months. Naturally, Jiang Qing's performance of *Nora* received particular attention by the Shanghai press. The *Shishi xinbao (Current Affairs Daily)* even published a special edition headlined *Xin Shanghai Nala (Nora of New Shanghai)* with a picture of Jiang Qing on the front page; Jiang Qing's performance style was critically acclaimed. At that time, the *Nora* theme had become an important topic on China's stages, so it was a distinguished honor to be invited to perform this role. (This has not always been the case, as will be discussed below). It is thus puzzling how Jiang Qing as an allegedly untalented actress managed to enter and even dominate the stage for a while as a Shanghai Nora.

All biographical sources agree that Jiang Qing was born into a poor family (regardless of whether her background was proletarian or not). Born in Zhucheng, Shandong Province, she left there with her mother after her father's death in 1926 to live with relatives in Jinan. Due to Jiang Qing's poor education, she always lacked both job opportunities and money. During her early training as an actress in Jinan and Qingdao she had to support not only herself but at times also her mother.

Her first professional encounter with modern Chinese drama was in Jinan, where she entered the Experimental Drama Academy of Shandong Province *(Shandong shengli shiyan juyuan)*, directed by

---

[13] Wei Heling is said to have invited a group of well-known actors and dramatists, including Zhao Dan, Gu Erji, Tang Na and Zheng Junli to Jiang's performance in O'Neill's *The Firmament (Tianwai)* (Wei Shaochang 1987:59).

Zhao Taimou.[14] Zhao Taimou had studied with Wen Yiduo in the United States and was married to Yu Shan, a prominent actress who was closely associated with Tian Han and his progressive South Nation Society (*Nanguoshe*) (ibid. 89). In Shandong Jiang Qing worked together with the aforementioned Wei Heling, a graduate of this academy and later famous film actor in Shanghai (Guo Hua 1998, 1:44-49), and Wang Baosheng, who led the theater department of the academy and succeeded Zhao Taimou as its director in 1934 (Eberstein 1983:214). When the academy in Jinan was temporarily closed for political reasons in 1931, Jiang followed Wang Baosheng to Beijing to enter the Dark and Light Drama Troupe (*Huiming jushe*) and perform in the opera *Yu Tangchun (Yu Tangchun)*, albeit with little success. Some sources say she married the student Pei Minglun upon returning to Jinan and lived together with him for two months.[15] More sources agree that she followed Zhao Taimou to Qingdao, where he gave her a job in the Qingdao University library, which he headed at the time. There she heard lectures by Wen Yiduo and Shen Congwen and started to write some pieces by her own, a fact she elaborates on rather extensively in her autobiography and ironically comments on as her participation in the "upper strata of culture" (Witke 1977:1-62).

During this period, she befriended Yu Qiwei, brother of Yu Shan and propaganda chief of the Communist underground in Qingdao. It is generally accepted that through Yu Qiwei Jiang Qing made

---

[14] Zhao Taimou was an active promoter of modern drama since the early 1920s. Together with Wen Yiduo and Yu Shangyuan of the Crescent Moon Society (*Xinyuepai*), he promoted a "national theater" that combined Western drama with traditional Chinese forms and was not entirely subjected to political goals (Eberstein 1983:81).

[15] Most sources do not mention Pei Minglun, yet it is assumed (mainly through the account of Xu Zhucheng) that she had had two husbands before Tang Na, her husband prior to Mao Zedong. Some identify the first one as Pei Minglun (Ye Yonglie 1992:7; Wang Suping 1993:280). The marriage must in any case have been a very short one (Guo Hua 1998, 1:169; Ye Yonglie 1993). Wei Shaochang identified the first husband as Wei Heling, Jiang's colleague in Jinan (Wei Shaochang 1987:48). One major problem in determining the correct number of "husbands" (or "wives," respectively) in this period is the fact that sources sometimes do not differentiate between "cohabitation" (*tongju*) and being officially married.

her initial contacts to the CCP, although sources disagree whether she was already a regular party member at that time. She also established contact to the League of Left-Wing Dramatists (*Zuoyi xijujia lianmeng*).[16] Many biographical sources mention Yu Qiwei as Jiang Qing's first husband.[17]

During her stay in Qingdao she joined the Seagull Drama Troupe (*Hai'ou jushe*) of Qingdao University, a group with close ties to the League of Left-Wing Dramatists in Shanghai, where she performed together with Yu Qiwei (Ye Yonglie 1993:37-38).[18] Very likely due to Yu Qiwei's arrest in spring 1933, Jiang had to leave Qingdao. She went to Shanghai through connections of Yu Shan, who introduced her to Tian Han's house, where she lived for a while and met Liao Mosha (ibid. 41-43).[19]

Tian Han's brother arranged a job for her in Tao Xingzhi's school Chengeng Work Study Group (*Chengeng gongxuetuan*), lead by the Communist Xu Mingqing.[20] According to Ye Yonglie and Jiang herself, Jiang lived for about a year on the outskirts of Shanghai

---

[16] The League was founded in 1930 as a merger of smaller groups (among them Tian Han's branch of the *Nanguoshe*) and in reaction to increased pressure on progressive arts and literature of the GMD government.

[17] Jiang Qing makes no mention of Yu Qiwei at all and Witke rejects a sexual relationship between them as "rumors" (see Witke 1977:495, n. 1).

[18] Yu Qiwei was later named Huang Jing and became mayor of Tianjin after 1949. Edgar Snow interviewed Huang Jing in 1935 (ibid.; see also ibid. 502, n. 2).

[19] Ye Yonglie gives a very negative description of this visit to Tian Han's house. His comments about Jiang Qing's allegedly impertinent and outrageous behavior were taken from memories of Liao Mosha. Given the undeniable hostility between Liao Mosha, Tian Han, and Jiang Qing in the later years of the PRC, the question whether the hostilities produced these memories or whether her behavior produced the hostilities cannot be answered here.

[20] In this respect, Jiang Qing had very negative comments about Tian Han's and his brother's attitude towards her. Moreover, she stressed that Tian Han and others visited her and offered her different options in the film and theater realm, from which she modestly chose the "lowest" one, to do grassroots work among the masses in this school (ibid. 71-73). There are many different stories about Jiang Qing's relation to Xu Mingqing and it should suffice to note on Xu Mingqing here that her case was also investigated after Jiang Qing's arrest in 1976.

and spent her time teaching, singing and acting in different theater groups.[21]

When the Chengeng School was revealed to be a Communist base after demonstrations in Shanghai in January 1934, Jiang fled with Yu Qiwei, who had been released from prison, to Beijing. She returned soon after to Shanghai, where Xu Mingqing arranged a job for her as a teacher in the night school of a tobacco factory.[22] When Jiang Qing was imprisoned by the Guomindang (Nationalist Party, GMD) in September 1934 it was also Xu Mingqing and her connection to the foreign community in Shanghai through the Young Women's Christian Association (YWCA) that helped get her released in January 1935.[23] After a short sojourn with Yu Qiwei's family in Shanghai, she followed him again to Beijing, where he had assumed a job as an instructor at Beijing University. Shortly after their arrival she was invited to play Nora, which made her return to Shanghai in April. At the same time she joined the Diantong Film Co. (*Diantong yingpian gongsi*), one of the large film corporations in Shanghai, which had engaged famous actors and actresses such as Yuan Muzhi, Zhou Boxun, and Wang Ying.

---

[21] Other sources mention her as member of the Old Shanghai Society (*Hushe*) theater troupe in 1933, to which Wei Heling introduced her (Guo Hua 1998, 1:171) and of the New Voice Amateur Drama Troupe (*Tuosheng yeyu jutuan*), where she played in O'Neill's *The Firmament (Tianwai)* (ibid.; Wei Shaochang 1987:59) on 1 January 1934. According to Guo Hua, Wei Heling brought Zhao Dan, Gu Erji, Zheng Junli and Tang Na to see the play (Guo Hua 1998, 1:171), but Guo Hua gives no sources. Jiang Qing is also mentioned as the lead in *Locked Box (Suozhe de xiangzi)* of the Anonymous Drama Group (*Wuming jushe*) in January 1934 (Wei Shaochang 1987:60), an association of dissolved theater troupes that mainly played for worker audiences. According to Wang Suping this performance was in October 1933, by the League of Left-Wing Dramatists, where she met Zhao Dan, Gu Erji, Zheng Junli, etc. through Wei Heling (see Wang Suping 1993:281).

[22] At that time Xu was affiliated with the Shanghai YWCA, which organized these night schools for women. It is also in these night schools that the Blueshirt Drama Group (*Lanshan jutuan*) of the League of Left-Wing Dramatists performed their revolutionary pieces to educate (especially female) workers.

[23] Other versions declare that she was released after having betrayed the CCP, but as far as I know there is no evidence of this.

Her performance as Nora attracted great public attention. Numerous articles, stage photographs, and interviews with Jiang Qing appeared in Shanghai papers, mainly the *Minbao (The Minpao Magazine), Shishi xinbao, Shenbao (Shanghai News)* supplements and film magazines, all commenting on her performance in a very positive tone.[24] As she became known as a new star, rumors started about her private life and it is said that at that time she was already the object of quite a few prominent men's fantasies.[25] This was not at all exceptional in view of the fact that many actresses had relationships with prominent producers, directors, etc., who functioned as their patrons and promoters, and at the time Jiang was new and still unattached in the film scene.

When Jiang Qing performed *Nora*, she had already been engaged in different activities of leftist "progressive" drama troupes, educational institutions of leftist reformers, and underground institutions of the CCP under the very repressive political climate of the GMD regime. Yet *Nora* was also only a starting point for a more consistent career in the Shanghai film and theater scene, not least also because she was now more firmly settled in Shanghai. Her film activities brought her in contact with the literary critic Tang Na, a prominent journalist in Shanghai with a leaning toward writing "progressive" or leftist articles and critiques,[26] a fact that attracted considerable public attention.[27]

---

[24] See below.

[25] Guo Hua gives some concrete examples of how some men chased after her, but of course he cites no source for this (Guo Hua 1998, 1:172).

[26] Her first film for the Diantong Film Co., which was rehearsed in July and August 1935, was *Spirit of Freedom (Ziyoushen)*, a piece by the well-known author Xia Yan. Jiang Qing played only a minor role alongside the much more renowned actresses Wang Ying and Zhou Boxun. In October she had a role in *Sceneries from the Capital (Dushi fengguang)*, written and directed by Yuan Muzhi. Tang Na also acted in this film (as well as, among others, Zhou Boxun and Zhang Xinzhu). Born in Suzhou, Tang Na was a graduate of St. John's University in Shanghai and had become a regular writer for the *Beiping Chenbao (Beiping Morning Post)*, but also contributed to papers such as the *Shishi xinbao*, Shanghai *Shibao* and *Xinwenbao (Sin Wan Pao)*.

[27] See Ye Yonglie 1993:619-635, who lists about two hundred articles on Lan Ping: *Guanyu Lan Ping de baodao mulu* (List of Reports on Lan Ping).

Jiang Qing continued to appear in plays by the League of Left-Wing Dramatists, in November 1935 in Gogol's *Revisor* and, more prominently, in Ostrowski's *The Tempest* in the leading role of Katharina in February 1937, as well as many other films and plays.[28] In May 1936 she joined the Lianhua Film Co. (*Lianhua yingpian gongsi*), after the Diantong Film Co. was closed down. She allegedly competed with Wang Ying a few months later for the role of Sai Jinhua in a production by the Shanghai Amateur Drama Association but did not get the part.[29] Zhang Min is said to have asked her to play Katharina, the lead in *The Tempest*, in order to compensate for her not getting the role of Sai Jinhua.[30] From April to May she rehearsed *Wang Laowu (Wang Laowu)*, also written by Cai Chusheng, who had invited her to play the leading role.[31] One month later, in June 1937, her contract with the Lianhua Film Co. was cancelled. The last play in

---

[28] She played in Chekhov's *Jinianri (Commemoration Day)* in the drama group of the Diantong Film Co. in January 1936. Two months later she played in *Ying'er shalu (Baby Murder)* by Yamamoto Yūzō, translated by Tian Han, on the occasion of a March Eighth celebration by the Woman's Association; Jiang Qing appeared in *Fugui (Father's Return)* by Kikuchi Kan in her old school, the Experimental Drama Academy of Shandong Province in Jinan, during a short stay there in May 1936. In the summer rehearsals for *Blood on Wolf Mountain (Langshan die xueji)* started, a film directed and revised as a screenplay by Shen Fu, Fei Mu and Zhou Daming and released in November 1936. A month later, in December 1936, she took a small role in Cai Chusheng's *Twenty Cents (Liangmaoqian)*.

[29] Together with the Yihua Film Co. (*Yihua yingpian gongsi*) and Mingxing Film Co. (*Mingxin yingpian gongsi*), the Lianhua Film Co. was one of the three film companies that were largely dominated by left-wing playwrights and actors. Because of its Communist propaganda the Yihua studio was even violently attacked by the fascist Blueshirt Drama Group in 1933.

[30] The play was also staged in Nanjing in February and taken up again in Shanghai in March 1937.

[31] See, for example, Cai Chusheng xuanyong Lan Ping wei Wang Laowu zhujiao de yuanyin (The Reason Why Cai Chusheng Chose Lan Ping as the Main Protagonist in Wang Laowu), in: *Ying yu xi (Film and Drama)* 2 (17 December 1936). Title quoted from Ye Yonglie 1993:628. The film was censored by the GMD and released only a year later in 1938.

which she appeared in Shanghai was *Abandoning the Child (Qi'er)* by Zhang Min, staged by the People's Life Troupe (*Minming jushe*).³²

Given Jiang's strong official rejection of foreign cultural products during the Cultural Revolution, it is not surprising that she hardly mentioned the many roles she played on Shanghai's stages or downplayed them as bourgeois theatre, as almost all plays in which she appeared were translations from European or Japanese authors. As for her film, according to Witke she did not mention a single film title in her account, "even in response to several direct questions" (Witke 1977:131).³³

An Actress in Distress

Jiang Qing had entered the Shanghai film scene at a time of change in the cultural policy toward the "progressive" actors in the cultural sector. Whereas the film industry had been largely dominated by imported Hollywood productions, the release of films produced in China (*guochan* films) had become increasingly popular after the bombing of Shanghai by the Japanese in 1932 and the increasing political pressure of the GMD (Lee 2001:85). A new official CCP cultural policy fostered the orientation of dramatists and literati such as Tian Han, Xia Yan, and Hong Shen from theater to film (especially in the Lianhua and Mingxing Film Companies), in order to gain a broader and less educated audience. Also, film tickets were far more accessible for the lower strata of the Shanghai society, which was the intended audience of their propaganda message. In terms of content,

---

[32] The sources for this mosaic of her various activities were mainly Wei Shaochang 1987; Ye Yonglie 1993; Wang Suping 1993; and Guo Hua 1998.

[33] The following discussions in the Shanghai papers are therefore also entirely excluded from Witke's narrative. At those points where she alludes to these issues she rejects them as unfounded rumors invented in order to harm Jiang Qing (Witke 1977:139). Whereas Witke may be partly right (even if it seems a bit exaggerated) to identify such gossip as part of a general "misogyny and sadism," I think it would not do justice to Jiang Qing as an individual person to reduce the whole affair to an intrigue to which Jiang Qing was only passively exposed. Quite the contrary, Jiang Qing played an active role, not only in creating this gossip but also in defending her case as a modern woman in public.

there was a new orientation towards social problems with laborers as the lead protagonists.

Women held a particular position in this public cultural environment: women were not permitted as actresses on stage until 1911; and until the late 1920s the government still issued regulations that prohibited mixed seating in the theaters (it was generally permitted in the major big cities only since the 1930s). Thus the appearance of individual women in public was still a controversial topic.[34] On the other hand, women quickly dominated the commercial realm by advertising a whole new consumer culture, fashion, clothes, and household consumer goods in films as well as in women's magazines and the new print culture that was oriented towards women as consumers. The new film magazines, advertisements and film critiques in the newspapers also fostered curiosity and gossip about the private lives of the stars, as an inevitable part of the emerging system of glamorous movie stars. Yet Leo Ou-fan Lee has also observed how the new role of the Chinese public women in film differed from the mainly sexualized "fashionable femininity" exhibited by Hollywood stars, as it also stressed certain new qualities that a "new woman" should possess apart from good looks to please the male gaze (Lee 2001:93-94).[35] Because of this merging of political and commercial spheres, even in political propaganda films female actors had to satisfy demands other than merely conveying a revolutionary message.

Jiang Qing's participation in political films was most likely as much an expression of her individual political dedication as it reflected the general trend of a growing popularity of and interest in such films. It was also a reaction to an official Communist cultural policy articulated by those in the cultural scene with whom she closely associated.[36] Jiang Qing illustrated how the "new woman" on stage or

---

[34] On the position of women/actresses in the Peking opera see Goldstein 2000, chap. 8.
[35] Similar observations can be made for the transformation of the Japanese cultural scene through the engagement of female actors on the stage and their fictionalization for a national discourse (Kano Ayako 2001).
[36] This fact is emphasized here because in many accounts the reason for her turn to the film world is seen as evidence of her ambitions to find a broader audience

screen had to tackle the different expectations that a woman in public had to meet: She had to be strong-willed, intellectual, politically engaged and yet appear in public in a way that did not offend or directly confront traditional moral values. This public negotiation of new roles and expectations is reflected in the historical judgments of some specific instances in Jiang Qing's life as an actress that will be dealt with here.

One such instance is her sudden break with the Lianhua Film Co., which seems surprising, given her diverse activities in the Shanghai cultural scene. She thus lost a stable link to a cultural institution, and consequently, she left Shanghai soon after in August 1937.[37] One reason why she was expelled from the Lianhua Film Co. is said to have been her impertinent insistence to play Sai Jinhua.[38] According to these accounts, Jiang Qing allegedly stirred up so much trouble among the members of the Shanghai Amateur Drama Association that it split up, and finally dissolved.[39] Only Wei Shaochang questions this narrative rather convincingly. In his view, Jiang Qing was never a real

---

and become a famous film star, similar to those engaged in Hollywood productions.

[37] Although the attack by Japan and subsequent collapse of the cultural world in Shanghai would be a rather rational reason for her to leave this city, such a simple explanation is not given.

[38] When the script by Xia Yan was completed, the Shanghai Amateur Drama Association advertised a search for suitable actors for the play. The two most prominent actors of Shanghai, Jin Shan and Zhao Dan, competed for the role of the male lead, as did Wang Ying and Jiang Qing for the role of Sai Jinhua. Guo Hua explained that the directors tried to find a compromise by giving the A roles to Jin Shan and Wang Ying, and the B roles to Zhao Dan and Jiang Qing.

[39] Jin Shan, Wang Ying and other members subsequently reorganized themselves as The Forties Troupe (*Sishi niandai jushe*) and performed Sai Jinhua with enormous success (Guo Hua 1998, 1:175-176; Ye Yonglie 1993:113-116). According to Guo Hua and Ye Yonglie, as well as many other historians, this fight for the Sai Jinhua role was the reason why Wang Ying was persecuted during the Cultural Revolution. This serves as evidence that Jiang Qing persecuted only her personal enemies during the Cultural Revolution. I might add here that I am certainly not attempting to make a case for Jiang Qing's actions during the Cultural Revolution or to defend anything she had done as right. The sole reason for these comments is to show the extent to which the evaluation of her "political actions" deviates from those of her male counterparts in the Cultural Revolution.

option for the role of Sai Jinhua and the split in the theater group was instead caused by internal disputes, triggered when some members opposed the selection of Wang Ying as Sai Jinhua.[40] These later historical accounts have of course to be read with care, as this play was later labeled "traitorous." Jiang Qing's involvement therefore serves as additional evidence of her incorrect political behavior. Not surprisingly, Jiang Qing herself denied any involvement in this struggle. Even Wei Shaochang, when explaining these historical circumstances, felt compelled to explicitly emphasize that he did not intend to defend Jiang Qing as a person, but wanted to observe historical fact as a historian. This shows that it is still very difficult for a historian to write against the mainstream historiography on Jiang Qing.

Another reason for Jiang Qing's leaving the Lianhua Film Co. is said to have been her affair with actor and journalist Tang Na, a close friend of her colleagues Zheng Junli and Zhao Dan. As mentioned, this very complicated love affair was widely covered by the Shanghai press. Their relation started in September 1935, yet according to Guo Hua they were already separated in spring 1936. When Tang Na received a position as playwright for the Mingxing Film Co. (*Mingxing yingpian gongsi*), they got back together; Jiang Qing had an abortion and went to his family in Suzhou to convalesce (Guo Hua 1998, 1:173). The first separation (though not the abortion) was confirmed by Jiang Qing (Lan Ping) in her "A Public Letter" (*Yi feng gongkai xin*), in which she explained that Tang Na had threatened to commit suicide if they separated (Lan Ping 1980-1981:83-91).[41] Their

---

[40] This version is supported by the fact that the Shanghai Amateur Drama Association itself produced a Sai Jinhua piece and searched for an external actress, whereas Jiang Qing was only given the role of a minor prostitute (Wei Shaochang 1987:14-18). Without attempting to find out the "true" story of the background to the Sai Jinhua dispute, it should be mentioned that an article written under the pseudonym *Moge* (A Brother) in the *Shishi xinbao* mentions that there were plans to ask Lan Ping to perform the role of Sai Jinhua. Ye Yonglie has claimed that Jiang Qing fabricated this news in order to create facts before the decision was made (Ye Yonglie 1993:114-115).

[41] Jiang Qing alluded to this abortion just before she assumed the role of Nora in June 1936 in her articles "From 'Nora' to 'The Tempest'" (*Cong "Nala" dao "Da leiyu"*) (Lan Ping 1977a:312-315) and "A Public Letter" (*Yi feng gongkai xin*) (Lan Ping 1980-1981:83-91). The latter was also republished in 1992 as

reunion was publicly affirmed when they participated in a social event in April 1936, which sparked great public interest in newspapers and came to be known as the joint "Wedding at the Liuhe Pagoda."[42] Yet by the end of the same month, Jiang went to Jinan to escape Tang Na and look for her former husband Yu Qiwei. After receiving her farewell letter from the hands of Zheng Junli, Tang Na immediately followed her to her family in Jinan, but was not allowed to see her. He later received news that she had already left Jinan. At this point he attempted suicide for the first time by swallowing matches and drinking pure alcohol. Tang Na was rescued and news of his attempt of suicide quickly reached Shanghai; word even spread to Beijing and Nanjing in the *Zhongyang ribao (Central Daily).*[43] Subsequently, Jiang Qing and Tang Na returned to Shanghai and lived (and quarreled) together for almost a year.

During this time Jiang Qing was busy performing in films and theater, among them the role of Katharina in *The Tempest* and a role in *Juno and the Paycock (Zuisheng mengsi)* by the Irish dramatist Sean O'Casey. Both of these plays were either directed or translated by Zhang Min, former director of *Nora*. Jiang Qing now started a love affair with this most renowned director in Shanghai, after having separated from Tang Na for the second time. When learning about this affair, Tang Na attempted suicide again, this time by drowning himself in the waters of the Huangpu in the middle of the day, from which

---

"Why I Have Parted with Tang Na" in Li Yu-ning's collection *Chinese Women through Chinese Eyes*.

[42] At this event six Shanghai actresses and actors organized a joint wedding in Suzhou as a typical case of self-styling in the Shanghai film world. The ceremony of Zhao Dan and Ye Luxi, Gu Erji and Du Xiaojuan, and Tang Na and Lan Ping was conducted by the prominent lawyer Shen Junru and covered widely with photos and comments by the Shanghai media. After returning to Shanghai the event was celebrated with three hundred personages from the cultural sphere. Among those invited were Jin Shan, Hu Die, Wang Ying, Chen Bo'er, and many other best-known actors (Wei Shaochang 1987:24-34; Ye Yonglie 1993:83-89; Wang Suping 1993:193-202).

[43] For specific references to these articles see Ye Yonglie 1993:106.

he was hindered by a close friend.[44] Teacher and actress Xiao Kun, Zhang Min's wife and mother of their child, immediately divorced him after news of his new affair reached Shanghai; consequently, the press blamed Jiang Qing for having destroyed the lives of two men at the same time.

For Ye Yonglie and others, these events clearly reveal Jiang Qing's tactics to use men to further her career. She had seduced Tang Na in order to get a prominent role in a movie when she had no stage engagements. When it turned out that Tang Na's connections were not all that helpful, she abandoned him and turned back to the stage, supported by her new "victim" Zhang Min.[45] Apart from the fact that these narratives depict entirely passive males which had but to surrender to the sexual allures of an evil woman – not a very positive picture for the male counterparts, yet a stereotype of male fears of powerful women in Chinese literature[46] – the articles about Tang Na and Lan Ping in the contemporary press revealed a somewhat different and more complex picture. They show how the different values of a new social behavior, of revolutionary or progressive ideas and "traditional" remnants were negotiated in a seemingly "modern relationship" in the public press.

When Lan Ping left Tang Na and went to Jinan she sent him a farewell letter in which she explained her motives in leaving him. One reason was that she had discovered his relationship with another actress, with whom he had exchanged love letters, some of which were found by Jiang Qing. The other reason, which according to her

---

[44] According to Ye Yonglie, Tang Na learned about this relationship through the *Ying yu xi* newspaper, in which it was reported that a friend visited Lan Ping and discovered Zhang Min in her bed (Ye Yonglie 1993:129).

[45] Such a depiction can also be found in a newspaper article that was extensively cited by Ye Yonglie, although he admitted that this journalist was not very well-informed about Jiang Qing's actual doings (see Lan Ping xiang chu fengtou 1993:131-133).

[46] Classical sources such as the *Lienüzhuan (Exemplary Biographies of Virtuous Women)* see the negative influence of women in politics mainly in their supposed sexual voraciousness that the Emperors cannot resist, testifying to a male fear of an apparently unresolvable tension between power and sexual desire. Another example in popular literature of the threat exerted by female sexuality would be the motive of the seductive fox-ghost.

letter was the main reason for their constant quarrels, was her wish to leave the cinema and theater world in Shanghai and pursue a somewhat more meaningful life. Tang Na, on the other hand, was addicted to the seduction of the movie world and constantly tried to convince her to stay with him. They had apparently found a temporary compromise, that she would leave the movie world after making one good movie. But Jiang realized that he would continue to cling to this life, which seemed to her to be hopeless, frustrating and self-destructive. She decided to leave the tempting life of prominence and position for a job in a school, which she received through someone in the CCP who could not be named in the letter (Jiang Qing xie gei Tang Na de jueqingshu 1980-1981:77-82).[47] After leaving Tang Na, Jiang actually did go to Jinan to take up her old connection with Wang Bosheng, and subsequently to Beijing to reestablish contacts with CCP activist Yu Qiwei.

Before his suicidal attempt in Jinan, Tang Na wrote a letter responding to Jiang Qing and her descriptions of the situation. He does not show any signs of reproach or rage against her, neither did he style himself as a victim of her evil doings. Instead, he expressed admiration of her strong-willed devotion to the national cause and declared his intention to follow her on this path of a truthful and sincere struggle against imperialism. Among many romantic memories and words of desperation and self-critique he depicted her as an upright, outspoken, and sharp person and ended the letter with his support for her strenuous efforts to gain independence and liberty for the whole nation. Interestingly, this aspect of their personal differences – their different attitudes towards the world of movies and political activism – is not discussed in the accounts on Jiang Qing's life, most likely because it does not fit into the intended picture of an ambitious actress seeking fame on the silver screen. Tang Na explained his sui-

---

[47] Unfortunately the original source of this letter is not mentioned. The letter, written on 23 June 1936, is quoted in Ye Yonglie 1993:97-99 and cited in passages in Min Anchee 2000:93ff. Interestingly, Ye Yonglie leaves out the important passages in which Jiang Qing wrote about her decision to leave the movie world.

cide with his weakness to live up to Jiang Qing's ideals, a failure he was not able to bear.[48]

Suicide is a topic frequently taken up in discussion of their love affair, which is partly a self-styling and self-dramatization of the actors in public and partly a traditional way of "resolving" love problems. In her farewell letter to Tang Na, Jiang Qing admitted that she had thought of suicide but had rejected the idea because she did not want to follow the tragic role of a Lin Daiyu (Jiang Qing xie gei Tang Na de jueqingshu 1980-1981:77-82) or, as she admitted in her public letter, even the more real model of Ruan Lingyu, the famous actress who committed suicide in March 1935 (Lan Ping 1980-1981:83-91).[49] Suicide in China was a traditional archetypal solution to problems for a woman in distress, especially when female virtues were in question. It had become part of May Fourth emancipation rhetoric to rebel against this solution of female surrender. Had Jiang Qing committed suicide like Ruan Lingyu, her fate would most likely have been commented on as "tragic" and "unjust," as in the case of Ruan Lingyu, and public opinion would have been made responsible for the "murder." This of course did not hinder the – male-dominated – press from accusing other actresses in the same way and for the same reasons as Ruan Lingyu. Jiang Qing's open rebuttal of this option instead seems to have confused parts of the public opinion at that time, as well as contemporary historians today, as her outspoken appearance is now interpreted as part of her shameless, egoistic, self-centered character.

Conventional gender relations were turned upside down in this affair, since it was Tang Na who committed suicide and apparently took over the traditional female part. Yet Jiang Qing repeatedly went back to him because of his threat and her compassion and pity for him.

---

[48] The letter is quoted in Ye Yonglie 1993:92-94 and Wang Suping 1993:213-226. There are indications that it had been published in Shanghai at the time, though I have not yet been able to locate it.

[49] Ruan Lingyu, who according to Jiang Qing was the best actress at the time in China (and therefore a model for her in professional terms), had been scorned for her divorce from Zhou Daming and her subsequent open affairs with other men. She was driven to suicide by the public criticism of her supposedly immoral behavior. Her suicide was covered widely by the media in China as a tragic event.

Male suicide – quite opposite to traditional female suicide – thus again became a means of oppression and forceful implementation of a man's individual interests.

This was also negatively appraised and Tang Na was reproached for his "selfish," romantic and unprogressive behavior represented by his suicide attempt. Tao Xingzhi, for instance, founder of the Chengeng School, where Jiang Qing had taught in 1934, published a poem to Tang Na entitled *Songgei Tang Na xiansheng (To Mr. Tang Na)*, in which he told him that "Lan Ping is Lan Ping, she does not belong to you. [...] How can you take possession of her?" and admonished him to give his life for more meaningful purposes required by the new times.[50]

One of the main motives for public exposing these private affairs was certainly to gain attention. Attention-getting is one of the fundamental survival principles in the world of media, and the Shanghai critics of the time also realized that. One article about Jiang Qing starts with the comment that the most important condition for survival in the metropolis (*da dushi*) is to gain attention. Therefore everybody seeks attention; the affair between Tang Na and Lan Ping also served this particular function. According to this article, both of them had de facto a legitimate motive for seeking attention. While it was claimed that Jiang had to do so because she lacked professional qualifications (which was "defined" as the necessary good looks), however, Tang Na's need for seeking attention through his dramatic public suicide was not explained further (Lan Ping xiang chu fengtou 1993:131-133).

The obviously different evaluations of public statements made by men or women were also perceived and reacted to by the social actors, which in this case is reflected in the public letters exchanged between the two partners. When Jiang Qing published her last explanation of the whole affair with Tang Na in her public letter of 31 May 1937, on the one hand she was strongly defending her case from the perspective of an individual and independent woman:

> [...] I'm certainly not going to be like Ruan Lingyu and kill myself because I'm "afraid of what people might say." Nor will I retreat. [...] No!

---

[50] Tao Xingzhi, *Xingzhi shige ji* (Collected Poems of Xingzhi), Shanghai 1947, cited in: Ye Yonglie 1993:108-110.

> Lan Ping is a human being and will never retreat [...]. Since in his eyes I had already turned into such a shameful female, he certainly did not need to worry about me anymore [...]. (Lan Ping 1980-1981:90)

On the other hand, she argued from the perspective of a deceived, hurt woman who was wronged, when lamenting about Tang Na's secret love affair with another person (the actress Zhang Xingzhu), thus legitimizing her conduct with public morals. At the same time she presented herself as a self-confident woman mocking her male colleagues who were attempting to "destroy" her:

> At the same time I heard that Tang Na's friends were going to use force in dealing with me. Ha, ha! Good Heavens! If they would be so brave in fighting against XX, then, really, China would definitely not be defeated! Unfortunately, to use it against one young woman, ha, ha [...]. (ibid. 91)

Lan Ping and Jiang Qing as "Nora"

Emphasizing that "Lan Ping is a human being" in this last public letter, Jiang Qing took up the *Nora* theme, which certainly did not escape the eyes of the readers. Yet this role was also more than ambivalent and her performance of the role of Nora added another, more sensitive dimension to these negotiations, as *Nora* had (and still has) very special status on Chinese stages.

When Hu Shi, one of the first to introduce Ibsen and Nora in his famous article "Ibsenism" (*Xin Qingnian*, 1918), attempted to perform his own adaptation of the *Nora* theme *A Great Event in Life (Zhongshen dashi)* in Beijing in 1919, no female actor was willing to play this apparently indecent role on a public stage (Eberstein 1983:49-50).[51] Even more than a decade later, the "Nora incident" that took place in Nanjing is an indication that the content of the play was reason for discriminating against women who played this role.[52] Thus

---

[51] There are nine different *Nora* translations in Chinese, and the *Nora* theme was adapted in numerous plays by other dramatists (for examples, see Hsüeh 1981). A public performance of *Nora* was still prohibited in Beijing in 1925.

[52] This refers to a widely discussed incident of a schoolteacher Wang Ping, who was dismissed from office for her performance of *Nora* in a Nanjing amateur

the representation of a figure such as Nora on stage was directly linked to the social position of the actress in society. Such a reaction mirrors the contradictory claims brought forward by a society which demands new qualities for women formulated in theoretical debates and at the same time reproaches the same persons for carrying out such demands. Jiang Qing herself criticized the identification of the actresses' life on stage and in private, when she emphasized that acting is "art, not life" (Lan Ping 1977c:322).

This inherent contradiction is visible also in social comments on the *Nora* performance by Jiang Qing. The ambivalence of the perception of an attractive actress playing a strong-willed woman who wants to leave home might perhaps best be reflected in the unusual use of the metaphor of a "little bird" (*xiao niao*) in the following interview with Jiang Qing. It is commonly known that Ibsen's *Nora* on stage rebels against being a "bird in a cage" and demands being treated as a human being. Jiang Qing picked up this theme, stating that "one should not be like a 'little bird,' acting like a slave or plaything of men, and one should not offer one's own life for men – as women we have to be independent (*zili*) and not parasites." However, the interviewer from the *Minbao (The Minpao Magazine)*, Ji Cheng, used the same metaphor when emphasizing Jiang Qing's attractive and refined behavior and expression by comparing her to a small bird with a clear positive connotation: "When Miss Lan heard the sound of my leather shoes, she immediately turned around like a 'little bird' and ran over to welcome me" or "while she was speaking increasingly engaged [about *Nora*] she could not abandon her natural and girlish attitude like a 'small bird'" (Ji Cheng, quoted in: Ye Yonglie 1993:68-74).

It was therefore still problematic to present oneself as a Nora, although the theme combined the most important features of debates on China's emancipation of women. As such, the play gained significant, positive status among progressive and politically engaged actors, authors and critics. The year 1935 was called the "Nora Year" by Tian Han, and later also by A Ying and Mao Dun, because of the numerous

---

group in January 1935, as it was regarded as unseemly behavior (Eide 1987:95-96).

times it was performed on the stages of China's major cities (Eide 1987:88). The aforementioned confusion between the representational space on stage and the social space in the actresses' actual life was not entirely arbitrary, but also fostered by a specific and increasingly limited perception of the function of drama (and literature) as realist literature by these intellectuals.

Their emphasis on interpreting *Nora* as a realist play had a political connotation, which is most clearly revealed in the discussions that followed the *Nora* hype.[53] Restating Lu Xun's famous question of 1923 "What happens after Nora leaves home?," a lively theoretical debate started in 1934 in journals such as the *Guowen zhoubao (National News Weekly)* and others about the role of Nora in the emancipation of Chinese women, which emphasized the importance of female economic freedom, as gained through their participation in the production process. In the official ideological view, realism, the most important lesson to be learned from Ibsen's play, was seen in his propagation of individualism. This meant a rebellion against feudal family structures and individual liberation and fulfillment. Nora's rebellion was represented in the sound of her shutting the door, a radical and thorough break with her past. As was observed by Wang Zheng, however, for the male intellectual part, Nora functioned more as a figure to express one's own frustrations with the Chinese hierarchical and patriarchal family, to reaffirm one's own superiority by "identifying an 'oppressed' and 'inferior' social group – women" (Wang Zheng 1999:59).

Actress Jiang Qing, however, formulated the "problem of Nora" in a much more poignant and radical way, addressing questions of female liberation, which were not welcome in the political scene of the underground CCP:

---

[53] For Chinese critics, the most salient problem inherent in the reception of *Nora* in China was the unresolved ambivalence in the conflict between Nora and Helmer, an ambivalence that was intended by Ibsen but not welcomed by writers who attempted to create a new, modern literary canon and increasingly oriented themselves toward socialist realism – which does not allow for ambivalences. Thus the main emphasis in the reception of Ibsen was laid on his "realism," a realism which meant a true reflection of real-life problems and not a dramatic technique (Tam Kwok-lam 1986:388).

> I played *Nora* in 1935, and more recently *The Tempest,* and both plays have the woman question as their central themes. Moreover, the performances had great significance. [...] But, since not long ago a young girl was violently kissed by a foreign seaman on the trolley bus, and reports that a woman worker of such and such company was raped by such and such foreman circulate widely in the newspapers [...] – we have to endure all this violence without resisting. In fact, we are living under such conditions of oppression. A single Nora leaving – can that be enough? No, it's absolutely not enough! We need more practically oriented, more awakened women! [...] From the position of a woman and an actress, I demand that the authors [...] represent us, and produce scripts for the suffocating women! (Lan Ping 1977b:310-311)

As Xu Huiqi has recently argued, male discourse on the *Nora* theme contained the attempt to desexualize Nora in order to present her "door-shutting" as a human act of individual liberation (Xu Huiqi 2002). Jiang Qing was resexualizing it against this dominant *Nora* discourse. The salient issue of women's liberation, in Jiang Qing's view, is not the question of political liberation through active participation in the production process but first and foremost a question of liberation from physical male oppression. By this Jiang addressed the question of female sexual liberation in a direct and public way that transgressed even the "liberal" social norms and values of her political comrades. Jiang repeatedly explained that she rejected marriage and that it was an open and accepted truth between her and Tang Na that at some future time they would separate and find other partners.[54] As the values of individualism propagated by Hu Shi via Ibsen were not equally valid for men or women, in public interpretation there was only a fine line between a radical strong will and an alleged fake selfishness.

This can be seen most clearly in judgments about the specific historical person Jiang Qing alias Lan Ping playing Nora. Also, her performance was directly linked to her "real-life" personality and not

---

[54] It was probably mainly because of her liberal sexual life (and her open affirmations about it) that she was so eager to destroy any evidence of her activities in Shanghai during the Cultural Revolution, a time in which sexuality had been restricted and erased from people's lives most extremely, a policy which Jiang Qing herself had actively promoted.

seen as acting. Reviews of Lan Ping's performance always highlighted her fluent, natural and highly convincing acting of *Nora*.[55] As Zhou Huiling has recently shown in a study on the role of actresses as "social actors," this identification was strongly promoted by the left-wing social campaigns on actresses in the mid-1930s (Zhou Huiling 2002). Although frequently insisting on the artistic and professional component of the work of an actress, Jiang Qing herself was following this strategy of identifying her representational role with her actual social role by repeatedly drawing comparisons between herself and Nora. For instance she emphasized how close Nora was to her own character, which made it so easy for her to play this role (Ji Cheng 1993:68-74). This shows how Jiang Qing oscillated between her desire to keep her private and public identities separate and the necessity to satisfy the opposite demands of a film industry that did not distinguish between "acting *well*" and "acting *good*" (Chang 1999:159).[56]

Jiang Qing presented herself as threatening, on the one hand, and she herself created the image of a birdlike "good-girl" Nora, on the other.[57] This *Nora* metaphor was then applied to her life in many subsequent accounts and she could never shed the name of Nora in her later life. Ross Terrill referred to this theme in his prologue by stating

---

[55] Kanguo "Nala" yihou (After Having Seen "Nora"), in: *Minbao*, 28 June 1935, quoted in: Ye Yonglie 1993:63-64; Guan "Nala" yanchu (Seeing the Performance "Nora"), in: *Chenbao*, 2 July 1935, quoted in: ibid.

[56] Michael G. Chang identifies three generations of actresses from the 1920s to the 1930s and the different demands posed on them by society's expectations, concluding that "the artifice and posturing inherent in acting well (as opposed to acting good) in movies should have allowed for the separation of cinematic art and the daily lives of those women who worked as actresses; but such a separation into private and public personae tore at the ideal of a unified and unifying subject position (called the 'good girl') that is easily knowable and non-threatening to urbanites living in the vibrant but volatile milieu of 1930s Shanghai" (Chang 1999).

[57] See, for example, Lan Ping, "Wo yu Nala" (I and Nora), in: *Zhongguo yitan huabao*, 13 September 1935, quoted in: Ye Yonglie 1993:64-65; Lan Ping 1977a:312-315. There are more than twenty articles of Lan Ping written in the 1930s on topics such as domestic life, professional experience and political issues, which are never quoted, among them the above-cited articles on International Women's Day (Lan Ping 1977b:310-311) or on the art of acting (Lan Ping 1977c:319-324).

that "Mao treated Jiang Qing as Nora, his playmate and supporter. Jiang accepted the role, biding her time." Terrill continued: "The theater, politics – for Jiang the two realms were not very different" (Terrill 1984:17). According to Ye Yonglie and others, Jiang Qing played a "fake" Nora by functionalizing the role for her own selfish purposes – as she did with any other ideology. Only Shanghai author Sha Yexin introduced a different perspective in his *Jiang Qing he ta de zhangfumen (Jiang Qing and Her Husbands)* written in 1990 (Sha Yexin 1991), by staging Mao Zedong in the role of Helmer and letting him explicitly act as this person. By this Sha was for the first time presenting the inner conflicts of Jiang Qing as an oppressed woman in relation to her lovers and husbands; insofar he is much closer to the original version of Ibsen's *Nora*, which leaves the oppositional forces in a dramatic conflict without resolving it.[58] Jiang Qing's radical rebellion against society's demands for conformity and subjugation were interpreted as ruthless and selfish mainly from a historical perspective by later historians. The comparison between Jiang Qing and Nora was perhaps too tempting not to be taken up time and again in Jiang Qing's subsequent narratives. At any rate it was functionalized in the same way as Nora was functionalized on China's stages.

---

[58] Sha Yexin was only able to present this interpretation by emphasizing that his play did not deal with Jiang Qing as a historical person, but that she only served as a typical example of a woman in China (interview with Sha Yexin in summer 1990). His play, which for the first time gives a slightly more negative interpretation of Mao Zedong's role in the Cultural Revolution, was published in Hong Kong and to today has not been performed in mainland China. For a detailed analysis of this play see Vittinghoff 1995; on this aspect see pp. 127-150. For an annotated German translation see ibid. 195-341.

Conclusion

Discussion on Jiang Qing's activities on and behind Shanghai's stages is a complex one because it involves different layers of perception. The theater realm itself represents a complex merger of social and representational spaces, which is extremely revealing in terms of gender aspects. On the one hand, new roles for women can be imagined, performed and tested on stages and film screens; on the other hand, however, these actresses are evaluated according to social standards apart from their fictional roles, which can clearly differ. Discussions of Jiang Qing's involvement in the Shanghai cultural scene reveal this complex intertwining of social and fictional personae. Treatment of her self-presentation in the Shanghai artistic world reveals constant negotiations between these different expectations, claims, and demands for a "new woman" in public, as articulated through a highly commercialized culture, politically radicalized literature, and a widening social sphere that allows for individual searches for personal fulfillment.

At the same time, these negotiations were not accepted or understood as such by a large part of the audience or readership at the time and – especially in the case of Jiang Qing – by later historians. This is most evident in historical accounts that evaluate her activities from the *ex posto* perspective of her life as Mao Zedong's wife and prominent leader of the Cultural Revolution. All aspects attributed to her in an effort to undermine her political authority in the CCP leadership can be traced back to her professional beginnings in Shanghai: unrestrained desire for public attention, sexual seduction of useful men, functionalizing of political slogans for private interests and using "feminism" to pursue selfish goals. To substantiate this point, stories, quotations, and historical facts were arbitrarily selected and combined.

What I have attempted to show is the unreliability of all these depictions in terms of historical evidence, on the one hand, and the ideological narrative behind all these depictions, on the other. Jiang Qing seems to be a person who cannot be examined without some historical judgment, and this might be true (or politically correct) from a post-Cultural Revolution perspective. Because of the political sensitivity of the case, Jiang Qing is perhaps not the most suitable person by which to study the complex struggles of actresses to defend a social and political position. Yet it is also precisely her outstanding historical position that brought forth such extreme evaluations. This makes her a rewarding object for studying the complex process of maintaining a public social position, on the one hand, and to show the variety of different possible interpretations of her appearance (to today), on the other.

Most striking in respect to historiography on Jiang Qing is the narrational parallelism between her career as an actress and her career as a political leader. For all authors it seemed a given that there was no separation between social and representational spaces. For Jiang Qing, apparently, every act was performance, every space was a stage. This is also the reason why the starting point in her professional career on Shanghai's stages is taken as the starting point of her transformation into an evil demon on the political stage. Such an underlying assumption reveals more about the authors than about Jiang Qing, as it shows their own confusion in distinguishing between a historical and a fictional person. An "authentic," reasonably thinking and acting Jiang Qing might be very difficult to imagine, as her "performances" and activities during the Cultural Revolution are difficult to explain in rational terms. Yet this problem is not singular to Jiang Qing; it applies to a large part of the society involved in Cultural Revolution activities – but it is discussed there in quite a different manner.

References

Bodard, Lucien, *Die zehntausend Stufen*, Berlin 1992.
Brief Introduction of Comrade Chiang Ch'ing, in: Guanyin hongqi, 29 October 1967, reproduced in: *Survey of China Mainland Press* 4089, 29 December 1967, pp. 1-2.
Chang, Michael G., The Good, the Bad, and the Beautiful: Movie Actresses and Public Discourse in Shanghai, 1920-1930s, in: Zhang Yingjin (ed.), *Cinema and Urban Culture in Shanghai, 1922-1943*, Stanford 1999, pp. 128-159.

Cheng Jihua (ed.), *Zhongguo dianying fazhan shi* (History of the Development of the Chinese Film), Beijing 1981.

Cui Wanqiu, *Jiang Qing qianzhuan* (Jiang Qing's Early Years), Hong Kong 1987.

Ding Wang, *Jiang Qing jianzhuan* (Short Biography of Jiang Qing), Hong Kong 1967.

Eberstein, Bernd, *Das chinesische Theater im 20. Jahrhundert*, Wiesbaden 1983.

Eide, Elisabeth, *China's Ibsen: From Ibsen to Ibsenism*, London 1987.

Goldstein, Joshua, *Theatrical Imagi-Nations: Peking Opera and China's Cultural Crisis, 1890-1937*, PhD Dissertation, San Diego 2000.

Guo Hua, *Lao dianxing, lao dianpian* (Old Stars, Old Films), 2 vols., Beijing 1998.

Hsüeh, Daphne, Why Nora? – Ibsen's "A Doll House" in China and Its Early Imitations, in: *Journal of the Chinese Language Teacher Association* 16:3 (1981), pp. 1-17.

Jiang Qing shi qishi daoming de zhengzhi bashou (Jiang Qing Is a Deceitful Impostor and Political Usurpator), comp. by Renmin wenxue chubanshe pipanzu (Critique Group of the People's Literature Publishing House), Beijing 1976.

Jiang Qing xie gei Tang Na de jueqingshu (Jiang Qing's Farewell Letter to Tang Na), in: Mingbao yuekan 166 (October 1979), pp. 42-43, translated as: Chiang Ch'ing's "Farewell Letter" to T'ang Na, in: *Chinese Studies in History* 14:2 (1980-1981), pp. 77-82.

Ji Cheng, Lan Ping fangwen ji (An Interview with Lan Ping), in: Minbao, 28 August-1 September 1935, in: Ye Yonglie 1993, pp. 68-74.

Kano Ayako, *Acting Like a Woman in Modern Japan: Theater, Gender and Nationalism*, New York 2001.

Lan Ping, Cong "Nala" dao "Da leiyu" (From "Nora" to "The Tempest"), in: Xin xueshi 1:5 (5 April 1937), in: *Zhang Chunqiao, Jiang Qing sanshi niandai de heiwen* 1977a, pp. 312-315.

Lan Ping, San ba funüjie (March Eighth, Women's Day), in: Shishi xinbao, 8 March 1937, in: *Zhang Chunqiao, Jiang Qing sanshi niandai de heiwen* 1977b, pp. 310-311.

Lan Ping, Women de shenghuo (Our Life), in: Guangming 2:12 (25 May 1937), in: *Zhang Chunqiao, Jiang Qing sanshi niandai de heiwen* 1977c, pp. 319-324.

Lan Ping, Yi feng gongkai xin (A Public Letter), in: Lianhua huabao, 5 June 1937, reproduced as: Wo weishenme he Tang Na fenshou (Why I Have Parted from Tang Na), in: Mingbao yuekan 166 (October 1979), pp. 44-46, translated as: Why I Have Parted from Tang Na, in: Chinese Studies in History 14:2 (1980-1981), pp. 83-91, republished as: Chiang Ch'ing, "Why I Parted with Tang Na," in: Li Yu-ning (ed.), *Chinese Women through Chinese Eyes*, Armonk 1992, pp. 216-227.

Lan Ping xiang chu fengtou, yong de shi meiren ji (When Lan Ping Seeks Attention, She Uses the Tricks of Beautiful Women), in: Shidaibao, 14 June 1937, in: Ye Yonglie 1993, pp. 131-133.

Lee, Leo Ou-fan, *Shanghai Modern: The Flowering of a New Urban Culture in China, 1930-1945*, Cambridge ^{2}2001 (^{1}1999).

Li Fengming, Jiang Qing shilüe (Biographical Sketch of Jiang Qing), in: *Zhonggong shouyao shilüe huibian* (Collection of Important Biographical Sketches of the CCP), Taipei 1969, vol. 1, pp. 129-156.

Min Anchee, *Becoming Madame Mao*, New York 2000.

Resolution über einige Fragen zur Geschichte der KP China seit 1949, Beijing 1981.

Sha Yexin, *Jiang Qing he ta de zhangfumen* (Jiang Qing and Her Husbands), Hong Kong 1991.

Tam Kwok-lam, From Social Problem Play to Socialist Problem Play, in: *Journal of the Institute of Chinese Studies of the Chinese University of Hong Kong* 17 (1986), pp. 387-402.

Terrill, Ross, *The White-boned Demon: A Biography of Madame Mao Zedong*, London 1984 (Chinese translation: Luosi Telier [Ross Terrill] [Ma Yuande, trans.], *Jiang Qing zhengzhuan* [Authentic Biography of Jiang Qing], Beijing 1988).

The Criticism Group of the Movie School of Central May 7 College of Art, How Chiang Ch'ing's Tooth Was Lost, in: *Chinese Studies in History* 12:3 (1979), pp. 54-55.

Vittinghoff, Natascha, *Geschichte der Partei entwunden – Eine semiotische Analyse des Dramas Jiang Qing und ihre Ehemänner (1991) von Sha Yexin*, Bochum 1995.

Wang Hongwen, Zhang Chunqiao, Jiang Qing, Yao Wenyuan fandang jituan de zuisheng (cailiao zhi yi) (Evidences for the Crimes of the Anti-Party Clique Formed by Wang Hongwen, Zhang Chunqiao, Jiang Qing and Yao Wenyuan [Material 1]), ed. by Wang Zhang Jiang Yao zhuan'an zu (Investigating Committee for the Cases of Wang Hongwen), n.p. 1976.

Wang Suping, *Ta hai mei jiao Jiang Qing de shihou* (When She Was Not Yet Named Jiang Qing), Beijing 1993.

Wang Zheng, *Women in the Chinese Enlightenment: Oral and Textual Histories*, Berkeley, Los Angeles, London 1999.

Wei Shaochang, *Jiang Qing waishi* (Unofficial History of Jiang Qing), Hong Kong 1987.

Wen Ping, Feng Chen, Confession of an Old-Time Capitulationist – Critique of Chiang Ch'ing's Sinister Article "Our Life," in: *Chinese Studies in History* 12:3 (1979), pp. 56-61.

Witke, Roxane, *Comrade Chiang Ch'ing*, Boston, Toronto 1977.

Xu Huiqi, Quxinghua de "Nala": Wu si xin nüxing xingxiang de lunshu celüe" (Desexualized Nora: Strategies on Discoursing Chinese New Women in the May Fourth Period), in: *Jindai Zhongguo funüshi yanjiu* 10 (2002), pp. 59-102.

Ye Yonglie, *Jiang Qing zai Shanghai tan* (Jiang Qing on the Banks of Shanghai), Hong Kong n.d. (preface 1988).

Ye Yonglie, Jiang Qing: Cong Shanghai dao Yan'an (Jiang Qing: From Shanghai to Yan'an), in: *Haishang wentan* 11 (September/October 1992), pp. 4-23.

Ye Yonglie, *Jiang Qing zhuan* (Biography of Jiang Qing), Beijing 1993.

Zhang Chunqiao, Jiang Qing sanshi niandai heiwen: Gongpi shiyong (Black Materials of the 30s by Zhang Chunqiao and Jiang Qing: Use for Criticism), n.p. 1977.

Zhong Huamin, *Jiang Qing zhengzhuan* (Authentic Biography of Jiang Qing), Hong Kong 1967a.

Zhong Huamin, Kōsei seiden (Authentic Biography of Jiang Qing), in: *Chūō kōron* 82 (1967b), pp. 302-324.

Zhong Huamin (Arthur C. Miller, trans.), *Madame Mao – A Profile of Chiang Ch'ing*, Hong Kong 1968.

Zhongguo funü mingren lu (Biographical Dictionary of Famous Chinese Women), n.p. 1988.

Zhou Huiling, "Xinggan yemao" zhi geming zaoxing: Chuangzuo, hangxiao, dianying nü yanyuan yu Zhongguo xiandaixing de xiangxiang (1933-1935) (Masquerading the Revolutionary Cats: Marketing, Actresses, and Chinese Film Industry [1933-1935]), in: *Jindai Zhongguo funüshi yanjiu* 9 (August 2002), pp. 57-120.

Zhu Shan, *Jiang Qing yeshi* (Unofficial History of Jiang Qing), Hongkong 1980.

Zhu Shan, *Jiang Qing mizhuan* (Secret Biography of Jiang Qing), Hong Kong 1988a.

Zhu Shan, *Nühuang meng – Jiang Qing waizhuan* (Dream of an Empress – Unofficial Biography of Jiang Qing), Beijing 1988b.

Gender, Religion and Little Traditions: Henanese Muslim Women Singing *Minguo*

Maria Jaschok and Shui Jingjun

> Memory does not sew the past back to the present. Or the present back to the past. Experiential time is all broken up. Memory is an acknowledgment of that fragmentation. It is the knowledge that an absence has to be bridged with words. Schwarcz, *Bridge across Broken Time: Chinese and Jewish Cultural Memory* (1998), p. xi.

Growing attention has been given by scholars to Chinese women's organizing activities which, however, move in the main within the "large traditions" of All-China Women's Federation history and its variously positioned Others, whether as affiliated or self-supporting popular organizations (Frick et al. 1995; Hsiung Ping-chun et al. 2001; Li Xiaojiang 1999; Li Xiaojiang et al. 1999; Perry 2001; Wesoky 2001; Yang 1999, among others). Our purpose is to explore "little traditions" of women's public engagement, secular and religious, in which women build on familiar role models and relate in patterns of association which are structured by a multiplicity of forces, whether by kinship or extra-kinship association, whether by institutionalized authority or individual charisma. The deeply religious nature of much of rural and provincial society in China, the prominence of women in all major religious traditions (and the number of female religious believers is on the increase) make a study of women's religious organizations and of their relationship with secular women's organizations an investigative imperative (Hsiung Ping-chun et al. 2001; Jaschok/Shui Jingjun 2000; Shui Jingjun/Jaschok 2002).

We are researching in two different urban milieus, Kaifeng and Zhengzhou in Henan Province, each at different times occupying a distinct place in the history of religious women in Islamic, Christian and Buddhist traditions. Here we shall focus in particular on Kaifeng, during *Minguo*[1] the locale of a dynamic and diverse religious culture. At the heart of our discussion is the unique Muslim women's culture of Central China, the women's mosques (*Qingzhen nüsi*, hereafter referred to as *nüsi*) as its most central religio-cultural "linking institution" (Antoun 1989) and the congregations of women under the religious guidance of a female *ahong* (*nü ahong*),[2] a female religious responsible for religious/ritual/social duties, usually resident at a women's mosque, attached to *nüsi* numerous both in and around Kaifeng.

In this article we shall first attempt to discuss the relationship of Muslim women's conception of *Minguo* in relation to official chronology and extant scholarship as a way of historicizing the multifarious inequalities that structure scholarly priorities and official memory. We shall then summarize issues in writings by those Muslim women intellectuals during the Republican era who joined their male counterparts in debates on Islamic concepts of women's liberation, on the state of female education, and on their relevance to secular ideas and movements.

In this article, we are only beginning to state the perplexing questions we face in the theorization of "the past" and of "past-ness" of things and people. How investigation of the tradition of *jingge* (popular songs with a religious and also social context) as a central, defining part of women's mosque culture might provide the "crevice in the wall" (Schwarcz 1998:92) of historical master narratives that left no written documentation. In this act of salvaging of the *jingge* tradition, we are suggesting its significance to the retrieval of women's history and also the difficulty that is involved in reconstruction of its likely origin and evolution, diversity of styles and of non-Islamic cultural borrowings.

---

[1] *Minguo* is used here to convey two different meanings: (1) official chronology – the era of Republican Government which lasted between 1911 to 1949; (2) religious chronology – our informants, elderly Muslim women, use the term *Minguo* to talk about a golden time of relative political non-interference in religious affairs which lasted well into the late 1950s when persecution of religious leaders and organizations began in earnest.

[2] For a discussion of the title of *ahong* when applied to leading female religious, see Jaschok/Shui Jingjun 2000.

We conclude this paper with an illustration of one of the many local variations of *jingge,* the *kuhua* (grieving songs), sung in Henanese women's mosques.

The Islamic New Culture Movement and the New Chinese Muslim Woman: Debates over "Women's Liberation"

In the process of reconstituting women's fragmented and elusive memory of *Minguo*, we ask also how their lives were shaped by the local playing out of national debates and events – some remote or peripheral, others infused into local major themes of reform and traditionalism, Western ideas and Confucian renewal. An active intellectual and diverse religious milieu in Kaifeng was intimately connected with the participation of male Muslim scholars, *Hui* intellectuals, and a number of Muslim women intellectuals in general discourses over modernity, Islamic faith, gender and national identity, creating thereby a dissenting voice in the larger national debates. However, these ultimately can be said to have also shared in the limitations of the majority of Chinese intellectuals whose idealism was shaped by conversations in urban and Western contexts. They thus failed to turn to those who were equally passionate in their quest for identity and belonging, but wrote their narratives in different languages and inflections. The development of women's mosques cultures, the focus of our historical reconstruction, remained unwritten, because disconnected from other discourses. In this light, it might also be argued that the failure on the part of a small elite of educated religious female intellectuals to connect with the culture of women's mosques, the majority in townships and villages, contributed to their ultimate marginality in the evolution of a unique religious institution.

At the turn of the twentieth century, not only China's domestic weaknesses and international humiliations, but also the ever-growing presence of Christianity and deepening influence of Western ideas and political ideologies led Chinese intellectuals to profound individual and collective self-assessment through hard-hitting intellectual and philosophical debates. They asked how were cultural renewal and political change to be facilitated? Among those Chinese intellectuals who engaged in an incisive questioning of their past and the search for national solutions were also Muslim intellectuals reappraising their own history, the place of Islamic culture and of Muslims in a modernizing Chinese society. According to the influential scholar Ma Songting, Islamic practice and institutions at the turn of the twentieth century were in a state of unprecedented inertia. Traditional mosque-based education had failed to move with the times and widened the gap between Muslim Chinese and *Han* Chinese (Ma Songting 1985b:1033-1054). Their dual identity as Muslim and Chinese should inspire, so another Muslim scholar, Sun Shengwu, urged, to reinvigorate fellow Muslims' renewed dedication to the Islamic and to the national cause. Sun Shengwu observed in the *Huimin yanlun banyuekan (Huimin Affairs Bi-Monthly)*, in 1939, that "any contribution to society must start from a cultivation of self" (Sun Shengwu 1985:1769). These aims to reform Islam and Muslim culture and bring Muslims into line with the rest of the reform movement informed debates and cultural projects which commenced in the final years of the Qing dynasty and lasted several decades, sweeping the entire Muslim population with it. Scholars went abroad to learn and investigate; they returned to embark on projects of translation, language and educational and curriculum reform. They published journals and magazines for the dissemination of Islamic knowledge, and set up schools to teach a scientific Islam outside their old mosque traditions. Muslim history in China and evolution of an indigenized Chinese Islam became the object of study and of numerous publications.

Sharing in the general spirit of investigation and reform, *Minguo Hui* scholars also turned their attention to the predicament of women and children, advocating education of girls, the unbinding of feet, the liberation of women and equality between the sexes. But in their conception of the liberation of women, they differed in certain respects from other Chinese thinkers whose arguments bore increasingly the imprint of the secular bias of intense anti-Christian sentiments.[3] Muslim writers on the whole saw no conflict between attainment of equal rights of the sexes, the liberation of women and religious belief. On the other hand, it can be argued that the reformist

---

[3] See Lutz 1971, on the *Shouhui jiaoyu quanli* (Restore Educational Rights) movements of the 1920s.

agenda of Muslim intellectuals did not receive widespread popular support among Muslim communities because of the irritation aroused by "the women's question." Ma Songting *ahong* noted that "this is an unprecedented innovation, and not many share these ideals. Those who have understanding of Islam are still fewer in numbers and regard this as *yiduan* (heterodoxy). As for those who possess knowledge, they are filled with outrage, but in the face of so much opposition, seeking subsidies from the government is out of the question" (Ma Songting 1985b:1036). Muslim reformers had to tread cautiously, confining themselves to general observations on the situation of women and on their vital contributions to eradicating ignorance and backwardness in society.[4]

According to Wang Zengshan's investigation of the Xi'an Muslim Community, published in 1933 in *Yuehua (The Bright Crescent)*, the violence of Muslim opposition to female education then was such that local educationalists were forced to set rules which instructed girls above twelve years of age not to attend school. Older girls were therefore prevented by their families from leaving home (Wang Zengshan 1985:1382). The author, although sympathetic to the women's cause, was constrained by a strict code of gender segregation to remain a distant observer. He noted:

> Women amongst Xi'an Muslims are confined to attending household tasks and raising children. I have never seen a woman in public. Although this whole issue is of interest to me, the constraints imposed by social boundaries mean that I can only imagine what the scope of women's problems might be. It is only in quiet back-lanes and through the cracks of doors that I have caught a glimpse of one or two [women]. And from what I observe, their lives are not natural; they cannot learn, they cannot move. Their lives are as controlled as if they were subject to medieval religious rule. Allah's gift of human potential for learning and work has not been utilized and realized by women. Themselves unaware,

---

[4] For example, Dai Pengliang blamed the inferior state of female education in Jiaohe Potou Township, Hebei Province, on poverty, with parents unable to afford the expense of education, but also on religious traditionalists who opposed female education on the basis of their erroneous reading of the Koran. Although the Prophet Mohammed himself exhorted that "it is the duty of both Muslim men and women to advance their knowledge" (Dai Pengliang 1985:1303).

the women have wasted their abilities and potential. This is sad and a great pity. There are also a number of old and young women who follow blindly the ways of the West [Arab Muslim countries], and their behavior is the result of listening to such teachers who unthinkingly and blindly copy the customs of the Muslim West [Arab countries]. That is, these teachers only know how to add to Chinese Muslim women's burden of bound feet a further burden, a length of cloth with which to cover their heads, instead that they would release women's bound feet. They do not know the difference between virtue and evil, instead they turn things upside down. Aren't they the real sinners here? (ibid. 1383-1384)

For Wang Zengshan, these women were the real victims. His disapproval targeted those Islamic teachers who compounded women's burden of confinement and ignorance, turning misery into moral deficiency. Another writer, Zhao Bin, argued in 1926 in "Random Notes from an Islamic Study" (*Jiaojingshi suibi*), that observation of religious dress must be subjected to rational and enlightened discussion (Zhao Bin 1985:1126-1127).

Very clearly, Muslim scholars sought a balance between Western women's liberation perceived as negation of religious faith and of harmonious family life, on the one hand, and on the other hand, women's liberation as grounded in educated faith, social engagement, and mutual respect between men and women. Blind learning from "the West" was considered as fallacious as rigid adherence to traditionalist conceptions of gender relations. A number of articles appeared in which male scholars praised those women who study the scriptures and who engage themselves in society without forsaking their religious belief and Islamic way of life. An interesting source entitled "On the Good Practices among Chinese Muslims" (*Zhongguo Musilin zhi liangfeng meisu*) highlights in particular the advantage to society of educated women. Guan Yu refers to women scholars in Guangzhou and in Hong Kong, knowledgeable in many languages and adept in comparative textual criticism, who are setting praiseworthy standards of erudition. "Women from the Pearl River delta, because of their wide knowledge, take a keen interest in public affairs large and small, displaying much interest in national concerns. This demonstrates the virtue of women, something also true of the Boai Society of Muslim women in Hong Kong" (Guan Yu 1985:1747-1748).

In the Sichuan Muslim community, where universal education of children after four years of age at the mosque ensured a general level of ritual and doctrinal Islamic knowledge including a basic mastery of Arabic and Persian, women played a more active, visible and often exemplary role in the wider Muslim community (ibid. 1750). In Chengdu, Guan Yu observed, Muslim women are known to compete with each other to keep domestic or commercial premises spotlessly clean. The high level of hygiene, the author points out, comes from a Chinese tradition rather than a copying of foreign standards (*xiren youdian, zao wei wo you*) (ibid. 1752). Indicative of the quality of education of women in Chengdu, the old lady Wang was renowned and respected for both her profound knowledge of Islam and of the Confucian Classics.

Women's activities outside their home were also viewed with approval by some writers. In regard to Tianjin and the employment of Muslim women there, Mu Yigang notes, "there are also *Hui* women wanting work to attain independence (*zili qiusheng*) in this regard it may be said that Tianjin's *Hui* women excel through their particular strength" (Mu Yigang 1985:1346). Scholars were, however forthright when criticizing what they considered un-Islamic conduct and activities. A female religious instructor, from Linqing in Shandong, was roundly taken to task by Yi He for allowing women to participate in Fatima Day religious celebrations without having performed the necessary ablutions and for permitting young girls to spend excessive time and effort on their appearance, instead of purifying the inner person (Yi He 1985:1530).

We can ascertain also from these writings that Republican scholars viewed the development of both *nüsi* (women's mosques) and *nüxue* (women's Koranic schools) as perfectly attuned to the contemporary reformist zeitgeist. The emergence of modern Arabic-Chinese girls' schools (*Awen nüxue*), a trend noted in Heilongjiang Province, was seen as furthermore facilitating the emergence of outstanding women (Wang Junpu 1985:1366). Whilst it appears that some women's mosques were close to dissolution, as reported in 1937 in Yangzhou, elsewhere, so the writer Qing maintains, ordinary Muslim women were congregating in women's mosques, on their own initiative, whenever time allowed, in order to increase religious knowledge and also debate current affairs (Qing 1985:651).

It appears that even traditionalists among scholars saw the development of women's mosques as fulfilling essential needs. Commenting in 1936 on the situation of Islam in Beijing with its women's mosques and women's Koranic schools, Wang Mengyang says that whilst "it is not appropriate for women to congregate" there are however special needs to be taken into consideration, such as ordinary women's requirement for a place for ablution and for an educated *ahong* to lead them in prayer (Wang Mengyang 1985:1325).

Only a small number of male scholars gave attention to women's mosques and to the modern girls' Arabic schools (*nüzi Awen xiaoxue*). For instance, in regard to Kaifeng, Henan, Lu Zhenming noted the number of women's mosques and their location, but otherwise confined himself to two sentences on the educational role of the older women in these mosques as mentors and teachers of young girls. No reference was made to the daily life in such mosques and their service to adult women (Lu Zhenming 1985:1619). The presence of female *ahong* is equally ignored. In regard to Taiyuan, You Cheng identifies the *ahong* as sixty-year-old Ma Wushi from Henan, resident in the mosque for over ten years, a strict follower of Islamic rules and of comprehensive knowledge of the scriptures (You Cheng 1985:1359). This is the extent of the written documentation on a leading female religious.

Where we assess cultural reforms initiated, supported and documented by Islamic activists and *Hui* intellectuals between late Qing and Republican China from a gender perspective, it can be stated that this was a cultural movement initiated by men, importantly conducted by men, with educated men assuming leadership and authority. This leadership, similar to characteristics of Chinese intellectuals in general, was based on certain important factors: the relative privileged status and educational level of intellectuals and reformers in relation to ordinary Muslims and Muslim women; and the location of these initiatives in the more developed urban centers of Beijing and Shanghai. Generally speaking, in the period between late Qing to Republican China, innovative ideas, educational and social projects as well as new Muslim organizations, originated first in Beijing and Shanghai and only subsequently spread to the rest of the country.

Although national debates, linking concepts of women's liberation with that of national liberation inspired many Muslim scholars to incorporate the presence of women into fact-finding surveys, although a few Muslim women who had benefited from modern education took part in the debate over the scope of the Islamic cultural movement, it can be argued that the lives of Muslim women were appraised from a vantage point of social, educational and gender privilege distant from the sphere inhabited by women. Many writers' description and analysis of women's lives, of women's spiritual quest or of any positive social initiatives tended to be vague, generalized and not uncommonly marked by sentimentality. Their discourses allow only the most fleeting impressions of women's presence, of their individual subjectivity and of their collective self-expressions.

To summarize: with the rare exception of a few documented, because outstanding, *Hui* women intellectuals, the lives of ordinary Muslim women during the Republican era remain shrouded in obscurity – and thus their spiritual and social quest which created the unique culture of women's mosques.[5]

Muslim Women Intellectuals: Discourses on Status, Identity and Liberation

From late Qing onwards, for the first time, a number of educated Muslim women, supported by progressive male scholars, emerged into the public domain of debate, writing for newsletters and broadsheets.[6]

---

[5] Contemporary scholarship on aspects of Muslim women's lives during Republican China – the most important works emerged after the 1980s – demonstrate little divergence from approaches and methodologies characterizing *Minguo* scholarship: women as active, thinking, interventionist and strategizing beings and collectivities remain elusive (Shui Jingjun/Jaschok 2002).

[6] Although the following discussion confines itself to the Islamic circle, it may be useful to keep in mind the numerous publications put out by female intellectuals from a Christian background, with the "Chinese Young Christian Women's Association" playing an important facilitating role: see *Gongjiao funü jikan*

The earliest evidence of active religious women intellectuals indicates that they joined organizations founded by men, such as the first *Huizu* (*Hui* nationality) overseas student Yang Qidong who joined the *Liu dong Qingzhen jiaoyuhui* (Association of Islamic Education for Overseas Students) in Tokyo (Li Xinghua et al. 1998:740). In 1928, seven female members (and eighty-nine men) were members of the *Yisilan xueyouhui* (Islamic Friendship Association) organized by *Hui* students from Beiping's various universities (Zhao Zhenwu 1985:963). From the 1920s onwards, we have evidence of religious women scholars publishing and writing in their own voice. The earliest such women-initiated religious periodical is the Christian *Nü qingnian yuekan (Young Women's Monthly)*,[7] brought out by the National Editorial Committee of the "Chinese Young Christian Women's Association" (*Zhonghua jidujiao nü qingnianhui*). Around the mid-1930s, Muslim and Buddhist women scholars also appeared in print. For example, in June of 1936, the "Shanghai Muslim Women's Association" (Shanghai Yisilan funü xiehui) set up *Yisilan funü zazhi (Magazine for Islamic Women)*; a few months later, on 3 July 1937, Buddhist women in Wuchang printed the first issue of *Fojiao nüzhong (Buddhist Women)*. These periodicals were short-lived, lasting only until about the middle of 1937, the commencement of the Sino-Japanese War. In January of 1945, the *Zhongguo Huijiao xiehui* (China Islam Association) brought out in Chongqing *Huijiao funü (Muslim Women)*, but it too did not last long. At this point we have been able to discover only these few religious women's periodicals, but their scarcity renders the insights they afford into women's perspectives, visions and viewpoints of great value, however partial.

The most prominent theme dominating the years between late Qing and the early Republican era concerned the benefit Islam had brought to women. In all aspects, economically, socially, legally, educationally, Islam "brought equality" (*huade yilü pingdeng*), and should be seen as "the originator of women's liberation" (*jiefang*

(Religious Women's Periodical), 1934-1939, Beijing Library; *Shanghai nü qingnian (Shanghai Female Youths)*, and other like periodicals in Guangdong, Kunming, Nanjing, Chongqing, and so on.

[7] The magazine was first published in 1927.

funüde bizu). Indeed, the case was made by Li Rongchang in 1931 (see Li Rongchang 1932) that Chinese Muslim women had "been contaminated by *Han* culture" (*shoule hanzu fengsu de xunran*) and, so Xue Lan asserted in 1935, only the message from the Koran could really liberate women with benefits unmatched by rights for which women in the West were clamoring (Xue Lan 1935).

In the course of the 1930s, discussions of the nature of Muslim femininity were linked to the fate of Islam in an era of social change. Modernity, equated in these articles with the conduct and fashion of women in Europe and in America, was seen as dangerous and could only be countered by advocacy of a "reinvigorated Neo-Confucian morality" (*huifu jiu daode*). Scholars expressed their concern that Muslim women would succumb and "forsake their religion" (*paoqi jiaofa*) (see Ma Jigao 1935). The politicization of "the women's question" led to preoccupation with the female body and feminine conduct. An article in *Shanghai Yisilan xuesheng zazhi (Shanghai Islamic Students' Magazine)* put forward the argument that in the absence of direct Islamic instruction it must be up to women to decide how to dress, and to display their hair. Such an attitude was immediately denounced for harboring heretical ideas.

In 1935, Ma Hongyi felt compelled by the perceived danger posed to a Muslim way of life to elaborate three guidelines he thought should be more widely propagated among Muslim women: *xiuti* (concealment of women's shameful body) observation of worship, and dedication to learning (Ma Hongyi 1935:7-10). This article sounded a sympathetic chord with other writers, so Ma Xiang admitted, thus "I read, I wrote" (*you gan er xie*). And Ma wrote with particular venom about "the modern woman" who, influenced by Western Europe, illustrated the destructive consequences of a most troubling trend, that is, "in particular the way men face demands for liberation from women in general" (*youqi shi yiban funü dui nanzi de yaoqiu jiefang*). Indeed, in 1935 Ma Xiang lamented, "[women's] conduct and ideas exceed the boundaries of reason" (Ma Xiang 1935:9). For him, a true Muslim woman, well instructed in religious knowledge, knew her central duty to be a "true chaste wife, virtuous mother" (*zhenzheng de xian qi liang mu*) (ibid. 13).

In turn, women intellectuals like Bi Yun castigated such writing as reactionary, as "backward thought" (*daotui sichao*), targeting the female body to undo hard-won achievements. She exhorted women, in an article published in 1935, to build on their successful struggle for rights which had begun with the May Fourth Movement, to fight in solidarity with each other, to view society in a critical manner and to examine their own shortcomings with continuous self-reflection (Bi Yun 1935:33).

Perusing the extant (eighteen) pages of the First Issue of *Yisilan funü zazhi* is to find passionate testimony on the questions women intellectuals asked of Islam, women's liberation and their identity of Muslim women in a modernizing age. They also raise issues of selfhood and meaning, equity in gender relations, rights of women, among other areas of concern expressive of the determination of Muslim women intellectuals to change their lives. As with male scholars, the centrality of women's destiny as "chaste wife, virtuous mother" (*xian qi liang mu*) remained intact. Thus He Shuyun wrote in 1936 that women's contribution to humanity must be seen to reside importantly in their "love as a mother" (*muxing de ai*). It is this which underpins women's role as teacher of religious knowledge and faith (He Shuyun 1936:5). At the same time, women writers stressed the importance of confronting the social implications of their rightful dual identity as *gongmin* (public citizen) and as *Huimin* (Islamic believer). Mu Changhua addressed women in a bold piece of writing, urging them to organize their collective strength to eradicate oppressive and unjust conventions so as to liberate women's innate wisdom and capabilities. She particularly encouraged women intellectuals to lead their sisters to become effective citizens, devout believers and conscientious wives and mothers. Whilst incorporating traditional duties of women into the new construct of Muslim womanhood, women's duties and contributions to nation, society and their religion were stressed as of equal importance (Mu Changhua 1936:8).

Another important insight afforded to us concerns the way Muslim women intellectuals defined their relationship with men, their fellow believers, against a complex constellation of influences: secular, religious, modern, traditional, Western or Arab. Women's road to progress and liberation is described by He Ru in 1936 as possible only in unison with men. As Allah's creatures women and men are as one materially and spiritually, thus they are as one in claim to dignity, equality and justice. He Ru stressed the rights and obligations of both women and men in relation to society, economy and family, their equality expressed in shared rights and shared duties rather than in autonomy: "On no account does this imply rivalry with men for power, because [women's obligations towards religion and society] are our responsibility and duty" (*Zhe bing bu shi he nanzimen zheng quanli, yinwei zhe shi women de zeren, women de yiwu*) (He Ru 1936:6). That this did not entail unquestioning acquiescence in their male colleagues' judgment is illustrated in the writings of Xun Zhi. She asks male scholars why it was that so suddenly they had come to regard footbinding and sexual equality as topical issues (Xun Zhi 1936:15). Women strive to be human, He Ru says, to be *ren*.

> We want to be "human," to be independent, to be whole "human beings," we want to become "human" in every way. We do not shrink with fear, nor do we turn back, we go forward enthusiastically and courageously to start taking action. We want to stand at the frontline of this age, pushing the gigantic wheel of history, sustained by our spirit, strength, we shall pursue our struggle ceaselessly. We will act for ourselves, and more so, we will engage ourselves for the masses. Act! Act! Act! (He Ru 1936:6)

Other writers like Ma Xiuzhen placed Muslim women at the forefront of the liberation of women – internationally, nationally, locally. In an article for *Yisilan funü zazhi*, written in 1936, she argued that it was up to Muslim women to lead women everywhere to where "authentic" (*zhenzheng de*) freedom and equality resided, that is, to the road which leads to Islam (Ma Xiuzhen 1936:13).

How much support did these considered arguments for change, for collective action, receive from male writers? No direct commentary exists on the *Yisilan funü zazhi*, from which we cited the assertive and thoughtful voices of various contributors. But Zhen Wu, in an article on the *Yisilan funü xiehui* (Islamic Women's Association) in Shanghai, allows us an insight into why distinct support came from certain male scholars for women's call for action: in the same way that wider debates over how to achieve modernity and international competitiveness entailed "the women's question," advocacy of rights for Muslim women was an indispensable factor in shifting Islamic reforms into the main frame of national cultural and social change. Zhen Wu notes approvingly the strategy pursued by Shanghai Muslim women activists. In their attempts to recover the progressive element in early Islamic thought in order to attain liberation, these Islamic activists could only compare favorably to the women's liberation movements elsewhere, whether in China or in the West (Zhen Wu 1936:1).

The periodical *Huijiao funü* brought out in Chongqing in 1945, appeared in an irregular fashion and for a short time span only. But the writing carries a general tone of determination to reclaim Islam as a source of liberation for women, to oppose religious traditionalists and to build on the Islamic principle of equality as well as to engage women and men jointly in furthering the cause of religion (Zhongguo Huijiao xiehui di'er zu 1945:1). Similar in content to *Yisilan funü zazhi*, other articles in the magazine profiled prominent Muslim women leaders, women's organizations and the Islamic women's movement in Egypt.

We see from these accounts that Muslim women of education and with the ability to turn their convictions into print were both a part of the general movement for gender change, and yet asserted their right to differ: opposition to "feudal" (*fengjian*) constraints and calls for equality were to make the case for women's realization of "natural abilities" (*tianfu caineng*), and thus to engage themselves, jointly with men, in the affairs of the nation, society, and of their religion. No contradiction, according to these women writers, stands between their religious impulses and secular concerns; to change society through their faith was to live in accordance with Allah's sacred will.

In a time of intense secular and religious debates, and of multifarious influences, these few Muslim women intellectuals whose writing we discovered always retained their own eloquent voice, their own position. Together with their like-minded male counterparts, they took part in the general debate at that time over applicability of

Western models of reform, and of means to achieve reform in line with national needs.

But, however eloquent and persuasive the writing, their audience and influence were limited; the majority of their contemporaries were women without education and access to the written word who expressed their histories in other, non-literary, ways. None of the texts we found so far make mention of the architecture and institutional life of women's mosques and schools, which can be found in largest concentration in *Zhongyuan diqu* (Central China: encompassing Henan, Shanxi, Shandong, Hebei) where a potent symbolic landscape of women's sites of communal faith had been evolving.

We now turn to a first tentative presentation of a central aspect of women's mosque cultures, *jingge* (Islamic songs), as a "bridge," however tenuous, across the distance which separated the printed word from the oral world of the majority of contemporary Muslim women. But we are also probing the limitations of our ability to bridge time. The researcher is compelled, in Vera Schwarcz's words, to "keep on redefining what history means if [one is] to do justice to the actual voices of remembering" (Schwarcz 1998:183), to the voices of those otherwise absent from the literary narratives of history.

Jingge as a Bridge to the Past

> [...] I can only imagine what the scope of women's problems might be. It is only in quiet back-lanes and through the cracks of doors that I have caught a glimpse of one or two [...]. (Wang Zengshan 1985:1383-1384)

How Stories Are Told

If stories are not allowed to be told, can history be said to have happened? In Jane Kilby's words, the power of history to "haunt is a function of the stories we tell and, perhaps more importantly, how they are told" (Kilby 2002:210).

When approached by us, the researchers, most informants' initial response is that they cannot remember, "what is in the past is past" (*guoqu jiu guoqule*). The past has become an abstraction filled with official speak of "the feudal," and "the backward" in which religion as "the old" has featured as a defining Other of Maoist liberation of women for the new China. Harrowing experience, both collectively and personally, of associations of religious identity with ignorance and ignominy before the institution of more liberal policies, from the 1970s onwards (Leung 1996; MacInnes 1972, 1989; Tong 1999; Uhalley/Wu Xiaoxin 2000), has transpired into a vague forgetfulness for many of the older women we are approaching. David Coplan refers to oral genres as "a people's autobiographical ethnography" (Coplan 1991:47, quoted in: Rees 2000:98). But a collective history of persecution and decades of suppression of religious practice has effectively muted many such traditions. "Abstraction is memory's most ardent enemy," Judith Miller says. "It kills because it encourages distance, often indifference" (Miller 1990:287, quoted in: Schwarcz 1998:23-24). When the researchers persist beyond initial protestations and prolonged pauses, then, sometimes, attitudes shift. Older women respond with embarrassment that alternates with excitement, with pleasure that gives rise to pain as the *jingge* are recalled. (And then we persuade, making reference to the preciousness of women's history, the importance of connecting to a tradition, which has to be told.) When the singer is positioned comfortably with the tape recorder placed close to her, the other women congregate around her, and the room falls silent, barely a hush to be heard. There must be "cultural forms and occasions for remembering," Laurence Kirmayer observes (1996:193). The singer, the group of listeners and the researchers together create this occasion, an instant of sacred time. When tears fall, younger women are ready with tissue paper to dry the wrinkled cheeks of their elders.

Jingge, *Introduction*

A term not to be found in ordinary dictionaries, the tradition of *jingge* nevertheless has a firm place in the popular culture of religious believers in Central China, as ubiquitous in Islamic as it is in Buddhist and Daoist traditions. Today, Chinese Catholics and Protestants tend to use the term *lingge* (song of the soul), but during *Minguo*, Christians too recited *jingge*.

Jingge has been considered by many scholars a sub-genre of *minjian gequ* (popular or folksongs) and is little studied.[8] Yet, as Daniel Neuman points out, reflecting on the relation between music and history, "music is the medium – the crucible in which time and its memories are collected, reconstituted, and preserved – and history, its message" (Neuman 1991:269, quoted in: Rees 2000:98). We are still ignorant of the cultural legacy that evolved within women's organized religious traditions in China, thus of the sentiments, knowledge and visions which women invested in them.[9]

Gender in Islamic or Buddhist *jingge* has inscribed performance, form, and transmission. Thus, certain Buddhist *jingge* or *miaohui jingge* (songs performed on temple feast-days) are performed only by women and taught only to other women. Transmission of *jingge* among Muslim communities in Central China is equally structured by gender. Whereas men copied down the lyrics, women tend to recollect through oral recital (but some female *ahong* resort to *xiaoerjing*[10] [use of Arabic or Persian characters to transliterate Chinese] to copy the lyrics), with some of the songs only recited in the ambience of women's mosques. This makes performance of religious songs (*nian jingge*) an integral and a unique part of the traditional women's mosque culture.[11]

---

[8] A recent study by Dong Xiaoping/Arkush 2000, is beginning to address this aspect of popular culture; see also Rees 2000.

[9] *Zhongguo minjian gequ jicheng, Henanjuan* (The Chinese Folksong Collection, Henan Volume), which came out in 1997, based on fieldwork largely conducted during the 1980s, treats only Buddhist popular chants, called *jingdiao* (scriptural tunes); there is no mention of Islamic or Christian traditions. This has been left in the purview of a few scholars in the field of religion and of *Hui* popular culture. Regarding the history of *geyao* (folksong), see Yu/Yang 1993; Liu/Qi 1996.

[10] We use *jing* rather than the more common *jin* to reflect the meaning attached by women informants to the sacred task of communion with God's words as transmitted by the Prophet; that is, *jing* (sacred scripture) rather than *jin* (beautiful). See Shui Jingjun/Jaschok 2002. *Xiaoerjing* as part of women's mosque culture forms a subject matter of current research by Jaschok and Shui Jingjun.

[11] Helen Rees, who studied Lijiang's *dongjing* music, remarks on the male dominance in Yunnanese local religious traditions, how age and gender determine performer, performance and context. Exceptionally, a few Buddhist laywomen's groups, such as the *mamahui* (women's group), "held temple meetings on the

Here it needs noting that *nü ahong* use exclusively the verb *nian* or *han*, as in *nian jingge* (reciting *jingge*) rather than the verb *chang*, ordinarily employed in connection with the act of "singing." *Nian* conveys the solemn religious character of *jingge* which, *nü ahong* are adamant, is a distinguishing mark of this tradition. The same careful use of terminology is true of Buddhist women's reference to recital of *jingge* (*Zhongguo minjian gequ jicheng, Henanjuan* 1997:351).

Jingge, *Women's Mosques and a Gendered Heritage*

A unique tradition of over two hundred years within a unique institution of female religious life, *jingge* have been largely "forgotten" and never, until recently, documented (Shui Jingjun/Jaschok 2002:135). Yet, this tradition speaks to the history of women, to their communal life and faith, to their relations with men and to male religious authority. And it does so most eloquently as the very terminology, so our erstwhile reconstruction suggests, is embedded in gendered meanings.

The evaluation of *jingge* as inferior didactic tools and association with deficient religious knowledge, as well as with social contexts of poverty and marginality, may be seen as emblematic of the difficult course of female religious organization in China's Islam. The use of common Chinese language and reliance largely on oral transmission appear in stark contrast with the highly regarded *shige* (sacred hymns), copied and transmitted by male scholars, and because in print preserved as representative heritage of Muslim religious life, its language and style considered appropriately elegant, refined and poetic. Equally popular among men and women Muslims, *shige* have become the acknowledged conduit of Islamic core beliefs, through which morality and human sentiments are invoked and ritualized. The importance of songs belonging to *jingge*, on the other hand, remain unacknowledged, classified as educational tools of the most rudimentary kind and serving the needs of the lowly educated.

---

first and fifteenth of each month, during which they recited Chinese-language sutras and ate vegetarian food" (Rees 2000:36).

The fate of the *jingge* tradition exposes multifarious inequalities: on the one hand, men's religious culture, emphasizing literacy and access to Islamic knowledge through the written word; on the other side, the tradition of women's mosques with their dependence on *nürenjing* (abridged Persian texts to convey teachings of the Koran considered pertinent to women's moral guidance), the use of *xiaoerjing* (Arabic/Persian transliteration of Chinese) and a core oral culture of instruction, worship and transmission.

Associations of the practice of *jingge* with illiteracy, rural backwardness, low spirituality, their exclusion from use for worship, worship as chanted recitals of *Sura* (chapters of the Koran) (*Zanzhu Zansheng*) have made *jingge* suspect both as vehicle of Islamic faith and of paradigmatic women's history. Younger generations of female *ahong* and ordinary believers reject these songs as embarrassing legacy and antithesis of modernity, their place relegated to the rustic courtyards of old women who do not know better.[12]

Diversity of Jingge

We have identified three broad types of *jingge* based on linguistic criteria: The "songs to instruct in pronunciation of Arabic" (alphabetically organized) to which belong *bianba* (pronounciation exercise of Arabic words in strict alphabetical order), *luanba* and *tiaozebu* (pronunciation exercise of Arabic words in random order). We surmise that *bianba* or *luanba* emerged as important educational tools during the first important Islamic cultural movement (late Ming/early Qing), when its major educational initiative for the first time targeted all ordinary Muslims, including women (Jaschok/Shui Jingjun 2000; Shui Jingjun/Jaschok 2002), and that many are the creation of contemporary Muslim scholars. Considered suitable for the level of children, they remain educational tools in women's mosques until the present. We know that before the early 1950s, mixed classes

---

[12] Since the 1980s, mosques have printed their own religious materials, including *jingge* we described above as having been shaped by male scholars during *Minguo* into what is now a highly popular and esteemed corpus of religious hymns (Musilin changshi 1994; Jingwei Zhenzhu zhi lu n.d.; Liu Fuli 1993). Excluded are, as ever, the *jingge* of women's mosques, and knowledge of these is close to extinction.

were taught *bianba* or *luanba* in individual men's mosques (for example, in Hai*zhuang*, Fengqiu*xian*, Henan); it is, however, no longer the practice today (interview with Liu Jingwu, June 2002, Kaifeng, Henan). This class of songs is now a feature exclusive to women's mosques.

Songs in Arabic and Persian. The long history of their transmission and influence of diverse local dialects have obscured the linguistic and often semantic origins. In this case, it is the memory of the individual *nü ahong* which becomes the guide to pronunciation, to the tune and to interpretation. From the point of women singing these *jingge*, their sacredness transcends the opaqueness of meaning as little of the text is comprehended. For *nü ahong*, they are effective sources of inspiration, vital to aid in instruction in the core precepts of faith, principal Muslim duties, the lives of saints and ritual knowledge. They also tell of women martyrs, of female paradigms of Muslim virtue, and of salvation through submission to God. *Ahong* in the course of interpretation translate their meaning first into *jingtangyu* (religious linguistic medium used by Muslims which fuses Arabic, Persian and Chinese into a unique form of communication) and then into ordinary Chinese. Whilst the narrative sweep and basic plots of songs have changed little over time, local differences, however, are noted in details of interpretation and emphasis, related to an individual *ahong's* learnedness, subtlety of understanding and pedagogical skills.

Most numerous and rich in content are *Chinese-language jingge*. They provide ritual and doctrinal knowledge and exhort Muslims to fear God, fulfill their duties and remain pious and obedient. Ballads also narrate women's morality (*funü daode*) virtues and women's spiritual and emotional life. Only in rare cases do we know the author, in the majority of these *jingge* anonymous interpreters and singers have over generations preserved, shaped and, wherever they felt it was called for, altered phrasings and words to reflect changed realities.

Whilst content and form of *jingge* show much continuity and only minor adaptations to reflect personal or collective circumstances, their evaluation by women has shown more radical changes. For example, a well-known *kuhua* (grieving song), in which a woman laments the loss of her husband, was seen by the more than seventy-year-old Li Xiangrong as a "real" and profound account of courtship, "making the whole world shed tears" (*bai shi bai yang de hua dou kudaole*) (interview, June 2002, Kaifeng). The narrative concerns a young woman who meets a young man at a mosque. He persuades her to read the scriptures, and their attraction develops into mutual love. Before the marriage can take place, he leaves for Weihe County in Gansu Province to study Islam; there he dies. The young girl weeps at night, shedding secret tears, lamenting her loss. She is overheard, so says the story, her lament recorded, and thus it has come to be familiar to many women. Li Xiangrong remembers that neither maidens nor young married women were allowed to take part, it was to be for the ears of middle-aged and old women only. She was allowed by her parents to learn these *jingge* at the women's mosque during the 1940s.

In contrast, the eighty-year-old Ding *nü ahong* dismisses the same *kuhua* with much contempt as "pointless" (*mei yisi*). After much prompting (interviews, June 2002, Zhuxian*zhen*), she tells her version of the narrative of loss of the beloved as involving a woman's loss of a husband who died of drinking cold water, but here a widow's mourning turned into rejection of tears and religion. In a more cynical turn of events, she ends up marrying a man who pursues a commercial trade. Perhaps Ding *ahong's* criticism of the excessive sentiment in these laments cannot be understood unless one understands her biography. Deserted when young by her husband, left to care for an infant and to support herself through her religious work as *ahong*, she only retired at the age of eighty. When we visited her again in the summer of 2002, she lived in degrading poverty, dependent on the kindness of believers.

Another informant, Dan *nü ahong*, locates her story in Weihe County in Gansu Province (interviews, June/July 2002, Zhuxian*zhen*). In her version of the *kuhua*, a most intelligent young girl, Lan Ying, starts reading the scriptures at thirteen years of age. Two years later, she marries Zhang Mingzhi, an *ahong*, tragically he dies shortly after. This forms the prelude to the recital of the *jingge*. Dan *ahong* knows this song by heart, but she too judges the tradition as "pointless." Yet when Dan *ahong* recites, it is rare if at least some of the listeners do not weep.

This last class of *jingge*, transmitted from early Qing and in continuous use in women's mosques until the beginning of the 1950s, demonstrates a certain infusion from local *Han* folksongs, both in style and content. Often of a solemn and didactic nature, religious songs praising filial piety (*quan xiaoge*) or hailing virtuous women *xiao gu xian* (virtuous sister-in-law), testify to shared gender prescription and the fluid intermingling of diverse local traditions (Dong Xiaoping/Arkush 2000).

The History of Jingge

Muslim women's own knowledge of the origin and place of *jingge* in women's mosque culture is vague and ranges between "several generations" to "more than two hundred years." Based on an analysis of content and characteristics of the songs, judging also from the scope of transmission of the work of the renowned Qing scholar, Liu Zhi (ca. 1655-1745),[13] we suggest that their origins lie in the emergence of Islamic female education in the early Qing era, when popular tunes must have appeared the most appropriate means of spreading rudimentary religious knowledge. With the development of women's Koranic schools and mosques, the influence of *jingge* would have also spread (Jaschok/Shui Jingjun 2000). Such beginning might explain why *jingge* have always been considered inferior to sacred hymns, part of worship in men's mosques. As "rudimentary" educational tools, and given perceptions of women's spiritual deficiencies, *jingge* were tainted by the gender of those who utilized them.

Whilst Arabic recitals of chapters of the Koran have unvarying tunes, this is not the case with *jingge*; in particular Chinese-language *jingge* have borrowed heavily from folk-tunes, popular in society at large.[14]

To summarize the major uses of *jingge*: (1) They were used as an educational tool to teach young girls basic Islamic knowledge and

---

[13] For example *Wu geng yue* (Brightness of Dawn), *Qingzhen sanzijing* (Islamic Primer).

[14] The complex confluence of religious with popular and Confucian traditions that shaped the evolution of *jingge* in Henanese culture is the subject of on-going investigation by the authors.

the scriptural languages; (2) they added animation and pleasure to the discipline of learning, much like the function of music lessons in modern school curricula; (3) they were considered useful, because accessible and easy methods of instructing mature women in religious knowledge; (4) they brought release, speaking to women's emotions, suffering and expectations, to their sense of loss and their unhappiness; (5) they enhanced communal life in a women's mosque by the pleasure they provided, and they reinforced a more emotional identification with women's own site of congregation, making the mosque community a family of like-minded women; (6) the recital of Arabic and Persian *jingge* had the effect of strengthening Islamic faith, and identity, by evoking suffering in exile, and by sustaining the collective memory of a spiritual origin in Muslim ancestry and an Islamic homeland.

Women's Mosques, Competition for Women's Souls and *Quanjiaoge* in Kaifeng, Henan

When the older generation of Muslim women, in particular the older *nü ahong*, recollect life during *Minguo*, Wang Chunli (also known as Wang Letian) features as their teacher and as an authority figure of towering importance. He bequeathed to Muslim women the enduring legacy of the *quanjiaoge* (songs for religious instruction). The songs today are still copied by hand by the older generation of women *ahong*. The affection and respect with which Wang Chunli is remembered acknowledges the profound impact on succeeding generations of Muslim believers of the Islamic cultural movement in which he played an important part. A closer examination of the *quanjiaoge* also allows for a tentative understanding of how, and to what extent, Muslim women during the years of the Republic might have participated in social change. In places as different as Kaifeng, Zhoukou and Jiaozuo, a collective memory translates *Minguo* into an era, which saw a dynamic, reinvigorated Islam – and its vanguard of pious, erudite scholar/activists, who spread the faith so that all could hear and comprehend.

Local Context: Many Faiths and the Christian Factor

Henan Province had consistently been an exception to the inroads made into Chinese society elsewhere by Christian missionaries; taking even longer to enter urban Henan society (see accounts in: The Christian Occupation of China 1987). Yet, comparatively speaking, despite its many problems with corruption, gambling, drugs and prostitution that loomed large in Kaifeng society before and during the Japanese invasion (Shi Xiaoyan 1993), the city of Kaifeng appeared a haven from the harsh conditions which prevailed in the surrounding countryside. Apart from anti-foreign sentiments so prevalent among Henan's rural population, missionaries complained about danger to life and property, as criminal gangs were especially active in remote areas (Zhou Mingyi 1983:130-133); general poverty and dislocation were exacerbated by particularly calamitous years of natural disasters and locust plagues (see accounts for the 1930s/40s, in: Henan wenshi ziliao (Henan Historical Source Materials), for example Bai Wentian 1994).

It had been the British vice-consul's successful petition to the Qing court, in early 1901, which opened up Kaifeng to vigorous missionary proselytizing and ambitious, and competitive, missionary projects in the fields of education and health (see The Christian Occupation of China 1987). In this local context of tense competition between rival religious denominations, the issue of "the women's question" became important: that is, access to the soul and religious allegiance of women as ensuring access to family and society. Moreover, given the close link missionaries made between the "betterment" of women, and the "betterment" of the nation, female education was seen as a strategy for addressing many urgent social issues afflicting Chinese society.[15]

It can also be argued that as a result of local missionary competition as well as an assertion of political control by the Chinese government over Christian educational institutions in the 1920s (Gra-

---

[15] For an eloquent case, see Mai Nüshi 1983:79.

ham 1995; Lutz 1971), women in Kaifeng suddenly experienced a flourish of educational activities.[16] Not only Christian religions were spurned into activity. For example, Taixu *fashi* (Revered Teacher) of the Chinese National Buddhist Association proposed the slogan "doctrinal, organizational and property reform" (*jiaoli geming, jiaozhi geming, jiaochan geming*) to propel Buddhism into a period of renewal. In 1925, the Shi Jingyan *fashi*, and others, initiated the *Henan Foxueshe* (Henan Buddhist Society) and established the *Henan Foxueyuan* (Henan Buddhist College) in the local Tieta Temple. In keeping with the general interest in women's education, and in view of a large female congregation, the Nüzhonglin Temple (still continuing today) was built (Zhao Jiazhen 2000:146, 150). Not only a site of religious activity, women were also provided with employment in the textile industry (ibid. 167).

The reforms in Islam relevant to our discussion are therefore not only to be seen in relation to national and local intellectual, reformist discourses, but they also have to be seen with regard to a general and intensely competitive acceleration of religious activities which, in Kaifeng, also produced beneficial results from the local

---

[16] In 1920, a Catholic girls' school, *Huamei nüxiao* (Chinese-American Girls' School), was set up in Kaifeng, thus the *Kaifeng minzu zongjiaozhi* (Local History of Kaifeng Folk Religions) reports (Zhao Jiazhen 2000:234). In 1932, a lower middle-school for girls followed, *Henan sili Jingyi nüzi chuji zhongxue* (Henan Jingyi Private Lower Middle School for Girls); and four years later, in 1936, a girls' senior middle-school was added (ibid. 235, 258-259). The "Protestant China Inland Mission" began to develop women-targeted work in 1903 (ibid. 265), in 1907 the "Fuyin Hospital" was built, and in 1929 the "Fuyin Senior Nursing School" was also set up (ibid. 276). The Baptists began their work in 1905 with a girls' primary school, continued in 1915 with a girls' middle school, and opened an embroidery factory which employed over one hundred women (ibid. 277). In 1920, women were able to attend a bible class on the *bangong banxue* (part-work/part-study) principle (ibid. 278). The "American Free Methodist Mission" added in 1918 the "Panshi Primary School," the "Panshi High School" and "Peide Girls' Middle School" (ibid. 279-280). The Hong Kong-based "Bible, Book and Tract Depot Society" opened in 1912 the doors of their girls' school, followed in 1913 by the "Saint Mary Girls' School," in 1915 by a kindergarten and "Yude Girls' School," in 1916 by the "Mingxin Primary School," and in 1920 a women's literacy class was organized (ibid. 283-285).

women's point of view. Education at all levels was suddenly no longer outside their own, or their daughters', reach.

Islam was proving itself to be a serious claimant to successful work among women. It is said that a meeting organized in Kaifeng, in the 1920s, had led to Christian clergy finally taking note of a vigorous Islamic presence. The objective of this meeting had been to bring together leaders of local religious institutions, and the highly erudite Henan-born *ahong* Ma Zicheng from Shanxi was among those who followed an invitation from the influential Jesuit Li Jiabai. From Ma *ahong's* impressive performance, it became clear to all participants that Islam was a force to be reckoned with (narrated by Pang Shiqian, from Jin Jitang 1985:644).

Around the time of the meeting, the "China Continuation Committee" (*Zhonghua xuxing weibanhui*) published, in English and Chinese, findings from a comprehensive survey, which had been conducted between 1901 and 1920. It appeared in 1922 under the title of *Zhonghua gui zhu (The Christian Occupation of China)*.[17] This invaluable historical source indicates an early interest in Muslim institutions because Christian missionaries sought to understand coexisting religions which might hinder or facilitate their entry into local society (see Mees 1984). Thus Islam in Henan, the detailed survey of rival religious institutions reveals, must be seen as modernizing, dynamic and growing fast. Henan Province had about three hundred mosques, and the city of Kaifeng demonstrated its importance as a religious center with its numerous sites of worship; in the 1910s, seven mosques for men and eight women's mosques were listed. More than thirty *ahong* and over 120 *hailifan* (students of Islam preparing to be ordained as *ahong*) were at the service of a community of over 3,500 Muslim households (Zhonghua gui zhu 1985:735, 741; also see Shui Jingjun/Jaschok 2002:133-142). Women's mosques in Henan were cited as an illustration of the flourishing state of Islam. However, as no close research of these women's institutions was undertaken, observations were confined to drawing attention to such mosques as indicative of the advancement of Islamic religion. (Mention was made

---

[17] For the debate among Chinese intellectuals over the publication title, see Graham 1995:174.

also of women's mosques in the provinces of Gansu, Shanxi, Henan and Shandong.)

Wang Haoran, the imam of Kaifeng's important Dongda Mosque, organized scriptural classes, so-called *jingfang* and instructed by a *hailifan*, which placed these classes in the midst of the people (Zhao Jiazhen 2000:221). The active participation on the part of Henanese Muslim scholars in the Islamic cultural movement led to the setting up of a Henan branch of the *Zhongguo Huijiao jujinhui* (Society for Advancement of Islam in China). At a more popular level, between the turn of the twentieth century and the Republic, Islamic tracts and widely-known religious songs were published and distributed among Muslim believers.

How did these activities relate to women? Carried by a reformist spirit and openness in relation to women's rights and quest for betterment, during the early twentieth century, the building of women's mosques had become a common sight in *Hui* Muslim *fang* (mosque-centered communities). These communities were particularly influenced by the spread of a popular culture of songs and recitals, such as *jingge* which appeared in *Mumin quanshange (Muslim Songs for Religious Instruction)*, compiled in 1918 by the Shangqiu *ahong* Li Fuzhen. These *jingge* constituted the staple of worship for Muslim female congregations (Li Fuzhen 1935).

The most effective popularizer of Islamic popular songs during the years of *Minguo* is considered Wang Chunli. Wang's conversion to Islam, during its dynamic growth in China, his association with famous reformist Muslim intellectuals, such as Wang Jingzhai (Wang Jingzhai 1985:1097), his unorthodox and unprecedented ways of spreading Islam, his charisma and engagement in popular educational causes, have made him the stuff of legends. No other *ahong* had ever stood in crowded streets on market-days to preach the Koran. Wang Chunli fell back on popular ballads and tunes to attract attention to the message of Islam. Muslims, men and women, liked, and retained, what they heard. The most influential were the songs called *Qingzhen quanjiaoge*, in short, *quanjiaoge* (Islamic songs for religious instruction).

In the 1920s, a growing number of publications of all these popular Islamic songs accelerated their nationwide dissemination among China's Muslim population (Qingzhen quanjiaoge 1922; Qingzhen tongsuge 1924; see Yu/Yang 1993:598-600). In 1934, Wang Chunli's compilation of *Jingjie alin xuanyan lüe* (Guidelines for *ahong*) came out in Shanghai (Yu/Yang 1993:357-359). His fame was such that when the *ahong* Ma Songting lectured in Egypt during that time on the achievements of the *Zhongguo Hujiao jujinhui* (Society for the Advancement of Islam in China), its Henan branches, including Zhengzhou, were given special mention (Ma Songting 1985a:83).[18]

Impressive religious developments, intense rivalries among diverse religious traditions, the rapid growth of popular education including female education, a burgeoning mass production of didactic materials, social welfare projects, but also unchecked poverty, corruption and political volatility – these are impressions of Kaifeng society during *Minguo* which convey a culture that was buzzing with energy and tension, with the possibility of change and social mobility, but also with uncertainty over the nation's political directions.

Where are the women in this vibrant scene? What part was played by women's mosques under their female *ahong* in the religious and social developments of Kaifeng? How did reforms and innovations shape the way women organized their religious and social life? We have only a fleeting glimpse of their hopes and hard labor, of the effect of reforms they experienced, and how relations with Muslim and Kaifeng society at large were evolving.

We know that *nü ahong* brought so-called *funü quanjiaoge* (songs to instruct women in Islam) from among the *quanjiaoge* then circulating among Muslims, from the streets to the women's mosques, teaching them to be receptive believers. Some female *ahong*, illiterate in Chinese, used Persian or Arabic to transliterate (a method of transmission known as *xiaoerjing*) the lyrics, copying them for future transmission.

---

[18] The positive impact of Wang Chunli on a hitherto inert religious scene in Zhengzhou during the late 1930s is detailed in Zheng Daoming 1985:1313.

We asked elderly informants what they remembered from their childhood. One afternoon in June of 2002, we were joined by three old women from the "Wangjia Hutong Women's Mosque" in Kaifeng to listen to their memories of *Minguo*. All in their late seventies, one old lady knitting as they talked, they slowly returned to girlhood in their old women's mosque. From her earliest years, Li Xiangrong remembers with emotion that she loved *jingge*. Her natal home, as well as her husband's home, are located close to the mosque, and she has lived here all her married life. At the time that she learned about Islam, how to recite and to chant, the mosque was inhabited by the senior *ahong* and three subordinate *ahong*. Each room was pointed out to us as Li Xiangrong recalled who had resided in which part of the mosque. Between twenty to thirty girls were instructed in Islam, the youngest six or seven years old, the oldest between sixteen to seventeen years. The education was as in other schools regulated by strict discipline and days filled with instruction, with the resident *ahong* teaching basic Islamic knowledge and *jingge*. After some time of instruction would have passed, an *ahong* would say, Girls, now how about reciting a *jingge*! And then everyone would join in the singing. In those years, women's mosques were filled with women and girls. It had felt good. She was happy then.

Lamenting Loss, Remembering Words

Kuhua (Grieving Song)[19]
Ai! Yearning for you, I am yearning for a man of true knowledge. They say there is no comfort sitting on a wooden bench, studying the holy books. I have never sought possessions, sought riches and honor; for you, I have not married the official, I have married the honorable *erlin* [scholar with profound knowledge of the Islamic scriptures].
I thought when the roses bloom, we will be together, the roses are blooming, but we are apart.

---

[19] The first lament was recorded in the women's mosque of Zhuxian*zhen* and recited by Dan *ahong* (June 2002). The second lament was recorded in "Wangjia Hutong Women's Mosque" and recited by Li Xiangrong (June 2002). Questionmarks indicate our current uncertainty over meaning as the performers are illiterate.

I thought when the peony unfolds its petals, your studies are done, but like the *luomi* [?] only loneliness and sadness abound.

I thought when the cockscomb blossoms, it would break into smiles, but you have given me sunflowers instead, their heads drooping.

I thought that pomegranate would drench the courtyard in red, but you gave me flower-petals from the pear tree, shivering in white. Compassionate God, oh miserable me!

I thought that when *baila* [?] flowers bloom, all the people would like them well, but I did not know that when your *gaizheng* [?] flowers opened, there was no one to gaze upon them. Compassionate God, oh miserable me!

I thought that when the phoenix descends on the parasol tree, skipping from branch to branch, happiness would fill us; I did not know that you'd give me prickly branches on which the phoenix caught, lacerating the heart.

I thought that as the *juzheng* [?] opens its petals, we shall grow old together, but I did not know that you'd give me orchids and never reach the end of the road.

I thought that you would ride your horse up and down the main street, I did not know that your horse would gallop over the wall and never return.

I thought that the geese and duck would happily swim along the river, I did not know you would will them into the mouth of death.

I thought that the peach blossom would bring forth fruit, I did not know that the peanut plant would blossom, but its seeds end up scattered on the ground. Compassionate God, oh miserable me.

Kuhua

Ai! I yearn for you! Ai, [my beloved] who has gone to Weihe [to study Islam]! They say there is no comfort in sitting on a cold wooden bench reciting the holy books!

I hoped that you would be ordained as *ahong*, I did not know you would give me a bamboo basket in which to fetch dripping water. Compassionate God, oh miserable me.

I thought you would come home to me ever so often, I did not know that you would be lost to me when you departed. Compassionate God, oh miserable me.

I thought when the peony unfolds its petals, your studies are done, but like the *luomi* [?] only loneliness and sadness abound.

[remaining refrains as above]

A women's mosque has been, continues to be, women's spiritual and social universe, the site of communal activity. During *Minguo*, the relationship of women's mosques with Muslim and local society was marked by reforms in political, intellectual and religious spheres of society. In this sense, the religious culture of these women's communities partook also in aspirations for progress, which marked society at large. They benefited from educational initiatives and individual intervention that made their mosque, as the old women remember it, alive with hope and curious to learn about the outside world. In this sense, *Minguo* is a golden age to those who speak at a time of ageing mosque populations and intense debates over the relevance of an inert and traditionalist women's mosque education to the twenty-first century. The current situation is however also a legacy of *Minguo* society. The history of these *jingge* illuminates some of the unique features that Muslim made their own; their history also illuminates their inter-dependence with reform movements in which gender prescriptions were questioned by an elite of reformers, including women Muslim intellectuals, whose class, education and social milieu allowed them only a glimpse of the majority of rural women in back alleys and through "the cracks of gates."

Jingge are an integral part of the Islamic female culture, in this identity they also reveal the problems which beset those who wish to prompt memories: *jingge* have retained their separate characteristics, they are the vehicles of a women's mosque tradition, and they are also steeped in conservative Islamic morality. Yet they are not an expression apart or closed off from other meaning systems. We can trace certain commonalities, for example, not only with *jingge* in Buddhism and *lingge* in Christian religion but also with certain popular folksongs. The history of *jingge* is emblematic of the changing place and relevance of women's mosques culture in relation to Chinese society, to local society, to Muslim communities and, ultimately, to their own congregation of believers. The *Minguo* era, so golden in the remembering of the old Muslim believers as a vibrant era of women's mosque culture, is also a bridge to sadness, because it has come to represent loss, the "past-ness" of their culture and the fragmentation of what they had once been.

Notes and Reflections from *en route*

Vera Schwarcz talks about memory "which won't leave us alone" (1998:184) and, until it is confronted, troubles, disturbs and interrupts. Memory traumatized has no access to the past. A past that has not been taken into the present has as yet to happen, says Jane Kilby. "[...] where a turn to the future is figured as a turn away from the past (or an overlooking of the past), memories of trauma are put at risk, for I am less certain that we know all we need to know of history, or, more precisely, I am not confident that we know all the histories of history. Is there not a chance that memories still elude us?" (Kilby 2002:205). The peculiarity of trauma as elusive remembering, its defiance of chronology of remembering and experience, make the gathering of "historical evidence" a difficult and imprecise and seemingly random process.

For Vera Schwarcz, memory does no more, and no less, than acknowledge the fragmented nature of all human time, it neither "restores" continuity of narrative nor does it bring enlightenment. Memory "is the knowledge that an absence has to be bridged with words" (Schwarcz 1998:xi), troubling, and destabilizing, the oppressive hold of what Schwarcz calls the "lexicon of public events" that is official historiography over personal remembrance.

The "futural grammar" is strong in the lived religious faith. The presence of God, of Allah, who even when women are faced with glaring injustices and oppression makes sense, makes meaning, of living. The heavier the weight of unnamed (unnameable) past, the more intense the embrace of the life after death (*houshi*). The flight from the trauma is the greater as the very modernity of a socialist state, with its revolutionary legacy and thus an identity locked in the "myth of origin" (Jabri 1996), of unfettering from "feudalism" (including backwardness of religious belief), is built on the back of religion (Harding 1991). There the paradigm of progressive *Zhongguo funü*[20]

---

[20] See Tani E. Barlow's historicization of *Zhongguo funü* (Chinese woman) as "national woman, or, more precisely, national woman under a Maoist-Communist state inscription" (Barlow 1994:345).

was predicated on the dismantling of the old dependencies on clan and religion. In this case, the unretrieved trauma is also the celebrated phase of Maoist laws of unilinear progress in which the transition from "the old" to "the new" era is commemorated.

Memory's relation to the past is one both of knowledge and of action, so says Paul Ricoeur (1999). The uses made of memory, and its abuse, entail ethical dimensions that can affirm or erase collective and personal identity. How much do the *jingge*, the chanted *kuhua* reveal, how much do they evoke and how much obscure? Is it possible, especially in the case of what Ricoeur calls "the founding events which are the ground of a collective memory" (Ricoeur 1999:9), to retrace shared events for telling other histories?[21] We are seeking in our on-going study to tell Muslim women's histories of the origin of their liberation for too long marginalized as otherwise.

References

Antoun, Richard T., *Muslim Preacher in the Modern World*, Princeton 1989.

Bai Wentian, 1943 nian Henan huangzai qin liji (Personal Chronicle of the Locust Plague in Henan 1943), in: *Henan wenshi ziliao* 3 (1994), pp. 216-220.

Barlow, Tani E., Theorizing Woman: *Funü, Guojia, Jiating* (Chinese Woman, Chinese State, Chinese Family), in: Angela Zito, Tani E. Barlow (eds.), *Body, Subject and Power in China*, Chicago, London 1994, pp. 263-289.

Bi Yun, Funü dui shidai yingyou de renshi (Women's Proper Understanding of Their Times), in: *Nü qingnian yuekan* 14 (1935), pp. 33-35.

Blum, Stephen, Philip V. Bohlman, Daniel M. Neuman (eds.), *Ethnomusicology and Modern Music History*, Urbana, Chicago 1991.

Bradshaw, Sue Sister, Religious Women in China: An Understanding of Indigenization, in: *The Catholic Historical Revue* 68:1 (1982), pp. 228-245.

---

[21] See Ye Hanming's (1999) discussion of the "search for female subjectivities."

Cooke, Maeve, Questioning Autonomy: The Feminist Challenge and the Challenge for Feminism, in: Kearney/Dooley 1999, pp. 258-282.
Coplan, David B., Ethnomusicology and the Meaning of Tradition, in: Blum et al. 1991, pp. 35-48.
Dai Pengliang, Hebei Jiaohe Potouzhen Huimin zhuangkuang (The Situation of Muslims in Potou Town, Jiaohe County, Hebei), in: Yu gong banyuekan 7:4 (Beijing, n.d.), reproduced in: Li/Feng 1985, vol. 2, pp. 1302-1304.
Dong Xiaoping, R. David Arkush, *Xiangcun xiqu biaoyan yu Zhongguo xiandai minzhong* (Rural Popular Opera Performance and China's Modern Populace), Beijing 2000.
Frick, Heike, Mechthild Leutner, Nicola Spakowski (eds.), *Frauenforschung in China: Analysen, Texte, Bibliographie*, München 1995.
Graham, Gael, *Gender, Culture, and Christianity: American Protestant Mission Schools in China 1880-1930*, New York 1995.
Guan Yu, Zhongguo Musilin zhi liangfeng meisu (On the Good Practices among Chinese Muslims), in: Yisilan 3:4 (n.d.), reproduced in: Li/Feng 1985, vol. 2, pp. 1746-1752.
Harding, Susan, Representing Fundamentalism: The Problem of the Repugnant Cultural Other, in: *Social Research* 58 (1991), pp. 373-393.
He Ru, Yisilanjiao yu funü (Islam and Women), in: *Yisilan funü zazhi* 1 (1936), pp. 5-6.
He Shuyun, Duiyu Yisilanjiao de guoqu yu zhanwang (On Islam's Past and Prospects), in: *Yisilan funü zazhi* 1 (1936), pp. 2-5.
Henan wenshi ziliao (Henan Historical Source Materials), ed. by Zhongguo renmin zhengzhi xieshang huiyi Henansheng weiyuanhui wenshi ziliao weiyuanhui (Chinese People's Political Consultative Session, Henan Provincial Committee, Historical Source Materials Committee), Zhengzhou 1993-1995.
Herman, Judith Lewis, *Trauma and Recovery: From Domestic Abuse to Political Terror*, London 1994.
Hsiung Ping-chun, Maria Jaschok, Cecilia Milwertz, with Red Chan (eds.), *Chinese Women Organising: Cadres, Feminists, Muslims, Queers*, Oxford 2001.

Jabri, Vivienne, *Discourses on Violence*, Manchester 1996.

Jaschok, Maria, Shui Jingjun, *The History of Women's Mosques in Chinese Islam*, Richmond, Surrey 2000.

Jian Qiao Zhongguo wan Qing shi 1800-1911 (The Cambridge History of China, Late Qing 1800-1911, vol. 11), ed. by John K. Fairbank, Liu Kwang-Ching, translated by Fei Zhengqing, Liu Guangjing, vol. 2, Bejing 1993.

Jin Jitang, Ma Zicheng *ahong* zhuan (Remembering Ma Zicheng *ahong*), in: *Yuehua* 7:14 (1935), reproduced in: Li/Feng 1985, vol. 1, pp. 644-645.

Jingwei Zhenzhu zhi lu (Respecting the Path of Allah), ed. by Zhengzhou Yuyuanli Mosque, n.d.

Kearney, Richard, Mark Dooley (eds.), Questioning Ethics: Contemporary Debates in Philosophy, London 1999.

Kilby, Jane, Redeeming Memories: The Politics of Trauma and History, in: *Feminist Theory* 3:2 (2002), pp. 201-210.

Kirmayer, Laurence J., Landscapes of Memory: Trauma, Narrative, and Disassociation, in: Paul Antze, Michael Lambek (eds.), *Tense Past: Cultural Essays in Trauma and Memory*, London 1996, pp. 173-198.

Kristeva, Julia, Revolt Today, in: Kearney/Dooley 1999, pp. 220-229.

Leung, Beatrice (ed.), *Church and State in State Relations in 21st Century Asia*, Hong Kong 1996.

Li Fuzhen, *Mumin quanshangge* (Muslim Songs for Religious Instruction), first copied by hand in Shangqiu, Henan, 1918, reprinted by Beiping Chengda shifan xuexiao chubanbu (Beiping Chengda Normal School Printing Section), Beiping 1935.

Li Rongchang, Funü jiefang shengzhong zhi wo gan (Musing on Women's Liberation), in: *Chengda wenhui* (Chengda Anthology), ed. by Beiping Chengda shifan xuexiao (Beiping Chengda Normal School), Beiping 1932, pp. 95-97.

Li Xiaojiang, With What Discourse Do We Reflect on Chinese Women? Thoughts on Transnational Feminism in China, in: Yang 1999, pp. 261-277.

Li Xiaojiang, Zhu Hong, Dong Xiuyu (eds.), *Zhuliu yu bianyuan* (Center and Margin), Beijing 1999.

Li Xinghua, Feng Jinyuan (eds.), *Zhongguo Yisilanjiaoshi cankao ziliao xuanbian* (The History of Chinese Islam, Selected Source Materials), 2 vols., Ningxia 1985.

Li Xinghua, Qin Huibin, Feng Jinyuan, Sha Qiuzhen, *Zhongguo Yisilanjiaoshi* (History of Chinese Islam), Beijing 1998.

Liu Fuli (ed.), *Liu Zhisan lao ahong shiji* (Collected Chants of the Revered *ahong* Liu Zhisan), Xi'an 1993.

Liu Yihong, Qi Qianjin (comps.), *Yisilanjiao yishu baiwen* (Comprehensive Introduction to Islamic Art), Beijing 1996.

Lu Zhenming, Kaifeng Huijiao tan (Talking about Islam in Kaifeng), in: Yu gong banyuekan 7:4 (Bejing, n.d.), reproduced in: Li/Feng 1985, vol. 2, pp. 1618-1628.

Lutz, Jessie Gregory, *China and the Christian Colleges 1850-1950*, Ithaka 1971.

Ma Hongyi, Xianzai Zhongguo Huijiao funü yingdang zhuyi de san jianshi (Three Things Modern Chinese Muslim Women Must Observe), in: *Yuehua* 7:2 (1935), pp. 7-10.

Ma Jigao, *Funü you jia waichu* (Women Leaving Home) in: *Yuehua* 7:1 (1935), p. 13.

Ma Songting, Zhongguo Huijiao de xianzhuang (Current Situation of Islam in China), in: *Yuehua* 16:18 (n.d.), reproduced in: Li/Feng 1985a, vol. 1, pp. 77-87.

Ma Songting, Zhongguo Huijiao yu Chengda shifan xuexiao (Chinese Islamic and Chengda Normal School), in: Yu gong banyuekan 5:11 (Beijing, n.d.), reproduced in: Li/Feng 1985b, vol. 2, pp. 1033-1054.

Ma Xiang, Xiangei xianzai Zhongguo Huijiaode xin nüxing (For Modern China's New Islamic Woman), in: *Yuehua* 7:5 (1935), pp. 9-13.

Ma Xiuzhen, Yisilan funü de juewu (Awakening of Islamic Women), in: *Yisilan funü zazhi* 1 (1936), pp. 12-13.

MacInnes, Donald E., *Religious Policy and Practice in Communist China: A Documentary History*, London 1972.

MacInnes, Donald E., *Religion in China Today: Policy and Practice*, Maryknoll/NY 1989.

Mai Nüshi, Jidujiao nüzi jiaoyu (Christian Female Education), in: *Zhonghua Jidujiaohui nianjian, 1914* (China Christian Association Yearbook, 1914), reprint Taipei 1983, vol. 1, pp. 79-80.

Mees, Imke, *Die Hui – Eine moslemische Minderheit in China: Assimilationsprozesse und politische Rolle vor 1949*, München 1984.

Miller, Judith, *One by One by One: Facing the Holocaust*, New York 1990.

Mu Changhua, Cong qunian shengdanjie tandao funü xiehui (Talking about the Women's Association since Last Year's Celebration of the Birth of the Saint), in: *Yisilan funü zazhi* 1 (1936), pp. 8-9.

Mu Yigang, Tianjin Huimin gaikuang (Situation of Tianjin's Muslims), in: Yuehua 7:12 (1935), reproduced in: Li/Feng 1985, vol. 2, pp. 1345-1348.

Musilin changshi (Muslim Common Reader), ed. by Zhengzhou Beida Mosque, 1994.

Neuman, Daniel M., Epilogue: Paradigm and Stories, in: Blum et al. 1991, pp. 268-277.

Peng Yaqian, Das feministische Erwachen chinesischer Christinnen, in: *Berliner China-Hefte* (Free University Berlin) 16 (1999), pp. 125-128.

Perry, Susan H., Celeste M. Schenck (eds.), *Eye to Eye: Women Practicing Development across Cultures*, London 2001.

Qing, Yangzhou Xianhesi Yang Zhechen *ahong* fangwen ji (Visit to Yang Zhechen *ahong* of the Xianhe Mosque in Yangzhou), in: Tu jue yuekan 4:5 (1937), reproduced in: Li/Feng 1985, vol. 1, pp. 651-653.

Qingzhen quanjiaoge (Islamic Songs for Religious Instruction), n.p. 1922.

Qingzhen tongsuge (Islamic Popular Songs), printed by Beiping Qingzhen shubanshe (Beiping Islamic Printing Press), Beiping 1924.

Rees, Helen, *Echoes of History: Naxi Music in Modern China*, Oxford 2000.

Ricoeur, Paul, Memory and Forgetting, in: Kearney/Dooley 1999, pp. 5-11.

Schwarcz, Vera, *Bridge across Broken Time: Chinese and Jewish Cultural Memory*, New Haven, London 1998.

Shi Xiaoyan, Kangzhan shiqi Lunxianqu de du du chang (Opium, Gambling, and Prostitution in Lunxian District during the Anti-Japanese War Period), in: *Henan wenshi ziliao* 3 (1993), pp. 186-192.

Shui Jingjun, Maria Jaschok, *Zhongguo Qingzhen nüsi shi* (The History of Women's Mosques in China), revised and translated edition, Beijing 2002.

Sun Shengwu, Sanshi nian lai de Zhong A wenhua guanxi (Thirty Years of Contact between Chinese and Arabic Culture), in: Huimin yanlun banyuekan (1939), reproduced in: Li/Feng 1985, vol. 2, pp. 1768-1775.

The Christian Occupation of China (Zhonghua gui zhu), ed. by China Continuation Committee, Special Committee on Survey and Occupation (Zhonghua xuxing weibanhui diaocha teweihui), 1922, reprint Beijing 1987 (see Zhonghua gui zhu, Chinese version).

Tong, Joseph, *Challenges and Hope: Stories from the Catholic Church in China*, Taipei 1999.

Uhalley, Stephen, Wu Xiaoxin (eds.), *China and Christianity: Burdened Past, Hopeful Future*, New York 2000.

Wang Jingzhai, Wozhi Yijing xiaoshi (My Humble History of Translating the Koran), in: Yiguang 101 (1939), reproduced in: Li/Feng 1985, vol. 2, pp. 1093-1103.

Wang Junpu, Heilongjiang quansheng Musilin zhi zhuangkuang (Situation of Muslims in the Province of Heilongjiang), in: Yuehua 7:16 (1931), reproduced in: Li/Feng 1985, vol. 2, pp. 1366-1371.

Wang Mengyang, Beipingshi Huijiao gaikuang (Situation of Muslims in Beiping), reproduced in: Li/Feng 1985, vol. 2, pp. 1323-1340.

Wang Zengshan, Chang'an Huicheng xun li ji (Record of Customs in Chang'an's Hui Quarter), in: Yuehua 5:1-14 (1933), reproduced in: Li/Feng 1985, vol. 2, pp. 1372-1390.

Wang Zheng, *Women in the Chinese Enlightenment: Oral and Textual Histories*, Berkeley, Los Angeles, London 1999.

Wesoky, Sharon, *Chinese Feminism Faces Globalization*, London 2001.

Xue Lan, Yisilan duoqizhi lilunde jie da (Theorizing Islamic Polygamy), in: *Yisilan* 5 (1935), pp. 9-13.

Xun Zhi, Women de mubiao (Our Goal), in: *Yisilan funü zazhi* 1 (1936), pp. 14-15.

Yang, Mayfair Mei-Hui (ed.), *Spaces of Their Own: Women's Public Sphere in Transnational China*, Minneapolis 1999.

Ye Hanming, *Zhuti de zhuixun: Zhongguo funüshi yanjiu xilun* (In Search of Subjectivities: Historical Studies of Chinese Women), Hong Kong 1999.

Yi He, Linqing Huimin zhuangkuang (Situation of Hui People in Linqing), in: Yuehua 7:16 (1935), reproduced in: Li/Feng 1985, vol. 2, pp. 1530-1533.

Yisilan jiaoyi ge (Islamic Chants), ed. by Zhengzhou Yuyuanli Mosque, n.d.

You Cheng, Taiyuan Huijiao gaikuang (Situation of Islam in Taiyuan), in: Chen xi xunkan (Dawn of Day Periodical) 1:12-13 (n.d.), reproduced in: Li/Feng 1985, vol. 2, pp. 1356-1361.

Yu Zhengui, Yang Huaizhong, *Zhongguo Yisilanzhuyi tiyao* (Topical Outline of Chinese Islam), Ningxia 1993.

Zhang Fengwu, Meiguo chuanjiaoshi zai Jigongshan (American Missionaries in Jigongshan), in: *Henan wenshi ziliao* 1 (1995), pp. 212-215.

Zhao Bin, Jiaojingshi suibi (Random Notes from an Islamic Study), in: Zhongguo Huijiao xiehui yuekan 1:2-7, 9-12 (Shanghai, 1926), reproduced in: Li/Feng 1985, vol. 2, pp. 1126-1127.

Zhao Jiazhen (comp.), *Kaifeng minzu zongjiaozhi* (Local History of Kaifeng Folk Religions), privately printed, Kaifeng 2000.

Zhao Zhenwu, Sanshi nian lai zhi Zhongguo Huijiao wenhua gaikuang (Situation of China's Islamic Culture these Last Thirty Years), in: Yu gong banyuekan 5:11 (Beijing, 1936), reproduced in: Li/Feng 1985, vol. 2, pp. 947-965.

Zhen Wu, Yisilan funü xiehui (Islamic Women's Association), in: *Yuehua* 8:18 (1936), p. 1.

Zheng Daoming, Henan Zhengxian Huimin gaikuang (Situation of Muslims in Zhengzhou County, Henan), reproduced in: Li/Feng 1985, vol. 2, pp. 1306-1315.

Zhongguo Huijiao xiehui di'er zu (China Islam Association, Second Division), Xie zai qianmiande jihuhua (A Brief Foreword), in: *Huijiao funü* 1 (January 1945), p. 1.

Zhongguo minjian gequ jicheng, Henanjuan (The Chinese Folksong Collection, Henan Volume), ed. by Zhongguo minjian gequ jicheng Henanjuan bianji weiyuanhui (The Chinese Folksong Collection, Henan Volume Editorial Committee), Beijing 1997.

Zhonghua gui zhu (The Christian Occupation of China), ed. by Zhonghua xuxing weibanhui diaocha teweihui (China Continuation Committee, Special Committee on Survey and Occupation), 1922, reprint Beijing 1985 (see The Christian Occupation of China, English version).

Zhou Mingyi, Wunian lai jiaohuizhi xiangcun gongzuo (Christian Association's Rural Work these Last Five Years), in: *Zhonghua Jidujiaohui nianjian 1929-1930* (China Christian Association Yearbook 1929-1930), Shanghai 1931, reprint Taipei 1983, vol. 11, part 1, pp. 130-133.

Contemporary Discourses on Homosexuality in Republican China: A Critical Analysis of Terminology and Current Research

Jens Damm

There is no doubt that many of the terms and expressions used in the Chinese language today to describe same-sex desire were first coined and introduced toward the end of the Qing dynasty and the beginning of the Republican period in China. It was at this time that terms such as *nanfeng* (literal translation: male custom or southern custom)[1] and *mou doufu* (literal translation: rubbing tofu), *duanxiu pi* (literal translation: passion of the cut sleeve) and *ai shimo* (literal translation: rubbing the mortar) passed out of common currency, giving way to *tongxinglian* or *tongxing'ai* (literal translation: same-sex love).

But what were the underlying changes which led to the rapid spread of these newly coined terms? Did these new terms really signal a totally different understanding of sex, gender and sexuality or were they simply linguistic changes without any deeper intrinsic meaning? Did these terms herald wholesale Westernization, or had indigenous developments in Chinese society already taken place which had led to a new understanding of gender and sex in general and of same-sex relations in particular? Did connotative differences exist between the Western term "homosexual" and the Chinese term *tongxinglian*?

The starting point of my reflections on this topic is the question of how the relationship between the expressions used to refer to same-sex desire, identity and culture in different theoretical approaches has been described, leading on to a consideration of the extent to which cultural and historical influences have shaped the present view of homosexuality in Chinese societies. Republican China

---

[1] Nanfeng: "southern" and "male" are homonyms in Chinese, but are written with different characters.

was the period when traditional discourses on gender and sexuality were rapidly replaced by theories which were described as global, international and modern. Most of the expressions used today could be found in the 1920s and 1930s in very different types of publications ranging from medical journals to women's and life-style magazines. Questions still remain, however, as to how far these new discourses have influenced the current discourse in general and to what measure the "former," that is the traditional, discourse has left traces which are still obvious today. Two contrasting opinions on this topic predominate at present: first of all, there is the view that the Western model of same-sex desire with its homo-hetero dichotomy and a specific homosexual (or gay/lesbian or queer) identity has become the dominant form world-wide. From this perspective, the Republican period is seen as the time when an increasingly less indigenous Chinese discourse was "colonized" by Western values and discourses, and when Chinese intellectuals, for example the May Fourth generation, were only too ready to accept values which they perceived as Western and progressive. In postmodern discourses linked with the role of the colonizer and the colonized, the current situation in Hong Kong, since the departure of Great Britain, the "colonizer," is seen as offering opportunities for revitalizing and modernizing a tradition which is regarded as being more tolerant and also more appropriate for any Chinese society. Western models are now considered to be "confrontational" and deriving from a model of an individualistically organized Western, that is "alien," society. In addition, Hong Kong, with its more lively discourse on same-sex life styles, is seen as a model for the People's Republic of China (PRC) which is regarded less as a Communist society than as a society where, despite forty years of Communist rule with many campaigns against "feudal tradition," many traditional values have survived. In particular, the relaxation of controls in the private sphere is regarded as providing the necessary space for a revival of traditional ethics. Here, postmodern ideas deriving from the West, put forward, for example, by the Chinese *Tongzhi* Conference, the Hong Kong Chou Wah-shan and other activists,[2] are used to criticize Western influences and to reevaluate

---

[2] See, for example, the Manifesto of 1996 Chinese Tongzhi Conference (1996).

the past. Proponents of the other widely held view speak of "hybrid discourses," regarding an observed world-wide convergence of "gay/lesbian" or "queer identities" as the result of glocal interaction and the economic convergence of life-styles, thus clearly rejecting theories that the modernization of China only occurred in "response to the West" (Fairbank 1954) and that China in the role of the colonized would eventually become totally "Westernized." For them, the newly-evolved hybrid discourses are not seen as shaped by any societal meta-narratives or grand narratives but in the context of a postmodern understanding of society where "a self does not amount to much, but no self is an island; each exists in a fabric of relations that is now more complex and mobile than ever before" (Lyotard 1984). They are equally critical of any attempts to revitalize or even "glorify" traditional elements. For them, it is impossible for the old tradition, whether regarded as more tolerant or more repressive, to be rationally revitalized. In the process of absorbing ideas from the "other," the "self" also changes and the influence of tradition is also multi-faceted: a tradition can live on, but the rejection of some elements of that tradition may create a new understanding which can nevertheless only be fully understood in the context of the original tradition. Thus, it is not possible to describe current hybrid discourses in terms of "global" or "traditional," or "Western" vs. "Chinese," they can only be understood as constantly changing, reacting and fluid discourses in a postmodern world, that is, a pluralistic and individualistic world, in which personal feelings play a decisive role. The Republican period here is also treated as a key period when the forces of "glocalization" – to use a modern expression – gained strength for the first time in China; the heated debates within intellectual circles are seen as symbolizing the active involvement of the Chinese in shaping the modern discourses. The proponents of this view, who include Deborah Sang (Sang Zilan), and many Taiwan-based activists such as Chi Ta-wei (Ji Dawei), Mickey Chen (Chen Junzhi) and Jo Ho (He Chunrui),[3] also point out

---

[3] See, for example, Chi Ta-wei 1997a, b; Mickey Chen expresses his views quite clearly in his film *Bu zhi shi xiyan (It Is Not Only the Wedding Banquet)* (1998) and in Chen 1998.

that these debates spread rapidly to other strata of society, for example, to the growing number of students in local teacher-training colleges.

From the Present to the Past: Looking Back at Republican China

In this essay, I am going to present an analysis of the female homosexuality discourse in Republican China seen from today's perspective to show how any perception of the past differs according to one's own understanding of the present. This is achieved by examining current perceptions of Republican China and also by drawing on some original sources written between 1910 and 1930. It will be demonstrated that the discourse during the Republican period was highly controversial and that the integration of popular Western ideas can only be understood within the context of traditional ways of thinking (see Lin Yu-sheng 1973, 1979).

The first part deals with questions regarding essentialist and constructivist views of homosexuality and the so-called emergence of the "homosexual" in the nineteenth century as described by Foucault, and also with questions regarding the transferability of "homosexual identities" to other cultures (Müller 1988). The question of historicizing "queer" theory will be considered: that is, can the current postmodern queer theory (Jagose 1996; Berry/Martin 2000) be extended to historical questions. It has been claimed that queer theory in general is "without history" and only deals with contemporary developments (Hawley 2001:4), thus neglecting other historical experiences. Queer theory, although it acts as a counter-discourse in the Western world, is restricted to the contemporary Western capitalist world. Secondly, the political and social situation regarding the view of gender during the second part of the Qing dynasty is subjected to examination as this was the groundbreaking stage when discourses of sex, gender and also of class differences changed and the foundations were laid for the far more wide-reaching changes in Republican China. Thirdly, there is a general discussion of the discourses on (female) homosexuality in Republican China as found in contemporary interpretations and with special regard to the influence of the Republican period on contemporary China: the interpretations of these discourses offered by Frank Dikötter and Chou Wah-shan are compared with that presented by Deborah Sang. Fourthly, the specific details of the public discourse of homosexuality in Republican China are revealed through a targeted examination of the media where the public discourse took place and also through an article, published in a "modern urban journal" in 1911, which was the first to deal with the topic of same-sex love and also gives an indication of the ways in which new expressions began to form and develop. Finally, the conclusion shows that theories referring to wholesale Westernization should be treated with a degree of reserve, and that the emergence of a new understanding of same-sex behavior has to be regarded as an ongoing process which necessarily includes elements of indigenization and elements of Westernization.

Theoretical Background

Carrying out research into same-sex desire or homo-eroticism places the researcher in a very difficult position, since current terms referring to identities and views of same-sex desire cannot be projected onto the past. The first researchers still assumed the existence of an essentialist "homosexual being," who was believed to have existed in every historical age and in every cultural context. This essentialist view that "presume(s) the existence of a biologically unchanging sexual minority prior to history" (Sang 1996:1), however, is no longer acceptable. Nowadays, the researcher is expected to reconstruct historical narratives and discourses, to question the source material and place it in a broader political and social context.

The essentialist view, deriving from a positivistic scientific approach which began to influence the Western academic world toward the end of the nineteenth century is, however, still of major importance as most of the terms such as "homosexual" (or the Chinese *tongxinglian*) which we use today have their origin in this approach. Michel Foucault, for example, described the emergence of the term and of the "homosexual" identity for the Western world as follows:

> The nineteenth-century homosexual became a personage – a past, a case history and a childhood, a character, a form of life; also a morphology,

with an indiscreet anatomy and possibly a mysterious physiology. Nothing in his total being escapes his sexuality. (Foucault 1978:43)

Two academic disciplines in particular, ethnology and history, paved the way for a different understanding: for a historical approach, the basis for a constructivist view was first established as early as 1968 by Mary McIntosh who, regarding the problems of research into the etiology of homosexuality, stated:

> There has been much debate as to whether the condition is innate or acquired. [...] Yet, after a long history of such studies, the results are sadly inconclusive and the answer is still as much a matter of opinion as it was when Havelock Ellis published *Sexual Inversion* seventy years ago. The failure of research to answer the question has not been due to lack of scientific rigor or any inadequacy of the available evidence; it results rather from the fact that the wrong questions have been asked. (McIntosh 1968:183)

In addition to the varying visibility of homoerotic desire, another crucial issue is that of the differing quantity of references to male vs. female found within materials available. This leads to the issue of the relationship between discourse and practice and the ways in which reference is made to women. The reasons for the differences in visibility between men and women in the specific cultural and historical context should be taken into account and women should not only be mentioned in appendices and epilogues, as is the case in many "gay and lesbian historical works" (for example Boswell 1980).

Some more recent strategies were offered by Bravmann (1997), who uses the analytical term "queer heterosociality" to deal with these phenomena: This term allows for multiple differences among the subjects of the research and also tries to take into account the systematic oppression that is common to them all. For Bravmann, who was influenced by social constructivists and also by the historian Hayden White (1973), it is the task of research to reveal how certain historical narratives have been constructed, which individuals have been included or

288

excluded, which points of view were privileged and which constructs of power were developed.[4]

The more recently developed queer theory, which deals specifically with a variety of different identities ranging from gay and lesbian, to transgender and "everything in between," and might, therefore, be considered a powerful tool for dealing with non-Western identities, has been accused of "historical amnesia" (Hawley 2001:4).[5] Postcolonial approaches which are used to examine the introduction of Westernized terms and ideas into the historical process might be accused of suffering from a "mystifying amnesia of the colonial aftermath" (ibid.).[6] Although during the last decade, the issues of same-sex desire, gender and sexuality in China have been studied more extensively, the approaches employed have varied greatly: most researchers have completely disregarded questions related to identity, to self-

---

[4] See also the relation between "inner" and "outer," that is *nei* and *wai*, in the Chinese tradition and the overlapping spheres of *nei* and *wai* as described by Bray (1997) and Furth (1999).

[5] A short definition for "queer theory" is given by Jagose 1996: "Broadly speaking, queer describes those gestures or analytical models which dramatise incoherencies in the allegedly stable relations between chromosomal sex, gender and sexual desire. Resisting that model of stability – which claims heterosexuality as its origin, when it is more properly its effect – queer focuses on mismatches between sex, gender and desire. Institutionally, queer has been associated most prominently with lesbian and gay subjects, but its analytic framework also includes such topics as cross-dressing, hermaphroditism, gender ambiguity and gender-corrective surgery. Whether as transvestite performance or academic deconstruction, queer locates and exploits the incoherencies in those three terms which stabilise heterosexuality. Demonstrating the impossibility of any 'natural' sexuality, it calls into question even such apparently unproblematic terms as 'man' and 'woman.'" See Hawley 2001 for a more detailed discussion of a "globalized queer." For the relationship between gender and history in a poststructuralist approach, see, for example, Scott 1988.

[6] In addition, Carolyn Dean (1999:129) asks the following questions: "How does the historian or the 'historizing project' theorize the relationship between culture (collective representation or memory) and social experience? Or more implicitly, how do they demonstrate the ways in which that relationship is mediated by institutions (the state, the family, etc)? How do such projects and their authors account for transformation within structures or representation over time? What, moreover, is the relationship between cultural formation and identity formation?"

perception and to the specific view of society on sexuality.[7] Much of the research carried out into Chinese history has even fallen into the "essentialist trap," that is, modern homosexual identities were merely transferred to the past without an appropriate understanding of the specific historical context. Although other researchers have claimed that they were well aware of social constructivism, admitting that the "modern homosexual" is a product of certain developments within the medical discourse of the nineteenth century, a more essentialist approach is still prevalent in their works. This is exemplified in *Passions of the Cut Sleeve* by Bret Hinsch, who writes "the field of Chinese history in the West has all too often involved an imposition of our own priorities and intellectual framework onto a different culture!" (Hinsch 1990:5). It is his aim "to present an interpretative framework for understanding the Chinese homosexual tradition that is as free as possible from Western preconceptions" (ibid.).[8] Hirsch's work, still regarded as the most comprehensive work on male same-sex desire in traditional China, has been described as an adaptation of *Zhongguo tongxing'ai shilu (Historical Records of Homo-Eroticism in China)* by the Hong Kong author Samshasha (Xiaomingxiong) (1994). Neither Hinsch nor Xiaomingxiong, however, pay much attention to female desire. The essentialist approach is also employed by Ruan Fang Fu, who in his work *Sex in China* (1991), seems to be totally unaware of any constructivist approaches, suggesting that "gays and lesbians" have existed throughout Chinese history. He also focuses almost exclusively on male sexuality.

---

[7] This, of course, is not only true for research on the Chinese world; the "essentialist" view that "gays and lesbians" have always existed and that they were only "hidden in the past" was also claimed for US history by Duberman, Vicinus, and Chauncey in: *Hidden from History: Reclaiming the Gay and Lesbian Past* (1989). These works offer interesting stories, but the authors' efforts to "reveal the truth" are subject to doubt, because they did not examine the specific historical narratives which shaped the lives of the subjects of the research.

[8] Nevertheless, his work is in general essentialist and bears great resemblance to Boswell's ground-breaking *Christianity, Social Tolerance and Homosexuality* (1980).

The Semantic Field

One of the major problems facing historical research into same-sex attraction is the need to be aware of the cultural and historical context of the terms used in the limited supply of source material available, and how this may have led to differences in the present understanding of these terms; this applies to the language in which the research is carried out, in this case, English, or to the language of the culture being researched, in this case, Chinese. Postmodern and poststructuralist expressions, such as "queer" or "same-sex desire," which are used in current gender studies, are also heavily value-ridden and cannot be used without taking into account the historical and cultural context from which they have derived. This also applies to the more essentialist terms "gays" and "lesbians," which have nevertheless always been important within a more political and social movement, and the term "homosexual," which, although often found in older academic publications, is not as value-free and neutral as it often seems.[9] An alternative might be to use the Chinese expressions, and examine the ways in which these expressions were used in their specific historical and cultural contexts – whether by taking a look at the old, classical expressions or at the more recent loan-words and neologisms which shaped the discourse in the twentieth century. Best known for representing the difference between the West and China are the more classical expressions which are structured differently from Western expressions, and which have to be seen within a very specific cultural and social context. These expressions, in general, emphasize the biological differences between men and women, and describe actions and emotions, but not identities. In the male context, these expressions have often derived from relations within the court and the

---

[9] The first social constructivists argued that "homosexuality" was a Western product of a very specific historical time; it seems that in postmodern criticism, "'queer' has replaced 'homosexuality' as a uniquely Western construct, and 'homosexuality' has become the general term for any indigenous same-sex sexual behaviour" (Hayes 2001:82). For an introduction to the more recent *tongzhi*-discourse, see Damm 2000.

nobility, while in the female context, they are more frequently related to descriptions of specific actions. The most well-known expressions for describing male homosexual desire are *fentao* (to share the peach, deriving from a story of Mizi Xia and Duke Ling of Wei, 534-493, see Hinsch 1990:20), *Long Yang* (Long Yang was the name of a lord who desired the King of Wei, ibid. 32), *hao nanse* (liking men's beauty and sex, see Sang 1999:279) and *duan xiu* (cut sleeve, an expression deriving from a story of the Han Dynasty, see Hinsch 1990:53).

Another problem is the prevalent emphasis on the written, and thus, urban discourse of homosexuality in the 1920s. Only a few, sometimes not very reliable, reports on expressions for same-sex love and desire exist in the oral history. Ke Ruiming (1991), focusing on Taiwan, refers to folk tales which mentioned the idea that seduction could take place without taking into account the biological sex of the people involved (ibid. 115). Although not subject to any legal provisions, female-female relations were very often described in negative terms (Sommer 2000:15; Damm 2003:54-60) and, in these tales, were often linked to criminal acts. Ke Ruiming (1991:118) also reports that – at least in the southern coastal provinces and in Taiwan – folk operas existed where women played men's roles, referring to the popular belief that wealthy women used to offer private invitations to these actresses (called *xiaosheng*).[10] For sex between women, more vivid descriptive terms were used, such as *mou doufu* (rubbing doufu) and *ai shimo* (grinding the mortar) (Sang 1999:279) or *dunduidun* (stump to stump).

Today, other expressions are used which are useful for describing the present, but attempts to extend their use to descriptions of the past can give rise to many problems, comparable with the problems arising from the use of "gay and lesbian" in the Anglo-Saxon world to describe historical situations where implied identities did not exist (see Padgug 1990). Historical works in the Chinese language by

---

[10] It is more widely known that the male actors at the Peking opera played female roles, and the expression xianggong, which meant actor, became synonymous with "male concubine" (see Karsch-Haack 1906:16). The quoted expressions derive from holo or Taiwanese; due to the lack of a standard romanization, Hanyu pinyin is used.

Samshasha (1994) and by Weixingguanzhaizhu (1994) used the expressions *tongxinglian* for descriptions of the past. This term *tongxinglian* – and also *tongxing'ai* – was taken from the Japanese term *douseiai* (literal translation: same-sex love), the same characters being used for both terms; *douseiai* itself was a loan-translation deriving from the German "homosexuell" (Sang 1996:110-111). Some contemporary authors use the expression *tongzhi* (comrade, literal translation: same will), to refer to homosexual relations in the past, disregarding the fact that this meaning of *tongzhi* is very modern and that *tongzhi* in the past had a different connotation: *tongzhi* was used in Republican China and in the later PRC to signify "party comrade", and only in the 1990s did the use of the new meaning become prevalent (see, for example, Wu Ruiyuan 1998:97). Other expressions used today are *ku'er* (the onomatopoeic reproduction of "queer" or *guaitai* (literal: strange being), which can be found in postmodern writings and also in some historical essays; the use of these terms is, however, for the most part restricted to Taiwan and the same problems that arise in connection with "queer history" arise with the use of *ku'er* (Damm 2000). It would, therefore, seem appropriate to begin with the semantic perspective and ask how a shift from classical terms such as *fentao* or *ai shimo* to *tongxinglian* could have taken place, and by whom the new terms were used and first brought into the public discourse. The detailed usage of the new terms could also be examined and possible differences between *tongxinglian* and "homosexual" could be discussed in order to ascertain whether the terms themselves have contributed to the existence of a homosexual identity, as is usually assumed for the West.[11]

---

[11] In this particular context, Sang (1999) dealt with the role of the translators as "mediators." John D'Emilio (1983), in a post-Marxist approach, also put forward a hypothesis, which claimed that a free labor market and growing urbanization were the basis for a homosexual identity, so that a similar development could be expected in any society where such a free-labor system develops.

Historical Developments in Qing Dynasty

The discourse of same-sex desire in Republican China must be viewed in the light of the tremendous changes which occurred in China during the Qing dynasty. The May Fourth Movement of 1919, the most well-known symbol of the dramatic changes which took place in China in the twentieth century, was only the outward manifestation of profound social upheavals rooted in much earlier times. While for many years, researchers highlighted the inconsistencies and differences between the "traditional" and the "modern" China, newer approaches seek to emphasize the continuity aspect, seeing the emergence of Western terms and a leaning toward the West only against the backdrop of dramatic change which took place during the Qing dynasty. Concerning the shifts in gender-roles, for example, Matthew H. Sommer writes:

> Qing innovations (especially of the eighteenth century) represented a fundamental shift in the organizing principle for the regulation of sexuality: from *status performance*, whereby different status groups had been held to distinct standards of familial and sexual morality, to *gender performance*, whereby uniform standards of sexual morality and criminal liability were extended across old status boundaries and all persons were expected to conform to gender roles strictly defined in terms of marriage. [...] These measures implied a new anxiety about female chastity, as well as a new imperative that males act as husbands and fathers, corresponding to the imperative that females act as wives and mothers. (Sommer 2000:5, 10)

The terms "woman" (*nü*) and "man" (*nan*) gained new meaning, and while for many centuries class and hierarchical structures were crucial for the legitimation or non-legitimation of sexual relations, it was now the biological sex which was believed to define the appropriate gender role within society. Another interpretation of these changes is offered by Frank Dikötter (1995). Dikötter regards "sodomy" and "prostitution" as representing the two extreme forms of non-procreative sex which it was necessary to eliminate for the sake of the family and the nation (Dikötter 1995:137). He assumes that the regulations of the

Qing dynasty were intended to work against wide-spread prostitution, and sees a great similarity to the developments in the West in the eighteenth and nineteenth century (ibid. 138). He fails, however, to offer any convincing explanation for the sudden appearance of legislation aimed at homosexuals or for the fact that homosexuality, after being ignored for many centuries, was suddenly perceived to be a threat to family and nation.

The Discourse in Republican China

From the very beginning of the Republican period, from 1911 onward, female same-sex desire started to achieve new visibility; popular magazines started to publish articles related to this topic which indicates that far-reaching changes were taking place in the economic, social and political status of women in Republican China – at least for the newly-emerging middle class.

There was an increasing interest in everything dealing with "sexuality," and many terms in connection with "sexuality," "gender" and the concept of the individual had already undergone a tremendous shift in meaning: *xing*, to take one of the best known examples, which had meant "character" and "nature" in the past, at some time during the Qing dynasty came to be used to describe the linguistic term "gender" with reference to Western languages, and also "sexuality" or "sexual intercourse" (in terms such as *xingjiao*) in general (see Chou Wah-shan 2000:13-14; Sang 1999:278-279).

Articles about *tongxing'ai* and love between women started to appear in various kinds of publications which had only one common characteristic: they were all aimed at the new urban middle class which was now able to afford them. This shows the limitations of such a discourse, but at the same time indicates the potential scope of the topic. The educated middle class of the 1910s and 1920s who could afford these publications was not only geographically limited to the urban centers but also constituted only a tiny proportion of the urban population in general. Nevertheless, the fact that these articles were printed not only in medical journals but also in women's and life-style magazines provided a far broader context for the discourse which was thus not restricted to the medical world alone. This contrasted directly with the situation in the West: the Chinese authors of these articles were never specifically named as medical experts, whereas in the West at that time, homosexuality, at least male homosexuality, was prohibited by law in most countries so that only medical experts were able to write on homosexuality without running the risk of being accused of homosexuality themselves. In the Chinese context, however, legislation against homosexuals did not exist and the authors were not accused of being homosexual.[12] In the West, when the topic of homosexuality was not referred to in medical terms, it was often discussed in connection with the law, such as paragraph 175 in Germany or the Oscar Wilde trial in England.

Although the urban discourse of same-sex love appeared in a variety of different publications, it should not be assumed that the urban discourse was able to spread rapidly and easily over the entire country. As I have already pointed out, these magazines were only accessible to the newly-emerging middle class so that the segmentation of society into rich and poor and the gap between rural and urban China clearly operated as restricting factors on the spread of the discourse. I shall nevertheless concentrate on the urban developments since the discourse first occurred in the large conurbations. Of particular interest are articles published in women's magazines at that time, which had an influence not only on women, but also on their large number of male readers (Nivard 1984). One of the first of these articles was "Same-Sex Love between Women" (*Funü nü tongxing zhi aiqing*) which appeared as early as 1911, that is to say, even before the Chinese Republic was founded. There were also other articles related to female same-sex desire, some of which were translations, in *Funü shibao (Women's Times)*, and *Funü zazhi (The Ladies' Journal)*, in *Xin nüxing (New Woman)*, and also in *Xin wenhua (New Culture)*.[13]

---

[12] During the Qing dynasty, there was some legislation against male homosexuality. The Constitution of the Chinese Republic, however, did not only stress the equality of men and women, it also did not include any legislation against homosexual acts per se (Damm 2003:52).

[13] Sang 1996:100 mentions Mao Yibo 1928:1257-1258 and Yan Shi 1923:14-15. See also Furuya/Wei Sheng 1925 and Xie Se 1927.

In addition, educational journals, such as *Jiaoyu zazhi (Chinese Educational Review)* (Shen Zemin 1923), mentioned same-sex love between women, as did some sensationalist works which could be described as an early form of the yellow press (Tao Wu 1918, quoted in: Sang 1996:103; Jie Chen 1939, quoted in: Sang 1996:106). Only toward the end of the Republican period did specific translations of longer works on homosexuality appear – works which would later become the standard for every Chinese translation of Western sexology, the best known example of this being the translation of Havelock Ellis by Pan Guangdan in the early 1940s.[14]

Theories of Westernization: Dikötter and Chou Wah-shan

The two authors, Chou Wah-shan and Frank Dikötter, maintain that the whole concept of sexology in China today is the result of a process where the aspect of Westernization has played an important role. They both argue that, as a result, the concept of homosexuality as a deviant pattern of behavior with pathological traits took root in China, but there are, however, fundamental differences of opinion between the two authors regarding the underlying causes of this Westernization: according to Frank Dikötter, the Chinese did not "understand" the more "progressive and scientific aspect" of new Western science so that, in his opinion, homosexuality was treated even more negatively than in the West, while Chou Wah-shan differentiates between an intellectual and academic discourse which describes wholesale Westernization and the continuity of a traditional discourse within the broad masses of the people.

In his work *Sex and Modernity in China*, Frank Dikötter describes homosexuality or the emergence of a medical discourse in a chapter named "A Filthy Habit: The Inverted Homosexual" (Dikötter

---

[14] Sang (1996:296-297) assumes that the more medically-oriented translation by Pan Guangdan showed that "the range of Chinese discourses on homosexuality narrowed after the 1920s, in which process Ellis's medical theory of homosexuality, premised on a dichotomy between sexual normality and deviation, gained hegemony through repeated citations and translations into Chinese" (see Pan Guangdan/Havelock 1987).

1995:137-145). He regards the discussion of *tongxinglian* as belonging within the broader spectrum of extramarital sexuality, which was seen – in his opinion – as a threat to the social order. Dikötter writes that, in China, sexual science was used by the modernizing elites only "to consolidate the widespread distinction between procreative and non-procreative sexual acts" (ibid. 139), while in the West, he views the medical discourse in a much more positive light: "Although the dissolution of the idea of heterogenitality as a natural need and the recognition of a plurality of individual desires was a very gradual and uneven cultural development in Europe, no similar tendency took place in China" and "the emphasis on sexual preference gradually led to the recognition of the potential equality of heterosexual and homosexual desires" (ibid.). For China, he says: "The concept of 'sexuality' never made a significant impact [...]. Instead of conceptualizing 'homosexuality' as a sexual preference distinct from 'heterosexuality,' it continued to be interpreted as a non-procreative act which should be condemned as a form of extramarital sexuality" (ibid.).

Dikötter does not, however, explain why non-procreative sex should suddenly have been seen as a threat to the social order where for centuries homosexuality and the extramarital affairs of men had not been considered non-procreative and had therefore been disregarded; he also has difficulty in explaining why, suddenly, the sexuality of women should have been described in medical terms and equated with the sexuality of men.

Dikötter is also mainly concerned with male homosexuality; regarding female homosexuality he assumes "a discursive silence which can probably be ascribed to the overwhelming concern with regulating male extramarital sexuality" (ibid. 141). He further assumes that a "homosexual identity" for women did not exist and "a lack of concern for female homosexuality indicates that sodomy was condemned as an occasional non-procreative sexual act which threatened married harmony" (ibid.). His rather negative view of the Chinese discourse leads to the conclusion that: "Sexual variations were not seen [in Republican China] as an expression of human diversity which needed to be catalogued and investigated, but rather as a mark of the uncivilized 'other'" (ibid. 144). Dikötter's basic flaw is that, in principle, he regards the Western medical discourse as positive, not sharing the view that the medical discourse led the way to a pathological classification of homosexuality; he also disregards the problems arising from the strict categorization of sexuality in the West (see Müller 1988). Sang (1999) observed that Dikötter focuses exclusively on the medical discourse, and is thus unable to explain to what extent the medical discourse had become the mainstream discourse.[15]

Coming from a different background, the Hong Kong sociologist, Chou Wah-shan, attests to the wholesale adoption of Western ideas within the more academic discourses, describing the public discourse on homosexuality as highly Westernized. He does make a clear distinction, however, between the academic discourses and the general attitude and sees the latter as being much less influenced by Western discourses; he is convinced that traditional discourses of sexuality, gender and body have to a great extent survived in the PRC and in Hong Kong.

He states that popular opinion regarding homosexuality had, until the 1990s, been shaped by the traditional views of a Chinese *yin-yang* cosmology, thus rejecting the thesis of Matthew H. Sommer (Chou Wah-shan 2000:14ff.) who refers to the Qing Dynasty as the time when the fundamental changes had taken place and "people were expected to conform to gender roles strictly defined in terms of marriage" (Sommer 2000:5).

Chou Wah-shan, as a sociologist, is less interested in history than in contemporary *tongzhi* politics, and he is a committed proponent of the notion of a specific *huaren tongzhi*, a Chinese *tongzhi* which, in terms of culture and historical developments, he defines as being fundamentally different from the West. He regards culture as the basis for a different understanding of sexuality, completely discounting the effects of the very different political developments in Hong Kong, the PRC and Taiwan. In his postcolonial approach, Chou

---

[15] Dikötter (1995) mentioned the following sources for his observations: handbooks such as Wang Chengpin 1939, Cheng Hao 1934, Zhu/Yi 1923:22151, 22161, and also the works of Zhang Jingsheng, the well-known Chinese sexologist who was nevertheless emphatically against any kind of non-heterosexual sex, see Zhang Jingsheng/Levy 1967.

Wah-shan fiercely attacks the West and regards the homophobia in modern Chinese society (in particular, in Hong Kong and the PRC) as deriving from a Western model of the homo/hetero dichotomy. He regards the Republican China years as the time when medical and Western approaches began to shape the modern image of homosexuality in Chinese societies, and he is deeply concerned that, even now, Hong Kong is still undergoing "wholesale Westernization," which in his view is not appropriate for any Chinese society.

Chou Wah-shan distinguishes between a traditional concept which he regards as still influencing the view of sexuality among normal people (*laobaixing*) and the concept of sexology, which he sees as part of the public discourse, belonging to a more academic world and influencing parts of the homosexual-movement. For Chou Wah-shan, traditional China was a "world without homo-hetero duality" (Chou Wah-shan 2000:13) and the "whole modern concept of sexuality in China" was imported from the West during Republican China (ibid.). Traditional *yin-yang* cosmology was replaced "in the name of modernity, and replaced by a biological determinism that medicalizes a woman's body as weak and passive, in contrast to the male body, which is said to be active and strong" (ibid. 14). For him, "sexual identity politics first entered China during the May Fourth Movement, at a time when the new urban intellectuals were appropriating the newest Western ideologies of individualism, democracy and scientism. Chinese *funü* in the twentieth century appropriated the colonial sign 'woman' (*nüxing*) and sexual binarism (masculine vs. feminine) to subvert the Confucian patrilineal construction of *funü*, who was situated historically in *jiating* (family). Intellectuals began to use the term *nüren* (female person) and *nüxing* (woman) in a generic sense" (ibid. 22). In his work *Houzhimin tongzhi* (Postcolonial *Tongzhi*) (1997), Chou Wah-shan describes his view of Westernization in more detail:

> The Christian white people, convinced of their superior civilization and progress, brought the Western anti-sex (*fan xing*) and abstinence (*jin yu*) culture to China; this occurred just at the end of the Qing Dynasty when the Chinese race was suffering from a lack of self-confidence, which led to a blind admiration of the West. Western sexology, a newly developing science, had invented the term "tongxinglianzhe," and regarded it as a deviant disease. The May Fourth Movement, which deified Western

science, immediately adopted free love (*ziyou lian'ai*) and the one husband, one wife (*yi fu yi qi*) system, accepting Western homophobia unquestioningly and learning from Western science that the Chinese same-sex sexual tradition was shameless and a sign of backward, corrupt public morality (*shangfeng baisu*). The May Fourth Movement regarded the Chinese tradition as "feudalistic" (*fengjian*) and "backward" (*luowu*), and the Chinese themselves began to feel ashamed of their own Chinese culture and to disregard it. When they saw that Western science had already "proved" that homosexual love (*tongxing'ai*) was "deviant and pathological," this gave them the confidence to reject the Chinese same-sex sexual tradition under the banner of scientism and at the beginning of the Republican era, the still popular male custom (*nanfeng*) began to suffer condemnation. (Chou Wah-shan 1997:345)

Chou Wah-shan, however, is uncertain of the extent to which this "new view" has been accepted: "[E]ven up to the 1990s, none of the categories homo, hetero, or bisexual have taken root in the general population" (Chou Wah-shan 2000:22) and he states for Chinese society in general: "Sex is simply not the grounds on which to classify people" (ibid. 13). The contradiction in Chou Wah-shan's work lies in the fact that although he accepts Dikötter's thesis that "human bodies were seen as purely biological mechanisms through which hierarchical gender differences are naturalized and biologized" (ibid. 45), he also claims a very different cultural pattern even when he talks about Chinese *tongzhi* in present times and regards the classical tradition as still being alive. For Chou Wah-shan, the whole understanding of sexuality (*xing*) is a kind of Western import, inappropriate for describing not only the Chinese past but also of limited value for the Chinese present day.

There are, of course, many contradictions in his understanding of the historical discourse of same-sex desire: he concludes "it is only since the Republican period that China's long history of cultural tolerance of same-sex eroticism began to fade" and "Chinese intellectuals have accepted [...] a scientific discourse of biological determinations that marginalizes and pathologizes all non-reproductive sexuality" (ibid. 55); on the other hand he states "it is dangerous to romanticize traditional Chinese culture, as the cultural tolerance of same-sex eroticism appeared only within a classist and sexist hierarchy of unequal social relations – it is the male elite who have enjoyed the class-gender privilege of sexually dominating their social inferiors of both sexes" (ibid. 7).

Deborah Sang: Hybrid and Indigenous Discourses

Deborah Sang, with her research, challenged the findings of the previous authors: she claims that there was a much wider variety of discourses in Republican China, and that the pathologizing of homosexuality only occurred much later, particularly in the PRC (Sang 1996:246ff.):

> [Dikötter] assumes that discriminatory medical writings dominated or monopolized the modern discourse of homosexuality in Republican China. But the actual texts I've unearthed from this period speak to the contrary. The Republican discourse of homosexuality was, accurately speaking, characterized by a vibrant diversity in terms of genre, discipline, conceptualization and political stance. (ibid. 111-112)

In her PhD thesis, *The Emerging Lesbian: Female Same-Sex Desire in Modern Chinese Literature and Culture* (1996), in which she describes the discourse of female homosexuality in Republican China, Deborah Sang also refers to a significant Westernization: "Because of the massive Westernization of China on many fronts, which included the movement for women's liberation, lesbian desire in modern Chinese public discourse acquired the status of the sexual, and at the same time that of depravity" (ibid. 10). She later revises this view, becoming more involved with indigenization approaches. She describes the specific characteristics of the discourse in her article "Translating Homosexuality: The Discourse of *Tongxing'ai* in Republican China" (Sang 1999). One of her hypotheses regards the general involvement of male intellectuals with women's sexuality in Republican China, which she describes as an "attempt to grasp, contain and regulate female sexuality with conceptual means in the face of women's growing access to education and profession, as well as their increasing economic independence from the patriarchal family" (Sang 1996:11). That is, only when women finally gained recognition as "persons with integrity" (ibid.) during the Republican era did this lead to a counter-reaction on the part of men.

Deborah Sang points to the growing influence of sexual science as the main rationale for the discrimination against same-sex love in Republican China, describing the cultural interaction which took place when Western texts were introduced to a Chinese audience; this interaction could be divided into three dimensions, semantic levels, choice of sources with explanations (which Western sources/materials were translated/referred to; which were omitted), publishing units (medical journals/women journals/yellow press etc.).

Regarding the choice of sources, she writes: "It is precisely at a moment of choice, when a Chinese translator had the freedom to cite and appreciate certain materials rather than others, that we witness the possibility of cross-cultural understanding and coalition, rather than bleak, whole-scale [sic] Western cultural imperialism and imposition in the name of universality" (Sang 1999:276-277). At the semantic level, Sang emphasizes that *tongxinglian* or *tongxing'ai* both differ from the Western term "homosexual" in that they replace "sex" with "love" (*lian* or *ai*) (ibid. 278-279).

On the third point, Sang points out that many publications which dealt with love, sexuality and women, were not specialized medical journals but to a large degree "major urban journals on women, gender, education, love, relationships, and sex" (ibid. 281). Sang mentions, in addition, that "the material that Chinese intellectuals chose to translate covered a fascinating variety" (ibid. 282-283). She also makes clear that discourses which derived from the writings of Edward Carpenter and which appeared as Chinese translations in the 1920s, should not be described as counter-hegemonic discourses (as they were in the West) but that up to the 1920s and 1930s a broad variety of discourse could be observed which left "much room for the maneuvers of Chinese intellectuals who had access to theories of homosexuality written in other languages" (ibid. 282).

Shan Zai's "Same-Sex Erotic Love between Women"

In order to clarify the ways in which same-sex desire or love were treated in the public discourse in Republican China when the new terms such as *tongxing'ai* or tongxinglian appeared, it is essential to examine the different kinds of publications which dealt with the topic.[16]

One of the earliest articles to introduce the Western scientific terms, but which still differed from the Western discourse, was published in 1911 in the women's journal *Funü shibao*, one of the first glossy magazines for women. This article, entitled "Same-Sex Erotic Love between Women" (*Funü tongxing zhi aiqing*), was written in the vernacular but the author, Shan Zai, also included many modern expressions. One of the first striking differences in content from the traditional discourse is the equating of women's same-sex affection with men's same sex affection right at the beginning of the article; while classical terms differentiated strictly between the sexes, Shan Zai states: "When a woman falls in same-sex love with another woman, it is in reality the same as a man being fond of men's beauty and sex" (*funü yu nü tongxing zhi xiang lian'ai shi tongyu nanzi zhi hao nanse*) (Shan Zai 1911:36). It seems that the attribution of strict gender roles to men and women was no longer seen as an essential part of Chinese society; but although it is obvious that the role of women was gaining more respect in society in general, there was no sign of any growing tolerance toward same-sex relations among women. By using the well-known classical expression *nanse*, a fairly positive statement is made right at the beginning of the article, a sign perhaps that at the beginning of the twentieth century, same sex affection was not imbued with any particularly negative connotations. This does not mean, however, that Western terms, which require a more

---

[16] In spite of the previously mentioned limitations of the written urban discourse, the ways in which early articles dealt with the topic of female same-sex desire illustrate the background to these discussions: whether an assumed tolerance had existed before the "arrival of the Western discourse," what parts of the Western discourse were highlighted and which parts were rejected.

negative interpretation than that offered by Dikötter, had not already found their way into China: in the next paragraph, we can already find translations of Western concepts such as *qingyu zhi diandao* ("Inversion des Sexualtriebs" or inversion of sexual desire), *jibing* (disease) and *bianchang* (abnormality) which do not correspond to the term *nanse* or *nüse* but show that "the overall assumption about homosexuality is already negative" (see also ibid. 283).

Shan Zai goes on to speculate about homosexual love in schools, which is described as a "fashion" (*feng*) and advises the staff to consider ways of preventing such a "custom" even if "to prevent this fashion by abolishing the dorms in women's schools is easy to say but difficult to carry out." It is not, however, regarded as a terrible vice and the author, Shan Zai, states that such behavior, described as a "bad custom" (*e'xi*) (Shan Zai 1911:37), often occurs in prisons and in schools. In addition, the article also refers to the idea of a homosexual identity which defines an unchanging gay or lesbian existence and which did not exist at all in Chinese society: "Those females who have inverted erotic desire have no romantic feelings even if they see beautiful men" (ibid. 38). It is quite clear that, by 1911, new terms and ideas were being adopted, but this might have been due less to the dominance of Western science than to the new gender role models and the abolition of a more class-oriented society: "This new attention to gender performance among ordinary commoners went hand in hand with the project of status leveling, which extended [...] 'formal commoner equality' to include practically everyone in the empire" (Sommer 2000:310). There is nothing in this early article, however, to indicate that same-sex love was perceived in an extremely negative light as Dikötter would have us believe. And yet another author, Shen Zemin, whose translation of an article by Edward Carpenter "Affection in Education" from his work *The Intermediate Sex* in 1923 was published in the *Jiaoyu zazhi*, remarked "Why don't we gather the courage to recall our own school days! We have all gone through life in the schools" (Shen Zemin 1923:221-223, quoted in: Sang 1999:285).[17]

---

[17] In 1923, however, another article by Yan Shi which contained similar comments came to a very different conclusion: "All of us who had experience of living in a

Conclusion

The political and societal changes which shaped the first years of the Republican era led thus to new visibility for women and the striving for equality by urban middle-class women contributed towards the equating of male with female same-sex love/homosexuality. It would appear that there is a distinct correlation between the status of women in general and the social perception of women's same-sex relations, but in the 1920s, the rising awareness of female same-sex relations was described, using a medical and male-dominated approach, in terms ranging from the more "neutral" (nevertheless highly value-ridden) *nüzi de tongxing'ai* to the very derogatory, *yichang* and *biantai*, that is "abnormal" and "perverted." It could be argued that the efforts of the May Fourth generation to "liberate" opposite-sex relations led to a further weakening of the traditional acceptance of same-sex bonding, where the emphasis was on same-sex friendship and not on physical desire, with the result that same-sex love gradually came to be regarded in medical/sexual and negative terms. Sang also states that

> [w]hereas in previous ages, Chinese men were largely content to contain female homo-eroticism within women's quarters rather than prohibit it, in the Republican period male intellectuals found that it was no longer possible to contain it within inconsequential domestic seclusion, and that increasingly they had to explicitly criticize, regulate, or inhibit women's same-sex attraction. (Sang 1999:297)

and

> Female homo-eroticism broke out of its former negligibility and insignificance in the patriarchal familial organization of traditional China, to become distinctively associated with feminism on the one hand and psycho-biological abnormality on the other. (Sang 1996:2)

The newly coined terms show that a new understanding of same-sex love was developing. Both in the West and in China at the beginning

---

school could observe it. [...] However, people usually respond to such things with ridicule, and no one is seriously interested in studying the matter or in thinking of a remedy. This is very strange. We should be aware that same-sex love is a perversion of love (lian'ai de biantai)" (Yan Shi 1923:14-15).

of the nineteenth century, important changes regarding same-sex love and desire had taken place. In the West, a medically-oriented approach replaced religiously motivated discrimination against every form of non-marital sexuality. In China, however, in the past, a certain tolerance toward male same-sex sexuality had existed so long as this remained within the confines of a strictly class-oriented society. In Republican China, males and females achieved partial equality but the liberation movement which had led to this was directed against the old arranged forms of marriage, did not include homosexual love and was not considered part of legal marriage so that same-sex relations were marginalized.

The changes in Republican China should thus not be seen as resulting from a wholesale adoption of Western ideas, whether within the context of the imperialist enforcement of these ideas, or in terms of a more voluntary acceptance of them in an attempt to carry out technological and political reform in China; we may, however, assume that the contact with the West, even if seen as enforced, acted as a catalyst which accelerated some developments and slowed down others.

The discourse of "free love" led to the creation of the term *tongxinglian* in which the character for "love" (*lian*) appeared and not that for "sex." There is no evidence to suggest that it was the wholesale adoption of Western ideas which led to the later discrimination against homosexual love; this was rather more due to the ending of a specific Chinese tradition. It should also be remembered that these changes were most prevalent in regions shaped by global capitalism in pre-Communist China. The situation in the rural areas was entirely different, whether these areas were controlled by the Guomindang (Nationalist Party, GMD), by warlords or whether they were the so-called "liberated" areas under the rule of the Communists. The discourse of same-sex love in the 1920s and 1930s appeared in some well-known urban journals which had a high proportion of – male and female – readers among the young, educated middle class, but the economic hardships and the high rate of illiteracy existing at the time meant that these publications did not find a wide readership among the Chinese people in general.

References

Berry, Chris, Fran Martin, Queer'n'Asian on- and off- the Net: The Role of Cyberspace in Queer Taiwan and Korea, in: David Gauntlett (ed.), *Web Studies: Rewiring Media Studies for the Digital Age*, London 2000, pp. 74-81.
Boswell, John, *Christianity, Social Tolerance and Homosexuality*, Chicago, 1980.
Bravmann, Scott, *Queer Fictions of the Past: History, Culture and Difference*, Cambridge 1997.
Bray, Francesca, *Technology and Gender: Fabrics of Power in Late Imperial China*, Berkeley, Los Angeles, London 1997.
Chen, Mickey (Chen Junzhi), Tongzhi yingxiang yangwei guoji: Guonei baoshou qishi (The *Tongzhi*-Films are Gaining an International Reputation, but are Discriminated against within the Country), in: *China Times*, 4 April 1998, online-edition: http://www.chinatimes.com/news/papers/ctimes/cforum/87040405.htm (accessed 4 April 1998).
Cheng Hao, *Renlei de xing shenghuo* (The Sexual Life of Mankind), Shanghai 1934.
Chi Ta-Wei (Ji Dawei) (ed.), *Ku'er kuanghuanjie* (Queer Carnival: A Reader of the Queer Literature in Taiwan), Taipei 1997a.
Chi Ta-Wei (Ji Dawei) (ed.), *Ku'er qishilu* (Queer Archipelago: A Reader of the Queer Discourses in Taiwan), Taipei 1997b.
Chou Wah-shan (Zhou Huashan), *Houzhimin tongzhi* (Postcolonial *Tongzhi*), Hong Kong 1997.
Chou Wah-shan, *Tongzhi Politics of Same-Sex Eroticism in Chinese Societies*, New York, London, Oxford 2000.
Damm, Jens, *Ku'er* vs. *Tongzhi* – Diskurse der Homosexualität: Über das Entstehen sexueller Identitäten im glokalisierten Taiwan und im postkolonialen Hongkong, in: *cathay skripten* (Ruhr University Bochum) 16:2 (2000).
Damm, Jens, *Homosexualität und Gesellschaft in Taiwan, 1945-1995*, Münster 2003.

Dean, Carolyn, Scott Bravmann, Queer Fictions of the Past: History, Culture, and Difference, in: *History and Theory* 38:1 (1999), pp. 122-131.

D'Emilio, John, Capitalism and Gay Identity, in: Ann Barr Snitow, Christine Stanswell, Sharon Thompson (eds.), *The Powers of Desire: The Politics of Sexuality*, New York 1983, pp. 100-113.

Dikötter, Frank, *Sex, Culture and Modernity in China: Medical Science and the Construction of Sexual identities in the Early Republican Period*, London 1995.

Duberman, Martin, Martha Vicinus, George Chauncey, *Hidden from History: Reclaiming the Gay and Lesbian Past*, New York 1989.

Fairbank, John K., Teng Ssu-yu, *China's Response to the West: A Documentary Survey, 1839-1923*, Cambridge/MA 1954.

Foucault, Michel, *The History of Sexuality*, vol. 1 (An Introduction), New York 1978.

Furth, Charlotte, *A Flourishing Yin: Gender in China's Medical History*, Berkeley, Los Angeles, London 1999.

Furuya Toyoko (Wei Sheng, trans.), Tongxing'ai zai nüzi jiaoyu shang de xin yiyi (The New Meaning of Same-Sex Love in Women's Education), in: *Fünu zazhi* 11:6 (1925), p. 1065.

Hawley, John (ed.), *Postcolonial Queer: Theoretical Intersections*, Albany/NY 2001.

Hayes, Jarrod, Queer Resistance to (Neo)-Colonialisms in Algeria, in: Hawley 2001, pp. 79-97.

Hinsch, Bret, *Passions of the Cut Sleeve: The Male Homosexual Tradition in China*, Berkeley, Los Angeles, London 1990.

Jagose, Annemarie, Queer Theory, in: *Australian Humanities Review* (December 1996), online-edition: http://www.lib.latrobe.edu.au/AHR/archive/Issue-Dec-1996/jagose.html (accessed 7 July 1997).

Jie Chen, Ga pengyou zhi e'xi (The Evil Habit of Bonding with a Friend), in: Wang Shubi (ed.), *Shanghai heimu yiqian zhong* (One Thousand Secret Dealings in Shanghai), Shanghai ^{4}1939.

Karsch-Haack, Ferdinand, *Das gleichgeschlechtliche Leben der Ostasiaten: Chinesen, Japaner, Koreer*, München 1906.

Ke Ruiming, *Taiwan fengyue* (Taiwanese Customs), Taipei 1991.

Lin, Yu-sheng, Radical Iconoclasm in the May Fourth Period and the Future of Liberalism, in: Benjamin I. Schwartz (ed.), *Reflections on the May Fourth Movement: A Symposium*, Cambridge/MA 1973, pp. 23-58.

Lin, Yu-sheng, *The Crisis of Chinese Consciousness: Radical Anti-Traditionalism in the May Fourth Era*, Madison 1979.

Lyotard, Jean-François, *The Postmodern Condition: A Report on Knowledge*, Manchester 1984, online available: http://www.marxists.org/reference/subject/philosophy/works/fr/lyotard.htm (accessed 1 June 2003).

Manifesto of 1996 Chinese Tongzhi Conference, 8 December 1996, http://sqzm14.ust.hk/hkgay/news/manifesto.html (accessed 5 August 2001).

Mao Yibo, Zai lun xing'ai yu youyi (Yet Again on Sexual Love and Friendship), in: *Xin nüxing* 3:11 (1928), pp. 1257-1258.

McIntosh, Mary, The Homosexual Role, in: *Social Problems* 16 (1968), pp. 182-193.

Müller, Klaus, Sprachregelungen: Die Codierung des „Homosexuellen" in der Sexualpathologie des 19. Jahrhunderts, in: *Forum Homosexualität und Literatur* (April 1988), pp. 75-92.

Nivard, Jaqueline, Women and the Women's Press: The Case of the Ladies' Journal (Funü Zazhi), 1915-1931, in: *Republican China* 10:1 (1984), pp. 37-55.

Padgug, Robert, Sexual Matters: On Conceptualizing Sexuality in History, in: Radical History Review 20 (1979), pp. 3-23, reproduced in: Stein, Edward (ed.), *Forms of Desire: Sexual Orientation and the Social Constructionist Controversy*, New York 1990, pp. 43-67.

(Pan Guangdan, trans.) Havelock, Ellis, *Xing xinlixue* (The Psychology of Sex), Beijing 1946, reprint Beijing 1987.

Ruan Fang Fu, *Sex in China: Studies in Sexology in Chinese Culture*, New York, London 1991.

Samshasha (Xiaomingxiong), *Zhongguo tongxing'ai shilu* (Historical Reports on Homo-Eroticism in China), revised edition, Hong Kong ²1994 (¹1984).

Sang, Tze-lan Deborah, *The Emerging Lesbian: Female Same-Sex Desire in Modern Chinese Literature and Culture*, PhD Dissertation, Berkeley 1996.

Sang, Tze-lan Deborah, Translating Homosexuality: The Discourse of *Tongxing' ai* in Republican China, in: Liu, Lydia H. (ed.), *Tokens of Exchange: The Problem of Translation in Global Circulations*, Durham 1999, pp. 276-304.

Scott, Joan W., *Gender and Politics of History*, New York 1988.

Shan Zai, Funü nü tongxing zhi aiqing (Same-Sex Love between Women), in: *Funü shibao* 1:7 (1911), pp. 36-38.

Shen Zemin (trans.), Tongxing'ai yu jiaoyu (Same-Sex Love and Education), in: *Jiaoyu zazhi* 15:8 (1923), pp. 221-223.

Sommer, Matthew H., *Sex, Law and Society in Late Imperial China*, Stanford 2000.

Tao Wu, Mo jing dang (The Mirror Rubbing Gang), in: *Shanghai funü nie jingtai* (A Mirror of Shanghai Women's Sin) (Shanghai 1918), pp. 60-65.

Wang Chengpin, *Qingchun de xing jiaoyu* (Sex Education for Youth), Shanghai 1939.

Wang Shunu, *Zhongguo changji shi* (The History of China's Prostitution), Shanghai 1988.

Weixingshiguanzhaizhu (pseud.), *Zhongguo tongxinglian mishi* (The Secret History of Homosexuality in China), Hong Kong 1964.

White, Hayden, *Metahistory: The Historical Imagination in Nineteenth-Century Europe*, Baltimore, London 1973.

Wu Ruiyuan, *Niezi de yinji: Taiwan jindai nanxing "tongxinglian" de fuxian, 1970-1990* (As a "Bad Son": The Emergence of Modern "Homosexuals" in Taiwan, 1970-1990), MA thesis National Central University, Hsinchu 1998.

Xie Se (trans.), Nü xuesheng de tongxing'ai (Same-Sex Love among Female Students), in: *Xin Wenhua* 6 (1927), pp. 57-74.

Yan Shi, Nan nü de geli yu tongxing'ai (The Segregation between the Sexes and Same-Sex Love), in: *Funü zazhi* 9:5 (1923), pp. 14-15.

Zhang Jingsheng (Levy, Howard S., trans.), *Xing shi* (Sex Histories: China's First Treatise on Sex Education), Yokohama 1967.

Zhu Yunying, Yi Jiayue, Zhongguo de xing yu jiaoyu wenti (The Problem of Sex Education in China), in: *Jiaoyu zazhi* 15:8 (1923), pp. 22151-22161.

Wanting Some: Commodity Desire and the Eugenic Modern Girl

Tani E. Barlow

The educated, Chinese, urban consumer class created a means of self-expression in the 1920s that I call vernacular sociology. In vernacular sociology, modernists conveyed their novel experiences of body, mind, emotion, eros, and social life. A sophisticated expression of internationally viable social theories, vernacular sociology's categories formed an "adaptable platform" (Smith/Sako Teruhito n.d.), rationalizing what became familiar Republican-era, colonial-modernist class and gender norms. Vernacular sociology explained and legitimated the ascendant elite's new social relations and social practices. It also provided the medium where academic sociological projects thrived. Vernacular sociology and academic sociology (the relation of vernacular and professional is historically complex) stabilized the claim that human behavior has its roots in natural evolution. Both high and low sociology consequently presumed that the female of the human species was a product of natural evolution and was particularly open to social remolding or social evolutionary restructuring. But vernacular sociology particularly dwelt on a social scientific ideology of "natural manhood" and "natural womanhood" that would pervade elite social opinion in the 1920s.

The intellectual content of Chinese vernacular sociology is consequently this essay's central concern. A decade before the canonization of progressive feminism, vernacular sociology had already laid down its distinctive intellectual claims.[1] Particularly in the

---

I would like to thank Carola Krüger, Brian Hammer, and Kristy Leissle for their editorial support and Ruri Ito, sociologist, for providing an insider perspective.

[1] The ideological subject "woman" under consideration here is not the woman of theoretical feminism as such. Arguments for women's liberation did eventually come to rest on social scientific justifications similar to these during the late 1920s and more centrally in the 1930s. See my chapter 3, "Progressive Chinese

heroic era of the 1920s, in the United States, China and elsewhere, the intellectual category of women in sociology formed a matrix where, theorists held, nature and culture may once have fitted into a seamless entity. In women, the question of how natural development and social development mesh together could be hypothetically resolved. What women want and what essential contributions women make to social evolution informed many of the new social sciences that educated people and intellectuals, male and female, found useful. Though distinctive in relation to older traditions, the idea that women's social being is mediated through their natural essence is commonplace in popular sociological traditions everywhere, not just in China. After all, as sociologist Lester Ward, possibly the most regularly cited US social theorist in China during the 1920s, put it, in social evolutionary terms life *is* woman (Ward/Xia Gaizun n.d.).

Complicating any intellectual history of colonial modern social life is the fact that sociology's hallmark is the commodity. The iconic woman who appears in transnational corporate[2] copy and in images that advertise commodities like Kotex, Moddess, and Comfort pads marketed in Chinese cities is, I will contend, the "natural woman" sociologists and particularly vernacular sociologists were describing. Eventually it will be possible to link commodities, advertising images, and the consumer herself to everyday practices like shopping in the department store or going to the beauty parlor. The social history of elite female consumption, however, has an intellectual and ideological as well as a social content. That intellectual content is vernacular sociology. A brief look at the natural woman in Chinese transnational advertising suggests that the commodity advertising image and vernacular sociology mutually reinforced a class ideology formation.

Feminism," Barlow 2003. Some of my interest in sociology derives in fact from my investigation into foundational Chinese feminism.

[2] A typical "Index of Advertisers" in *Funü zazhi (The Ladies' Journal)*, October 1930, listed twenty-three sponsors, eighteen of which are transnational corporations. They are Allen & Hanburys Ltd., Charles Bahond, Crème Simon, Colgate-Palmolive-Peet Co., Crescent Baking Powder, Dr. Williams Medicine Co., Eastman Kodak, Eibb's Dentifrice, Horlicks Malted Milk, Melchers & Co., Mrs. Winslow's Syrup, Modess, Pepsodent Co., Society of Chemical Industry in Basle, Staycomb, Tangee, Victor Talking Machine, and Viyella.

Foundational Social Science

What are Sociology and Vernacular Sociology?

Sociology is the science of modernity. Of the social sciences it particularly expresses the view that "society" is real, tangible space which individuals occupy and where norms, conflicts and relationships are mediated in family and other social institutions. This is a circular definition since sociology relies for proof on a ground that it assumes. Circularity does not deter its usefulness. In this regard sociology is the modernist's tool. It substantiates the theoretical claim that society is an *a priori* and that the social contract among individuals regulates it. The professional sociologist's academic work – the social survey, for instance – not only gives information about everyday life. It also illustrates substantially how the constituent forces of societies, e.g., class, gender, social pathology, race and ethnicity, and existing social institutions can be scientifically ascertained and described. Because we still presume the reality and tangibility of society and draw on the insights of sociologists past and present, my pointing out the instability of sociology's core assumptions does not deny its effect on us. This section of the paper suggests working definitions for what sociology is in relation to other conventions of thinking.

Yung-chen Chiang has correctly argued that "social science research in China during the 1930s constituted part of a larger phenomenon that occurred simultaneously in the United States and Western Europe" (Chiang Yung-chen 2001:1). Chiang focuses on the canonization, institutionalization, and legacy of Chinese- and US-sponsored Chinese client enterprises that linked social science to social engineering projects. It is a great story. Chiang reveals a well-financed Rockefeller Foundation effort to make the modern Chinese social science disciplines into instruments of policy and social engineering. Chiang is not concerned in his study with the question of how earlier sociological presuppositions colored social and intellectual or ideological norms in the 1920s. But his focus on the history of sociology's institutionalization opens up a related question of what it was that – prior to the infusion of Rockefeller Foundation funds – fascinated Chinese intellectuals so much. What ideas in sociology did they find so valuable that they were willing to struggle hard against many odds to institutionalize the university discipline of sociology in the 1930s?

Posing this question is another way of asking what modern intellectuals meant when they said "sociology" and of distinguishing general social theory (or vernacular sociology) from the professional sociology that Chiang writes about. This is a problem in historical genealogy of knowledge and the way it coalesces into differential positions. The example of Yan Fu (and nineteenth-century Chinese social theory generally) will illustrate what I mean. Evaluating Yan's importance in the 1920s and 1930s provides a way of understanding how Chinese sociology came into focus historically. In 1933, as academic sociology was flowering into what Chiang calls an era of "academic entrepreneurship and social engineering," the eminent sociologist-anthropologist Lin Yaohua (Lin Yueh-hua) published a long article. Entitled "Yan Fu's Social Thinking" (*Yan Fu shehui sixiang*), it appeared in the Yanjing University journal, *Sociology Scholarly World (Shehui xuejie)* (Lin Yaohua 1933). In part, Lin's article explained how and why Yan Fu had come first to translate T.H. Huxley's *Evolution and Ethics (Tian yan lun)*, J.S. Mill's *System of Logic* (translated into Chinese as *Mill's Logic [Mule minxue]*), Herbert Spencer's *Study of Sociology (Qunxue yiyan)*, J.S. Mill's *On Liberty (Qun yi quan jie lun)*, Adam Smith's *Wealth of Nations (Yuan fu)*, Montesquieu's *L'esprit des Lois (Fa yi)*, E. Jenk's *A Short History of Politics (Shehui tongquan)*, and W.S. Jevons *Primer of Logic (Mingxue qianshuo)*. The article's second objective was to elaborate the great ideas in contemporary European social thinking – evolutionism, positivism, utilitarianism – Yan Fu had absorbed and transmitted. And a third object was to differentiate between Yan Fu's theories of Chinese history and Europe's, where the theories had originated. At issue was the question of how Yan Fu's social theory had contributed to Chinese sociological thought in the 1930s. Lin Yaohua suggests that the gulf separating Yan Fu's utopian anticipations from the actual modern university system that had sprung up in the China was too vast to bridge (ibid. 77).

Apparently, then, the effort to establish a history of the origins of "real sociology" in China originated at least as early as the 1930s. The effort to nail down the origin probably coincided roughly with the growth period of professional sociology. No doubt a detailed history of the attitudes that professional sociologists in the 1930s held toward Yan Fu's thinking will help to clarify the perceived stakes. But the point I want to draw here, provisionally at least, is that measuring the impact of Yan Fu's evolutionism, positivism, and utilitarianism on Chinese social science has continued to divide historians of sociology right down to the present.

The standard work on the history of Chinese sociology is Yang Yabin's *Modern Chinese Sociology (Jindai Zhongguo shehuixue)* published in 2001 (Yang Yabin 2001). She simply asserts without too much discussion that having been the first Chinese thinker who truly understood Western theory, Yan Fu is the de facto pioneer of the Chinese sociological tradition (ibid. 7, 29). Yang rests her case on a number of factors. First, she stressed Yan Fu's anti-feudalism and Darwinian evolutionism, and his grasp of Herbert Spencer's social evolutionary theories. Second, her rationale for making Yan the founder of Chinese sociology, as opposed to simply an important innovator, grows out of priorities which Yan himself established. Yan accorded the individual an *a priori* status and made the individual into the foundation of social groupings, including the nation. He also directly linked social evolution of groups to natural evolution, which set up a chain reaction in which social progress, wealth, power, and democracy were causally linked. Finally, he began the process of translating the analytic English term "society," the central concept in "sociology" however it is defined. Yang follows Feng Youlan closely. She stresses Feng's emphasis on the importance of Yan Fu's concept of *qunxue*, a precursor term for *shehuixue*. She argued further that because each term embodies a contradiction between individual and collectivity typical of all sociologies, Yan Fu is a sociologist. Finally, Yan Fu's *qunxue* and latter-day *shehuixue* share the classic contradiction of subject and object. While the object of social science is "society," society is not objective; social scientists are both disinterested scientific observers and the foundational social elements, subject and object of their own investigations (ibid. 44-48).

Arguing a different view on Yan Fu is Zheng Hangsheng and Li Yingsheng's *Twentieth Century Chinese Sociology (Ershishiji Zhongguo de shehuixue)* (Zheng/Li 1999). In this volume, Zheng and Li rethink some of the inherited, core problems in the history of sociology (lamenting at how few studies exist at all)[3] and introduce new materials for consideration. Their primary concern lies with reorienting the terms of the study of Chinese sociology's history. To do this they ask questions that are both theoretical and historical. When, they point out, you ask "what is society?" and "what is sociology?" simultaneously, you cannot disregard the complexities of historical periodization. Also you cannot get around the stumbling block that sociologists are both the composite members of society (classical Comteanism) and social scientists. Zheng and Li's objective when they seek to trouble the fit between theory and history in sociology is that, like me, they are particularly interested in the context for ideas and particularly what historical context conditioned how sociology entered the world of Chinese intellectual life and who is responsible for the shape which sociology took in the early twentieth century. These are, I would say, questions about the conditions for thinking as much as the content of thought. At the very least, they situate the content of thinking in relation to the conditions of thinking.

As for Yan Fu, Zheng and Li point out that Zhang Taiyan's translation of Kishimoto Yoshii's *Sociology* had already established the term *shehuixue* in Chinese before Yan introduced the notion of *qunxue*; and, moreover, given Yan Fu's general level of scholarship it was impossible for him to have been unaware that a standard term existed already in Chinese, and among Japanese sociologists. In other words, though Yan may have been the most prominent introducer of Western ideas, contemporaries including Zhang Taiyan and Han Xianshou had as early as 1889 already been involved in the transplantation

---

[3] Ibid. 4. They note Sun Benwen, *Contemporary Chinese Sociology (Dangdai Zhongguo shehuixue)* for pre-Liberation and Han Mingmo, Chinese Sociology *(Zhongguo shehuishi)* in addition to Yang Yabin, *Modern Chinese Sociology (Jindai Zhongguo shehuixue)* for the post-Mao era.

of sociology into Chinese learned circles (ibid. 63-64). Rather than fetishizing Yan Fu as the founder of sociology, that is, Zheng and Li refer to his work as "theoretical activity" (*lilun huodong*) and Yan Fu as the first to systematically promote sociological *styles* of thinking in China. They qualify Yan Fu's impact. They situate him within a larger intellectual history, focusing on his old school tendency to transplant a style of sociological inquiry that would be accessible to traditional scholars.[4]

Yan's conservative strategy, according to Zheng and Li, means that Chinese sociology must trace its roots not just from Yan Fu's Anglo-Saxon ideas but also Zhang Taiyan and the Japanese tradition which Zhang, like many others, was also promoting (ibid. 63).[5] In the late 1880s the influence of Toyama Masakazu, Ichikawa Genzo, Kōtoku Shūsui, Fukui Jun, Nishikawa Kojiro, and Murai Tomoyoshi into Chinese and Chinese social theory means that the Japanese discussions of "society" have to be considered as contributors to the Chinese canon.[6] The Chinese sociological tradition was multipolar. Players other than Yan Fu, in translations made from languages other than England's English, make the direct line of descent merely a convenient fiction.

It may be more accurate then to say that in the 1920s, sociology, in the crude sense of a mode of thinking about society, represented a richly heterogeneous intellectual world in the process of coalescing into institutional modernity. Pre-professional thinking is crucial. As the discipline of sociology coalesced, it did so, in other

---

[4] For a discussion of Yan Fu's preference for making up neologisms in spite of the existence of standard terms, see Wright 2001. See particularly p. 245 which notes that "Yan Fu's use of neologisms had little influence on the terminology which flowed, in contrast to the *ideas* in his translations, which were enormously influential."

[5] Zheng and Li are interested in the translation, institutionalization, and basic schools of Chinese sociology. They are particularly convincing regarding the basic difference between the Marxist schools and the Comtean or bourgeois sociologists. Their remarks on Yan Fu are a small element of their argument.

[6] According to Smith and Sako four competing words for "society" were in play in theoretical Japanese between 1860 and the 1880s, when "shakai" (*shehui*) came to prevail. These were "nakama" (*zhongjian*), "yononaka" (*shizhong*) and "kousai" (*jiaoji*) (Smith/Sako Teruhito n.d.).

words, not in agonistic defiance of traditionalism but rather in relation to a rather wildly divergent set of theories all claiming somehow to be sociological. Or at the very least, it took shape in a situation where "society" had already become the presumptive platform for truthful generalization and a sturdy means of making analytic sense of the chaotic political and economic changes that semi-feudal, semi-colonialism represents. The ideas in play were most certainly sociological in nature, as the problem of how to classify Yan Fu makes clear. The immediate question for me is what to call material that Lin Yaohua, Yang Yabin, and Zheng and Li might all disdain to include in the canon of Chinese sociology's founding documents. They belong in the category of "theoretical activity," in other words, but I find it useful to collect them under the umbrella term of "vernacular sociology."

The discipline of Chinese sociology mushroomed in a larger medium of modernist vernacular thinking about society and social life. This medium, like rich compost, nurtured professionalization. But it also slightly preceded academic sociology and continued independently around it, forming a preserve where educated people who did not read these new professional sociologies or who turned away from Comtean sociology could engage with social theories and social truths. Commodity advertising texts and images ratified the platitudes and branded them with a progressive stamp of approval. Vernacular sociology is, in other words, quite "sociological" in the sense that Comte, Spencer, J.S. Mill, Adam Smith, Montesquieu as well as Endo, Marx, Toyama, Ward, Nishikawa, Robinson, Key, Bogardus, Blackmar, Thompson – the famous and the infamous – were all promiscuously available to intelligent and literate men and women in Chinese treaty port society, particularly in the 1920s.

The media of vernacular sociology's dissemination were journals of enlightened opinion. Looser, less focused on professionalizing the social sciences, and providing an outlet for major transnational advertising campaigns, the commercial media of mainstream elite journals formed a lively matrix where Pan Guangdan, for instance, began his publishing career. Pan, a Qinghua University graduate and eugenic sociologist, became one of China's most influential social scientists. Pan published his first major paper, "Feng Xiaoqing: A

Study in Narcissism" (*Feng Xiaoqing: Yijian ying'ai zhi yanjiu*) in 1922 in *The Ladies' Journal (Funü zazhi)* under the title "Study of Feng Xiaoqing" (*Feng Xiaoqing kao*) (Pan Guangdan 2000:1-66). The piece was a historical psychoanalytic case study modeled on Freud's investigations of Leonardo and Moses, but using a Chinese, historical female figure. Later when the essay came to the attention of professional academic Liang Rengong at Qinghua University, Pan revised and expanded it. The relationship between the venue of mainstream elite publications like *The Ladies' Journal* and the professionalization of intellectuals like Pan is significant. (So is the haunting commercial quality of the essay's illustration of a woman gazing into a vanity mirror.)[7]

In the years between 1898 when Yan Fu's translations began appearing and the founding and gradual consolidation of major university sociology programs at Yanjing (1922), Fudan (1925), Guanghua and Qinghua (1926), Central Zhonghang (1927), Dongbei (1928), Shanghai Laodong (1929), and in particular Nankai (1927-1931), the difference between what qualified as sociology and what did not qualify seems to have shifted.[8] If we draw a line between general ideas about society and the profession of academic sociology, (many beholden to US joint ventures with elite sociology projects in the United States) then perhaps pre-sociology or vernacular sociology is the true descendent of Yan Fu-style "theoretical activity," and professional sociology is more indebted to the international model. By international model I mean missionary social service organizing and curricular and research imperatives emphasizing social control. Vernacular sociology seems on the other hand to have retained an elite general interest focus on racial improvement, national characteristics, the great abstractions of enlightened social thought (e.g. subject and object, human nature, etc.), and the question of women's will and personality.

---

[7] The connection of the scholarly topic of narcissism, this erotic image and its resemblance to popular advertising images of women looking into the hand mirror indicate the spectral commodity, as well.

[8] For a discussion of the processes of institutionalization, see Zheng/Li 1999:70-71 and Chiang Yung-chen 2001:46-128.

Where are Women in Sociology?

The woman question (*funü wenti*) played a key role in May Fourth cultural politics. Yet over the 1920s, as sociology was institutionalized, the woman question did not transit out of vernacular and into professional sociology. Free-wheeling vernacular sociology and its big-picture philosophic discussions of eroticism, women's will and emotions, its emphasis on liberation and subjectivity, its concern with woman at the intersection of natural and social evolution, eventually gelled into a systematic doctrine, a "progressive feminism." By the 1930s, progressive feminism had become public policy and statecraft in the social process, which Christina Gilmartin has documented in her *Engendering the Chinese Revolution: Radical Women, Communist Politics, and Mass Movements in the 1920s* (Gilmartin 1995). The iconography of the *xin chao nülang* (new wave girl), which I will argue is the ideal female model for most sociological projects, out-survived the apotheosis of professional sociology.

The commercial canon of progressive feminism, published at the end of the 1920s and particularly the early 1930s, is Mei Sheng's *Zhongguo funü wenti taolunji (Collected Discussion of the Woman Question)* (Mei Sheng n.d.). This huge collection consolidated the canon of common sense feminism of the era, indicated by its commercial success, which is to say that people bought enough reprints of key articles to keep a press reprinting it. But it is noteworthy that in 1925, five years earlier, Gao Ersong and Gao Erbai (central figures in the progressive sociology movement) contributed an important summary to *Sociology Magazine (Shehuixue zazhi)*, then in its second year of publication. The Gao brothers' stated objective was to systematize the vast and chaotic archive on women that had accumulated since 1920 (Gao/Gao 1925). In their annotated and selected bibliography, the brothers laid out the typology that Mei Sheng's gigantic mainstreaming project would later recycle with additions in the form of the *congshu* (compendium), to retail selected canonical texts. The 1925 Gao bibliography is the only systematic discussion of the category woman in social terms that I have yet found in a professional sociology publication, that is a journal attached to a formal, academic university department of Sociology.[9]

Not surprising in light of core arguments in Chinese progressive feminism, the Gao bibliography selected to annotate the work of standard figures like Luo Jialun, Feng Fei, Li Da, Gao Shan, Se Lu, Xia Gaizun, and Gao Xian. Along with professional sociologists like Pan Guangdan and Sun Benwen, the work of Luo, Feng, Li, and the others is abundantly represented in *The Ladies' Journal* and then again in Mei Sheng's republication project.[10] But vernacular sociology's formal interest in erotic desire, marriage and divorce, love, and women's rights were hived off into progressive feminism. In professional sociology, a new set of questions took center stage. These scholarly preoccupations did presume along with popular social evolutionary theory that the question of sexual difference was central to social organization. But professional sociological studies recoded the institutions of social life. Instead of desire, sociology considered population. Sociologists wrote histories of Chinese attitudes toward widow chastity instead of first-hand accounts of the injustices widows experienced. Surveys of social attitudes and theories of socialization preoccupy the professionals. In 1925, the Gaos were bemoaning the fact no one had yet organized the huge volume of writing about the centrality of women in social life published in the previous half decade and were politely groaning that the responsibility had fallen on them. They surveyed hundreds of pertinent articles. They noted the existences of thousands of potential bibliographic entries that should be considered sociology in the future. To my knowledge it never was.

Vernacular Sociology and the Idiom of Modern Subjectivity

Vernacular sociology in the 1920s is the idiom of modern subjectivity. By idiom of modern subjectivity I mean that vernacular

---

[9] *Shehuixuekan (Sociology Journal), Shehuixue zazhi (Sociology Magazine), Zhongguo shehuishe (Chinese Sociology Press), Shehuixuejie (Sociology World)* etc.

[10] Only Luo Jialun continued on to become a professional sociologist so far as I know; also I have not uncovered any of these other figures in sociology journals as yet.

sociology structured modernists' foundational understanding of personality, social reality, historical processes, the role of natural processes and natural science in social relationships and institutions. Characterizing it as such helps to explain why in vernacular sociology we find the woman question a persistent presence even after professional sociologists appear to have sidelined it. I think we underestimate in a formal sense the ideological content of elite preoccupation with theories of social processes. *The Ladies' Journal* for example delivered five special topic issues in 1922 and 1923, each focusing on a key social question. Marriage, the women's movement, prostitution, family reform and free mate selection, as many critics have pointed out, were pressing matters for the young men cultural revolutionaries of the May Fourth generation and were a staple issue in vernacular fiction, too.[11] Particularly in the marriage and mate selection issues (as in the later issue on divorce), a mix of genre is apparent. Contributions range from personal testimonials to biographical accounts of social tragedies, from descriptions of model social relations which educated elite women and men were establishing to fiery indictments of socially devolutionary practices like prostitution, bride purchase, child wedding, deficiencies in the breeding populations and so on.

Certainly literary writing also famously conditioned self-expression. Yet at the foundation of modern literature, you find many of the same presuppositions regarding natural and social evolution that structure vernacular sociology or elite commonsensical norms. Reading fiction or vernacular sociology as exclusively the projection of self-interest, leaves out the larger social and ideological forces that actually conditioned the thinkable, factors that constrain and enable thought and self-invention. The preeminent position of Qu Qiubai, a founder of Marxist sociology and Maoist literary theories of popular culture is one example. Another example is Zhou Jianren, who is both a literary theoretician and a vernacular, eugenic sociologist. My point

---

[11] They are as follows: *Funü yundong hao* (Issue on the Women's Movement) 9:1 (1923), *Jiating gexin hao* (Issue on Family Reform) 9:9 (1923), *Changji wenti hao* (Issue on Prostitution Problems) 9:3 (1923), *Pei'ou xuanze hao* (Issue on Free Mate Selection) 9:11 (1923), and *Hunyin wenti hao* (Issue on Marriage Problems) 8:4 (1922).

is simply that the vehicle of vernacular sociology offered educated elites a means for rethinking foundational social verities in relation to economic and social currents in the immediate post-Imperial decades. The new intellectuals reevaluated core experiences. When they did so, they drew on the natural scientific and social scientific categories that the translators Yan Fu, Tan Shougong (who rendered Endo Ryukichi into Chinese in 1920), and many others had made available in their synthetic interpretations of evolutionism, positivism, and utilitarianism. Vernacular sociology is the ideological framework conditioning literary self-expression.

In this respect, the "self" that fiction writers and theoreticians speculated about and described may also have been grounded in that flexible platform of vernacular sociology. For instance, there is no doubt that mate selection, marriage, divorce, birth control, and prostitution are matters that particularly concerned ambitious young men in the 1920s. As new institutions (e.g., universities, commercial careers, modern governmentality) offered career and social possibilities unheard of before the Republican era, social exigencies made it difficult to marry and procreate in the old ways. The self-interest of young men, however, does not exhaust the problem of why the patterns of citation draw so regularly on the same set of speculative social theorists: Letourneau, Gobineau, Lester Ward, E.S. Bogardus, William J. Robinson, Nagai Sen, Comte, Huxley, Ellen Key, Ellwood, Havelock Ellis, and Sanger, among others.[12] Social Darwinism and its associated "social sciences" of eugenics, speculative or "cosmic" sociology à la Lester Ward, anthropology, social reform, and so on define avenues of self-interest. Qiao Feng, Se Lu, and Zhou Jianren were intellectuals. They immersed themselves in the diffuse ideas of social science that had been unfolding in a global theatre of academic racism for decades. They spoke in the idiom of social science about social processes like "socialization" itself. They understood human attributes in naturalistic terms. They took positions for or against theories about heritable IQ, sexual instincts, primary and secondary sexual characteristics, hormones, criminality, deviant sexuality, childhood

---

[12] A useful list of standard translations of sociologist's names is Sun Benwen 1930:1-13.

development, sexual maturation and, reproductive psychology. They positioned themselves in relation to social structures, social functions and so on (see Burgess 1925). In other words, as much as they were ambitious men on the make, they were also positioned and defined within governing ideas of their day. They understood themselves in those modernist terms.

Taking an overview of vernacular sociology in 1920s Chinese urban elite publications reveals several core preoccupations. These included (1) the relation of social and natural sciences in evolution, (2) eugenic science, and (3) the primal relationship between individual and society (the social contract). Vernacular sociology is not confined to these topics. Nor do these topics apply exclusively to it, for they also trouble the foundational characteristics of the discipline of sociology. But these were key concerns in the ongoing discussions over how modern social norms should be justified. Like moderns everywhere, Chinese popular elite opinion justified newness in relation to social evolution. Their near obsessional concern with demonstrating how personal choices were consistent (or inconsistent) with biological and social norms took on a vernacular tone. In these preoccupations, young men and some women spoke authoritatively. At times they wrote directly, under their own name. Many times they wrote through a translation, for translators frequently listed themselves as the "author" of an essay and assigned what they called the "original" author an inconspicuous second billing.

A simple example of the relation that vernacular theorists struck between social and natural sciences in the dogma of evolutionism is Wei Xin's interpretation of Letourneau's thoughts on the evolutionary production of divorce. This argument that social institutions are correlated to natural evolutionary drives appeared in 1922 under Wei's name rather than the "original author's" name and was titled "The Evolution of Divorce" (*Lihun de jinhua*) (Letourneau/Wei Xin 1922). Another essay of Wei Xin, "The Material Basis of Life" (*Shengming zhi wuzhi de jichu*), appeared in the same year. It explains regards how to theorize life itself from the ground base upward, from nature into social order, from natural sciences into sociological truth

(Wei Xin 1922).[13] Another good example which puts women into the position of social agents of social evolution is Ke Shi's essay "The Responsibility of Women in Evolution" (*Funü zai jinhua zhong de renwu*) (Ke Shi 1922). Ke drew widely on familiar authorities from Marie Stopes to Thompson's *The Evolution of Sex*. In these popular social evolutionary arguments, the starting point is a truism. The truism holds that natural science, i.e. Darwinian science, has already demonstrated how evolution is both natural (since humans belong to the mammal family which propagates bisexually) and social. Attached to this truism is the belief that good natural selection and sexual selection create the conditions for rapid species development.

Essays like these comfortably invoke natural science as a means of explaining how social processes work and why they work on the analogy of chemistry, biology, and physics. Evolution of species becomes an analogy for explaining the evolution of social institutions like marriage and divorce. Certainly this sort of vernacular sociological argument relied on popular renditions and translations of the views of early sociologists like Thomas Huxley (Huxley/Gao Xingruo 1923). But it drew as well on explicitly naturalistic or natural science expositions like the long running translation of William J. Robinson's volume on female physiology, as well as the work of Wei Xin (Robinson/Wei Xin 1923). In fact, I find virtually no generalizations about the social responsibility of modern women, or new wave women, without the corresponding natural science justification. Counter-arguments outside the mainstream press must certainly exist, but they remain for me to discover. It is not surprising that even a discussion of women's need for physical exercise is cast in relation to popular natural science (Yan Wei 1923).

A second core truism of vernacular sociology was eugenics. The fuzzy line separating and linking natural science and social science is precisely the place where eugenics flourishes. This is clarified in Gao Junzhe's 1930 descriptive analysis in the professional journal *Sociology World (Shehui xuejie)* of the so-called "biological schools of sociology" (Gao Junzhe 1930). Ms. Gao's exposition of main topics in the history of biological or physical sociology argued that Darwin-

---

[13] The piece is canonical.

ian and neo-Darwinian strands in Spencer's organicism gave rise to theories of "social selection." Three subtopics within the general problem of social selection she listed as the race-war question, eugenics, and the population question. Less systematic and historically schooled commentators than Ms. Gao were not scrupulous about historical origin or theoretical influences. The elite adopted eugenic concepts in China as thoroughly as elites did in the United States, Britain, and Mexico; anywhere one finds relations of modern domination of heterogeneous populations it appears that eugenics is also to be found.[14] As ossified social dogma, eugenics was, Hiroko Sakamoto has recently made quite clear, a key element in Chinese elite ideologies from the beginning of modern speculation and can be found throughout the thought of the nation's founding fathers (Sakamoto Hiroko 1999/2004).[15] US-centered scholarship has produced incontrovertible arguments and evidence that eugenicist ideas, the idea that the human race can and should be improved through reproductive engineering, suffuse social evolutionary thinking in the United States and Britain at the turn of the nineteenth century (Ryan 2001). Furthermore, I have argued in *The Question of Women in Chinese Feminism* (Barlow 2003) that indeed scientific racism is a core element of progressive feminism.

Zhou Jianren is a useful example of a literary figure enabled and constrained in the taxonomies of speculative, vernacular social science. In his famous essay "The Meaning and Value of Love" (*Lian'ai de yiyi yu jiazhi*), for instance, Zhou takes positions that might be called eugenic poetics since he describes in literary language the vernacular social scientific truism that heterosexual love is an evolutionary norm and an index of social development. For one thing, love separates humans from ordinary mammals who rut promiscuously and without emotion. But what distinguishes the natural from the social in human beings is a secondary matter, by and large an assumption. Zhou's primary concern in this article is the argument that where personal selection is the norm, love freely sought and given improves racial health and racial quality; as an index, it measures race

---

[14] See Dikötter 1992, 1998, 1995; Dikötter/Sautman 1997; Stern 1998.
[15] I wish to thank Rebecca Jennison for translating this difficult essay.

against race in the battle of the fittest, since Zhou assumes that the fittest races are the ones that tolerate the highest levels of personal choice in romantic and erotic life (Zhou Jianren 1922, 1923). Zhou was, of course, a figure of key importance at *The Ladies' Journal*. He takes the same positions as the canonical theorist Gao Xian, in other words. I make this point because in current intellectual history Gao has been considered an eccentric theorist. But just like Gao does, Zhou draws a relationship between social practices that limit eugenic racial health, such as parents choosing spouses, and Chinese racial inferiority or cultural degeneracy. Zhou also proposes that the woman's power to select her spouse is valuable because it will improve the race. For Zhou as for Gao, social selection and sexual selection are the motors driving eugenic improvement. Gao Xian was preoccupied with the core problem for progressive feminism of "personality" or *renge* and how despite their historically devolutionary plight, Chinese women should retool themselves around a personality that would make possible individual choice. Zhou's interest is organized around the Lester Wardian question of women's will. The effect is similar.

Before we turn to a discussion of vernacular preoccupation with individualism, it may be useful to make a subordinate point about the expression of self in the 1920s. A common contention in critical analysis of writing in this era has been that the self of men was consolidated around the "other" of women. This could happen because, theoretically speaking, men could "voice" themselves in the contemporary cultural Imaginary, whereas women could not. This is the conundrum of the subaltern and her speech.

In much very stimulating and often brilliant work, the operating thesis in this argument in the context of Chinese Republican thought has been that desire is the desire of the other. The subject's desire to be the other, or to own the other or contain the other in one's self, gets pulled into the psychic machinery that makes possible the consolidation or voicing of "self" in the first place. This psychodynamic thesis is argued strenuously as a way of understanding why particularly in the 1920s male intellectuals were at such pains to liberate women. As Stephen Chan argued a decade ago, men tried to liberate women because they imagined that the harm they were doing to women was in fact a kind of harm to themselves: men had no way to understand women independent of their own projections in other words. No doubt still useful in attenuated form, these psychodynamic arguments have as yet not come to terms with the theoretical world in which Zhou Jianren, like his famous brothers and countless other literary figures, operated. Elite intellectuals got a sense of self from writing about sexual selection, natural selection, social selection, racial improvement, natural instincts, and the whole baggage of eugenic and sociological theory sketched out here. In the psychic theater, they may have become coherent selves through the medium of a female "other," but that possibility cannot override the constraints and explicit arguments that raged around these new men and new women. The governing ideology (if I am correct) was vernacular sociology, and it had little to do with intrapsychic realities. Discussions of "desire" can be found scattered throughout the body of vernacular sociology, in the Freudian eugenic theories of Pan Guangdan as well as discussions or references to August Comte, Lester Ward, and Herbert Spencer, who are the foundational figures for sociology in China (particularly vernacular sociology). But these are exegeses on vernacular sociology. They speculate on desire because, as I will demonstrate shortly, desire is one of the categories of speculative sociology. My subordinate point here, in other words, is that creative writers lived under the same conditions as intellectuals who wrote social theory. The shape of wanting, its origins and capacities, were theorized in countless ways in the theoretical fever of the 1920s (see also Zhou Jianren 1922, 1923, 1925).

Vernacular Sociology, Natural Woman's Menstrual Products and Her "Look"

Who was the woman at the center of vernacular sociology? This iconic drawing by Ding Hao, one of Shanghai's best known commercial graphic artists of the era, is a mature version of what natural woman looked like (see figure 1).[16] An advertising campaign

---

[16] *Shenbao (Shanghai Journal)*, 29 January 1948, Shanghai Public Library holding, reproduced in: Zhao Shen 2000:125.

for Kotex sanitary napkins, started in the mid-1920s, explicitly addressed menstruation and hygiene in relation to a commodity. Kotex is by definition an industrial object that replaces "unhealthful, self-fashioned" menstrual products with "new style, scientific, sanitary" pads that absorb fluid and can be thrown away. This usage is itself hygienic since, as the second ad points out, home-made and reusable menstruation products are potentially harmful to female reproductive health (see figure 2).[17] Kotex also dispels odor and anxiety. Kotex is "brand named" for easy purchase at the drug store or by mail order, and Kotex is a modern, medically sound product. The advertising graphic of one woman buying the branded menstrual commodity from another woman renders all these scientific, hygienic facts visible (see figure 3).[18] The repetitive invocation of the sanitary healthful qualities of machinemade, brand-identified, septic menstrual products found explicit scientific reinforcement in articles appearing alongside the ads in journals of opinion like *Funü zazhi* where I first discovered this ad campaign[19] (see figures 4 and 5).[20] The link of menstruation to hygiene could not be more explicit, for instance, in Wei Xin's translation in 1923 of William Robinson's work on eugenic improvement (Robinson/Wei Xin 1923).

The significant element at this juncture is that in both print culture and advertising culture, the scientifically revalued fact of menstruation was now a biological life-event. Menstruation possessed the ability to centrally define the social evolutionary capacity of every natural woman. The progressive woman knew that her body was defined physiologically and that was a reason she used Kotex. Only devolutionary women reused dirty rags. Scientific menstruation is not a familial, ritual, or even a purely medical event. It became in advertising campaign a public event, publicly trumpeted and measured for menstruating women's scientific contribution to modern progress. For preoccupation with menses in product advertisement and caution-

---

[17] *Funü zazhi* 14:8 (August 1928).
[18] *Funü zazhi* 14:6 (June 1928).
[19] See *Funü zazhi* 6-8 (June-August) 1928.
[20] *Jiating (Family)* 5 (June 1939); *Shanghai shenghuo (Shanghai Life)* 3 (August 1939).

ary writing suggested that women's contribution to modern social progress lay in personal hygiene. A hygienic, modern woman bathes regularly. Unlike her unenlightened sisters, she bases her life practices on clinical scientific truths about female sexual maturation, menstrual cycles, conception, pregnancy, and post-delivery self-care (see Y. S. 1930).

Advertising historian Zhao Shen's claim that new consumer goods like Kotex liberated more women than theoretical debates ever did may require some adjusting. His implicit point, that representing liberated women iconically in commercial advertising arts affected daily life practices, seems less debatable (Zhao Shen 2000:165-204).[21] Shanghainese advertising culture in the 1920s particularly targeted young, female urbanites in the process of family formation. Sensitive to the effectiveness of the earlier and popular "calendar ad" (*yuefen pai*) traditionalistic styles in the struggle to establish their branded commodities, the sales directors in transnational corporations and the advertising artists working for them developed specific icons that were supposed to attract post-traditional, young urban women. Virtually the same woman who in the Kotex ads is selling, using, and buying menstrual pads appears, for instance, in a long-running advertising campaign for Sincere Department Store (*Xianshi gongsi*). In this ad the Sincere Girl is gazing raptly at a bundle of female hygienic and cosmetic goods which she has purchased by mail order; other versions of this same ad have her unwrapping foodstuffs (see figure 6).[22] The Sincere icon is a version of what Zhao Shen calls the "new wave girl" (*xinchao nülang*). Although Ding Hao was too young in the 1920s to have drawn the Sincere Department Store icon, the new wave girl is a precursor of his highly successful, anatomically explicit commercial iconography of "It Girls" that came to predominate advertising culture later in the decade (see figures 7 and 8).[23]

---

[21] I wish to thank Jing Wang for recommending Zhao Shen and note her new project to trace the reemergence of China's advertising industry in the post-Mao order and its implications.
[22] *Funü zazhi* 17:8 (August 1931)
[23] *Shenbao*, 21 February 1948, Shanghai Public Library holding, reproduced in: Zhao Shen 2000:129; *Shenbao*, 23 October 1947, Shanghai Public Library holding, reproduced in: Zhao Shen 2000:127

At one level the repetitive linking of the visual icon and progressive or patriotic messages was simply instilling brand loyalty, of course. At another level image and rhetoric were associating sociological platitudes about women's perfectibility with her biological-scientific body.[24] Written copy consolidated the link of modernity and evolution implicit in the graphic iconography. The Sincere advertising campaign, for instance, exploited the bodiliness of a "modern" female type, while the commercial culture associated body with menstrual and other commodities, physical hygiene, and the modern notion that evolutionary bodies are animal bodies since beneath social improvement lies the "natural" body that all mammals share. For humans the natural body is the eugenic race body.[25] Image and message in the Sincere ads confirm this complex cluster of associations. Its simple rhetoric links the consumer who chooses up-to-date commodities at the most up-to-date department store to national-racial improvement.[26] See for instance, Sincere Department Store's "Shrinking space" (*Suodi*) campaign, extolling mail marketing and the long distance purchase of commodities.[27] People who are agents of the progressive drive to develop China's "material civilization," it seems, buy Kotex, and Quaker Oats, Horliks, Tangee lipstick, Palmolive soap, Pepsodent toothpaste, and Kodak film.[28]

---

[24] Hygiene commodities are presented as being universal. Literally they blanket the map. They are natural, because they ameliorate the natural physiological mess of femininity, sanitizing and improving it. Kotex is social, too, because new wave girl's consumption habits improve self, civilization, country, and in the idiom of the day, make good evolution.

[25] A US-based discussion of this contemporary association of body and race is Berg 2002:1-31.

[26] "Material civilization finds new ways to do things on the basis of older theories. Not a single day passes that we are not in progress. That is why our company is specializing in offering the most contemporary commodities to the society. Thus, if you need the most up-to-date commodities you need to choose our store." See Sincere Department Store ad campaign, in: *Funü zazhi* 17:8 (August 1931) for this ubiquitous ad.

[27] See *Funü zazhi* 16:10 (1930).

[28] See Barlow et al. (forthcoming) for a discussion of image and globalization around skin products.

The future-oriented new wave girl is vernacular sociology's ideal woman. She is a consumer of modernity. She is emotionally engaged with commodity culture. Even when new wave girls (like my mother-in-law, for instance) could not actually afford to buy at Sincere, advertising reinforced their longing for commodified self-expression. Lacking the wherewithal to buy, she consumed and wanted nonetheless. This ideal woman who wants things is physically or eugenically perfect. Short hair, young and fertile, slender and curvaceous, vernacular modern woman is clean and bright. The new wave girl has her bob styled in a mechanized beauty parlor. She read *The Ladies' Journal* or books on natural science, modern etiquette, evolutionary social science. She is perhaps a co-ed or office worker, a housewife, an agent of national racial improvement, the trigger of social evolution and the indispensable element in transvaluation of all social values. She consumes evolutionary commodities. She has evolutionary babies. She makes evolutionary choices. She has liberated the Nature within her from an old and stultifying Confucian culture, and she promotes social development when cultivating her own natural essence. Certainly there is no image more central to the theoretical natural woman and her social development than the Kotex icon.

My theoretical point here is that the hygienic menstrual commodity, the new wave advertising icon, and vernacular sociology created an ideologically significant unity or closed circuit. No doubt examining other commodities will yield similar conclusions. Here the result is an ideology of scientific, modern womanhood. This ideology of womanhood is a hegemonic formula. The eugenic health of modern women redefining themselves in scientific terms as units of reproductive physiology are linked to a commodity representing the antiseptic scientific ideal celebrated in vernacular social norms and reinforced in advertising copy. Advertisements make explicit prevailing assumptions about gender and class norms. When Kotex links fashion, scientific sepsis, asepsis, and disposable commodities, it publicly reinforces the defining power of reproductive physiology. Anatomical sex is given a social face. Closing the circle that links advertising image – social theory – commodity is the way hegemonic forces operate. Tacit assumptions become incontrovertible because they are now self-evident. The Kotex pad is an ideological entity. It links social improvement to the scientific reality of woman's sexed body (Yi Bin et al. 1995-2000; Song Jialin 1997-1999). Keeping in mind this circuit and particularly what the new wave girl of advertising and vernacular sociology looked like, this essay considers the intellectual foundations legitimating her existence (Wang Jian 1997).

I have indicated in the discussions above that one reason for the intense importance new intellectuals accorded to vernacular sociology had to do with the recoding of social values. Norms inherited from the past were rethought in light of modern knowledge of evolution and science. In the previous section I argued that the commodity form and the ideology of the natural woman in progressive natural and social evolution actually kept this redefinition in motion. Here is an example. To modernists, and vernacular sociology is a modernism, divorce is a "social problem" and not primarily a religious, legal, ethical or ritual matter.[29] Modernists may appreciate the religious, ethical or ritual *implications* of divorce, but modernist writing on "the evolution of divorce" makes society (and social evolution) into the basic foundation or platform. Atop the platform of society, theories about the social significance or social importance of divorce are then developed. *Society* is the level where cause and effect occur and where causes are sought and found. And as we have seen, vernacular sociology in China in the 1920s collapsed social development and natural evolution together into the same process.

The final point in this discussion of vernacular sociology is that "the individual" is a core element of social science theory. The centrality of individualism in popular elite writing in the 1920s resonates with foundational claims not just in vernacular but in professional sociology, and in the Enlightenment anthropologies that form the touchstone of much international nineteenth-century theory about social development. The individual, like women, is another place where society and nature allegedly meet. In general social theory, the individual secures a place in society through the so-called social contract where, in exchange for safety and social development, everyone

---

[29] See, for instance, Rao Shangda 1922.

gives up their will to the collectivity or general will. This notion of the contract binding all individuals into a society which distinguishes man from beast is a foundation of thinking about society in the abstract. Allegedly the individual is the person who expresses all of the interior feelings, desires, will, intellect and needs of our animal nature. Sexuality is allegedly an animal instinct: in good societies this instinct leads to eugenic progress and in bad societies it is repressed into febrile culturalism and leads to devolution. Such Comteanism pervades most non-Marxist writing on sociology and social science in vernacular sociology.

My example of how this theoretical matrix legitimates "the individual" in the idiom of vernacular sociology (and forms the parameter of the thinkable, I suspect) is Endo Ryukichi's *Sociology in Modern Times* (Endo/Tan Shougong 1920). Published in Japanese in 1903 it appeared in Chinese translation in 1920. The book lays out in a powerful general argument summarizing what became, over the course of the 1920s, foundational assumptions in vernacular sociology. Endo is concerned with both the basic theories of general sociology, which means primarily French, German and USA scholarship, and with how these theories measure up in relation to East Asian social forms. The outline and execution of the book is systematic and social scientific. It begins with a general introduction to the types of sociology and their contents, materials and methods, their major problematics and systems. It moves to chapters on precursors, sociological method and its relation to natural sciences, the subjective factors in sociology (desire, subject, ideation), statistics and statistical categories, the study of social development, primitive society and matrilinearity social systems, key figures in social theory (Ward, Durkheim, JHW Stuckenberg, Spencer etc.), and foundational problems in sociology. Endo's particular concern, however, appears to be the question of individual subjectivity and inside that preoccupation Endo singled out the problem of will.

Provisionally at least, it would appear that Endo builds on Ward's theories about material foundations of human life detailed in, among other volumes, Lester Ward's 1898 volume *Outlines of Sociology* (Ward 1898). Out of the materialism of the primal matter which

Ward theorized to be a kind of plasma humans are an assertive and self-evolving species. The importance of will (*yizhi*) is that it, of all the complex elements that make up the individual and social condition, the individual compels and organizes action. Such activities include, it appears, the activity of self-evolution. Thus, for instance, in a detailed discussion of the relationship between desire (*yuwang*) and will, Endo develops a complex argument regarding the relationship between desiring, willing and compelling the other in relation to one's self. Each quality of personhood, willing and desiring, is a separate capacity or function within individuals (Endo/Tan Shougong 1920:212). How the will is exercised in relation to desire or the psychology of emotions and, very importantly, Spirit (*jingshen*) and so on is through consolidation (*jiehe*), a complex process that will not concern me here. Now I only want to stress that every aspect of the will is thoroughly aired, including the question of "free will" and its conditions. Citations build. Arguments are complex and lengthy. Most Enlightenment figures and a host of late nineteenth-century German and French social theorists are invoked on the question of the centrality of will and its relation to feelings, emotions, desire, volition, and from the individual psyche up through the social processes (association, socialization and so on) that shape and condition the unit called "society" and that, through individual and collective efforts, propel human history forward. Endo is quite definite that the unit of all of these calculations is the individual (*geren*) (ibid. 245). And Endo brings out all of the major social collectivities (nation, race, etc.) that one would expect in late nineteenth- early twentieth-century evolutionary sociology no matter where in the world one encounters it.

This is not professional sociology. It is far more speculative and philosophical. Although it is clearly built on the foundation of European and United States sociological theory, it is also refracted through the sensibility and concerns of a self-identified East Asian. What concerns me about Endo's generalizing project at this juncture are two things. First, the connection between the natural sciences and the social sciences – or Nature and society – that consolidated vernacular sociology's foundation gave the new social categories that Endo draws on, e.g. individual, society, desire, evolutionary social institutions not just a universal quality but a totalizing one. There is no room in these generalizations for alternatives to the individual in his relation to society. The modernist recognizes the implications of different social origins and histories, but all history will lead in only one direction because beneath historical change is evolution or the natural foundation of history. Consequently, Endo's arguments bear very much on the anatomically correct figures of the natural man and natural woman that Ding Hao, for instance, used to successfully model advertising icons, and advertisers routinely invoked. Second, a major question for Endo – because of the centrality in his thinking of the "individual" as the suturing point between Nature and culture – is volition. Standing behind the question of will and willed behavior, somewhat in the shadows, is the matter of what people want and why they want menstrual pads and permanent waves, Parker pens and Victrola brand record players and Ponds vanishing crème. How people manage in their social lives to balance the elements alleged to make individuals human – e.g. will, desire, and emotion – is the philosophic version of the question of what people want and how they get what they want. The question preoccupying progressive Chinese feminism in the next decade, of *renge* (personality) does not appear in a prominent position in Endo's text. But the theory that human individuals live in societies together as collectivities (races, nations, communities, etc.) and in exercising their individual wills, forward the aims of the race, nation, community, and self, is very much present.

Philosophy and Vernacular Sociology

There is no evidence at this point that Endo Ryukichi was a particularly influential sociologist. There is every evidence that the sociologists he drew on, from Spencer to Ward, were widely influential in the 1920s among the coterie particularly of intellectuals around the opinion journal *The Ladies' Journal*. Many of the preoccupations of vernacular and professional sociologists – prostitution, female criminality, abnormal sexuality, family reform, the women's movement, social reproduction cycles (choice, marriage, childhood socialization, divorce) – were thoroughly informed by the same starting assumptions that I am claiming are well represented in Endo, however. I have suggested that the general argument in Endo and the elements of his system (individual, society, will, emotion, spirit) were generally available to theorists who were re-evaluating the truths of social life through vernacular sociology. I gave the commonplace example of advertising for menstrual products as a way of suggesting that even at the level of female cycles, vernacular sociology offered a new understanding. Reproductive physiology did not invent human sexuality or tell women in 1920 anything new about what it feels like to reach reproductive maturity or how to get pregnant. What it did do is connect the menstrual cycle to the natural science of physiology, the social values of sepsis and hygiene, and the commodity world where public sanitation, disposability, and machine tooling are valued over frugal re-use, hand making, and privacy.

There are several points where Endo's philosophic voicing of the ideology of individualism and ongoing vernacular revaluations of social values in popular sociological writing overlapped. One of them was eugenics. I raise this in conclusion because it brings back into the analysis the "black box" or mysterious zone where all social evolution is revealed to depend on women and particularly on the smooth working of their erotic drives and procreative choices. As has become increasingly clear in other national or regional traditions, racialism is inextricably knit up with the modern recasting of women. Specifically, a debate between Pan Guangdan and Sun Benwen, Pan who began as a vernacular sociological critic and Sun who would become a dean of non-Marxist professional sociology, highlights the importance that both popular writers and professionals gave to the problem posed in modernizing the production of the race. Pan, of course had begun quite early to voice the problem of racial degeneration of Chinese in relation to European and US "races" (Pan Guangdan 1925). But in a classic nature-nurture debate with Sun over the validity of what Pan called "the young science of eugenics," Pan scored points that echoed throughout the prior decade of debate. What eugenics and its claims that natural drives, heredity, and intelligence were linked to evolutionary development really advocated, Pan claimed, was the right of people to free will participation in selection. In other words, when people – women, for instance – were able to select their mates, as animals in the wild selected the fittest among the herd for reproduction, then the quotient of superior people in the civilization would rise. Sun Benwen made the stronger case. His counter-attack was devastating. But he did not confront the interesting paradox that Pan had introduced. That was the paradox of women's need to choose (Pan Guangdan 1929; Sun Benwen 1929).

On Sun's hand the question of how a cultural sociology explained for transvaluation of women's value to the society went unanswered, although in relation to modernity women clearly played a central role in key social processes. On Pan's hand the lack of evidence that intelligence and virtue were hereditary did not completely defeat the strong argument that a mark of modern racial improvement would be the more humane regulation of social reproduction. My point is simply this: in each theoretical positioning, the female reproductive body was a central (if in non-feminist writing like this, largely unspoken) reality. By 1929, the centrality of female fecundity, female will to choose, females as the switchpoint between the processes of human reproduction and the human sciences and civilizational achievements was so foundational in vernacular and in professional sociology that it could be safely ignored.

References

Barlow, Tani E., *The Question of Women in Chinese Feminism*, Durham 2003.
Barlow, Tani E., Madeleine Yue Dong, Uta G. Poiger, Priti Ramamurthy, Lynn M. Thomas, Alys E. Weinberg, *The Modern Girl Around the World: A Research Agenda and Preliminary Findings*, in: *Gender and History* (forthcoming).
Berg, Allison, *Mothering the Race: Women's Narratives of Reproduction, 1890-1930*, Urbana, Chicago, 2002.
Burgess, J. S., The Problem of Prostitution, in: *Shehuixue zazhi* 2:4 (1925), pp. 1-12.
Chiang Yung-chen, *Social Engineering and the Social Sciences in China, 1919-1949*, Cambridge 2001.
Dikötter, Frank, *The Discourse of Race in Modern China*, Stanford 1992.

Dikötter, Frank, *Sex, Culture and Modernity in China: Medical Science and the Construction of Sexual Identities in the Early Republican Period*, London 1995.
Dikötter, Frank, *Imperfect Conceptions: Medical Knowledge, Birth Defects, and Eugenics in China*, New York 1998.
Dikötter, Frank (ed.), Barry Sautman (consulting ed.), *The Construction of Racial Identities in China and Japan: Historical and Contemporary Perspectives*, London 1997.
Endo Ryukichi (Tan Shougong, trans.), *Jinshi shehuixue* (Sociology in Modern Times), Shanghai 1920.
Gao Ersong, Gao Erbai, Zhongguo xuezhe funü wenti zhi yanjiu (Research of the Woman Question by Chinese Scholars), in: *Shehuixue zazhi* 2:2-3 (1925), pp. 1-56.
Gao Junzhe, Shehuixue de shengwu xuepai (Biological Schools of Sociology), in: *Shehui xuejie* 4 (1930), pp. 87-139.
Gilmartin, Christina K., *Engendering the Chinese Revolution: Radical Women, Communist Politics, and Mass Movements in the 1920s*, Berkeley, Los Angeles, London 1995.
Huxley, Thomas H. (Gao Xingruo, trans.), Xing he xing de jueding (Sex and the Determination of Sex), in: *Funü zazhi* 9:8 (1923), pp. 32-41.
Letourneau, Charles (Wei Xin, trans.), Lihun de jinhua (The Evolution of Divorce), in: *Funü zazhi* 8:4 (1922), pp. 106-114.
Lin Yaohua, Yan Fu shehui sixiang (Yan Fu's Social Thinking), in: *Shehui xuejie* 7 (1933), pp. 1-82.
Ke Shi, Funü zai jinhua zhong de renwu (The Responsibility of Women in Evolution), in: *Funü zazhi* 8:8 (1922), pp. 9-11.
Mei Sheng (ed.), *Zhongguo funü wenti taolunji* (Collected Discussion of the Woman Question), Shanghai n.d.
Pan Guangdan, Shengyu xianzhi yu youshengxue (Limiting Fertility and the Field of Eugenics), in: *Funü zazhi* 11:10 (1925), pp. 1560-1569.
Pan Guangdan, Yousheng yu wenhua: Yu Sun Benwen xiansheng shangque de wenzi (Eugenics and Culture: A Discussion on the Writings of Sun Benwen), in: *Shehui xuekan* 1:2 (1929), pp. 1-19.

Pan Guangdan, Feng Xiaoqing: Yijian ying'ai zhi yanjiu (Feng Xiaoqing: A Study in Narcissism), in: *Funü zazhi* 1 (1922), reproduced in: Shen Ji, Zhang Xichang (eds.), *Pan Guangdan wenji* (Collected Writings of Pan Guangdan), Beijing 2000, pp. 1-66.

Rao Shangda, Lihun wenti de jiujingguan (A Final Observation on the Divorce Question), in: *Funü zazhi* 8:4 (1922), pp. 23-29.

Robinson, William J. (Wei Xin, trans.), Nüzi zhi xing de zhishi (Knowledge of Female Sexuality), in: *Funü zazhi* 9:4 (1923), pp. 110-114; 9:7 (1923), pp. 106-113; 9:8 (1923), pp. 116-122; 9:9 (1923), pp. 111-116.

Ryan, Frank X., *Darwin's Impact: Social Evolution in America, 1880-1920*, Chicago 2001.

Sakamoto Hiroko, Ren'ai shinsei to minzoku kairyo no kagaku: Goshi shinbunka disukosu toshiteno yuseishiso (The Cult of "Love and Eugenics" in May Fourth Movement Discourse), in: *Shiso* 894 (1999), pp. 4-34, and in English translation as The Cult of "Love and Eugenics" in May Fourth Movement Discourse, in: *positions: east asian cultures critique* 12:2 (2004).

Smith, Jeremy, Sako Teruhito, *"Society" and "Sociology" in the Meiji Era Japan: 1860s-1880s*, n.d., http://www.lian.com/SAKO/papers/SHAKAI.doc (accessed 8 July 2002).

Song Jialin, *Lao yuefenpai* (The Old Yuefen Brand), Shanghai 1997-1999.

Stern, Alexandra, Unraveling the History of Eugenics in Mexico, in: *Archive: Institute for the Study of Academic Racism*, 1 August 1998, http://www.ferris.edu/isar/archives/sources/ mexico.htm.

Sun Benwen, Zai lun wenhua yu youshengxue: Da Pan Guangdan xiansheng shangque de wenzi (Further Discussion on Culture and the Field of Eugenics: A Response to the Writings of Pan Guangdan), in: *Shehui xuekan* 1:2 (1929), pp. 1-45.

Sun Benwen, Shehuixue shang waiguoren minghanyi shangque (A Discussion of the Chinese Names of Foreign Sociologists), in: *Shehui xuekan* 1:3 (1930), pp. 1-18.

Wang Jian, From Four Hundred Million to More than One Billion Consumers: A Brief History of the Foreign Advertising Industry in

China, in: *International Journal of Advertising* 241 (1 November 1997), online version.

Ward, Lester, *Outlines of Sociology*, New York 1898.

Ward, Lester (Xia Gaizun, trans.) (from Japanese translation by Sakai Toshihiko), Nüxing zhong xing shuo bu guo qu (What to Say about the "Sex" [xing] in "Women" [nüxing]), in: *Funü pinglun* (n.d.), pp. 1-24.

Wei Xin, Shengming zhi wuzhi de jichu (The Material Basis of Life), in: *Funü zazhi* 8:3 (1922), pp. 78-83.

Wright, David, Yan Fu and the Tasks of the Translator, in: Michael Lackner, Iwo Amelung, Joachim Kurtz (eds.), *New Terms for New Ideas: Western Knowledge and Lexical Change in Late Imperial China*, Leiden 2001, pp. 235-256.

Y. S., Renshenqi zhong funü yingzhi zhi changshi ji qi weisheng (Hygienic Commonsense that all Women Ought to Know during Pregnancy), in: *Funü zazhi* 16:10 (1930), pp. 77-79.

Yan Wei, Nüzi tiyu yanjiu (Research on Women's Athletics), in: *Funü zazhi* 9:7 (1923), pp. 6-12.

Yang Yabin, *Jindai Zhongguo shehuixue* (shang) (Modern Chinese Sociology), vol. 1, Beijing 2001.

Yi Bin, Liu Youming, Gan Zhenhu, *Lao Shanghai guanggao* (Advertisements in Old Shanghai), Shanghai 1995-2000.

Zhao Shen, *Zhongguo jindai guanggao wenhua* (China [sic] Modern Advertising Culture), Changchun 2000.

Zheng Hangsheng, Li Yingsheng, *Ershishiji Zhongguo de shehuixue: Zhongguo shehuixue de fazhan; lishi, xianzhuang yu qianzhan* (Twentieth Century Chinese Sociology: Development of Chinese Sociology; History, Current Status and Prospects), Beijing 1999.

Zhou Jianren, Lian'ai de yiyi yu jiazhi (The Meaning and Value of Love), in: *Funü zazhi* 8:2 (1922), pp. 2-6.

Zhou Jianren, Funüzhuyi zhi kexue de jichu (The Scientific Foundation of Feminism), in: *Funü zazhi* 9:4 (1923), pp. 1-7.

Zhou Jianren, Hafuluoke Ailusi (Havelock Ellis), in: *Funü zazhi* 11:5 (1925), pp. 732-736.

Figure 1: Shenbao (29 January 1948, Shanghai Public Library holding), in: Zhao Shen 2000:125.

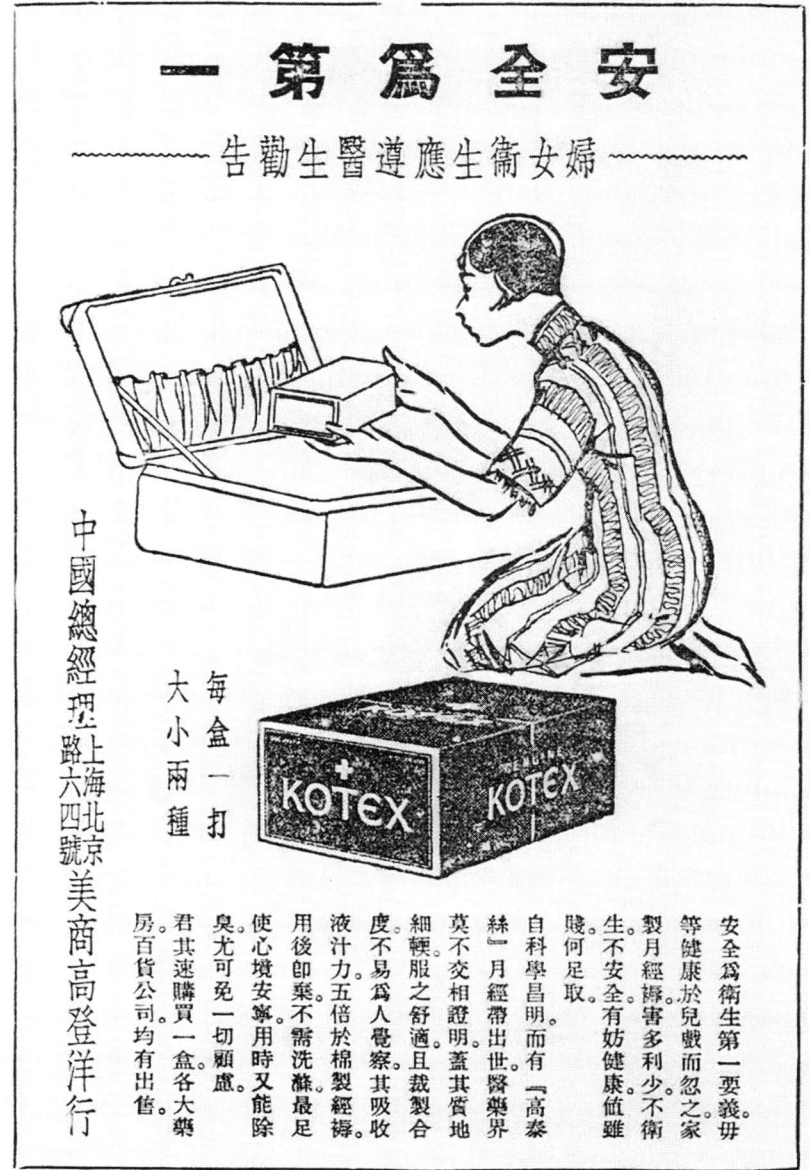

Figure 2: Funü zazhi (The Ladies' Journal) 14 (August 1928).

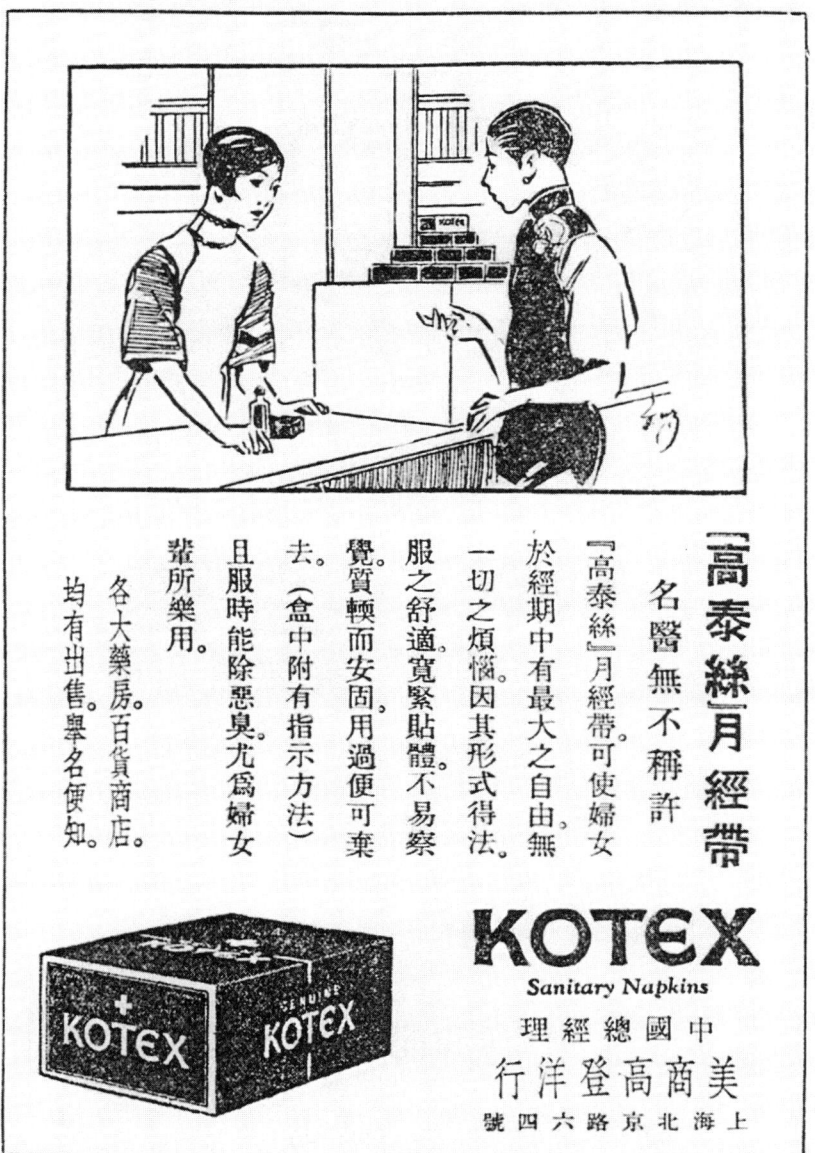

Figure 3: Funü zazhi (The Ladies' Journal) 14 (June 1928).

Figure 4: Jiating (Family) 5 (June 1939).

Figure 5: Shanghai Shenghuo (Shanghai Life) 3 (August 1939).

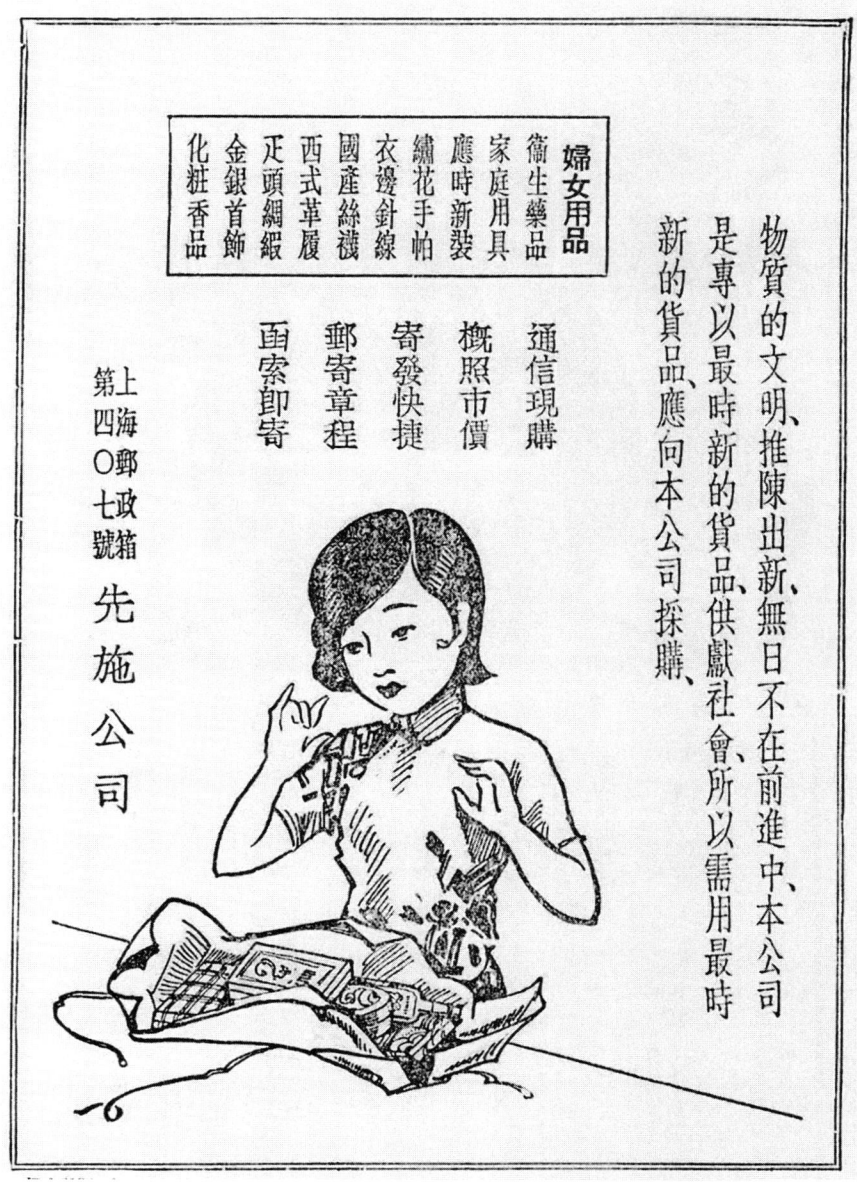

Figure 6: Funü zazhi (The Ladies' Journal) 17 (August 1931).

Figure 7: Shenbao (21 February 1948, Shanghai Public Library holding), in: Zhao Shen 2000:129.

Figure 8: Shenbao (23 October 1947, Shanghai Public Library holding), in: Zhao Shen 2000:127.

Unvirtuous Exchanges: Women and the Corruptions of the Shanghai Stock Market in the Early Republican Era

Bryna Goodman

In his social novel, *The True Nature of the Stock Market (Jiaoyisuo xianxing ji)*, serialized in the periodical *Xingqi (The Week)* in late 1922 and early 1923, the New Culture writer Jiang Hongjiao painted a scene of social and economic devastation (Jiang Hongjiao 1994). An array of suicides punctuates the plot: a former revolutionary, a doctor, a family elder, a wife, a student. The several doctors who did not abandon their practice to invest in the market are called from suicide to suicide in efforts to revive those who determined to escape their debts and loss of face through death. Within this panorama of greed, death and destruction, the author highlights one suicide in particular. This one took place at the "Midnight Exchange" (*Banye jiaoyisuo*):

> Business flourished at the "Midnight Exchange" after it opened. [...] Other exchanges did not permit women to buy and sell. Only the "Midnight Exchange" had female employees. But how could women understand the subtleties of the business of speculation? They only thought to buy when prices rose. When they saw prices fall they quickly sold. Naturally their losses were high and their earnings low. Most pitiful was the suicide of the wife of the Western medical doctor, Pan Huzhen. [...] She did not begin with much money, just some private savings, no more than 3,600 *yuan*. When she saw stock prices rising, she relied on someone to purchase 100 shares, and in four days she earned 700 *yuan*. [...] So she thought it was easy to make a profit on the market. [...] Who would know that a month later prices would suddenly dive? Not only did she lose her earnings but her blood capital as well. She resolved to wait until prices rose. Her private savings were depleted, and her jewelry sold as well, and still the prices didn't rise. Finally she decided to cut her losses

---

I am indebted to Cynthia Brokaw, Ted Huters, Wendy Larson and Monika Übelhör for comments and suggestions. I am also grateful for a research fellowship from the Center for the Study of Women in Society at the University of Oregon.

and sell. Who would guess that when she sold the price suddenly rose? Agitated, she borrowed money and invested. [...] Who could have known that four brokers had cornered the market? [...] Pan Huzhen's wife not only had no earnings, but lost everything and also sold her clothing. In less than two months she lost a total of 17,000 *yuan*. At first she didn't tell her husband, but when he found out she couldn't think what to do. She went to the "Midnight Exchange" and hid herself in a dark corner. After midnight, when the exchange closed and the people went home, she tiptoed onto the trading floor. There she took out a cloth, fastened it on a post in the brokers' section and hung herself. At daybreak the next day she was discovered by a custodian who finally brought her down. Exchange director Wang Zongfa quickly acted to cover up the matter, finding a way to settle quietly with Pan Huzhen. Nonetheless several people on the outside heard of the suicide. Because of this, it became known that the directors had organized a phoney company to cheat people of their money. (ibid. 155-156)

This passage is cited at length because it highlights common themes in contemporary public perceptions of the stock market, as found in newspaper reportage at the time and in popular literature in the early 1920s. These include the unfathomability and secret corruption of the market, a problematization of the relationship between women and money, female weakness, and the illustration of market evils through a narrative focus on suicide, particularly a spectacular and poignant female suicide. To these themes, it is necessary only to add sex, specifically, imaginative connections drawn between monetary greed and excessive and disorderly sex. For a full sense of the imaginative possibilities of this theme – which is hinted at, but not indulged, in Jiang's novel – one may refer to Lu Shouxian's identically titled, but more culturally conservative book, another *True Nature of the Stock Market (Jiaoyisuo xianxing ji)*, also published in 1922 (Lu Shouxian 1922).[1] Lu's mostly fictional vignettes mix tales of extravagant greed on the market with the improper presence in places of business of prostitutes, concubines and female students, making stock markets and even stock exchange personnel training schools, into "secret dens of lascivious pleasures" (*yinle zhi miku*) (ibid. 39).

---

[1] This is not a novel, but a stock market miscellany in the popular "dark secrets" (*heimu*) literary genre.

China's experimentation with stock markets in the most recent decade of the reform era has stimulated renewed historical study of China's early stock market experiences, particularly in the commercial city of Shanghai. Recent work has illuminated China's economic history, but has generally avoided inquiry into the cultural meanings of this new capitalist institution as it emerged, fitfully, in the first decade of the Republican era (Jiu Shanghai de zhengquan jiaoyisuo 1992; Zhu Yingui 1998; McElderry 2001). This period of early discussion of the stock market is interesting, in contrast to the better-known late 1920s and 1930s, because of the relative freshness of the topic in public discussion. Public understandings of the market were not, at this point, dictated by the terms of an ideological debate between Communists and members of the Guomindang (Nationalist Party, GMD), and they do not generally reflect either a fully articulated concept of capitalism or a Marxist critique of capitalist institutions.

In the context of the new Chinese Republic, before journalists instinctively thought in categories of class or economics, the project of creating a Chinese stock exchange had a variety of different cultural meanings. Against the backdrop of foreign economic interventions in China, market entrepreneurs promoted a Chinese exchange as a nationalist assertion of economic autonomy (Wang Enliang 1921; Goodman 2002). Against older models of business networks and social networks more broadly, networks which featured hierarchical interactions with known associates, reinforced by kin or native place ties, stock markets offered more anonymous and potentially more democratic interactions. (If, in the old system, one knew whom one was dealing with, in the new system, transactions were remote and impersonal.) For those uneasy with the rapid transformations of the commercial city and nostalgic for aspects of an older, literati-based moral and political order, the stock market emblematized the rude intrusions of business relations governed by amoral profit-making. Stock markets were understood to be foreign to Chinese cultural traditions. A Chinese stock exchange presented the familiar conundrum of Chinese modernity – the problem of retaining Chinese identity while adopting foreign institutions, values and modes of behavior (Goodman 2002). When Chinese stock markets failed, on the other hand, the experience seemed emblematic of larger failures of Chinese modernity, or the impossibility of escaping the corruptions of Chinese culture.

It is not surprising that the cultural narratives that invested the early Chinese stock market with meaning were infused with competing – and gendered – visions of power and morality. The ways in which new modes of economic relations necessarily intertwine with gendered understandings of politics and power have been fruitfully explored in the contexts of modern French and English history (Felski 1995; Searle 1998; Thompson 2000; Andrew/McGowen 2001). In the case of nineteenth-century France, for example, as Victoria Thompson has persuasively argued, participation in the stock market paralleled shifting ideas of citizenship. The prominence in French popular literature of the prostitute-like Lorette, who speculated in her feminine charms, embodied cultural concerns about unhealthy speculative tendencies on the market. The formal banning of women from the French stock exchange (on the basis of their imagined speculative tendencies) accompanied women's increasing political exclusion after the 1848 revolution (Thompson 2000:137-139, 150). In nineteenth-century England, in contrast, if John Stuart Mill's support for middle-class female suffrage was not yet generally accepted, women faced no legal or even social obstacles to playing the stock exchange. Nonetheless, moralists were disturbed by what G. R. Searle aptly calls the "social promiscuity" of the market, and expressed repugnance at the sight of women who strayed from their homes to try their luck on the stock market. J.G.A. Pocock, writing about eighteenth-century British political discourse, argued that capitalism was initially perceived in terms of speculation rather than calculation, and, as such, was thought to inhabit a "'feminine' world of fantasy" (Searle 1998:85, 164). In China, as elsewhere, prior to the articulation of an ordering language of class, concerns for the morality of the market were expressed through gendered imagery. The specific gendered narratives of the market that one finds in the early Republican era, of course, reflect the particular historical trajectories of the stock market, women and the state in China, differences in the relation of the early stock market to the state, and differences in women's historical relationship to commerce and the state.

In the context of foreign economic penetration of China, it was not women, but the Japanese, who appear in both fiction and reportage of popular rumors as feared manipulators of the market (Goodman 2002). Women were more commonly depicted as innocents and victims of the stock exchange, though their innocence and the danger of their victimization also served to exclude them. Gendered imagery surrounding the market in China also reflected a textual tradition of recounting exemplary or repugnant female behavior as an aesthetic mirror for the contemplation of male virtue (Goodman 2005a). This tradition found new resonance in the modern period as women became icons and repositories of cultural identity and value, as well as markers of cultural progress (or decay) in the modern era.

This essay examines the ways in which public discussion of the early Republican experience with the stock market was informed by old and new discourses of money, commercialization, cultural identity and models of female behavior. My sources include contemporary stock market fiction, archival material, stock exchange regulations, guides and other commentary, as well as newspaper reportage, reader poetry, and intellectual commentary surrounding a real-life 1922 suicide of a female investor on the Shanghai market (ibid.). Fiction and non-fiction accounts of the stock market are juxtaposed here as constituent elements of public discussion. They were similarly juxtaposed on the pages of Shanghai newspapers, in which reports of the stock market appeared together with serialized popular fiction.

A Brief Sketch of the Early History of the Shanghai Stock Market

The early Shanghai stock market developed in the context of the semi-colonial political and economic structure of the city. This meant (1) that the project of the creation of a Chinese stock market in the city would necessarily be understood in nationalist terms, (2) that the nationalist imperative of economic (and capitalist) transformation would necessarily raise questions of Chinese cultural identity, and (3) that in the early Republican era (prior to the rise of the GMD to national power) when the Chinese government initially permitted the creation of Chinese stock markets in Shanghai, the diminished sovereignty of the state led to an uncontrollable proliferation of Chinese stock markets that mirrored the fragmentation and multiplicity of political powers governing the city.

Prior to 1920, the stock exchanges that operated in Shanghai were foreign, with the exception of a short-lived flurry of stock purchasing in Chinese joint-stock companies in 1883 (Zhu Yingui 1998; Jiu Shanghai de zhengquan jiaoyisuo 1992:263-265). The foreign shares market in Shanghai formalized with the establishment of a Shanghai Stock Exchange in 1905. From its inception, discipline was lax, records were loose, and speculative forward transactions were common, as were short sales. Insider trading was rife. Whereas in most countries stock markets formed as a means of financing mounting national debts, in Shanghai, speculation alone was a primary motivating factor (Thomas 2001:103). This speculative market attracted numerous Chinese investors. Indeed, Chinese capital made up 40 percent or more of the total in major joint-stock enterprises launched from the 1860s by Jardine's, Russell's and other leading firms (ibid. 71-90, 112).

This early Shanghai stock market experienced the bubbles and depressions that make stock market history interesting for cultural historians and frustrating for those economists who imagine the possibility of economic rationality. In 1910, Shanghai investors leapt into the global rubber boom. When the rubber bubble burst, many Chinese *qianzhuang* went bankrupt (Zhu Yingui 1998:62-65; Thomas 2001:153, 162; Shanghai qianzhuang yinhang shiliao 1978:74-78).

Despite such painful experiences, Chinese businessmen and modernizers agitated for the formation of a Chinese stock exchange. Writing in 1910, Liang Qichao praised the joint-stock company over the still-dominant family or partnership style of Chinese business organization, and advocated the establishment of a Chinese stock market as a necessary mechanism of modernization and national strengthening (Liang Qichao 1992).

In 1914, persuaded that stock exchanges were essential to China's future, the Beijing government promulgated a law providing for the legal registration and regulation of Chinese stock exchanges.

The immediate stimulus for the creation of a full-fledged stock exchange in Shanghai was the 1918 establishment of a Japanese exchange in Shanghai's International Settlement. (Quyinsuo yu Jiaoyisuo zhi zhengzhu 1918; Zhu Zhenlu 1994). At the end of 1919, symbolically striking at this iconic site of Japanese economic penetration, the powerful Ningbo businessman, Yu Xiaqing, purchased the land under the Japanese exchange and expelled the Japanese (Japanese Exchange Loses its Quarters 1920; Chinese Form Stock Exchange 1920).

Yu then established a Chinese exchange on this site in July 1920. It was immensely profitable. A second Chinese exchange opened in early 1921.[2] But initial profitability swiftly led to rampant speculation. By the summer of 1921 the city was gripped by a stock-exchange frenzy. As many as 150 stock exchanges were established in the city, together with numerous trust companies (which also traded in stock). Though technically limited in number by Chinese law, the operation of extraterritoriality in the city enabled exchanges to register with foreign consulates in the city. Once established, the new exchanges – most of which traded stock only in themselves – competed in an atmosphere of gross speculation and popular ignorance. In terms of capital, the figures were fabulous. A November 1921 report prepared for the "Conference of British Chambers of Commerce" in Shanghai calculated that, whereas the average amount held by all of the Shanghai native and foreign banks during 1921 totaled $75 million, the total capital tied up in Shanghai's stock exchanges far exceeded that sum, amounting to as much as $163 million (Public Record Office FO 228/3175).[3]

In certain respects, these new economic institutions were remarkably accessible and open to investment from members of soci-

---

[2] Yu established the "Shanghai Securities and Commodities Exchange" (*Zhengquan wupin jiaoyisuo*). The second exchange was the "Shanghai China Merchants' Securities Exchange" (*Shanghai Huashang zhengquan jiaoyisuo*) (Qi Liang 1994).

[3] George Sokolsky provided the figure of $169 million invested in the ninety-eight exchanges in Shanghai for which figures were available, estimating a total sum of $200 million for 140 exchanges in existence at the end of 1921 (Sokolsky 1921).

ety who had even a small bit of capital. Competition led small exchanges to entice small investors of the petty urbanite class. At least twenty of the new exchanges operated in the evenings, after the end of the business day (Shanghai jiaoyisuo yi lan 1922:1-4, 63). But in a fashion resembling the workings of Chinese politics at the time, there was little regulation, transparency or accountability, and small groups behind closed doors manipulated outcomes and absconded with funds at the expense of the larger population. The rapid collapse of all but six of these exchanges followed shortly after their inception. The widespread trauma of this whirlwind stock market experience provided social commentators with only more evidence of the weakness of the Chinese state, the corruptions of capitalism, and the failures of the Chinese Republic (US Department of State Archives 893.52/37). In retrospect, the businessmen who had promoted stock markets as tools for nation-building were now reviled as "poisonous snakes" and greedy, "traitorous merchants" (Ru Yin 1922; Cui Weiru 1922, 1:16).

In contemporary accounts, the imaginative connections between Shanghai's traumatic experience of investment in stock exchanges and women are striking. Women do not appear in accounts of Shanghai stock market history, no doubt because their aggregate economic importance in market behavior was minimal. In both fictional accounts and in stock market commentary, however, women are given a disproportionately important role in the functioning (or dysfunction) of the market. Both the actual experiences of women and broader notions of gender – which fed a gendered reading of the stock market – are relevant to understanding the role of women in public discourse. Though it is not possible to quantify their investment, a variety of factors limited women's ability to greatly influence the behavior of the market. Women – lumped together with foreigners and a variety of criminal and civil offenders – were prevented by law from being brokers or officers of exchanges (Zhengquan jiaoyisuo fa 1921). Although a few women rose in the early Republican era to positions of surprising prominence in banking and business (Chu 2001), women generally had less access to capital than men and were not clearly recognized as independent economic agents by law or society (Bernhardt 1999; Lu Shouxian 1922:40). Indeed, economic independence for women was a central goal of feminists in this period, who produced volumes of rhetoric dedicated to the creation of vocational women, very few of whom existed yet in reality (Goodman 2005b). Nonetheless, more than a few women were investors in the new Shanghai stock market. Certainly the stock market offered women a radically new kind of transactional anonymity with money, opening an important new avenue for economic investment for a group with still quite limited ability to engage in public social intercourse. A variety of women (if only women who had some money) appear prominently in both contemporary newspaper and fictional discussion of the new economic institution. Among female investors, one finds discussion of wives, concubines, prostitutes, old-style women as well as new-style educated working women.

But only a portion of the public discussion of women and the stock market reflected women's actual interactions with exchanges. Much of the discussion had to do with the conjuncture between the moral imagination of the market and cultural ambivalence regarding changing views of women at the time, particularly the controversial feminist goals of women's "public social intercourse" (*shejiao gongkai*) and "female vocations" (*funü zhiye*). In this early period of acquaintance with the stock market, there was relatively little public interest in the petty details of economic accounting and the day-to-day procedures of issuing stock receipts and certificates. There was little interest, in general, in economic arguments or understandings of the new economic institution (Goodman 2002). Rather, the stock market was apprehended on moral terms. Just as the author of the Ming novel *Jinpingmei (The Plum in the Golden Vase)* may have been motivated to focus on the evil effects of the unrestrained desires of "lasciviousness" and "greed" (*se* and *cai*), as David T. Roy has persuasively argued, by a conservative orthodox Confucian desire to diagnose the evils of commercialized Ming society (Roy 1993:xviii, xxiii, xxxviii-xxxix) the modern tales of the stock market that were woven in the early Republican period were commonly organized around critiques of these two fundamentally disturbing elements of Shanghai modernity. In this regard, the early Republican-era discussion of *se* and *cai* in discussion of the stock market resonated deeply with earlier cultural critiques of commercial society. This said, amid what were rather conventional moral narratives (narratives which are striking in the context of the New Culture Movement and the avowed feminism of many of the authors), here and there plots were complicated by changing understandings and experiences of women. If women appear frequently as magnets and manipulators of *se* (and *cai*), they occasionally depart from such roles. Added to the familiar elements of older moral tales one finds occasional evidence of new preoccupations (positive and negative) with the possibility of moral or economic agency on the part of women, particularly new, educated women, who could venture into new arenas of society and depart from stock female roles.

Innocents in the Whirlpool of Market Corruption

A common concern of both stock market fiction and stock market reportage was the corruption of innocent young men, perhaps the likeliest group to foolishly lose money on the market. A *Shenbao (Shanghai Journal)* cartoon representing the dangers of the stock market, captioned "Swept into the Whirlpool" (*Juanru Xuanwo*), depicts young male elementary school teachers, too caught up in a frenzy of bidding to realize their imminent destruction (Juanru xuanwo 1921).

In the simplest of stock exchange stories, the main characters are innocent young men. Women figure only as emblems of virtue or descent into corruption. Such stories follow tropes found in turn-of-the-century and later Shanghai novels of wide-eyed young men who come from literati centers outside Shanghai and gradually lose their virtue in the Westernized, commercial city. One tale which transposed the familiar country-boy-comes-to-Shanghai narrative onto the Shanghai stock market was entitled, appropriately enough, *The Evils of the Stock Market* (*Jiaoyisuo de zui'e*) (Ai Zi 1922). The story concerns a youth from Suzhou (his name, Ziliang, combines the characters for "good" and "son"), who goes to Shanghai with family money. Upon his arrival in the city, Ziliang is fascinated with the "half-Chinese and half-Western buildings." He immediately enters one labeled "Stock Exchange." Inside, he notices the people all wearing Western suits, hurrying about. Enchanting new Westernized friends soon persuade him to invest and to join them in founding a new exchange. The man who serves as Ziliang's guide in Shanghai encourages him to meet business acquaintances in brothels. Once Ziliang is hooked on a life of dissipation it goes without saying that he forgets his elderly mother's parting words of caution and ceases to pay attention to his business affairs. The end of the tale is swift and predictable. Surrounded by creditors and filled with remorse at losing his family's money, Ziliang commits suicide with a pistol. Not only does he commit suicide, but so does his wife's brother, who enters the stock market through Ziliang. The account of the brother-in-law's death, which takes place at the end of the story, clarifies the mistaken desires that lead to his demise, in the event that an inattentive reader has missed the moral message: "after entering the stock exchange he wore the Western suits and glasses [he had coveted], and he frequented prostitutes with his co-workers."

Such cautionary tales repeat familiar tropes. Disorderly sex naturally accompanies the waste of fortune and the destruction of family property. Both result from improper or excessive desires, for money, for women, for what is foreign. Women are tangential to the narrative, though they play important iconic roles, poignantly invoking the duties of filiality (the mother) or inciting lasciviousness (the prostitutes). (None of these women – nor the male protagonist for that matter – can be said to be individual.)

A variation on this theme substituted female investors for men in the moral tale. The story of the doctor Pan Huzhen's wife, whose fictional suicide was recounted at the beginning of this essay, should be included in this category.

When a female investor named Xi Shangzhen committed suicide in a newspaper office in 1922,[4] her death stimulated moral

---

[4] Xi Shangzhen was a young female secretary who hung herself in the office of the *Shangbao (Journal of Commerce)* in September 1922 after giving her employer, Tang Jiezhi, five thousand *yuan* to purchase stock in his newly-established "China Trust Company." Xi's sister-in-law also purchased stock. Both of them lost their money in the stock market collapse. The case stimulated extensive commentary in the Shanghai press. I have explored the commentary generated by the case in the contexts of the cultural meanings of suicide in the early

commentary along these lines (Cui Weiru 1922; Chen Wangdao 1979; Dan Weng 1922). In such accounts the novelty of a female investor – and the riveting public spectacle of a captivating female suicide – heightened readers' impressions of vulnerability and innocence, destroyed by the unhealthy desires elicited by the corrupting influence of the market. The pioneering film director Zheng Zhengqiu, for example, explained unusual public interest in Xi's suicide in the following fashion:

> Those who fail in trust companies and the stock market and kill themselves are many. Those who are pressed by debt and kill themselves are also numerous. Those who experience economic difficulty and kill themselves are also many. If Xi Shangzhen were male, I believe her death would not have occasioned a similar social uproar. It is because Xi Shangzhen is a female secretary in a newspaper office that people take such unusual notice. [...] Under an unhealthy economic system, the heat of her desire to buy stock was naturally not easy to repress. At the boom of trusts and stocks, even very famous scholars could not restrain themselves. To blame Miss Xi and say she should not have "speculated unto death" (*touji zhi si*) is unfair. [But] to use Miss Xi's death to advise people not to engage in speculation is fine. (Zheng Zhengqiu 1922:2-8)

The logic of Zheng's argument suggests the psychological impact of a female suicide on the reading public. Xi's combined modernity (as a working woman), susceptibility and vulnerability (as a woman) highlighted the corruptions of the market in a manner more poignant than narratives devoted simply to the embarrassment of educated men losing money in the market.

Republican era (Goodman 2005a) and in regard to the issue of female vocations (Goodman 2005b).

Women's Weakness, Financial Promiscuity and Confusions of *Nei* and *Wai*

If some morality tales of the market exploited the spectacle of imagined or real female suicides in order to broadly warn of the dangers of the market for the (mostly male) investing public, some of the cautionary tales were also literally about women. In such stories, the market is an emblematic location for the expression of anxieties concerning new avenues for women's independence and financial mobility.

Cultural conservatives argued against women's participation in stock market activity because of women's inherent vulnerability. Conservative commentators suggested that women needed shelter from "the foulness of society, in which hundreds of frauds emerged" (Sheying,[5] quoted in: Cui Weiru 1922, 2:66). (Here the stock market emblematizes the broader corruptions of the troubled Chinese Republic.) Writing in a similar vein, Lu Shouxian, in his fictional vignette, "The Suicide Hanging of a Woman Who Failed" (*Shibai funü zhi touhuan*), suggested that women were natural targets for manipulative brokers, who understood that "women's money could be easily loosened from their grasp, with promises of profit." This story tells the tale of a broker's financial seduction of an insufficiently guarded wife, whose husband was periodically away on business in Hankou, unaware of her secret and ultimately disastrous financial relations with the broker. The narrative presents the impersonal economic consequences of the woman's speculative market activity entirely in terms of the interpersonal relations between the woman and the broker: "Not only did she have to sell her clothing and jewelry, but she had to borrow money to repay the debt. Early and late the broker demanded payment, not permitting even a slight postponement. Madame Hu begged the broker for mercy [...]." In her growing desperation Madame Hu, "not ashamed," goes to the office of the stock market director and kneels down humiliatingly before him. Even though the fictional Ma-

---

[5] Social Hero, pseud.

dame Hu was not sexually promiscuous, her financial transactions appear as marital improprieties (Lu Shouxian 1922:41-42).

Other conservative narratives used the dangers of the stock market to argue specifically against free-choice marriages and the entrance of women into places of male business (what was clearly *wai*), where, unprotected, they could become entangled in risky social and financial interactions. After the stock market collapse, the "mosquito paper" *Jingbao (Crystal)* published a serialized novella, entitled, "An Admonition to New Women."[6] The story featured a female secretary who lived with her widowed mother. Rather than marry a student from an old family, she pursued a free-choice engagement to a modern man who worked in a stock market. Her choice unfortunately led to her downfall. Her boyfriend visited her office, used her key to open a safe, and "borrowed" a large sum of money intended for medical research. Despite his promise to return the money the next day with profits from the stock market that they could share together, the money he took to invest was lost. After the girl was sent to jail, her mother died of grief. Finally, through an unpersuasive set of coincidences, once the girl fully appreciated the errors of her ways she was united in marriage with the man her parents originally chose for her (Ma Er 1923).

In the case of Xi Shangzhen's suicide, commentators decried "girls who were intoxicated with liberation" and who worked together with men: "They can't avoid discrediting their families and attracting social ridicule. [...] If Miss Xi had not taken work at the newspaper office she wouldn't have lost her money and her life. [...] She could have achieved happiness within women's quarters" (Nong,[7] quoted in: Cui Weiru 1922, 2:66-77). The writer Jiang Hongjiao, whose stock market novel is quoted in the introduction to this essay, was among those clearly disturbed by the implications of Xi's suicide for women with "upright professions": "That this concerns a woman with a vocation and that it took place in a newspaper office influences women's social intercourse and livelihood. The glory of women and the

---

[6] *Xinnü jie*, a play on the classical *Nü jie (Admonition to Women)* by the female scholar Ban Zhao.
[7] Farmer, pseud.

advancement of their future are at stake." He railed against those who opposed women's liberation and used female suicides to argue that women were unable to act positively and with integrity in public: "I dare to shout that the suicide of Xi Shangzhen provides instead a clear lesson for every woman today, politically awakening today's society. Everywhere in all respects women's sacred souls and bodies are undermined. Caution and care must be exercised, everywhere, and a glorious future will be achieved" (Jiang Hongjiao 1922:30-31).

Jiang was specifically concerned with conservative tendencies to equate women's entry into male professions with a degradation of female virtue. Women who worked were tainted by their motivation to earn money, particularly if earning money involved mixing with men. This is a prominent theme in poetic elegies written by newspaper readers in response to Xi Shangzhen's suicide, which contain phrases like, "She was cheated because of her wish to be in a gold chamber," "To die for money, her folly was extreme. How pitiful her white haired mother," "How worthless that she ruined her life through money. Being unwise she herself is to blame," and again, "Making a living damages your life. Money brings a thousand evils" (Shibao, 14, 16, 18 October 1922).

Stock markets served conservative moralists as iconic sites of particularly virulent moral contamination. In such arenas, women's leap to liberation exposed them to moral deterioration. This happened as quickly as the new exchanges "turned what was formerly gold and silver into paper with characters on it," and then ultimately "waste paper" (Lu Shouxian 1922:54, 74). In a farcical chapter entitled, "Breaking New Ground with Female Exchange Employees" (*Yong nü suoyuan zhi bie kai shengmian*) Lu Shouxian mocked contemporary journalistic celebrations of women's integration into male arenas of work:

> The average fashionable person sings of liberation and equality between men and women. From this followed the proposition to have female stock exchange employees. A certain exchange's preparatory director fancied himself a "modern man" (*xin renwu*). He raised the strange proposal of having male and female exchange employees. [...] The female exchange employees [...] were like a certain female short-story writer in Shanghai, or one of her characters. Or like the physical educa-

tion graduates of a certain school. Most comically, they were like someone's concubine. So in short form, they were transformed from female students to prostitutes and from prostitutes to concubines. (ibid. 145-146)

Such conservative accounts give witness to anxieties provoked by the new phenomenon of educated women's entrance into formerly exclusively male workplaces and arenas of business. Significantly, female stock exchange employees appear in several fictional accounts, whereas I have found no evidence that they existed in reality. As mentioned, women were prevented by law from functioning as brokers, officers or employees of exchanges (Zhengquan jiaoyisuo fa 1921). These injunctions are repeated in the published regulations of individual exchanges (Wupin jiaoyisuo tiaoli 1921; Shanghai zhengquan 1921). Lu's anecdotal stock market miscellany reported that "women were not permitted to enter stock exchanges to conduct trade, even if their husband or family head gave permission" (Lu Shouxian 1922:40). It is possible, of course, that some of the smaller, fly-by-night, exchanges may have employed women in some capacity. Whether female stock market employees were entirely invented or whether they had some basis in reality, their ability to fascinate is perhaps not surprising. Such a juxtaposition of money-tainted work and disordered gender relations epitomized the incongruence and impropriety of women's entrance into male arenas.

Public concern over the confusion of *nei* and *wai* that occurred in modern social and economic life reveals anxieties, not simply over women's growing access to male realms of society, but over the disturbing development of a broadly accessible new arena for the creation of wealth, where people of established backgrounds and morality unsuspectingly mixed with distasteful parvenues. Another of Lu's satirical stories, this one entitled, "Husband-and-Wife Stock Exchange Preparation Office" (*Fu qi jiaoyisuo zhi choubei chu*), concerns one such petty upstart, who clearly had no sense of propriety. The main character's inability to decorously maintain spatial gender divisions provides a central clue to his bad character and to the fraudulent nature of the economic enterprise he engages in. The story concerns a petty swindler who seizes upon the advent of stock exchanges as an opportunity to defraud unsuspecting investors. He gathers together a few likeminded people and sets up a tiny "Candle and Soap Stock Exchange Preparation Office." Soon he is engaged in "mad whoring and excessive gambling," funded by investments in his "exchange." The unholy nature of this office is underlined by the fact that it is established, not in a business office, but in a home, or rather, in one room of a home. Despite the brevity of the vignette, the specifics of the site are described in some detail, suggesting the significance of the improprieties they disclose. A curtain is hung across the center of the room, dividing it incompletely into two sections. One section housed the so-called stock exchange preparation office. The other section was the family residence. "Such was the brilliant such-and-such stock exchange preparation office" (ibid. 143-144).

Resistant Women and Unvirtuous Financial Upstarts

In some stories, the unrestrained greed and fraudulent actions of such upstarts who violate normative social hierarchies appear to call forth a counter-balancing confusion of *nei* and *wai*, in the form of women who enter shockingly into the male domain of the stock exchange and effectively expose the immorality of the men. These women – in contrast to those who are only victims and dupes – are remarkable for their ability to act effectively in their own interest.

One vignette, entitled, "A Pack of Females Makes a Show of Strength in the Director's Office" (*Lishi shi qunci yaowu*) relates a stock investment venture on the part of a group of prostitutes. Here the prostitutes ultimately succeed in ruining the reputation of the man, "a certain Lu," responsible for their losses by presenting themselves at his workplace, effectively destroying his reputation (ibid. 74). Their topsy-turvy revenge seems especially welcome because of Lu's identification with foreign customs and his ridiculous pretense of Western attire, even though he was too poor to be convincing:

> He had learned a bit of pidgin English [...] and bragged that he would be the compradore of a certain foreign company. He was slippery. [...] All year he wore a Western-style suit to demonstrate his civilized style. [...] Unfortunately he had only one set of clothes. In winter and summer this

was inconvenient. When it was hot he sweated [...] and when it was cold he wore a Chinese jacket on top. (ibid.)

As Lu makes money on the market he dons gold spectacles and a watch and gallops off to the brothel district. Lu did not earn enough to cover his extravagances, so he began to prey on high-class prostitutes who had some jewelry and cash. Gender roles here appear reversed as Lu "entices and lures" the prostitutes, finally "moving their hearts" with his promises. They sell their gold and jewelry to purchase his stock certificates, which quickly decline in value. As the prostitutes ask to sell their certificates he refuses, and then he avoids them by ending his visits to the brothel. Rather than accept their fate, the prostitutes leave the brothel and head for the stock exchange, where, with "long and slender jade hands" they drag out the hiding Lu and pull him outside. The spectacle destroys his professional reputation: "His fellow workers knew Lu had called this disaster upon himself. No empty words could resolve the matter. All of his energy could not restore his lost face" (ibid. 74-76).

In the above story, the conservative Lu Shouxian used the revenge of the prostitutes (a group of women he evidently found more sympathetic than the "new women" so cherished by feminists) as a fitting fate for a reprehensible figure like the fictive, socially mobile Lu. By making prostitutes the agents of justice here, he strengthened his indictment of the stock exchange and the social upstarts it engendered. The moral message of his tale is emphasized by the idea that even prostitutes could see the problems with the market. The fictional Lu is humiliated by low-status women who live in violation of the *nei/wai* divisions that governed basic propriety.

Stock market parvenues were also distasteful to New Culture writers like Jiang Hongjiao, who was equally eager to provide them with their fictional comeuppance. Unlike the conservative Lu Shouxian, however, Jiang did not embrace an old-fashioned propriety which enforced the separation of *nei* and *wai*. The difference in the two writers' ideologies of gender accounts for Jiang's choice of a "new woman" as the agent rendering justice.

It was not long after Jiang Hongjiao wrote his unpersuasive comments on the glorious future of women (in reaction to the real-life suicide of Xi Shangzhen) that he began to publish installments of his stock market novel. In writing fiction he had greater control of his plot than he did in his newspaper commentary. Significantly, his fictional stock market narrative does not contain such a contradictory and conflicted character as a "new woman" who commits suicide. Instead two women figure significantly in the novel as investors. Both create shock waves when they are seen at the stock exchange. One is the more traditional, poorly comprehending wife of the doctor Pan Huzhen, who creates such a spectacle by hanging herself on the stock market trading floor. This woman, identified only by her husband's name, registers for the reader the horrors of the stock market. The other is a "new woman," a Miss Tang, who, by virtue of her education and her free-choice engagement is clearly marked as a "new woman." This fictional "new woman" refuses to become a victim, successfully exerting herself where the real Xi Shangzhen had failed. Her opponent is an unscrupulous upstart broker who used to be a lackey at her father's home, when her father (now diminished in fortune) was still an eminent official. When this man, Ruifu, gets hold of her money and attempts to invest it unwisely for his own profit she is not too shy to come to the stock exchange to confront him in front of his male colleagues:

> Miss Tang stiffened her face and was not especially polite, asking him straight out, "Where is the deposit book I entrusted to you? Give it back to me immediately. There can be no mistake!" Ruifu thought to himself, "You little slave girl, aren't you fierce now? I thought you would be bashful and wouldn't dare ask about the money. Who would know that after three months she would come to demand it?" (Jiang Hongjiao 1994:40-41)

It is not accidental that the women in both these stories – prostitutes and a "new woman" – are outside the norms of traditional female virtue. But in Jiang Hongjiao's New Culture narrative the resistant female becomes a kind of hero. By virtue (one is tempted to say, by the new virtues) of her education and ability to handle her money and herself in male society, Miss Tang is the only female character in Jiang's novel who manages to escape the broadly metaphoric evils of the stock market. Jiang both focuses the reader's attention on her violation of the *nei/wai* division (her shocking appearance in the stock market ends one chapter and opens the next) and emphasizes that this is a good thing.[8] This said, Miss Tang serves a double function. Even as she upholds Jiang's political commitments with regard to new women, one is tempted to note that she also serves the purpose of defending the family fortune of an old scholarly line against new upstarts like Ruifu who lack her scholarly lineage.

Conclusion

This essay has explored gendered depictions of Shanghai's early stock market experience in reportage, commentary and popular fiction, to understand some of the cultural meanings of the stock market, an emblematic economic institution in a city already identified with rampant capitalism and disorderly sex. Female figures served a variety of purposes in a broad discussion of disturbances caused by the specific corruptions of the market, the intrusion of Western tastes and institutions and other modern transgressions of normative values, and social transformations associated with the new economic opportunities of the city and feminist advocacy of gender equality. If many of the anxieties reflected in this discussion had been in play since the late Qing, their poignancy was heightened by a new publicness, conveyed in the vehicle of the rapidly expanding press, a commercial press which fed on spectacle. The press was also a vehicle for the swift rise and fall of the new securities exchanges, bearing publicity, inciting desires, reporting rumors, spreading scandals. The newspapers created a new space for the contemplation of women and the transformation of gender roles, through reportage, advertisements, cartoons and serialized fiction. Amid cautionary narratives of fortune and virtue lost in the pursuit of empty, selfish, Western-style profit (in

---

[8] Jiang's comment in his contrasting description of Pan Huzhen's wife ("How could women understand the subtleties of the business of speculation?") should not be taken as a contradiction in his portrayal of women. Jiang has divided women into two categories, the old and the new. Old-fashioned women are seen negatively and "new woman," positively. In this case he is making a disparaging comment about an anonymous, house-bound, traditional woman.

which women serve as markers of virtue lost), the stories serialized in the newspapers conveyed as well the preoccupation of both cultural conservatives and New Culture radicals with the emergence of "new women."

The discussion here provides a preliminary excavation of a body of literature that could certainly bear examination in greater depth and across a longer period of time. The trajectory of Chinese stock market literature (and public understandings of the stock market) may nonetheless be indicated with reference to Mao Dun's much better known and more comprehensively analyzed stock market novel, *Ziye (Midnight)*, published in 1933. The early stock market literature from the early 1920s reflects a world quite different from that depicted in Mao Dun's novel. In the later novel, if women are still markers of virtue lost, educated (bourgeois) women's work and women's investment are out of the picture, and generalized (elite) morality, as opposed to the morality of particular classes, is not the overriding preoccupation. Commercial society is taken for granted and understood as a necessary constituent of progress. In the Nanjing decade, in contrast to the early 1920s, the stock market was dominated by the state. Accordingly, the later novel (and, of course, in the context of the ideological commitments of the author) is correspondingly preoccupied with the corruptions of the Nanjing regime and the revolutionary project of class analysis. Though women of dubious virtue serve as (problematic) conduits of bits of market information they get from their male lovers, class, not gender becomes the focus, and the stock market appears as a more closed, exclusive and resolutely male arena.[9]

---

[9] The one partial exception in Mao Dun's novel is the female figure Liu Yuying, whose family background also provides the novel's only reference to Shanghai's earlier stock market experience (we are told that Liu's father committed suicide a decade earlier in a great upheaval on the exchange). Liu is portrayed as a modest investor. In one scene which emphasizes the spectacle of Liu's sexuality in a male arena (she wriggles her hips and her breasts show rosily through the gauze of her dress), Liu presses herself into the sea of men on the exchange floor as part of a plan to capitalize on her market knowledge.

References

Ai Zi (pseud.), Jiaoyisuo de zui'e (The Evils of the Stock Market), serialized daily in: *Xianshi leyuan ribao*, 19-28 September 1922.

Andrew, Donna T., Randall McGowen, *The Perreaus and Mrs. Rudd: Forgery and Betrayal in Eighteenth-Century London*, Berkeley, Los Angeles, London 2001.

Bernhardt, Kathryn, *Women and Property in China, 960-1949*, Stanford 1999.

Chen Wangdao, Xi Shangzhen nüshi zai Shangbao guan li diaosi shijian (The Suicide Hanging of Xi Shangzhen in the Journal of Commerce), in: Fünu pinglun (supplement to the Minguo ribao), 20 September 1922, reproduced in: *Chen Wangdao wenji* (Collected Writings of Chen Wangdao), ed. by Fudan daxue yuyan yanjiu shi (Fudan University Linguistic Research Section), Shanghai 1979, pp. 162-169.

Chinese Form Stock Exchange: Institution Formally Inaugurated after Twenty Years of Agitation, in: *China Press*, 3 February 1920.

Chu, Margaret, Biographical Notes on Lady Xie Yao Zhilian – A Banker of the First Instance, in: Monika Übelhör (ed.), *Zwischen Tradition und Revolution: Lebensentwürfe chinesischer Frauen an der Schwelle zur Moderne*, Marburg 2001, pp. 218-222.

Cui Weiru (ed.), *Xi Shangzhen* (Xi Shangzhen), 2 parts, Shanghai 1922.

Dan Weng, Wan Shangbao guan Xi Shangzhen nüshi lian (Elegy for Miss Xi Shangzhen of the Shangbao Office), in: *Jingbao*, 12 September 1922.

Felski, Rita, *The Gender of Modernity*, Cambridge/MA 1995.

Goodman, Bryna, *Semi-Colonialism, "Empty Enterprise," and the Cultural Meanings of Shanghai's Early Stock-Exchange Fever*, paper delivered at "Repositioning Hong Kong and Shanghai in Modern Chinese History," University of Hong Kong, Hong Kong, 11-12 June 2002.

Goodman, Bryna, The New Woman Commits Suicide: The Press, Cultural Memory and the New Republic, in: *Journal of Asian Studies* (2005a).

Goodman, Bryna, The Vocational Woman and the Elusiveness of "Personhood" in Early Republican China, in: Bryna Goodman, Wendy Larson (eds.), *Gender in Motion: Divisions of Labor and Cultural Change in Late Imperial and Modern China*, Lanham 2005b.

Japanese Exchange Loses its Quarters to Chinese Combine, in: *China Press*, 1 January 1920.

Jiang Hongjiao, Duiyu Shangbao nü shuji ziyi zhi ganxiang (Thoughts about the Suicide Hanging of the Shangbao Female Secretary), in: Cui Weiru 1922, part 2, pp. 29-31.

Jiang Hongjiao, Jiaoyisuo xianxing ji (The True Nature of the Stock Market), originally serialized in: Xingqi, 1922-1923, reproduced in: Tang Zhesheng (ed.), *Jiaoyisuo zhenxiang de tanmizhe – Jiang Hongjiao* (Jiang Hongjiao: Sleuth of Secret Stock Market Truths), Nanjing 1994.

Jiu Shanghai de jiaoyisuo (Stock Markets in Old Shanghai), ed. by Zhongguo renmin zhengzhi xieshang huiyi Shanghai shi weiyuanhui wenshi ziliao weiyuanhui (Shanghai Municipal Cultural and Historical Materials Committee of the Chinese People's Political Consultative Committee), Shanghai 1994.

Jiu Shanghai de zhengquan jiaoyisuo (Securities Exchanges in Old Shanghai), ed. by Shanghai shi dang'an guan (Shanghai Municipal Archives), Shanghai 1992.

Juanru xuanwo (Swept into the Whirlpool), in: *Shenbao*, 17 September 1921.

Liang Qichao, Jinggao guozhong zhi tan shiye zhe (Notice to Those of Our Nation Who Speak of Industry and Commerce), in: Guofengbao, 2 November 1910, reproduced in: *Jiu Shanghai de zhengquan jiaoyisuo* 1992, pp. 265-273.

Lu Shouxian, *Jiaoyisuo xianxing ji* (The True Nature of the Stock Market), Shanghai 1922.

Ma Er (pseud.), Xinnü jie (An Admonition to New Women), in: *Jingbao*, 6, 9, 12, 15 March 1923.

McElderry, Andrea, Shanghai Securities Exchanges: Past and Present, in: *Occasional Paper Series in Business History* 4 (2001), Asian Business History Center, University of Queensland, pp. 1-19.

Public Record Office FO 228/3175, Report of A. L. Anderson, Enclosure No. 1 in Sir E. Fraser's Despatch No. 284 of 28 November 1921 to Peking.

Qi Liang, Shanghai Huashang zhengquan jiaoyisuo gaikuang (Overview of the Shanghai China Merchants' Securities Exchange), in: *Jiu Shanghai de jiaoyisuo* 1994, pp. 39-42.

Quyinsuo yu Jiaoyisuo zhi zhengzhu (Competition between the Quyinsuo and Jiaoyisuo), in: *Shenbao*, 17 September 1918.

Roy, David T., Introduction, in: David T. Roy (trans.), *The Plum in the Golden Vase, or, Chin P'ing Mei*, Princeton 1993, vol. 1, pp. xvii-xlviii.

Ru Yin (pseud.), Xi Shangzhen nüshi zisha hou zhongzhong de duanpian ganxiang (Brief Thoughts after the Suicide of Miss Xi Shangzhen), in: *Shishi xinbao*, 18 September 1922.

Searle, G. R., *Morality and the Market in Victorian Britain*, Oxford 1998.

Shanghai jiaoyisuo yi lan (A Look at Shanghai Exchanges), ed. by Jinbu shuju (Progressive Book Company), Shanghai 1922.

Shanghai qianzhuang yinhang shiliao (Materials on Shanghai Old-Style Banks), ed. by Shanghai renmin yinhang Shanghai shi fenhang (Shanghai Municipal Branch of the Shanghai People's Bank), Shanghai 1978 (reprint of 1960 edition).

Shanghai zhengquan wupin jiaoyisuo gufen youxian gongsi yingye xize (Detailed Business Regulations of the Shanghai Securities and Commodities Exchange Company, Limited), in: Wang Enliang 1921.

Shibao, 14, 16, 18 October 1922.

Sokolsky, George (writing under the pen name G. Gramada), The Gambling in Produce Exchanges, in: *North China Daily News*, 6 December 1921.

Thomas, William A., *Western Capitalism in China: A History of the Shanghai Stock Exchange*, Aldershot 2001.

Thompson, Victoria E., *The Virtuous Marketplace: Women and Men, Money and Politics in Paris, 1830-1870*, Baltimore, London 2000.

US Department of State Archives 893.52/37, Shanghai's Stock and Produce Exchanges, in: *The Chinese Engineer and Contractor Bulletin*, supplement (January 1922), pp. 2-9.

Wang Enliang (ed.), *Jiaoyisuo daquan* (The Complete Stock Exchange), Shanghai 1921.

Wupin jiaoyisuo tiaoli (Regulations of the Commodities Exchange), in: Wang Enliang 1921.

Zheng Zhengqiu, Cong Xi nüshi zisha delai de jiaoshun (Lessons from the Suicide of Miss Xi), in: Cui Weiru 1922, part 1, pp. 1-15.

Zhengquan jiaoyisuo fa (Securities Exchange Law), 1914, reproduced in: Wang Enliang 1921.

Zhu Zhenlu, Zhengquan wupin jiaoyisuo jianshu (Short History of the Securities and Commodities Exchange), in: *Jiu Shanghai de jiaoyisuo* 1994, p. 13.

Zhu Yingui, Jindai Shanghai zhengquan shichang shang gupiao maimai de sanci gaochao (Three Peaks of Stock-Purchasing in Modern Shanghai's Security Markets), in: *Zhongguo jingjishi yanjiu* 3 (1998), pp. 58-70.

"Women Returning Home" – A Topic of Chinese Women's Liberation

Zang Jian

"Women returning home" (*funü huijia*) is a topic that has been discussed for nearly a century in the modern history of Chin a.

The transformation of society and the accompanying modernization of China that started in the early twentieth century greatly eroded the traditional family values embodied in the expression, "men are responsible for outside matters, women are responsible for domestic matters" (*nan zhu wai, nü zhu nei*). This became most apparent after 1919 during the New Culture Movement associated with the May Fourth Movement, when an increasing number of women began working outside of their homes. Equality between men and women and the moral principles relating to changing family values became central concerns for the Chinese women's liberation movement.

Subsequently, there have been three large-scale debates in society related to the topic "women returning home." The first debate took place in the mid-1930s, the second at the beginning of the 1940s and the third debate, which has been most influential and longest lasting, took place in the period from the early 1980s into the 1990s. Each debate followed times of turbulence and broad transformation in Chinese society, and in each of these debates the proposition was raised that women should return home and become "good wives and mothers" (*xianqi liangmu*). This led to extensive discussions about the role of Chinese women in society in general, about women joining the workforce, about gender equality and about the road to women's liberation. Within these debates concerning women's return to a traditional role, there were two distinct, opposing positions: women

---

The author would like to express her thanks and appreciation to Luo Yan for translating this essay and Helen Young for correcting it.

"returning home" to assume traditional roles and the new "good wife and mother" theory.

1933-1937: The First Debate about Women Returning Home

The first debate on the topic "women returning home" took place in the mid-1930s, mainly from 1933 to 1937, a time when the whole capitalist world was undergoing the economic crisis that began in 1929. In China after the Mukden Incident,[1] the Japanese imperialists accelerated the invasion of China, and the Chinese people were faced with national calamity. The invasion and the accumulation of capital by the imperialists brought continuous strikes and bankruptcy to the already weak Chinese national industries, such as the manufacture of silk, matches, flour and cigarettes. The majority of workers were women, hundreds of thousands, and they bore the brunt of the job losses.

The first debate was initiated by Lin Yutang with a speech about "Marriage and Women in the Workforce" (*Hunjia yu nüzi zhiye*) given in June 1930 at the "Shanghai Chinese-Western Girls' School" (*Shanghai Zhong Xi nüshu*), and later published on 13 September 1933, in the *Shishi xinbao (Current Affairs Daily)*. Lin Yutang argued that due to a lack of jobs the occupation most suitable for women was marriage:

> The present economic system is extremely unequal for both sexes. [...] Both at home and abroad, there have always been fewer professions accessible to women than for men. Hence, the only occupation without any male competition is marriage. Marriage is the best, most suitable and most satisfying occupation for women. (Lin Yutang 1933:4)

In the same issue of the *Shishi xinbao*, Jiang Yue raised doubts about Lin Yutang's point of view in the article "Is Marriage the Best Occupation for Women?" (*Hunjia shi bu shi nüzi zui hao de zhiye?*),

---

[1] This incident occurred in northern Manchuria on 18 September 1931 when a bomb of unknown origin blew up a section of a Japanese railroad. Japan accused Chinese terrorists of being responsible, and used this incident as an excuse for the annexation of Manchuria.

asking critical questions such as: Can a woman "change" a bad husband in the same way a man can change a job he cannot abide? (Jiang Yue 1933)

In later issues of the *Shishi xinbao* other authors also became involved in the debate: In the article "Is Employment Unnecessary for Women after Marriage?" (*Nüzi chujia hou jiu bu bi you zhiye ma?*), Zha Shiji argued that the traditional idea that men should "provide for women" (*nanzi yang nüzi*) endured. The article also discussed the inconvenience for a woman in the workforce, who also is bearing and rearing children and taking care of her home. Letters from the readers demonstrated the importance of this issue, and a letter written by Chen Xiang called for an intensive discussion of this problem, and for opinions from the women's sphere.[2]

A rather radical response to Lin Yutang was offered in Yi Fan's article "The Opinion of a Woman" (*Yige nüzi de yijian*) on 16 September 1933. The article held that the reason why there are fewer women as successful as men in the various professions is not because women are not as smart as men, but because society failed to provide them with opportunities.

> We should devote ourselves to overthrow this economic system. The present society maintains this system, thus, we shall seek to overthrow this society. [...] Mr. Lin Yutang accepts this society. We do not. We want to get rid of it. (Yi Fan 1933:2)

Another opponent of Lin Yutang was Qian Taisheng, who, in his article "Good Wife and Mother" (*Xianqi liangmu*) on 24 September, argued that the idea of being a "good wife and mother" was not the narcotic that women needed. Instead, they should share the whole world with men (Qian Taisheng 1933).

Slogans such as "women should return home" and "women should become good wives and mothers" spread rapidly. The call for "women returning home" now became a powerful trend that was opposed to the opinion which had been promoted since the May Fourth Movement that "women should have the same responsibilities as men" (*funü yao he nanzi fu tongyang de zeren*). This trend was

---

[2] For Chen Xiang's letter see Zha Shiji 1933.

depicted in an article published in the *Shidai funü (Modern Women)* supplement of the *Dazhong ribao (Dazhong Daily)* from 1934: "[To be a] 'good wife and mother' again becomes the ultimate goal of female education. The one-sided virtue is again encouraged. The theory that women are born imperfect is being revived" (Beiping shidai funü wenti yanjiushe 1990a:540-541). The same opinion was also proposed in 1935 in the *Shidai funü* supplement. The article, "What is Women's Vocation?" (*Shenme shi funü de tianzhi?*), denounced the opinion that "women's vocation is that of wife and daughter," proposed by Fan Zhongyun, a prominent figure in the intellectual world of Beijing at that time (Beiping shidai funü wenti yanjiushe 1990c).

The women's liberation movement after the May Fourth Movement faced the threat of being defeated and being beaten back by this trend of returning to the past.

There also existed, however, critical voices coming from progressive women's associations and women's periodicals, which attributed the debate to larger economic and social problems within society, which had deepened and deteriorated with the economic panic under the capitalist system.

An article, entitled "Should Women Return Home?" (*Nüren huidao jiali qu ma?*), also published in *Shidai funü*, claimed:

> The first who had proposed the idea that "women should return home" was the German Hitler; he believed that "women should return home" in order to support a male-dominated society and to prevent the "imminent collapse of private ownership." (Beiping shidai funü wenti yanjiushe 1990b:541)

Another article which equated the call for "women returning home" with fascism was "Where Shall the Chinese Women Go?" (*Zhongguo funü wang nali qu?*), published in 1936 in *Beiping funü (Beiping Women)*.[3] The author asked:

> Where shall the women go? To fight for gender equality in the narrow sense, or to come home obediently and give up all their previous efforts, like the women in the fascist countries? (Jiang 1990:564)

---

[3] The journal was first issued in 1936 and ceased publication only after two issues.

We can see that the women's movement in China was closely related to the situation of women in international society, and many articles described women's life abroad; the weekly publication *Funü (Women)* of the *Beiping xinbao (Beiping Newspaper)*, for example, presented the life of German women in the articles "Lessons from the Life of German Women" (*Deguo nüzi shenghuo jiyu women de jiaoxun*) (Ruo 1990a) and "German and Italian Women under the Rule of a Pair of Fascist Twins" (*Yi dui Faxisi luanshengzi tongzhi xia de De Yi funü*) (Ruo 1990b).

Another line of argument was brought forward from 1935 to 1937, linking the role of women in China with the Chinese movement against Japanese aggression. In the weekly publication, *Funü* of the *Beiping xinbao*, several articles successfully denounced the argument that "women should return home."[4] The article, "Where Shall the Chinese Women Go?" (*Zhongguo funü wang nali qu?*), for example, related Chinese women's problems to the problems Chinese society was facing at the time:

> Women's problems are part of larger social problems. As long as the contradictions of the society remain unsolved, women's problems will remain forever. [...] Chinese women have only one correct choice, that is to hold on to the anti-imperialist and anti-feudalist stand, to strive for national liberation, and only when the poor and working people attain complete liberation will women's liberation be won. (Jiang 1990:564)

It may be concluded that the first debate on "women returning home" mirrored the conflicts between Chinese domestic and foreign politics, and between new and old forces within Chinese society. The debate begun in 1933 not only focused on the question "should women return home," but was also heavily shaped by resistance against forces wanting to revive old ways. In a later phase of the debate, approximately in 1937, the subject focused on the question of whether women should

---

[4] See, for instance, "Women's Liberation Movement Today" (*Dangqian de funü jiefang yundong*) by Li Ge (1936/1990), "The Revival of the 'Good Wife and Mother Theory'" (*'Xianqi liangmu' zhuyi de fuhuo*) by Yi Ding (1936/1990), "Which Road Shall We Take?" (*Women yinggai zou na yi tiao lu?*) by Shan Zi (1936/1990), and "New Trends of the Women's Liberation Movement" (*Funü jiefang yundong xin qushi*) by Bai Jixiong (1936/1990).

be allowed to take part in the Chinese Anti-Japanese Resistance Movement and thus perhaps gain their own liberation through the liberation of the whole nation.

1940-1943: The Second Debate about Women Returning Home

The second debate took place in the early 1940s. At that time, Japan had already invaded large parts of Northeast, Southeast and Southwest China, enslaving about one hundred fifty million Chinese people. The invasion by Japan also had severe economic effects, and a large number of women workers were now without jobs. The debate was initiated by the article "A Little Darkness in Blue" (*Weilan zhong yi dian an dan*), published in the Shanghai *Dagongbao (Dagong Newspaper)* on 6 July 1940. The author, Duanmu Luxi, also referred to the impact of the May Fourth Movement:

> From the May Fourth Movement until the twenty-third year of the Republic of China […] we cannot see what kind of liberating effect this movement had on the minds of ordinary women. Under the present social system and organization, we cannot deny that nine out of ten of our two hundred million women have to stay at home and assume the responsibility of being a mother. (Duanmu Luxi 1940:3)

Duanmu Luxi's article reiterated the "good wife and mother" slogan which she had already promoted in the mid-1930s and called upon women to "be content to manage the household within the home" (*zai xiao wo de jiating zhong, an yu zhili yi ge jiating*) (ibid.). The article, however, aroused an intense debate immediately after it was published. Yu Peihou criticized the article directly with his response "A Discussion of 'A Little Darkness in Blue'" (*'Weilan zhong yi dian an dan' zhi shangque*). The author argued for an "awakening of women" by promoting women's independence and stressed that women should not rely on anyone else (Yu Peihou 1940). On 28 July 1940, the *Dagongbao* published an essay by Xia Yingzhe, entitled "How to Understand the Chinese Women's Movement at the Present Stage – A Reading of 'A Little Darkness in Blue'" (*Zenyang renshi xianjieduan de Zhongguo funü yundong – 'Weilan zhong yi dian an dan' du hou gan*). In the article, the author gave details on his ideas regarding the nature, development and direction of the women's movement (Xia Yingzhe 1940).

The topic was then taken up by other journals such as *Funü xinyun (New Women's Movement)*, a supplement of the *Zhongyang ribao (Central Daily)*, which published Mo Ying's essay "After Reading 'A Little Darkness in Blue'" (*Du 'Weilan zhong yi dian an dan' hou*) (Mo Ying 1940). She claimed that Duanmu's proposal that "the substance of women's liberation was to be satisfied with one's small family and preserve it well" could never be the answer to this question. Mo Ying again put the focus on linking women's liberation with national liberation:

> What is more, we have struggled hard against the enemy for three years, most families suffered losses from enemy gunfire, many women lost their homes and were displaced and had to leave their children behind. Only national liberation can make women's liberation possible. (ibid. 4)

Mo Ying considered the following points as essential steps for implementation of the women's liberation movement:

> Women cadres have the task of motivating the intellectual women in the middle and upper classes and to mobilize the great number of rural women to participate in the war against Japan. Efforts have to be made to promote production, husbands and sons have to be encouraged to go to the front instead of returning back to the cozy life of the "private family." (ibid.)

An accompanying article by Ju Zi, entitled "Talking about a 'Good Wife and Mother'" (*Tantan 'xianqi liangmu'*), also criticized the "good wife and mother" theory. The article called upon the women to get rid of such shackles and devote themselves – as men were doing – to the fight for the well-being of the nation and the people (Ju Zi 1940).

Lin Feng regarded the strife of women for more equality as deriving from Western influences. In the article "The New Form of a Good Wife and Mother" (*Xianqi liangmu de xin xingshi*) (Lin Feng 1940), also published in the *Funü xinyun*, the author argued – by comparing Chinese tradition and Western influences – as follows: "When the capitalist forces of Western Europe together with the theories of civil rights, liberty and equality intruded into China, it was natural for women to awake and demand liberation" (ibid.). He continued that, however, there were still some people crying out: "'Women should go home,' which was nothing other than to drive women into the trap of a new form of being a 'good wife and mother'" (ibid. 4).

In the second debate, there was also strong influence of the Chinese Communist Party (CCP), with Deng Yingchao as one of the leading proponents. She wrote, also referring to "A Little Darkness in Blue," an article in *Funü zhi lu (The Road of Women)*, a supplement of the *Xinhua ribao (Xinhua Daily)* (Deng Yingchao 1940), in which she argued that the discussion of "women returning home" and the idea of a "good wife and mother" contained significant problems. She distinguished four essential points:

> First, the basis, direction, task, content, and goal of the Chinese women's liberation movement. Second, the development and evaluation of the history of the Chinese women's liberation movement. Third, perseverance in the fight against the Japanese and opposition to the reactionary trend of surrender. Fourth, the problems of women's education and profession. (ibid. 4)

Deng Yingchao called for everyone to participate:

> Today the people of China, both men and women, are oppressed in this semi-feudal and semi-colonial country. In the past three years during the blood and gunfire of invasion, they all, men and women, have been enslaved and lived miserable, inhuman lives. How could one then enjoy independence and human dignity? How could one enjoy a happy family life? (ibid.)

Deng Yingchao believed that at the time of national crisis, "the problems of women's education, profession, and liberation movement had to be related to the task of liberating China from the burden of being a semi-colonized country" (ibid.).

The same supplement also published articles written by Zhou Enlai, Zhang Xiaomei, and Pan Zinian.[5]

---

[5] For instance, "About a 'Good Wife and Mother' and Mother's Vocation" (*Guanyu 'xianqi liangmu' yu mu zhi*) (Zhou Enlai n.d./1990), "How to Solve the Problem of Women's Profession" (*Ruhe jiejue funü zhiye wenti*) (Zhang Xiaomei 1940/1990), and "The Problem of Conscience for Women's Liberation" (*Funü jiefang de yizhi wenti*) (Pan Zinian n.d./1990).

From 4 February to 8 March 1941, the supplement *Xin kendi (Virgin Land)* of the *Libao (Power News)* published more than fifty articles with different points of view on the debate about "women returning home" (Lu Fangshang 1994). This specific part of the debate was started by advocates of the theory "nation and country first" (*minzu zhi shang, guojia zhi shang*), referring to Nietzsche, admiring fascism, and were against the Soviet Union and communism. These authors included, for example, Fei Xiaotong, Zhu Guangqian and Shen Congwen.

Two articles by Shen Congwen were most remarkable: "Talking about Family" (*Tan jiating*) and "Equality between Men and Women" (*Nan nü pingdeng*) (Shen Congwen 1994, 1929), in which he stressed the existence of "natural differences between men and women." He thought that women's striving for equality would lead to conflicts between men and women; that the best place for women is at home (*jia*), and if women provide a good home, the problems of women will be greatly simplified. Only those feminists "with some physical abnormalities, who want to imitate men," are the ones who "want a family and cannot get one" (Shen Congwen 1929:4).

The editor of the *Libao*, Nie Gannu, published more than fifty related articles, of which more than two thirds showed disapproval of Shen Congwen's view. Shen Congwen was not only accused of promoting the restoration of ancient ways, but even of persuading women to fall into the "trap of the Confucian ethic" (*lijiao laolong*). Even more arguments were raised which demonstrated the reality of the inequality between men and women in society. These clearly pointed out that the women's question was crucial for the entire society: "no national liberation without women's liberation" (*meiyou minzu de jiefang, jiu meiyou funü de jiefang*) and "no national liberation without the participation of women" (*meiyou funü de canjia, ye jiu meiyou minzu de jiefang*).

In 1942, Nie Gannu edited a book about the discussions between *Libao* and *Zhanguoce (Strategies of the Warring States)* entitled *Nüquan lunbian (Discussion about Feminism)* and wrote a foreword for this book (Nie Gannu 1942).

Chinese intellectual women again were very interested in the situation of the women in Europe and in Russia, and the experience of the women's movement in the West. On 18 October 1940, *Funü zhi lu* published an article by Mu Ning, "Revealing the Life of German Working Women during the War" (*Zhanshi Deguo laodong funü de shenghuo*) (Mu Ning 1940), which argued as follows:

> Whether the ruling class of a nation is good or not can be determined by its attitude to women. In Germany, for example, Hitler said at a German women's conference that the men's sphere is the country, the women's sphere is her husband, her relatives, her children and her family. [...] Hence the subject of the women's movement in the NSDAP is only one, that is, [to have] two children. A Nazi woman leader also said that the biggest goal of women was to give birth to children for her country and her nation. (ibid. 4)

The Chinese women's movement has always closely watched the development of the women's movement in the West, which is one of the characteristics of the Chinese women's movement not only recently but also from the very beginning. Conversely, the women's movement in the West rarely paid attention to women in China.

The second debate took place at the beginning of the Anti-Japanese War, continuing the previous debate as well as expressing the political conflict between the supporters of resistance and those supporting surrender.

Women's organizations (*funü zuzhi*) under the leadership of the CCP shared the belief of all progressive women's organizations that the concept, "women should return home" equaled a backward step for women's liberation. At the same time they regarded the liberation of women as inseparable from the liberation of the nation. Thus the direction of the Chinese women's movement, i.e. the recognition that women should seek liberation through the liberation of the country and the nation, had become even more evident by this time.

1980-1990: The Third Debate about Women Returning Home

The third debate took place in the early 1980s and continued into the 1990s. It was the longest and the most influential among those three debates.

The Chinese government, after the establishment of the People's Republic of China (PRC) and the socialist planned economy in the 1950s, called upon the large number of urban women to take on the responsibility of finding jobs in production. With the slogans "times are different, men and women are the same" (*shidai bu tong le, nan nü dou yiyang*), and "women can do anything men can do" (*nanren nenggou zuo dao de, nüren ye neng zuo de dao*), a new trend was born. A great number of women turned from being housewives to becoming employed and entering the social arena – this had never happened before in the history of China. Now women had the same rights and opportunities in regard to occupation as men had.

The equalization process of women and men was implemented in the public fields by the administrative forces of the nation from top down to bottom. Although it could effectively efface the gender difference in system and ideology, it could neither radically solve the problem of gender equality nor thoroughly transform traditional gender roles. Since this gender difference was reduced during a time of poverty, it could only be possible during a limited time and in a limited space. While poverty provided an opportunity for achieving gender equality, eventually it became a barrier to it.

The third debate on "women returning home" took place after 1979 when China was facing the most serious unemployment pressure since 1949. There were two main reasons for this: on the one hand, the beginning of the transformation of the economic system had led to a great surplus of labor. On the other hand, about 17 million educated urban youth who had been forced to work in the countryside during the Cultural Revolution came back to the cities and were in urgent need of employment. Although almost every family in the cities was affected by this situation, it was most difficult for young women.

The third debate was also initiated in Shanghai. In May 1980 Li Fan wrote an article entitled "A Discussion about Women's Problems of Finding Employment in Shanghai" (*Shanghai funü jiuye wenti tantao*) (Li Fan 1980). The article stated that when making arrangements for women to find employment, one must consider that China had a large population and limited resources, and that therefore, the employment of women had to be coordinated with the establishment of a reasonable labor structure. This article questioned the full employment women had been enjoying in China for more than thirty years. These opinions had a great impact on the women's sphere in Shanghai (ibid.).

In the same year the Shanghai Women's Federation held a symposium and agreed that Li's article catered to the social trend of believing that "women should return home," which they regarded as an attack on women's liberation. On 6 August 1980, the *Guangming ribao (Guangming Daily)* introduced this debate to a larger audience with an article entitled "Two Opinions about Women Finding Employment" (*Guanyu funü jiuye wenti de liang zhong kanfa*) and caused a discussion which continued for several years (Guanyu funü jiuye wenti 1980). The evolution of this debate, which may be divided into three stages, is parallel to the reform of the economic system.

The first stage of the debate lasted from 1980 to 1985; it gradually extended to the whole society and reached a climax in the year 1984. From the very beginning this debate closely related women's employment to the transformation of the economic system. On 14 August 1980, Quan Fuxuan published an article in the *Guangming ribao*, proposing that the reason why there were so many people waiting for employment was not the high percentage of women in the workforce, but resulted from the lasting effects of "leftist" policies, such as the restrictions of the collective enterprises and the elimination of individual enterprises, which had closed the door to opportunities for employment (Quan Fuxuan 1980).

In June 1984, Xing Hua published an article in the *Beijing ribao (Beijing Daily)*, "The Women of Our Country Should Implement Employment in Stages" (*Woguo funü ying shixing jieduan jiuye*), arguing that women should rest the entire period from the seventh month of pregnancy until the child turned three years old, and then return to work (Xing Hua 1984).

This policy was adopted by many enterprises in the beginning of the 1980s. This preliminary reformation of the women's employment system did not break away from the old system of distribution of labor. It temporarily eased the burden of excessive personnel and solved the problem women face during pregnancy and lactation; thus, it could not be called "employment in stages" in the strict sense. The opposition to "women returning home" gained the upper hand for two reasons. First, the economic reform and the reform of the system of labor distribution had just begun, and people were still accustomed to the equal distribution of labor between the two sexes. Second, after the establishment of the socialist system in China, it had become an irrevocable fact that women widely participated in the society. The opinion that women "should return home" did not fit the expectations of both men and women from either an ideological or an individual point of view.

The second stage of the debate was the period from 1986 to 1989, and can be characterized by the fact that a large number of women had been laid off because of the ongoing economic reform and the influence the reform had on the large state-owned enterprises. At the same time, it was also becoming more difficult for women college graduates to find appropriate jobs. This led to a radicalization of the debate with an increasing focus on theoretical and analytical questions. In this context, a debate that was started in 1988 with a series of special columns on women's unemployment problems entitled "1988 – The Way Out for Women" (*1988 – Nüren de chulu*) and "May We Ask Which Direction We Should Take?" (*Gan wen lu zai hefang?*), published from January to November in the magazine *Zhongguo funü (Chinese Women)*, was of particular interest (1988 – Nüren de chulu 1988; Ganwen lu zai hefang? 1988). The involvement of the society was demonstrated by a special forum on the topic offered by the state-run TV channel CCTV (*Zhongyang dianshitai*) and many special seminars organized by women's and labor unions of various levels.

The last phase of the debate began after 1989. The debate not only centered on "women returning home" and "women's employment," but also looked at the changed course of the economy after many of the beneficial policies for women under the old planned economy had disappeared. It also looked at the disadvantageous status of women caused by the new competitive system, the new opportunities for women's employment and professional skills introduced by the reform, and how the skills and qualifications of women themselves might be improved in order to adjust to the new demands of the economy and to broaden the field of women's employment in general. On 20 July 1990, the *Zhongguo funübao (Chinese Women's Newspaper)* published an article by Shen Lirong, "Women in Urban Areas Face New Difficulties in Finding Employment" (*Chengzhen nüxing jiuye mianlin xin kunjing*), which analyzed aspects such as women's high expectations for finding good jobs on the one hand, and the low level of their competence on the other (Shen Lirong 1990). In 1992, Tao Tiezhu published an article in the second issue of *Nüxing yanjiu (Women's Studies)*, entitled "Market Economy and Women" (*Shichang jingji yu funü*), which predicted five changes that economic reform would bring to women:

1. The employment structure for women will change and they will turn to occupations "more naturally suitable for women."
2. The professional competence of women will remarkably improve.
3. For a predictable period, employment for women will become increasingly difficult.
4. Women and men may be paid different wages for the same labor.
5. A social class of housewives will develop (Tao Tiezhu 1992:11-12).

In the 1990s, the debate about whether "women should return home" gradually merged into the broader debate concerning women's employment and related problems, and the original debate disappeared. After the mid-1990s, and especially in the beginning of the twenty-first century, women's employment was no longer regarded as the only criterion of women's liberation; the debate had thus lost its original significance and had finally become history. The debate on women's liberation however is still bound up with the relation of women and family.

The development of modern society today has enabled women to participate in the society, and to implement their own independent individual social value. One cannot deny, however, that traditional social psychology and expectations today still require women to do household duties and to be devoted to their husband and children. Women are still "sandwiched between tradition and modernity."

From the perspective of women, their two-fold involvement in family and society illustrates that women still have double role-expectations to fulfill. The majority of women expect to participate in the workforce and at the same time to become good wives and mothers. This double role and double devotion to duty exhaust women physically as well as psychologically. Social expectation tends to "solve" this problem by the traditional pattern of division of labor expressed by "men responsible for outside matters, women responsible for domestic matters." In traditional society, the conflict between women's double role is conceived of as women's own private problem, not a public one. Hence the conflict between women's double role still remains a contradiction that is difficult to solve in an increasingly developed society.

Conclusion

In a review of the three debates about "women returning home," many similarities are apparent, although the debates took place in very different decades of the twentieth century.

If "women returning home" is the focus of the discussion, the early struggles regarding Chinese women's liberation – whether concerned with women entering school, running newspapers, or joining the workforce – are all characterized by women going out of their homes and entering society. Hence "women returning home" (*funü huijia qu*) and "women stepping out of their homes" (*funü zouchu jiamen*) have become the defining factors of "modern women" and "traditional women," and the criterion of women's liberation in more than a century.

The opponents of "women returning home" all agreed that the central question was not only women participating in the workforce, but women's involvement in an anti-imperialist, anti-feudal national democratic revolution in a society characterized as semi-feudal and semi-colonial. In the socialist society, it was widely acknowledged that the women's liberation movement should be merged into the fundamental national policies of reform, opening and modernization.

All three debates originated in Shanghai, the largest industrial city in the country, and the place where the foreign imperialist invasion forces had been concentrated. It was an appropriate place for the debates to arise, both because of the spread and infiltration of the West's women's movement, and because of the large number of educated and working women in various professions.

In all three debates there was an extremely close relationship with the development of the international women's movement. In the 1930s and 1940s, the initiation of the debate was consistent with German women's resistance against Hitler's women's policy and incorporated the model of the women of the Soviet Union. After the 1980s, the Western feminist movement influenced the debate, and there was a focus on raising women's consciousness and the search for women's self-fulfillment.

The three debates proved that women have never ceased their struggle against traditional concepts that opposed their taking part in social activities. Yet, to realize the goal of gender equality, there is still a long way to go. The previous women's movements urged women to step out of their families and to act like men, that is to seek success in a male-dominated society. But this kind of a "women's liberation" remained too "masculine," and often created a backlash. "Returning home," however, is also not a solution, as the women's liberation movement regards this as the source of oppression. Then what does women's liberation mean? Women's relation to the family and women seeking equality between men and women, are the most pressing theoretical blind spots in regards to women's liberation.

References

Bai Jixiong, Funü jiefang yundong xin qushi (New Trends of the Women's Liberation Movement), in: Funü 63 (weekly publication of the Beiping xinbao), 26 November 1936, p. 2, reproduced in: *Beijing funü baokan kao* 1990, p. 525.

Beijing funü baokan kao (Beijing Women's Newspaper and Periodical Review), ed. by Beijingshi funü lianhehui (Beijing Women's Federation), Beijing 1990.

Beiping shidai funü wenti yanjiushe (Society for Research on Beiping's Modern Women's Problems), Funü ying you de juewu (Women's Appropriate Consciousness), in: Shidai funü 3 (supplement to the Dazhong ribao), 8 October 1935, p. 3, reproduced in: *Beijing funü baokan kao* 1990a, pp. 540-541.

Beiping shidai funü wenti yanjiushe (Society for Research on Beiping's Modern Women's Problems), Nüren huidao jiali qu ma? (Should Women Return Home?), in: Shidai funü 3 (supplement to the Dazhong ribao), 8 October 1935, p. 3, reproduced in: *Beijing funü baokan kao* 1990b, p. 541.

Beiping shidai funü wenti yanjiushe (Society for Research on Beiping's Modern Women's Problems), Shenme shi funü de tianzhi? (What is Women's Vocation?), in: Shidai funü 7 (supplement to the Dazhong ribao), 5 November 1935, p. 3, reproduced in: *Beijing funü baokan kao* 1990c, p. 541.

Deng Yingchao, Guanyu "Weilan zhong yi dian an dan" de pipan (About the Critic of "A Little Darkness in Blue"), in: *Funü zhi lu* 7 (supplement to the *Xinhua ribao*), 12 August 1940, p. 4.

Duanmu Luxi, Weilan zhong yi dian an dan (A Little Darkness in Blue), in: *Dagongbao*, 6 July 1940, p. 3.

Ganwen lu zai hefang? (May We Ask Which Direction We Should Take?), ed. by Zhongguo funü zazhi bianjibu (Editorial Committee of the Magazine *Zhongguo funü*), in: *Zhongguo funü* 1-11 (1988).

Guanyu funü jiuye wenti de liang zhong kanfa (Two Opinions about Women Finding Employment), in: *Guangming ribao*, 6 August 1980, p. 3.

Jiang (pseud.), Zhongguo funü wang nali qu? (Where Shall the Chinese Women Go?), in: Beiping funü 1 (1 March 1936), pp. 8-10, reproduced in: *Beijing funü baokan kao* 1990, p. 564.

Jiang Yue, Hunjia shi bu shi nüzi zui hao de zhiye? (Is Marriage the Best Occupation for Women?), in: *Shishi xinbao*, 13 September 1933, sec. 3, p. 4.

Ju Zi, Tantan "xianqi liangmu" (Talking about a "Good Wife and Mother"), in: *Funü xinyun* (supplement to the *Zhongyang ribao*), 22 July 1940, p. 4.

Li Fan, Shanghai funü jiuye wenti tantao (A Discussion about Women's Problems of Finding Employment in Shanghai), in: *Guangming ribao*, 6 August 1980, p. 3.

Li Ge, Dangqian de funü jiefang yundong (Women's Liberation Movement Today), in: Funü 50 (weekly publication of the Beiping xinbao), 27 August 1936, p. 2, reproduced in: *Beijing funü baokan kao* 1990, p. 524.

Lin Feng, Xianqi liangmu de xin xingshi (The New Form of Good Wife and Mother), in: *Funü xinyun* (supplement to the *Zhongyang ribao*), 29 July 1940, p. 4.

Lin Yutang, Hunjia yu nüzi zhiye (Marriage and Women in the Workforce), in: *Shishi xinbao*, 13 September 1933, sec. 3, p. 4.

Lu Fangshang, Kangzhan shiqi de nüquan lunbian (The Debate about Women's Rights during the War of Resistance), in: *Jindai Zhongguo funü shi yanjiu* (Research on Women in Modern Chinese History), ed. by Jindai Zhongguo funü shi bianji weiyuanhui (Editorial Committee of Women in Modern Chinese History), Institute of Modern History, Academia Sinica, Taipei 1994, vol. 2, pp. 81-115.

Mo Ying, Du "Weilan zhong yi dian an dan" hou (After Reading "A Little Darkness in Blue"), in: the *Funü xinyun* (supplement to the *Zhongyang ribao*), 22 July 1940, p. 4.

Mu Ning, Zhanshi Deguo laodong funü de shenghuo (Revealing the Life of German Working Women during the War), in: *Funü zhi lu* 12 (supplement to the *Xinhua ribao*), 18 October 1940, p. 4.

Nie Gannu (ed.), *Nüquan lunbian* (Discussion about Feminism), Guilin 1942.

1988 – Nüren de chulu (1988 – The Way Out for Women), ed. by Zhongguo funü zazhi bianjibu (Editorial Committee of the Magazine *Zhongguo funü*), in: *Zhongguo funü* 1-11 (1988).

Pan Zinian, Funü jiefang de yizhi wenti (The Problem of Conscience for Women's Liberation), in: Funü zhi lu (supplement to the Xinhua ribao), n.d., reproduced in: Tian/Zheng 1990, pp. 117-118.

Qian Taisheng, Xianqi liangmu (Good Wife and Mother), in: *Shishi xinbao*, 24 September 1933, sec. 4, p. 2.

Quan Fuxuan, Guanyu funü jiuye wenti (About the Problems of Women's Unemployment), in: *Guangming ribao*, 14 August 1980, p. 3.

Ruo (pseud.), Deguo nüzi shenghuo jiyu women de jiaoxun (Lessons from the Life of German Women), in: Funü 17 (weekly publication of the Beiping xinbao), 29 December 1935, p. 2, reproduced in: *Beijing funü baokan kao* 1990a, p. 526.

Ruo (pseud.), Yi dui Faxisi luanshengzi tongzhi xia de De Yi funü (German and Italian Women under the Rule of a Pair of Fascist Twins), in: Funü 54 (weekly publication of the Beiping xinbao), 17 September 1936, p. 2, reproduced in: *Beijing funü baokan kao* 1990b, p. 526.

Shan Zi, Women yinggai zou na yi tiao lu? (Which Road Shall We Take?), in: Funü 55 (weekly publication of the Beiping xinbao), 1 October 1936, p. 2, reproduced in: *Beijing funü baokan kao* 1990, p. 525.

Shen Congwen, Nan nü pingdeng (Equality between Men and Women), in: *Zhongyang fukan* (supplement to the *Zhongyang ribao*), 17 October 1929, p. 4.

Shen Congwen, Tan jiating (Talking about Family), in: Zhanguo ce 13 (October 1929), reproduced in: Lu Fangshang 1994, vol. 2, p. 103.

Shen Lirong, Chengzhen nüxing jiuye mianlin xin kunjing (Women in Urban Areas Face New Difficulties in Finding Employment), in: *Zhongguo funübao*, 20 July 1990, p. 3.

Tao Tiezhu, Shichang jingji yu funü (Market Economy and Women), in: *Nüxing yanjiu* 2 (1992), pp. 11-12.

Tian Jingkun, Zheng Xiaoyan (eds.), *Zhongguo jin xiandai funü baokan tonglan* (Review of Women's Periodicals in Modern China), Beijing 1990.

Xia Yingzhe, Zenyang renshi xianjieduan de Zhongguo funü yundong – "Weilan zhong yi dian an dan" du hou gan (How to Understand the Chinese Women's Movement at the Present Stage – A Reading of "A Little Darkness in Blue"), in: *Dagongbao*, 28 July 1940, p. 4.

Xing Hua, Woguo funü ying shixing jieduan jiuye (The Women of Our Country Should Implement Employment in Stages), in: *Beijing ribao*, 1 June 1984, p. 4.

Yi Ding, "Xianqi liangmu" zhuyi de fuhuo (The Revival of the "Good Wife and Mother" Theory), in: Funü 52 (weekly publication of the Beiping xinbao), 10 September 1936, p. 2, reproduced in: *Beijing funü baokan kao* 1990, p. 524.

Yi Fan, Yige nüzi de yijian (The Opinion of a Woman), in: *Shishi xinbao*, 16 September 1933, sec. 4, p. 2.

Yu Peihou, "Weilan zhong yi dian an dan" zhi shangque (A Discussion of "A Little Darkness in Blue"), in: *Dagongbao*, 22 July 1940, p. 3.

Zha Shiji, Nüzi chujia hou jiu bu bi you zhiye ma? (Is Employment Unnecessary for Women after Marriage?), in: *Shishi xinbao*, 15 September 1933, sec. 3, p. 4.

Zhang Xiaomei, Ruhe jiejue nü zhiye wenti (How to Solve the Problem of Women's Profession), in: Funü zhi lu 17 (supplement to the Xinhua ribao), 13 December 1940, p. 4, reproduced in: Tian/Zheng 1990, pp. 117-118.

Zhou Enlai, Guanyu "xianqi liangmu" yu mu zhi (About a "Good Wife and Mother" and Mother's Vocation), in: Funü zhi lu (supplement to the Xinhua ribao), n.d., reproduced in: Tian/Zheng 1990, pp. 117-118.

Women and Gender in the Rural Modernization Movement: A Case Study of Ding County (1912-1937)

Du Fangqin

> The rural areas should reform, the state urgently needs to be reconstructed, the nation must be revived. People with lofty ideals have not only realized their importance, but have also transformed theoretical discussion into practical movements everywhere.
> Yan Yangchu, *Zhonghua pingmin jiaoyu cujinhui Dingxian shiyan gongzuo tiyao* (1990b).

At the intersection of the nineteenth and twentieth century Mi Digang and Yan Yangchu,[1] men with lofty ideals, carried out many experiments related to modernization and reform, ranging from urban to rural areas, from south to north for the purpose of creating a prosperous country and reviving the nation. This essay focuses on the gender issue against the background of the twenty-five-year-long reform of the Village Self-Government Movement (*Xiangcun zizhi yundong*) and the Mass Education Movement (*Pingmin jiaoyu yundong*) in Ding County, North China from early Republican China until the outbreak of the War of Resistance Against Japan.

Emphasis will be put on the following questions: (1) What is the relationship between the goals and the plans of the reform led by male elite, and women and gender? How did the male elite design and implement gender relationships in their modernization reform? (2) What did the modernization movement mean to rural women? How did they participate in the movement? What changes did the move-

---

The author would like to express her thanks and appreciation to Fang Fengxia, Wang Xiangxian and Cai Lingping for translating this essay and Helen Young for correcting it.

[1] Mi Digang was born in Zhaicheng Village of Ding County. After having studied in Japan he returned to China and became leader of Village Self-Government Movement; Yan Yangchu (1890-1990), was born in Bazhong County, Sichuan Province. He studied in the United States and obtained a PhD. After his return to China he became leader of the Mass Education Movement.

ment bring for their lives? What remained unchanged? And what implications do the reform of self-government and mass education have for today?

There are two reasons why this topic is of great interest. First, few villages have undergone such a continuous modernization movement as has Ding County, and in no other places are there so many existing records and discussions written by participants and others at that time. The *Annals of Zhaicheng Village (Zhaicheng cun zhi)*, for example, records the process of reconstruction in Zhaicheng, Ding County, during the early period of Republican China (Yi Zhongcai 1925). *Ding County: A Social Survey (Dingxian shehui gaikuang diaocha)* is another well-known work dealing with Ding County mass education and county reconstruction experience in the 1920s and 1930s (Li Jinghan 1986). Moreover, there are many work notes, commentaries and articles from that time, which offer valuable historical material for the study (see Li Jidong 1990). Second, from 1994 to 1997, with funding provided by the Ford Foundation, the Women's Studies Center of Tianjin Normal University (*Tianjin Shifan daxue funü yanjiu zhongxin*) implemented a research and training project with rural women in Ding County.[2] One objective of the project was to explore the way the cultural changes in society affected the life of rural women during the past one hundred years.

An Outline of Village Self-Government in Zhaicheng Village

The early twentieth century reforms in Zhaicheng Village represented the beginning of the modern reform movement in rural North China toward the end of the Qing dynasty. Influenced by an increasing interest in education at that time, a member of the Zhaicheng Village gentry, Mi Jiansan in 1902 built a modern village school, a part time school and an old-style private school for girls in the village. Meanwhile, he also initiated plans for village self-governance. In 1914, Sun Faxu, the magistrate of Ding County, after an inspection trip to Zhaicheng, reported that the local people were good

---

[2] Ding County is now named Dingzhou City.

and honest and demonstrated a strong interest in education. His report was the basis for the decision to make Zhaicheng a model village. The government officials at the county and province level honored Zhaicheng and provided funds many times. Zhaicheng even received support from the central government in Beijing. In 1914, the village self-government program was officially implemented. A village self-government council, lecture hall, and library were built, and societies such as the "Patriotic Society" (*Aiguo she*) were organized. Beginning in 1915, a higher primary school, a primary school for girls and a higher primary school for girls were set up (Yi Zhongcai 1925:45-46, 68-69). Mi Digang, the son of Mi Jiansan, finished his studies in Japan and brought back his experience with self-government in the rural areas of Japan. Mi Digang and Mi Jiansan were also deeply influenced by the Yan-Li school of thought,[3] under the training of the teacher Jia Peiqing. They regarded social reform and village reform as their duty. They believed village reform should be carried out according to the "three guiding principles" (*san gang*)[4] and "eight items" (*ba mu*)[5] of the *Da xue (The Great Learning)* and Lü Dazhong's *Lüshi xiangyue (The Local Rules of Lü's Clan)* of the Song dynasty (ibid. 67).[6]

Mi Digang was convinced that only by developing self-government in the villages could the families and – subsequently the nation – be united. As the village government stands between the families and the county and provincial governments, improvement in village self-government was regarded as the foundation that would ensure the integrity of the families, the proper government of the state and bring peace and harmony to the country. In addition, Mi Digang

---

[3] Yan Yuan (1635-1704) and Li Gong (1659-1733) of the early Qing belonged to a philosophical school that stressed practical knowledge.

[4] *San gang* includes *mingming de, qin min, zhiyu zhishan* (to illustrate illustrious virtue, to be kind to people, and to rest in the highest excellence).

[5] *Ba mu* includes *gewu, zhizhi, zhengxin, chengyi, xiushen, qijia, zhiguo, ping tianxia* (investigate things, extend knowledge, make the will sincere, rectify the mind, cultivate the person, regulate the family, govern the state well and bring peace to the world).

[6] Its brief points are *de ye xiang li* (to encourage each other in morality and vocation), *guoshi xiang gui* (to admonish each other not to be mistaken), *li su xiang jiao* (to treat each other with manners), and *huannan xiang xu* (to pity and help each other in trouble).

emphasized the specific role for the development of village self-government. In his opinion village reform should fill the gap that exists between "upholding the family" (*qijia*) and "governing the country" (*zhiguo*), according to *The Great Learning*, and described village reform as "caring for the neighbors in the village" (*qin xiang*). Mi Digang considered the country and the world as abstract, but the village as existing in reality. Since the village depended on the clan, if the village were well run, then the clans were united and the family was in good order. Thus, Mi Digang's reform was based on village self-government and he intended to make Zhaicheng a model village according to the system of "official and teacher combined in one (person)" (*guan shi heyi*), so that the administrative head of the village was the chairman of education. He hoped that these examples would spread to the whole of China in order to "solve the problems of education and to educate more people" (ibid. 44). Mi Digang attempted to establish new villages, for example in Inner Mongolia and to reform old ones at the same time. He wished to train many capable, honest and candid representatives through village self-government. These representatives then would become the male elite who would "get rid of peacockery," would be "happy living in a village," would "dedicate themselves to the cause of reform," and simply "serve the masses without selfish purposes" (ibid. 66-68). The process of training the village community elite should also produce the citizens (*guomin*) urgently needed by the newly founded Republic. Beginning in 1914 rules and regulations for village self-government were enacted that helped this kind of government run normally and smoothly, and also made possible the building of many new village schools.

In 1924 the Chinese Mass Education Association (*Zhonghua pingmin jiaoyu cujinhui*) set up a "Rural Education Department" (*Xiangcun jiaoyubu*). Yan Yangchu, the general secretary of the association agreed to carry out further experimental reforms in Zhaicheng Village, after he was enthusiastically invited by Mi Digang. In the winter of 1927, the Rural Education Department moved to Zhaicheng and the village self-government and the mass education there entered a new stage.

The Position of Women in Village Self-Government

Going further, we confront the following questions: Which reforms and restructuring did the village self-government implement combining local and foreign experiences? How did these reforms affect women? How did it influence the social position of women and men, and the relationship between them? How did it construct new models of femininity and masculinity?

Reformers such as Mi Digang substituted the expression *guomin*, meaning citizens with a modern identity, for the imperial era term *baixing* (common people). It may be asked, however, to whom *guomin* actually referred. There is no doubt that *pifu* (ordinary men) who were also responsible for the rise and fall of a nation had been changed into *guomin*, but what about the *pifu* (ordinary women),[7] who had been excluded from public and official affairs for the previous three thousand years? If "ordinary women" also should become qualified *guomin*, this would create an unavoidable problem for the reformers.

In Zhaicheng's village self-government system, the conflicts between women and *guomin*, and tradition and modernity, could be solved by using the two ambiguous, unclear terms, *guomin* (citizen) and *renmin* (people). In fact, however, in the context of village self-government, both *guomin* and *renmin* referred to males, that is male household heads and male adults. Every position in each organization – including the village self-government committee, the village assembly, the economic organization, and the education organization – was *de facto* occupied by a male. The village self-government in the beginning was completely controlled by the male elite. Only later, after the establishment of the Republic of China, were women granted more opportunities regarding education by order of the central government. As a model village, girls' education in Zhaicheng, however, had already made great progress. Women were organized into different groups to receive adult education, whereby modernity and tradition were combined, but this special education for women was still limited and differed from education for men. From some incidents related to

---

[7] The characters for *fu* in *pifu* are those for "man" and "woman" respectively.

education and custom in Zhaicheng Village, it can be concluded that women were given limited and different education from men and were particularly required to be models and examples of virtue and morality, and to "uphold the family" and "keep the village customs in good order." The ambiguous and uncertain meaning of *guomin* reflected the unequal rights and obligations of males and females during the village self-government period.

The ideal model of Zhaicheng's village self-government – as designed by Mi Digang and other key members – was a bottom to top government with great emphasis on morality, designed according to Confucian principles. The 330 families, that is 2,071 inhabitants of the village, were divided into five groups, named after the five Chinese virtues, "benevolence" (*ren*), "righteousness" (*yi*), "propriety" (*li*), "wisdom" (*zhi*) and "faith" (*xin*). The reformers also calculated the ratio of men and women, and the ratio of pupils who were actually attending school, according to their sex (ibid. 55-57).[8]

The Organizational Rules of Self-Government of the village were described as follows:

6. The village self-government is managed by all villagers.
7. The villagers select one village head and two deputy heads.
8. The village is divided into eight self-governing districts with an elected head in each district.
9. A Village Public Service Bureau (*cun gong suo*) is set up to deal with all affairs of the village.
10. The village routine work is separated into two sections: a) the general affairs section and b) the financial affairs section.
11. The officers of each section are in charge of the affairs of the respective section.
12. The Village Public Service Bureau organizes village assemblies (*cun hui*) to discuss the important affairs of the village. When holding an assembly, the village head is the chairman of the assembly, and the two deputy heads, the officers of the above two sections and each head of the eight districts form the committee members.

---

[8] See the official statistics of 1927: Before 1927, 60 percent of the seven- to fourteen-year-old-children attended school, of which 20 percent were girls.

13. Special committees and societies are set up to issue regulations for education, philanthropy, sanitation, business and transportation, and for the "Benefit Society" (*Yin li xie she*).
14. All the expenses of the self-government should be covered by all the villagers.
15. The budget and the final financial accounts of the self-government are decided upon by vote of the village assembly and submitted to the county level government to be audited and placed on record.
16. The charter of this organization will be published and placed on record at the county level government (ibid. 59-60).

Although there was a completely new organizational system and centralization of power in village self-government, the elite politics could be described as a redistribution of power among the male elite in accordance with the traditional clan and familial relationships. Mi Digang himself stated frankly that the development of Zhaicheng's village self-government was greatly stimulated and assisted by members of the Mi families. Mi Jieping, the third younger brother who had worked in the Ministry of Foreign Affairs, became a key person in the village. Mi Xiaozhou, the second younger brother was once the head of the village. Mi Shuping, his nephew, was elected director of the Benefit Society – in spite of the fact that he was illiterate – on the basis of a single good proposal he had submitted. The male elite of the Mi family occupied most of the positions in the village. According to the *Annals of Zhaicheng Village* of 1920, out of the fifteen members in the Village Public Service Bureau, eight were from the Mi family, including the head of the village, the deputy head, and the officers of the general affairs and financial affairs. Furthermore, the Mi clan occupied forty-nine positions, and each person held seven or eight different posts (ibid. 49-51).[9] The redistribution of power among males took place first according to the social stratum, then the clan, and finally according to the residential area. In brief, men monopolized public power in the village and women were unable to participate in public affairs and were granted no access to power. The situation changed, however, in 1928, when the Nationalist forces reached

---

[9] According to the table of employees in Zhaicheng Village (*Zhaicheng cun zhiyuan yilanbiao*) from May 1920.

North China and promulgated a new law concerning the organization of the village government that required the village heads to be elected by both men and women at a village meeting. Representatives of the county level government attended the meeting to ensure that the election was properly conducted and to prevent wealthy and influential families, such as the Mi and Qin in Zhaicheng, from again gaining control over the village government. From then on, the women of Zhaicheng Village had the right to vote (Gamble 1968:150).

Education and Gender

The origin of self-government in Zhaicheng Village can be traced back to the initiation of girls' schools (*nüxue*), which were promoted from 1907, the 33rd year of the Guangxu reign, when the Qing government published *Nüxuetang zhangcheng (The Rules for Girls' Schools)*. After that, the establishment of schools for girls quickly gained popularity. In Zhaicheng, a private school for girls opened shortly after the establishment of a school for boys by Mi Jiansan in 1894. Soon after the founding of the Republic, Mi Jiansan, who had been developing plans for village reform since 1902, at his own expense organized a girls' primary school and a higher primary school for both boys and girls. As a model village, Zhaicheng emphasized education in the process of the self-government movement. In 1914, a Village Education Committee was set up to administer the village schools and to discuss the problems of school budgets, school subjects, and the improvement of education. By 1915, the names of the schools were changed to "citizens' primary schools" (*guomin xiaoxue*) or "citizens' higher primary schools" (*guomin gaodeng xiaoxue*). The Education Committee Acts were intended to make village education free and universal, to improve family education, community education and moral education for young people.

School Education

It was believed that education was the key factor for both village self-government and national development, and the popularization of primary school was fundamental in fostering "new citizens" (*xin guomin*) and talents. Every child between six and fourteen years should receive at least a primary school education. The purpose of primary school should be to build up common qualifications for citizens and to teach them basic knowledge for everyday living, such as how to organize a group. "Whether male or female, rich or poor, each school-aged child should be educated. That means that education must be compulsory for every child" (Yi Zhongcai 1925:90-91).

The most important breakthrough for female education in the village was that girls departed from the tradition that had kept them at home: females "have to learn in schools outside their homes" (*bu neng bu jiu wai fu*) (ibid. 89-91). The acts of the Village Education Committee made village education free and universal, but public education for girls only meant primary school, including higher primary school, a total of seven years including four years primary school and three years higher primary school. Enrolment of girls in school also remained much lower than for boys; from 1904 to 1930, enrolment of boys grew from forty-five in 1904 to many more than one hundred in the 1920s, but until 1930 there were only ninety-five girls:

School Enrolment in Zhaicheng Village[10]

year	total	girls	boys
1904	-	-	45
1912	-	-	57
1913	-	-	87
1916	211	36	175
1917	-	-	136
1920	-	-	172
1922	-	-	178
1923	-	-	178
1929	-	-	146
1930	248	95	153

[10] Gamble 1968:160-161; Yi Zhongcai 1925:139, 13.

Although the rules of the village self-government provided that a girl under fourteen years old could go to a girls' primary school, but they were ambiguous concerning whether she could enter middle school afterwards. Fourteen-year-old girls, even if they had potential, would not be encouraged by the Village Education Committee to continue formal education, while excellent but poor male students could apply for education loans, according to the rules. This was different from regulations for primary school, which stated that both girls and boys from poor families could apply for loans. The Village Education Committee also encouraged the father and brothers of such intelligent boys to support them to continue their education. Another crucial difference in education for boys and girls was that although boys were required to be resident in school to train their team spirit, girls were not allowed to live at school with the boys since it was considered "improper behavior for girls" (ibid. 97-98, 102, 138).

In Zhaicheng, there were obviously differences between girls and boys regarding the purpose of training, organization of curriculum, and regulations. Regarding the purpose of education, requirements for boys were high and focused on the development of morality, intelligence, learning and physical education, while for the girls the requirements were lower and more ambiguous. Boys were rated according to their good nature, wisdom, persistence and tolerance. They were taught to be warm-hearted, tidy, diligent, disciplined, quick in action, concise and logical in expression. Boys whose scores were high or who showed potential would be encouraged to continue their education. The school required students to do physical exercises to strengthen their bodies. With clear training aims and punishment threatened for those boys who did not follow the rules or obey their teacher's orders, boys were encouraged to make progress so that they would be able to use their talents to carry on the village self-government and to perform their social duties.

The most important requirements for girls, however, were to become obedient, gentle, faithful and peaceful. They should respect each other and obey their teachers' instructions. They must wear school uniforms everyday and were not allowed to bind their feet. There were no definite requirements and objectives for girls' studies, nor explicit encouragement and awards. There were many rules and most of them were trifling. "Enter and leave the classroom in an orderly manner," "be prepared for lessons," "do not change seats randomly," and while listening to the lesson "do not look around in class," "do not talk or leave your seat during class," "raise your hand before speaking." In addition, there was one rule particularly made for girls: "girls should return home immediately after school and review their lessons" (ibid. 114-124, 138-143). One of the reasons for the great differences between boys' and girls' rules could be that male leaders thought girls were immature and could not control themselves.

The *Annals of Zhaicheng Village* reported that as early as 1909 Mi Chunming had built a private girls' school (ibid. 46). In February 1915, the public girls' school was opened on the site of the old-style private girls' school, admitting thirty-six girls divided into two classes. In September of that year, new schoolhouses were built at the old temple in the south of the village, and girls' classes at the higher level were added and taught by male teachers. In 1916, this was expanded and named "Zhaicheng Village National Higher Primary School of Ding County" (*Dingxian Zhaicheng cun li guomin gaodeng xiao xuexiao*). There were strict rules to ensure that males and females were strictly separated: girls were not allowed to visit boys' schools and girls were taught by women teachers. Mi Chunming was headmaster of the girls' school (ibid. 140-141). According to the *Annals of Zhaicheng Village* the required courses for the primary schools for girls were ethics (*xiushen*), Chinese language, mathematics, needlecraft (*nügong*) and gymnastics (*ticao*), and the optional courses were drawing and music. In higher primary school two hours of history, geography and natural science were added. The subjects in primary schools and higher primary schools for boys were different from those in girls' schools. As stated in the second part of the *Rules of Lower and Higher Primary School* (*Guomin gaodeng xiao xuexiao zhangcheng*): "The courses in primary school were ethics, Chinese language, mathematics, gymnastics, handicrafts (*shougong*), drawing and singing. Courses in higher primary school are ethics, Chinese language, mathematics, Chinese history, geography, science, gymnastics, handicrafts, drawing, singing and English language" (quoted in: ibid. 112-115).

The subjects of ethics, Chinese language, arithmetic and gymnastics, while taught both at boys' and girls' schools, differed in content, quantity and extent of training. The teaching of English in boys' schools was regarded as a sign of modernity for boys and as a chance for social advancement allowing men to leave the small village; but English was not taught in girls' schools. There was a wide variety of subjects included in boys' handicraft classes, but girls' needlecraft (*nügong*) classes focused on the skills needed for the private sphere. They learned sewing, design and cutting and mending. In the higher grades, the hours of *nügong* were extended, that is two hours every week from the third school year, and an additional five or six hours every week for higher primary school students (Shu Xincheng 1961:805-808). In the girls' school of Zhaicheng Village, there were two sewing-rooms in addition to the nine classrooms. This demonstrates that the skills girls learned in the private sphere before had been incorporated into the new education system.

Community and Family Education

Apart from the formal school education, the reformers in Zhaicheng Village also emphasized community (*shequ*) and family education. For example, they provided "half-day school" for male adolescents who were poor and beyond school age, to study ethics, Chinese language, arithmetic and gymnastics two hours per day, so that they would learn basic knowledge for everyday living (Yi Zhongcai 1925:125-127).

Adult education was intended to enlighten people, reform customs, blend old ideas with new and unite the villagers. The "Patriotic Lecture Society" (*Aiguo xuanjiang she*) was organized in 1915 to help foster patriotism in the villages, and the magistrate Sun Faxu himself came to Zhaicheng to give lectures on patriotism (ibid. 128-131). In addition, the village established a library, a newspaper-reading room, an Institute for the Training of Village Self-Government Personnel (*Zizhi jiangxisuo*) and the "Society of Admiring the Virtuous" (*Le xian hui*).

One of the first tasks undertaken by the Institute for the Training of Village Self-Government Personnel was to encourage male villagers to participate in village self-government, to "study the nature of self-government, cultivate the character of citizens (*gongmin xingge*) and become model villagers." The first students were officials of the villages and districts. The content of the lessons was based on teaching materials of the Institute for the Training of Citizens in Ding County (*Dingxian gongmin jiangxisuo*) and on the history of self-government in three model villages in Japan (ibid. 134). Thus, it is clearly demonstrated that the community education of village self-government was male-oriented. The Society of Admiring the Virtuous was organized by teachers to encourage the people to learn from "wise people of the past." The Mi brothers and other prominent men gave lectures at the one or two meetings the society held every year. The Society of Admiring the Virtuous was established in order to serve as a bridge between different educational forms. This society emphasized the affinity between fathers and sons, older brothers and younger brothers. It advocated that fathers and older brothers should not only supervise their sons and younger brothers, but should also be in touch with schools and teachers from time to time, thus allowing them to learn about the family and daily life of the students in order to train and discipline them in a better way (ibid. 137-138). That meant the guardianship of mothers was ignored as well as mothers' rights concerning the education of their sons.

Zhaicheng's village self-government could be considered an extension of family and community education and a series of organizations were established. These included the "Society for the Implementation of Morality in Business" (*De ye shijianhui*), the "Improvement of Customs Society" (*Gailiang fengsuhui*), the "Thrifty Savings Society" (*Qinjian chuxuhui*), the "Friendliness Society" (*Jimuhui*) and the "Patriotic Society" (*Aiguohui*).

The Society for the Implementation of Morality in Business was organized in 1914. Its meetings were regularly attended by some 150 men, while women held separate meetings. The purpose of this society was to organize and encourage villagers to conduct business with virtue. It was based on Lü Dazhong's *The Local Rules of Lü's Clan* and the old "customs of drinking etiquette in a village" (*xiang yinjiu li*), which meant that in their spare time men would gather according to age and seniority and discuss agriculture, issues of morality and etiquette, and that women would receive premarital counseling from the head of their clan.

In Zhaicheng Village, the head of the village mobilized all villagers older than fifteen to join the Society for the Implementation of Morality in Business and divided them according to occupation and status. First, villagers were divided into two groups by sex. The men met in the higher primary school, and the women in the higher primary girls' school. Heads and deputy-heads of the village acted as the chairmen and vice-chairmen. Each group elected four men as secretaries, and the women were also supervised by men. Discussions in the men's group concentrated on a few topics, such as conforming to morality, advocating frugality, encouraging new business and the development of the organization. Discussions in the women's group varied – they were further divided into an unmarried female group (*chunü bu*) (fifteen to twenty-five years old) and a women's group (*funü bu*) (married women and women over twenty-five) – and each had their own important issues to study. The unmarried females dealt with the virtue of a woman, and once a month the headmaster or a teacher taught female virtues and family education. The women's group emphasized learning household management, methods and skills of family education, household economy, and child care, in order to perform "women's duties" perfectly. Each year two outstanding women were selected from each group. They received awards and prizes, their names were recorded in the village "Book of Good Conduct" (*Shanxing bu*), and subsequently sat at the front during meetings (ibid. 145-148).

According to the reformers,

> Westernized women who were used by ambitious politicians were morally bad, and only women educated by Confucianism were suitable role models. Thus, the traditional gender divisions – men in charge outside the home and women in charge inside the home, men being strong and women being weak – were strengthened and redefined by Zhaicheng's male elite. The underlying motivation for that was not only to maintain morality in the village, but also to oppose the feminist movement in China and abroad at that time. (see ibid. 145)

Mass Education

Although there has been some criticism of the way the Mi family and other people in Zhaicheng's village self-government organized according to gender, in my view they were still admirable for their great imaginative power and creativity. One of their achievements was the introduction of the Mass Education Movement led by Yan Yangchu and the Chinese Mass Education Association in Zhaicheng and Ding County through a model project which lasted over ten years. If the Lugouqiao Incident in 1937[11] had not occurred and the eight years of the War of Resistance Against Japan could have been prevented, the history of the rural modernization movement would have gone another way.

"Mass education" (*pingmin jiaoyu*) was advocated by intellectuals influenced by the New Thoughts Movement who were concerned about the fate of China and the life of common people. They promoted "eliminating illiteracy and becoming new citizens" (*chu wenmang, zuo xinmin*). In 1921, Yan Yangchu, who had returned from studying in the United States, began his survey on mass education with the support of Yu Rizhang, the general secretary of the Young Men's Christian Association (YMCA) in Shanghai. At the same time, others were carrying out their own experiments in Changsha, Yantai and Jiaxing, and mass education organizations were also founded in Nanjing and Wuhan. In August 1923, the Chinese National Mass Education Association (*Zhonghua pingmin jiaoyu cujinhui zonghui*) was initiated and established by Xiong-Zhu Qihui, Wang Boqiu and Tao Xingzhi. Xiong-Zhu Qihui was elected as chairman of the board and Yan Yangchu became the general secretary. The next year, Yan Yangchu invited Fu Baochen, who had studied rural education in the United States at Cornell University, to become the director of the Rural Education Department. This was the starting point of village mass education. In the winter of 1927, the "Rural Education Department" (*Nongmin jiaoyubu*) was established by the Mass Education Association in Zhaicheng by invitation of Mi Digang. Afterwards Yan

---

[11] The Lugouqiao Incident marked the beginning of the Second Sino-Japanese War (1937-1945).

Yangchu invited a group of PhD's in agriculture, education, medicine, literature and engineering from Europe and America, to move to Ding County to begin research on and implementation of village mass education. They carried out social surveys, compiled teaching materials and institutionalized organizations. In autumn 1929, the headquarters of the Mass Education Association moved to Ding County and started the mass education program throughout the whole of Ding County. In 1931, the Mass Education Association began to cooperate with the Hebei Research Institute of County Political Reconstruction (*Hebei sheng xian zheng jianshe yanjiuyuan*). In 1932, because of the success of both the system and the methodology of mass education, the experiment was vastly extended. In 1935, Yan Yangchu wrote and published a series entitled *The Chinese Mass Education Association: A Summary of the Experimental Work in Ding County (Zhonghua pingmin jiaoyu cujinhui: Dingxian shiyan gongzuo tiyao)* (Yan Yangchu 1990b). Unfortunately, in 1937 the Japanese invasion and the War of Resistance Against Japan interrupted the Mass Education Movement of Ding County.

To obtain a picture of how mass education in Ding County related to women, the mission, objective, content, steps and methods of the mass education advocated by Yan Yangchu should be analyzed in detail. Mass education differed from the "national education" (*guomin jiaoyu*) of Zhaicheng's village self-government, as it focused on "eliminating illiteracy and producing new citizens." The "new citizen" (*xinmin*) referred to the "new national citizen" (*xin guomin*) of the Republic of China. The new concept of "country" (*guo*) also transformed the *guo* of Confucius's *xiushen* (to cultivate oneself), *qijia* (to uphold the family), *zhiguo* (to rule the country), which referred to a traditional concept of an empire, into the meaning of the modern national state. Associating new concepts and new meanings with old words was a strategy commonly used by modern intellectuals.

Yan Yangchu also believed in the Confucian idea that "people are the foundation of a country, and only if this foundation is strong can the country be at peace" (*min wei bang ben, ben gu bang ning*). Therefore, his ideology of "people as foundation" (*minben*) was based on the lowest and largest stratum of grass root peasantry, and not on an abstract idea of "people".

He tried to enrich the country and to strengthen people through changing their lives and their fate. He also advocated penetrating deeply among the people to understand them, to establish relationships with them, to learn from them, and to discuss the reconstruction of the village with them. He firmly believed that through mass education the peasants could empower themselves to change their lives and become "new citizens" (*xinmin*).[12]

Yan Yangchu hoped to use education to overcome the problems of China's peasants: "To prevent ignorance through literacy and art education, to prevent poverty through vocational education to prevent disease through health education and to prevent selfishness by citizen education (*gongmin*)" (ibid. 186).

Mass education also included women: "Any citizen (*guomin*) of Republican China, whether male or female, rich or poor, who did not receive an education during childhood or who lack the common knowledge of citizens even if he or she were educated, all of these people are the target of mass education" (Yan Yangchu 1990a:22). Obviously, there was no gender limitation in mass education and women were included in the term "new citizens" (*xinmin*).

There were three steps in the shaping of new citizens according to the plans of the Mass Education Association. "The first step is to eliminate illiteracy (*shizi jiaoyu*), the second step is citizen education (*gongmin jiaoyu*), and the third step is education for earning a living (*shengji jiaoyu*)" (ibid. 24). This education was implemented by means of the three spheres of school, family and society. For education in school, boys' and girls' primary schools, high schools and mass vocational schools (*pingmin zhiye xuexiao*) (later changed into "training school for common people" [*pingmin yucai xuexiao*] mainly training the leading talents in the villages) were established. Education in school was the foundation of mass education, and female education was an important part of it.

---

[12] See the tape transcription of the interview with Yan Yangchu in Ding County, September 1984, in: Li Jidong 1990:2-9.

The first school for the masses (*pingmin xuexiao*) was built in Zhaicheng. In 1926, the Mass Education Movement established a training school for higher primary graduates and others, in which men and women were segregated. In the fall of 1927 the Mass Education Movement also organized four experimental schools, two for boys and two for girls; two at the higher primary level and two at the lower primary level. The Mass Education Movement established several schools in Zhaicheng, both to improve education in the village and to experiment with a rural education program. There were forty-five students in the men's school and thirty-seven in the women's.

Family education was defined as the mode which brought together family members holding the same position in each family and granting them identical training organized by the Mass Education Movement. According to age and role, family members were grouped by heads of household (*jia zhu*), housewives (*zhufu*), young boys (*shaonian*), young girls (*guinü*) and children (*youtong*). The "social" education mode also replicated Zhaicheng's practices, organized various friendship and charity activities for associations of classmates, published magazines, sent books to the countryside, and broadcast programs to educate the public.

We can see from the description above that all the activities and the content of these three modes of education were related to both men *and* women.

Women were involved in the mass education program in many aspects. The next part of this essay will deal with questions concerning the way gender relations was handled in the mass education designed by Yan Yangchu and his colleagues, the extent to which women participated over the ten year period, and in what way mass education influenced women.

The basic objective of mass education was to create "new citizens" with the "spirit and attitude of a citizen" (*gonghe guomin ying you de jingshen he taidu*) who is patriotic, public-spirited, and has the skill and knowledge to make a living. From this we might conclude that no gender differences existed in regard to the design and implementation of the Mass Education Movement.

Within the Mass Education Movement four kinds of education (*si da jiaoyu*), "elimination of illiteracy," "citizenship education," "livelihood education" and "health education" (*sao mang, gongmin, shengji he jiankang jiaoyu*) were combined with the aforementioned three modes, with school education being the most important.

Women's education was considered an important part of the Mass Education Movement, and women and men obviously enjoyed the same rights and opportunities in regard to education, yet the aim, content, and method of education for women were different from those for men.

The first Training School for Common People (*Yucai pingmin xuexiao*) set up in 1926 by the Mass Education Association, separated the school by sex. The men's school offered classes for two hours in the evening; women's classes lasted for three hours in the morning and two hours in the afternoon.

The subjects for men included art and literature, citizenship (*gongmin*), letter writing, geography, history, village self-government, and general knowledge. In addition to these subjects, the women's classes also included home economics (*jiazhengxue*), "home handicraft industry" (*jiating shougongye*), Sun Yatsen's "Three People's Principles," calculation with the abacus, writing, and games (*youxi*). In 1927 the Mass Education Movement set up experimental schools for boys and girls, which also offered classes for two hours in the evening for boys as well as two hours in the morning and two hours in the afternoon for girls. The curriculum of the boys' lower primary classes included the "thousand characters textbook" (*qian zi keben*), that is simple texts with the primary aim of eliminating illiteracy, calligraphy, calculating with the abacus, and the phonetic alphabet (*pinyin*). The boys' higher primary courses were "advanced Chinese reading" (*gaoji guowen duben*), letter writing, citizenship, history, calculating with the abacus, and agriculture. The girls' school substituted home economics for agriculture. The Mass Education Movement also established the Thousand Characters School to Eliminate Illiteracy (*Qianzi saomang xuexiao*) for boys and girls with the primary aim of eliminating illiteracy (Gamble 1968:162-163).

The leaders of the Mass Education Movement and the local staff in charge considered women's education to be a part of family reform and the main focus for women was still the family, with housework their most important activity. For example, in December 1930, when Yan Yangchu and other core members of the Mass Education Movement talked with the two hundred villagers of Gaotou Village, Yan Yangchu said: "The villagers of Gaotou [...] can voluntarily attend the meeting and go on to develop agriculture, education and improve the family. Then we will have a model for the village, county, province and country [...]."

The village head Duan Xinshan, voiced his opinion about women's education:

> The Mass Education Association coming to Ding County and advocating mass education in every village convinced us that mass education was both necessary and easy to implement; therefore, we established a village people's school and a women's school. The women's school was set up to improve families [...]. Only by having good families can we build a good village [...]. (Li Jidong 1990:254-255)

The people in charge of mass education distrusted and looked down on women's ability to deal with public affairs, but the real capacity of females was beyond their imagination and often surprised them. For example, one purpose for setting up experimental higher female schools in 1933 was to explore whether it was possible to train and educate rural women to become educators. The Mass Education Movement advocated the four skill areas of giving smallpox vaccinations, health care, sewing and spinning and weaving, and included them in the curricula. But all in all, women's education for earning a living was still within the sphere of the family (ibid. 172).

The Mass Education Movement had a special "Research Committee on Young Women's Education" (*Qingnian funü jiaoyu yanjiu weiyuanhui*). They divided women's education into vocational training and home economics, but they did not take into account a solution for women's great double burden. Apparently, the Mass Education Movement did not draw a clear line between women's education in the three modes of school, family and society and did not overcome the gender role division of labor derived from traditional society. The leaders of the Mass Education Movement were convinced that the main concern of women was sewing and childcare. However, they also wanted women to obtain skills in earning their living as new female citizens (*xin guomin de funü*); thus, they designed their women's education program as a combination of education for earning a living with housework. Therefore, on the one hand, they provided a "modern education" (*xiandai jiaoyu*) and "technical training" (*jishu peixun*) for sewing and childcare in the Village People School for Girls and thus moved women's housework into the classroom and the communities. On the other hand, the Mass Education Movement emphasized six kinds of vocational education and training for young females, which were writing and calculating, childcare, sewing, spinning and weaving, animal husbandry and gardening. The intention of this education was to produce new female citizens who could support themselves by their own labor and could create wealth for the society. The Mass Education Movement included both males *and* females in the objective of livelihood education to show the importance of the function of women, but this kind of recognition still did not go beyond the sphere of women's old family responsibilities.

Participation and Implementation: Women in the Mass Education Movement

How did women participate in the Mass Education Movement? What role did they play and what influence did they have? The core members of the Mass Education Movement were academics who had studied in Europe and the United States and had given up their comfortable lives abroad to come to Ding County with their wives and children to implement the unique experiment and fulfill their ideals.

By having a closer look at the wives and daughters behind the professional male elite, we are able to evaluate more clearly gender relations and the gender division within the Mass Education Movement as it was designed by the core members of the Mass Education Movement. These women maintained traditions and supported their husband's careers as wives, partners and assistants. Xu Yali, the wife of Yan Yangchu was known as "a virtuous and supportive wife" (*xian nei zhu*). She devoted her life to her husband and stayed permanently in Ding County with him; she was the host for guests of the Mass

Education Movement, but she never joined the association as a volunteer. Many professional women who had received higher education, including some foreign women followed their husbands and fathers to Ding County and did behind-the-scenes voluntary work there.

Coincidently, several interviewers' records reveal some limited information. For example, Chen Hengzhe visited Ding Xian and recorded a few women's experiences, such as those of Dr. Chen Zhushan's wife and the two daughters of his former wife, who were responsible for citizen education. They put greatest emphasis on women's education in the family. They organized the heads of households, housewives, boys, girls and children, taught systematic household management, taught the spirit and methodology of team work, helped villagers learn handicraft skills, introduced the wool textile profession, and taught unmarried girls how to educate children.

The wife of Dr. Zhao Shuicheng, who had previously been a teacher at the Nankai Middle School for Girls in Tianjin, taught hygiene to women. Additionally, Miss Ding and Mrs. Zhang, the daughter of Chen Zhushan, were volunteer teachers for the Mass Education Movement.[13]

How did the local women participate in the Mass Education Movement and how did they benefit from it? First, let us examine the data. Before the Mass Education Movement came to Ding County, only a few girls attended primary school and the illiteracy rate was over 94 percent. In 1928 Li Jinghan collected the following data relating to women aged fourteen to fifty in sixty-two villages:

Literacy Rates in 62 Villages (1928)[14]

sex	absolute illiterates	half-illiterates	literates	total
men	560 (51.2%)	71 (6.5%)	463 (42.3%)	1094 (100%)
women	619 (94.1%)	3 (0.5%)	36 (5.4%)	658 (100%)

---

[13] Chen Hengzhe, Dingxian nongcun zhong jiandao de pingjiaohui shiye (Mass Education in the Villages of Ding County), in: Li Jidong 1990:357.
[14] Li Jinghan 1986:236.

The Mass Education Movement began with the experiment in mass education in 1928; by the end of 1931 there were mass education schools in 453 villages and in nineteen satellite villages and more than 20,000 students were enrolled. By 1934 there were 844 classes in 416 villages with an enrolment of 21,170 students, i.e. 14,080 males and 7,090 females. In Zhaicheng the male and female literacy rate was highest among the eleven- to twenty-four-year-olds: 65 percent of all males and 36 percent of all females were literate; the respective rates for Dongting Village were 60 percent and 37 percent (Gamble 1968:186-187).

In Ding County today, old women of around seventy years still recall their experiences in mass education. This is the story of Xu Airu of Zhaicheng Village:

> Xu Airu was born in a landlord family in 1916. Her parents had only two daughters. Both she and her sister attended school. After graduating from Zhaicheng Girls' Normal School, her sister became the head of a school in Baoding. She herself entered school in 1925 at the age of nine but dropped out one year after her brother's birth. She resumed studying after her brother's death two years later. She also attended the normal school in her village and even became captain of the basketball team. Since she was literate, she became a cadre of the Women's Salvation Association (*Fujiuhui*) during the War of Resistance Against Japan. She married at the age of twenty-three, her husband marrying into her family and living with them. After their child was born, her husband would not permit her to work in public affairs, and said she should stay at home and care for the children. He assumed her job and she taught him how to use the abacus. Today she is teaching her grandson how to use the abacus [...].

She Ruichang of Zhaicheng Village still remembered the song of the Mass Education Movement:

> Mass education, the root of Republican China,
> Not only reduces illiteracy, but it also creates new citizens.
> 400 million Chinese all equal and bright,
> Make China strong and carry on the spirit of the nation.[15]

---

[15] These texts are based on interviews carried out in Zhaicheng Village by Wang Qi and Du Fangqin respectively.

Another example of women's participation in the Mass Education Movement is the female tutors who were trained to spread mass education during the last period of the movement. Most of these tutors were excellent, articulate students and efficient organizers. They were first taught by teachers, then passed on their knowledge to other pupils or to family members. They were praised not only for being conscientious in their work but also for continuing to teach even during harvest time. In Wuyao Village, the experimental unit for the tutorial system, sixty-nine female tutors graduated on 28 May 1935, after three months of training, and five of them, aged fourteen to twenty-four, gave reports on their achievements. Although they had been illiterate and the villagers had many doubts about their ability, they delivered excellent speeches in front of an audience of five hundred people.[16]

A representative and heroine of the Mass Education Movement in Ding County was Zhang Jinping from Xipingzhugu Village. She acted as head of the female student union and initiated preschool education by setting up kindergartens in some villages. Chen Hengzhe mentioned her in a report:

> We came to a village called Xipingzhugu where an experimental girls' school [...] held a special meeting for us. Ms. Zhang, the head of the female students union of that village welcomed us. Although she was only sixteen or seventeen years old, her speech was eloquent and elegant, demonstrating intellectual capacity and broad knowledge.[17]

Zhu Ruoxi also recorded the achievements of Zhang Jinping:

> In Xipingzhugu there was a training course for kindergarten teachers, which was established on the site of the primary school. There were about twenty children who were taught and cared for by five to six young women. These women were all graduates of the common school and had come there to learn how to care for children. The equipment was really poor. [...] During my visit [Ms. Zhang] led the children in playing

---

[16] See Report on the Public Speeches of Female Tutors of the Tutors' Instruction Class at Wuyao Village (Wuyao cun daosheng xunlianban nü daosheng gongkai yanjiang de baogao), materials arranged by Wang Deliang, head of an experimental normal school in Hengshan County, Henan Province.

[17] Chen Hengzhe, quoted from Li Jidong 1990:359.

various games. They were lively and full of vigour. This spirit of serving the community is really admirable.[18]

Zhang Jinping died early but there was a memorial set up for her that praised her achievements in the field of kindergarten education.

Although men organized the Mass Education, women participated, learned and improved their abilities within it. The women in Ding County became the first women in North China to receive mass education. Some of them became key members of the Mass Education Movement, rural education specialists and women activists who called for more women to join the Mass Education Movement. The Mass Education Movement provided a wide public sphere for rural women, allowing them to break free from the confines of their homes, become educated and participate in the public affairs of the village. Therefore, women's participation in the Mass Education Movement was a great improvement over the male-dominated village self-government of Zhaicheng.

References

Du Xueyuan, *Zhongguo nüzi jiaoyu tongshi* (Comprehensive History of Women's Education in China), Guiyang 1996.
Gamble, Sidney D., *Ting Hsien: A North China Rural Community*, Stanford ²1968 (¹1954).
Li Jidong (ed.), *Yan Yangchu yu Dingxian pingmin jiaoyu* (Yan Yangchu and the Mass Education of Ding County), Shijiazhuang 1990.
Li Jinghan, *Dingxian shehui gaikuang diaocha* (Ding County: A Social Survey), Beijing 1986.
Luo Suwen, *Nüxing yu jindai Zhongguo shehui* (Women and the Modern Society of China), Shanghai 1996.
Lü Meiyi, Zheng Yongfu, *Zhongguo funü yundong (1840-1921)* (The Women's Movement in China [1840-1921]), Zhengzhou 1990.
Shu Xincheng (ed.), *Zhongguo jindai jiaoyushi ziliao* (Modern Chinese Education History Data), Beijing 1961.

---

[18] See Zhu Ruoxi, Visiting the Mass School of Ding County (Dingxian pingmin xuexiao guangang), in: Li Jidong 1990:375-376.

Yan Yangchu, *Pingmin jiaoyu de yiyi* (The Meaning of Mass Education), 1927, reproduced in: Li Jidong 1990a.

Yan Yangchu, *Zhonghua pingmin jiaoyu cujinhui: Dingxian shiyan gongzuo tiyao* (The Chinese Mass Education Association: A Summary of Experimental Work in Ding County), 1935, reproduced in: Li Jidong 1990b, pp. 147-231.

Yi Zhongcai (comp.), *Zhaicheng cun zhi* (Annals of Zhaicheng Village), Tianjin 1925.

Marriage Reform, Rural Women and the Chinese State during World War II

Christina K. Gilmartin and Isabel Crook

The impact of war in the twentieth century on gender transformations has become a major subject in Western scholarly literature.[1] In contrast, the absence of scholarly work on the impact of World War II on Chinese women is striking. To be sure, a handful of excellent studies of the women's programs of Communist base areas during the 1930s and 1940s could be seen as fitting into this genre, but their focus on socialist revolutionary dynamics and agendas is more central to their analyses than the causal relationship of war and gender reform. These works helped to create a strong sense that the gender policies of the Nationalist Government during the World War II era compared very unfavorably with Communist initiatives in their rural base areas. Such sentiments, for instance, were expressed by the prominent gender scholar, Delia Davin, when she wrote: "Such [Nationalist] legislation as might have been expected to affect women,

---

We greatly appreciate the support of Carola Krüger in the preparation of this article for publication as well as the work of Ma Wenqin, a graduate student in the History Department at Northeastern University, Boston, and Liu Jing, an archivist at the Chongqing Municipal Archives (*Chongqing dang'anguan*), in helping to find some relevant Chinese archival materials for this study. As always, Yu Xiji has contributed immensely to this study by searching through Chinese sources and providing valuable personal insights and assessments.

[1] The relevant scholarship is quite extensive. In past decades, many studies have argued that wartimes brought significant changes to women, such as suffrage rights, new work opportunities, etc. More recent works have questioned such sweeping generalizations, showing that shifts in gender roles have usually not brought about a fundamental. Regardless of their arguments, these studies have primarily used the experiences of Western women as their yardstick. See, for instance, Arthur Marwick, *The Deluge: British Society and the First World War* (1975); Margaret Higonnet et al., *Behind the Lines: Gender and the Two World Wars* (1989); and Penny Summerfield, *Reconstructing Women's Wartime Lives: Discourse and Subjectivity in Oral Histories and the Second World War* (1998).

notably the marriage law and the law on equal inheritance, was not only unheeded, but in rural areas was even largely unknown" (Davin 1975:243).

Davin was hardly alone in her negative assessment of the Nationalist Government during the war era. Until relatively recently, most studies of wartime China had little positive to say about Chiang Kai-shek's regime. This paradigm was altered by William Kirby when he argued that certain aspects of the state-building efforts of the Nationalist Government laid the basis for much subsequent development under the aegis of the Chinese Communist authorities after 1949. Thus, in many ways 1949 should not be viewed as a watershed, but rather as part of a continuum that existed between the Nationalist and Communist state-building efforts (Kirby 1990). Joseph Esherick extended this analysis to the realm of society, conjecturing that "social changes of the long 1940s [were] a harbinger of the early years of the PRC [People's Republic of China]" (Esherick 2001:19). To be sure, Esherick was less confident about the likelihood of significant changes for women, but his general message was that scholars need to examine the continuities between Nationalist and Communist social change initiatives during the end of the Chiang era and the beginning of the Mao era.

Our contribution in this essay is small in comparison with what is necessary to gain a comprehensive understanding of social changes during the 1940s. We seek only to examine the efforts of the Nationalist Government to alter marriage practices in the rural Sichuan township of Prosperity (*Xinlongxiang*) located in Bishan County through its implementation of directives, laws and political campaigns during the war years, which in China lasted from 1937 until 1945. We examine the relationship of rural women to the state primarily from the bottom up rather than taking the more common approach of proceeding from the top down by relying primarily on archival materials produced by state institutions and functionaries. This bottom-up approach has been made possible by the availability of an unusual set of anthropological materials – the field notes, texts, and survey results of Isabel Crook and Yu Xiji, who were working on a Christian-sponsored reform project to improve the economic well-being of rural communities through the establishment of a salt cooperative, a health clinic, and an embroidery project as well as lending educational assistance in the new elementary public coeducational school.[2] This unique body of anthropological materials provides valuable understandings of the dynamics of social change and of resistance at a local level, thereby providing an instructive corrective to the limited views that are derived from a total reliance on state-generated sources, such as county court records, government records, government newspapers, and gazetteers, all of which were also utilized for this essay.

The Perimeter Becomes the Political Center: Sichuan in World War II

When Japanese invaders seized most of the country in 1937 and 1938, the Nationalist Government transferred its capital from the relatively prosperous and commercialized eastern coastal area of Jiangnan to the hinterland city of Chongqing in the province of Sichuan. Until quite recently the Nationalist Government had had little influence in the southwestern part of China, which had been wracked by internecine struggles of warlords for control of its rich resources. From the mid-1920s onward, seven warlords fought one another intermittently to expand and protect their territories. Warlord

---

[2] The ethnographic materials used in this essay are taken from Isabel Crook's unpublished manuscript (1994) entitled *A Community Called Prosperity*. The two chapters that were used most extensively were chapter 21 "Marriage Making in Middle and Better Off Families" (twenty-one pages) and chapter 22 "Marriage Making among the Poor" (thirteen pages). This manuscript has circulated among interested scholars for more than a decade and has been cited in several books, including Gregory Ruf's *Cadres and Kin: Making a Socialist Village in West China, 1921-1991* (1998). The fieldwork was part of a rural reconstruction project in 1940-1941 that ran out of funding before a final report could be written. When Isabel Crook retired from her teaching profession in the early 1980s, she took up the project of writing up the field notes with the help of Yu Xiji, producing a massive text of approximately 1,500 pages. This manuscript is being used as the basis for a scholarly study by Isabel Crook, Christina Gilmartin, and Susan Ridgon with Yu Xiji on the theme of rural community and its response to outside efforts of reform during World War II.

administration was carried out through the "garrison area" system, whereby the major warlords staked out their territory, assigning portions of it to lesser officers who received no pay for themselves or their troops but were given the freedom to raise taxes, recruit troops and maintain security by whatever means they could. Due to the ravages of this system, banditry had become endemic and the merciless attempts to crush it added to the insecurity and violence throughout rural areas.

The invasion of Japan sparked a very different war than the one that had gripped Sichuan in the past decades. The resurgence of nationalist sentiment support for the Nationalist Government provided a strong basis for support among urban people in the province. Most importantly, Sichuan was suddenly the destination point for a large migration of "downriver" people as the transferal of the capital to the far southwestern part of the country brought with it a flood of institutions and people from the occupied cities of the coastal provinces, including many industries, universities, hosts of urban dwellers, as well as secular and religious reformers. Many of these "downriver people" fanned out into rural areas and greatly livened local communities.

A farming community of approximately 1,500 families, the standard marketing town of Prosperity was experiencing the full force of outsiders in its midst by 1940. Recurrent Japanese aerial bombings of the Nationalist capital city of Chongqing, less than forty miles away, prompted many downriver refugees to seek the safety of this remote rural retreat.[3] This downriver influx included professionals, students, and secular and religious reformers, such as the educator Liang Shuming, the sociologist Jiang Zi'ang and the well-known James Yen (Yan Yangchu), who had headed up the Mass Education Movement in Dingxian, Hebei Province, before the war and now chose to relocate his new projects in the neighboring community of Xiemachang. Some of these immigrants brought with them urban notions about the importance of free-choice or voluntary marriages, as well as more relaxed

---

[3] According to the *Bishan Gazetteer (Bishan fangzhi)*, more than sixty thousand downriver people found their way to Bishan County during the war (Bishan fangzhi 1996:106).

ways of dealing with people of the opposite sex that had some impact on the social practices of those residing in the county town of Bishan.

The main foray of downriver immigrants into the rural township of Prosperity were connected to the experimental center for alleviating rural poverty that was set up by the National Christian Council (NCC) in 1939. This decision to locate the center here, no doubt, was influenced by the fact that Christian reformers had been working on and off in this township since 1924 when the American Methodist Episcopal Mission (AMEM) set up the first coeducational school in this locality. Although the school only lasted for four years, the AMEM continued to hold a three-week Bible School session to educate girls twice a year. These classes served as an occasion for propagating Christian values, including ideas about how a Christian home should be run. Some students may well have been influenced by these classes, but they were unable in large part to defy the main requirements of the traditional marriage system, including their parents' rights to determine their spouses.[4]

When the Nationalist Government moved its capital to Sichuan in 1938, it did not make marriage reform in the rural areas a central element of its modernizing agenda. To be sure, its power over rural society was relatively weak, in large parts because it was a relatively new political actor in the province that was not able to wield considerable influence until 1935. When it moved its capital to Chongqing in 1938, the government chose to place its main focus on reforming local government to make it more responsible to the central government's wartime directives than to the interest of the local elites. In particular, it sought to control the selection of township heads, collect taxes, to secure sufficient amounts of rice to feed its armies, and conscript sufficient manpower for its armed forces. Nevertheless, it did articulate a modernist program that envisioned the curtailment of traditional marriage practices. Nationalist Government directives, laws and political campaigns serve as a useful lens for examining gender changes in the society. These government initiatives were applicable to almost all women and most men in rural Sichuan as marriage was

---

[4] Interview with Cao Hongying, a participant in the Bible Classes in Prosperity in the 1940s, in Daxing Township on 22 January 2004.

all but compulsory. In short, the institution of marriage was generally regarded as a socially sanctioned norm for all Chinese and it was considered a great misfortune for any individual to remain unmarried. In Prosperity no daughters were ever left unmarried beyond their early twenties, with the sole exception of two Buddhist nuns, women who had come from comfortably well-off pious families. In contrast to this compulsory marriage patterns for females, many poor males remained bachelors, not out of desire but because they could not afford the required bride price.

Specifically, the marriage codes in the Nationalist Family Laws clearly stipulated that the decision to marry should be made by the individuals involved and that it should be monogamous, though some contradictory articles also indicated concubines could be acquired if the first wife did not object. The Nationalist code specified that an engagement should not take place until a woman was fifteen years of age (*xiu sui*) and a man, seventeen years of age. Most importantly, it devoted much more attention to the nature of the marriage contract than the engagement contract. These laws asserted the state's authority to set the terms of marriage, including stipulating a minimum age (age sixteen for women and eighteen for men), expanding the degree of relatives that had to be excluded from consideration, with the result that maternal first cousins were now prohibited from marriage, and setting the basis on which a marriage could be terminated. Most importantly, women now had the right to divorce their husbands. Thus, according to the Nationalist Civil Law, both parties enjoyed the freedom of divorce and were not compelled to provide strong reasons for this request.

At a local level, these Nationalist legal codes vied with customary laws. In some cases, the differences between the two sets of legal practices were huge. Most importantly arranged marriages were the norm in rural Sichuan. Free-choice marriages occurred in urban areas, but were very rare in rural Sichuan before the war. Engagements were usually contracted well before children reached their teenage years, and were considered binding. Significantly, marriage age was one area where the codified laws were fairly close to long-standing customary laws that regarded a girl over sixteen (*er ba*) and a boy over eighteen (*ruo guan*) as having reached adulthood. Already by the 1930s most urban women married in correspondence with the marriage law age, though 10 percent were less than fifteen years of age by the traditional way of reckoning, or fourteen by present-day calculations of age (Zang Xiaowei 1999). But in many respects marriage rather than age in Chinese rural society was the determinant of adulthood. Those who married early were thus considered as adults. Early marriages were more common in some parts of China than others. Martin Yang found that early marriages were virtually unknown in the village of Taitou, Shandong.[5] In contrast, early marriages in many Sichuan rural communities including Prosperity were evident.

As the force of law was generally weak in rural Chinese communities, the government used several means to educate the people of Prosperity about its provisions: articles in its party newspapers, government ordinances, and social movement organizations. The *Zhongyang ribao (The Central Daily)* in Chongqing carried many articles advocating the end of arranged marriages, the holding of group marriages to be conducted in a frugal manner, and expanding voluntary marriages. The local Bishan newspapers also carried a few articles calling for gender reform. For those issues of greatest concern, directives were issued from the central ministries in Chongqing to the county governments, who then usually passed them along to the township government, in order to require enforcement of certain laws.

Government Mandates on Footbinding and Early Marriage

Government directives on reforming marriage practices began with the issuance of an order to rural townships in 1938 and again in 1940 to eliminate the "evil" custom of footbinding, a practice that had once served as an important condition for marriage (Bishan

---

[5] In Taitou a young bride was not desired because she was not yet capable of taking on a heavy work load. As a result, no woman in this community married before the age of seventeen. The average age of a couple at the time of marriage was twenty (Yang 1945:113).

dang'anguan 1940).⁶ The Nationalist Government argued that this atrocious practice should be terminated in order to increase female involvement in the anti-Japanese war effort. This directive instructed township heads to impose fines on all families whose women had bound feet. However, it also noted that this practice could only be found in remote areas of the county, as is confirmed by the observations of Isabel Crook and Yu Xiji. They saw no evidence that young girls' feet were being bound in 1940, and from what can be reconstructed, it seems that this practice was rarely practiced in this community after 1929, though there is some evidence that it continued into the late 1930s in some mountainous communities on the edges of Bishan County.⁷ Thus the Nationalist Government chose to target a marriage related practice that was definitely on the wane and would not be difficult to secure further compliance.

A more difficult issue was addressed in December 1942, when the Sichuan Provincial Government issued a mandate calling on each county to restrict the incidence of early marriages in its areas and to write up a report about its prevalence (Jiancha bao zaohun 1943). Once again it used the rationale that early marriages were bad for ones health, and thus detrimental to the war effort. Some county reports indicated that the incidence was fairly high, as much as 50 percent of the marriages in Dazu, for instance. It seemed to be the sense of the various county officials that it was impossible to use law to eradicate early marriages as it clearly was a survival strategy of the poor and desperate. One report suggested that the government should hire these poor young girls in its textile factories as a way to delay their marriages (ibid.).

Crook and Yu found that many girls in Prosperity married around the age stipulated by the civil code, that is sixteen (*xu sui*). To wait much beyond this age caused great concern, for with every

---

[6] These Bishan County archival materials were provided to us by Liu Jing, an archivist at the Chongqing Municipal Archives. Unfortunately, it was not clear what files these documents were pulled from and we are still waiting for that information.

[7] This assessment was reached through a combination of observations by Isabel Crook and Yu Xiji in 1940 and 1941, and interviews with fifty elderly people in the community in late January 2004.

passing year her "worth" was considered to have diminished except in the case of more educated peasant families.

However, it was also true that occasionally a girl in Prosperity reached her twenties still unmarried. The reason was often that her family was dissatisfied with the candidates put forward by matchmakers, believing they fell short of the "matching doors" principle that guided families to seek spouses for their children from families of an equivalent social and economic standing. But this was not the only reason for delay. Parents could be loath to lose a daughter who was a major income-earner. Such cases were chiefly found in comfortable and middle farm families who supplemented their income through cottage weaving, for the weavers were often their unmarried daughters.

The most extreme case of putting off a daughter's marriage was that of Sun Yichang, another of the young women who attended the Bible School sessions. A skilled weaver, good-looking, healthy, industrious, and from a comfortably-off farm family, she was still not engaged at the age of twenty-three. The explanation given by friends of Yichang was that in "matching doors and households," the Suns over-rated themselves: candidates they considered appropriate were not satisfied while those who sought their daughter were not good enough (*gao buchang: di bujiu*). But there was an equally compelling reason. The longer the Suns postponed their daughter's engagement, hoping for a better match, the longer her family could enjoy the income from her skilled labor. Yichang herself was in no hurry to give up her current status of favorite daughter in a loving home for the status of daughter-in-law in an unfamiliar and possibly uncongenial family. This is a sign with opportunities appearing for young women to obtain an education. There was a beginning of some new thinking of women's potential outside of reproduction.

A similar case which turned out differently was that of Cao Ziyun's daughter, another one of the Bible School girls. The Caos owned eight *dan*[8] of riceland and had a thriving cottage-weaving

---

[8] A *dan* is a volume measurement for grain, amounting to ten lbs. *Dan* was used as a measurement of land based on the historical yield, that is the amount of land needed to produce one *dan* of unhusked rice. These amounts were set by the census in the 1940s. As a liquid measurement, a *dan* was ten liters.

industry with two standard looms. One of the weavers was the seventeen-year-old daughter. The parents were forward-looking people who had sent their son to secondary school in Bishan, after which he had taken a job in Chongqing. After two years there, he had just returned to Prosperity to take up the post of clerk of the township government office. When he found his parents had not arranged a match for his competent, young sister, he remonstrated with them saying, "If you're going to be new-fashioned, then send her to school to get a regular education; if you're going to be old-fashioned, then arrange the match and marry her off." The parents took the advice and, choosing to be modern, they sent her to school. As the farm was eight *li* (three miles) from the village, they rented a room for her in the home of Zhang Yunheng, whose daughter was the same age and attending the same school. The brother, as village clerk, lived in the village and kept an eye on his sister.

In theory, as a daughter grew older her marriage "value" decreased and it would become more and more difficult for the family to arrange as advantageous a marriage as they wished. In the end the girl might find she was worse off than she might have been if her family had accepted an earlier offer. But this did not necessarily hold if the young woman was a substantial money earner or if she was literate.

Crook and Yu found that these instances of delayed marriage stood out much more than the early marriages for their rarity. According to their survey of families in Prosperity, early marriages were not as common as in Dazu or as was reported by John Buck in his surveys of Sichuan, but they were nonetheless somewhat common (see Buck 1937). Among nine- and ten-year-old girls, one in forty-two was married; among eleven- and twelve-year-olds, one in eighteen was married; and among thirteen- and fourteen-year-olds, one in three was married. Moreover, at least some of these girls had already been married for a number of years.

Although girls were more likely than boys to be subjected to an early marriage, cases show that several well-off families in the community chose to arrange the marriage of their sons under the age of fifteen. One example is the marriage between the fourteen-year-old son of a prosperous family, Su Shaoliang, and the sixteen-year-old daughter of Cao Guoliang, whose family fortunes fell short of Sun's. Another example is the remarkable marriage between Zhengbi, the fifteen-year-old son of a powerful landowner, Wang Junliang, and a daughter of the landowning Zhang family of Zhongxin Market.

Although the above two cases of early marriage were not driven by dire financial reasons, quite a number of families who opted to marry their children early were motivated by desperate economic or personal situations. For instance, two middle farmer families who were neighbors, the Xiangs of Gaoyuan Temple Corners (*Gaoyuan sijiao*), and the Yangs of Yangjia Bend (*Yangjia wan*), betrothed their children when the Xiang's boy was three, and the Yang's girl, two. When the girl was four her mother died. Not long after, the father went on business to Guizhou, leaving her in the care of his brother. The father was never heard from again and when the girl was eight her uncle was conscripted, leaving her on her own. To provide a home for the child, the boy's mother (who had been widowed the previous year) celebrated the marriage of the children, aged eight and nine. Six months later she too died and the juvenile couple was taken in by relatives. When Xiang was fifteen, they helped him rent a small farm of one *dan* of upland fields with a tiny three-room cottage. With less and less help from his relatives, the boy and girl were able to support themselves. By the time Crook and Yu knew them, they were twenty-two and twenty-three years old, had been married fourteen years, and had a two-year-old baby daughter who they treasured.

In short the promulgation of marriage codes prohibiting early marriages had little impact on curbing this practice in Prosperity. Families who vied from the customary practices of marrying children off after they had reached the age of sixteen mostly did so out of economic necessity. It was a strategy for survival that could not be altered by law alone.

Curtailing Wedding Extravagances

Another issue that warranted a government directive was group marriages. This idea had been adopted by the Nationalist Party in 1934 as part of its "New Life Movement" which included the belief that marriages should be simple and frugal rather than the normal practice of extravagant and elaborate. After it had set up its capital in Chongqing, the government once again promoted this as a kind of new marriage style during the war. It furnished the food and space for these weddings, thereby enticing many young urban couples who lacked the money to hold a wedding party. In 1941 Chongqing tried to spread this practice to the county towns and the townships by telling local officials that they needed to promote frugal group weddings among their citizenry. This practice did not attract many followers in Bishan or Prosperity as weddings were still seen as the occasion for display, for affirming or enhancing the standing of the family in the community and the honor due to it. They also served to publicize and document the event through having many witnesses in the community. This occasion provided a more immediate legality than could be afforded by written document dispensed by the county.

Symbolically, too, both scale and style mattered. Crowds, bustle and noise augured prosperity, happiness and many sons. The greater the furor the more auspicious the occasion. In a community starved for cultural life, any wedding attracted some attention. But when leading families were involved they provided entertainment and excitement, livening the social scene and remaining a major topic of conversation in the neighborhood for days.

When the day of the wedding arrived, the bride was carried in a sedan chair to her new home, escorted by relatives and bringing a dowry. If she came from a family of substance the wedding procession included a whole set of furniture together with chests of clothes and quilts and other items borne along by young relatives, friends or tenants. The ceremony itself was the familiar honoring of the ancestors and kin, with the young couple kowtowing in turn to the ancestral tablets, to the groom's grandparents, his parents, to the bride's relatives, and all the honored guests, in strict order of precedence. The ceremony combined formality and furor.

A marriage connecting two prosperous and/or influential families could be a social affair involving hundreds of guests and many more onlookers. Few received invitations to the wedding. Most came unbidden to honor the family because they were duty-bound to do so as relatives, friends, secret society brothers, neighbors or tenants. The greater the number of guests banqueted, the greater was the honor bestowed on the families involved. Since the host could only guess at the number of guests, it was necessary to underestimate, for empty places would discredit the host. Underestimation had the additional advantage that a pleasant furor was created as more tables were set up and more cured pork brought down from the kitchen rafters, bringing attention to the size of the crowds.

When Wang Junliang hosted a betrothal party for his son, he prepared thirty tables of guests, but six extra tables were required to seat all the well-wishers. When the time came for the wedding party for his son, it had to be on an even greater scale. Such crowds came to honor him that there was no counting them until they sat down to eat. By the time the banqueting was over, Wang had fed one hundred tables of guests – eight hundred people in all. The strain on Wang's financial resources was heavy, but such extravagance was obligatory. Wang Junliang at the age of forty-five was one of Prosperity's most prosperous and influential citizens, with an estate of one hundred *dan* of riceland and a high rank in the most powerful local lodge of the gowned brothers secret society.

Apart from the scale of ceremonials, the rituals and formal codes could be utilized to achieve certain objectives. This was particularly important for women in well-off families who led comfortable but circumscribed lives and who lacked the economic leverage that women in a working farm family could exert. The celebration of family rituals of passage gave such women a chance to display their talents in public, project their personality and exert the power so generated to achieve a desired goal. Furthermore, a skilled and determined woman under attack could use them to defend herself or others.

Gentry women were more confined to their homes than women in working farm families; they also had more idle time at their disposal. Attention to codes of conduct, family ceremonials and the minutiae of their circumscribed social intercourse gave them some scope of interest and some opportunity to exercise their talents. They also provided these women with tools to strengthen their position in male-dominated families. Older women in gentry families often acquired considerable skill in these matters, as is well illustrated by Wang Junliang's wedding party for his son.

Resilience of Arranged Marriage Practices

Although the Nationalist Government invested its resources and energies into promoting group marriages, ending footbinding and early marriages, it did little to enforce or educate its populace about the legal provisions to terminate arranged marriages. In Prosperity, there was no indication in the early 1940s that voluntary marriages contracted by the couple themselves as stipulated in the Nationalist Civil Law were happening. The silence of the government on this issue constituted a recognition of its inability to use state mandates and laws to transform this family practice. Free-choice marriages did not exist in Prosperity where marriage-making continued to be seen as the responsibility and right of parents. In many ways, it is not surprising that the government did not make a strong effort to enable young people to make betrothal decisions on their own accord as there was little economic or social basis for voluntary marriages. In short, most young people were dependent on their families for their livelihood. Unlike the process of ending footbinding, the better-educated and more open-minded families in Prosperity were not willing to tolerate free-choice marriages in the early 1940s. Crook and Yu did learn of one attempt that was undertaken by Dr. Yang Huaqing's adopted son, who had been set up in business in Bishan County town by his family when he had reached adulthood. In due course the man became interested in a stylish modern young woman who sent a matchmaker to him suggesting marriage. As he was willing, he brought the young woman and her matchmaker to Prosperity to obtain his parents' approval. The Yangs held a dinner and the parents and the matchmaker negotiated late into the night. The following morning the young woman and her matchmaker departed for Bishan in style, riding in litters paid for by theYangs. When no engagement ensued, it was understood that the negotiations that had transpired that night were not to set the terms of the marriage but rather to fix the amount of compensation to be given to the young woman for a rejection of the suit. Word later spread that the young woman had doomed her cause when she tried to create a favorable impression by saying, "I'd like you to know I have high-ranking friends in the 29th Army." Contrary to her expectations, instead of indicating her high connections, it suggested to the Yangs that she was a woman of questionable virtue. The young man appeared to accept his parents' verdict calmly. With an inheritance at stake, it was highly improbable that a young man in Prosperity would have disregarded his parents' disapproval.

Arranged marriage practices took into account a number of considerations when making a match. One was the much-spoken-of principle of "matching doors and households" – meaning that the socioeconomic status of the two families should be equal. But a second was the scarcely-mentioned principle of adjustments for special positive or negative qualities in the individuals involved. On the positive side, a girl might be valued for special household or production skills or her beauty or education. A young man might be valued for his special capabilities, his education or prospects. On the negative side, flaws of one kind of another – physical or mental – would be taken into account, though each family did its best to hide these.

Orthodox marriage-making practices started with the aid of a matchmaker approached by one party or the other. This third party was important since, for reasons of face, it was inconvenient for the two parties to deal directly with each other. The matchmaker, often a woman, could be a relative of both sides who matched up cousins of different surnames. Among influential landowners, however, the initiator might be a member of a power faction, proposing a match between eminent families in order to consolidate property and strengthen a political alliance.

Once the initial approach had been made and tentatively accepted by both families, the horoscopes of the proposed couple were checked. While this was a necessary procedure, a competent horoscopist (*bazi xiansheng*) could accommodate any match that might have been decided upon by influential families, Crook and Yu were told by a skeptic. Likewise he could be persuaded to declare horoscopes incompatible should one family wish to avoid a match without offending the family seeking the marriage link. Once the horoscopes were found compatible, the matchmaker helped the two families reach agreement on guidelines for the dowry and gifts to the bride. A banquet sealed these agreements and made them almost as binding as the wedding itself. No matchmaker would dare suggest alternative matches and if either side backed out at this point, a legal case could result with demand for compensation. When the entire family decided it was time for the wedding, the matchmaker was again approached to put forward the request to the other party. If agreeable, the horoscopist was again consulted to determine an auspicious date for the wedding. The bridegroom's family now presented gifts to the girl's. If these were up to expectations, everything moved forward smoothly.

Betrothals traditionally took place when children were small, as parents were eager to seal a good match as early as possible. This meant that in difficult times families of similar economic and social standing at the time of betrothal might more easily find themselves in drastically different financial situations by the time the marriage was consummated a decade or more later. Perhaps for this reason, betrothals in the early 1940s often took place not long before the marriage when the young people were already in their early or mid-teens.

Although the traditional marriage system remained quite vibrant, one marriage-related custom that was beginning to show signs of alteration among the well-to-do was the easing of the strong prohibition against the couple seeing one another before the wedding day. In many cases, the engaged young people would be allowed to catch a glance of their future mate from afar. In a few cases, an "accidental meeting" of the couple was concocted before the wedding day in order to win the enthusiasm of the two teenagers designated for betrothal. Importantly, these meetings had to be set up in a fashion that made them seem to have happened as a coincidence, as is revealed in the chance meeting one January morning in 1941 between Wang Junliang's eighteen-year-old daughter, Wang Zhengbi (the prospective bride), and her fiancée. Wang Zhengbi joined a group of eight of her female relatives who were making an unexpected call on the wife of Mr. T.H. Sun, the director of the National Christian Project in Prosperity. The party filed straightaway upstairs to the surprise of the hostess, who followed them up. At this moment a second party of unexpected guests arrived, led by the wife of the biggest landowner, Mrs. Cao Yuexian, with her sixteen-year-old nephew (the prospective groom), who was heir to the large Zhang estate. She was accompanied by Commander Cai Xunqing's wife, as well as three of her own daughters. The Wang party upstairs took this as their cue to file downstairs in full sight of the Cao party below. As the boy and girl came face-to-face, Mrs. Cai introduced them. The girl bowed to the boy and he reciprocated. The girl and her party left while the boy's party lingered, but only briefly for the mission was accomplished. This little operation not only succeeded in winning the support of the two teenagers who were highly satisfied with each other's appearance, it exhibited style. The practice of "accidental meetings" deviated sharply from the traditional conventions which prohibited social contact between unmarried adolescents of the opposite sex. Yet this type of premarital encounter was beginning to be accepted by Prosperity's better-off families who showed some modern influences.

However, these erosions in betrothal customs were limited. Wang Zhengbi's orchestrated outing was not an indication that a significant loosening had occurred in the strict taboos against immoral conduct by young unmarried women. Any hint of impropriety could undermine modern-minded cultural rebels. There existed in Prosperity a strong sense that it was unseemly for engaged women to have a visible presence in public, as Cao Hongying sadly discovered when she tried to attend the three-week Bible Classes offered by Mabel Proctor as part of her regular bi-annual circuit around Sichuan. These classes were appealing to a select group of young educated women like Hongying because they offered an opportunity to both increase literacy skills and to learn about modern ways of managing a family. However, soon after these classes began, an anonymous note was found pasted on the wall opposite the South Gate of the village, stating that Hongying had been seen attending market, an oblique but unambiguous way of saying that she was meeting a boyfriend. Although Hongying had always been careful not to use the public street when attending these meetings, but rather to arrive discretely by the back gate, she and her family took the warning seriously. She gave up the literacy classes and stayed at home until her wedding.

Minor Marriages Not Illegal

The Nationalist legal codes pertaining to marriage did not outlaw the practice of minor marriages. Termed *tongyangxi*, this arrangement was widespread in the entire county of Bishan.[9] Stark poverty made it impossible for poor farm families to follow standard practices in arranging marriages for their sons and daughters. The most common solution was taking a young girl to raise as a future daughter-in-law, a little "foster fiancée" (*tongyangxi*). Finding a child fiancée for a son was commonly adopted by poor families by taking a young girl to raise as a future daughter-in-law. However, a large number of girls moved into the homes of their future husbands when they were quite young, perhaps even babies, and were raised by their future mothers-in-law. Contradictory reports from Bishan County show that some government officials confused early marriage with the *tongyangxi* (foster daughters-in-law) form of marriage. *Tongyangxi* were girls from poor families who were taken at a very young age and brought up as foster fiancées in the home of another family as a future bride for a young son, with the marriage mutual agreement between the parents. If the girl was two or three years old the boy's family might give a small sum to the girl's parents in recognition of what her parents had spent on feeding her; if she was older, they would give somewhat more; if she was already ten or twelve and able to earn her own keep through work around the house or in the fields, they would have to present a more substantial sum. Despite the transfer of money, the system was not spoken of as purchasing a girl.

This method of contracting a marriage had advantages for both families involved. For the boy's family, it ensured them a daughter-in-law in good time in a community where boys outnumbered girls by

---

[9] The 1996 Bishan Gazetteer did not provide any exact figures for *tongyangxi*, merely stating that it was very common (Bishan fangzhi 1996:74).

fifty-five to forty-five.[10] And it also reduced the expense to the relatively small initial payment and spread out the cost of feeding the youngster until she was old enough to pull her own weight. As for the girl's family, it relieved them of the expense of raising a daughter and provided her with a dowry. Both sides also suffered a loss. Unlike the standard marriage which forged a link between two families, with this type of marriage there was rarely an ongoing link. Poverty steadily broke up scores of poor and landless families causing them to disperse. Even where both families remained, the tie between a girl and the parents who had not brought her up often weakened.

In 1940/41, there was a slight trend away from the foster fiancée pattern of marriage. The price of rice, which before the Sino-Japanese war had sold at 1.40 *yuan* a *dou*, by December 1941 was up to 120.00 *yuan* a *dou*.[11] Calculating the monetary cost of feeding a girl, some poor families decided against taking an extra mouth to feed. Others regretted having already brought in a foster fiancée and if they had not had her long might look for an excuse to return her.

Life could be exceedingly harsh for these little fiancées. They formed the special section of the child population of the community that led the hardest lives. They were typically overworked and underfed. Often by the time these girls had reached their mid-twenties and thirties, they had become the mainstay and even the family head, having lost their parents-in-law or even their husbands.

While this form of marriage-making was typical of the poor, some better-off families also took foster fiancées. This was often the case where a farm family had several sons and could not afford a traditional marriage for all of them. Since Crook and Yu's questionnaire was not designed to study internal family relations, they had no precise statistics on the prevalence of this form of marriage. But based on fourteen months of field research in Prosperity Crook estimates that foster fiancées made up the majority of brides in any given year.

---

[10] This ratio was determined by Crook and Yu and is included in table 3 of chapter 1 in Isabel Crook's manuscript.
[11] A *dou* is ten liters.

Codified and Common Forms of Divorce

Equally difficult to institute in the community of Prosperity was the notion that the state had the power to determine the terms for ending marriages. Although the municipal courts in the large cities of Beijing and Shanghai and Chongqing had been issuing divorces for a number of years, legal divorces in Bishan were quite rare before 1940. One of the few suits filed with the Bishan Court in the early 1940s was brought by a woman from a wealthy family, as was evident by the fact that she was willing to hand over the very large sum of 1,000 *yuan* in the settlement, more than enough to enable her ex-husband to find another wife. She wrote in her divorce statement that there had been no happiness in the five years that the couple was married. But what is most interesting about this case is that she did not seek a judgment from the court. Rather she just wanted to register her divorce agreement with them as a way of legitimating it. This action was similar to her decision to buy an advertisement in a Chongqing newspaper publicizing the fact that the couple had decided to divorce.

Few people in Bishan seemed interested in obtaining a legal divorce. What is striking in the few cases that discussed marriage difficulties is that the plaintiff did not seek a divorce, but rather asked the court to make a wandering wife to come home. In another case a woman who remarried for financial reasons after her husband had been away in the army for several years was charged with polygamy (*chong hun*).[12]

The few cases brought before the Bishan Court that were connected to marriage issues were not primarily about divorce but rather were related to the complications connected with executing or enforcing a marriage agreement, with wartime disruptions adding to the difficulties. In one fairly contentious case the forty-three-year-old Chen Nanxuan from Taihe Township petitioned the Bishan Court to stop Luo Xingwei of Zitong from pestering him, sometimes in a belligerent manner, about honoring the marriage agreement they had

---

[12] This case was included in materials Xeroxed from the Bishan County Archives (*Bishan dang'anguan*) by Liu Jing, archivist from the Chongqing Municipal Archives. Unfortunately it did not have a case number attached to it.

entered into some years earlier. As Chen's son had been conscripted into the army in August of 1938, he was reluctant to incur the expense of the bride price plus the upkeep of the prospective daughter-in-law until his son returned home. The court in effect decided in favor of Chen by ordering the township authorities to prevent Luo from continuing to badger Chen, but it also indicated that there was no basis in the law for determining the validity of the marriage contract (Bishan shiyan difang fayuan n.d.). In another case Gan Xiangquan, a Daoist priest, filed a petition with the court claiming that his wife had run off with another man who was quite wealthy, leaving him with two kids to raise. He sought to call the integrity of his wife into question by asserting in his statement to the court that his wife had a history of being unfaithful to him. While he asked the court to force his wife to come back to him, in fact he seemed more interested in gaining compensation for his loss, including the jewelry that he had given her. In yet another case, relatives of a man who had been conscribed into the army asked the court to take action against his wife who had gotten a job in a small textile workshop in Danfeng in order to make ends meet after her husband went away to the war and then moved in with a male co-worker. Her incensed husband's relatives succeeded in having her imprisoned (Bishan shiyan difang fayuan 1941).

There were numerous examples in Prosperity of women who walked out of their marriages and found another spouse. Commonly referred to as runaway wives (*taoqi*), these women were compelled to flee because of unbearable ill-treatment or poverty. Though many young women put up with exceedingly unhappy circumstances, others ran away, preferring to gamble on the chance of making a better match. They would travel a distance of an hour or two walk from their fiancée's or husband's home, and then begin loitering along the way, lingering especially on the outskirts of a market village, waiting to be picked up by someone looking for a partner either for himself, for a son or for a poor relative. If the fugitive was not picked up in one place she moved on to another, keeping a distance from her partner's home for she was family property and a valuable source of labor.

The appearance in the village of a runaway fiancée or wife aroused the eager interest of those seeking a partner. Still they were viewed with uneasiness. Might the woman be a perennial runaway and perhaps even run off taking some of the family's meager possessions? Or might she be the quarrelsome type? Might she commit some crime for which the new husband would now be held legally responsible? Yet despite these apprehensions the fugitives found partners – for women were in short supply.

In September 1940 a young woman appeared in Prosperity Market and hung about for a day or two. She freely replied to questions posed her. Soon everyone knew that she was the daughter-in-law of Wu Hailu, a small farmer up the hill at Xueyakou, that her husband had been conscripted the previous year and not been heard from since, that her parents-in-law maltreated her and that she was determined to leave them for good.

Immediately a number of people were interested. Peng Shaohui, a twenty-nine-year-old laborer in the village still unmarried because of poverty, asked his widowed mother for permission to marry the woman. She refused. She had come from a prosperous farm family bankrupted only a decade earlier and could not relinquish hopes of a standard marriage for her eldest son. He reluctantly dropped the matter.

In another poor household in the village, Wu Chunzhi and his wife were on the lookout for a bride for their eighteen-year-old son, the eldest of three. They agreed that the woman looked promising, so Wu invited her to live with them and marry their son. The young woman on her part thought the prospect satisfactory and moved in. But she had no sooner done so than her father-in-law, Wu Hailu, arrived in Prosperity and compelled her to return to his farm.

The young woman, however, did not submit to her forced retention and quarreled unremittingly. After a whole month of this Wu Hailu and his wife could stand it no longer. The father-in-law himself brought the young woman to the village and negotiated with Wu Chunzhi for compensation. A sum was agreed upon, Wu Hailu relinquished his claim to the woman, and she was publicly recognized as Wu Chunzhi's daughter-in-law. During the following year the young woman made a name for herself in the village as a quiet, industrious, well-behaved daughter-in-law. People commented on the Wus' good fortune and even Peng Shaohui's mother berated herself for having thrown away such a golden opportunity.

This example was not unusual. Families who lost a daughter-in-law or wife would seek to track her down, for her disappearance represented an economic loss and they were legally entitled to seize her and take her home. But often they found it preferable to settle for compensation instead. For the new husband, even if he had to pay compensation, the cost of the marriage with a fugitive was greatly reduced.

Among the poor the accepted practice of marriage with a runaway wife meant that in reality a woman could divorce her husband. And her remarriage became legal when her new partner paid compensation to her former husband. This practice went counter to the accepted marriage codes that permitted only men to seek divorce. It was a reflection, on the one hand, of the crucial economic role played by women in poor families and the shortage of women in the community. On the other, it was a reflection of the harshness of the life for women among the poor. Unlike women in better-off families, they had little to lose.

While taking in a runaway was primarily a marriage stratagem of the poor, well-off families were also known to adopt such tactics in order to avoid expensive marriages for second or third sons. Such a case occurred in 1938, two years before Crook and Yu arrived in Prosperity. It all started when a woman stranger arrived in the village. As she refused to say who she was or where she came from, someone suggested she must be a fugitive from the law and forthwith she was placed in the township lockup. No one turned up to lay any accusations against her, so after a few days she was released. She then went to Prosperity's cheapest inn, where she unaccountably stayed for another couple of days before disappearing as mysteriously as she had come.

Not long after this the thriving but thrifty butcher Wang Chang'an announced that his twenty-five-year-old second son, Wang Haiyun, was engaged and soon to be married, the matchmaker being the young man's older married sister who lived in Bishan. On the appointed day the bride arrived in a red wedding sedan chair, clad in red and with a modest dowry. Guests and onlookers were impressed until one of them recognized the bride as the stranger of a few weeks before. Clearly Wang's subterfuge had enabled him to greatly scale down the cost of his second son's marriage. But it caused a storm of gossip and further confirmed Wang Chang'an's reputation as a miser. People speculated that Wang's daughter in Bishan had found (or enticed away) an unhappily-married woman and had sent her to Prosperity to look over and be looked over by the Wangs and that a secret agreement had been reached while she was staying in the inn.

This bride, like her new father-in-law, was the subject of unfavorable gossip. She was categorized as a brash woman and a perennial runaway type. But two years later the marriage was still holding, despite incessant quarrels between the couple in which neither side had any sympathizers for both were considered equally at fault. Proof that the marriage was nevertheless acceptable to all concerned came when the Wangs paid a sizeable indemnity to the woman's previous husband when he finally managed to track her down after a two-year search.

Wang Chang'an had made a decent traditional marriage for his eldest son. But he begrudged this expense for his other three sons. In addition to providing this mock-traditional marriage for his second son, he left his third soldier son unmarried and his fourth son he allowed to marry out of his family and into a farm family with a daughter but no sons. While this type of marriage was considered very demeaning to the man, it provided him with an inheritance and relieved his family of an expensive wedding party.

The neighbor across the street was Zhou Dongchang, a forty-year-old laboring man, who earned his living by helping the restauranteur, Zhang Yunheng, with such heavy jobs as butchering and carrying water. He had obtained the job through the offices of Zhang's wife who was also of the Zhou lineage. In 1939 Zhou Dongchang had picked up a runaway wife and was considered a lucky man for she turned out to be a quiet hardworking woman who contributed to the couple's livelihood by hiring herself out by the day as a farm laborer.

But no one in the village, even Zhou, learned anything of her background, for she hardly spoke at all.

Then in October 1940, Zhou's wife disappeared without explanation. Two months later she returned, saying only that she had taken employment as a live-in domestic. But a few weeks later, three men seized her in front of her home and took her to the township office where she was charged with having stolen a peddler's stock of needles and thread. She was put in the village lockup to await the hearing of her case by the township head. Throughout the incident, Zhou stood in his doorway, apparently an indifferent spectator, though his kinswoman negotiated the woman's release, promising to stand guarantor.

In the course of the hearing next day, the following story came out. One market day back in October, a couple of fortune tellers from Shizi Market town came to Prosperity to set up their stands. When the pair returned home at the end of the day, Zhou's wife went with them. She stayed with the couple for a time but could find no way to earn her living, so she suggested that they arrange a match for her with their bachelor neighbor, a peddler named Lai. This was done. Lai was highly satisfied with his new wife, who even on occasion accompanied him on his rounds, carrying his wares for him. After two weeks the wife suggested they move to a safe place in the countryside, saying she feared that living in town she might be recognized by people who knew her husband in Prosperity. Lai agreed. A week after the move, the wife sent her husband off on an errand. When he returned he found she had absconded with his stock-in-trade. The woman had in fact returned to Shizi Market town to the home of the original couple of fortunetellers. But they in turn ran off with the needles and thread, leaving her stranded. It was at this point that she returned to Zhou. Lai, having lost his precious stock, now peddled cheap gourd dippers. As he traveled around the countryside he kept on the lookout for the wife who had robbed him. It took a month or more before he set up his stall in Prosperity and happened to catch sight of her. He immediately accosted her but she insisted it was a case of mistaken identity and Lai let the matter rest. However that very night when he returned home he rounded up two young men friends and the three of them came to Prosperity where they put up in the cheapest inn to watch for the woman. But each morning before dawn she rose and went into the countryside to work as a farmhand, so it was not till the third day that they finally caught her.

When the hearing was over, the township head ruled that the woman was guilty of robbing Lai of his stock-in-trade valued at thirty *yuan*; he ordered Zhou to pay the sum to Lai; then he advised both Zhou and Lai to disown the woman publicly so as to clear themselves of responsibility for any future crimes she might commit. Zhou paid the indemnity without a murmur, the two men disowned her and the woman departed for an unknown destination.

Six weeks later, the disowned wife returned to Prosperity. She walked into Zhou's house and set about tidying the place, ignoring Zhou who stood in the doorway loudly ordering her to clear out. Next she prepared a meal. When it was ready and set out on the table, she took a hoe and went into the back garden to tend the vegetable patch. After some delay and seeming reluctance, Zhou sat down and ate the food. Toward evening the woman gathered some twigs and heated water for her husband and Zhou enjoyed the rare luxury of washing in hot water. The following morning Zhou and his ex-wife could be seen silently hoeing the vegetable garden side-by-side. As one neighbor commented, "He would be a fool not to take her back. Where could he find another woman who is so quiet, able and hardworking?"

Anyone could see that the quality of Zhou's life was immeasurably better when his wife was with him. But what of the woman? Why had she run away from Zhou? What was she seeking? She never gossiped or quarreled or even talked much. No one knew where she had come from, what sort of life she had led, or what she thought. And few, if any, knew her name or if she had one. Such self-effacement was a much-praised virtue in a woman.

Conclusion

The merging of anthropological and historical research materials has allowed for a fairly intensive examination of the implementation of Nationalist marriage reforms in a rural community during the war era. The war stimulated some major changes in Chinese politics and society, including marriage practices in the rural township of Prosperity, but they were limited and more connected to indirect influences than to the efforts of the government to enforce its legal codes. The large influx of downriver people who brought many new ideas and practices facilitated some minor shifts, as did the rapidly shifting economic realities. The arranged marriage system remained unchanged. This study finds that the gap between what the government aimed to achieve and what it was actually able to accomplish was quite great. To be sure, government directives, laws, and propaganda campaigns to alter marriage practices were based on a bold vision of Nationalist reformers to modernize the family that was influenced by Western models and received support from Christian and secular reformers. But in large part, the Nationalists failed to implant their urban based vision in rural society, as it was unable to create social legitimacy and support for its proposed reforms, particularly in its efforts to replace customary marriage practices with codified laws.

References

Bishan dang'anguan (Bishan County Archives), Minzhengting (Office of Civil Administration), document no. 102, March 1940.
Bishan fangzhi (Bishan Gazetteer), ed. by Bishan fangzhi bianjizu (Editorial Group of the Bishan Gazetteer), Chengdu 1996.
Bishan shiyan difang fayuan (Bishan Experimental Regional Court), document no. 41-46, n.d.
Bishan shiyan difang fayuan (Bishan Experimental Regional Court), document no. 3450-447, 12 July l941.
Buck, John L., *Land Utilization in China*, Nanjing 1937.
Crook, Isabel, with Yu Xiji, *A Community Called Prosperity*, unpublished manuscript, 1994.
Davin, Delia, Women in the Countryside in China, in: Roxane Witke, Margery Wolf (eds.), *Women in Chinese Society*, Stanford 1975, pp. 243-273.

Esherick, Joseph, War and Revolution: Chinese Society during the 1940s, in: *Twentieth Century China* 27:1 (2001), pp. 1-38.

Higonnet, Margaret R., Jane Jenson, Sonya Michel, Margaret C. Weitz (eds.), *Behind the Lines: Gender and the Two World Wars*, New Haven, London 1989.

Jiancha bao zaohun (An Investigation into the Situation of Early Marriages), Chongqing dang'anguan (Chongqing Municipal Archives), file 5, document no. 10, 15 August 1943.

Kirby, William C., Continuity and Change in Modern China: Economic Planning on the Mainland and on Taiwan, 1943-1958, in: *The Australian Journal of Chinese Affairs* 24 (1990), pp. 121-141.

Marwick, Arthur, *The Deluge: British Society and the First World War*, London 1975.

Ruf, Gregory, *Cadres and Kin: Making a Socialist Village in West China, 1921-1991*, Stanford 1998.

Summerfield, Penny, *Reconstructing Women's Wartime Lives: Discourse and Subjectivity in Oral Histories of the Second World War*, Manchester 1998.

Yang, Martin C., Chinese Village: *Taitou, Shantung Province*, New York 1945.

Zang Xiaowei, Family, Kinship, Marriage, and Sexuality, in: Robert E. Gamer (ed.), *Understanding Contemporary China*, Boulder, London ²1999 (¹1998), pp. 267-292.

Gender, Higher Education, and the "New Woman": The Experiences of Female Graduates in Republican China

Harriet T. Zurndorfer

> "There, you see," said Miss Wu, "we must be able to earn our own living, or we shall remain in our fetters for ever."
> "Miss Wu," said I, and hesitated. "Our forerunners in women's 'freedom' used to talk that way. But things are not so easy as that. You in China seem to think every English and American woman is happy and contented. Because she has had a better chance of education than Chinese women and can therefore usually earn her own living if put to it, you think all is well with her. Think now of many of our unmarried women in the West, teaching when perhaps wearied to death of their profession, being typists and secretaries in cramped offices year after year, washing dishes in restaurants; and often leading very lonely lives, going home to a small bedroom or a cheap woman's club. These are the facts you know [...]. Perhaps you do not realize how lonely the life of a single woman earning her living can be."
> Lady Hosie, *Portrait of a Chinese Lady* (1930), pp. 115-116.

> While I regard the increased knowledge and education as an improvement and approaching the ideal of womanhood, I wager that we are not going to find, as we have not yet found, a world-renowned lady pianist or lady painter. I feel confident that her soup will still be better than her poetry and that her real masterpiece will be her chubby-faced boy. The ideal woman remains for me the wise, gentle and firm mother.
> Lin Yutang, *My Country and My People* (1938), p. 155.

Despite the fact that the role of schooling and higher education has long been appreciated as an important element in the construction, representation, and transmission of gender identities, this topic has only begun to receive its due attention in modern scholarship on Republican China. Recent research building on earlier compilations of education materials (Cheng Zhefan 1936; Shu Xincheng 1962; Taga Akigoro 1972; Li/Zhang 1975; Chen Xuexun 1981) has revealed a plethora of contending and contradictory impressions and reflections.

In a society bent on nation-building while maintaining social stability, women's education formed one more contending element in the broader intersection of forces open to change and continuity. Both the late Qing and early Republican governments saw education as a means to cultivate women into virtuous housewives as well as high-minded citizens. And as such, female access to education proved both a barrier and a gateway in the first decades of the twentieth century.

Reviewing contemporary writings on women and education originating from the 1920s and 1930s, we may also recognize certain other disparities, such as the (mis)representation of women as "national virtue" in Guomindang (Nationalist Party, GMD) campaigns to encourage nationalist fervor, or the loopholes in the Chinese Communist Party's (CCP) master narrative of Chinese women's liberation. These political histories deflect the complexity of the changing circumstances that influenced how women themselves considered their education in relation to their own lives; the instances of discrepancy between what male intellectuals, government officials, and revolutionaries wrote about higher education for women, and what women themselves communicated on this topic, stimulate further investigation. In this essay, I attempt to follow up these conflicting images as they emerge out of education debates, journal articles, and first-person accounts that relate to the question of what meaning higher education had for Chinese women in the Republican era.

Issues of Women and Education Prior to the Republican Era

Late Qing reformers concerned themselves with the situation of women after China's defeat in the 1894-1895 Sino-Japanese War, and cast the need to promote education for girls in terms of ideas on state-building and the advancement of the Chinese nation. On 1 June 1898 a gentry-official Jing Yuanshan, with the support of the reformers Kang Youwei (1858-1927) and Liang Qichao (1873-1929), opened the first Chinese-run girls' school in Shanghai (Lewis 1919:25; Wang Zheng 1999:172). But the establishment of this particular school (which endured only one year), and other female-only educational institutions, was part of a general campaign to reduce "economic wastage and genetic deterioration" (Borthwick 1985:72); these schools were not meant to be academies for cultivating girls' talents. As Liang Qichao announced on the occasion of the Shanghai school's opening: "the new woman 'above, will be a helpmate to her husband, and below a source of instruction for her sons; in her immediate surroundings, she will give ease to the family, and in a wider sphere, she will improve the race'" (quoted in Borthwick 1985:72). The argument for female education from the 1898 reformers was neatly summarized in the expression *qiangzhong baoguo* (to strengthen the Chinese race and defend the nation) (Wang Zheng 1999:173). Education for girls and women formed part of a general reformist view that women should contribute to the productive power of the Chinese state by becoming "erudite" mothers who in turn would produce better-informed sons and thereby a stronger body-politic. And so, by the late 1890s, China's women became part of a broader nationalist discourse "to mobilize the energies of women to service the nation [...]" (Judge 2001:770). For the first time in China's long history, education for women became a matter of "public concern."

The idea of cultivating "good wives and wise mothers" (*liangqi xianmu*) originated in Meiji Japan, the same nation against which China had fought the 1894-1895 war that resulted in the ruptures in Qing visions of government and society in the first place. According to Joan Judge, Japanese nationalists had been promoting this concept (in Japanese, *ryōsai kenbo shugi*) since the early 1890s. "Merging ancient Chinese female ethical principles with contemporary nationalist concerns," the *liangqi xianmu* concept proved attractive to both Chinese conservatives and radicals alike (*ibid.* 771). But the phrase originated several decades earlier with the Japanese education reformer Nakamura Masanao in the mid-nineteenth century, and was picked up by late Qing advocates of Japanese-style education for girls (Higuchi Keiko 1982). Lu Xun (1881-1936) recorded in his 1925 essay "The Grave: Widowism" (*Fen: Guafuzhuyi*), how the Chinese students who had had teacher training in the late Qing era returned home with a certain eagerness to popularize the "good wives and wise mothers" philosophy among their contemporaries (Lu Xun 1980:212).

Although Chinese militant nationalists disdained the thought of encouraging erudite mothers merely for the sake of men, they also recognized the possibilities that their endorsement opened for women who might want to pursue formal education in Japan. And, as Weikun Cheng has written in a recent study on education in early twentieth-century Beijing, the Japanese-owned (but Chinese-staffed) publication *Shuntian shibao (Shuntian Times)* helped disseminate the work of the most effective Japanese female proponent of the "good wives and wise mothers" ideology, Shimoda Utako (1854-1936) (Cheng Weikun 2000:111; see also Judge 2001:772). A teacher to the overseas Chinese female student community in Tokyo, and the founder of the publishing house *Zuoxin she* (Society for Renewal) in Shanghai, Shimoda sought to convince others how educating Chinese women did not mean their relinquishing "feminine virtues." Her "pedagogical philosophy" elevated the study of domestic science, and the value of physical education which ultimately would foster a stronger nation (Judge 2001:776).

During the first decade of the twentieth century both men and women commentators on the future of Chinese women's education revealed their disapproval of the antecedent of the new educated woman, i.e. the *cainü* (talented woman) of the imperial era. As *the* representative of the literate woman of the past, in the eyes (and words) of Liang Qichao, she was "useless" because she was closely married to traditional high culture and divorced from the practical learning needed for the advancement of modern China (Hu Ying 2001:202; cf. Hu Ying 2000:4-6). Radical female nationalists also expressed their criticism of the talented women in China's past. The Tokyo-based activist He Xiangning (1877-1972), also known as "the mother of the Chinese revolution," had little sympathy with the literate women of the past. She saw them

> indulging their emotions rather than serving the nation: Upper-class women would wallow in their own compositions of sentimental prose-poems set to music (*ci*) and descriptive prose interspersed with verse (*fu*), and the sound of lamentation would fill the inner chambers. While their poems on the spring flowers and the fall moon yielded nothing but confusion, these women did not know what the nation was. (Judge 2001:800)

Such disparagement of China's female literary legacy was part of the radical women's agenda to distance themselves from writings of women they considered "self-consciously emotional and purposefully apolitical" (*ibid.*).

The Qing government only reluctantly enacted legislation for schooling for girls as it initiated a program of "New Policy" reforms during the first decade of the twentieth century in the wake of the Boxer rebellion. Zhang Zhidong (1837-1909), the architect of China's 1904 regulations for its first modern school system, specifically excluded girls from access to basic instruction, and recommended that they continue to be educated in the home (Borthwick 1985:77; Bailey 2001:318-319). Supported by other powerful officials Rong-qing (1854-1912), and Zhang Baixi (1847-1907), Zhang Zhidong feared the effects Western-style ideas of education could have on young women, and in particular, the notion of their choosing their own husband (Borthwick 1985:77). But once the Empress Dowager's negotiating efforts to bring Shimoda to China, in order that she could propagate her ideal, "the beauty of East Asian female virtue," became known in 1906, it did not take long for the Qing government to issue the *Nüzi xiaoxuetang zhangcheng* (Regulations of the Ministry of Education on Elementary Schools for Girls) and the *Nüzi shifan xuetang zhangcheng* (Regulations of the Ministry of Education for Women's Normal Schools) the following year which sanctioned the establishment of the first Chinese-run girls' schools (see Li/Zhang 1975, 2:974-989; Shu Xincheng 1962, 3:800-819). The first teaching training institution, the Beiyang First Girls' Normal School (later known as the Zhili First Women's Normal School), located in Tianjin, also opened in 1906 (McElroy 2001:349).

The new regulations prescribed a single-sex, two-tiered system: primary education and normal school. The primary education had two phases, junior and senior, totaling eight years. At the junior elementary level, instruction focused on ethics, the Chinese language, arithmetic, needlework, and gymnastics, while at the senior level, the subjects of geography, physics, history, painting and music were added. Girls were excluded from learning foreign languages, the Confucian classics, or business (Cheng Weikun 2000:118). In contrast, boys could attend the equivalent of middle-school education of five years, and had the option to compete for a place in a three-year high school and three-year college. For girls, four years of normal school was the highest level of education available to them (Du Xueyuan 1995:340).

Late Qing texts for use in these institutions continued to teach the value of "virtuous wives and mothers" with didactic instruction emphasizing ethical principles, exemplary models, and appropriate life-cycle roles (Judge 2000). The endorsement of such manuals in these new schools indicates that the authorities were actively constructing and perpetuating a particular view of femaleness very much linked to the Qing vision of womanhood. Although a number of the texts included the biographies of some foreign women, the insertion of the stories of these Western lives was intended "to mark the possibility of transformation from within existing cultural traditions [...]" (*ibid.* 130). *Nügong* (women's work) was also incorporated into the curriculum of normal schools. Embroidery, sericulture, sewing, and handicrafts along with household management were part of the prescribed study (Bailey 2001:319). The Republican scholar Cheng Zhefan, surveying the educational structure during the late Qing, concluded it was a "two-track" system based on gender inequality (Cheng Zhefan 1936:96). And in his recent study Paul Bailey has argued that "the entire *raison d'être* of women's education [...] was the cultivation of diligent, compliant, and frugal household managers [...]" (Bailey 2003:355).

These domestic-orientated goals of girls' education were confirmed in the emerging female press during the decade preceding the revolution of 1911. The issue of China's first periodicals for women, e.g. *Nübao (Women's Journal)* and *Nüzi shijie (Women's World)*, was an important marker in the history of Chinese women, and one may well ask what role did this new journalism play in the promulgation of education for women.[1] In practice, these journals had a limited readership, a tiny group of literate, elite women, but they did give practical guidance for school enrollment. And most important, the contents of some of these magazines deviated from the usual educational hand-

---

[1] See Nivard 1986a and 1986b for bibliographical information.

books available to women; the new publications featured biographies of non-Chinese women, utopian feminist fantasies, reports of Chinese women's achievements in émigré communities, and thus provided "alternatives to the traditional Confucian ideals of womanhood" (Dooling/Torgeson 1998:6-7).

Female Education in the Early Republic

The end of the Qing empire did not bring any real radical change to the scenario that legitimated women's education in terms of national well-being. Although anarchists like Jin Tianhe (1874-1947) with his 1903 pamphlet *Nüjie zhong (Women's Bell)* advocating *nüquan* (women's rights) (Edwards 1994), and the feminist revolutionary Qiu Jin (1879-1907) with her ideas of women asserting their own female agency, might have stirred ripples among political extremists,[2] the tenor of the early Republic remained distinctly conservative, and female access to education moved slowly. According to one analysis of the available statistics for government-sponsored schools:

> The number of female students increased from 1,853 (0.21 percent of the school-age population) in 1907 to 141,130 (4.81 percent of the school-age population) in 1912-1913. By 1922-1923 the total had reached 417,820 (6.32 percent of the school-age population). At the primary level the number of girls increased from 130,808 in 1912-1913 to only 164,719 in 1916-1917 (the number of boys at primary school increased from 2,662.825 to 3,678.736 in the same period). By 1922 primary school enrollment for girls totaled 403,742 (6.19 percent of the total) [...]. Also, whereas the number of schools for boys increased from 84,883 (2,792.257 students) in 1912 to 117,658 (3,801.730 students) in 1916, the number of schools for girls rose from 2,389 (141,130 students) to only 3,461 (172,724 students) during the same period. (Bailey 2001:320)

These statistics indicate that educational opportunities for girls were still limited in the first decade of the Republic. But, as Wang Zheng argues, for those girls born in the early twentieth century, "education

---

[2] As Peter Zarrow has remarked in his study of anarchism and feminism, "until 1907 virtually all Chinese feminism was nationalistic" (Zarrow 1988:796).

was no longer a luxury that only women born in elite families could enjoy" (Wang Zheng 1999:174). The pervasive nationalist discourse, it would seem, made girls' education an important ingredient in the forging of the nation. And slowly, the number of girls attending secondary school increased, from 10,066 in 1912 to 11,824 in 1922 (Bailey 2003:331 n. 10).

The question remains to what extent these modernizing influences reached beyond modern cities into the hinterland where the bulk of the population lived. By 1918-1919, almost a third of China's 1,819 counties still had no girls' schools (Borthwick 1985:82). In rural regions, the old-style *sishu* (private schools), dependent on locally rich families or lineage funding, continued to function and to serve as a bastion of traditional values (where the secondary education of girls had no place) (Mackerras 1985:162-164). In some locations, missionary-run schools provided facilities for a small percentage of the school age population: by the early 1930s, some 1.7 percent of the total number of pupils (both male and female) attended Catholic primary schools, while some 2.5 percent of the same population frequented Protestant primary schools. In a certain sense these Christian institutions, particularly in the poorer regions of China, were no more innovative than their secular counterparts. The curriculum in Protestant mission schools for girls offered religious studies, maybe some mathematics, but domestic skills such as sewing dominated the instruction, and were obligatory. Apparently, the teaching of English was problematic: it was found that the girls' acquisition of English could lead them to becoming mistresses or "protected women" of Western merchants (Lutz 2002:20).

Even the most famous private school in Shanghai, "McTyeire" (also known as *Zhongxi nüshu* [Chinese-Western Girls' Academy]), which opened in 1892 could not escape the potential clash between private domesticity and public responsibility that students were likely to confront at some stage in their development. This school's role "in training future wives and mothers to 'be the center of Christian influence in the sphere of power with which Christ has gifted them [the family]' *and* its goal to train young women to use their study of English and the Bible, as well as history, science, mathematics, and Chinese, to become leaders in their communities, moved Chinese women into non-traditional roles" (Ross 1996:216). "McTyeire" was well-known for its challenge to traditional cultural patterns of subservience, early betrothal, and duty to one's mother-in-law. But the institution's teachers who were unmarried, strong-willed, and highly educated women may not seem to offer an alternative, ideal, viable role model to follow for these young, and protected girl students from wealthy, and probably somewhat conventional homes. Lu Xun also commented on these women educators in his essay "The Grave." He suggested that childless, unmarried women could not be good teachers because they have no love in their lives: "[...] to give single women the task of training wise mothers and good wives is like asking a blind man to travel on a blind horse [...]" (Lu Xun 1980:215).

As for primary and secondary education for girls in early Republican state-run institutions, a contemporary study of these schools reveals that the curriculum focused on three main areas: the teaching of female virtues, literature and language, and basic calculation. A certain amount of attention was also paid to singing, sewing and mending, and manual labor (Lin Paotchin 1926:45-47). In the last phase of elementary schooling, girls received instruction, in addition to these subjects, in Chinese history, geography, and natural history (biology). It is noteworthy that no foreign language was offered at this stage of the teaching program; in contrast, girls attending missionary schools might have been exposed to at least one European language. In government-sponsored schools, English as a subject of instruction was offered only at the secondary-school level (*ibid.* 90-94).

The early Republican popular periodical press also sent out mixed messages about the importance of female education. It attempted, on the one hand, to create a modernized *zhufu* (housewife) well-adapted to "modern" ideas of good hygiene, efficiency, thrift in the home, and, on the other hand, to communicate the value of women's work (outside the home?) in terms of the nation's well-being (Orliski 2003). The *Funü zazhi (The Ladies' Journal)*, which began publication in 1915, published in its first issue an article by a female contributor, Ma Enshao, endorsing factory work as suitable employment for women: "[...] industrial labor benefits the state, provides a means of improving family finances, and lends itself to female autonomy, allowing women 'to become free' (*ziyou*) and 'independent' (*zili*)" (*ibid.* 46-47). But this same publication, in its articles on women's education, situated the aims of women's learning in only one of two major themes: women's education as integral to the construction of modern nationhood, or women's education as a remedy for the poor quality of Chinese women. And it would seem that this second theme had the louder voice in *The Ladies' Journal* (Wang Zheng 1999:71). During its first five years, *Funü zazhi* became a vehicle for those male writers who judged Chinese women responsible for the ills of the nation.

Even Chen Duxiu's radical *Xin qingnian (New Youth)*, also founded in 1915, propagated the value of women's education in terms of overcoming China's backwardness and China reaching modernity (Cini 1986). Despite the fact that this journal gave voice to writers arguing for a woman's right to attend university and earn the same degree as men, it also discriminated the abilities of the sexes: "women were suited to the arts, while men had an aptitude for science" (quoted in McElroy 2001:362).[3] One publication, *Jiaoyu zazhi (Educational Journal)* endorsed the value of European and American models of womanhood so unconditionally that a 1914 article celebrated the virtues of the Swedish feminist Ellen Key "who argued that marriage and the family were the central focus of a woman's life and that work outside the home made women sterile or incapable of bringing up children" (quoted in Bailey 2001:331). In general, popular journals in the early Republic considered education a panacea for all of China's ills: with education, China's problems would be solved. But the role of women in this process remained somewhat murky, and would continue to do so throughout the 1920s and 1930s.

---

[3] And, as Cini (1986) points out in her important study of this journal, the editors of *Xin qingnian* never afforded its readers even a glimpse of what "growing up female" meant – there were no personalized accounts by women writers in these first years of issue.

The Beginnings of Higher Education for Women in China

At the time of the birth of the Chinese Republic, there were no government-sponsored institutions of higher learning for women. The national universities were all male-only establishments. The first four-year higher institution of learning for women was the missionary-run Jinling College in Nanjing; it opened in 1916. It was followed in 1918 by the first Chinese-run institution, the Beijing Women's Normal School which was upgraded to tertiary status in that year (Borthwick 1985:82). Only one university in China offered coeducation before 1920; the missionary school at Canton (Guangzhou) known as Lingnan University had been coeducational since 1905 (Ono Kazuko 1989:109). By the end of the second decade of the twentieth century Beijing University did admit female students, and notably, in reaction to women's own behest. The story of Gansu-born Deng Chunlan's demand "to abolish the gender barrier in universities" in 1919 is well-known (*ibid.*; Wang Zheng 1999:77). In that year, when the Beijing University authorities did not answer her request for admission, she turned to national newspapers and *Funü zazhi* to call on other like-minded women to demand the right to enter universities.

The publicity must have helped because the Fifth Congress of the *Quanguo jiaoyuhui lianhehui* (National Federation of Educational Associations) held in October 1919 agreed that universities might become coeducational. A quick, positive response followed, allowing nine women in February 1920 to enter Beijing University to audit classes (McElroy 2001:366). Six registered to study philosophy, two to major in English, and one to study Chinese. By 1922, not counting missionary-run colleges and universities, 665 women were attending Chinese institutions of higher learning, although they represented only 2.1 percent of the total university population, and it would take until the late 1920s before all the public institutions went coed (Yeh Wen-hsin 1990:225). Lin Paotchin's study of post-1911 female education claims that for academic year 1923-1924, there were 847 women students attached to Chinese universities or specialist schools. This number of women students represents 2.5 percent of the total 33,880 students attending institutions of higher learning (Mackerras 1985:171). But by 1928-1929, the total number of women enrolled in higher education institutions (excluding missionary ones) had risen to 1,485 (or 8.59 percent of the total number of students) (Bailey 2003:331 n. 10). By the 1920s, there were also substantial numbers of women studying abroad, some of whom were financed by indemnity scholarships (Ye Weili 1994).

These changes, however positive at the time, should not disguise certain lingering problems. The number of secondary school institutions either for girls or coeducational was still limited. In 1923 there were in the entire country only twenty-five state-sponsored women's middle schools with a total of 3,249 students (compared to over 100,000 male students in middle schools) (McElroy 2001:367). If women were to enjoy the benefits of higher education, they still needed to access secondary-level education first. And outside the larger metropoles, good quality schools were not easy to find. How typical the conditions of the Jinan (Shandong) Girls' School that the social commentator Deng Enming (1901-1931) described for the journal *Lixin (Promote the New)* in 1921 is unclear, but his remarks lucidly articulated the poor curriculum and teaching as well as the "high-handed" school administration (see Lan/Fong 1999:130-141). One of his most critical remarks concerns the female students' lack of purpose: "Even if they were sent by their parents to get an education, they still do not understand what the purpose of an education is. The best of these kinds of girls can go on to Beijing Women's College, but they still do not realize why they are getting educated or what the purpose of an education is" (quoted in Lan/Fong 1999:139-140).

The "New Woman": Social Housekeeper or Career Professional?

The Birth of the "New Woman" and the Cult of Domesticity

Deng Enming's observations here concerning these pupils' lack of vision may be considered in relation to another widely-debated issue in the 1920s among educators, officials, and the students themselves: what purpose should higher education for women serve? For Liang Qichao, who by the early 1920s did favor the higher education of women, tertiary instruction was meant to prepare them for entrance into the professions. In a lecture "My Views on Women's Higher Education," delivered at Beijing Women's University in 1922, Liang proposed that women were best disposed toward four particular professions: the study of history, accounting, librarianship, and journalism. He justified these choices on the basis of gender differentiation: "Historical research requires patience and putting things in order. Men generally do not have the patience, they do not like history;" as for accounting – "Women are more efficient than men in accounting which should be a woman's profession; they should be at least the main work force in this field;" as for librarianship, again "Librarianship is meticulous work. Women can handle meticulous and careful work;" and finally, as for journalism, women possess three characteristics to make them good journalists: "A woman's observation of society is more penetrating than a man's; she is impartial and has little political partisanship; and people are more polite to women" (quoted in Chang Peng-yuan 1993-1994:52-53).

For other (male) commentators, writing in the popular press about women's motives for choosing to attend college or university, higher education was not necessarily a stage for gaining knowledge for the professions. Louise Edward's recent study of female-orientated journals of the 1920s and 1930s points to the negative conclusions of these correspondents. For example, Qiao Zhi in a 1927 article in *Funü zazhi* wrote that too often women considered their education as a form of "recreation." Five years later, another writer, Wang Xiyan, reviewing the public dispute about women in universities, indicated why some gauged female higher education "a waste." "We all know such girls [...] who regarded the university campus as a hunting ground for husbands and a place where they could increase their market value before selling themselves in marriage. Their main education aspiration was to marry a wealthy businessman so that they could relax and busy themselves with perming their hair" (all quotes from Edwards 2000:136-137). And certainly, as Yeh Wen-hsin has recorded in her publication on Republican era college life, there were plenty of opportunities for men and women "to intermingle" outside the classroom, during "church services, athletic meets, public lectures," and so on (Yeh Wen-hsin 1990:225). The point is that these first female university students probably themselves had difficulties to reconcile the conflict between their duty to become good citizens (still, the principal justification for studying in the first place) and their privilege to associate with men in a legitimate setting, a kind of social intercourse absolutely denied their mothers or grandmothers. Moreover, female graduates had anxieties about how they could fulfill individual aspirations such as economic independence with the goal of personal happiness and motherhood.

Interestingly, it would seem that for those women who were among the first Chinese to study abroad in institutions of higher learning, beginning in the 1880s, this question of what purpose should education for women serve was easier to answer than for women college students during the 1920s. Many women of the earlier generation, the majority of whom were the adopted children of missionaries or the daughters of Chinese Christians, attended medical schools and upon graduation, returned to China to care for the needs of women and children as physicians. Because their profession "emphasized the feminine qualities of service and sacrifice," these women practitioners also personified the feminine virtues that the late Qing and early Republic reformers had prescribed (Ye Weili 1994:324; see also Ye Weili 2001:114-152).

However, the later generation of university-trained women, faced a number of dilemmas unknown to those who had studied thirty to forty years earlier. In her story, "The Problem of Louise" (*Luoyisi de wenti*), Beijing University's first woman professor, the American-educated Chen Hengzhe (1890-1976) expressed her own problem, the conflict between her commitment to her independence and her career, as well as her desire for a happy marriage (Ye Weili 1994:337-339; Ye Weili 2001:146-149; Chen Hengzhe 1938). In the story, Louise is an American philosophy professor who rejects her boyfriend's marriage proposal because she does not wish to sacrifice her intellectual interests to domesticity. Years later she imagines herself with children at her side and, with regret, thinks about the impossibility of having both a family and a career. Chen herself escaped Louise's fate when at the age of thirty she found "Mr. Right," Ren Hongjun, but it would seem "the debate with herself about the pros and cons of married life" for a woman intellectual was never really far from her mind (Ye Weili 1994:338). There may have been many professional women like Chen, but there were probably also many others like Buwei Yang Zhao (1889-195?), a medical doctor, and graduate of "McTyeire," with training in Japan and a practice in Beijing in the early 1920s, who eschewed her own vocational commitments to follow her husband, the famed linguist Zhao Yuanren (1890-1969), first around locations in China, and then to America. Her *Autobiography* is full of experiences in which she makes clear that making use of her medical knowledge and experience could not compete with the services demanded from a husband singularly occupied with his own career (Zhao Yang Buwei 1947).

The first Chinese women in the second and third decades of the twentieth century to encounter the choices, between self and others, were also the earliest generation to perceive the changing vocabulary used to denote the female gender. Whereas imperial China had no generic category for women: females were either daughters in the family (*nü*) or wives (*fu*) and/or mothers (*mu*), the sex identity politics of the May Fourth Movement created the neologisms, *nüxing* and *xin nüxing*. *Nüxing* (woman) was a Western-inspired concept used by anti-Confucian male reformers "to name the newly discovered transcendent category of women" (Barlow 1994:254). She was "discovered" when the reformers, in search of a reason for China's underdevelopment, realized that the seclusion of *nü*, *fu*, and *mu* from public life as well as footbinding, both practices representative of purity and morality during the imperial era, were in fact the symbols of China's backwardness (Brownell/Wasserstrom 2002:28). The *xin nüxing* (new woman) emerged in the early Republic, as a general fascination with "new styles" ("new-style women," "new-style students," "new-style learning") penetrated the print and film industries (Link 1981:196-235; Lee 1990:110). The *xin nüxing's* appearance was particularly striking: her clothing was determined by "fashion" – she wore high-heeled shoes, Western-style undergarments, hats, bobbed her hair, and realigned the skirt length, type of fabric, and the kinds of sleeves, collars, and so on according to what she considered "right" for the time. Despite successive attempts by the early Republican Government to define "proper attire" (including a patriotic campaign to "to buy Chinese," i.e. to stop women from purchasing foreign-made textiles) urban, middle-class women determined their own sense of fashion (Laing 2003).

More specifically, the concept of "new woman" was introduced to Chinese intellectuals by Hu Shi in 1918 in the journal *Xin qingnian*. For Hu, this "new woman" was *not* someone with political goals, unlike her counterpart in the United States, European countries, and Japan. There, the "new woman" referred "primarily to educated, politically active public women with women's rights agendas such as suffrage, labor, or birth control" (Harris 1995:65). In Hu Shi's vision of the Chinese "new woman," we encounter "a woman who could maintain her positive 'extremes' of independence and selfhood (*zili*) in marriage" (*ibid.*). But by 1923 when a translation of Ibsen's *A Doll's House* had seen publication, with the title *Nuola (Nora)*, the writer Lu Xun could speculate in an address to Beijing Women's Normal College, "What Happens after Nora Leaves Home?", that women's independence is a matter of economic independence – "what she needs is money" (Lan/Fong 1999:176-181). By casting women's future in this way, Lu Xun also recognized the economic tie that continued to bind women to their fathers, husbands, and sons in what was nothing less than the age-old patriarchal family system.

To be sure, one of the issues of the New Culture Movement was family reform.[4] New Culture radicals claimed the dependency and poverty of the Chinese people were due to the patriarchal extended family, and urged the Western conjugal family (*xiao jiating*) as a remedy. This model, consisting of a husband and wife and their children, operating as an independent economic unit, was based on the ideal of a companionate marriage in which partners freely chose each other. *Funü zazhi* picked up on this theme by 1917 and began publishing on

---

[4] The New Culture Movement (1915-1923) refers to the new literature and new thought that predated the May Fourth Incident. The New Culturalists (or radicals) were the first generation of modern intellectuals, many of whom had been shaped by Confucian *and* Western (or Japanese) models of education; from an urban base, either in universities or publishing houses, they rebelled against the dominant culture (Wang Zheng 1999:10-11).

the virtues of domesticity within the structure of the middle-class nuclear family. The editor of *Funü zazhi* at this point, a woman well-traveled in Japan and the United States, Zhu-Hu Binxia, commented on how American women's domesticity exemplified the Confucian teaching on family and nation (Wang Zheng 1999:73).

But more radical voices about this matter originated from two Beijing University male students, Luo Dunwei (1901-1964) and Yi Jiayue (1899-1972) who founded the short-lived journal *Jiating yanjiu (Family Research)* in 1920 (see Glosser 2003). Their standpoint was basically an attack on the concept of Confucian family patriarch (*jiazhang*), which they considered a hindrance to China's industrializing economy that separated home and work place (*ibid.* 128, 140). "Rejecting the traditional family ideal that celebrated 'five generations under one roof,' condemning the authority of elders who subordinated the happiness of the individual to the well-being of the family and determined each member's education, occupation, and marriage in light of its impact on the larger group, these radicals expressed their dissatisfaction with 'old ways,' and proposed new concrete solutions" (*ibid.* 9). Nevertheless, in spite of the rhetoric, Glosser maintains, these men were more interested in finding a new identity for themselves in these changing circumstances rather than revolutionizing the structure of Chinese society. The premise of the nuclear family ideal was to fulfill the needs of the "individual" (*geren*), and by implication, the male individual in this new model. This point becomes clearer, as Glosser convincingly demonstrates, when one reads how they and their readers considered the role of women in the *xiao jiating* – the quality of a wife (as well as the quality of the marriage) was an essential ingredient to the man's self-image. If a man considered himself educated and enlightened, then his mate should have the same degree of advancement. In essence, the aspirations of these young men and their followers only reshaped the prescriptive roles of women, without changing the centrality of marriage and family to the social and political order in which they lived (*ibid.* 139-140). *Jiating yanjiu* may have concerned itself with such issues as age of marriage, family organization, and family hierarchy, but the publication never overcame the general conviction that connected women with a well-run family and a well-run state.

But even as the romantic individualism of the New Culture Movement faded, interest in family reform continued. The campaign for *xiao jiating* was featured in the journal *Shenghuo zhoukan (Life Weekly)*, a popular and "progressive" publication for "old and new" middle-classes (Yeh Wen-hsin 1992:191). By the late 1920s, the famed publisher of this magazine, Zou Taofen (1895-1944) promoted in its pages the ideal of marriage built upon emotional bonds and joint ownership and disposition of the couple's properties. In his view, which was widely propagated among the newly educated urban classes, the ideal husband would be a full-time provider, while his ideal wife would *not* take up employment outside the home until the children were fully grown (*ibid.* 211). This wife, who would have acquired the benefits of literacy in a new-style school, would also possess training in home economics, and skills in child rearing, home beautification, and not least, the social talents of an attractive hostess (*ibid.* 210). In short, Zou was attempting to replace the sanctity of the many-generated joint family with the cult of domesticity.

The cult of domesticity is not something unique to China. As Susan Mann has written, in Victorian England and nineteenth-century America, the popularity of the cult of domesticity may be explained as an attempt by these respective societies to affirm and strengthen a grip on high status during a period of rapid social and economic change (Mann 1994:194-195). Other scholars have offered views on the cult's popularity: as a foil, "to police" women in the face of male anxieties over their own place of power in a rapidly commercializing and militarizing society (Edwards 2000:123),[5] or the outcome of a long-term process that commodified the family and "appropriated women's

---

[5] Duara (1998 and 2000) argues how Chinese nationalists tended to depict women as embodying the "eternal" Chinese civilizational virtues of self-sacrifice and loyalty, and to elevate them as national exemplars. By "freezing" women into time this way, Chinese intellectuals cast them into the role of guardians of history.

reproductive labor for family and state" (Glosser 1995:108).[6] Whatever the reason, it is significant that the cult of domesticity took hold just as more and more women were beginning to make inroads into higher education and the professions. At this point in our discussion we need to turn to consult the voices of university-educated women who experienced the conflicts of this era.

"The Virtuous Transaction"

One of the most articulate spokespersons of the quandaries facing "new" women in Republican China was Ling Shuhua (1900-1990).[7] Although she received the dubious distinction of being named a new *guixiu* (gentlewoman) writer – "a slightly derogatory term which at the time denoted a highly 'feminine' style of writing on narrow domestic subjects" (Dooling/Torgeson 1998:177), Ling was an acute observer of the dilemmas beset the educated female graduate, as well as any girl or woman who dared challenge subordinate roles. The literary critic Yi Zhen dubbed Ling a *xin guixiu* (new gentlewoman) in his 1933 study of her work (Yi Zhen 1933:1-36; and in response Chow 1988:72),[8] but more recent analyses of her fiction, in which issues of domesticity and triviality seem vital, point to its subversive message (Shih Shu-mei 2001:215-228; Holoch 1985:379-393; Dooling/Torgeson 1998:175-195; Laurence 2003:82-99, 246-293).

Ling studied at Yanjing University from 1921 to 1924, just when the institution was beginning to achieve its reputation as an oasis of "ease and tranquility enjoyed by the privileged and Westernized cosmopolitan elite [...]" in the northwest Beijing suburbs (Yeh Wen-hsin 1990:207; see also West 1976). Born into a well-to-do and well-connected Beijing family, Ling went to Japan with siblings at the

---

[6] The central role of consumption and commodification in Republican China's modernization is well-noted in a recent compilation. See Yeh Wen-hsin 2000:1-28.

[7] Named Ling Ruitang at birth, and also known as Su Hua Ling Chen in her publications.

[8] Yi also considered the writers Bing Xin (1900-19?) and Su Xuelin (1897-1998?) further examples of the gentlewoman group of writers (*guixiupai zuojia*), since they depict a love that stays comfortably within feudal manners (*zai lijiao de fanwei zhi nei*) (Yi Zhen 1933:4).

age of seven for three years. In her autobiography, *Ancient Melodies*, written in increments in English during the 1930s, with Virginia Woolf's encouragement, and published in 1953 with a preface by Woolf's good friend Vita Sackeville-West (Shih Shu-mei 2001:215), Ling relates how her family and friends took notice of her talents as a painter and poet from an early age. In the chapter "Great Uncle," she recounts the impact of her uncle's story of the achievements of Empress Wu of the Tang that left her with the idea there should be a "court examination" for women (Ling Chen 1953:151). After completing her studies in foreign languages, Ling married Chen Yuan (1896-1970), a professor at Beijing University. In 1928, the couple moved to Wuhan University where Chen became dean of the Department of Foreign Languages, and Ling wrote full time, continuing to publish her short stories in popular literary journals and magazines, *Xiandai pinglun (Contemporary Review)*, *Xinyue (Crescent Moon)*, and *Xiaoshuo yuebao (Short Story Monthly)*. One of the central events in her life was her two-year affair with Julian Bell (1908-1937) who had come to Wuhan in 1935 to teach English literature as a visiting professor. After Bell's death, she maintained a steady correspondence with Julian's mother Vanessa and his aunt Virginia Woolf to whom both she expressed her desire to succeed as a writer (Laurence 2003).[9]

The setting of Ling's stories is usually inside an urbanized middle-class household of contemporary China, with a female as the main character and marriage as the principal theme. These features have led one modern critic to claim that "the modernity of the stories lies in the social relations" (Holoch 1985:381). While the women are not idealized, the men invariably demonstrate negative qualities such as rigidity, deviousness, self-indulgence, self-pity, or opportunism (*ibid*. 390 n. 9). Ling's fiction indicates that contemporary marriage, however "updated" for the "new woman," is really not much better than the earlier model: wives should expect anomie, frustration,

---

[9] Recently, Ling Shuhua's love affair with Bell was fictionalized in the novel *K: The Art of Love* by the London-based writer Hong Ying. The novel became the subject of a well-publicized lawsuit launched by Chen Xiaoyang, Ling's daughter, another London-based resident, who claimed the book slanders her parents Chen Yuan and Ling Shuhua. Tried in a Chinese court in Manchuria, the case won for the plaintiff. See Lancaster 2003 for details.

desperation, and betrayal; "[...] even beneath a bourgeois veneer, Confucian and feudal values are concrete and lethal presences in the roast duck, the needlework, and the small talk" (*ibid.* 388-389). Her stories, scrutinizing such matters as the predicament of a young woman facing marriage – damned if she does, damned if she does not (*Xiuzhen*), finding a husband (*Chahui*), or career versus marriage (*Zaijian*), among other subjects, are more than sentimental narratives of personal experience. As Rey Chow points out, Ling's fiction illustrates how women engage in "virtuous transactions": "Chinese women learn to give up their own desires in exchange for their social 'place' [...] it's not that Chinese women want to be victimized, but alternatives [according to Ling], are unavailable" (Chow 1988:75-76). In other words, Chinese society during the first decades of the twentieth century had still not found a way to consolidate the potential and the achievements of the educated "new woman."

Ling was not a lone voice, and as we review episodes in the lives of other articulate women, we may observe the same lingering sense of disappointment and frustration. In her recent book, Shu-mei Shih refers to the 1936 correspondence between the writer and architect Lin Huiyin (1904-1955), wife of Liang Sicheng (the eldest son of Liang Qichao), and the American Wilma Fairbank, wife of the American scholar John K. Fairbank, where Lin "expressed how she felt oppressed by housework which prevented her from engaging in literature" (Shih Shu-mei 2001:209). In her account of Lin's life and career, W. Fairbank discusses her predicament: despite having help in their Beijing household, Lin was "the prisoner" of at least ten persons – her baby daughter, her husband, her mother, and six to seven servants who turned to her for every decision. "No period at desk or drawing board was safe from interruption by children, servants, or mother" (Fairbank 1994:60). When Lin Huiyin did write, she expressed in modernistic style the dilemmas of those women in what Fairbank calls "the transitional generation" (post-May Fourth and pre-Liberation). In Lin's 1934 story "Ninety-nine Degree Heat" (*Jiushijiu du zhong*), one of the story lines concerns the female character Ah Shu who must concede to an arranged marriage; her problem is that Ah knows all about "free love," so well publicized in books and magazines. As Shu-mei Shih observes, Lin here touches upon "the contradiction between the May Fourth rhetoric of emancipation and the present reality of oppression" (Shih Shu-mei 2001:214).

Both Ling Shuhua and Lin Huiyin are associated with the *Jingpai* (Beijing) group of May Fourth writers who could "flaunt a new kind of bicultural cosmopolitanism" (*ibid.* 206). Both women had traveled extensively outside of China, already as children. Nevertheless, they both grew up with a certain awareness of how skewed the post-May Fourth China's program for cultural rejuvenation cast women's role. And their own ambivalent relationship to "tradition" – on the one hand, socially "secure" in marriages with men of prestige and transnational sophistication, and on the other hand, conscious and highly articulate of the limitations of their own personal milieus, makes them exemplars of the "virtuous transaction."

Other Personal Accounts

Ling's and Lin's experiences as female graduates in Republican China may or may not have been "typical." And as modern scholars both in Euro-America and East Asia attempt to reread and rewrite Chinese history beyond grand narratives and comprehensive explanations, the significance of their stories (and life histories) may become even more difficult to comprehend. For one thing, the concerns of these two writers indicate the continuities in attitudes toward women between past and present. Although statistics inform us of the "progress" that women made by the 1930s and into the 1940s with regard to university admission and attendance – the proportion of women in institutions of higher learning by 1934 was 15.02 percent, and by 1947, 17.8 percent of the total university enrollment (Mackerras 1985:171) – their presence in colleges and universities did not mean a change in attitude that would have revolutionized what equal access to education should have meant. In his study of education during the Nationalist regime, Colin Mackerras quotes the 1929 Ministry of Education guidelines for education for girls: "Education for girls must pay great attention to moulding a sound and healthy morality in them, to preserving the special qualities of motherhood, and also to building up good family life and social life" (from *Jiaoyu faling* [Education Statutes] quoted by Mackerras 1985:173). From other statistics, it is clear that women did not make much inroad into certain professions such as law or engineering (Mackerras 1985:172). In her study of the legal profession during the Republic, Alison Conner reports a comment of a contemporary legal historian, Chang Yu-chuan made in 1938, that "women lawyers were still as 'scarce as morning stars'" (quoted in Conner 1994:232).

We also know now that the CCP program for female members did not venture much beyond the rhetoric of a feminist agenda. Christina K. Gilmartin's recent monograph, *Engendering the Chinese Revolution*, tells how the "blooming" Communist subculture of the short-lived Shanghai University (1923-1927) played a certain role in the young adult lives of such well-known female activists as Yang Zhihua (1900-1973), Ding Ling (1904-1986), Li Yichun (1899-1984), and Zhong Fuguang (1903-?); the CCP tapped the feminist aspirations of these women and aligned itself into the organizations these women founded in order to achieve its own legitimation (Gilmartin 1995; on Shanghai University, see Yeh Wen-hsin 1990:129-165).

Gender discrimination among educated women in Republican China pervades the oral histories Wang Zheng collected for her remarkable book, *Women in the Chinese Enlightenment: Oral and Textual Histories*, in which she reports the monologues she created out of interviews with five women all born around 1900. The life stories are complex, and sometimes seemingly contradictory in terms of the women's movement of the times. One of the interviewees, Wang Yiwei (1905-1993), a graduate of Fudan University, founded the journal *Nüsheng (Women's Voice)* in 1932, not to participate in the women's movement but to promote nationalism: "I just thought we should act and be patriotic together" (quoted in Wang Zheng 1999:230). Eventually, the same publication also became known for its "exposés of unfaithful men and philanderers" (*ibid.* 256). Another university graduate interviewed by Wang Zheng, Chen Yongsheng (1900-1997), after study in the United States, became the first female principal of Shandong Number One Women's Normal School, and later, the physical education teacher and deputy supervisor of female students at the (rejuvenated) University of Shanghai.[10] There, she related, "women had no status. A male professor was able to have his whole family live in a nice house, but a single woman was treated differently. I and another single woman who taught chemistry and had studied in Germany lived in the dorms with the students" (quoted in *ibid.* 269). It would seem that the "new woman" as career professional had neither stature nor access to material benefits without her having a husband.

But, if she did have a husband, her fate might not have been much better either. As Pearl Buck recalled, among her students attending her classes at the University of Nanking in 1927 was a young man who wrote in an essay about what problems an educated wife could bring:

> I should like to marry a college woman who would be mentally stimulating. But my friend married one, and [...] he is compelled to rise in the morning and fetch water for her tea. She is imperious and she says: "I am educated. I need not work like a slave. If you cannot support me, I will leave you and support myself." Now I do not wish to fetch water for my wife. I still believe she should fetch it, if not for me, at least for herself. Shall I marry for my mind or for my comfort? (Buck 1927:653)

Buck commented that the young man's demands were incompatible: "a college graduate who in the evening with fascinating intelligence will stimulate his mind, and in the morning with sweet stupidity will fetch him his tea" (*ibid.*).

The professional woman who did not want "to fetch tea" or get "sidetracked into one of the three respectable white collar jobs of the educated woman, i.e. Young Women's Christian Association (YWCA) work, teaching, or clerkship" (Zhao Jizhen 1941:493) usually paid a price for her ambitions. This is clear from the personal account of Zhao Jizhen, an economics and political science graduate of Beijing University, who writes in 1941 of her disappointment, after having

---

[10] In her interview, Chen clearly refers to the University of Shanghai, but given the closure of the institution with the same name in 1927, it is not obvious from her account to which school she refers. According to the list displayed in Yeh Wenhsin 1990:286-287 there was no such college or university by that name for the 1927-1937 period.

achieved a certain level of security and independence as a career woman, to face pressure and even ridicule from her family about her bachelor status. Although her father had encouraged her to pursue higher education, and even profited from the financial support she gave to him and her brothers, he disdained her unwed state. She reported that he considered her a "mental burden" and said to her: "You cared for us all, but you have no son [...]" (*ibid.* 495).

Conclusion: The Problem of Experienced History and Gender History

"History is neither the whole nor even all that remains of the past. In addition to written history, there is a living history that perpetuates and renews itself through time" (Halbwachs 1980:64). These personal reflections, in some cases recollected seventy years after the experiences occurred, form what the British historian Peter Burke has labeled "a social history of remembering" (Burke 1989:100). The testimonies to which we have referred are in a sense "unauthorized representations of the past," but they also constitute windows through which we may seek to understand the effects of higher education on the lives of women during the Republican era. Behind the official statistics, GMD rhetoric, and Communist propaganda, lies every woman's story which does not necessarily conform to the master narratives of "communism is the only true outcome of the May Fourth Movement" or "China's struggle to attain a prosperous and independent nation-state." These highly personal memories might be dismissed by those seeking to write a history of higher education in twentieth century China. But as the conceptualization of modern Chinese history increasingly drifts away from that one figuring the centrality of the nation-state toward one where "structural tension, spatial fragmentation, temporal duality, and unintended consequences, along with unsuspected links of continuity" (Yeh Wen-hsin 2000:3) becomes more common, the implications of such depositions also seem all the more pertinent for understanding the Republican era. It is known there were numbers of women students and graduates who simply did not fit male-defined frameworks in which general nationalistic goals were central. The biographies of those persons who did *not* in some way contribute directly to the legitimacy of government policy may be just as meaningful as those whose stories are better known. The significance of these "unapproved" memories is that they form the basis upon which another (or new) history of higher education in Republican China might be formulated.

In effect, the testimonies make clear the relevance of a gendered history of education in the context of this "new" way of considering China during the first fifty years of the twentieth century. We need to ask how did the ideas and practices associated with the modernization of education, at all levels, have such different outcomes for men, and for women? On what basis did influential publicists, men like Zou Taofen, continue to foster a separate identity for men and women that ultimately supported only men's potential for self-realization? Why did "foreign models" which did endorse women's higher education, and which in so many ways, did serve as a guide to reform for May Fourth intellectuals, fail to capture the potential importance of women's contributions to Chinese society? At what point did the discourse of the "new woman" and her economic independence become swallowed up in the "cult of domesticity?" We might conclude that in their concern with preserving their own rank and status in a changing society, men would not, and probably could not, offer women a place in the public sphere. But we need to know more about how the actions, or passivity, of the "new woman" figured in this containment process. Like many studies in gender history, the investigation of Chinese women and their experience of higher education during the Republican era is not yet resolved. The multiple-identities thrust upon the "new woman" left her stranded in a sea of changes from which Chinese society was only in the midst of emancipating itself; and thus, the rescue operation afforded her little room to maneuver.

References

Bailey, Paul, Active Citizen or Efficient Housewife? The Debate over Women's Education in Early-Twentieth Century China, in: Peterson et al. 2001, pp. 318-347.

Bailey, Paul, "Unharnessed Fillies": Discourse on the "Modern" Female Student in Early Modern Twentieth-Century China, in: Lou Jiu-jung and Lu Miaw-fen (eds.), *Women and Culture in Modern China (1600-1950), vol. 3 Voices amid Silence*, Taipei 2003, pp. 327-357.

Barlow, Tani E., Theorizing Woman: *Funü, Guojia, Jiating*, in: Angela Zito and Tani E. Barlow (eds.), *Body, Subject and Power in China*, Chicago and London 1994, pp. 253-289.

Borthwick, Sally, Changing Concepts of the Role of Women from the Late Qing to the May Fourth Period, in: Pong and Fung 1985, pp. 63-91.

Brownell, Susan and Jeffrey N. Wasserstrom, Introduction: Theorizing Femininities and Masculinities, in: Brownell and Wasserstrom 2002, pp. 1-46.

Brownell, Susan and Jeffrey N. Wasserstrom (eds.), *Chinese Femininities/Chinese Masculinities: A Reader*, Berkeley and Los Angeles 2002.

Buck, Pearl, New Modes of Chinese Marriage, in: *Asia: The American Magazine on the Orient* (1927), pp. 650-653.

Burke, Peter, History as Social Memory, in: Thomas Butler (ed.), *Memory: History, Culture and the Mind*, Oxford 1989, pp. 97-113.

Chang Peng-yuan, The Tenacity of Tradition: Liang Qichao and Gender Relations, in: *Journal of the Oriental Society of Australia* 25-26 (1993-1994), pp. 42-54.

Chen Hengzhe, Wo younian qiuxue de jingguo (My Youthful Search for Education), in: Tao Kuangde (ed.), *Zizhuan zhi yizhang* (Chapters of Autobiography), Guangzhou 1938, pp. 70-83.

Chen Xuexun (ed.), *Zhongguo jindai jiaoyu dashi ji* (Chronicle of Events on Modern Chinese Education), Shanghai 1981.

Cheng Weikun, Going Public through Education: Female Reformers and Girls' Schools in Late Qing Beijing, in: *Late Imperial China* 21:1 (2000), pp. 107-144.

Cheng Zhefan, *Zhongguo xiandai nüzi jiaoyu shi* (A History of Contemporary Women's Education in China), Shanghai 1936.

Chow, Rey, Virtuous Transactions: A Reading of Three Stories by Ling Shuhua, in: *Modern Chinese Literature* 4:1-2 (1988), pp. 71-85.

Cini, Francesca, Le "problème des femmes" dans *La Nouvelle Jeunesse*, 1915-1922, in: *Études chinoises* 5:1-2 (1986), pp. 133-156.

Conner, Alison, Lawyers and the Legal Profession during the Republican Period, in: Katherine Bernhardt and Philip C.C. Huang (eds.), *Civil Law in Qing and Republican China*, Stanford 1994, pp. 215-248.

Dooling, Amy and Kristina M. Torgeson (eds.), Introduction, in: *idem., Writing Women in Modern China: An Anthology of Women's Literature from the Early Twentieth Century*, New York 1998, pp. 1-38.

Du Xueyuan, *Zhongguo nüzi jiaoyu tongshi* (History of Chinese Women's Education), Guiyang 1995.

Duara, Prasenjit, The Regime of Authenticity: Timelessness, Gender, and National History in Modern China, in: *History and Theory* 37:3 (1998), pp. 287-308.

Duara, Prasenjit, Of Authenticity and Woman: Personal Narratives of Middle-Class Women in Modern China, in: Yeh Wen-hsin 2000, pp. 342-364.

Edwards, Louise, Chin Sung-ts'en's *A Tocsin for Women*: The Dextrous Merger of Radicalism and Conservatism in Feminism of the Early Twentieth Century, in: *Jindai Zhongguo funü shi yanjiu* 2 (1994), pp. 117-140.

Edwards, Louise, Policing the Modern Woman in Republican China, in: *Modern China* 26:2 (2000), pp. 115-147.

Fairbank, Wilma, *Liang and Lin: Partners in Exploring China's Architectural Past*, Philadelphia 1994.

Gilmartin, Christina K., *Engendering the Chinese Revolution: Radical Women, Communist Politics and Mass Movements in the 1920s*, Berkeley and Los Angeles 1995.

Glosser, Susan, The Business of Family: You Huaigao and the Commercialization of a May Fourth Ideal, in: *Republican China* 20:2 (1995), pp. 80-116.

Glosser, Susan, "The Truths I Have Learned": Nationalism, Family Reform, and Male Identity in China's New Culture Movement, 1915-1923, in: Brownell and Wasserstrom 2002, pp. 120-144.

Glosser, Susan, *Chinese Visions of Family and State, 1915-1953*, Berkeley and Los Angeles 2003.

Halbwachs, Maurice, *The Collective Memory*, New York 1980.

Harris, Kristine, *The New Woman*: Image, Subject, and Dissent in 1930s Shanghai Film Culture, in: *Republican China* 20:2 (1995), pp. 55-79.

Higuchi Keiko, Ryōsai kenbo kyōiku no imi surumono (On the Meaning of the Good Wife, Wise Mother Education), in: Aoki Yayoi (ed.), *Sensō to onnatachi* (War and Women), Tokyo 1982, pp. 71-88.

Holoch, Paul, Everyday Feudalism: The Subversive Stories of Ling Shuhua, in: Anna Gerstlacher, Ruth Keen, Wolfgang Kubin, Margit Miosga, and Jenny Schon (eds.), *Women and Literature in China*, Bochum 1985, pp. 379-393.

Hosie, (Dorothea [Soothill]), Lady, *Portrait of a Chinese Lady and Certain of Her Contemporaries*, New York 1930.

Hu Ying, *Tales of Translation: Composing the New Woman in China*, Stanford 2000.

Hu Ying, Naming the First New Woman: The Case of Kang Aide, in: *Nan Nü: Men, Women and Gender in Early and Imperial China* 3:2 (2001), pp. 196-231.

Judge, Joan, Meng Mu Meets the Modern: Female Exemplars in Early Twentieth Century Textbooks for Girls and Women, in: *Jindai Zhongguo funü shi yanjiu* 8 (2000), pp. 129-175.

Judge, Joan, Talent, Virtue, and the Nation: Chinese Nationalism and Female Subjectivities in the Early Twentieth Century, in: *The American Historical Review* 106:3 (2001), pp. 765-803.

Laing, Ellen Johnston, Visual Evidence for the Evolution of "Politically Correct" Dress for Women in Early Twentieth Century Shanghai, in: *Nan Nü: Men, Women and Gender in Early and Imperial China* 5:1 (2003), pp. 69-114.

Lan Hua R. and Vanessa L. Fong (eds.), *Women in Republican China: A Sourcebook*, Armonk and London 1999.

Lancaster, John, Looking for Trouble in China, in: *The New York Review of Books* 50:4 (2003), pp. 25-27.

Laurence, Patricia, *Lily Briscoe's Chinese Eyes: Bloomsbury, Modernism, and China*, Columbia/SC 2003.

Lee, Leo Ou-fan, In Search of Modernity: Some Reflections on a New Mode of Consciousness in Twentieth-Century Chinese History and Literature, in: Paul Cohen and Merle Goldman (eds.), *Ideas across Cultures: Essays on Chinese Thought in Honor of Benjamin I. Schwartz*, Cambridge/MA 1990, pp. 109-135.

Lewis, Ida Belle, *The Education of Girls in China*, New York 1919.

Li Youning and Zhang Youfu (eds.), *Jindai Zhongguo nüquan yundong shiliao* (Source Materials on the Women's Rights Movement in Modern China), 2 vols., Taipei 1975.

Lin Paotchin, *L'instruction féminine en Chine (après La Révolution de 1911)*, Paris 1926.

Lin Yutang, *My Country and My People*, New York 1938.

Ling Chen, Su Hua, *Ancient Melodies*, London 1953.

Link, E. Perry, *Mandarin Ducks and Butterflies: Popular Fiction in Early Twentieth Century Chinese Cities*, Berkeley and Los Angeles 1981.

Lu Xun, Fen: Guafuzhuyi (The Grave: Widowism), in: *Selected Works of Lu Hsun*, trans. by Yang Hsien-yi and Gladys Yang, Beijing 1980, vol. 2, pp. 212-218.

Lutz, Jessie Gregory, *Mission Dilemmas: Bride Price, Minor Marriage, Concubinage, Infanticide, and Education of Women*, New Haven 2002.

Mackerras, Colin, Education in the Guomindang Period, 1928-1949, in: Pong and Fung 1985, pp. 153-183.

Mann, Susan, The Cult of Domesticity in Republican Shanghai's Middle Class, in: *Jindai Zhongguo funü shi yanjiu* 2 (1994), pp. 179-201.

McElroy, Sarah Coles, Forging a New Role for Women: Zhili First Women's Normal School and the Growth of Women's Education in China, 1901-1921, in: Peterson et al. 2001, pp. 348-374.

Nivard, Jacqueline, L'évolution de la presse féminine chinoise de 1898 à 1949, in: *Études chinoises* 5:1-2 (1986a), pp. 157-184.

Nivard, Jacqueline, Bibliographie de la presse féminine chinoise, 1898-1949, in: *Études chinoises* 5:1-2 (1986b), pp. 185-236.

Ono Kazuko, *Chinese Women in a Century of Revolution, 1850-1950*, Stanford 1989.

Orliski, Constance, The Bourgeois Housewife as Laborer in Late Qing and Early Republican China, in: *Nan Nü: Men, Women and Gender in Early and Imperial China* 5:1 (2003), pp. 43-68.

Peterson, Glen, Ruth Hayhoe, and Lu Yongling (eds.), *Education, Culture, and Identity in Twentieth Century China*, Ann Arbor 2001.

Pong, David and Edmund S.K. Fung (eds.), *Ideal and Reality: Social and Political Change in Modern China, 1860-1949*, Lanham and London 1985.

Ross, Heidi, "Cradle of Female Talent": The McTyeire Home and School for Girls, 1892-1937, in: Daniel H. Bays (ed.), *Christianity in China: From the Eighteenth Century to the Present*, Stanford 1996, pp. 209-227.

Shih Shu-mei, *The Lure of the Modern: Writing Modernism in Semicolonial China, 1917-1937*, Berkeley and Los Angeles 2001.

Shu Xincheng (ed.), *Zhongguo jindai jiaoyushi ziliao* (Materials on Modern Chinese Educational History), 3 vols., Beijing 1962.

Taga Akigoro (comp.), *Kindai Chūgoku kyōiku shi shiryo* (Materials on the History of Education in Modern China), Tokyo 1972.

Wang Zheng, *Women in the Chinese Enlightenment: Oral and Textual Histories*, Berkeley and Los Angeles 1999.

West, Philip, *Yenching University and Sino-Western Relations, 1916-1952*, Cambridge/MA 1976.

Ye Weili, *"Nü liuxuesheng"*: The Story of American-Educated Chinese Women, 1880s-1920s, in: *Modern China* 20:3 (1994), pp. 315-346.

Ye Weili, *Seeking Modernity in China's Name: Chinese Students in the United States, 1900-1927*, Stanford 2001.

Yeh Wen-hsin, *The Alienated Academy: Culture and Politics in Republican China, 1919-1937*, Cambridge/MA 1990.

Yeh Wen-hsin, Progressive Journalism and Shanghai's Petty Urbanites: Zou Taofen and the Shenghuo Weekly, 1926-1945, in: Yeh Wen-hsin and Frederic Wakeman, Jr. (eds.), *Shanghai Sojourners*, Berkeley 1992, pp. 186-238.

Yeh Wen-hsin, Introduction: Interpreting Chinese Modernity, 1900-1950, in: Yeh Wen-hsin 2000, pp.1-30.

Yeh Wen-hsin (ed.), *Becoming Chinese: Passages to Modernity and Beyond*, Berkeley and Los Angeles 2000.

Yi Zhen, Jiwei dangdai Zhongguo nüxiaoshuojia (A Few Contemporary Chinese Fiction Writers), in: Huang Renying (ed.), *Dangdai Zhongguo nüzuojia lun* (Contemporary Chinese Women Writers), Shanghai 1933, pp. 1-36.

Zarrow, Peter, He Zhen and Anarcho-Feminism in China, in: *Journal of Asian Studies* 47:4 (1988), pp. 796-813.

Zhao Jizhen, Being an Old Maid in China, in: *Asia: The American Magazine on the Orient* 41 (1941), pp. 492-496.

Zhao Yang Buwei, *Autobiography of a Chinese Woman*, New York 1947.

Female Physical Education and the Media in Modern China

Yu Chien-ming

Female participation in sports did not begin in modern China but made its appearance early in traditional Chinese society. According to the literature, traditional Chinese women usually practiced sports that consumed little energy, such as swinging, flying kites, and shuttlecock kicking. Only a few women exercised more rigorous sports, including football, polo, *buda* ball (using a stick to hit a ball, quite similar to present-day golf), wrestling, tug-of-war, martial arts (*wushu*), and boxing (Liu Bingguo 1987:4-23, 35-37, 46-51, 120-127, 130-132). Nevertheless, in every kind of women's sport, the main purpose was to entertain the performer herself or her audience, and was not practiced for competitive purposes.

Beginning in the late Qing, however, many different kinds of sports for women came from the West; in addition to providing a great variety of sports, the meaning of sports changed tremendously from that of the past. Sports were no longer for performance or entertainment; there was greater emphasis on the idea of "competition." Furthermore, physical education for females in modern China was deliberately planned and administered by the government. Through exercising state power, the government required the female students in modern women's schools to receive physical education. In this way, they could transform female bodies in order to enhance the prestige of the state and the society, breaking away from the image of China as "the sick man of East Asia" (*Dongya bingfu*). At the same time, the government hoped to nurture healthy females who would give birth to a stronger new generation. Therefore, the idea of "strengthening the nation and protecting the race" (*qiangguo baozhong*) made women's

---

The author would like to express her thanks and appreciation to Han Ling for translating this essay and Helen Young for correcting it.

sports no longer uncomplicated, and it became a gambling chip in the competition between China and other countries.

One thing that must be mentioned here is that females who participated in sports in this period were mainly students, and school was where female physical education took place. Moreover, school sports activities were not only limited to inside the campus; students could also practice sports in sports arenas outside of school. Essentially, modern Chinese women's sports were built on the foundation of physical education in the schools. Therefore, it is more correct to use the term "physical education" (*tineng jiaoyu*) for this kind of sports training. For the purpose of discussion in this essay, which covers the period from the late Qing to 1937, the term "female physical education" (*nüzi tiyu*) rather than "women's sports" (*nüzi yundong*) is used.

In order for female students to receive physical training, schools employed progressive methods for advocating physical education. In addition to continuing to encourage students to eliminate the practice of footbinding, they also presented light, yet interesting activities such as gymnastics, games and dance to attempt to stimulate student interest in learning. For schools that did not have large campuses, ball games provided another way to promote physical education, one that was loved by the students (Yu Chien-ming 1999:65).

Since schools used physical education to display educational achievement, they held sports tournaments to give the students the opportunity to demonstrate what they learned. Since the tournaments were open to visiting parents and guests, the tournaments showed them the achievements in female physical education. These sports competitions were originally held on campus. With the gradual rise in the popularity of physical education, there were regular sports competitions between the schools, the districts, the regions, and within the whole country and internationally. Consequently, female physical education moved from providing limited interest to public performance and competition. This was particularly apparent after the Nationalist Government settled in Nanjing.

In order to unify the nation, the Nationalist Government undertook many reforms. It gradually passed a series of educational laws and also regulated physical education methodology in the schools

(Zhongguo jindai tiyu shi 1989:193; Su Jingcun 1994:158-164). Moreover, the Ministry of Education became more concerned with the realm of physical education for both sexes and, with recommendations from experts, undertook various reforms in this field. More importantly, the government not only cared about physical education in the schools, it also emphasized developing physical education for citizens. In doing so, the government promulgated the "Law on the Physical Education of Citizens" (*Guomin tiyu fa*) which required each county and municipality to provide at least one public sports field (Wu Wenzhong 1967:209). In addition, the government held larger sports tournaments each year that were always very popular. Fundamentally, the implementation of this policy by the Nationalist Government was an important reason why physical education flourished in the 1920s and 1930s.

In addition to advocacy by the government, the media, which arose in the late Qing, was one of the great contributors to the upsurge of enthusiasm for physical education. The media provided information regarding physical education that profoundly influenced the public. Setting aside negative effects of the media, it is clear that the media had its own special role in transmitting information, teaching and leading the public in gaining knowledge, providing entertainment, and covering business activities. In other words, the media not only provided services for the government, certain organizations and intellectual authorities, it also catered to the tastes of the general public. The media provided coverage on sports in both of these aspects.

In order to allow the general public to appreciate the importance of physical education, the media acted as the government spokesperson in providing physical education coverage and publicity. The media introduced information about physical education topics such as sports rules and competition strategies in order to educate the public about physical education. It conveyed these messages in a more formal manner, creating certain values and standards that were accepted by the general public. However, it was difficult to attract the public with this formal kind of coverage, and it was also difficult for the media to enlarge the readership. Therefore, the media also adopted a different style in catering to the general public, using an attractive layout to stir up the interest of the public on the subject of physical education; the entertainment element of sports competition fitted the purposes of the media well. Hence, when the media provided coverage for each competition, it did not only focus on who won or lost the game, but the characters of the sport stars, their game strategies, and even their sensational actions became the focus of media coverage. This not only satisfied public curiosity but it also led the public into the world of sports. From this one can discern that the media had relatively much flexibility in conveying messages to the public since it did not need to be supervised by the government, and that the news also appealed to the public. This kind of information about physical education, constructed and chosen by the media, not only took into account the interests of the consumers but it also transferred the intent of those in power to promote physical education.

Since the media played a large role in influencing public understanding of and attitudes toward physical education, this essay analyzes the media coverage of sports and investigates how the media conveyed the message of physical education in the period from the late Qing to 1937. The goal of the government in promoting physical education was to reconstruct women's bodies in order to achieve the purpose of *qiangguo baozhong* and to revive the nation; how the media fused this consciousness into media coverage of sports needs further investigation. At the same time, with rapid changes in politics, economy, and in the society during this period, the essay inquires into the way the content of media coverage changed over time. Moreover, it examines the attitude of the media in viewing female students exercising in public activities at sports arenas, and the way the media portrayed these female athletes' lives on and off the sports field in order to appeal to the public. In short, this investigation reveals that not only the government but also the media took part in shaping modern Chinese female physical education and demonstrates the strategies that media used in controlling females.

Starting from the late Qing, Chinese media sources included newspapers, journals, novels, advertisements, and pictorials, and also electronic media such as movies and broadcasting. Among these media sources, newspapers and journals were more widely available to the public, and therefore this essay uses these two kinds of reference material for analysis.

Manifestation of Nation and Race through Physical Education

Intellectuals were the first to unite the concept of nation with physical education. Because China had lost the Sino-Japanese war, intellectuals initiated the idea of *qiangguo baozhong*. They felt that nurturing an intelligent and strong nation was the only way to save China, and that physical education was the main path for achieving this purpose and that both men and women should undergo this kind of training.

Late Qing reformer Liang Qichao pointed out that Westerners used female gymnastics to strengthen the nation and the military, based on a belief in prenatal education (Liang Qichao 1960:41). Yan Fu also raised the argument that "a strong mother will give birth to a stronger baby; nurturing the present generation will produce better progeny" (*mu jian er hou er fei, pei qi xiantian er zhong nai jin ye*) from an eugenics point of view. He also emphasized that physical education should not ignore women (Yan Fu 1971:55). After the establishment of the Republic of China, internal revolt and foreign invasions never stopped. The idea of "the destruction of the state and the extinction of the race" (*wangguo miezhong*) haunted many intellectuals; therefore, the belief that "physical education will save the nation" (*tiyu jiuguo*) became their hope.

In addition to the call from the intellectuals, the government also understood the important concept that "a strong body will save the nation" (*shenqiang jiuguo*). Therefore, when the new form of education was promoted all over China, every school included physical education classes in the curriculum. Moreover, under the influence of militaristic nationalistic education, the campuses were filled with military spirit, even in the girls' schools. In 1915 the media reported that the "Girls' Cansang School" (*Nüzi cansang xuexiao*) created a physical education song full of military spirit:

> In twentieth-century sports stadiums there is competition for wealth and power.

Is there a way to save the feeble and the poor? The responsibility rests on our party.
We will carry out our own careers in silk. Train our bodies to become like steel.
The merits of Leizhu [the goddess who invented silk] cannot be forgotten.
When will Mulan's aspirations be fulfilled?
Classmates, classmates come and promote physical education.

In twentieth-century sports stadiums, women should not concede victory.
Wash away the makeup and change into military uniform.
Female soldiers walking gallantly, with high spirits,
Strengthen our regiment with a whetstone.
Always bring glory to our school.
We will carry on the heritage, pave the way for future generations with no idleness or negligence. (Fan Yao Yunsu 1915:2)

In 1916 when the "Second Women's Normal School of Jiangsu Province" (*Jiangsu sheng di'er nüzi shifan xuexiao*) held its sports competition, there were many militaristic slogans on the walls of the campus; for example, "Do not only speak eloquently of heroines; there are also dutiful wives and loving mothers," "Training military citizens relates to education," "Not only the males can try out their skills at sports competitions; female students also have the same spirit," and "Now the world has changed, do not only stress the idea of 'valuing male over female,'" "Nowadays physical education is given to everyone; females can become stronger, too" (Song Jilan 1916:18-20).

Although after the end of the First World War the schools no longer advertised a militaristic kind of physical education, the spirit of nationalism embedded in this sort of education did not fade away; it grew in strength due to the nationalist movement in the May Fourth period. When the government engaged in the Northern Expedition and in the war to resist Japanese aggression, nationalism rose and flourished. Since the government and its party promoted the nationalist movement as a strategy and, as the Japanese invasion of China gradually increased in severity a nationalist consciousness permeated all of Chinese society (Li Guoji 1981:19-25).

Therefore, people were concerned with the relationship between physical education and revitalizing the nation, and this kind of discussion often appeared in the media. In 1930, Dai Jitao's speech made at the "Third National Sports Tournament" (*Di san ci quanguo yundonghui*) was in the headlines of every newspaper. In his speech, Dai emphasized, "Only when one possesses a strong and healthy body, can one have a strong healthy spirit. Strong and healthy citizens can form a strong and healthy nation" (quoted in: Jiang Xiangqing 1933:13). Also, journals often published papers written by famous scholars and politicians on the subject of *tiyu jiuguo*. Although the main readership of these articles was the general public, some articles spoke especially to female readers and their central principle was identical. The authors of these articles generally thought that as one part of the nation, women should possess a healthy physique in order to save the nation and give birth to a healthy new generation. Moreover, some of the media provided successful examples of foreign women in physical education in order to encourage Chinese women (Wu Cheng 1934; Lu Hanjuan 1931:38).

One thing worth noting here is that while most media sources cooperated with the government in calling on females to use their healthy bodies to save the nation, there were some media sources that displayed a different view of physical education. They claimed that having a healthy body could facilitate the process of gender equality, and these sources encouraged the idea of "the healthy beauty." These arguments mainly came from women's journals or were written by women (Yu Chien-ming 1996:138-144). The reason that the media covered reports on the importance of physical education departing from the idea of "saving the state" arose from the influence of the women's movement at that time; it used the idea that "all women love beauty" in order to attract more females to accept physical education (Yu Chien-ming 2003). However, when the Japanese invasion occurred, many discussions in the media gave first priority to the belief of *tiyu jiuguo* and gender equality was secondary. At the graduation exercises of the "Shanghai Zhonghua Women's Theological Seminary" (*Shanghai Zhonghua nüzi shen xueyuan*), physical education specialist Zhang Zhijiang told the female students to nurture healthy bodies to achieve gender equality. On the other hand, he said that women should accept the fate of being the mothers of the nation and undertake responsibility for the nation's glory and decline (Zhang Zhijiang 1931). Xiao Zhongguo pointed out in the article "Advocating Female Physical Education and Reviving the Chinese Nation" that female physical education was advantageous in achieving state revitalization, and assuming the responsibility for state revivification was more important than prattling on about female emancipation or female freedom (Xiao Zhongguo 1937:145-147). There were also women supporting this kind of argument, and they appeared most commonly in writings in campus publications. In ads calling for papers for an essay contest in *Zhonghua nüzhong xiaokan (Zhonghua Girls' High School Journal)* in 1936, papers were solicited on the topics "My views on saving the nation" and "Women during a time of national calamity." From the winning writings, one could perceive that female students generally felt that they should fulfill the tasks of saving the nation through physical education since resistance toward the Japanese rested on the shoulders of both men and women (Zhonghua nüzhong xiaokan 1936).

The media not only conveyed the importance of *tiyu jiuguo* through in-depth discussion, it also covered the actual development of physical education. For example, *Tiyu banyuekan (Physical Education Bimonthly)* reported in 1933 that the "Zhejiang Province Fourth High School" (*Zhejiang shengli di si zhongxue*), in response to government advocacy of *tiyu jiuguo*, required female and male students to choose at least two different kinds of physical education activities each semester and that once the students decided which activities to join, they could not make any changes. The students were classified and divided into groups by the Physical Education Department, and given fixed times for practices at an assigned location (Zhejiang shengli di si zhongxue 1933:116). However, the media was more engrossed in covering exhibitions of patriotism by athletes. After the Shanghai female ball players established the "Young Western Women's Basketball League" (*Xiqing nü lanhui*), they often played ball games with foreigners or foreign diplomats living in China. In 1929 the League defeated the foreign team for the first time, and the media covered it widely. *Shenbao (Shanghai Journal)*, a popular newspaper with wide circulation, used the headline, "Chinese Women's Military Spirit Worth Celebrating," to describe the great ball-playing skills of Chinese women (Zhong Xi nüzi lanqiusai 1929). Moreover, the famous "Two Rivers" (*Liangjiang*) female ball team was invited by overseas Chinese in Southeast Asia to participate in a competition. That was during the time that the Japanese seized northeastern China; the female ball players' performance overseas played a big role in encouraging people in the homeland, and the media did a series on their competition schedule and activities at the game (Liangjiang landui nanyou jingguo 1935). This kind of media coverage on the combination of physical education achievements and national pride appeared in reports on missionary schools too. After the triumphant return of the ball team to "Shanghai Chongde Girls' School" (*Shanghai Chongde nüxiao*), the school not only welcomed them in grand style, they also dedicated Chinese couplets to them: "For God, for the country, for Chongde" (*Wei shen wei guo wei Chongde*) and "With all your heart, with all your energy, with all your loyalty" (*Jin xin jin li jin zhongcheng*) (Deyin banyuekan 1932:39). Student publications accordingly reported these physical education stories.

Undeniably, the act of enforcing *tiyu jiuguo* for women contained the idea of equal gender rights. In other words, it meant that when the nation was in a calamitous situation, saving the nation was not only high priority for the males, but females also had the responsibility of sharing the burden. However, strictly speaking, this kind of equality with nation as the basis, did not actually touch upon the true essence of gender equality, nor did it take into account the concept of gender equality of the feminists at that time. Nevertheless, looking at it from a different angle, rather than criticizing the media's promotion of *tiyu jiuguo*, ignoring women's rights and fawning on the government, one should consider how the media could possibly have stayed in its own world and not serve the government since from the late Qing, China had been suffused in an atmosphere of patriotism and the need to revitalize the nation.

Conveying Moral Standards through Physical Education

Besides publicizing the central spirit of physical education, the media also played the part of the instructor in introducing different rules and regulations in sports competition and the concept of good sportsmanship, giving the general public a basic knowledge of physical education. This section focuses on what conditions surrounded female athletes, and what kind of sportsmanship and rules were required; through in-depth observation, one can detect how the media displayed these standards. One thing worth noting here is that female ball games were an attraction during that time; additionally, because the games were group activities many of the regulations were related to ball games. Using the way a ball team was organized as an example, *Tiyu banyuekan* printed a news report concerning how the "Zhejiang Jiaxing Girls' High School" (*Zhejiang Jiaxing nüzi zhongxue*) established their ball team. Since the school felt that selected players represented the school when the team went outside for competition, the name, flag, team leader, and training of the team should all be approved by the school. Academic grades and the conduct of the ball players needed also to correspond to the school's standards. "Students receiving failing grades in one third of their academic subjects and showing bad behavior," and "students who do not respect sports rules and regulations" could not become ball players representing the school (Jiaxing xianli nüzi zhongxue 1933:140). From reading these regulations of Zhejiang Jiaxing Girls' High School, one can perceive that before the school's athletes could become public figures, the school expected the representative athletes to have both sports skills and academic proficiency.

When the athletes became representatives of a region or the nation, the team sponsors demanded even more strict regulations for athletes. In the 1935 Shanghai Women's Basketball Team training measures promulgated before the "National Sports Tournament" (*Quanguo yundonghui*), one can see the general outline of the situation. According to the Shanghai *Shibao*, there were sixteen ball players receiving training, and the training period was divided into two phases. The first phase was half of a month, three times each week, and after three weeks the athletes began participating in friendly matches in order to strengthen the spirit of collaboration among the ball players. After the formal training, ten people were chosen as representatives to participate in the competition in Shanghai and began their second phase of training, which continued until the opening ceremony of the National Sports Tournament (Benshi canjia quanyunhui 1935:7). The second phase of training included training four times a week, and if the budget permitted, they planned to have the players lodge together. In this way, they could receive strict scientific training under a regular daily routine in order to allow the skills, stamina, and spirit of each ball player to reach a state of perfection. Additionally, there were specific training regulations for each player to obey, including following the orders of the instructor, punctual arrival for practice, no absence without excuse, and acute awareness of one's personal health, daily life, and having a positive attitude towards learning (ibid.).

One interesting fact is that when the Shanghai *Shibao* stated the content of the National Sports Tournament measures in the newspaper, there were six codes of conduct: (1) Each team member must obey absolutely the orders and regulations provided by the instructor. (2) Each team member must punctually attend practice for every compulsory exercise and specially arranged contest. (3) Each team member should fill out a formal excuse form before an absence due to special circumstances. (4) If a team member has an unexcused absence one or more times, after investigation by the instructor, the team member will receive appropriate punishment or warning. (5) Each team member should pay close attention to her personal health and habits of daily life. (6) If a team member does not possess the spirit of wanting to make progress, she should be given a warning at the first offense, and if she continues this habit, her qualifications should be revoked by replacing her with a new member (ibid.).

Although these regulations were for ball playing team members, the general public could also perceive the strict training required for ball players.

As public enthusiasm rose, many sports associations appeared in schools and in the society during the 1920s and 1930s, and each school and local sports group required different measures for regulating athletes. The most difficult situation during that time was the paucity of sports sites with conflicts arising between ball team members who were fighting for each site. Because of this, some schools set up time schedules for practice, and the media also did coverage on this particular subject. For example the Basketball Department at Jiaotong University separated practice times for male and female students, and also arranged special practice hours for the basketball team (Jiaoda nüsheng zuijin de yundong 1930:4). The "Zhejiang Yin County Private Xiaoshi High School" (*Zhejiang Yinxian sili xiaoshi zhongxue*) even promulgated "Regulations for Ball Team Practice" (*Qiudui lianxi dengji jianzhang*) to regulate the number of practice games, the practice times, and to create a priority list of the ball teams (Yinxian sili xiaoshi zhongxue 1933:68-69).[1]

The local sports associations were established for the purpose of playing in sports tournaments; therefore, their regulations were very strict. According to the report in *Shenbao* on the regulations of ball teams, almost every ball team had detailed regulations concerning the organization of the association, membership fees, game rules, attire, membership qualifications, and the number of team players. These rules not only facilitated the proceedings of the games, but also had the effect of governing the ball team and the players. Moreover, since the attendance of each ball team had a tremendous affect on the competition schedule, each organized association set up rigid rules. In 1929 the Shanghai Women's Basketball Game Committee told the ball teams that if they encountered special circumstances that would result in an absence from the game, they should, with the agreement of the opposing team, write up a formal excuse for the committee and apply for a change of date. If the team did not do this, they would forfeit the game, and if the team continued to be absent, their cash deposit would also be confiscated (Shanghai Zhonghua nüzi lanqiuhui

---

[1] The regulations stated: "Each team can only register for a time spot three times a week at most," "If the same kinds of teams register for the same date, the team arriving first gets the earlier time opening," and "A team will be dismissed if it does not practice in the registered week" (Yinxian sili xiaoshi zhongxue 1933:68-69).

zhangcheng 1929). In 1933, the committee amended this regulation, stating that "if a ball team forfeits their right to play once, the deposit will be confiscated; and if a team forfeits their right to play twice, its membership will be revoked" (Shanghai nüzi lanqiuhui 1933:13).

There were also clear regulations for participating teams and athletes in sports tournaments. Using the women's basketball game's regulations as an example, besides a clear requirement for using "balls produced in our own country in the competition" to ensure the fairness of the game, there were also strict measures concerning the status and qualifications of the athletes. In most cases, to ensure fair competition, qualifications for athletes received special attention and usually amateur players could not enter a professional contest. Some sponsoring committees even enforced regulations such as the following:

> Team members who do not register for the game and do not turn in their photos, cannot participate in the competition and will be dropped from the team. If a team member withdraws midway through the game or is ordered out of the game due to penalty for a foul, the cash deposit for that team will not be returned, and points gained in the game will be canceled accordingly. (Nülanhui bimu 1933:12)

Sanitation concepts were also included in the regulations: "One should provide one's own towel for showering after the game" (ibid.).

One thing that must be mentioned here is that athletes' moral standards were being regulated, too. At the "Fifth National Sports Tournament" (*Di wu ci quanguo yundonghui*) the committee promulgated a measure named "Ten Dos and Don'ts for Athletes" (*Yundongyuan shi bu yao yu shi yao*): (1) Do not stay up too late; one should go to sleep early and wake up on time. (2) Do not overeat; one should eat less and chew more. (3) Do not start out as hardworking and end up slackening; one should persevere to the end. (4) Do not be afraid of difficulty; one should always move forward. (5) Do not only vie to win; one should have real skills and strength. (6) Do not be hasty; one should progress gradually. (7) Do not drink or smoke; one should live a simple life. (8) Do not indulge in lust; one should lead a quiet life. (9) Do not be greedy for material goods; one should be incorruptible. (10) Do not be secretly happy about getting away with a foul; one should obey the morals in sportsmanship and the rules of the game (Yundongyuan shi bu yao yu shi yao 1933).

The common characteristic of all the above regulations is that they do not contain the idea of gender difference. In other words, both female and male athletes should always obey the same rules at the sports arena. These regulations were very extensive; some taught the athletes how to become modern citizens through participating in group sports, requiring punctuality, obeying laws, practicing good sanitation, obeying moral and patriotic concepts.

The media not only widely covered the regulations for athletes, it also covered actual examples of sports rules violations. The newspapers reported the terrible incident in which the "Number Two Team" (*Liang liang dui*) of Liangjiang was asked to withdraw from a competition due to being about a quarter of an hour late (Nülanhui bimu 1933). Also popular in the media was the coverage on the disqualification of ball players. The media reported two incidents, one in 1930 with Liangjiang ball team member Xi Jun, who was a former physical education instructor, and the other in 1933 with Haixing volleyball team member Guo Xiaoping, who violated the amateur qualification (Zuo lanqiu jieguo 1930; Hushi yundonghui qiusai 1933; Wuben de nüzi paiqiu jinbiao 1933).

According to the various regulations listed above, one can detect that in order to become an athlete or a selected contestant, sportswomen and sportsmen needed to follow many codes. The main characteristic of these codes was that the athletes must possess the spirit of teamwork while obeying the rules, and at the same time they must have good conduct and be patriotic. The media not only conveyed these messages to the athletic contestants to keep them vigilant about various regulations, it also taught the general public about physical education. Physical education was not only about performance or entertainment but was actually about striving for amending social practices and establishing good discipline and order based on teamwork.

Lifestyles of Female Athletes

In order to gain a greater readership, the media not only played the part of spokesman for the government or opinion-maker, it also needed to select entertaining topics to appeal to the general public. Therefore, the media tried to probe into the lives of female athletes, reporting on their practice before games, performance at the tournaments, and activities outside of the sports arenas.

Selected female athletic contestants continually received training to sharpen their skills. They also disciplined themselves in addition to regular practice, and these activities outside of the routine were the focus of the media. The following report gives a glimpse at the female athletes' sports practices:

> When the women's basketball team joined the Basketball League, they practiced diligently daily. At dawn, there were many heroines practicing on the court preparing to win the tournament. (Jinan nüsheng ai lanqiu 1929:7)

More interestingly, the media also compared female athletes with the males: "At dawn, the male students were still sleeping, and the heroines were already practicing in the gym" (Zhonggong nüzi lanqiudui 1929:7).

Besides extra practice, a friendly match before the game was also a method for training. For these matches, the media of course grasped every opportunity to find fascinating material about the game to report. Since the match was a practice game, sometimes the two teams' strengths were not compatible and many hilarious situations occurred. The media did not miss any opportunity to capture these incidents. For example, when the "Zhonggong Women's Basketball Team" (*Zhonggong nüzi lanqiudui*) and "Fudan Women's Basketball Team" (*Fudan nüzi lanqiudui*) played a friendly match, there were many faults during the game. The media wrote an accurate report of the Zhonggong Women's Basketball Team at the game saying "they were befuddled and often passed the ball to the opponents" (Zhonggong nüzi lanqiu liang da zhan 1929:7). In addition, since a friendly match was not a real game, there were no restrictions on the qualifications of the competing opponents. The teams played with members of the same sex and even of the opposite sex, and these scenes that could never be seen at a formal tournament attracted public attention. Shanghai *Shibao* reported a friendly volleyball match between female and male volleyball players:

> The two competing teams were Chenzhong and Dongyan. One was the never-yielding female team, and the other one was the awe-inspiring male team. At the match, the female team was in full power, winning over the male team by a score of three to one. Their success brought glory to the world of women's sports. (Yimu nan nü paiqiusai 1934:8)

Many matches between the sexes were played in an easy and free manner. After the opening ceremony of the 1933 "Zhejiang Province Jianshe Sports Tournament" (*Zhejiang jianshe yundonghui*) in Hangzhou, many journalists from different newspaper offices in Shanghai, at the invitation of the chair, formed a ball team with the chair and competed against the two female ball teams of Dongnan and Liangjiang. Since this was an entertaining performance, the match was hilarious and very different from the regular games (Hangzhou Zhejiang jianshe yundonghui kaimu 1933).

However, the media did not only present coed games in a positive way. The coed match during the Zhejiang Province Jianshe Sports Tournament brought great attacks from the media. During the twenty minutes of game time, the male team headed by the chair did not gain any points, and the closing banquet was delayed due to this match, causing complaints from many guests. Some journalist ridiculed this game as being not for learning but only for fun (Jiang Jun 1933). Conservative Beijing was even more intolerant of this kind of situation. In 1932 an author named "Si'ai" (sometimes "Aisi") published a paper titled, "One Scene of Close Combat between Men and Women" in the Beijing *Chenbao*. He described the embarrassing episode at the coed basketball game, and described male ball players as hungry tigers pouncing on their prey during the entire game; moreover, the audience even made vulgar gestures during the game. Therefore, Si'ai pointed out that basketball was a very violent sport, and because of differences in physiology between male and female, coed games were not only harmful to women's physiology, but they also prevented the males from bringing their ball playing skills into full play. Si'ai also emphasized that close combat between male and female was inappropriate and could even give rise to lewd and despicable acts. He wrote with sincerity that whether these acts were intentional or not, they could damage the reputation of the beloved ball players (Aisi 1932; Si'ai 1932).

Strictly speaking, not all audiences watched sports competitions in a peculiar way. Many already had considerable understanding of sports competitions, such as Si'ai. Therefore, when the media recounted a live sports competition, in addition to analyzing and commenting on the game, it provided the general public with a deeper understanding of how to watch the games. To satisfy the sports fans, it also described the skills of the players. When commenting on the game, the reporter not only evaluated the personal ability of each athlete, the performance of the entire team, and whether the sports regulations could be applied to female athletes, they also reviewed the fairness of the judge (Yu Chien-ming 1999:99-102). When describing athletic skills, the media used a masculine vocabulary for the female athletes, to make them appear to be heroines on a battlefield. In portraying these athletes, the media used such words as "courageous and skillful in battle" (*yonggan shan zhan*), "appearing and disappearing mysteriously like ghosts" (*shen chu gui mo*), "a crack shot" (*bai fa bai zhong*), "brave in offense and defense" (*yong yu gongshou*), "powerful as a flying dragon" (*jiao ruo you long*) and "undefeatable" (*wan fu mo di*) (ibid. 98-99). Nevertheless, some athletes were given romantic titles, such as "mermaid" (*meiren yu*) for the top-notch swimmer Yang Xiuqiong.

Another topic that caught the interest of the media was the athletes' appearance and their little gestures during the game. Because athletes and actors were both public figures, the audience was very curious about them, and also liked to judge them; therefore, the media grasped this mindset of the general public and revealed the lives of the athletes when catering to the public. The media not only used words to describe the athletes, they also used the modern technology of the camera to reveal different ways athletes looked, showing some of their facial expressions in the sports arenas or their appearance when not wearing sports outfits. This kind of portrayal of the athletes through words and images deeply impressed the audiences. For example, although it was somewhat of an exaggeration when the media used masculine words and phrases to describe the techniques of the female athletes, there were actually some female athletes who liked to exhibit masculinity in their looks. They dressed themselves like handsome young boys, which was made evident when observing the appearance of the athletes in real life. It was difficult to distinguish whether these athletes were male or female when they dressed like boys. In one incident, the Shanghai *Shibao* reported that when the female ball player, Chen Jinchai, attended the National Sports Tournament, she intentionally dressed like a handsome young boy. Her appearance fooled everyone, to the point that she was prevented from entering the female dorm (Dongya jinguo liezhuan 1936).

More interestingly, the media liked to catch the sudden facial expressions and gestures of the female athletes. Most commonly, the media especially liked to depict athletes shedding bitter tears due to careless errors (Nüzi lanqiu juesai 1930; Nüzi paiqiu gongkai biaoyan 1934; Zeng Naidun 1936:45).[2] For instance, special actions by many female athletes such as not wearing glasses during the game, or tying a red handkerchief on their hands while playing ball were displayed before the eyes of the audience (Ping Dongwu daxue nüsheng lanqiudui de qiuyi 1929; Laoda de nüsheng lanqiudui 1929). Moreover, the media would not even omit intentional gestures of female athletes, as reported in 1933 by *Shijie ribao (World Daily Newspaper)*:

> When the opponents passed the ball, a female athlete followed swiftly, but, because the male audience was shouting, she tried to catch the ball in a flamboyant manner, but failed to catch it. The female athlete suddenly broke out laughing leading the male audiences at the game to shout louder and start clapping (Qiu Ying 1935:6).

Apparently, this female athlete was intentionally flirting with the male audience at the game, using her body language to appeal to them. This

---

[2] *Shenbao* and Tianjin *Dagongbao (Dagong Newspaper)* covered the athletes' grieving after losing a game in the "National Sports Tournament" (*Quanyun*) in 1930 and in the "Far-Eastern Sports Tournament" (*Yuanyun*) in 1934. Moreover, Zeng Naidun also pointed out that female athletes' tears due to defeat were often seen in the newspaper.

could also be understood as the way a female manipulates a male (Yu Chien-ming 1996:143). However, coverage of the kind written by Qiu Ying was a serious attack on this female athlete, reproving her for debasing herself and destroying female dignity. Qiu Ying even added that this confirmed the fact that "the female is a male sex toy" (Qiu Ying 1935:6). There were quite a few reporters who were also unhappy with this kind of misbehavior of female athletes. An author using the pseudonym "Liao Xing" wrote an article titled "What For?" in *Nü qingnian yuekan (Young Women's Monthly)*. She suspected that some athletes seemed to forget the real goal of physical education, and that they thought vanity was more important than actual problems. Therefore, "they need to make themselves up especially alluringly in order to show off during each game and catch the attention of the public" (Liao Xing 1934:34).

Though there was continual criticism, it could not stop public figures from being in the spotlight and wanting to lead the fashions of the time. For instance, in 1930 it was popular among the new urban clique of female students and new women to have short hair, permed hair, to expose their arms and legs, and to wear makeup. Female athletes reflected this fashion too, bringing the most popular fashions to the audience to fulfill the public's desire to peep at the female body. Undoubtedly, the media acted as a go-between in this fad. In addition, the reason that the media emphasized this kind of coverage was related to the social currents of the 1920s and 1930s. During that time though nationalism continued to permeate the public, sexual expression also emerged, and objectification of the female body was common. Displaying the female body and using makeup were often a part of people's daily lives, and were made more popular through the displaying and exhibiting of fashionable women with beautiful well-trained physiques.

In addition to the careers of female athletes, their love lives or married lives could not avoid the pursuit of the media, and even retired players received media attention. The reason the media brought retired players back into public view was apparently to increase sales. Marriage break-ups were also extensively covered in the reports. In April 1934 the famous retired female basketball players Shao Jinying and Gao Zhaolie, who graduated from Fudan University, were engaged and were a perfect match in the eyes of the public; however, Shao unexpectedly became engaged to Liu Xuesong, the chair of the Jiangda Physical Education Department. This incident shocked the entire public. Thus, the *Tiyu pinglun (Sports Commentary)* used the title, "Female Basketball Player Changes Wedding Plans" (*Nü lanqiu jianjiang hunbian ji*). Since media coverage began, the general public became increasingly interested in gossip about sports players' personal life (Cang Sheng 1934:271). This situation became even worse in the 1930s, when the famous actress Ruan Lingyu was sacrificed to this atmosphere of *renyan kewei* (gossip), and as public figures the athletes constantly lived under this kind of situation.

The media widely revealed the lives of these female athletes to the general public for the purpose of causing a public sensation in order to attract business, also a win-win strategy. Since the media brought the public to a deeper understanding of the athlete's sports techniques and personal lives, it also indirectly promoted the athletes and brought them an opportunity for exhibitionism. Undeniably, exaggerated reporting was in fact damaging to the female athletes' image and also affected the true essence of sports. Fortunately, the media had a conscience, and it made moral judgments about certain inappropriate or erroneous representations, which kept media sports coverage from being overly biased.

Conclusion

Since female physical education was put into the curriculum as a required course in modern schools, female physical education progressed under systematic planning and administration. Besides the established sports regulations, course, and content, the female students needed to do actual practice; therefore, the general public saw a group of female students, wearing T-shirts and shorts, dancing, running, and jumping. This was something rarely seen in traditional society, but the media brought this new modern fashion into public view, allowing an increasing number of people to have the chance to observe this activity.

For the older generation, women's sports was like a vaudeville show, but for the newer generation, it was like a Western opera. No matter what, through its machinations, the media lured the readers to hold a view that the media chose and constructed. In the foregoing analysis, one can understand that the media paid great attention to the subject of physical education, and that it tried to exhibit female physical education from different angles. At the same time, the media tried to set up moral standards, the most conspicuous being the combination of physical education and the idea of nation. Since modern China was weak, the government hoped to promote the idea of *qiangshen baoguo* (strengthening the body will save the nation), and the media felt the responsibility to be the megaphone of the government to call upon the public to save the nation through physical education. In addition, the media also conveyed the modern concepts of order and discipline through the discussion of sports regulations. However, the interesting aspects of sports also allowed the media to reveal a different side, entertaining the public with various rumors, especially in the 1920s and 1930s when urban lives in China became modernized. The media used these two extremes of sports reports to reflect modern Chinese society, which was still full of vitality in the midst of foreign invasion and civil war.

References

Aisi, Yi mu liang xing roubo ji: Duiyu nan nü hunhe lanqiu zhi shangquan (One Scene of Close Combat between Men and Women: About the Negotiation of Power in Coed Basketball Games), in: *Chenbao*, 24 January 1932, p. 9.

Benshi canjia quanyunhui (Shanghai Joins the National Sports Tournament), in: *Shibao*, 24 July 1935, p. 7.

Cang Sheng, Nü lanqiu jianjiang hunbian ji (Female Basketball Player Changes Wedding Plans), in: *Tiyu pinglun* 81 (21 April 1934), p. 271.

Deyin banyuekan (Deyin Bimonthly) 1:5 (November 1932), pp. 38-39.

Dongya jinguo liezhuan (Biographies of East Asian Heroines), in: *Shibao*, 14 March 1936, p. 7.

Fan Yao Yunsu, Tai jiao (Prenatal Education), in: *Zhonghua funüjie* (Chinese Women's World) 1:6 (1915), pp. 1-2.

Hangzhou Zhejiang jianshe yundonghui kaimu (Opening Ceremony of the Zhejiang Province Jianshe Sports Tournament in Hangzhou), in: *Shenbao*, 7 January 1933, p. 18.

Hushi yundonghui qiusai (Ball Game at the Sports Tournament in Shanghai), in: *Shenbao*, 19 September 1933, p. 14.

Jiang Jun, Suowei Zhesheng jianshe yundonghui (On the Zhejiang Province Jianshe Sports Tournament), in: *Tiyu pinglun* 14 (7 January 1933), p. 1.

Jiang Xiangqing, Xuexiao tiyu zhi miaowu qushi jiyi xiuzheng (The Absurd Trend of Physical Education in Schools Needs to be Corrected), in: *Dongfang zazhi* 30:20 (1933), pp. 13-15.

Jiaoda nüsheng zuijin de yundong (Latest Sports Activities of Women Students at Jiaotong University), in: *Shenbao*, 12 April 1930, p. 4.

Jiaxing xianli nüzi zhongxue (Jiaxing County Girls' High School), in: *Tiyu banyuekan* 32-33 (May 1933), pp. 131-160.

Jinan nüsheng ai lanqiu (Jinan Women Students Love Basketball), in: *Shenbao*, 19 April 1929, p. 7.

Laoda de nüsheng lanqiudui (Laoda Women's Basketball Team), in: *Shenbao*, 16 June 1929, p. 7.

Li Guoji, Jiawu zhanhou zhi kangzhan yiqian woguo minzu zhuyi de fazhan (1985-1936) (The Development of Nationalism between the Period of the Sino-Japanese War and the Chinese War of Resistance (1985-1936)), in: *Zhonghua minguo jianguo shi taolunji* (Collection of Articles on the History of Nation-building in the Republic of China), ed. by Zhonghua minguo jianguo shi taolunhui bianji weiyuanhui (Editorial Committee for the Collection of Articles on the History of Nation-building in the Republic of China), Taipei 1981, vol. 2, pp. 2-30.

Liangjiang landui nanyou jingguo (The Two Rivers Basketball Team's Tour South), in: *Shenbao*, 27 May 1935, p. 12.

Liang Qichao, Bianfa tongyi: Lun nüxue (On Reform: Women's Education), in: *Yinbingshi wenji* (Collected Writings from the Yinbing Studio), Taipei 1960, vol. 1, pp. 37-44.

Liao Xing, Weide shenmene? (What For?), in: *Nü qingnian yuekan* 13:6 (June 1934), pp. 33-34.

Liu Bingguo, *Zhongguo gudai tiyu shihua* (The History of Physical Education in Ancient China), Beijing 1987.

Lu Hanjuan, Jinshi Ouzhou nüquan yundong yu Zhongguo funü wenti (The Feminist Movement of Modern Europe and the Chinese Women's Question), in: *Jindai funü* 30 (1931), pp. 38-39.

Nülanhui bimu (Closing Ceremony of Women's Basketball Game), in: *Shenbao*, 28 November 1933, p. 12.

Nüzi lanqiu juesai (The Women's Basketball Finals), in: *Dagongbao*, 17 April 1930, p. 5.

Nüzi paiqiu gongkai biaoyan (Open Performances of the Women's Volleyball Team), in: *Shenbao*, 14 May 1934, p. 15.

Ping Dongwu daxue nüsheng lanqiudui de qiuyi (Comments on the Skills of Dongwu University Women's Basketball Team), in: *Shenbao*, 27 July 1929, p. 3.

Qiu Ying, Yougan yu mou xiao nüsheng saiqiu (Remarks on a Women Students' Ball Game), in: *Shijie ribao*, 22 April 1935, p. 6.

Shanghai nüzi lanqiuhui ding benyue shiyi ri kaimu (Shanghai Chinese Women's Basketball Game Planned to Have Opening Ceremony on the Eleventh This Month), in: *Shenbao*, 6 November 1933, p. 13.

Shanghai Zhonghua nüzi lanqiuhui zhangcheng (Rules of the Shanghai Zhonghua Women's Basketball Association), in: *Shenbao*, 19 March 1929, p. 11.

Si'ai, Yi mu liangxing roubo ji: Duiyu nan nü hunhe lanqiu zhi shangquan (One Scene of Close Combat between Men and Women: About the Negotiation of Power in Coed Basketball Games), in: *Chenbao*, 22 January 1932, p. 9.

Song Jilan, Jizai: Ji benxiao di'er ci yundonghui huichang de buzhi (Record: Record on Our School's Second Sports Tournament Arrangement of the Sports Site), in: *Jiangsu shengli di'er nüzi shifan xuexiao xiaoyou huikan* (Periodical of the Second Women's Second Normal School Alumni of Jiangsu Province) 2 (1916), pp. 18-20.

Su Jingcun (ed.), *Zhongguo jindai xuexiao tiyu shi* (History of Physical Education in Chinese Schools Today), Beijing 1994.

Wuben de nüzi paiqiu jinbiao (Wuben Wins the Women's Volleyball Tournament), in: *Shenbao*, 25 September 1933, p. 15.

Wu Cheng, Deguo nüzi tiyu zhi xunlian (Physical Education Training of German Women), in: *Nü qingnian yuekan* 13:6 (1934), pp. 39-43.

Wu Wenzhong, *Zhongguo jinbainian tiyu shi* (History of Physical Education in China in the Past One Hundred Years), Taipei 1967.

Xiao Zhongguo, Tichang nüzi tiyu yu Zhonghua minzu zhi fuxing (Advocating Female Physical Education and the Reviving the Chinese Nation), in: *Tiyu jikan* (Physical Education Quarterly) 3:2 (1937), pp. 145-147.

Yan Fu, Yuanqiang (Source of Strength), Shanghai 1922, reproduced in: Jiang Zhenjin (ed.), *Yan Jidao wenchao* (The Collected Works of Yan Jidao), Taipei 1971, vol.1, pp. 6-27.

Yimu nan nü paiqiusai: Chenzhong sheng Dongyan (Men versus Women in a Volleyball Game: Chenzhong Beats Dongyan), in: *Shibao*, 26 June 1934, p. 8.

Yinxian sili xiaoshi zhongxue (Yinxian Private Xiaoshi High School), in: *Tiyu banyuekan* 32-33 (May 1933), pp. 49-69.

Yu Chien-ming, A Probe into Views on Women's Physical Education in Modern China, in: *New History* 7:4 (1996), pp. 119-158

Yu Chien-ming, Female Ball Game Players in Eastern China (1927-1937): A Discussion Based on Newspapers and Journals of That Period, in: *Bulletin of the Institute of Modern History at Academia Sinica* 32 (1999), pp. 57-122.

Yu Chien-ming (You Jianming), Jindai Zhongguo nüzi jianmei de lunshu (1920-1940 niandai) (Discourse on Women's Health and Beauty in Modern China [1920s-1940s]), in: Yu Chien-ming (ed.), *Wu sheng zhi sheng: Jindai Zhongguo de funü yu shehui (1600-1950)* (Voices amid Silence: Women and Society in Modern China [1600-1950]), Taipei: Institute of Modern History, Academia Sinica, 2003, vol. 2, pp. 141-172.

Yundongyuan shi bu yao yu shi yao (Ten Dos and Don'ts for Athletes), in: *Shenbao*, 10 October 1933, p. 35.

Zhang Zhijiang, Haomian nü tongzhi ying zhuzhong tiyu guoshu (To Urge the Female Patriots to Pay Attention to Physical Education), in: *Nüduo* (Female Bell), 20:3-4 (1931), pp. 91-92.

Zhejiang shengli di si zhongxue (Zhejiang Province Fourth High School), in: *Tiyu banyuekan* 34-35 (May 1933), p. 115-163.

Zeng Naidun, *Nü xuesheng shenghuo sumiao* (Sketches of Women Students' Lives), Shanghai 1936.

Zhonggong nüzi lanqiu liang da zhan (Zhonggong Women's Basketball Team's Two Fights), in: *Shenbao*, 16 June 1929, p. 7.

Zhonggong nüzi lanqiudui (The Zhonggong Women's Basketball Team), in: *Shenbao*, 10 June 1929, p. 7.

Zhongguo jindai tiyu shi (History of Physical Education in Modern China), ed. by Guojia tiwei tiyu wen shi gongzuo weiyuanhui, Zhongguo tiyu shixuehui (National Committee of Physical Education History, Association of Modern Chinese Physical Education History), Beijing 1989.

Zhonghua nüzhong xiaokan (Zhonghua Girls' High School Journal) 10 (1936), pp. 1-52.

Zhong Xi nüzi lanqiusai: Qiangnan zhansheng Xiqing (Chinese versus Western Women's Basketball Game: Qiangnan Defeats Xiqing), in: *Shenbao*, 8 December 1929, p.11.

Zuo lanqiu jieguo (The Outcome of Yesterday's Basketball Game), in: *Shenbao*, 15 March 1930, p. 15.

Contributors

Tani E. Barlow teaches in the departments of History and Women's Studies at the University of Washington, Seattle. She is the author most recently of *The Question of Women in Chinese Feminism* (2004) and "The Pornographic City," in: Jing Wang, David Goodman (eds.), *Locating China: Space, Place and Popular Culture* (2005). Barlow is the founding senior editor of *positions: east asian cultures critique* published by Duke University Press.

Isabel Crook is a Professor (retired) at the Beijing Foreign Studies University. Publications (with David Crook) include *Revolution in a Chinese Village – Ten Mile Inn* (1959), *Ten Mile Inn – Mass Movement in a Chinese Village* (1979), and *The First Years of Yangyi Commune* (1966).

Jens Damm is a Research Associate at the Seminar of East Asian Studies of the Free University Berlin. His research interests include gender studies and identity politics in Chinese societies. He is the author of *Homosexualität und Gesellschaft in Taiwan (Homosexuality and Society in Taiwan)* (2003), and co-editor and co-author of *Chinese Cyberspaces* (2005).

Du Fangqin is a Professor of History at the Classics Research Institute and Director of the Women's Studies Center at Tianjin Normal University. Her research focuses on women's history and the current situation of women and gender questions in China. She has been involved in establishing women's studies as a scientific discipline in China. She is co-editor of *Lishi zhong de funü yu shehui xingbie (Engendering History Studies)* (2000), and author of *Funüxue yu funüshi de bentu tansuo (An Exploration of Women's Studies and Women's History from a Chinese Perspective)* (2002).

Louise Edwards is a Reader at the China and Korea Centre at the Australian National University. Her most recent publications include *Men and Women in Qing China* (1994, 2001), *Women in Asia:*

Tradition, Modernity and Globalisation (2000) (ed. with Mina Roces), and *Women's Suffrage in Asia* (2004) (ed. with Mina Roces).

Christina K. Gilmartin is an Associate Professor at Northeastern University, Boston. She is the author of *Engendering the Chinese Revolution: Radical Women, Communist Politics and Mass Movements in the 1920s* (1995), and a co-editor of *Engendering the Chinese Revolution: Women, Culture and the State* (1994) and *Feminist Approaches to Theory and Methodology: An Interdisciplinary Reader* (1999).

Bryna Goodman is Associate Professor of History at the University of Oregon. She is the author of *Native Place, City and Nation: Regional Networks and Identities in Shanghai, 1853-1937* (1995), and co-editor of *Gender in Motion: Divisions of Labor and Cultural Change in Late Imperial and Modern China* (2005).

Sabine Hieronymus finished her PhD entitled *Frauenbilder: Über fiktive und reale Heldinnen in der späten chinesischen Kaiserzeit am Beispiel von Meng Lijun und Qiu Jin (Female Role Models: Fictional and Actual Heroines of the Late Chinese Empire with Reference to Meng Lijun and Qiu Jin)* at the University of Kiel in 1999. She lives in Heidelberg as an independent scholar.

Hsiung Ping-chen is the Dean of the College of Liberal Arts for National Central University, Taiwan, also a Research Fellow at the Institute of Modern History, Academia Sinica. As a specialist in the cultural and intellectual history of Late Imperial China, she has published monographs and articles on provincial intellectual life, history of infants and children, as well as Chinese paediatrics. She is the author of *A Tender Voyage: Children and Childhood in Late Imperial China* (forthcoming), *Tongnian yiwang – Zhongguo haizi de lishi (Reflections on Childhood in the Past – A History of Chinese Children)* (2000), and *An yang: Zhongguo jin shi ertong de jibing yu jiankang (In Peace or in Discomfort: Diseases and Health of Young Children in Late Imperial China)* (1999).

Maria Jaschok is Director of the International Gender Studies Centre, Queen Elizabeth House, and Senior Research Scholar at the Institute for Chinese Studies, University of Oxford. Her recent publications include (co-authored) "Contexts, Sources and Methods for Research on Women and Islamic Cultures in China, 1700-1900," in: *Encyclopedia of Women and Islamic Cultures* (2003), (co-authored) *The History of Women's Mosques in Chinese Islam/Zhongguo Qingzhen Nüsishi* (2000/2002), and (co-edited) *Chinese Women Organizing: Cadres, Feminists, Muslims, Queers* (2001).

Mechthild Leutner is Professor of Sinology at the Seminar of East Asian Studies of the Free University Berlin. Her publications include *Geburt, Heirat und Tod in Peking. Volkskultur und Elitekultur vom 19. Jahrhundert bis zur Gegenwart (Birth, Marriage and Death in Peking: Elite Culture and Popular Culture in China from the Late Nineteenth Century to the 1980s)* (1989) (Chinese version 2000), and she is editor of the monographical serial *Berliner China-Studien*, and co-editor of the periodical *Berliner China-Hefte*.

Gotelind Müller-Saini is Professor of Sinology at the University of Heidelberg. Major publications include *Buddhismus und Moderne: Ouyang Jingwu, Taixu und das Ringen um ein zeitgemäßes Selbstverständnis im chinesischen Buddhismus des frühen 20. Jahrhunderts (Buddhism and Modernity: Ouyang Jingwu, Taixu and the Quest for a Timely Self-Definition of Chinese Buddhism in the Early Twentieth Century)* (1993), and *China, Kropotkin und der Anarchismus: Eine Kulturbewegung im China des frühen 20. Jahrhunderts unter dem Einfluß des Westens und japanischer Vorbilder (China, Kropotkin and Anarchism: A Cultural Movement in Early Twentieth Century China under the Influence of the West and of Japanese Models)* (2001).

Shui Jingjun is an Associate Research Fellow at the Henan Academy of Social Sciences and the Director of the Centre of Islamic Culture Studies. Her publications include (co-authored) "Contexts, Sources and Methods for Research on Women and Islamic Cultures in China,

1700-1900," in: *Encyclopedia of Women and Islamic Cultures* (2003), (co-authored) *The History of Women's Mosques in Chinese Islam/Zhongguo Qingzhen Nüsishi* (2000/2002), and "In Search of Sacred Women's Organizations," in: *Chinese Women Organizing* (2001).

Nicola Spakowski is a Professor of History at International University Bremen. Her main fields of interest are historiography, social history and women's history of twentieth century and contemporary China. She is author of several articles on feminism in contemporary China, and is writing a book on the military participation of Chinese women in the Communist movement in China from 1925 to 1949.

Natascha Vittinghoff (Gentz) is Junior Professor of Sinology at Frankfurt University. She is author of *Die Anfänge des Journalismus in China 1860-1911 (The Rise of Modern Journalism in China)* (2002) and *Geschichte der Partei entwunden – Eine semiotische Analyse des Dramas* Jiang Qing und ihre Ehemänner *(1991) von Sha Yexin (History vs. Party Historiography and Sha Yexin's Drama* Jiang Qing and Her Husbands*)* (1995), and co-editor of *Mapping Meanings: The Field of New Learning in Late Imperial China* (2004) as well as *Cultural Identities and Media Representations* (2004).

Wen-hsin Yeh is Professor of History at the University of California at Berkeley. Her current projects explore the urban history of modern Shanghai and the writing of Chinese history in Mao's China.

Helen Praeger Young is an Associate Scholar at the Center for East Asian Studies, Stanford University doing research in modern Chinese women's history in the Republican period. She is author of *Choosing Revolution: Chinese Women Soldiers on the Long March* (2001).

Yu Chien-ming is an Associate Research Fellow at the Institute of Modern History in Academia Sinica, Taipei, and served as the chief editor of the annual journal, *Research on Women in Modern China*

(1993-2002). Women's history in modern China and Taiwan is her research interest. She is author of *Rikang shiqi Taiwan de nüzi jiaoyu (Women's Education in Taiwan under Japanese Rule, 1895-1945)* (1988), and *Qingting tamen de shengyin: Nüxing koushu lishi de fangfa yu koushu shiliao de yunyong (Listening to Their Voices: Methodology of Female Oral History and the Use of Oral Historical Sources)* (2002).

Zang Jian is an Associate Professor at the Center for the Study of Premodern Chinese History, and at the Department of History at Peking University. Her research interests include the history of Chinese women, especially women and the household during the Song dynasty and girl's education in the poor areas of Northwest and Southwest China. Her publications include "Women and the Transmission of Confucian Culture in Song China," in: Ko, Dorothy, Jahyun Kim Haboush, Joan R. Piggott (eds.), *Women and Confucian Cultures in Premodern China, Korea, and Japan* (2003), and "Songdai jia fa de chansheng ji dui jiazu zhong de nannü xingbie juese de rending" (The Emergence of Song Family Laws and Determination of Male and Female Roles), in: Deng Xiaonan (ed.), *Tang Song nüxing yu shehui (Tang and Song Women and Society)* (2003).

Harriet T. Zurndorfer is Associate Professor of Chinese History at Leiden University. She is the author of *Change and Continuity in Chinese Local History* (1989), *China Bibliography* (1995; paperback edition 1999), and editor of the compilation *Chinese Women in the Imperial Past: New Perspectives* (1999). She is founder, and editor-in-chief of the journal *Nan Nü: Men, Women and Gender in China*, published since 1999.

Berliner China-Studien
hrsg. von Prof. Dr. Mechthild Leutner
(Freie Universität Berlin)

Heike Frick; Mechthild Leutner;
Nicola Spakowski (Hg.)
"Die Befreiung der Kinder"
Konzepte von Kindheit im China der
Republikzeit
Bd. 34, 1999, 392 S., 35,90 €, br.,
ISBN 3-8258-3910-9

Nicola Spakowski
Helden, Monumente, Traditionen
Nationale Identität und historisches
Bewußtsein in der VR China
Bd. 35, 1999, 232 S., 35,90 €, br.,
ISBN 3-8258-4117-0

Kathrin Ensinger
Leben und Fiktion
Autobiographisches im erzähleri-
schen Werk der chinesischen Autorin
Lin Bai
Bd. 36, 1999, 104 S., 15,90 €, br.,
ISBN 3-8258-4421-8

Heike Frick
"Rettet die Kinder!"
Kinderliteratur und kulturelle Erneue-
rung in China, 1902 – 1946
Bd. 37, 2002, 288 S., 25,90 €, br.,
ISBN 3-8258-5166-4

Mechthild Leutner;
Klaus Mühlhahn (Hg.)
Deutsch-chinesische Beziehungen im 19. Jahrhundert
Mission und Wirtschaft in interkultu-
reller Perspektive
Bd. 38, 2001, 408 S., 35,90 €, br.,
ISBN 3-8258-5736-0

Heike Schmidbauer
Aufbruch aus den Dörfern
Chinesische Migrantinnen zwischen
Modernisierung und Marginalisierung
Bd. 39, 2001, 200 S., 20,90 €, br.,
ISBN 3-8258-5385-3

Jens Hürter
Tang Caichang (1867 – 1900)
Reformer, Denker und Rebell in Chi-
na an der Schwelle zur Moderne
Bd. 40, 2002, 344 S., 17,90 €, br.,
ISBN 3-8258-5857-x

Joachim Krüger (Hg.)
**Beiträge zur Geschichte der Bezie-
hungen der DDR – VR China**
Erinnerungen und Untersuchungen
Bd. 41, 2002, 264 S., 25,90 €, br.,
ISBN 3-8258-6149-x

Jens Damm
**Homosexualität und Gesellschaft
in Taiwan**
1945 bis 1995
Bd. 42, 2003, 288 S., 25,90 €, br.,
ISBN 3-8258-6674-2

Martina Wobst
**Die Kulturbeziehungen zwischen
der DDR und der VR China
1949 – 1990**
Kulturelle Diversität und politische
Positionierung
Bd. 43, 2004, 280 S., 29,90 €, br.,
ISBN 3-8258-7422-2

LIT Verlag Münster – Berlin – Hamburg – London – Wien
Grevener Str./Fresnostr. 2 48159 Münster
Tel.: 0251 – 62 03 22 – Fax: 0251 – 23 19 72
e-Mail: vertrieb@lit-verlag.de – http://www.lit-verlag.de